Growing Pains:
Adapting Copyright for Libraries,
Education, and Society

Growing Pains:
Adapting Copyright for Libraries, Education, and Society

Laura N. Gasaway, editor

Fred B. Rothman & Co.

Littleton, Colorado 80127
1997

Library of Congress Cataloging-in-Publication Data

Growing pains : adapting copyright for libraries, education, and
    society / Laura N. Gasaway, editor.
        p.   cm.
    ISBN 0-8377-0654-8 (cloth : alk. paper)
    1. Fair use (Copyright)—United States. 2. Copyright—
United States. I. Gasaway, Laura N.

KF3030.1.G7   1997
346.7304'82—dc21   97-1727
                                                        CIP

Printed in the United States of America

Dedication

This book is dedicated to those librarians and educators who struggle daily with the complexities of the copyright law as they try to provide library services to users and to teach students at all levels of education. Too few copyright publications focus on the needs of students and the users of libraries; this work aims to remedy that situation.

Contents

Section II
Libraries and Copyright

Section III
Education and Copyright

Appendices

Foreword

Librarians and teachers find their jobs increasingly difficult in today's world. They face a myriad of challenges: inadequate financial support for their institutions, overcrowded facilities, violence in the classroom and in the workplace, lack of respect in the community, and low salaries, just to name a few. Yet, the work they perform in educating students and meeting the information needs of an increasingly sophisticated community is vital. Although different in scope from these problems, teachers and librarians also must find ways to provide materials to students, scholars, and researchers alike. Teachers and library users rely on copyrighted works as the basis of their teaching materials and research sources. The material on which they depend now embraces a wider array of types of works than in the past. Not many years ago, there were few educational audiovisual works, yet today there are thousands of such works embodied in a variety of formats. In using copyrighted works even for research and scholarship or in the classroom in a nonprofit educational institution, librarians, library users, teachers, and students must deal with copyright law.

One hallmark of U.S. copyright law is that it seeks to balance the rights of copyright holders with those of the users of copyrighted works. Although neither the user community nor the owner community was completely happy with the Copyright Act of 1976, it apparently struck a reasonable balance between competing interests. During the past two decades since the law was enacted, however, a series of court decisions seems to favor the rights of copyright owners and publishers over important rights and interests of the users of copyrighted works. The recent report from the Task Force on the National Information Infrastructure, *Intellectual Property and the National Information Infrastructure* (the White Paper) further recommended advancing the rights of copyright holders to the detriment of the public. Those of us who are knowledgeable about copyright law and who work in the public interest see fair use under serious attack in both the print world and certainly in the emerging digital environment. Too often we have been silent or ineffective when owners challenge fair uses of copyrighted works in libraries and education. This has begun to change: We are silent no more!

This book consists of 20 chapters written by a variety of scholars with expertise in the fields of copyright law, education, and librarianship who advocate changes in the copyright statute, in interpretations of the law, and in school and library practices so that librarians and educators can meet their obligations. The book will have served its purpose if it encourages librarians and teachers to exercise their fair use rights fully.[1]

The book has its genesis in a telephone call from a colleague who serves as editor of a respected library science journal published by a well-known commercial concern that publishes a number of library science journals. His request to me was to edit a double or triple issue of the journal on copyright law for librarians which then also would also be published as a monograph. I produced an overview of the issues and proposed a list of authors and topics which the journal editor liked very much. I was given the go ahead to contact the proposed contributors. All but two of authors accepted the invitation to write for the journal. Alas, however, it was not to be.

I reviewed the journal's copyright release and found it unacceptable. Basically, the publisher required a complete transfer of all rights. I tried to work with the publisher to develop a more reasonable

---

1.   While there continues to be disagreement about whether fair use is a right or a privilege, section 108(a)(4) calls fair use a right.

copyright release, but there was no willingness to alter the agreement. I then shared the copyright agreement with the prospective authors, each of whom refused to serve as a contributor under these conditions. Thus, I contacted Paul Rothman, president of Fred B. Rothman & Co., who expressed interest in the project and agreed that Rothman would own the copyright in the book but that individual authors would own the copyright of their chapters. This will permit authors to make their works available electronically after publication of the book, to use it in future works, to update the chapter for later use, and to use their work however they choose. I am personally grateful to Paul Rothman for his forward thinking and willingness to embrace this project.

I want to thank the contributors for their outstanding work. It was a pleasure to receive their chapters and work with them. Also I am grateful to Christopher Humphreys, my research assistant, for his excellent work on the chapters including the difficult task of cite checking, Priscilla Fulcher, my secretary, for preparation of the manuscript, and Terri Saye for indexing this book. Sheila Jarrett at Fred B. Rothman & Co. provided outstanding editorial assistance.

The chapter authors and I hope this work will make an important contribution to copyright scholarship and will present clearly the users' perspective which too often is missing from the literature. On May 19, 1997, the Conference on Fair Use held its supposedly final meeting. None of the CONFU guidelines was found to have garnered sufficient support to be adopted generally. Participants are continuing to talk and will meet again in May 1998.

Laura N. Gasaway
May 1997

Section I
Copyright Issues:
The Changing Landscape

Chapter One
Copyright and the Invention of Authorship[*]

by
Professor James Boyle
Washington College of Law
American University

So far I have argued that, because of the contradictions and tensions described here, there are certain structural pressures on the way that a liberal society deals with information. When we turn to the area of law conventionally recognized as dealing with information—intellectual property law, and in this case copyright law—I claim that we will find a pattern, a conceptual strategy which attempts to resolve the tensions and contradictions in the liberal view of information. On one level, understanding this pattern will help us to make sense (if not coherence) of the otherwise apparently chaotic world of copyright. On

---

[*]   James Boyle, *Copyright and the Invention of Authorship,* in SHAMANS, SOFTWARE, AND SPLEENS (President and Fellows of Harvard College 1996). Reprinted by permission of Harvard University Press.

another level, I claim that the conceptual strategy developed in copyright is important to understand because parts of it can also be found in most, if not all, of the areas where we deal with information—even if those areas conventionally are understood to have nothing to do with copyright.

From what I have argued previously it should be apparent that, although intellectual property has long been said to present insuperable conceptual difficulties, it actually presents exactly the same problems as the liberal concept of property generally. It merely does so in a more obvious way and in a way which is given a particular spin by our fascination with information. All systems of property are both rights-oriented and utilitarian, rely on antinomian conceptions of public and private, present insuperable conceptual difficulties when reduced to mere physicalist relations but when conceived of in a more abstract and technically sophisticated way, immediately begin to dissolve back into the conflicting policies to which they give a temporary and unstable form. In personal or real property, however, one can at least point to a pair of sneakers or a house, say "I own that," and have some sense of confidence that the statement means something. In fact, it is not at all clear that such confidence is justified, but at least property presents itself as an *apparently* coherent feature of social reality, and this is a fact of considerable ideological and political significance. In intellectual property, the response to the claim "I own that" might be "what do you mean?"

As Martha Woodmansee discovered, this point was made with startling clarity in the debates over copyright in Germany in the eighteenth century. Encouraged by an enormous reading public, several apocryphal tales of writers who were household names living in poverty, and a new, more romantic vision of authorship, writers began to demand greater economic returns from their labors. One obvious strategy was to lobby for some kind of legal right in the text—the right that we would call copyright. To many participants in the debate, the idea was ludicrous. Christian Sigmund Krause, writing in 1783, expressed the point pungently.

> "But the ideas, the content! that which actually constitutes a book! which only the author can sell or communicate!"—Once expressed, it is impossible for it to remain the author's property. . . . It is precisely for the purpose of using the ideas that most people buy books—pepper dealers, fishwives, and the like and literary pirates excepted. . . . Over

and over again it comes back to the same question: I can read the contents of a book, learn, abridge, expand, teach, and translate it, write about it, laugh over it, find fault with it, deride it, use it poorly or well—in short, do with it whatever I will. But the one thing I should be prohibited from doing is copying or reprinting it? . . . A published book is a secret divulged. With what justification would a preacher forbid the printing of his homilies, since he cannot prevent any of his listeners from transcribing his sermons? Would it not by just as ludicrous for a professor to demand that his students refrain from using some new proposition he had taught them as for him to demand the same of book dealers with regard to a new book? *No, no it is too obvious that the concept of intellectual property is useless. My property must be exclusively mine; I must be able to dispose of it and retrieve it unconditionally.* Let someone explain to me how that is possible in the present case. Just let someone try taking back the ideas he has originated once they have been communicated so that they are, as before, nowhere to be found. All the money in the world could not make that possible.[1]

Along with this problem go two other, more fundamental, ones. The first is the recurrent question of how we can give property rights in intellectual products and yet still have the inventiveness and free flow of information which liberal social theory demands. I shall return to this question in a moment. The second problem is the more fundamental one. On what grounds should we give the author this kind of unprecedented property right at all, even if the conceptual problems could be overcome? We do not think it is necessary to give car workers residual property rights in the cars that they produce—wage labor is thought to work perfectly well. Surely, an author is merely taking public goods—language, ideas, culture, humor, genre—and converting them to his or her own use? Where is the moral or utilitarian justification for the existence of this property right in the first place? The most obvious answer is that authors are special, but why? And since when?

Even the most cursory historical study reveals that our notion of "authorship" is a concept of relatively recent provenance. Medieval church writers actively disapproved of the elements of originality and creativeness which we think of as an essential component of authorship:

---

1. Christian S. Krause, *Uber den Buchernachdruck*, 1 DEUTSCHES MUSEUM 415–17 (1783), *quoted in The Genius and the Copyright Economic and Legal Conditions of the Emergence of the "Author"*, 17 EIGHTEENTH-CENTURY STUD. 425, 443–44 (Martha Woodmansee ed. & trans., 1984) (emphasis added) [hereinafter Woodmansee].

They valued extant old books more highly than any recent elucubra-
tions *and they put the work of the scribe and the copyist above that of the
authors.* The real task of the scholar was not the vain excogitation of
novelties but a discovery of great old books, their multiplication and
the placing of copies where they would be accessible to future generations of readers.[2]

Martha Woodmansee quotes a wonderful definition of "book"
from a mid-eighteenth-century dictionary that merely lists the writer
as one mouth among many—"the scholar . . . the paper-maker, the
type-founder and setter, the proof-reader, the publisher and book-
binder, sometimes even the gilder and brass worker"—all of whom are
"fed by this branch of manufacture."[3] Other studies show that authors
seen as craftsmen—an appellation which Shakespeare might have
accepted—or at their most exalted, as the crossroads where learned
tradition met external divine inspiration.[4] But since the tradition was
mere craft and the glory of the divine inspiration should be offered to
God rather than to the vessel he had chosen,[5] where was the justification for preferential treatment in the creation of property rights? As

---

2.   ERNST P. GOLDSCHMIDT, MEDIEVAL TEXTS AND THEIR FIRST APPEARANCE IN PRINT 112
     (1943) (emphasis added).

3.   Georg H. Zinck, *Allgemeines Oeconomisches Lexicon* col. 442 (3d ed. n.p. 1753),
     quoted in Woodmansee, *supra* note 1, at 425.

4.   *See* James Boyle, *The Search for an Author: Shakespeare and the Framers*, 37 AM.
     U. L. REV. 625, 628–33 (1988).

5.   A view which persisted for some time:

     Nevertheless, I had to be told about authors. My grandfather told me,
     tactfully, calmly. He taught the names of those illustrious men. I would
     recite the list to myself, from Hesiod to Hugo without a mistake. They
     were the Saints and Prophets. Charles Schweitzer said he worshipped
     them. Yet they bothered him. Their obtrusive presence prevented him from
     attributing the works of Man directly to the Holy Ghost. He therefore felt
     a secret preference for the anonymous, for the builders who had had the
     modesty to keep in the background of their cathedrals, for the countless
     authors of popular songs. He did not mind Shakespeare, whose identity
     was not established. Nor Homer, for the same reason. Nor a few others,
     about whom there was no certainty they had existed. As for those who
     had not wished or who had been unable to efface the traces of their life, he
     found excuses, provided they were dead.

     JEAN-PAUL SARTRE, THE WORDS 61–62 (1964).

authors ceased to think of themselves as either craftsmen, gentlemen,[6] or amanuenses for the Divine spirit, a recognizably different, more romantic vision of authorship began to emerge. At first, it was found mainly in self-serving tracts, but little by little it spread through the culture so that by the middle of the eighteenth century it had come to be seen as a "universal truth about art."[7]

Woodmansee explains how the decline of the craft-inspiration model of writing and the elevation of the romantic author both presented and seemed to solve the question of property rights in intellectual products:

> Eighteen-century theorists departed from this compound model of writing in two significant ways. They minimized the element of craftsmanship (in some instances they simply discarded it) in favor of the element of inspiration, and they internalized the source of that inspiration. That is, inspiration came to be regarded as emanating not from outside or above, but from within the writer himself. "Inspiration" came to be explicated in terms of *original genius* with the consequence that the

---

6. I use the male form deliberately. It is true that, despite the obstacles placed in their way, a number of women authors established themselves on the literary scene. To say, however, that they participated in the "invention" of romantic authorship, or to claim that such a notion accurately reflected the parts of their own creative practices which they thought most valuable, seems to me to be going too far. In this historical analysis, gender-neutral language might actually obscure understanding. *See* Sandra M. Gilbert & Susan Gubar, The Madwoman in the Attic: The Woman Writer and the Nineteenth Century Literary Imagination (1988); *see also* Ann Ruggles Gere, Common Properties of Pleasure: Texts in Nineteenth Century Women's Clubs 647 (1992); Marlon B. Ross, The Contours of Masculine Desire: Romanticism and the Rise of Women's Poetry (1989); Martha Woodmansee, *On the Author Effect: Recovering Collectively*, 10 Cardozo Arts & Ent. L.J. 279 (1992).

7. For an early but more comprehensive development of these ideas, see Boyle, *Search for an Author, supra* note 5. The original hints for this line of thought can be traced back to Michel Foucault, *What Is an Author? in* Textual Strategies: Perspectives in Poststructuralist Criticism (J. Harari ed., 1979). Woodmansee, *supra* note 2, provided the paradigm for actual research, and her article gives a marvelous account of the "rise" of intellectual property in Germany. For the linkage between romantic authorship and intellectual property in England, see Mark Rose, *The Author as Proprietor: Donaldson v. Becket and the Genealogy of Modern Authorship*, 23 Representations 51 (1988); *see also* Mark Rose's Authors and Owners: The Invention of Copyright (1993). *But see* John Feather, *Publishers and Politicians: The Remaking of the Law of Copyright in Britain, 1775–1842; Part II: The Rights of Authors*, 25 Pub. Hist. 45 (1989). For the same linkage in France, see Carla Hesse, *Enlightenment Epistemology and the Laws of Authorship in Revolutionary France, 1777–1793*, 30 Representations 109 (1990). And for the United States, see Cathy N. Davidson, The Revolution and the Word: The Rise of the Novel in America (1986).

inspired work was made peculiarly and distinctively the product—and the property—of the writer.[8]

In this vision, the author was not the journeyman who learned a craft and then hoped to be well paid for it. The romantic author was defined not by the mastery of a prior set of rules, but instead by the transformation of genre, the revision of form. Originality became the watchword of artistry and the warrant for property rights. To see how complete a revision this is, one need only examine Shakespeare's wholesale lifting of plot, scene, and language from other writers, both ancient and contemporary. To an Elizabethan playwright, the phrase "imitation is the sincerest form of flattery" might have seemed entirely without irony. "Not only were Englishmen from 1500 to 1625 without any feeling analogous to the modern attitude toward plagiarism; they even lacked the word until the very end of that period."[9] To the theorists and polemicists of romantic authorship, however, the reproduction of orthodoxy would have been proof they were not the unique and transcendent spirits they imagined themselves to be.

It is the *originality* of the author, the novelty which he or she adds to the raw materials provided by culture and the common pool, which "justifies" the property right and at the same time offers a strategy for resolving the basic conceptual problem pointed out by Krause—what concept of property would allow the author to retain some property rights in the work but not others? In the German debates, the best answer was provided by the great idealist Fichte. In a manner that is now familiar to lawyers trained in legal realism and Hohfeldian analysis, but that must have seemed remarkable at the time, Fichte disaggregated the concept of property in books. The buyer gets the physical thing and the ideas contained in it. *Precisely because the originality of his spirit was converted into an originality of form,* the author retains the right to the form in which those ideas were expressed. "Each writer must give his own thoughts a certain form, and he can give them no other form than his own because he has no other. But neither can he be willing to hand over this form in making his thoughts public, for

---

8.   Woodmansee, *supra* note 1, at 427.

9.   HAROLD O. WHITE, PLAGIARISM AND IMITATION DURING THE ENGLISH RENAISSANCE 120, 202 (1935).

no one can *appropriate* his thoughts without thereby *altering their form*. This latter thus remains forever his exclusive property."[10]

A similar theme is struck in American copyright law. In the famous case of *Bleistein v. Donaldson Lithographing Co.*,[11] concerning the copyrightability of a circus poster, Oliver Wendell Holmes was still determined to claim that the work could become the subject of an intellectual property right because it was the original creation of a unique individual spirit. Holmes's opinion shows us both the advantages and the disadvantages of a rhetoric which bases property rights on "originality." As a hook on which to hang a property right, "originality" seems to have at least a promise of formal realizability. It connects nicely to the romantic vision of authorship which I described earlier and to which I will return. It also seems to limit a potentially expansive principle, the principle that those who create may be entitled to retain some legally protected interest in the objects they make—even after those objects have been conveyed through the marketplace. But while the idea that an original spirit conveys its uniqueness to worked matter seems intuitively plausible when applied to Shakespeare[12] or Dante, it has less obvious relevance to a more humdrum act of creation by a less credibly romantic creator—a commercial artist in a shopping mall, say. The tension between the rhetoric of Wordsworth and the reality of suburban corporate capitalism is one that continues to bedevil intellectual property discourse today. In *Bleistein*, this particular original spirit had only managed to rough out a picture of energetic-looking individuals performing unlikely acts on bicycles, but to Holmes the principle was the same. "The copy is the personal reaction of an individual upon nature. *Personality always contains*

---

10. Johann G. Fichte, *Proof of the Illegality of Reprinting: A Rationale and a Parable* (1793), *quoted in* Woodmansee, *supra* note 1, at 445.

11. 188 U.S. 239 (1903).

12. In fact, of course, Shakespeare engaged regularly in activity that we would call plagiarism but that Elizabethan playwrights saw as perfectly harmless, perhaps even complimentary. Not only does this show the historical contingency of the romantic idea of authorship, but it may even help to explain some of the "heretical" claims that Shakespeare did not write Shakespeare. Most of the heretics use the fact of this supposed plagiarism and their knowledge of the timeless truth of the romantic vision of authorship to prove that someone else, preferably the author of the borrowed lines, must have written the plays. After all, the immortal bard would never stoop to copy the works of another. Once again, originality becomes the key.

something unique. It expresses its singularity even in handwriting, and a very modest grade of art has in it something irreducible, which is one man's alone. That something he may copyright."[13]

This quality of "uniqueness," recognized first in great spirits, then in creative spirits, and finally in advertising executives, expresses itself in originality of form, of expression.[14]

> Why is it that copyright does not protect ideas? Some writers have echoed the justification for failing to protect facts by suggesting that ideas have their origin in the public domain. Others have implied that "mere ideas" may not be worthy of the status of private property. Some authors have suggested that ideas are not protected because of the strictures imposed on copyright by the first amendment. The task of distinguishing ideas from expression in order to explain why private ownership is inappropriate for one but desirable for the other, however, remains elusive.[15]

I would say that we find the answer to this question in the romantic vision of authorship, of the genius whose style forever expresses a single unique persona. The rise of this powerful (and historically contingent) stereotype provided the necessary raw material to fashion some convincing mediation of the tension between the imagery of "public" and "private" in information production.

To sum up, then, if our starting place is the romantic idea of authorship, then the idea/expression division which has so fascinated and puzzled copyright scholars apparently manages, at a stroke, to do four things: First, it provides a *conceptual basis* for partial, limited property rights, without completely collapsing the notion of property into the idea of a temporary, limited, utilitarian state grant, revocable at will. The property right still seems to be based on something real—

---

13. *Bleistein,* 188 U.S. at 249–50 (emphasis added).

14. In the language of romantic authorship, uniqueness is by no means the only characteristic of the author. Originality may imply iconoclasm. The romantic author is going beyond the last accepted style, breaking out of the old forms. This introduces an almost Faustian element into the discussion. The author is the maker and destroyer of worlds, the irrepressible spirit of inventiveness whose restless creativity throws off invention after invention. Intellectual property is merely the token awarded to the author by a grateful society.

15. Jessica Litman, *The Public Domain,* 39 EMORY L.J. 965, 999 (1990) (footnotes omitted); *see also* David Lange, *Recognizing the Public Domain,* 44 L. & CONTEMP. PROBS. 147 (1981).

on a distinction which sounds formally realizable, even if, on closer analysis, it turns out to be impossible to maintain.

Second, this division provides a *moral and philosophical justification* for fencing in the commons, giving the author property in something built from the resources of the public domain—language, culture, genre, scientific community, or what have you. If one makes originality of spirit the assumed feature of authorship and the touchstone for property rights, one can see the author as creating something entirely *new*—not recombining the resources of the commons.[16] Thus we reassure ourselves both that the grant to the author is justifiable *and* that it will not have the effect of diminishing the commons for *future* creators. After all, if a work of authorship is original—by definition— we believe that it only adds to our cultural supply. With originality first defended and then routinely assumed, intellectual property no longer looks like a zero-sum game. There is always "enough and as good" left over—by definition. The distinguished intellectual property scholar Paul Goldstein captures both the power and the inevitable limitations of this very well. "Copyright, in a word, is about authorship. Copyright is about sustaining the conditions of creativity that enable an individual to craft out of thin air an *Appalachian Spring*, a *Sun Also Rises*, a *Citizen Kane*."[17] But of course, even these—remarkable and "original"—works are *not* crafted out of thin air. As Northrop Frye put it in 1957, when Michel Foucault's work on authorship was only a gleam in the eye of the episteme, "Poetry can only be made out of other poems; novels out of other novels. All of this was much clearer before the assimilation of literature to private enterprise."[18]

Third, the idea/expression division circumscribes the ambit of a labor theory of property. At times, it seems that the argument is almost like Locke's labor theory; one gains property by mixing one's labor with an object. But where Locke's theory, if applied to a modern economy, might have a disturbing socialist ring to it, Fichte's theory bases the property right on the originality of every spirit as expressed through words. Every author gets the right—the writer of the roman à clef as well as Goethe—but because of the concentration on originality of expression,

---

16.   By focusing on the truly exceptional work, one can even ignore the conceptual deflation that occurs in a case like *Bleistein*.

17.   Paul Goldstein, *Copyright*, 38 J. COPYRIGHT SOC'Y 109, 110 (1991).

18.   NORTHROP FRYE, ANATOMY OF CRITICISM 96–97 (1957).

the residual property right is only for the workers of the word and the image, not the workers of the world. Even after that right is extended by analogy to sculpture and painting, software and music, it will still have an attractively circumscribed domain.

Fourth, the idea/expression division resolves (or at least conceals) the *tension between public and private*. In the double life which Marx described, information is both the life blood of the noble disinterested citizens of the public world and a commodity in the private sphere to which we must attach property rights if we wish our self-interested producers to continue to produce. By disaggregating the book into "idea" and "expression," we can give the idea (and the facts on which it is based) to the public world and the expression to the writer, thus apparently mediating the contradiction between public good and private need (or greed).

Thus the combination of the romantic vision of authorship and the distinction between idea and expression appeared to provide a conceptual basis and a moral justification for intellectual property, to do so in a way which did not threaten to spread dangerous notions of entitlement to other kinds of workers, and to mediate the tension between the schizophrenic halves of the liberal world view. Small wonder that it was a success. Small wonder that the language of romantic, original authorship tends to reappear in discussion of subjects far removed from the one Fichte had in mind. Like insider trading. Or spleens.

A final question remains: Has the structure I have just described been rendered superfluous by economic analysis and public goods theory? An economist might say that the difference between the author and the laborer is that the author is producing a public good and the laborer is (generally) producing a good that can be satisfactorily commodified and alienated using only the traditional lexicon of property. The distinctions drawn from the idea of romantic authorship might appear to be surplus—unnecessary remnants of a conceptualist age.

It is certainly true that there are articles that decry the language of "idea" and "expression" and that offer the prediction that those terms will be used as mere summations of the underlying economic analysis[19]—in the same way that "proximate cause" is used as a way of expressing a conclusion about the desirable reach of liability. But this kind of response mistakes both the popular and the esoteric power of the language of romantic authorship. The romantic vision of authorship continues to influence public debate on issues of information—far beyond the traditional ambit of intellectual property. The language of economic analysis provides no neat solutions to the problems of information regulation—precisely because economic analysis is marked by the same aporias as the rest of public discourse. In this situation of indeterminacy and contradiction, it is the romantic vision of authorship that frequently structures technical or scholarly economic analysis—providing the vital initial choices that give the analysis its subsequent appearance of determinacy and "common sense" plausibility. Scholars may criticize the distinctions that flow from the romantic vision, but they should not imagine themselves to be free from its influence.

Before I go on, I would like to separate my project here from other critiques of the idea of authorship. Poststructuralist philosophy has produced a fair amount of author bashing. Literary criticism has been particularly hard on the idea of authorial intent. (Cynics would say that this is because the author's intentions are the last threat to the authority of the critic as the imperial interpreter of the text. Actually the truth is a little more complex.) Strange as it may seem, I would like to differentiate my project from full-court author bashing. I have no particular stake in the questions of whether literary authors are being presented as coherent, omniscient individual subjects; if they are, I wish them well. It's nice work if you can get it. I do not believe that authorship is a patriarchal, phallocentric plot; indeed, I am willing to agree that, as an abstract idea, it has great liberating potential. How could someone of even mildly "pinko" sensibilities fail to be attracted by a system in which workers get property rights in the objects they create, or by a property system built on originality, where iconoclasm is actually the warrant for ownership? The irony about many of the critics of the author is that they fix on qualities to revile—defiant individuality, transformation, noncommodifiable moral rights—which

---

19.   John Shepard Wiley, Jr., *Copyright at the School of Patent*, 58 U. CHI. L. REV. 119 (1991).

under a slightly different set of historical and social circumstances they would have been the first to celebrate.

The historical work on the actual development of authorship as both an interpretive construct and a repository for property rights has been much more important to me—indeed, I have tried in a small way to add to it. But nothing in my argument turns on whether authorship is something that law has unwisely borrowed from literature, something that literature has unwisely borrowed from law, or something in between, as seems most likely.

Finally, this chapter is not written out of hostility or condescension toward the authorial ideal or its adherents. Attachment to the idea of the individual transformative authorship is not a silly "mistake." First, it has a clear element of existential truth—our experience of authors, inventors, and artists who *do* transform their fields and our world, together with the belief (one I hold deeply myself) that the ability to remake the conditions of individual life and collective existence is to be cherished and rewarded. Second, as a basis for an intellectual property system, it seems to *work*, precisely because it makes a series of wrenching and difficult conflicts disappear—largely by defining them out of existence rather than solving them, however. It is possible to portray the fixation on originality and the neglect of sources and audience as a technical error made by the rational guardians of the legal system or as a deep plot by the multinationals. Instead, my argument has been that we need to see the romantic vision of authorship as the solution to a series of ideological problems. For those who do not like the word "ideology," at least as applied to any group of which *they* might be a part, we could call these problems deep-seated conceptual conflicts in our ideas of property and polity. The romantic idea of authorship is no more a "mistake" than classical economics was a mistake. It is both something more and something less than that. If one is critical of a system built on its presuppositions, one must begin by understanding both its authentic appeal and the deep conceptual itches it manages to scratch. Only then can one begin the critique.

Chapter Two

Applying Copyright History Lessons to Altering a Tight Jacket's Fit: Protecting Perception and the Uncopyrightability of Ideas in Digital Networked Environments[*]

by

Mary Brandt Jensen

Director of the Law Library and Assistant Professor of Law
University of Mississippi

The concept that use of a copyrighted work short of infringement should be encouraged is fundamental to copyright, so fundamental that it is rarely articulated, but it has been explicitly recognized from time to time by the Supreme Court and copyright scholars.[1] The reason

---

[1].   *See* Fortnightly Corp. v. United Artists Tel., Inc., 392 U.S. 390, 394 n.8 (1968); Teleprompter Corp. v. Columbia Broadcasting Sys., 415 U.S. 394, 399 (1974); BENJAMIN KAPLAN, AN UNHURRIED VIEW OF COPYRIGHT 57 (1967) [hereinafter KAPLAN];

for this basic principle is found in both the Statute of Anne (the first English copyright statute) and the copyright clause of the U.S. Constitution. The first words of the full title of the Statute of Anne are "An act for the encouragement of learning. . . . "[2] The patent and copyright clause of the Constitution gives Congress the power to "promote the Progress of Science and useful Arts" through the use of copyright and patent laws.[3] According to both Congress and the U.S. Supreme Court, encouraging the progress of science and the useful arts for the benefit of society is the primary purpose of copyright. This primary purpose is expected to be achieved by using the economic rewards that come from exploitation of copyright rights to motivate authors to create more works, but ensuring economic rewards to authors is not the primary purpose of copyright.[4] Promoting learning is what is most important. The value of additional works to society and the government's interest in encouraging the creation of additional works lies in what society can learn from them. Learning cannot occur if the authors' ideas are not transferred to the minds of individuals. Ideas cannot be transferred to minds and used to build more works if users do not have the rights needed to render imperceptible copies housing the ideas perceptible. Without this kind of use, imperceptible copies of works cannot promote learning. For these reasons copyright law historically has recognized an implied right of public access and an implied right of human perception. Other scholars, including Jessica Litman, L. Ray Patterson, Stanley W. Lindberg, and Paul Heald, have written on the implied right of public access.[5]

L. RAY PATTERSON & STANLEY W. LINDBERG, THE NATURE OF COPYRIGHT 69–70 (1991). *See also* Williams & Wilkins Co. v. United States, 487 F.2d 1345, 1362 (Ct. Cl. 1973).

2.   8 Anne, c.21 (1709).

3.   U.S. CONST. art 1, § 8, cl. 8.

4.   Berne Convention Implementation Act of 1988, H.R. REP. No. 100-609, 100th Cong., 2d Sess. 23 (1988); Feist Publications, Inc. v. Rural Tel. Serv. Co., 499 U.S. 340, 349 (1991).

5.   Jessica Litman, *The Exclusive Right to Read*, 13 CARDOZO ARTS & ENT. L.J. 29–54 (1995); L. Ray Patterson, *Copyright and the "Exclusive Right" of Authors*, 1 J. INTELL. PROP. L. 1, 37 (1993); Jessica Litman, *The Public Domain*, 39 EMORY L.J. 965 (1990); Paul Heald, *Federal Intellectual Property Law and the Economics of Preemption*, 76 IOWA L. REV. 959 (1991); L. RAY Patterson, *Americus Advocacy: Brief Amicus Curiae of Eleven Copyright Law Professors in Princeton University Press v. Michigan Document Delivery Services, Inc.: Editor's Foreword*, 2 J. INTELL. PROP. L. 183 (1994); L. RAY PATTERSON & STANLEY W. LINDBERG, THE NATURE OF COPYRIGHT: A LAW OF USER'S RIGHTS 52–55, 69 (1991).

This chapter focuses on the implied right of perception and its relationship to the uncopyrightability of ideas, facts, and material already in the public domain. Since the recommendations of the White Paper,[6] and the bill introduced to implement them,[7] threaten the historical perception right, this fundamental right and its historical legal basis must be brought to the attention of policy makers.

I. General Encouragement of Use by the Courts

The Supreme Court's history of encouraging use short of infringement runs a long and venerable course from at least *Wheaton v. Peters*[8] in 1834 to the recent decision in the 2 Live Crew parody case.[9] In *Wheaton*, the Court refused to hold a publisher of a condensed version of Supreme Court cases liable for infringing the copyright of an earlier reporter since the actual text of the opinions could not be copyrighted, and it was not clear whether the earlier reporter had complied with all the technicalities of copyright law to obtain and preserve whatever copyright he might have had in his edition. Forty-five years later, the Court refused to allow a copyright holder to restrict the use of an unprotected system of bookkeeping by claiming a copyright in the forms needed to use the idea.[10] In *Bobbs-Merrill v. Straus*,[11] the Court refused to stop the purchaser of copyrighted books from reselling them at prices below the minimum price established by the copyright holder. In the same term that *Bobbs-Merrill* was decided, the Court allowed the maker of piano rolls for player pianos to continue manufacturing the rolls despite the claims of copyright holders that the rolls violated their copyrights in the sheet music.[12]

By the 1960s and 1970s, the Court was encouraging the use of broadcasting technologies that did not infringe specific rights granted to copyright holders. In *Fortnightly Corp. v. United Artists Television*[13]

---

6. INTELLECTUAL PROPERTY AND THE NATIONAL INFORMATION INFRASTRUCTURE: THE REPORT OF THE WORKING GROUP ON INTELLECTUAL PROPERTY RIGHTS (1995) [hereinafter White Paper].
7. H.R. 2441, 104th Cong., 1st Sess. (1995).
8. 33 U.S. (8 Pet.) 591 (1834).
9. Campbell v. Acuff-Rose Music, Inc., 114 S. Ct. 1164 (1994).
10. Baker v. Selden, 101 U.S. 99, 107 (1879).
11. 210 U.S. 339 (1908).
12. White-Smith Music Pub. Co. v. Apollo Co., 209 U.S. 1, 18 (1908).
13. 392 U.S. 390 (1968).

and *Teleprompter Corp. v. Columbia Broadcasting System*[14] the Court refused to find that cable-access television (CATV) companies were engaging in public performances when they enhanced the ability of viewers to receive distant television signals. The Court also refused to allow copyright holders to require owners of restaurants and stores to pay license fees for turning on television and radio receivers for the enjoyment of their customers.[15] After Congress changed the definitions of copies and performances to include piano rolls and reception, the Court continued to rely on other reasoning such as fair use to encourage noninfringing uses of copyrighted works, including off-air home recording of television programs for time-shifted viewing purposes.[16] In recent years, the Court has also continued to protect even the right of commercial use short of infringement. It has refused to stop a commercial publisher of telephone directories from using factual listings laboriously and expensively collected by another directory publisher.[17] The Court has also encouraged the creation of parodies such as 2 Live Crew's version of "Pretty Woman" by finding that commercial parody frequently is a fair use.[18]

The balancing act of deciding when use should be encouraged and when it crosses the line to infringement is a difficult one. The courts have struggled for years to find tests that assist in determining how to divide unprotected ideas and facts, the use of which should be encouraged, from protected expression, the use of which is usually reserved to the copyright holder. The problem has not become any easier with time and experience. In the first half of the 20th century, courts struggled with issues such as how much of the general plot and characterization of novels and plays could be used in the creation of new novels, plays, and movies. Today, the same issues are litigated with little more clarity than in the past, and even more difficult issues have been added, such as when is the screen similarity between computer programs the result of providing functionality, which is to be encouraged, and when does it cross the line into taking the expressive elements of a program, which belong to the copyright holder. Making

---

14. 415 U.S. 394 (1974).

15. Twentieth Century Music Corp. v. Aiken, 422 U.S. 151, 162 (1975).

16. Sony Corp. of Am. v. Universal City Studios, 464 U.S. 417, 454–56 (1984).

17. Feist Publications, Inc. v. Rural Tel. Serv. Inc., 449 U.S. 340, 349 (1991).

18. *Acuff-Rose*, 114 S. Ct. at 1179.

decisions on where to draw the boundary lines for the scope of particular exclusive rights or the scope of particular limitations on those
rights is also difficult. Because the decisions are so inherently difficult,
and because careful balancing is a process that requires time and willingness to think, consider, and compromise, there is a natural tendency to grab onto anything in decisions that looks concrete and to use
those points as guideposts in formulating semi-bright-line rules.
Justice Kaplan stated the problem well in his well-respected lectures,
An Unhurried View of Copyright:

> [T]he rules of the game about plagiarism should respond at every
> point to the interacting policies. They do not. They tend to look in
> upon themselves and forget their public obligations. . . . [T]he intens-
> ity of the search to find what was the plaintiff's original contribution,
> then to judge whether that was somehow taken by the defendant . . .
> has sometimes driven out other considerations. When thus detached,
> the law of plagiarism drifts toward excessive protection, with recipro-
> cal excessive constraint, out of proportion to any needed incentive to
> the producer (the major consideration) and unjustified by any collat-
> eral objectives of copyright.[19]

This tendency is readily apparent in many copyright decisions. Occasionally, Congress and the Supreme Court send an explicit message
about the need to face the difficult balancing act.[20] But more often, the
subtle steps taken by Congress and the courts in support of the public
obligation side of the balance are not so explicit.

II. Historical Protection of Perception

Although it may not be obvious from the Supreme Court cases alone,
case law, legislation, and legislative history support the process of
rendering the ideas and facts contained in imperceptible copies perceptible as one of the uses short of infringement that definitely should be
encouraged. Under the 1909 Act and its predecessors, the content of
reproductions had to be humanly perceptible to infringe the copyright
holder's exclusive right to make copies. In *White-Smith Music
Publishing Co. v. Apollo Co.*,[21] the Supreme Court, emphasizing that

---

19. KAPLAN, *supra* note 1, at 76–77 (1967).
20. *Acuff-Rose*, 114 S. Ct. at 1164, 1171; *Sony*, 464 U.S. at 455 n.40; Harper &
    Row Publishers, Inc. v. The Nation Enters., 471 U.S. 539, 580 (1985).
21. 209 U.S. 1 (1908).

even skilled musicians could not perceive the melody from piano rolls, held that a tangible object which allowed a machine to convert the melody represented to the eye by sheet music into audible sound was not a copy of the sheet music.[22] Six decades after *White Music*, the Supreme Court again protected the public's right to use technology to render imperceptible forms of copyrighted works perceptible. In *Fortnightly Corp. v. United Artists Television*[23] and *Teleprompter Corp. v. Columbia Broadcasting System*,[24] the Supreme Court had to decide whether actions taken by CATV systems to amplify and enhance the delivery of signals from near and distant television stations met the definition of performance under the Copyright Act. *Fortnightly* reminded us that if a user "puts the work to a use not enumerated in [the copyright holder's exclusive rights], he does not infringe."[25] In *Teleprompter*, the Court explained that the viewer made a noninfringing use of a work when he reconverted electronic television signals "into visible images and audible sounds" with the aid of a television receiver.[26] Although the technology of CATV systems improved in the

---

22.   *Id.* The Court emphasized the fact that ordinary people skilled in the art of music could not perceive the melody from the perforated rolls as they could from sheet music. The Court accepted that the intellectual conception of the melody was embodied in both the sheet music and the rolls, but pointed out that the law did not provide for protection of the intellectual conception apart from tangible expression of the concept. Despite the fact that failure to protect the concept of the melody meant that the piano roll makers could commercially exploit the melody without paying any value to the creator of the concept, the Court refused to expand the interpretation of existing exclusive rights in a manner that would grant copyright holders control over an embodiment of the concept in a form perceptible only to machines. Throughout the decision there are many references to what is visible to the eye or audible to the ear. Much of the decision focuses on the copyrightable expression in terms that describe communication with another human being. Even Justice Holmes' concurrence, which called for a change in the law, focused on copyright as protecting the visible or audible expression of the product of the author's mind.

23.   392 U.S. 390 (1968).

24.   415 U.S. 394 (1974).

25.   392 U.S. at 394.

26.   415 U.S. at 405. The Court carefully distinguished the actions of the viewer in making the works perceptible again from the actions of the broadcaster in making the works available to the public. The broadcaster's action was the point at which the decision to make the expression available to the public was made, and thus was the point where the performance occurred. The viewer's action simply converted what was made available to the public in imperceptible form to perceptible form. Since the Court found that all a CATV system did was enhance the viewers'

six years between *Fortnightly* and *Teleprompter,* and CATV was providing access to a considerably larger area of television signals, the *Teleprompter* Court again focused on the viewer's privilege of receiving and converting electronic signals into the sights and sounds of the programs.[27]

In time, the rule of *White-Smith Music* that a copy had to be directly perceptible to the human senses was legislatively changed by a new definition of "copies" in the 1976 Copyright Act. In the 1976 Act, Congress also changed the definition of performance to include reception of electronic signals and the relay services provided by CATV systems. But Congress did not make either of these changes without carefully wording the definitions and enacting additional measures to make sure that society retained many rights to render the content of imperceptible formats perceptible. The current Act's definition of reproduction still requires that a copy must be fixed in a stable tangible medium of expression from which it "can be *perceived*" either directly or with the aid of a machine.[28] The expanded definition was explicitly limited to exclude "transient reproductions such as those projected briefly on a screen, shown electronically on a television or other cathode ray tube, or captured momentarily in the 'memory' of a computer."[29] Thus, the definition was tailored carefully to ensure that the uses necessary to perceive the uncopyrightable content of copies would remain noninfringing.

---

capacity to render signals perceptible, the Court found that the CATV system did not perform the works.

27.　*Id.* at 408. The Court pointed out that the CATV systems did not edit or change the copyrighted performances made by the broadcasters. They simply enhanced and relayed the reception so that the viewer had more capacity to exercise his right to render these signals perceptible. The Court reached this decision despite arguments by the traditional television networks that allowing the CATV systems to operate without having to obtain permission from copyright holders would have a negative effect upon the networks' ability to market licenses for performances of their works. These arguments are remarkably similar to arguments made by publishers and the White Paper that without enhanced protection, making copyrighted works available on the Internet will have a negative effect on their ability to collect sufficient royalties from the works to provide the necessary incentive to produce more works. The Court did not accept that argument with CATV systems, and CATV systems did not lead to the death of the television industry.

28.　17 U.S.C. § 101 (1994).

29.　H.R. Rep. No. 94-1476, 94th Cong., 2d Sess. 53 (1976) [hereinafter H.R. Rep. No. 94-1476].

The definition of performance was expanded in the 1976 Act to cover any act by which a rendition or showing was communicated to the public. The explanation of the definitions in the legislative history makes it clear that Congress intentionally was including the turning on of receiving devices and the retransmission of television signals by cable TV companies among the acts which constituted performances.[30] But the Act also made it clear that the new definition of the performance right did not apply to sound recordings or to private performances,[31] thus making sure that society would have noninfringing ways to render the imperceptible sights and sounds embodied in phonorecords, motion pictures, and other audiovisual works perceptible once the copyright holder had decided to release a work for public distribution. The legislative history clearly states that the intent in broadening these definitions was not to eliminate society's right to use performances of publicly released copyrighted works, but rather was to adopt the approach of many other countries by defining the right broadly and then limiting the right with specific limitations.[32]

Thus, while some of the means of implementing the policy of an implied right of human perception shifted with the enactment of the 1976 Act, the policy itself did not change. Instead, where display or performance was recognized as necessary to perceiving the ideas contained in a work, a series of specific limitations were enacted to ensure that the ideas embodied in a copy could still be perceived by society without infringing the performance or display rights. The 1976 Act kept the judicially created *Aiken* exception[33] in section 110(5) which permitted listeners and viewers to continue to turn on ordinary reception devices, like radios and televisions, in public places to render imperceptible broadcasts perceptible. The Act also substituted a series of narrowly drawn instructional and nonprofit performance and display exemptions for the wholesale exemption of nonprofit performances under the 1909 Act. Section 110(1) permits performances and displays of all types of works in the context of face-to-face teaching activities. The performance or display of religious works in the context of religious services is permitted by section 110(3). Section 110(4)

---

30.   *Id.* at 63.

31.   17 U.S.C. § 106 (1994).

32.   H.R. REP. NO. 94-1476, *supra* note 29, at 63.

33.   Twentieth Century Music Corp. v. Aiken, 422 U.S. 151, 162 (1975).

permits face-to-face, non-profit performances of nondramatic literary and musical works. Public performances of certain nondramatic musical works by government entities and at agricultural and horticultural fairs are permitted by section 110(6). Section 110(10) permits the performance of nondramatic literary and musical works at social functions of nonprofit veterans and fraternal organizations. Although a few additional even more narrowly drawn exceptions permit some transmitted performances, such as the exceptions which permit special transmissions to assist perception for the handicapped, most of the exceptions do not authorize transmission of public performances. As transmission becomes more essential to rendering any content of a particular format perceptible, the narrowness of these exceptions will create serious obstacles to the goal of encouraging the transfer of knowledge contained in copyrighted works.

The development of the definition and exceptions to the display right parallels that of the performance right. Prior to the 1976 Act, copyright law did not recognize a separate display right as one of the copyright holder's exclusive rights.[34] Thus, throughout most of the history of U.S. copyright law, the public had a right to use both direct and mechanically enhanced displays to perceive visually the contents of an imperceptible copy of a copyrighted work once access to a lawful copy was obtained. With the enactment of the 1976 Act, Congress took note of the fact that some limitation on the public's right to display copyrighted works might be needed to prevent displays in new media from replacing the old traditional reproduction right. On the other hand, Congress also noted that too broad a display right would interfere with society's need to perceive the content of works which had to be projected in order to be perceived, such as film strips, slides, and negatives.[35] So, Congress added a display right but limited it to public displays. Additionally, Congress enacted the limitation in section 109(c) as a means of balancing the two competing needs by permitting direct public display or indirect public display of no more than one image at a time when the physical copy and the audience were located in the same location. At the time of the enactment of this section, this balance did much to provide the public with the ability to perceive the

---

34. *See* Paul Goldstein, 2 COPYRIGHT § 5.10, at 5:219 (2d ed. 1996).

35. H.R. REP. NO. 94-1476, *supra* note 29, at 79–80.

contents of most works once lawful access had been obtained.[36] Precise drafting of the definitions of the rights and highly tailored exemptions, however, did not provide the flexibility needed to ensure that the ideas contained in future digital works such as computer programs would not be locked up inside of copyrighted imperceptible copies.

Although the 1976 Act settled the early computer cases which tried to determine whether computer programs were entitled to any copyright protection, the Act left open the issue of whether imperceptible object code was copyrightable or could be considered a copy. The court in *Apple Computer, Inc. v. Franklin Computer Corp.*[37] considered the fact that object code was not designed to be perceptible to humans as a factor that weighed against finding that object code contained the necessary expression for copyrightability.[38] In time, object code came to be recognized as a copy embodying copyrightable expression, but this result did not end the debate over the need to be able to perceive the uncopyrightable ideas and facts that were also included in binary or digital code.

Since computer programs stored in binary form cannot be perceived or understood directly by human beings, people who want to understand the ideas and other uncopyrightable elements of programs have to find a way to render the programs intelligible before they can build upon the ideas in them. Since all forms of reverse engineering computer programs require some type of duplication in the process of decompiling, it was perhaps inevitable that copyright holders would argue that such reverse engineering violated their copyrights. But the courts have recognized that allowing copyright holders to lock up the ideas of copyrighted works inside of imperceptible formats would defeat the primary purpose of copyright in furthering the progress of

---

36.   17 U.S.C. § 109(c) (1994). In the same section, Congress did much to insure the right of access by codifying the first-sale doctrine, which allows owners of legitimate copies to share them with others by selling, lending, or leasing them to others without permission from the copyright holder. Even when restricting the lease or lending of sound recordings and computer programs, Congress has recognized the need to preserve public access by preserving the right of libraries and educational institutions to lend, or in some cases even lease, these works.

37.   545 F. Supp. 812 (E.D. Pa. 1982).

38.   *Id.* at 821.

science and useful arts.[39] In response to the claims of copyright holders, the courts developed a line of cases holding that reverse engineering of copyrighted programs can constitute a fair use.

Atari Games Corp. v. Nintendo of America, Inc. [40] is one of two landmark cases which clearly hold that reverse engineering of a computer program for purposes of rendering the contents perceptible is not a copyright infringement. The *Atari* court relied heavily upon the idea/expression dichotomy, *Feist*, and the fair use doctrine when it said

> An author cannot acquire patent-like protection by putting an idea, process, or method of operation in an unintelligible format and asserting copyright infringement against those who try to understand that idea, process, or method of operation. The Copyright Act permits an individual in rightful possession of a copy of a work to undertake necessary efforts to understand the work's ideas, processes, and methods of operation.[41]

The *Atari* court found that "when the nature of a work requires intermediate copying to understand the ideas and processes in a copyrighted work, that nature supports a fair use for intermediate copying."[42]

In *Sega Enterprises, Ltd. v. Accolade, Inc.*,[43] the second landmark reverse engineering case, the court also focused on the fact that ideas embodied in digital copies are imperceptible to even the best trained experts without copying. Throughout the analysis the court focused less on whether each step was a technical infringement of an exclusive right and more on whether the end result of all the essential steps necessary to get to the ideas infringed upon the policies and reasons why the law gave rights to the copyright holder.[44]

In the latest case protecting the implied right of perception, *ProCD, Inc. v. Zeidenberg*,[45] the district court refused to allow copyright holders

---

39. Atari Games Corp. v. Nintendo of Am., Inc., 975 F.2d 832, 842 (Fed. Cir. 1992) (*citing Feist*, 111 S. Ct. 1282, 1290 (1991)).

40. *Id.*

41. *Id.* at 842.

42. *Id.*

43. 977 F.2d 1510 (9th Cir. 1992).

44. The analysis reaches the conclusion that reverse engineering game cartridges to learn what is necessary to produce compatible cartridges is a fair use.

45. 908 F. Supp. 640 (W.D. Wis. 1996). The district court opinion was reversed on appeal, 86 F.3d 1447 (7th Cir. 1996), on the grounds that Zeidenberg had agreed to the terms of the shrinkwrap license and that those license terms were not

to use copyright law to lock uncopyrightable data[46] into an imperceptible digital CD copy. ProCD produced a commercial CD-ROM product
which was a combination of copyrighted computer software and uncopyrightable telephone listing data. Zeidenberg purchased a copy of the
CD, used the software on the CD to extract the uncopyrightable phone
listings, wrote his own software to search the extracted data, and then
posted the listings and his new software on his Internet Web site. ProCD
sued Zeidenberg for copyright infringement. Since the court found that
section 117 gave Zeidenberg the necessary permission to use the copyrighted software to extract the uncopyrighted data stored in imperceptible form, it did not address Zeidenberg's argument that fair use also
permits the making of intermediate copies of a protected work to extract
the uncopyrighted parts.

The court, however, did decide that the preemption policies in
section 301 of the Act prevented ProCD from using contract terms to
avoid copyright limitations on tying up uncopyrightable information.
Although *ProCD v. Zeidenberg* is a decision that is based on access to
uncopyrightable data,[47] it is clear from the discussion in the case that
the court would apply the same reasoning to attempts to use infringement claims based on intermediate copying of imperceptible copies to
monopolize uncopyrightable ideas, facts, or other material already in
the public domain.

The reasoning behind this long line of precedent involving perception
is that people cannot learn from what they cannot perceive and cannot
use what they cannot perceive as building blocks in creating more
works. Often the need to perceive, and to use machines to aid perception,
is not even questioned. No one has yet claimed that using an electronic
hearing aid, binoculars, a telescope, a microscope, or a microform reader
infringes copyright. When a computer becomes involved, however,

---

preempted by copyright. The author believes that the court of appeals did not
consider the rarely articulated history of the right of perception and the impact of
the reversal on this right. The reversal demonstrates the great need to articulate the
history and make sure that the courts and Congress understand that such decisions
represent a departure from the previous law and public policy that will have far
greater ramifications than simply preventing some computer software vendors
from unfairly benefiting from the work of their predecessors.

46.　*Id.* at 647. The court determined that the actual telephone listings were uncopyright-
　　　able facts because of the earlier Supreme Court decision in *Feist*, 499 U.S. at 340.

47.　*Id.*

machine assistance to perception is not only being questioned but also attacked in the name of protecting commercial viability.

III. The Threat to Perception: The White Paper

The White Paper recommends that all transmissions of a work be considered to be reproductions of works when the result of a transmission is to fix a copy beyond the place from which it is sent. When combined with the White Paper's interpretation that a representation of a digital work in a computer's random access memory is sufficiently fixed to be a reproduction,[48] the effect of this recommendation is to make it impossible to use a networked computer or terminal to perceive the contents of a digital work without using the reproduction right. The White Paper and the implementing bill do not define what constitutes a place "beyond the place from which it is sent," but it is entirely conceivable that copyright holders could use the transmission definition and the interpretation of reproduction to argue that a digital work is transmitted and reproduced every time it is electronically transferred from the hard drive or other storage device to a computer's random access memory.

Indeed the White Paper appears to make that argument. No specific exception in the current copyright law or the bill introduced to implement the White Paper recommendations gives users of digital works the right to make the uses of the reproduction right that would be necessary to perceive the uncopyrighted parts of a digital work under these proposed interpretations and changes. The reproduction right, unlike the performance and display rights, is not limited to public reproductions. The direct display provisions in section 109(c) do not cover transmitted displays or reproductions in computer memory.[49] None of the other specific exceptions which apply to the reproduction right are clearly applicable. Only fair use would remain as a possible argument to authorize users with legitimate access to perceive the uncopyrightable material in digital works.

---

48. White Paper, *supra* note 6, at 65. The author and many other scholars believe that this interpretation is clearly wrong. But several recent cases quote this interpretation as accepted fact, so there is a very real danger that this incorrect interpretation will be used by copyright holders and the courts.

49. H.R. REP. NO. 94-1476, *supra* note 29, at 80.

It is by no means clear that fair use will be interpreted by everyone, especially copyright holders, to provide the necessary authority for society to perceive the works. Additionally, this particular combination renders licenses to use the performance and display rights alone totally ineffective as a means of acquiring access to perception of digital works. As the White Paper correctly points out, the separate rights are distinct and may even be owned by separate people. If a user obtains a public performance and display license for a digital work or has a right to perform or display the work under one of the existing exceptions, but does not have a specific right or obtain a license to make reproductions (or acquires the display or performance license from someone who does not have the right to sublicense reproduction rights), the user may have the right to display a digital work on a computer screen or monitor but not the right to get it from a lawful copy to the monitor or screen from which it can be perceived. Instead of electronic systems simplifying the process of obtaining permissions, the use of them could make it nearly impossible for a user to determine what kind of permissions would be needed just to be able to perceive the parts of a digital work that are not protected by copyright.

The problem concerning perception created by the White Paper recommendations will continue to worsen as many works become available only in digital form and as computers, computer memory, and digital transmission increasingly become a part of nearly every machine or device used to render imperceptible works perceptible. Currently, no one thinks of a hearing aid as a device that reproduces a copy of anything. But given the progress of technology, it is not likely to be long before the intelligent hearing aid will be developed that will make a copy of what the user wants to hear or one that will learn from the material to which its user listens. That learning function will require the use of some sort of microscopic computer with some sort of random access memory. Many microform readers still use a form of refractive or reflective display, but it is not likely to be long before some form of digital imaging and display is commonly used in microform readers that can produce better clarity in image magnification. That enhancement probably will involve computer chips, memory, and some sort of electronic transmission. Libraries already use videotape and disc players and electronic film projectors that use computer technology and memory to enhance the quality of the perceptible images they produce. In time, the bionic eyes and ears imagined in *The Six Million Dollar Man* and *The*

Bionic Woman will electronically simulate exactly what the human eye and ear now do biologically. These devices will be full of computer chips and memory and may engage in reproductive transmissions which, under the White Paper proposals, occur every time any interaction with a copyrighted work occurs. The White Paper and its proposed legislation do not consider these implications of the recommended approach to copyright in a digital world. For if they did, they would surely recommend some sort of essential step in perception exception similar to the essential step in use limitation that CONTU[50] recommended for computer programs.

The *Atari/Sega* reverse-engineering fair use approach makes far more sense than does the White Paper approach. If every bit of digital activity necessary to perceive the ideas housed in binary storage is analyzed to determine how many technical infringements occur, and copyright holders have the right to insist upon users obtaining specific authority for every one of those steps, society will not be able to use copyrighted digital works in a networked environment for the purposes for which they were clearly intended without fear of infringement. Even if the vast majority of copyright holders react reasonably, the fear that some will not, coupled with the lack of specific exceptions to cover the situation, may seriously chill the uses of digital works that the law claims to be encouraging. Copyright holders will be able to use copyright law and the fear of infringement suits to hold true monopoly power over ideas as well as expression. Such a result clearly is not intended by the law and is contrary to a very long history of copyright policy. Further, it contravenes the constitutional mandate but it is a likely result of recommendations in the White Paper.

To achieve the intent of the copyright law and to maintain a proper balance between society and the copyright holder, only the initial and perhaps the final performances, displays, distributions, broadcasts, and permanent reproductions from which users most directly perceive the content of copyrighted works need be considered. Uses of the exclusive rights which are necessary and essential steps to end-user perception of embodied ideas and other uncopyrightable elements ought not to count. And when those performances, displays,

---

50. FINAL REPORT OF THE NATIONAL COMMISSION ON NEW TECHNOLOGICAL USES OF COPYRIGHTED WORKS 32 (1987) (CCH edition).

distributions, broadcasts, and reproductions result in a similar number of people extracting and absorbing the ideas from a copyrighted work in a context similar to what the law authorized in the non-networked analog world, the law ought to reach a similar result in the networked electronic world.

IV. Protecting Perception for the Future: A Modest Proposal

Clarification is needed to ensure that copyright and a globally networked digital world can coexist and thrive. Any legislation designed to support the application of the constitutional principles of copyright to a digitally networked environment should include the following clarifications:

✦ Amend the definition of "fixation" to exclude transitory or temporary storage and embodiments on the surface of display devices. Fixation should be reserved for relatively permanent storage. This clarification could be achieved by adding the following language to the definition of copies and phonorecords:

> The term copy or phonorecord does not include temporary reproductions (such as reproductions in or on the memory, temporary files, or display components of machines or devices) incidental to the process of rendering lawfully made imperceptible copies perceptible or useable.

✦ Clarify fair use to specify that uses of the copyright holder's exclusive rights, including reproductions, public performances, displays, or distributions that are incidental to the process of making ideas perceptible or extracting ideas and other uncopyrightable elements from copyrighted works, are not infringements of copyright.

✦ Clarify the definition of fair use to the effect that uses of the copyright holder's exclusive rights, including reproductions, public performances, displays, or distributions incidental to the process of transmissions that ultimately result in the same number of end-user copies, performances, displays, and distributions that would be permitted by current law without transmissions are not infringements.

These clarifications would enable users of electronic works in a networked environment to use the works for the purposes for which the works were intended without fear of infringement. Such clarifications would also ensure that once a person had obtained lawful access to a copyrighted digital work, he would be able to learn from the work and build upon the ideas in the work without fear of infringement. Copyright holders still would have the ability to decide whether they want to disseminate information in the first place, just as they do in the print world and with telephone- and network-accessible databases now. They would have the same rights to control access as they do now.

These clarifications would not give users any more rights than they currently have to *keep* relatively permanent reproductions of works that they access through the networks. Users would have no more right to make a permanent copy of a part of a work or of a whole work on their hard drives, printers, or other permanent storage devices than they currently have to make a photocopy of material from a book or a copy of a videotape. Users would have no more right to copy materials and forward them to friends than they now have to photocopy something and mail or fax it. But users would have the same kind of access to information and ability to use information that they now have with print and non-digital audiovisual materials. Users would be able to browse, read what they are willing to read in one sitting looking at their screen, obtain information, learn, and generally operate with much the same balance that has existed in the analog/print world without fear of unknowing and unavoidable infringement. This clarification of copyright principles is precisely what the digital networked environment needs to continue growing and thriving.

The arguments of the NII Task Force in the preliminary report (Green Paper) and then later in the White Paper boil down to an argument that copyright must protect the time, effort, and money that copyright holders invest in creating digital works or such works will not be created and placed on the large networks of the national and global information infrastructure. With all due respect to the time and effort invested by the Task Force, this argument has already been correctly rejected at least twice by Congress and the Supreme Court as inconsistent with the Constitution and contrary to copyright policies for other industries that have continued to thrive.

For years, the motion picture industry tried to get an amendment to the law that would repeal the right under section 109 to rent, lend, or lease videos because it claimed that if the public could borrow videos without buying them, they easily could and would make millions of illegal copies which would make the industry so unprofitable that the number of movies being produced would decline. The motion picture industry had made a very similar argument in 1983 when it tried to stop the sale of video recorders by suing the manufacturers for contributory infringement, which was also rejected by the Supreme Court.[51] The motion picture industry did not win the suit or get the amendment, and instead of killing the movie industry, the ability to rent videos and watch them on VCRs spawned a whole new and very profitable side industry.

The database industry and publishers who reprint public domain material with small changes have also argued that their economic investment in collecting and redistributing unprotected facts and public domain material should be protected. The Supreme Court rejected this argument in *Feist* as inconsistent with the idea/expression dichotomy and the purpose of the copyright clause of the Constitution. The industries and many experts predicted that this decision would have dire consequences which would reduce the available products. But this has not happened either. Instead, two companies with major investments in such public domain-based databases have recently sold for $1.5 billion and $3.425 billion respectively.[52] While both companies also contain major print publishing components, neither would have sold for anywhere near the selling price without these large, primarily public domain-based databases. Both of these companies have been offering password-protected access to their services through the Internet for more than two years under current copyright law. Both have found this form of access so commercially advantageous that they have offered to forego a price increase to a major sector of their subscribers if the subscribers will switch from phone to Internet access.

Justice Kaplan's warning has not been heeded by the drafters of the White Paper and its implementing legislation. Their view of the law is drifting "toward excessive protection, with reciprocal excessive constraint, out of proportion to any needed incentive to the producer (the major consideration) and unjustified by any collateral objectives of copyright."[53]

---

51.   Sony Corp. of Am. v. Universal City Studios, Inc., 464 U.S. 417 (1984).

52.   These companies are Mead Data Central (LEXIS) and West Publishing Co. (WESTLAW).

53.   BENJAMIN KAPLAN, AN UNHURRIED VIEW OF COPYRIGHT 76–77 (1967).

Chapter Three
The Term of Copyright[*]

by
Dennis S. Karjala
Professor of Law
Arizona State University

33

I. Introduction

Congress is now considering legislation that would extend the existing terms of copyright protection by an additional 20 years. This chapter explains why the adoption of this legislation would deal a severe blow to the progress of United States culture and scholarship. If the bills have not become law by the time this appears, it seeks active support against the bills from everyone who, personally or professionally, is concerned with the maintenance of a vibrant and viable public domain as a basis for the creation of new works and unfettered scholarship. If, sadly, the bills have in fact become law, this chapter may at least stand as a requiem for the unnecessary and indeed wasteful death of a major portion of our public domain.

This book is aimed primarily at librarians. Therefore, while defeat of the extension legislation is of vital importance to nearly all scholars and other creative persons, a few words directed particularly to librarians are in order. Libraries and librarians collect, categorize, archive, maintain, and make available works whose primary function is to deliver information (including information in the form of entertainment). Many of these works are protected under copyright law. Compliance with copyright by librarians in carrying out their social role has become increasingly complex, especially in view of the rapid growth of digital networks.[1] Given the already very long term of copyright, however, it might appear that extension of the term would not greatly exacerbate these compliance difficulties. After all, the majority of works handled by libraries and librarians are likely to be under copyright even without any further extensions. Under this view, librarians may not feel overly concerned with the extension proposals.

This view, however, is both short sighted and fundamentally at odds with the traditional role played by librarians, both in the development of our social culture in general and with respect to copyright legislation in particular. Copyright legislation typically involves heavy negotiation between the interested private parties, with Congress largely playing the role of mediator.[2] This process can leave the general

---

1.   *See, e.g.,* Sandy Norman, *The Electronic Environment: The Librarian's View,* EUR. INTELL. PROP. REV. 71 (1996).

2.   Professor Litman has written broadly on the political dynamics underlying copyright legislation. *See* Jessica Litman, *Copyright and Information Policy,* 55 L. & CONTEMP. PROBS. 185, 196 (1992); Jessica Litman, *Copyright Legislation and*

public underrepresented when legislative compromises are made between owners' and users' rights.[3] Librarians and educators have traditionally been among the most vocal and most effective opponents of the trend toward ever broader, stronger, and longer copyright rights, not only, or perhaps even primarily because of direct professional interests in lower prices and freer use, but also because of a more fundamental commitment to the broader public interest.

A vibrant and growing public domain is a vital part of that public interest. Yet, the librarians as a group have been notably silent on the question of the copyright extensions. Apparently more immediately pressing are questions of copyright regulation in the digital network environment, the national information infrastructure, and the White Paper.[4] There is no doubt about the importance of these issues, but it is also true that we will almost surely be forced to rethink in a few years whatever solutions we come up with today, after the rapid development of the underlying technology settles down and we are able to see the issues with better clarity. The copyright extensions, however, if adopted, will result in a devastating and permanent 20-year loss to the public domain, with no public benefit and incalculable potential harm to the healthy progress of science and culture. Now, perhaps more than ever, these traditional effective voices on behalf of the public interest need to be heard by Congress.

II. The Proposed Legislation

Under the Copyright Act of 1976, as amended prior to the extension legislation,[5] copyright on post-1977 works lasts for 50 years beyond the death of the author, or for 75 years in the case of works made for hire.[6] Copyright on works published before 1978 continue for 75 years

---

Technological Change, 68 OR. L. REV. 275 (1989); Jessica Litman, *Copyright, Compromise, and Legislative History*, 72 CORNELL L. REV. 857 (1987).

3. Robert W. Kastenmeier & Michael J. Remington, *The Semiconductor Chip Protection Act of 1984: A Swamp or Firm Ground?* 70 MINN. L. REV. 417, 467 (1985) [hereinafter Kastenmeier & Remington].

4. INTELLECTUAL PROPERTY AND THE NATIONAL INFORMATION INFRASTRUCTURE: THE REPORT OF THE WORKING GROUP ON INTELLECTUAL PROPERTY RIGHTS (1995). Legislation has been introduced in both houses of Congress to implement the recommendations of this report. H.R. 2441, S. 1284, 104th Cong., 1st Sess. (1995).

5. 17 U.S.C. §§ 101–1101 (1994).

6. *Id.* § 302(a) & (c).

from publication.[7] Pre-1978 unpublished works remain under copyright for these same periods, but in no event does the copyright expire before the year 2003; if published before 2003, the copyright continues until 2028.[8] These works may be as old as our Republic or even older, such as letters or diaries of the founding fathers, provided they were never published prior to 1978 (when unpublished works were first brought into the federal copyright system).

The proposed legislation would extend the terms of all copyrights, including copyrights on existing works, by 20 years: for individual authors, the copyright term would continue for 70 years after the death of the author, while corporate authors would have a term of protection of 95 years. Unpublished or anonymous works would be protected for a period of 120 years after their creation. Copyrights in pre-1978 unpublished works will continue to the year 2003; if these already ancient works are published prior to 2003, their copyrights would continue in force through the year 2047.

III. Why Extension Is a Bad Idea

Various arguments have been offered in support of extension. Some say that the extension is necessary as an incentive for the creation of works. Others argue that the current period for individual authors—50 years after the individual's death—was intended to provide an income stream for two generations of descendants and that the longer human life span now requires a longer copyright term. Some maintain that we should adopt an extended term because the countries of the European Union have done so, in order to "harmonize" our law with theirs. Still others claim that the longer copyright term is necessary to prevent royalty inequality between United States and European copyright owners.

None of these arguments considers the costs to the public in this country of an extended copyright term. Moreover, as shown in more detail in later sections of this chapter, the arguments are either

---

7. *Id.* § 304(a) (1991). Copyrights on works published prior to 1964 expired 28 years after publication unless renewed. Renewal became automatic for post-1963 works pursuant to Pub. L. No. 102-307 (1991), which amended section 304(a) into its current form.

8. *Id.* § 303.

demonstrably false or, at best, without foundation in empirical data. If incentives were the issue, there would be no need to extend the copyrights on existing works, even if one were to accept the dubious proposition that the extra 20 years provide an incentive for the creation of new works. If we were worried about two generations of individual descendants, we should prohibit the first generation from selling the copyright outright, and we would have no need to extend the term for corporate authors. Harmonization, while overvalued in any event, is not achieved under the proposed legislation. The supposed royalty inequality, too, fails to provide a basis for extending the term—we do not blindly follow Europe's welfare legislation in other areas, and Europe's choice to supply extended welfare to "its" copyright owners provides no basis for our doing the same. (Because supporters of extension consistently and unjustly try to portray the bills as benefiting creators and authors,[9] it is particularly important to bear in mind constantly that extension benefits *copyright owners* and not creative *authors*, who will already have been dead for 50 years.) Moreover, the cost to the general public in the United States vastly exceeds even the gains to those relatively few copyright owners who would benefit from the extension, and the public receives no compensating benefits.

Once the errors in the arguments for increasing the term have been exposed, the real reason for the legislation becomes clear: the maintenance of royalty revenues from those relatively few works from the 1920s and 1930s that continue to have significant economic value today. The continued payment of these royalties is a wealth transfer from the U.S. public to current owners of these copyrights. These copyright owners are in most cases large companies and in any case may not even be descendants of the original authors whose works created the revenue streams that started flowing many years ago.

The works about to enter the public domain, absent this legislation, were created in 1922. At that time and for many years thereafter, society's "bargain" with the actual authors was a period of exclusive

---

9. Consider, for example, the statement of Senator Hatch in introducing S. 483: "The current term of copyright is . . . inadequate to perform its historic functions of spurring creativity and protecting authors." 141 CONG. REC. S3390 (Mar. 2, 1995). "By providing this across-the-board extension of copyright for an additional 20 years, I believe that authors will reap the full benefits to which they are entitled from the exploitation of their creative works." *Id.* at S3391.

rights under copyright for a maximum of 56 years. Those authors produced and published their works with the understanding that the works would enter the public domain 56 years later. Yet, notwithstanding that bargain, the period was extended by 19 years in 1976 to 75 years.[10] Then, 19 years later, these same copyright owners returned to Congress seeking yet another extension to continue the wealth transfer for another 20 years.

This wealth transfer from the general public in this country to copyright owners is, moreover, only a part—probably a small part—of the total cost that we and coming generations will bear if the extension is adopted. It is important to remember that the extension would apply to foreign works as well as those produced in the United States. Therefore, to maintain a flow of revenue to the owners of domestic copyrights, the general public will continue to pay on foreign copyrights from the 1920s whose terms must also be extended. No one has shown that there will even be a net international inflow of royalties from the works at issue.

Even worse, to maintain the royalty revenues on those few works from this period that have continued economic viability, the copyrights must be extended on *all* works. This includes letters, manuscripts, forgotten films and music, out-of-print books, and much more, all potential sources on which *current* authors and scholars could otherwise base new works. Copyrights can and usually do have very complicated multiple ownership so many years after an author's death. The transaction costs of negotiating for use can be prohibitively high, even for works that no longer have economic value. None of the arguments for extension take into consideration the loss to both revenue and culture represented by the absence of valuable new works that are *not* created because underlying works that would have served as a foundation remain under copyright. The magnitude of this loss, of course, can never be known, but that makes it no less real or substantial.

---

10. *Id.* § 304(a) (1991). The constitutionality of this unbargained for extension of existing copyrights has been questioned. MELVILLE B. NIMMER & DAVID D. NIMMER, 1 NIMMER ON COPYRIGHT § 1.05[A][1] at 1-44.35–1-44.36 (1995); Joseph A. Lavigne, *For Limited Times? Making Rich Kids Richer Via the Copyright Term Extension Act of 1995*, 73 U. DET. MERCY L. REV. 311 (1996) [hereinafter Lavigne].

Senator Hatch has offered as an argument in support of the extension the music of Walter Donaldson in the 1927 film *The Jazz Singer*.[11] The senator says, "The historical significance of that motion picture, the first sound film to be commercially released, can hardly be overstated."[12] It would, of course, be fatuous to assert that extended copyright is necessary as an incentive for the preservation of a film of such historical importance. Indeed, it is precisely the historical significance of the film that calls most strongly for allowing it to go into the public domain, so that film historians and others can make full and effective use of it. As long as it remains under copyright, many important uses of this cultural milestone will die aborning because of the transaction and royalty costs involved in obtaining permission from the copyright owners.

The creation of new works is dependent on a rich and vibrant public domain. Without good reason to expect a substantial compensating public benefit, we should not risk tying the hands of current creative authors and making them less competitive in domestic and international markets just to supply a financial windfall to owners of copyrights in works created long ago. Santa Claus and the Easter Bunny are justly part of the public domain that anyone can use every Christmas and Easter season. Eventually Mickey Mouse and Bugs Bunny should also join our freely available cultural heritage. That is a crucial part of the copyright "bargain" that the public made at the time these works were created.

---

11.   104 CONG. REC. S3390, S3392, 104th Cong., 1st Sess. (statement of Sen. Hatch, Mar. 2, 1995). According to Senator Hatch, Mr. Donaldson's daughter, now in her early fifties, continues to publish and exploit her father's works. Mr. Donaldson died in 1947, and this is one of those rare cases where a creative artist has children so late in life that the copyrights do not extend over the full life of the artist's children. Such extreme cases should not, however, constitute the basis for general policy, even if our goal were to insure royalty flow for the entire lives of all the artist's children. The music in question, assuming it was first published in 1927, will produce royalties until 2003, and of course any later works of Mr. Donaldson will go on longer. Royalties on very popular works can be the basis of a substantial estate that itself can be the source of income even after the expiration of the copyright in the underlying works. Even more important, however, is that 75 years is long enough. The goal of copyright is *not* to supply income to descendants for the full economic life of the work.

12.   *Id.* at S3392.

IV. United States Copyright Policy

Both Congress and the courts uniformly have treated U.S. copyright law as an instrument for promoting progress in science and the arts to provide the general public with more, and more desirable, creative works:

> The limited scope of the copyright holder's statutory monopoly, like the limited copyright duration required by the Constitution, reflects a balance of competing claims upon the public interest: Creative work is to be encouraged and rewarded, but private motivation must ultimately serve the cause of promoting broad public availability of literature, music, and the other arts. The immediate effect of our copyright law is to secure a fair return for an "author's" creative labor. But the ultimate aim is, by this incentive, to stimulate artistic creativity for the general public good.[13]

United States copyright tradition is in this respect philosophically different from that of many other countries that treat intellectual property as the natural right of individual creators. Under our system, Congress need not recognize intellectual property rights at all, but if it does, the purpose must be to promote innovation in science and the useful arts.

Our system of copyright protection is delicately balanced. We recognize exclusive rights in creators so that consumers have available an optimal number and quality of works, but want those rights to be no stronger than necessary to achieve this goal.[14] We do not recognize new intellectual property rights, or strengthen old ones, simply because it appears that a worthy person may benefit; rather, we do so only for a public purpose and where it appears that there will be a public benefit. The current statutory foundation of copyright protection, the Copyright Act of 1976, is itself the product of lengthy debate and represents innumerable compromises seeking to achieve the proper balance between private returns to authors and public benefit, including a broad public domain that permits current authors to build on the cultural heritage from those who have come before them.

Former Representative Kastenmeier, the primary architect of the current statute, recognized this point very clearly and has set forth the

---

13.   Twentieth Century Music Corp. v. Aiken, 422 U.S. 151, 156 (1975) (footnotes omitted).

14.   PAUL GOLDSTEIN, 1 COPYRIGHT § 1.1 (2d ed. 1996).

conditions that should be met by persons seeking change in the copyright balances: (1) The proponent should show that the new interest will not violate existing principles or basic concepts; (2) the proponent should present an honest analysis of all the costs and benefits; and (3) the proponent should show how recognizing the new interest will enrich or enhance the public domain.[15] In sum, "the proponents of change should have the burden of showing that a meritorious public purpose is served by the proposed congressional action."[16]

On these ground rules, the proponents of a life-plus-70-year period of copyright protection have not met their burden of proving that the change does not violate basic U.S. copyright principles, that the public benefits outweigh the costs, or that the public domain will be enriched. On the contrary, the public domain will not be enriched but rather will be diminished. If this loss to the public domain is not balanced by a greater incentive to create new works, the public benefits will not outweigh the costs. This means that we would be violating our basic principle establishing the general public good as the ultimate aim of the copyright system.

The extension proponents have made no effort to show that the public benefits from its enactment would outweigh the costs. Indeed, they have demonstrated no public benefit whatsoever and have barely attempted to do so. Yet, the public cost in the form of a diminished public domain is obvious. As demonstrated below, this public cost is not offset by any increased incentive to create new works; nor does international trade in intellectual property rights fill the gap between public costs and public benefits.

Europe, whose copyright law is based more on a natural rights tradition, has recently moved to a life-plus-70 regime for individual authors and a 70-year period of protection for corporate authors. That should not cause us to change our underlying intellectual property philosophy. Nor does it provide a reason for avoiding the careful cost/benefit analysis called for by that philosophy. The United States joined the Berne Convention for many good reasons, one of which was to become an influential leader in world intellectual property policy.

---

15. Kastenmeier & Remington, *supra* note 3, at 440–41. A fourth component of Mr. Kastenmeier's test is a clear definition of the new interest. That component is clearly satisfied for the proposal to extend the term to life plus 70 years.

16. *Id.* at 440.

Our underlying policy has served us well, as shown by our dominant position in the worldwide markets, particularly for music, movies, and computer software. Rather than following Europe we might better seek to persuade Europeans that our approach to intellectual property rules both rewards creativity *and* promotes economic efficiency.

V. Tangible versus Intangible Property

Given that the current extension proposals follow so quickly after the expiration of the 19-year extensions for pre-1978 works effected by the 1976 Act, we justifiably fear that these same copyright owners (or *their* descendants) will be back in 20 years with proposals to extend again—their ultimate dream, an essentially perpetual copyright term. Therefore, it may be worthwhile to say a few words about the nature of intellectual property in general and why we have always treated it differently from tangible property.

A pure natural rights theory does not distinguish between the two types of property. If I make a coffee table, it's mine until I or my heirs sell it, and then it belongs to the new owner, and so on ad infinitum (at least until the table disintegrates). In other words, property rights in tangible property are perpetual. If I write a song, natural rights theorists ask why the song isn't equally "mine" until transfer under a perpetual property rights system.

Of course, no country follows a pure natural rights theory for intellectual property. Under such a theory, not only would there be no limitations on the duration of patents, many of which are at least as intellectually creative as the bulk of copyright-protected works, but we would not distinguish between idea and expression in determining the scope of copyright protection. Often the most creative aspect of a work is its underlying "idea." Nothing in pure natural rights theory can tell anyone where to draw the line between protected and unprotected elements of works. This line-drawing problem is, in fact, one of the most important policy problems in copyright law, as judges and legislators seek to draw a balance between creation incentives and the social desirability of allowing others to make further developments. We have concluded that the free use of "ideas" results in more works from subsequent authors than we lose by failing to protect them. In any event, for present purposes it is sufficient to note that, for policy reasons, there are *some* unprotected elements of a copyright-protected work. To the extent these elements are, indeed, the product of a particular person's intellectual creativity, natural rights theory cannot tell us why they go unprotected.

The traditional cost/benefit analysis on which U.S. law is based does not have these problems. We protect works, and elements of works, to the extent necessary to maximize the public benefits. A copyright term no longer than that necessary to provide a creation incentive follows as a matter of course from the fundamenatal difference between tangible and intangible property: intellectual propery is a nondepletable commons. "The tragedy of the commons" for tangible property is that failure to recognize transferable property rights in tangible property leads inevitably to "overgrazing." Recognition of property rights leads to economic efficiency, because a rational owner will optimize the balance between present and future consumption.

There can be no overgrazing of intellectual property, however, once a work is created, because intellectual property is infinitely multipliable without destroying the original. No matter how many people copy or use someone else's idea or even "expression," the author still has it and, absent legal intervention recognizing exclusive rights of some kind, still can make full use of it. If works would be created in optimal numbers without the incentive of copyright, economic theory tells us that the period of protection should be zero. We believe, however, that many authors depend on the expectancy of being paid something for their works to earn a living, so without any protection we are unlikely to have available as many works as the natural talents of our authors would permit.

Therefore, the different rights we recognize in tangible and intellectual property are a matter of economic efficiency. Equating the two types of property for legal purposes requires justification for switching to an economically inefficient result. At a minimum, that requires the proponents of the extension to admit openly and forthrightly that they are seeking a new basis—presumably some form of natural rights basis—for our concepts of property rights.

The following sections consider in some detail the arguments put forward to oppose the extension. First, the very real and substantial costs to the public that would result from adoption of this legislation are considered—costs that are ignored by the arguments of its proponents. This is followed by a demonstration that the arguments in favor of the extension are either logically fallacious or unsupported by any plausible evidence.

VI. Costs of a Longer Protection Period

While the asserted public benefits of an extended copyright protection period range from speculative to nonexistent, two identifiable costs are real and substantial. The first is the economic transfer payment to copyright owners during the period of the extension from consumers or other producers who would otherwise have free use of works. The second is the cost to the public of works that are *not* produced because of the diminished public domain.

A. Economic Costs and Transfers

The direct economic costs of a 20-year-longer period of protection, although difficult to calculate precisely, include the higher cost to the consuming public for works that would otherwise be in the public domain. That these costs are substantial is shown by the very claims of the proponents of this legislation that they will miss out on the European windfall if we do not extend our term to that of Europe. This windfall does not arise out of whole cloth. Rather, it is ultimately paid by consumers, that is, by the general public. And if Europeans will be paying for the right to use U.S. works in Europe, the U.S. public will be paying for the right to use both domestic and European works here at home, increasing the windfall to copyright owners will be at the expense of U.S. consumers.[17]

In the legislative history of the Copyright Act of 1976, it was argued that the general public received no substantial benefit from a shorter term of protection, because the cost for works in the public domain was frequently not significantly lower than that for works still under copyright.[18] Even without the fervor of the special interest protagonists of this legislation, however, economic theory dictates that the price to the public for popular works must, through competition, decrease to the

---

17.   It stands to reason that we are greater users of U.S. works than citizens of other countries. Whatever the multiple is (for example, if foreign uses constitute 20% of the total use of U.S. works, the multiple is 4:1), the U.S. public will have to pay that multiple of dollars to U.S. copyright owners for every dollar paid by Europeans.

18.   H.R. REP. NO. 94-1476, 94th Cong., 2d Sess. 133 (1976).

marginal cost of producing the work. If the work is under copyright, the marginal cost of production would have to include the royalty owing to the copyright owner, even if there is general licensing to competing producers of the work. Moreover, if there is no general licensing of a copyright-protected work, the price can be expected to be set at the level that maximizes the return of the copyright owner. Consequently, any claim that the public pays the same for public domain works as for protected works is implausible, at least in general.[19] Educational and scientific uses would also seem to be large markets for public domain works. At a time of rising educational costs we should inquire into the effect on our schools of a reduced public domain due to an extended protection period. Something more than anecdotal evidence should be presented before we accept the claim that the consuming public will not incur higher costs from the longer period.

B. Cost of a Diminished Public Domain

An even more important cost to the public is that paid in desirable works that are *not* created because of the continuing copyright in underlying works:

---

19.   Of course, the market for many public domain works may often be inelastic but small, with the result that competition is thin, or even nonexistent. This can allow, say, a book publisher to charge a price for a republished public domain work that is consistent with prices for similar types of books that are under copyright. Given the thin market, such a price may be necessary for this publisher even to cover production costs. This does not mean that the public domain status is irrelevant, because if a royalty were required in addition, such a book might not be republished at all, or would have to be sold at an even higher price.

It may also be that the works in question are not public domain works at all but rather derivative works based on public domain works. A new derivative work is, of course, itself copyright protected and can be expected to sell at the same price that the public pays for other protected works in that category. In this case, continued copyright protection for the underlying work may require sharing of the profits generated by the new work. One of the parties sharing the copyright monopoly is, by hypothesis, the new author, whose creativity has resulted in the new derivative work. The other will be the owner of the copyright in the underlying work, who may or may not be distantly related to the original author. In this case, true concern for authors would seem to favor *not* lengthening the protection period, which would allow the current creative author to reap the full benefit.

Finally, as discussed below, when the underlying work remains under copyright, the most important cost to the public comes from those new derivative works that are *not* created because of the new author's inability to negotiate permission from whoever owns the copyright 50 years after the original author's death.

More than a nodding acquaintance with the concept of public domain is essential to comprehension of intellectual property law and the role of the United States Congress in creating that law. The addition of a creation to the public domain is an integral part of the social bargain inherent in intellectual property law.[20]

While primary control over the work, including the rights to refuse publication or republication and to create derivative works, properly remains in the author who has created it, giving such control to distant descendants of the author can deprive the public of creative new works based on the protected work. Artistic freedom to create derivative works from the public domain is a significant public benefit, as shown by musical plays like *Les Miserables*, *Jesus Christ Superstar*, and *West Side Story*, the recent spate of high production quality films based on the works of Shakespeare[21] and Jane Austen, satires like *Rosencrantz and Guildenstern Are Dead*, and even literary classics like James Joyce's *Ulysses*. Although these might not necessarily be considered infringing derivative works even if the underlying work were under copyright, or might be excused by the fair use doctrine if otherwise infringing, their authors must necessarily take a cautious approach if a license is unavailable. When copyright subsists long after an author's death and there is no provision for compulsory licensing, the creation of derivative works that closely track a substantial part of the underlying work can be absolutely prohibited by copyright owners who have no creative relationship with the work at all. Authors of histories and biographies can also be inhibited from presenting independent analyses of earlier authors and their works by descendants who, for whatever personal reason, use copyright to prevent the publication of portions of protected works.

An important cost paid by the public when the copyright term is lengthened, therefore, is contraction of the public domain. The public domain is the source from which authors draw and have always

---

20.   Kastenmeier & Remington, *supra* note 3, at 459; *see also* Peter Jaszi, *When Works Collide: Derivative Motion Pictures, Underlying Rights, and the Public Interest*, 28 U.C.L.A. L. REV. 715, 804–05 (1981) [hereinafter Jaszi].

21.   Of course, Shakespeare's own reliance on earlier works for essentially all of his theatrical masterpieces is well known.

drawn.[22] The more we tie up past works in ownership rights that do not convey a public benefit through greater incentive for the creation of new works, the more we restrict the ability of current creators to build on and expand the cultural contributions of their forebears. The public therefore has a strong interest in maintaining a rich public domain. Nobody knows how many creative works are *not* produced because of the inability of new authors to negotiate a license with current copyright holders, but there is at least anecdotal evidence that the number is not insubstantial.[23] Unless evidence is provided that a life-plus-70 regime would provide a significant added incentive for the creation of desirable works, the effect of an extension may well be a net reduction in the creation of new works.

This point may be highlighted by the rapid developments now occurring in digital technologies and multimedia modes of storing, presenting, manipulating, and transmitting works of authorship. Many multimedia works take small pieces of existing works and transform them into radically different combinations of images and sounds for both educational and entertainment purposes. The existing protection period, coupled with termination rights, may well be distorting or inhibiting the creation of valuable multimedia works because of the transaction costs involved in negotiating the number of licenses required. Ultimately, the rapid changes in the intellectual property environment for creating and disseminating works may necessitate a reassessment by

---

22. *See generally* Jessica Litman, *The Public Domain*, 39 EMORY L.J. 965 (1990); David Lange, *Recognizing the Public Domain*, 44 L. & CONTEMP. PROBS. 147 (1981). For an argument that copyright is also intended to accommodate users' rights, see L. Ray Patterson & Stanley W. Lindberg, THE NATURE OF COPYRIGHT (1991), which includes a Foreword by former Congressman Kastenmeier.

23. Nearly 50 years ago Professor Chafee pointed to examples in which the veto power of copyright in an author's descendants deprived the public of valuable works. Zechariah Chafee, *Reflections on the Law of Copyright: II*, 45 COLUM. L. REV. 719 (1945). There have been press reports of refusals by the estate of Lorenz Hart of permission to use Hart's lyrics to any biographer who mentions Hart's homosexuality and of censorship by the husband of Sylvia Plath of the work of serious biographers who wish to quote her poetry. There have also been reports of the Picasso estate's assertion of rights (apparently moral rights) to prevent the use of any of Picasso's pictures (even "look-alikes") in a biographical film of the artist with the content of which the estate disagrees. Anthony Haden-Guest, *Picasso Pic Has Heirs Seeing Red*, THE NEW YORKER, Aug. 21 & 28, 1995, at 53–54. Professor Jaszi has provided examples of derivative-work films whose continued distribution has been limited or even suspended because of conflicts with the owner of the copyright in the underlying work. Jaszi, *supra* note 20, at 739–40.

the international community of the underlying intellectual property rules. In the meantime, extending the protection period can only exacerbate this problem. The United States should be leading the world toward a coherent intellectual property policy for the digital age and not simply following what takes place in Europe.

VII. Rebuttal of Arguments in Favor of the Extended Copyright Term

A. Incentives for the Creation of Works

It does not follow that a longer term automatically drives creative authors to work harder or longer to produce works that can be enjoyed by the public. Indeed, there is necessarily a type of diminishing return associated with an ever-longer protection period, because the benefit to the author must be discounted to present value. As Macaulay observed more than 150 years ago:

> [T]he evil effects of the monopoly are proportioned to the length of its duration. But the good effects for the sake of which we bear with the evil effects are by no means proportioned to the length of its duration. . . . [I]t is by no means the fact that a posthumous monopoly of sixty years gives to an author thrice as much pleasure and thrice as strong a motive as a posthumous monopoly of twenty years. On the contrary, the difference is so small as to be hardly perceptible. . . . [A]n advantage that is to be enjoyed more than half a century after we are dead, by somebody, we know not by whom, perhaps by somebody unborn, by somebody utterly unconnected with us, is really no motive at all to action.[24]

Thus, while an additional year of protection has little or no incentive effect at the time of a work's creation, the *costs* are immediate and substantial if the extension is to apply to existing works, as provided in the proposed legislation.

The copyright industries are by their nature very risky, and no one in these industries makes financial decisions based on even 50-year, let alone 70-year, projections. Moreover, under the U.S. Copyright Act, most transfers of copyright by an individual author may be

---

24.   8 MACAULAY, WORKS 199 (Trevelya ed., 1879), *quoted in* Zecharia Chafee, *Reflections on the Law of Copyright II*, 45 COLUM. L. REV. 719 (1945), *requoted in* ROBERT GORMAN & JANE GINSBEURG, COPYRIGHT FOR THE NINETIES 307 (4th ed. 1993).

terminated 35 years after the grant.[25] The existence of these inalienable termination rights in individual authors makes it even more unlikely that anyone would pay an author more to exploit a work under the extended term than would be paid under the current life-plus-50 period.[26] The extension, therefore, holds little promise of financial benefit to individual authors.

The absence of any additional incentive for corporate authors from the extension of the copyright period to 95 years is also easily seen. Consider an *assured* $1,000 per year stream of income. At a discount rate of 10%, the present value of such a stream for 75 years is $10,992, while the present value of a 95-year stream is $10,999, a difference of less than 0.1%. Even at a 5% discount rate, the present values are only $20,485 and $20,806, respectively, a difference of about 1.5%. And these minuscule present value differences are for guaranteed streams of income. When risk is factored into the analysis, the present value of a 75-year stream and that of a 95-year stream must be considered essentially identical. The chance that a given copyright will still have nontrivial economic value 75 years after the work is created is very small—only a tiny fraction of all works retain economic value for such a long time. No company will take the "extra" 20 years into consideration in making a present decision to invest in the creation of a new work. In fact, an ongoing successful company

---

25.   17 U.S.C. § 203 (1994).

26.   No human author can possibly receive anything more in exchange for terminable rights in his work under a life-plus-70 regime than under the current life-plus-50 regime. The reason, quite simply, is that no purchaser of copyright rights will pay anything for the "extra" 20 years of the term, because those supposed extra years can be freely terminated, along with whatever remains of the current period, before they ever begin. An exception is the right to continued exploitation of derivative works, which cannot be terminated. Even in this case, however, the maximum "extra" value to the transferring author is the present value difference between a 50-year and a 70-year protection period. Even for guaranteed income streams, and assuming that the author is on his or her deathbed at the time of the transfer (otherwise the discount periods must include the life expectancy of the author), this difference is around 5.4% (at a very conservative assumed 5% discount rate). That is, a guaranteed income stream of $1,000 per year for 50 years has a present value of $19,256 while the same stream for 70 years has a present value of $20,343. The purchaser of the derivative work right, however, will not be willing to pay anything close to this difference in present value, because of the overwhelmingly high risk that the derivative work created pursuant to the purchased right will have an economic life, like most works, far less than even the life plus 50 years now afforded.

like Disney is more likely to be spurred to the creation of new works like *The Lion King* or *The Little Mermaid* because it realizes that some of its "old reliable" moneymakers, like Mickey Mouse, are about to enter the public domain.

Some have argued that the longer terms would give film companies more valuable libraries, the income from which could be used to finance new films. This superficially appealing argument, however, flies in the face of ordinary free-market economic theory. What film company is going to change its willingness to invest in risky projects just because it has more money in its pockets? Of course all film projects are risky, and many mistakes are made that require offsetting moneymakers to remain in business. But there is no reason to think that Disney, for example, will use whatever "extra" money it earns from extended copyrights on old works to make riskier new films rather than distribute the profits to its shareholders or increase the "perks" enjoyed by its management.

It is therefore extremely unlikely that an additional 20 years of protection tacked onto the end of a copyright protection period that is already very long will act as an incentive to any current author to work harder or longer to create works that would not have been produced in any event. What is certain, however, is that extension would seriously hinder the creative activities of future as well as current authors. Consequently, the only reasonable conclusion is that the increased term would impose a heavy cost on the public—in the form of higher royalties and an impoverished public domain—without any countervailing public benefit in the form of increased authorship incentives.

Indeed, if incentives to production were the basis for the proposed extension, there would be no point in applying it to copyrights in existing works. These works, by definition, already have been produced. Yet, if the extension were purely prospective (i.e., applicable only to new works), we could be certain that support for it would wither rapidly. Thus, the real issue is the continued protection of *old* works—not those that will enter the public domain 50 (or 70) years from now but rather those due to enter the public domain *today*. These works were originally published in 1922 (works published before 1978 have a flat 75-year copyright rather than the current life plus 50 for individual authors). At that time, the law afforded a maximum of 56 years of copyright protection. This period was expanded to 75 years in 1976, and now the descendants and assignees of these authors want yet another 20 years.

The very small portion of these works that have retained economic value have been producing royalties for a full 75 years.

To continue the royalty stream for those few copyright owners, the extension means that *all* works published after 1922 will remain outside the public domain for an extra 20 years. As a result, current authors who wish to make use of *any* work from this period, such as historians or biographers, will need to engage in complex negotiations to be able to do so. Faced with the complexities of tracking down and obtaining permission from all those who by now may have a partial interest in the copyright, a hapless historian will be tempted to pick a subject that poses fewer obstacles and annoyances.

B. Copyright in Works Never Published Prior to 1978

Until the effective date of the Copyright Act of 1976, works that had never been published were protected against publication without the author's permission under state or common law. Only published works were governed by the federal copyright statute. The 1976 Act, however, preempted state protection for unpublished as well as published works and, as a quid pro quo for the loss of perpetual state protection, recognized a copyright in these previously unpublished works until the year 2003. As an incentive to publication of these works, the current law also extends their copyrights through the year 2027, provided they are published prior to 2003. The proposed legislation would extend this period by 20 years, so that a previously unpublished work will be protected until 2003 and, if published prior thereto, it will remain under copyright through the year 2047.

An example is the recently discovered fragment from a draft of Mark Twain's *Huckleberry Finn*. The copyright on the published novel was registered in 1884, renewed by Twain's daughter in 1912, and expired in 1940. Even if a life-plus-70 system had been in place at the time of the work's creation, the copyright would have expired in 1980, along with everything else Mark Twain wrote (because he died in 1910). Because this story of Huckleberry Finn and Jim in the cave has now been published, however, current law recognizes the copyright until 2028. Under the proposed extension, the copyright on this story, already more than 110 years old, will continue until the year 2048.[27]

No arguments of any kind have been offered in support of this particular extension of the copyright period of protection.[28] In contrast to the Mark Twain fragment, most of these works have only scholarly value, because if they were readily available and had economic value, they would already have been published. Moreover, many of these works are truly ancient—letters and diaries from the founding fathers, for example—and constitute a vital source of original material for historians, biographers, and other scholars.

Obviously, the normal copyright incentive to creative authorship is not involved here. This is simply an incentive to current owners of copyrights in very old works to find the works and publish them so that they will be accessible to everyone. By the year 2003 we already will have afforded the very distant descendants of the authors of these works 25 years of protection, plus the possibility of 50 years of protection if they find and publish the works. There is no justification for extending their term of protection through 2047. Fifty years of copyright protection for such old works, in favor of people who have no creative relationship with the works at all, is more than enough.

---

27.   There have been recent newspaper reports that the manuscript of Louisa May Alcott's first novel, heretofore unpublished, has just been "discovered" in the Harvard Library. There are, of course, plans to publish it, so although it was written in 1849, it would under the extension remain under copyright until 2047—nearly 200 years later! Of course, it will be in the public domain nearly everywhere else in the world. So much for "harmonization"!

28.   Even the Copyright Office, speaking through the Register of Copyrights Marybeth Peters at both the House and the Senate hearings, opposes this aspect of the legislation. *Hearings on H.R. 989 Before the Subcomm. on Courts and Intellectual Property of the House Comm. on the Judiciary,* and *Hearings on S. 483 Before the Senate Comm. on the Judiciary,* 104th Cong., 1st Sess. (1995) (statements of Marybeth Peters, Register of Copyrights); *see also* 50 PAT., TRADEMARK & COPYRIGHT J. 589 (1995) (summarizing testimony at the Senate hearings). The bills before the 104th Congress would have extended protection of pre-1978 unpublished works through the year 2013. If published before 2013, protection would continue through the year 2048. The bills before the 105th Congress (1997–98) delete the extension of protection to 2013 for pre-1978 unpublished works. Such works published before 2003, however, under the current bills still will be protected through the year 2048.

C. Support for Two Generations of Descendants

It is also argued that the copyright protection period was initially designed to provide a source of income to two generations of descendants of creative authors. Given the longer life spans of today, the argument goes, a longer term is necessary to achieve this goal.

Far from requiring longer copyright terms to compensate for longer life expectancies, however, these actuarial changes are an argument for keeping the current term of life plus 50, or perhaps even reducing it, because the longer life expectancy of the *author* automatically brings about a longer period of copyright protection. A longer overall life expectancy, moreover, does not in itself imply that the second generation loses anything in comparison with earlier eras. The crucial age for the second generation is not the absolute number of years grandchildren may be expected to live but rather the number of years they survive after the author's (i.e., their grandparent's) death. The copyright period is measured from the death of the author, and if grandchildren are living longer, so too are authors themselves. Certainly no one has provided data to show that grandchildren of today have significantly longer life expectancies than today's grandparents, let alone 20 years longer. Consequently, we should expect the current cohort of authorial grandchildren to remain alive for roughly the same length of time after their grandparents' deaths as at other times in this century.

Second, protection of two generations of descendants is not the inevitable result of a longer protection period. The copyright in a work that has been exploited and become popular will often have been transferred by the author or his or her descendants. Any termination rights with respect to the transfer will have already been exercised before the descendants in question here ever come into the copyright picture.[29] It is very likely that the copyright will have been retransferred after any termination before the current life-plus-50-year period has expired. Unless these transfers provide for a continuing royalty, there will be no royalties for the author's descendants who are alive

---

29.   Termination rights accrue 35 years after a grant by an author and expire five years later. Because the extra 20 years that would be added by the extension to the protection period begin 50 years after the author's death, all termination rights with respect to any authorial transfer will either have been exercised or have expired.

thereafter. Moreover, even if the transferee is under obligation to pay a continuing royalty, it cannot be assumed that the royalty stream will accrue to distant relatives of the original author, such as great-grandchildren. The royalty may well be transferred outside the family, by will or otherwise, by earlier descendants. If sustenance to two generations of authorial descendants is really the goal, we should be considering prohibitions on transfers and/or stronger termination rights rather than a longer term of protection.

Third, even the "natural law" argument on behalf of such distant descendants of authors is very weak. These equitable claims to a continued income stream obviously diminish with increasing temporal distance of descendants from the creative author. More importantly, while one can understand the desire of authors to provide a substantial estate to their immediate offspring, one must question the economic efficiency of a system that, as a matter of policy, seeks to grant an easy flow of income to a group of people the majority of whom the actual author may never have known. The descendants themselves would probably be better off, and certainly the general public would be better off, if they were to engage in some productive activity. U.S. copyright policy is not and has never been designed as a welfare system. It is therefore not entirely flippant to say to these distant descendants of creative authors who died 50 years ago what many now say to current welfare recipients: "Get a job!"

Fourth, while the Directive in the European Union mentions protection for two generations of descendants as one of 27 "Whereas" grounds for the extension in Europe,[30] it has never been recognized as a goal of U.S. copyright law. Indeed, today's longer life expectancies were offered as a basis for the recent substantial extension of the copyright term in 1976, from 56 years to life plus 50 years, without any mention of a "two generation" goal.[31] Surely life expectancies have not increased since 1976 to justify an additional 20 years of protection on this ground. Going to our current life-plus-50 system was necessary for the United States to join the Berne Convention, and one could at least make a coherent argument that the benefits of joining Berne might outweigh the costs of the diminished public domain resulting

---

30.   Council Directive 93/98/EEC (Oct. 29, 1993).
31.   H.R. Rep. No. 94-1476, 94th Cong., 2d Sess. 133–34 (1976).

from the longer copyright. The "two generation" argument, however, is devoid of any relationship to a public benefit. This claim is therefore fundamentally at odds with basic United States copyright principles and the social bargain that places works in the public domain after the copyright has expired.

Finally, even if "two generations of descendants" were a valid basis for extending the copyright term for works of individual authorship, it provides no justification whatsoever for extending the term for corporate authors from 75 to 95 years.

In sum, the "two generations of descendants" argument is invalid on its face, advocates economic inefficiency, fails to comport with basic United States copyright principles, and is applicable at best to the term for individual authors. It cannot serve as a basis for the diminished public domain that the extension would effect.

D. "Harmonization" with European Law

The European Union has now directed its members to adopt a life–plus–70 term of copyright duration. Possibly because of the European natural rights tradition, neither the proposal in Europe nor its adoption was based on a careful analysis of the public costs and benefits of extending the term. Nevertheless, some argue that we must do the same to "protect" domestic copyright owners, against whom the "rule of the shorter term" may be used to provide a shorter period of protection in Europe for U.S. works (life plus 50) than is given to European works (life plus 70). They also argue that harmonization of the worldwide term of protection is a desirable goal in its own right and that failure to adopt the European term will have an adverse effect on the United States balance of international trade. This section considers the general harmonization goal. The next sections deal with the supposed "prejudice" domestic copyright owners and the balance of trade would suffer in Europe were we not to follow the European example.

Harmonization of worldwide economic regulations often can be useful, especially if differences in legal rules create transaction costs that inhibit otherwise beneficial exchanges. In some cases harmonization can be beneficial even if the uniform rule is in some sense less than ideal. We need not seek uniformity for its own sake, however, especially if it means compromising other important principles. If the United States determines that works should belong to the public domain after life plus 50 years, no transaction cost problem is posed to U.S. authors by the longer period in Europe. The ultimate owners of U.S. copyrights, of course, will be able to exploit them for a shorter period, in both Europe and the United States, but that is the result of our policy choice to make the works freely available and not because of the absence of harmonization.

Additionally, even if harmonization is desirable, the question remains, who should harmonize with whom? Although doubts were expressed about the constitutionality of a life-plus-50-year period of protection at the time the Copyright Act of 1976 was adopted,[32] that standard could then accurately be denominated international[33] and, in any event was necessary if we were ever to join Berne. Life plus 70 years is not an international standard today, notwithstanding recent actions in the European Union, nor will it become one without support from the United States. It was not even the standard in Europe until the European Council of Ministers, unilaterally and without international negotiation, directed that its member states adopt a uniform term of protection equal to the longest of any of its members. If the cost/benefit analysis required by our copyright tradition does not justify changing the social policy balances we have drawn, we would better use our influence to encourage the rest of the world to remain with our standard, and Europe to return to it, rather than follow a decision in Europe that was made without consideration of the factors we have always deemed crucial to the analysis.

Moreover, the proposed legislation is not really aimed at harmonizing U.S. and European law. It would, for example, extend the copyright period for corporate "authors" to 95 years (or 120 years if the work is

---

32. *E.g.*, 14 OMNIBUS COPYRIGHT REVISION LEGISLATIVE HISTORY, House Hearings 1975 (Pt. 1) 133–34, 141–42 (testimony of Irwin Goldbloom, Deputy Assistant Attorney General, Civil Division, Department of Justice). Some believe that special constitutional problems arise from an extension of the period of protection for works already under copyright, because it recaptures from the public domain works that should be freely available under the "bargain" made at the time the work was created and offers no countervailing public benefit. They argue that the constitutional term "limited times" must be interpreted in terms of the constitutional goal to promote the progress of science and the useful arts. *See also* Lavigne, *supra* note 10, at 354–58 (arguing that the extension would run afoul of the constitutional requirement that copyright legislation promote the progress of science as well as that protection last only "for limited times").

33. *E.g.*, 14 OMNIBUS COPYRIGHT REVISION LEGISLATIVE HISTORY, *id.* at 108 (testimony of Barbara Ringer, Register of Copyrights); *id.* at 120 (testimony of Joel W. Biller, Secretary for Commercial Affairs and Business Activities, Department of State).

unpublished). The European Union, by contrast, now offers corporate authors, for countries recognizing corporate "authorship," 70 years of protection, which is less than the 75 years we currently offer such authors. Consider also the works of Sir Arthur Conan Doyle, who died in 1930 and whose works were in the public domain in England and Europe since 1981, although the European extensions apparently have revivified the copyrights until 2001. Works first published before 1978 have a 75-year period of protection rather than the current life-plus-50 term, so those works of Conan Doyle published in the 1920s remain under U.S. copyright, while those published before 1922 are in the public domain. Because his last work was apparently published in 1927,[34] it is scheduled to go into the public domain in the United States at the end of the year 2002, about the same time as the revived European copyrights on his entire oeuvre. The extension would reintroduce "disharmony" for his later works until the year 2022.

There are many other features of copyright law that are not "harmonized" even within Europe, let alone between Europe and the United States, including moral rights and the important concept of fair use. "Harmonization" therefore is not in itself a valid ground for extending any of our current copyright protection terms. It is simply a high sounding word behind which the special interests supporting the U.S. extension bills are hiding—to keep the royalty streams flowing for another 20 years, during which time copyright holders will keep working toward their ultimate dream of perpetual copyright.

E. Unequal Treatment of United States Copyright Owners

In addition to lengthening the copyright term for individuals to life plus 70 years, the European Union has adopted the "rule of the shorter term," under which works are protected only for the shorter of the European term or the term in the country in which the work originates. Therefore, it is true that retaining the current term of protection would deny some U.S. copyright owners the financial benefit of this European windfall. But the mere fact that the European Union has

---

34. *The Adventure of the Veiled Lodger* was published Jan. 22, 1927, and *The Adventure of Shoscombe Old Place* was published Mar. 5, 1927. ROBERT BURT DE WAAL, THE WORLD BIOGRAPHY OF SHERLOCK HOLMES AND DR. WATSON 13, 23 (1974). This same source lists other Conan Doyle stories as having been published in 1921, 1922, 1923, and three each in 1924 and 1926.

adopted a bad idea does not mean that the United States should follow suit. France might elect in the future, for example, to give the works of Voltaire or Victor Hugo perpetual copyright protection, but that would be no reason for us to do the same with Mark Twain or Emily Dickinson. The European copyright tradition differs in important ways from that of the United States, primarily by treating copyright as a kind of natural entitlement rather than a source of public benefit. The European approach may on balance tend to discourage, rather than promote, new artistic creativity. We should not, therefore, assume that a policy giving a few U.S. companies and individuals an added financial windfall from works created long ago necessarily is one that promotes our long-term competitiveness in the production of new works.

This extension proposal is perhaps an occasion to consider the special character of U.S. copyright and the features that distinguish our law from its continental counterparts. The constitutional concept of a limited term of copyright protection is based on the notion that we *want* works to enter the public domain and become part of the common cultural heritage. It is worth noting that in this century the cultural productivity and international market share of the United States has been much greater than that of Europe. The genius of the American system is that it balances public and private rights in such a way as to provide a rich collective source on which to base new and valuable productions. This makes us wealthier not only culturally but in a hard-nosed economic sense as well.

We must ask whether we really wish to remake our cultural industries in the image of Europe. This is not, in fact, a conflict between Europe and the United States. The real conflict, in both Europe and the United States, is between the interest of the public in a richer public domain and the desires of copyright owners (who may or may not be relatives of authors) to control economic exploitation of the copyright-protected works that remain in their hands. That Europe has resolved the conflict one way does not mean that we should blindly follow suit.

The arguments for maintaining a rich public domain in the United States are not diminished by the withdrawal of works from the public domain in Europe, or even by the partial withdrawal of only "European" works. If Europe protects its copyright owners for a life-plus-70-year period, its public domain is reduced, and the European general public suffers a net loss. The United States public, however, as opposed to individual copyright owners, is not harmed by the absence of protection in Europe 50 years after the death of a U.S. author. Conversely, the public will pay a real cost, both as consumers and as potential creators of new works, to the extent the public domain is further reduced by the longer protection period.

Whether European or American, it should be borne in mind that we are no longer talking about authors of the works that would remain protected for the extra 20 years. Those authors will have been dead for 50 years. We *are* talking about current authors, however, who create new and valuable works based on the public domain. If the underlying work is unprotected in Europe as well as in the United States, those new U.S. derivative work creators, as authors, will reap the kind of economic benefits in both jurisdictions for which copyright is indisputably designed. There is real cultural value in allowing works to become part of the common heritage, so that other creative authors have the chance to build on those common elements.

In this context, therefore, the notion of international "harmonization" simply obfuscates the real issue: there is no tension here between Europe and the United States. The tension, rather, is between the heirs and assignees of copyrights in old works versus the interests of today's general public in lower prices and a greater supply of new works. Europe has resolved the tension in favor of the owners of old copyrights. We should rather favor the general public. It is *not* unfair to turn off the royalty stream at 75 (or life-plus-50) years and to allow then-current creators to have a go at making new and better works.

F. The Balance of Payments

Certain U.S. copyright owners will receive royalty payments from European users for a shorter period than will European copyright owners from European users, if the United States does not follow Europe in extending the copyright term. It does not follow, however, that this will have any net negative effect on the U.S. balance of trade, even in the short term and much less over the longer term.

Increasing the term in the United States means not simply that European users will pay longer, but that U.S. users will *also* pay longer, and not just to domestic copyright owners but to owners worldwide. Works that are about to enter the public domain were created in 1922, and while Europeans may take more of our current works than we take of theirs, that is not necessarily true of works from the 1920s and 1930s. Our use of European works of classical music and plays as well as art works from this era may outweigh the use Europeans make of our works from the same period. Short-term balance-of-trade analysis therefore requires an investigation of whether our use of such works that would remain protected under the proposed extension would cost more than we would receive in return.

Moreover, a shorter term of protection in the United States will encourage rather than discourage the production of new works for worldwide markets. We must recall that the public domain is the source of many of our finest and most popular works. The U.S. market is itself so large that, with both European and domestic works in the public domain here 50 years after the author's death, it alone serves as a strong creation incentive. If the new work is based on a U.S. work that is also unprotected in Europe, that new work should be a part of the continuing United States export engine in the world market. Even if the new work is based on a European work that remains under protection in Europe, popularity of the work in the United States will necessarily result in a license (to use the underlying work) in Europe, again with a net export gain to the United States.

The argument that U.S. copyright owners will unfairly "lose" royalty revenues from Europe is therefore both wrong and incomplete. It is wrong because it is not unfair that a work enter the public domain 50 years after the death of its author. It is incomplete because it does not consider that the royalties in question will be paid not just by Europeans but also by Americans, and not just to domestic copyright owners but also to copyright owners worldwide. Additional revenues to a few owners of old copyrights is not a public benefit justifying adoption of the legislation, and this remains true even though some part of those revenues would be paid by Europeans. The extension represents, rather, a heavy public cost, both in additional royalties paid by the U.S. public and in the loss of creative new works that will not be produced because the exclusive rights of copyright remain in full force on works that cost/benefit analysis would clearly place in the public domain.

VIII. Conclusion

The proposed copyright term extensions are a travesty that, if adopted into law, will become a tragedy. They are not based on the public interest but rather on private greed. Only the technical complexity of the issue and the diffuse nature of the public harm allows such proposals to move through the Congress essentially without public debate. They can be stopped, but not by a silent majority, or even a silent supermajority. Opponents of the extensions must be *heard* by Congress, with voices as loud as those seeking to prolong their parade of royalty welfare checks.

Chapter Four
New Copyright Paradigms*

by
Jessica Litman

Professor of Law
Wayne State University

The astonishing recent growth of digital networked technology has
challenged our thinking about information, authorship, and intellectual property. We've seen visionary predictions about how digital
technology could transform the ways we read, write, gain access to,
learn from, and use information.[1]

At the same time, we've witnessed parochial arguments about how
the language of copyright statutes written before the development of
the technology should be construed or revised to permit current

---

1.   *See, e.g.*, David Rothman, Teleread Home Page, URL <http://www.clark.net/pub/
      rothman/telhome.html>; David Lange, *At Play in the Fields of the Word: Copyright
      and the Construction of Authorship in the Post Literate Millennium*, 55 L. & CONTEMP.
      PROBS. 185 (Spring 1992); ETHAN KATSCH, LAW IN A DIGITAL WORLD (1995). *See also,
      e.g.*, WILLIAM GIBSON, NEUROMANCER (1984) (science fiction).

stakeholders to hang on to their current stakes in the information market. Content providers have argued that, since the copyright statute has always made commercial distributors of protected works strictly liable for infringing reproductions, online service providers should be strictly liable when their subscribers transmit infringing reproductions.[2] Representatives of copyright holders have insisted that since the privilege to loan, give, or sell a copy of a protected work has never permitted one to make additional reproductions, the privilege is and ought to be inapplicable to digital transmissions, since they, by necessity, involve the creation of temporary reproductions in computer memory.[3] Libraries and educators are not blameless here; they too have been arguing that we should reconfigure the language of the law to ensure that it continues to be legal for them to do all the things they now do, and their digital equivalents.[4]

---

2.   *See, e.g.*, William Cook, *Be Wary of Internet Casting Shadows on Copyright Holders,* CHI. LAW., April 1996, at 60; *Copyright Protection on the Internet: Hearing on H.R. 2441 Before the Courts and Intell. Property Subcomm. of the House Comm. on the Judiciary,* 104th Cong., 2d Sess. (Feb. 7, 1996) [hereinafter *Hearing,* Feb. 7, 1996] (testimony of Edward P. Murphy, National Music Publishers' Association) (available on LEXIS, NEWS Library, SCRIPT file; also at URL <http://www.cic.org/testimony/nmpa.html>).

3.   *See, e.g., NII Copyright Protection Act of 1995: Hearing on H.R. 2441 Before the Subcomm. on Courts and Intellectual Property of the House Comm. on the Judiciary,* 104th Cong., 2d Sess. (Feb. 8, 1996) [hereinafter *Hearing,* Feb, 8, 1996] (statement of Barbara A. Munder, Information Industry Association) (available on LEXIS, NEWS library, SCRIPT file). *See also NII Copyright Protection Act of 1995: Joint Hearing on H.R. 2441 and S. 1284 Before The Subcomm. on Courts and Intell. Property of the House Judiciary Comm. and the Senate Judiciary Comm.,* 104th Cong., 1st Sess. (Nov. 15, 1995) [hereinafter *Hearing,* Nov. 15, 1995] (statement of Mihaly Ficsor, WIPO) (available on LEXIS, NEWS library, SCRIPT file).

4.   *See, e.g., Statement on Behalf of the American Association of Law Libraries, the American Library Association, the Association of Research Libraries, the Medical Library Association and the Special Library Association on H.R. 2441: The NII Copyright Protection Act of 1995: Hearing Before the Subcomm. on Courts and Intell. Property of the House Comm. on the Judiciary,* 104th Cong, 2d Sess. (Feb. 8, 1996) (available at URL <http://www.ari.net/dfc/libraries.html#AALL>); *Public Hearing at Andrew Mellon Auditorium Before the Information Infrastructure Task Force Working Group on Intellectual Property Rights* 62–64 (Sept. 22, 1994) [hereinafter *Public Hearing,* Sept. 22, 1994] (testimony of Lucretia McClure, Medical Libraries Association); *Hearing,* Feb. 8, 1996, *supra* note 3 (testimony of Jeanne Hurley Simon, U.S. National Commission on Libraries and Information Science).

       I don't exempt myself from this criticism. I have made the same sort of balance arguments in opposition to pending legislation. *See, e.g., Public Hearing,* Sept. 22, 1994, *supra,* at 66–67 (testimony of Jessica Litman). Indeed, as a member of the

I want to offer a few (possibly incendiary) ideas in this debate. The first one is that if what we really want is to preserve the current legal balance among uses of protected works that are subject to the copyright holder's legal control, uses that are free to all comers, and uses that are privileged for a well-defined class of users, the problem is trivially easy to solve. Drafting legislative language to extend current proscriptions and privileges to cover their functional equivalents in networked digital environments on functionally equivalent terms is an easy task in any case in which we can agree on the scope of current proscriptions and privileges, and an achievable one even in most cases in which we can't agree. Most of the proposals that have been introduced under the aegis of mere clarification and extension, however, have been nothing of the sort; rather, they have been attempts to expand current stakeholders' preserves by annexing territory that seems not yet claimed. The characterization of those proposals as maintaining or restoring the preexisting balance is mere rhetorical flourish.[5]

If what we sought were merely to extend the preexisting balance, doing so would be straightforward. I don't think that's what anyone actually wants; rather, the status quo stands in here as a way to argue for what is really an improvement in one's position, and as a fall-back, compromise position to which one is willing to retreat. It seems likely that a critical mass of stakeholders will ultimately find themselves agreeing that they could live with something not too distant from the current balance. Something that at least *seems* akin to the present balance, then, is more likely to emerge from the political process than proposals that diverge further from current law. As of this writing, interest groups affected by copyright from all points along the spectrum are expending enormous reserves of energy to make the case that the proposals they support are the ones that most nearly capture the spirit of the status quo.[6] Let me suggest, however, that the legal status

---

steering committee of the Digital Future Coalition, I have helped to frame arguments that cast the dispute in these terms.

5. This criticism is explored more fully in James Boyle, *Overregulating the Internet*, WASH. TIMES, Nov. 14, 1995, at A17; Jessica Litman, *The Exclusive Right to Read*, 13 CARDOZO ARTS & ENT. L.J. 27 (1994); Pamela Samuelson, *The Copyright Grab*, WIRED 4.01, Jan. 1996, at 134.

6. *See, e.g.,* Creative Incentive Coalition Home Page, <http://www.cic.org/>; Digital Future Coalition home page, <http://www.ari.net/dfc>; Home Recording Rights Coalition home page, <http://www.access.digex.net/~hrrc/>; Jon Newcomb,

quo ought to be abandoned, and that copyright law should be replaced with something different from any actual copyright law this country has ever had on its books.

I. The Current Balance and How it Grew

The last several years have seen a flurry of activity directed toward revising the copyright laws to fit them around digital technology. Most of the effort thus far, both on the United States' national stage and in the international arena, has seemed to be aimed at making the Internet and its descendants safe for the current proprietors of copyrighted material. The U.S. Department of Commerce, egged on by a coalition of organizations representing copyright owners, released a White Paper report in September 1995 that argued that the copyright statute then on the books secured to copyright owners extraordinarily expansive control of uses of their works over digital networks. The White Paper recommended a few statutory amendments predicated on the assumption that modest changes in statutory wording would be all that was needed to nail those expansive rights down.[7] The suggested legislation was introduced immediately in the House and Senate, where it attracted bipartisan support.[8] As of this writing, it is uncertain whether the legislation will pass. Similar proposals have been introduced by the United States as the basis for an international treaty[9]; it is not currently clear whether the U.S. Department of Commerce can persuade the rest of the world to sign on to its vision.

The substance of the proposals is critiqued elsewhere in this volume.[10] It seems likely that they would result in a transformation of

---

Rants & Raves: The Copyright Grab Bag, WIRED 4.04, Apr. 1996, at 30 (letter to the editor from the president of Simon and Schuster).

7.   INTELLECTUAL PROPERTY AND THE NATIONAL INFORMATION INFRASTRUCTURE: THE REPORT OF THE WORKING GROUP ON INTELLECTUAL PROPERTY RIGHTS (1995) [hereinafter White Paper].

8.   S. 1284, 104th Cong., 1st Sess. (1995); H.R. 2441, 104th Cong., 1st Sess. (1995).

9.   *Hearing,* Nov. 15, 1995, *supra* note 3 (testimony of Mihaly Ficsor, WIPO); *Hearing,* Feb. 7, 1996, *supra* note 2 (testimony of Ed Black, Computer and Communications Industry Ass'n); *National Information Infrastructure: Hearing on S. 1284 Before the Senate Judiciary Comm.,* 104th Cong., 2d Sess. (May 7, 1996) [hereinafter *Hearing,* May 7, 1996] (testimony of Robert Oakley, Digital Future Coalition) (available on LEXIS, NEWS library, SCRIPT file).

10.   *See infra* Chapter Thirteen, "Building Partnerships for Change," by Prudence S. Adler (Appendix III, at p. 281).

the relationship our copyright law bears to our larger information policy. The supporters of the proposals endorse them without being willing, so far, to engage in discussion of their policy consequences. Instead, the strategy of copyright holders has been to insist that Congress made all the relevant policy choices twenty years ago, when the Internet was barely a gleam in the eye of the U.S. Department of Defense.[11] When policy questions are raised, the supporters of the White Paper have taken refuge in technicalities.

U.S. copyright law has long-standing, uncontroversial privileges and exemptions that, for example, allow one to read, view, listen or browse works without asking for permission, or allow one to lend, rent or resell copies of works one owns. The White Paper report interprets current law to subject activities like browsing documents on the Internet to the copyright holder's exclusive control, beyond the shelter of most exemptions and privileges.[12] Instead of addressing the significant policy concerns that would arise from expanding the copyright owner's control to encompass every act of reading, the White Paper and its supporters explain that the current copyright statute gives copyright holders exclusive control over reproduction of works in copies, and that each appearance of any work in the volatile memory of any computer anywhere is a reproduction in a copy within the meaning of the statute, and therefore the copyright owner's to license or forbid.[13] Instead of explaining the rationale for restricting the loan of electronic documents to exclude online transfers entirely, the White Paper and its supporters insist that any transfer of a document through transmission necessarily involves the reproduction of the

---

11. *See, e.g., Public Hearing,* Sept. 23, 1994, at 4–7 [hereinafter *Public Hearing,* Sept. 23, 1994] (testimony of Steven J. Metalitz, Information Industry Association).

12. *See* White Paper, *supra* note 7, at 64–100; *Hearing,* Nov. 15, 1995, *supra* note 3 (testimony of Bruce Lehman, Commissioner of Patents). The commissioner has conceded that the elusive privilege of fair use would continue to be available in appropriate cases. The White Paper, however, both interprets fair use very narrowly and suggests that the development of technological tracking and licensing systems will reduce the scope of the fair use privilege online. *See* White Paper, *supra* note 7, at 73–82.

13. *See, e.g., Hearing,* Feb. 8, 1996, *supra* note 3 (statement of Barbara A. Munder, Information Industry Association); White Paper, *supra* note 7, at 64–66.

document in volatile computer memory, and would therefore be illegal unless licensed.[14]

The consequences of the White Paper's vision of the law would be to give the owners of copyrights broad powers to license or prohibit a wide variety of uses that are not currently within their legal control. To the extent that the proponents of this view address its policy implications at all, they assert, without much justification, that without extensive control over the uses of their works, proprietors will decline to make their material available on the information highway.[15] For the most part, though, the defenders of the proposals have claimed that it is current law, passed by Congress lo these many years ago (rather than they), that strikes the balance where they insist it be struck.[16]

A number of commentators have addressed the vulnerabilities of these technical arguments on technical grounds—and there are many.[17] Some have criticized the proposals on policy grounds as well.[18] In response to the criticism, the White Paper's supporters have insisted that any policy consequences result directly from the language of the current law, and are therefore, one would gather, out of bounds. While I believe that the depiction of current law in the White Paper report is distorted, and that distortion is deliberate,[19] I also would argue that the aversion to serious policy discussion is a terrible mistake.

---

14. *See* White Paper, *supra* note 7, at 92–95; *Hearing*, May 7, 1996, *supra* note 9 (testimony of Kenneth R. Kay, Creative Incentive Coalition).

15. *See Hearing*, Nov. 15, 1995, *supra* note 3 (testimony of Bruce Lehman, Commissioner of Patents); *Hearing*, Feb. 7, 1996, *supra* note 2 (testimony of Frances Preston, BMI).

16. *See, e.g., Hearing*, May 7, 1996, *supra* note 9 (testimony of John Bettis, ASCAP); *id.* (testimony of Dan Burton, Novell).

17. *See, e.g.,* JAMES BOYLE, SHAMANS, SOFTWARE, AND SPLEENS: LAW AND THE CONSTRUCTION OF THE INFORMATION SOCIETY 135–39 (1996); J. David Loundy, *Bill to Amend Copyright Act Needs Work,* CHI. DAILY L. BULL., Oct. 12, 1995, at 6; Pamela Samuelson, *Legally Speaking: The NII Intellectual Property Report,* 37 COMM. OF THE ACM, Dec. 1994, at 12.

18. *See* James Boyle, *Is Congress Turning the Internet into an Information Toll Road,* WASH. TIMES, Jan. 15, 1996, at 24; Leslie A. Kurtz, *Copyright and the National Information Infrastructure in the United States,* 18 EUR. INTELL. PROP. REV. 120 (1996); Pamela Samuelson, *supra* note 5, at 137; Diane Leenheer Zimmerman, *Copyright in Cyberspace: Don't Throw Out the Public Interest with the Bath Water,* 1994 ANN. SURV. AM. L. 403.

19. *See* Jessica Litman, *Revising Copyright Law for the Information Age,* 75 OR. L. REV. 19, 20–25, 35–38 (1996); Litman, *supra* note 5.

Copyright lawyers are, among other things, technicians. We have invested huge resources in a process for drafting legislation that places a premium on arguing from precedent and technicalities, and seeking consensus among copyright owner and commercial user interests, whether or not that consensus makes sense. The proponents of the White Paper's proposals seem no longer to even understand objections of the form: "The rule you suggest would make lending libraries, or long distance teaching, or private browsing illegal." They have responded not with arguments explaining why lending libraries, or long-distance learning, or private browsing ought to be illegal, or at least licensed, in the brave new world, but instead by maintaining that that's the way the technicality crumbles: "That's not new, it's because of long copyright precedent," they've said, "it results in a 'reproduction,' you see, and copyright holders have control over reproductions."[20]

It is easy to be seduced by arguments like these. Copyright professionals have lived with the copyright law's peculiar collection of categories, divisions, and cubbyholes for so long that we often forget how little intuitive sense they make to the uninitiated, while copyright naifs can often be persuaded that they simply don't have a clue about the way the rules work. It's important to understand, though, that the current copyright balance is not the product of some magic process for discerning Truth and Beauty; we have arrived at our current law through a combination of accident and the self-interested efforts of copyright affected industries.

The history of copyright legislation has been characterized by multilateral bargaining among affected stakeholders. Some of the provisions in the current statute are there because affected interest groups asked for them, and other groups didn't object. Others are the result of hard-fought bargains among affected interests. The resulting law grew by accretion, as new groups showed up to propose new provisions, and affected interests struck new bargains among themselves. Often the lines were drawn where they were because those lines were most acceptable to the interests that showed up at the bargaining

---

20. *See, e.g., Hearing,* Feb. 8, 1996, *supra* note 3 (statement of Barbara A. Munder, Information Industry Association).

table.[21] When a statute reflects the results of private bargaining, though, it is instructive to pay attention to interests that were not well represented in the bargaining. Library groups were there; they asked for and got the reproduction privileges embodied in section 108 of the statute.[22] Educators were there; they asked for and got both specific (if very limited) privileges related to classroom performance and long-distance education,[23] and a detailed discussion, inserted in the statute's legislative history, of multiple copying for classroom use within the shelter of the fair use doctrine.[24]

The general public was not there, and a variety of entities purporting to speak on its behalf were busy with more specific concerns. Library groups and educators focused on threats to their common, everyday activities. Congress and the Copyright Office paid more attention to encouraging the diverse private groups to compromise on something, anything, than they did to asking how the details of the compromises would affect individual members of the public. Another large class of interests that couldn't be there were the copyright-affected businesses and institutions that did not yet exist, because they would be brought into being with the birth of new media. There were no commercial Internet service providers in the early 1970s. The World Wide Web was not yet a glimmer in Tim Berners-Lee's eye, and there could be no web page designers at the table. Finally, a careful analysis of the ways the current law meets and fails to meet the needs of interested parties, and the ways that it has done so through U.S. history, reveals that the interests who were at the bargaining table cannot even be deemed rough proxies for the interests not yet in being.[25] Instead, the upstart companies-to-be were routinely disadvantaged by the bargains, because the private parties crafting the statute understood that it was in none of their interests to give potential new competitors any sort of break.

---

21. This analysis is documented in detail in Jessica Litman, *Copyright Legislation and Technological Change*, 68 OR. L. REV. 275 (1989), and Jessica Litman, *Copyright, Compromise and Legislative History*, 72 CORNELL L. REV. 877 (1987).

22. 17 U.S.C. § 108 (1994).

23. *See* 17 U.S.C. §§ 110 (1)–(2), 112(b).

24. *See* H.R. REP NO. 94-1476, 94th Cong., 2d Sess. 66–72 (1976).

25. *See generally* Litman, *Copyright Legislation and Technological Change*, *supra* note 21.

If current stakeholders, then, report that they are well-pleased with the laws now on the books, it is hardly surprising. If they insist that under no circumstances should we think of replacing that law with a new one, it is what we ought to expect. When they characterize the provisions of current law, however, as embodying sacred policy concerns that make our country great, we should listen more skeptically than we do. The current balance embodied in the copyright law works fairly well, all things considered, but we arrived at it more by accident than by design. We ought at least to consider whether we might do better if we were willing to give it up.

II. A Couple of Easy Fixes

Having said that, I would like to offer a couple of examples to back up my argument that it would not be very difficult to arrive at language that writes specific aspects of the current copyright balance into the law by extending current doctrine to functionally equivalent activities in new media. The rhetoric coming from both sides in this debate invokes the gods of balance. Technological development is said to have altered the balance embodied in the law.[26] The White Paper's proposals are said to be designed to alter that same balance.[27] Both charges are well founded. If our principal goal were to maintain (or restore) the balance enacted by Congress in 1976, however, drafting responsive amendments would not be a difficult task.

The first-sale doctrine is exemplary: the doctrine terminates the copyright owner's control over distribution of a particular copy of a work after the first authorized distribution. It was devised by courts in the 19th century[28] in response to copyright owners' efforts to prohibit or control the resale of second-hand books. It provides a copyright exemption without which lending libraries, art galleries, videotape rental stores, and second-hand bookstores would all be illegal. The first-sale doctrine encourages the operation of secondary markets for

---

26. *See Hearing*, Nov. 15, 1995, *supra* note 3 (testimony of Bruce Lehman, Commissioner of Patents and Trademarks).

27. *See, e.g., Hearing*, Feb. 8, 1996, *supra* note 3 (testimony of Jeanne Hurley Simon, U.S. National Commission on Libraries and Information Science); *Hearing*, Feb. 7, 1996, *supra* note 2 (testimony of Edward Black, Computer & Communications Industry Association).

28. *See, e.g.,* Harrison v. Maynard, Merril & Co., 61 F. 689 (2d Cir. 1894).

access to copyrighted works, while preserving the copyright owner's opportunity to demand compensation for the first distribution of any given copy. The same limitation allows the purchaser of a newspaper to pass it on to a friend or drop it in the recycle pile; it permits the recipient of a letter to show it to a colleague or donate it to a library. The copyright owner is thus entitled to a reasonable opportunity to seek compensation without being able to control all uses of his or her protected work, and without being able to seek rents from all people who may see, hear, listen to, read, use, or own a copy of it.

The authors of the White Paper have been adamant that the first-sale doctrine should not apply in connection with digital communications. The problem, they've insisted, is a technical one. The first-sale doctrine has always permitted the owner of a copy to dispose of that copy by resale, by loan, and in most cases,[29] even by rental. It has not, however, permitted the owner of a copy to make reproductions of the legitimate copy and also dispose of them. Since it is not possible, as a technical matter, to transmit a copy of a document without causing a further digital reproduction, the first-sale doctrine cannot permit any transfer of documents by electronic transmission. Thus, while it may be legal under current law for a library patron to walk up the steps of the New York Public Library and read the library's copy of this book, or even check it out and hand carry it back home, it is not and should not be legal to dial up the New York Public Library and peruse the text online or borrow a copy via electronic transmission.[30]

Instead of accepting that the first-sale doctrine is inapplicable in the digital context because of a technicality, we might look for a functionally equivalent privilege that would permit the first-sale doctrine

---

29.　As enacted in 1976, the first-sale doctrine codified in 17 U.S.C. section 109 privileged rentals as well as other transfers of possession. In response to complaints from the record and software industry that rental of their works facilitated infringing reproduction on a broad scale, Congress enacted the Record Rental Amendments of 1984, Pub. L. No. 98-450, 98 Stat. 1727 (1984), and the Computer Software Rental Amendments Act of 1990, Pub. L. No. 101-650, 104 Stat. 5089, 5134 §§ 801–804. *See* Jessica Litman, *Copyright and Information Policy,* 55 LAW & CONTEMP. PROBS. 185, 188–89 (Spring 1992). The current version of section 109 restricts commercial rental of phonorecords and software, but not of other works.

30.　*Public Hearing,* Sept. 23, 1994, *supra* note 11, at 8–11 (testimony of Paul Aiken, Authors League of America). *See, e.g., Hearing,* Sept. 22, 1994, *supra* note 4, at 48–49 (testimony of Ann Harkins, Creative Incentive Coalition); White Paper, *supra* note 7, at 92–94.

to continue to operate so that the secondary market in access to protected works could be preserved. If the only barrier were the technical one that is so often mentioned, it would be trivial to overcome. One need only amend the statute to include a provision that transmission of a single copy is within the first-sale privilege so long as the transmitter destroys his or her original copy. In fact, such language has been proposed.[31] An influential group representing copyright holders, which has been one of the White Paper's most ardent champions, dismissed the proposal without analysis as "completely unworkable and virtually impossible to enforce."[32]

Another central tenet of copyright law is the distinction between unprotected idea and protected expression. Copyright protects only the expression embodied in a work and not the ideas, procedures, processes, systems, methods of operation, concepts, principles, or discoveries the work expresses.[33] To ensure that members of the public have access to the unprotected underlying ideas, methods, and processes contained in protected works, courts have privileged reproduction of the protected expression when it is necessary to reproduce or decipher the unprotected elements.[34]

Critics of the White Paper have argued that while the amendments on the table don't threaten the idea/expression dichotomy in terms, they

---

31. The Digital Future Coalition proposed that the following text be added to section 109:

> The privilege set forth in subsection (a) extends to any transmission of a single copy or phonorecord so long as the transmitter erases or destroys his or her copy or phonorecord at substantially the same time. The reproduction of a work, to the extent required to exercise this privilege, is not an infringement.

Hearing, May 7, 1996, *supra* note 9 (testimony of Robert Oakley, Digital Future Coalition).

32. *See Hearing,* May 7, 1996, *supra* note 9 (testimony of Kenneth R. Kay, Creative Incentive Coalition). It seems difficult to understand why the proposal would be any harder to enforce than a privilege to transmit works whenever the fair use doctrine would permit the transmission, something Mr. Kay insisted that the proposed amendments would in no way restrict. *See id.*

33. 17 U.S.C. § 102(b) (1994).

34. *E.g.,* Baker v. Selden, 101 U.S. 99 (1879); Sega Enters., Ltd. v. Accolade, Inc., 977 F.2d 1510 (9th Cir. 1992); Atari Games Corp. v. Nintendo of America, Inc., 975 F. 2d 832 (Fed. Cir. 1992).

promise to make it irrelevant.[35] A proposed new section of the copyright law would encourage publishers to use technological means to make their works unreproduceable, and would impose penalties for the manufacture or sale of devices, or the provision of services, that defeat copy protection—regardless of whether the users of such devices or services needed them to make copies that would have been privileged because of the idea/expression dichotomy.[36] While the public may continue to have a legal right to copy protected expression to decipher the ideas and facts it contains, the devices required to do so may be unobtainable. It would be easy enough to add language to the statute recognizing that the public has an affirmative right to gain access to, extract, use, and reuse the ideas, facts, information, and other public domain material embodied in protected works. That affirmative right should include a privilege to reproduce, adapt, transmit, perform, or display so much of the protected expression as is required to gain access to the unprotected elements. Yet, so far, even lobbies that style themselves as public advocates have not proposed language to that effect.

Indeed, if it were merely a technicality that threatened the public's longstanding assurance that it may browse, view, watch, and read copyright works without seeking permission, we could resolve that problem easily. The basis for the argument that any appearance of a work in the random access memory of any computer anywhere constitutes an actionable reproduction is a handful of cases, arguably misreading the statutory language in the context of commercial disputes. In search of a handle for liability, these courts relied on the exclusive reproduction right as a catch-all right that captures every appearance of any digital work in the memory of a computer.[37] The authors of the White Paper

---

35.   *See, e.g.*, Pamela Samuelson, *Technological Protection for Copyrighted Works*, EMORY L.J. (forthcoming, 1997).

36.   The Creative Incentive Coalition recently joined the chorus of copyright owner lobbies that have requested that circumvention of copyright protection technology be a crime. *See Hearing*, May 7, 1996, *supra* note 9 (testimony of Kenneth R. Kay, Creative Incentive Coalition); *see also Hearing*, Feb. 7, 1996, *supra* note 2 (testimony of Barbara Munder, Information Industry Association); *id.* (testimony of Jack Valenti, Motion Picture Association of America).

37.   *See* MAI Systems Corp. v. Peak Computer, Inc., 991 F.2d 511 (9th Cir. 1993); Triad Sys. Corp. v. Southeastern Express Co., 1994 U.S. Dist. LEXIS 5390 (N.D. Cal.), *aff'd in relevant part*, 1995 U.S. App. LEXIS 24426 (9th Cir.), *cert. denied*, 116 S. Ct. 1015 (1996); Advanced Computer Servs. v. MAI Sys. Corp., 845 F. Supp. 356 (E.D. Va. 1994). The opinions have been widely criticized. *See, e.g.*, Samuelson, *supra* note 17.

seized on this interpretation as the correct one. They insist that it applies to private individuals as well as commercial actors.[38] It seems obvious, though, that that cannot be what Congress meant when it enacted the language back in 1976.[39] It seems equally clear that the problem is easy to repair. Ephemeral reproductions in volatile computer memory need not be deemed "copies" under the statute at all, and clarifying language to that effect would be straightforward.[40]

The crux of the dispute is not, of course, that we can't solve the technical problems that threaten to upset copyright law's longstanding balance between owners and users of protected material. The controversy instead reveals a deep division over whether the current balance struck by the law is the appropriate one.

III. A More Basic Question

Current copyright stakeholders have their eyes on the size of their slices of pie. The question of what balance *should* be embodied in the copyright law is liable to get lost in the bickering. In the current scheme of things, it is nobody's job to look out for what "should" be the law.[41] But the question deserves to be asked more thoughtfully than the reflexive invocation it commonly receives as a prelude to an argument that the copyright law needs to be further clarified in the speaker's favor.[42] To determine what balance the copyright law should strike, we need to step back from seeking close analogues to activities and devices that current law deems lawful or infringing.

Rather than diverting our attention with debates over whether personal computers are indeed akin to printing presses, or copyright protection devices mere siblings to automobile door locks, we need to ask

---

38. *See* White Paper, *supra* note 7, at 64–66.

39. *See* Litman, *supra* note 5, at 40–43.

40. Congress could add the following sentence to the definition of copy in 17 U.S.C. § 101: "The ephemeral reproduction of a work in computer memory or temporary digital storage is not a copy." Alternatively, Congress could add a new statutory provision giving members of the public a privilege to make ephemeral copies. *See* Litman, *supra* note 19.

41. For a discussion of why this doesn't seem to be Congress's job, see Litman, *supra* note 5, at 53–54 (1994). For a discussion of what such an inquiry might look like, see Litman, *supra* note 19.

42. *See, e.g., Hearing*, Feb. 8, 1996, *supra* note 3 (testimony of Richard Robinson, Association of American Publishers).

more basic questions. Here is one: The essential balance embodied in the copyright law, which has been characterized variously by an assortment of actors, is a balance between giving copyright holders enough control over their works to permit them to exploit them commercially, and allowing the rest of the world sufficient access to those works to permit us all to read, see, listen to, use, reuse, learn from, and build on them, and thus promote the progress of science and useful arts. The copyright laws we have relied on until now pegged the owner's control to reproduction, because that made functional sense. In a digital world, it may not. If we want a copyright law that balances copyright owners' control with public access in a way that enables all of us to use copyrighted works and to create new ones, are there ways to define the nature of that control and access that are more suitable for a digital age?

IV. Current Law and Digital Technology

For those who spend their hours interacting with digital media, a surprising consensus has begun to appear that the copyright law doesn't make much sense in the digital environment, because it is based on the model of a reproduction, or copy, as the essential compensable unit (that's why we call it a "copy"right law), and, in a digital medium, a copy no longer measures anything very useful. Supporters of more expansive copyright laws have begun to call for new rights to "access" and "use" protected works to supplement rights to make copies; supporters of more measured copyright laws have suggested the express recognition of privileges to "browse" and "transmit," even if they result in the creation of temporary copies. Those who post grave pronouncements on the Internet to the effect that copyright is dead rest much of their argument on the fact that reproduction in digital memory is a crucial element in the functioning of digital technology.[43]

If we could put aside the frightening question of what we might devise to replace the basic copyright right to reproduce a protected work in copies (and momentarily exclude from the room all the people who have invested substantial capital in becoming more expert than

---

43.   See, e.g., John Perry Barlow, *The Economy of Ideas: A Framework for Rethinking Patents and Copyrights in the Digital Age (Everything You Know About Intellectual Property Is Wrong)*, WIRED, Mar. 1994, at 84.

most in the ins, outs, and arounds of the current system), we might find surprising agreement on the point that the basic reproductive unit no longer measures anything very important. What keeps us from recognizing that agreement is a longstanding polarization among communities interested in copyright, which leads each camp to distrust the other camps' agendas. Representatives of copyright holders, one suspects, will use any occasion as an opportunity to enhance their control over nearly all uses of their works. Representatives of schools and libraries, in contrast, might approach any proposal as an opportunity to enlarge the free-use zone they exploit without paying authors and publishers their due. Certainly if one reads the rhetoric emerging from opposing camps, it supports this view of reality.[44] The rhetoric suggests that the habit of distrust among opposing interests in realm of copyright lobbying is too ingrained to fade easily or soon.

Nonetheless, the group most drastically affected by the application of copyright law to the new digital technology is neither the publishers and their friends nor the libraries and their friends, but individual users making noncommercial, consumptive use of copyrighted works from their homes and offices. They have no formal alliances with any of the familiar stakeholders, although stakeholders have claimed to represent them for most of this century.[45] From the public's point of view, the most notable part of the copyright reinterpretation proposed by the White Paper is its insistence that rules that were drafted with the needs of commercial and institutional actors in mind, and that for 200 years applied principally to those actors, should henceforth control ordinary, private, noncommercial behavior as well.

Copyright law has always, officially, extended to all users of protected material rather than just commercial users. Even so, at least in the United States, copyright owners have rarely sought to enforce the law against individual end users. So long as the law, as a practical matter, constrains only copyright-intensive businesses and institutions

---

44. *See, e.g., Hearing*, Feb. 7, 1996, *supra* note 2 (testimony of Barbara A. Munder, Information Industry Ass'n); *Hearing*, May 7, 1996, *supra* note 9 (testimony of Kenneth R. Kay, Creative Incentive Coalition); David Rothman, Teleread Update #6: *Copyright Czar Threatens to "Destroy" Law Professor*, URL <http://www.clark.net/pub/rothman/update6.html>.

45. *See* Litman, *Copyright Legislation and Technological Change*, *supra* note 21, at 311–16; *Public Hearing*, Sept. 22, 1994, *supra* note 4, at 66–67 (testimony of Jessica Litman, Wayne State University).

who know that they need to hire copyright lawyers, it is unprob-
lematic for the law to be arcane, specific, detailed, technical, and
counter-intuitive. Just as digital technology promises and threatens to
permit any member of the public to act as his or her own publisher, it
also promises and threatens to subject every member of the public to
the provisions of a copyright law that was drafted by copyright
lawyers with no attention to the question whether it could make any
sense to the public at large, by which I mean folks who don't have and
don't yet realize they need a copyright lawyer. Anyone who curls up
in front of the fire for a cozy evening reading Title 17 of the United
States Code will soon conclude that the provisions of the current law
are unsuitable for that extension. If copyright rules are henceforth to
apply to everyday, ordinary behavior, we need to reformulate those
rules with that goal in mind. We need to make the rules much simpler.
We need to gauge copyright infringement in different terms. Most
fundamentally, I would argue, we need to fasten on some measure of
a copyright holders' rights other than the familiar reproduction. The
act of reproducing is no longer a useful proxy for the question whether
a copyright owner's incentives have been injured, or even insulted. We
need to consider alternatives to measuring copyright infringement in
terms of unauthorized copies.

V. Persistent Public Notions

There's another problem with merely extending a general rule against
reproduction to proscribe every unlicensed appearance of a copyrighted work in the memory of any computer anywhere. That rule
will strike the millions of individuals whose behavior it's intended to
affect as nonsensical. Very little systematic research about the public's
views of copyright has been conducted, because most of the entities
with sizable financial investments in copyright-affected activities have
already known what views they'd prefer the public to have, and have
therefore skipped directly to the guidance and instruction portion of
their agendas.[46]

---

46.   *See, e.g., Public Hearing at U.C.L.A. Before the Information Infrastructure Task Force*
       Working Group on Intellectual Property Rights 14–16 (Sept. 16, 1994) (testimony of
       Robert Simons, Dialog Information Services); *Public Hearing*, Sept. 23, 1994, *supra*
       note 11, at 17–18 (testimony of Heather Florence, Bantam, Doubleday, Dell); *Public*

Members of the public, however, appear to have formed their own views, and those views have been resistant to guidance and instruction.[47] There is not much empirical evidence showing what the general American public believes copyright laws to say, but there is some.[48] That evidence indicates that people have fairly well-formed views about copyright, and that they are stubborn about hanging onto them. Most notably, people appear to believe that copyright laws make sense— even when they don't. Sometimes, at least, people respond to copyright provisions that don't seem to make any sense by assuming that they can't really be the law.[49] In any event, such empirical evidence as I've seen indicates that, in the United States, there is a persistent sentiment that private, personal use of copyrighted works is outside of the copyright law's boundaries.[50] People insist that copyright law only covers commercial activities—that nonprofit or even consumptive private uses of copyrighted works are exempt from the law's reach.

People who assume that the folks who write laws try to make them make sense can be forgiven for supposing that copyright laws draw the lines where they draw them for good reason; and it is surely understandable that they believe that one of those lines separates noncommercial private activity from commercial uses. Noncommercial users are, after all, seldom sued. When they are sued, they frequently lack the resources to litigate, and simply roll over and play dead, generating no precedents for the casebooks. Those who find the resources to litigate often believe that they have compelling fair use arguments in their favor; sometimes they're right.

Implicit in most of the proposals on the table is that the public needs to be educated to understand that unlicensed individual, private,

---

Hearing, Sept. 22, 1994, *supra* note 4, at 49–50 (testimony of Ann Harkins, Creative Incentive Coalition); White Paper, *supra* note 7, at 201–10.

47.   *See* Litman, *supra* note 5.

48.   *See* OFFICE OF TECHNOLOGY ASSESSMENT, U.S. CONGRESS, COPYRIGHT & HOME COPYING: TECHNOLOGY CHALLENGES THE LAW 163–65 (1989); OFFICE OF TECHNOLOGY ASSESSMENT, U.S. CONGRESS, INTELLECTUAL PROPERTY RIGHTS IN AN AGE OF ELECTRONICS AND INFORMATION 121–23, 208–09 (1986); THE POLICY PLANNING GROUP, YANKELOVICH, SKELLY & WHITE, INC., PUBLIC PERCEPTIONS OF THE "INTELLECTUAL PROPERTY RIGHTS" ISSUE (1985) (OTA Contractor Report).

49.   *See* Jessica Litman, *Copyright Noncompliance (or Why We Can't "Just Say Yes" to Licensing)*, 29 N.Y.U. J. INT'L L. & POL. __ (forthcoming, 1997).

50.   *See* sources cited *supra* note 48.

noncommercial use is and ought to be illegal in most cases. Ambitious educational programs have been proposed to persuade the public of the rightness of such a view.[51] To the extent that the public's views are deeply held, we should, I would argue, try to work with them rather than bludgeoning them into submission. Since most end users have, until now, been effectively immune from copyright liability—either because the law privileges their uses of copyrighted works[52] or because copyright owners choose not to enforce their rights against individuals making private use of protected works, copyright holders lose little that they really own by shaping the rules that apply to individuals around existing expectations and copyright norms.

VI. A Right of Commercial Exploitation

I suggest that we begin by asking whether we could design a workable copyright-like law that accords with public perceptions rather than contradicting them. One of the most persistent misimpressions the public has is that copyright law only covers commercial activities— that nonprofit or even private consumptive uses of copyrighted works are exempt from the law's reach. That has never been the law, but people believe it anyway. And, in fact, if you look only at how the law has been enforced over the past 200 years, it's a pretty good description of actual outcomes, since very few noncommercial actors have been worthwhile lawsuit targets—lawsuits are expensive.

So, let's start there. If we are really trying to come up with a law that applies to the public at large, we could jettison the basic reproductive unit entirely, and recast the bundle of rights in a copyright as a right of commercial exploitation. (I concede that if copyright stops being about the right to make *copies* we might need to think up a different name for it.) Making money (or trying to) from someone else's work without permission would be infringement, as would large-scale interference with the copyright holders' opportunities to do so.[53] That

---

51. *See* White Paper, *supra* note 7, at 203–10.

52. *See, e.g.,* Sony Corp. of Am. v. Universal City Studios, 464 U.S. 417 (1984); 17 U.S.C. § 1008 (1994).

53. What I mean by "large-scale interference" is the sort of routine free use of educational materials by educational institutions, for example, that essentially vitiates copyright holders' commercial opportunities in substantial portions of their markets. We need some sort of exception of this ilk to avoid completely destroying

means that we would get rid of our current bundle-of-rights way of thinking about copyright infringement. We would stop asking whether somebody's actions resulted in the creation of a "material object . . . in which a work is fixed by any method now known or later developed,"[54] and ask instead what effect those actions had on the copyright holder's commercial exploitation.

One can't make a rule that's that general without relying on common-law lawmaking for a lot of embroidery. So one potential drawback of my proposal is that it would replace the bright lines in the current statute with a lot of uncertainty. The current set of statutory bright lines, through, while specific and detailed, are not particularly clear. The application of much of the statute's language to current activities is problematic.[55] The statute seems to make a variety of common, everyday, consumptive uses of copyrighted material illegal, but everyone knows that there is an undefined and largely unacknowledged free zone of people like your next-door neighbor who duplicates his wife's authorized copy of Windows 95® rather than buying his own from the computer store. Your neighbor's behavior is technically infringing and is very, very common. He is not at all likely to find himself the target of an infringement suit. It's not clear what a court would do with such a suit if it got one.[56]

---

the markets for works such as textbooks that are marketed primarily to non-commercial actors. At the same time, I would distinguish the sort of behavior that does not itself work a large-scale interference, but that might be argued to threaten one if it became widespread, like the computer bulletin board run by David LaMacchia. *See* United States v. LaMacchia, 871 F. Supp. 535 (D. Mass. 1994). While it may be the case that hundreds of bulletin boards like David LaMacchia's, if aggregated, might represent a large interference, there's no good reason to impose liability for the aggregate on Mr. LaMacchia. Common small-scale interference with commercial opportunities should not be actionable under this standard.

54.   *See* 17 U.S.C. § 101 (1994).

55.   *See, e.g.,* Barlow, *supra* note 43; Litman, *Copyright Legislation and Technological Change, supra* note 21, at 342–56.

56.   The mostly nearly analogous case is Sony Corp. of America v. Universal City Studios, Inc., 464 U.S. 417 (1984). In addition to suing the manufacturers, distributors, and retailers of videotape recorders, plaintiff motion picture studios joined an individual VCR user as a defendant, although without any intention of seeking to collect infringement damages from him. *See* James Lardner, *Annals of Law: The Betamax Case,* NEW YORKER, Apr. 6, 1987, at 45. Ultimately, the Supreme Court held that individuals' home videotaping was fair use.

I'm not at all sure that the existence of an unenforced and possibly unenforceable rule making common, everyday behavior illegal is much use to anyone, but, in any event, it's hard to argue that the lines currently drawn by the statutory language are either bright or predictable in their application to real-world activities. So we wouldn't lose much in the way of predictability or clarity by trading in the current detailed rules for a more general standard.

Moreover, the common law interpretive process, with all its faults, is better suited to discover privileges and limitations of general application than the usual copyright legislative process. Instead of relying on industry actors to craft workable bargains, it tries to draw lines that make sense.[57] Sometimes those lines may not work, but some of the current statutory lines don't work very well either. The public is more likely to be accepting of lines that are drawn by drafters attempting to make sense. And the public's involvement, through the jury process, in drawing those lines may—just may—give us an opportunity for expressing popular norms in where those lines end up.

Finally, and the thing I probably like best about this proposal, is that if we abolish all of the detailed, specific exceptions that we now have, the industries that have been able to rely on them will need to rely on the same general limitations to which everyone else is relegated. When established copyright companies tell us, as they always do, that they are *both* copyright owners and copyright users, so they are interested in a copyright law that is balanced,[58] they omit to mention that unlike users, unlike new start-up companies, and unlike small businesses who have no copyright lobbyists, they had the clout to negotiate and get Congress to enact some detailed copyright exemptions. Those exemptions, typically, give them what they need, but are

---

57.   Common law adjudication is responsible for the general privileges discussed earlier: the first-sale doctrine and the idea/expression distinction, as well as for the privilege of fair use. *See generally* Litman, *Copyright Legislation and Technological Change, supra* note 21, at 332–42.

58.   *See, e.g., Public Hearing on Intellectual Property Issues Involved in the National Information Infrastructure Initiative Before the National Information Infrastructure Task Force Working Group on Intellectual Property* 31 (Nov. 18, 1993) (testimony of Stephen L. Haynes, West Publishing Co.); *Hearing*, Feb. 8, 1996, *supra* note 3 (prepared statement of the Association of American Publishers); *Hearing*, May 7, 1996, *supra* note 9 (testimony of Dan Burton, Novell); *Public Hearing at U.C.L.A. Before the Information Infrastructure Task Force Working Group on Intellectual Property* 22 (Sept. 16, 1994) (testimony of William Barlow, Times-Mirror Company).

narrow enough that they are unlikely to prove useful to new competing media that might show up next year. I like the idea of harnessing all of that energy to devote to litigation designed to generate privileges that could be useful to the general public.

A variety of other new models might serve us as well. What is crucial, though, is that we recognize that our intellectual property laws form the basic *legal* infrastructure for our information policy in an online world. Interests that currently dominate intellectual property law would be delighted for our information policy to emerge as a byproduct of our intellectual property laws; that strategy is likely to leave them holding winning hands. Before we allow our intellectual property laws to dictate the terms of our information policy, though, we need to figure out whether the world that is likely to result is somewhere we really want to live. We cannot have an information policy that effectively promotes public access for the greatest number of people to the widest range of information unless our intellectual property laws give more than lip-service to the goal of public access.

Much of the control over access and use that current copyright laws give to copyright holders came to them not because of a congressional decision to enhance the copyright bundle-of-rights, but as accidental windfall benefits resulting from linguistic fortuity and technological change.[59] The unintended beneficiaries of these windfalls are understandably reluctant to relinquish them. Their success in retaining control until now over these new rights and new uses has persuaded many copyright holders that their destiny is to appropriate whatever surplus progress delivers in connection with the exploitation of copyrighted works. Suggestions that some of this surplus belongs to the public have recently been met with the objection that such a claim demands that copyright owners alone bear the burden of facilitating public access to works of authorship.[60] Any copyright historian would

---

59.   *See* Litman, *supra* note 29, at 206; Litman, *supra* note 5, at 39–43.

60.   *See, e.g., Hearing*, Feb. 7, 1996, *supra* note 2 (testimony of Barbara A. Munder, Information Industry Ass'n):

> The question of what constitutes fair use of the creator's exclusive rights is always an area of contention when copyright revisions are considered by Congress. No one—least of all those of us in the business of providing information—wants our society to devolve into segmented classes of information "haves" and "have-nots." However, ensuring that those who cannot afford to pay for information nevertheless have access to it is a

reply that such an objection misperceives the nature of copyright, since copyright owners have never been entitled to control all uses of their works—or even most of them. But even if the envoys of copyright holders had history on their side, it would be a mistake for the rest of us to allow the policy debate to proceed on those terms.

It may once have been the case that giving copyright owners the legal right to sue over any use of copyrighted works they could detect and prevent was an effective method to promote creation, distribution, access, use, reuse, and learning. That doesn't matter now. The question we need to concern ourselves with now is the degree to which that is an effective means today. We can't answer that question without identifying the needs of readers as well as writers, of listeners and players as well as composers, of learners as well as publishers and teachers. We are well on the way to adopting an information policy that is a byproduct of our copyright laws. I suggest that we need to do it the other way around.

---

broader societal responsibility, not one that should be borne primarily—let alone exclusively—by copyright owners.

In IIA's view, the current, vociferous push toward expanding fair use is little more than an attempt to create a new set of "user rights" that would place the burden of facilitating universal access to information resources solely on the shoulders of copyright owners. The fair use doctrine was never designed to carry this burden. I would point out that the White Paper addressed the issue of fair use with some thoroughness and emphatically rejected this approach.

It would be counterproductive to place information providers alone in a category with special obligations to fulfill an overall societal need. The building of our national highway system did not translate into demands or expectations that automobile manufacturers suddenly provide free cars to the underprivileged. Neither should content providers—if you will, the manufacturers of vehicles for the information superhighway—be required to bear the sole burden of providing information for free to the general public. Broad expansion of the current, workable fair use exceptions would decrease return on investment for information providers and would thereby diminish the incentive for the creation and distribution of the type of quality content products and services that online customers are demanding. In the end, there will be less, not more, information for all.

See also White Paper, supra note 7, at 84 ("The Working Group rejects the notion that copyright owners should be taxed—apart from all others—to facilitate the legitimate goal of 'universal access' ").

Chapter Five
Facing Facts:
The Database Protection Dilemma[*]

by
Jonathan A. Franklin
Reference Librarian
University of Michigan Law Library

I. Introduction

By the year 1998, the member states of the European Union will protect databases of factual information with a bold new right. This type of protection is in direct conflict with existing United States law. If U.S. database producers want their databases to be protected in the European Union and at home, then they will have to convince the United States to create such a right. Although such legislation would create a cause of action against data pirates, it would also severely limit database access for teachers, scientists, and the public at large.

This chapter provides a brief background of U.S. copyright law and the framework of the European Union's Legal Protection of Databases Directive, and addresses how this country should balance the competing interests of database producers and database users.

II. American Statutes and Jurisprudence

The roots of copyright law are found in the U.S. Constitution, which states that "The Congress shall have the Power . . . To promote the Progress of Science and useful Arts, by securing for limited Times to Authors and Inventors the exclusive Right to their respective Writings and Discoveries."[1] Pursuant to this clause, Congress passed the Copyright Act of 1976.[2]

The Copyright Act explicitly protects both underlying works[3] and original compilations of protected or unprotected works.[4] Creators can gain a copyright in text, visual creations, music, sound recordings, or many other types of works that meet this country's relatively low requisite level of originality.[5] Facts and other "ideas," as opposed to "expressions of ideas," are not copyrightable.[6] A copyright is also available for a sufficiently original compilation of works, whether the underlying works are copyrightable or not.[7] Thus, from a copyright perspective there are four types of compilations:

1. Copyrightable compilations of copyrightable works. An example of this is a selective compilation of poems; the individual poems are copyrightable as separate literary works, as is the compilation itself.
2. Copyrightable compilations of uncopyrightable subject matter, such as a selective compilation of license plate numbers.
3. Uncopyrightable compilations of copyrightable works. An example of this might be a comprehensive volume of all the poems of a

---

1. U.S. CONST. art. I, § 8, cl. 8.
2. 17 U.S.C. §§ 101–1101 (1994).
3. *Id.* § 102.
4. *Id.* § 103.
5. *Id.* § 102.
6. *Id.* § 102(b). Along with facts and other ideas, government information and copyrightable expression whose terms of protection have expired comprise the bulk of material in the public domain.
7. *Id.* § 103.

living poet, reproduced without any commentary and arranged chronologically by date of creation.

4. Uncopyrightable compilations of uncopyrightable subject matter, such as a comprehensive alphabetized list of license plates or a comprehensive list of the telephone numbers in a county organized alphabetically by the last name of the person linked to the number.

The Copyright Act of 1976 protects the underlying works (the poems) of types 1 and 3. The Copyright Act also protects the selective compilations in 1 and 2 based on originality.[8] If neither the underlying elements nor the compilation is sufficiently original, however, then the entire database is deemed unprotectable under U.S. copyright law.

An example of the application of this statute is the U.S. Supreme Court case of *Feist*,[9] in which the Court held that the white pages of a telephone book included neither protectable information nor sufficient originality to make the overall compilation protectable.[10] In *Feist*, the extraction of telephone numbers from the telephone white pages was permitted because there was insufficient originality in either the individual telephone numbers or the alphabetical arrangement of them to invoke the protection of the copyright law to prevent unauthorized duplication of the white pages.[11]

The plaintiffs in *Feist* argued that their compilation should be protected under the "sweat of the brow" or "industrious collection" doctrine, an artifact of the common law of copyright from the 19th century.[12] Under the sweat of the brow doctrine, a work or compilation was protected, regardless of its originality, because the creator invested an extensive amount of time, effort, or money in its creation. In other words, hard work to gather the material was sufficient to qualify the compilation for copyright protection. Although sweat of the brow previously had been rejected by the U.S. Supreme Court[13] where the Court relied on an unfair competition rationale to prevent

---

8. If the underlying elements of a copyrightable composition are unprotectable, then the elements may be extracted, but the resulting database must not infringe on the database from which the underlying works were extracted.

9. Feist Publications, Inc. v. Rural Tel. Serv. Co., 499 U.S. 340 (1991).

10. *Id.* at 363–64.

11. *Id.*

12. *Id.* at 352–53.

13. International News Serv. v. Associated Press, 248 U.S. 215, 234 (1918).

unauthorized extraction of unprotectable data,[14] other federal appellate courts continued to uphold copyrights based on the efforts of creation in preparing compilations.[15] The *Feist* opinion definitively eliminated the "sweat of the brow" doctrine as a basis for granting copyright protection.[16] The decision raised considerable concerns for database producers who feared they could no longer rely on copyright to protect their factual compilations.

III. European Situation

In contrast to the protections offered under American law, the Directive promulgated in the European Union[17] protects all four types of compilations if their creation required a sufficient amount of effort.[18] Thus, the sweat of the brow doctrine is alive and well in Europe. In the Directive on the Legal Protection of Databases,[19] the European Union requires all member states to adopt national legislation that parallels the tenets of the Directive.[20] Databases that consist of protectable components, such as poems, or sufficiently original compilations are protected by the copyright section of the Directive.[21] Nonoriginal compilations of unprotectable works, such as facts, are protected by a new *sui generis* right.[22] *Sui*

---

14. *Id.*

15. *E.g.,* Rosemont Enters. v. Random House, 366 F.2d 303 (2d Cir. 1966).

16. *Feist,* 499 U.S. at 359–60.

17. The European Union is a confederation of European countries that have banded together to promote social and economic benefits for its members, including free trade between members and becoming a greater force in global trade. Stephen Weatherhill & Paul Beaumont, EC Law 19–29 (2d ed. 1995). The Union uses directives to guide the member nations in drafting national legislation that parallels the directive, thereby facilitating Union-wide legal standards without needing an independent pan-European legal system. *Id.* at 137–38.

18. European Parliament and Council Directive 96/9/EC of 11 March 1996 on the Legal Protection of Databases, 1996 O.J. (L 77) 20 [hereinafter European Parliament & Council Directive 96/9/EC]. The text of the Directive is contained in the Appendix to this chapter, *infra* p. 101.

19. *Id.* Although the Directive has been on the drafting board for almost five years, and many drafts were produced, this chapter addresses only the final version because that is the form that the national laws of the member states of the European Union will take.

20. *Id.* at art. 16.

21. *Id.* at arts. 3–6.

22. *Id.* at arts. 7–11.

generis literally means "of its own" and in this context conveys the idea that the right is new, standing on its own, rather than part of an existing legal framework, in this case copyright law.

The European Union's effort to protect databases is driven by two concerns: the desire for harmonization of laws within the European Union, and the desire to gain ground on the more established United States database industry. First, the Directive acts to avoid conflicts in levels and types of protection of databases between the member states. Database protection is a fairly recent issue, and many member states are in the process of considering what type of protection databases should have. The Directive is, in effect, a preemptive strike, providing a blueprint for Union-wide standards before individual member states enact conflicting national legislation.

The rationale for drafting the Database Directive was that "databases are at present not sufficiently protected in all Member States by existing legislation; whereas such protection, where it exists, has different attributes. . . ."[23] Since databases are likely to cross borders, either in a fixed format such as CD-ROM or in an online format accessed via a modem or network, the differing treatments by the member states would thwart the European Union's goal of facilitating internal free trade.[24]

The second factor influencing the European Union's Database Directive is the American superiority in the database market. The Directive addresses the issue of American databases indirectly by stating that there is a great "imbalance" in the level of investment between the Community and other countries.[25] The Directive attributes this imbalance to the absence of a stable and uniform legal protection regime within the European Union.[26] To remedy this perceived imbalance, the Directive permits European database creators to protect their databases of public domain material and to extract public domain data from American databases, but not vice versa, unless the United

---

23.   *Id.* at recital (1).

24.   *See supra* note 17.

25.   European Parliament and Council Directive 96/9/EC, *supra* note 18, at recital (11).

26.   *Id.* Although there is no protection for unoriginally organized factual databases in the United States, there is sufficient infrastructure for the United States to maintain its lead in producing databases unprotected by copyright law. One of the major alternatives to relying on copyright law is relying on contract law in the form of a licensing agreement.

States adopts a parallel right.[27] Thus, under the guise of encouraging "investment," the Directive forces the United States to consider adopting "sweat of the brow" protection for databases of public domain material or risk losing control of these databases to extractors.

IV. The Specifics of the Directive

The Directive has two major substantive sections, copyright protection and *sui generis* protection.[28] The copyright section is roughly equivalent to U.S. law to the extent that it protects the original compilation of underlying works. The *sui generis* right is the section that conflicts with U.S. law by acknowledging "sweat of the brow" as a basis for protection.[29]

The *sui generis* right[30] protects databases from extraction and re-utilization.[31] Extraction means the transfer of a substantial part of the contents of a database, including physical duplication of the database's contents. Re-utilization means making the database physically or electronically available to third parties. The method of duplication could be electronic data transfer, photocopying, or handwriting. The final form of the protected database is not limited to electronic databases and could be a floppy disk, microfiche collection, or a piece of paper. In summary, the goal of the *sui generis* right is to prevent economic harm to the database producer caused by unauthorized reuse of the database, thereby theoretically increasing the incentive for European database makers to create databases of non-copyrightable information. An alternate

---

27.   *Id.* at art. 11(3).

28.   The Directive has four chapters: Scope (arts. 1–2), Copyright (arts. 3–6), *Sui Generis* Right (arts. 7–11), and Common Provisions (arts. 12–17). The scope section defines what legal areas the Directive will and will not affect. *Id.* at arts. 1–2. The common provisions are logistical issues such as terms of protection, dates for legislation to come into force, and the inability to contract out of certain copyright and *sui generis* rights and exceptions. *Id.* at arts. 12–17.

29.   Due to its divergence from American law, the *sui generis* right is the focus of the remainder of this chapter.

30.   The *sui generis* right is contained in five articles to the Directive, arts. 7–11 (*see* Appendix *infra* p. 101). This right includes sections on the object of protection, art. 7; rights and obligations of lawful users, art. 8; exceptions to the *sui generis* right, art. 9; term of protection, art. 10; and beneficiaries of protection under the *sui generis* right, art. 11.

31.   *Id.* at art. 7.

approach taken by rejecting sweat-of-the-brow protection is to create an incentive to generate original protectable value by making public domain data freely available to all competitors.

To counter the protectionist attitude of this right, the Directive offers member states the option of creating exceptions for the extraction of non-electronic databases for personal use, purely illustrative extraction in an educational context, and extraction for public security or administrative or judicial needs.[32] Although the educational exception would permit a professor to print a sample record to explain the database's structure, it would almost certainly not extend to the unauthorized educational use of the database or a substantial portion thereof, since that would constitute potential economic harm to the database maker.[33] The central problem with the *sui generis* right is that there is no exception for non-commercial access to electronic databases of public domain material, locking the public out of these databases for at least the initial 15-year term of protection.

V. Why the United States Must Consider Creating a Parallel Right

By protecting databases on the basis of the amount of work that went into a compilation, the European's Union's Directive subverts the basic tenet of American copyright law: originality. If the United States does not adopt such a right, however, then American databases of public domain material will not be protected from extraction and re-utilization, but those in Europe will be. The copyright infringement remedy will remain available for databases that have either copyrightable elements or copyrightable compilations, but there will be no recourse for the duplication of unoriginal compilations of factual or otherwise unprotectable data. Assuming that extraction from an American database constitutes a sufficient creative effort, the first European to copy an American database would even gain the 15-year term protection provided for in the Directive. Of course, as long as the United States does not have a similar right, a second European database maker could also extract from the original American database, but it could not extract it from its European competitor. In this environment,

---

32.   *Id.* at art. 9.

33.   *Id.* at art. 7(b).

American database creators doing business in Europe would be at a great economic disadvantage to the extent that their uncopyrightable compilations of facts would be unprotected from European duplication, but not the reverse.[34] Of course, the same database of public domain material would remain unprotected at home, as well.

The United States must consider the implications of creating a right that parallels the European Union's *sui generis* right.[35] Once the European Union and the United States have similar rights, American databases of public domain material will be protected in Europe and European databases of public domain material will be protected in the United States. This type of protection is known as "reciprocal treatment" because U.S. works in the European Union would be protected only to the extent that EU works would be protected in the United States. Therefore if the United States had a lower level of protection than the European Union, then American works in Europe would gain only that lower level of protection.[36] It is therefore not a surprise that the Information Industry Association, an American information industry trade group, is already calling for the adoption of a database protection right that parallels the EU Directive.[37] Furthermore, the

---

34. Although arguably once such a database has been transported out of the European Union and duplicated it would be unprotectable, it is unclear how far the jurisdiction statutes of each of the member states would reach.

35. Although this is logical when considering the United States and the European Union, it appears to conflict with the TRIPS component of the Uruguay Round of GATT in that it would force less developed nations to overprotect unoriginal computerized compilations. J. H. Reichman, *The TRIPS Component of the GATT's Uruguay Round: Competitive Prospects for Intellectual Property Owners in an Integrated World Market*, 4 FORDHAM INTELL. PROP., MEDIA & ENT. L.J. 171, 224–25 (1993).

36. European Parliament & Council Directive 96/9/EC, *supra* note 18, at art. 11(3).

37. *NII [National Information Infrastructure] Copyright Protection Act of 1995 (Part 2): Hearings on H.R. 2441 Before the Subcomm. on Courts and Intellectual Property of the House Comm. of the Judiciary*, 104th Cong., 2d Sess. 69–79 (1996) (statement of Barbara A. Munder, Senior Vice President, the McGraw-Hill Companies, on behalf of the Information Industry Association).

    If such a law is desirable to the information industry, it appears that Congress can enact the necessary legislation. One obstacle is that the U.S. Constitution provides that those rights not reserved for the federal government are reserved for the states, and because the *sui generis* right does not fit within the scope of the Patents and Copyrights Clause, Congress would have to rely on another part of the Constitution to enact this right in the United States. Even after hurdling the constitutional basis for such a right, Congress would have to avoid the preemption section of the Copyright Act. 17 U.S.C. § 301 (1994). This could be achieved by

Information Infrastructure Task Force suggests that the enactment of such a right be "carefully evaluated."[38]

VI. Major Issues In Existing Database Protection Proposals

The first database protection bill was introduced in Congress in 1996.[39] Although no action was taken on it, it is notable in that it suggests the form future legislation may take. Instead of amending Title 17 of the United States Code, addressing copyright, it amends Title 15, the title including commerce- and trade-related legislation. Furthermore, the centerpiece of the bill protects database producers from misappropriation, thereby circumventing the traditional balance between producers and consumers found in copyright legislation.[40]

Additionally, the European Union's Directive already has prompted the United States to draft a multilateral treaty to address the database protection issue.[41] This draft was presented to the World Intellectual Property Organization (WIPO), an international organization created to promote the protection of intellectual property throughout the world.[42] The U.S. proposal diverged from the EU Directive in expanding the term of protection from 15 years to 25 years. It also made explicit three points not discussed in the Directive. The U.S. draft treaty explicitly permitted contractual alteration of the rights protected by the treaty, exempted information created by the federal government,

---

basing its analysis on the economic injury caused to the original compiler. This was the rationale invoked in International News Service v. Associated Press, 248 U.S. 215 (1918).

38. INTELLECTUAL PROPERTY AND THE NATIONAL INFORMATION INFRASTRUCTURE: THE REPORT OF THE WORKING GROUP ON INTELLECTUAL PROPERTY 153 (1995).

39. H.R. 3531, 104th Cong., 2d Sess. (1996).

40. *Id.* § 3.

41. Proposal of the United States of America on *Sui Generis* Protection of Databases, May 20, 1996 (CRNR/PM/7) (drafted for the Preparatory Committee of the Proposed Diplomatic Conference (December 1996) on Certain Copyright and Neighboring Rights Questions and Received by the Director General on May 20, 1996). A proposal on the same topic from the European Union was also considered by a committee of experts who drafted a subsequent proposal that was tabled at the December 1996 WIPO Diplomatic Conference.

42. GIUSEPPE SCHIAVONE, INTERNATIONAL ORGANIZATIONS: A DICTIONARY AND DIRECTORY 276 (3d ed. 1992).

and granted national treatment to signatories.[43] In contrast to reciprocal treatment, national treatment grants foreign databases the same level of protection as domestic databases regardless of the laws of the foreign country, as long as they are signatories to the treaty. Thus, national treatment is preferable to reciprocal treatment for jurisdictions granting broader exceptions to the rights at issue. Although the Database Protection treaty has not yet been finalized, the existing drafts are likely to form the basis of future treaty efforts.

Given that this right is likely to be introduced in Congress as either a bill or a treaty in the next few years, information users including librarians, scholars, and scientists must consider how they want to influence this legislation. The first strategic question is whether such a right should be opposed. In an age of digitized information, where copying and downloading of factual information is simple yet vital for an informed populace, the enactment of such a right should not be taken lightly.[44]

A *sui generis* right would increase the cost of searching databases of public domain information. Instead of scanning or downloading information, competitors will be required to go back to the original source of the facts. In some cases the original source may be illegible, incomplete, or otherwise unavailable. In such cases, the original database compiler will have a virtual monopoly on the information for 15 years. Furthermore, for databases that are maintained and updated on an ongoing basis, the protection may extend indefinitely because it may not be possible to sever the unprotected portion from the protected portion.

The second problem with a *sui generis* right is that factual and governmental information is now being produced and distributed

---

43.   *See supra* note 41. *See also U.S. Treaty Proposal Would Create New WIPO Protection of Databases*, 13 INT'L TRADE REP. (BNA) 935 (June 5, 1996).

44.   For a scholarly work on the history and implementation of database protection, see J. H. Reichman & Pamela Samuelson, *Intellectual Property Rights in Data?* 50 VAND. L. REV. 51 (1997).

exclusively in the digital format.[45] Society is entering an era where there may be no way to obtain information other than by extraction. This will effectively grant the database maker a monopoly in public domain material. The European Union has built in a triennial review of the *sui generis* right to determine whether the right has led to an "abuse of dominant position."[46] While the remedy, "non-voluntary licensing," also known as compulsory licensing, would aid competitors and likely provide less-expensive access, it would not help those attempting to make the public domain facts freely available to the public.

Finally, current hardware, software, and data collection methods are unlikely to remain in use for more than five or ten years. As technology changes, the nature of databases will change, permitting still images, full-motion images, sound, text, and other digitized information to be easily stored, retrieved, and disseminated. One can imagine an electronic database of public domain audiovisual works that cannot be systematically duplicated for library use due to this *sui generis* right. Due to the speed of change, even the 15-year term of protection without an extension for updating or maintenance is too long to lock up otherwise unavailable public domain works.

VII. Strategic Decisions for American Information Users

The best initial position for American information users is almost certainly to oppose the creation of this new right. Economic interests in the American information industry are likely to try to persuade Congress that such a right is necessary to avoid losses to American jobs, sales of American databases to European corporations, and the general decline of the American information industry. Given the possibility of the adoption of such a right in some form, the primary reason to fight its adoption is to gain concessions for information users while encouraging the creation of copyrightable data and databases.

---

45. For a discussion of these issues in a scientific-data context, see COMMITTEE ON ISSUES IN THE TRANSBORDER FLOW OF SCIENTIFIC DATA, U.S. NATIONAL COMMITTEE FOR CODATA, COMMISSION ON PHYSICAL SCIENCES, MATHEMATICS, AND APPLICATIONS, AND NATIONAL RESEARCH COUNCIL, BITS OF POWER: ISSUES IN GLOBAL ACCESS TO SCIENTIFIC DATA (forthcoming 1997); a prepublication version is available at <http://www.nap.edu/readingroom/>.

46. European Parliament & Council Directive 96/9/EC, *supra* note 18, at art. 16(3).

This can be achieved through a combination of legal and economic approaches.

A. Legal Solutions

The only time that information users will have any leverage to influence the legislation is at the time of its drafting. After that, it will be very difficult to change whatever becomes status quo. Thus, information users must consider what types of exceptions would best balance this new right. If such legislation is deemed desirable, it must not deviate substantially from the Directive itself, hence avoiding the chance that the enacted right would fail to protect American databases in Europe while unnecessarily altering the American intellectual property law landscape.

1. Fair Use-type Defense. Under current U.S. copyright law, some un-authorized duplication of copyrighted works is permitted. "Fair use" is both a limitation on the copyright holder's exclusive rights and a defense in copyright infringement cases. Examples of uses that tend to be ex-empted from liability for copyright infringement include scholarship, teaching, research, criticism, news reporting, and the like.[47] The fair use analysis considers four primary factors in determining whether the fair use defense applies: the character of the use; the nature of the protected work; the proportion that was copied; and the economic impact of the copying (to the copyright holder).[48] These four factors are often weighted along with the copier's intent and First Amendment issues to determine whether the copying constituted fair use.

A similar type of exception could exist for certain types of database extraction and re-utilization. The problem with this approach in a non-treaty context is that if it is too broad, it will conflict with the very limited exceptions permitted in Directive, which in turn would prevent the United States from gaining reciprocal treatment. Fair use is not generally recognized in Europe, so the exact parameters of an appropriate fair use–type defense would have to be based on discussions between United States and European Union representatives who have the ability to determine what exceptions would still permit the American databases to be granted reciprocal treatment in Europe.

---

47.   17 U.S.C. § 107 (1994).

48.   *Id.*

The basic damage that the Directive addresses is the economic injury to the database maker as opposed to the nature of the use someone might make of the database. To that extent, a user extracting a subset of records and making them publicly accessible is depriving the maker of profits that would have been made but for the free access. Because the test focuses on the maker's loss, not the extractor's gain, the limitation would apply to libraries and competitors alike. One way to circumvent the economic analysis without creating an exception is to require the database maker to make a database of the unmodified public domain information accessible. Even if it was limited to one user per county or Internet domain, this would at least guarantee some form of ongoing, free access to the underlying data.

2. Change the Status of Information. Currently, the vast majority of government information in the United States is not copyrighted. This is unrelated to its inherent copyrightability and instead is based on the policy that the public should have access to government-generated information. Given that a substantial portion of the public domain information sought by database producers is generated by the federal government, the government could require the database creators using the federally generated data to make the raw data perpetually available for free extraction and reutilization. Alternatively, the government could start to request royalties for the overseas use of federal databases that would then be devoted to making such information publicly accessible within the United States. This is a complex solution that may not be feasible due to the cost of collecting the royalties and ensuring that those royalties are used for their intended purpose.

3. The Problem of Perpetual Protection. The Directive is overly protective to the extent that as long as the database is being continuously updated and maintained, no part of it enters the public domain, even if it is beyond the term of protection.[49] Although database producers may claim that the database is a single entity, it is also composed of distinct elements that can be independently protected for a fixed term and then moved into the public domain. Information users must eliminate the spectre of perpetual protection by lobbying to permit substantial extraction of individual elements once their term of

---

49.   European Parliament & Council Directive 96/9/EC, *supra* note 18, at art. 10(3).

copyright protection as a work has expired and they have been in the database for the 15-year term.

This would not be complex in either a legal or a technical sense because each element of the database could include a field indicating when it was added or loaded into the database; thus extraction of elements that had been loaded more than 15 years ago should be a simple matter. Although this does not address whether the individual work is in the public domain, at least it would permit the user to apply a traditional fair use analysis from that point forward. Eliminating the perpetual protection would further encourage ongoing competition between database producers to add different kinds of value to older material because no single database producer would be able to rest on the accumulation of older materials without ongoing efforts to add new value to the database beyond adding newer material.

B. Economic Solutions

It is difficult to "require" business to do things in the current political climate. Moreover, none of the above suggestions would alleviate the real problem, which is the effective shrinking of the public domain. For information to be truly accessible, it must be omnipresent and easily accessible. Fear of litigation decreases the number of intermediaries who are willing to make information available, and the cost of equipment limits the ability of institutions to make more technologically advanced products widely available.

What is needed is a nonprofit project to coordinate the gathering and storing of public domain information. Project Gutenberg is an example of an organization designed to gather, store, and provide access to public domain materials.[50] A Project Gutenberg for factual and governmental information should be initiated. The major drawbacks of this type of a project are the necessary financing and the need for ongoing support.

---

50.   Project Gutenberg is a cooperative volunteer venture started by Michael Hart in 1971 to make public domain writings electronically accessible. The Project serves multiple purposes, including data digitization, distribution, archiving, and certification of public domain status. Without any one of these pieces, the Project would not have its current level of effectiveness. Elizabeth Weise, *Building a Virtual Library*, S.F. EXAMINER, Jan. 23, 1995, at B1.

The reason such a Public Domain Data Preservation Project (PDDPP) must be considered prior to the creation of the *sui generis* right is that now is the time when such a project would have the best chance of gaining financial support either from the federal government, private foundations, or even the information industry itself. Assuming the PDDPP obtained financing, the next problem would be deciding what projects or fields to work on first. This could be determined by an advisory board. At some point in the future, the PDDPP might be able to include databases donated by the information industry in exchange for charitable tax deductions.

The Public Domain Data Preservation Project vision may seem idealistic and impractical, but a quick search of the World Wide Web reveals foundations, educational institutions, and individuals undertaking exactly this enterprise. The data digitization, distribution, and sometimes even copyright clearance are already underway. The main role of a PDDPP would be in archiving and organizing the information to make it accessible into the distant future.

The goal of such an enterprise is not to replicate the work of the database makers, but to ensure that public domain information remains accessible regardless of whether the web site disappears, the commercial database provider goes bankrupt, or the print copies decompose. Access must include both intellectual access such as cataloging, directory creation, and indexing for search engines, along with physical access such as preservation, standardized data storage, and ongoing hardware compatibility.

If such a project was funded by the American information industry, then databases would secure reciprocal or national treatment and information users would gain a long-term solution to the rights limitations to free access to public domain information. Depending on the specifics, the information industry might even be able to raise the funds by adding a surcharge for the overseas use of its databases.

VIII. Damned if We Harmonize and Damned if We Don't

There are no easy answers to the problems raised by the potential creation of this new right. Although the creation of such a right injures information users, it more substantially impedes competitors who currently are able to extract public domain information from other uncopyrightable commercial databases without the same collection costs as the original database producer.

If such a right is created in the United States, it should include a fair use-type defense and provisions for the extraction of public domain information. The greatest long-term benefit for end users would be reaped by gathering, organizing, and archiving information that is publicly available. This would permit widespread access to public domain information without injuring those database makers who are investing in adding value to the underlying public domain works.

Appendix
Directive 96/9/EC
of the European Parliament and
of the Council of 11 March 1996
on the Legal Protection of Databases[1]

Chapter I—Scope

Article 1—Scope

1. This Directive concerns the legal protection of databases in any form.
2. For the purposes of this Directive, "database" shall mean a collection of independent works, data or other materials arranged in a systematic or methodical way and individually accessible by electronic or other means.

---

1. 1996 O.J. (L77) 20. Text also is found at <http://www2.echo.lu/legal/en/ipr/database/text.html>.

3. Protection under this Directive shall not apply to computer pro-
    grams used in the making or operation of databases accessible by
    electronic means.

Article 2—Limitations on the Scope

This Directive shall apply without prejudice to Community provisions
relating to:
- (a) the legal protection of computer programs;
- (b) rental right, lending right and certain rights related to copyright in the field of intellectual property;
- (c) the term of protection of copyright and certain related rights.

Chapter II—Copyright

Article 3—Object of Protection

1. In accordance with this Directive, databases which, by reason of
    the selection or arrangement of their contents, constitute the
    author's own intellectual creation shall be protected as such by
    copyright. No other criteria shall be applied to determine their
    eligibility for that protection.
2. The copyright protection of databases provided for by this Direc-
    tive shall not extend to their contents and shall be without preju-
    dice to any rights subsisting in those contents themselves.

Article 4—Database Authorship

1. The author of a database shall be the natural person or group of
    natural persons who created the base or, where the legislation of
    the Member States so permits, the legal person designated as the
    rightholder by that legislation.
2. Where collective works are recognized by the legislation of a
    Member State, the economic rights shall be owned by the person
    holding the copyright.
3. In respect of a database created by a group of natural persons
    jointly, the exclusive rights shall be owned jointly.

Article 5—Restricted Acts

In respect of the expression of the database which is protectable by copyright, the author of a database shall have the exclusive right to carry out or to authorize:

   (a) temporary or permanent reproduction by any means and in any form, in whole or in part;
   (b) translation, adaptation, arrangement and any other alteration;
   (c) any form of distribution to the public of the database or of copies thereof. The first sale in the Community of a copy of the database by the rightholder or with his consent shall exhaust the right to control resale of that copy within the Community;
   (d) any communication, display or performance to the public;
   (e) any reproduction, distribution, communication, display or performance to the public of the results of the acts referred to in (b).

Article 6—Exceptions to Restricted Acts

1. The performance by the lawful user of a database or of a copy thereof of any of the acts listed in Article 5 which is necessary for the purposes of access to the contents of the databases and normal use of the contents by the lawful user shall not require the authorization of the author of the database. Where the lawful user is authorized to use only part of the database, this provision shall apply only to that part.
2. Member States shall have the option of providing for limitations on the rights set out in Article 5 in the following cases:
    (a) in the case of reproduction for private purposes of a non-electronic database;
    (b) where there is use for the sole purpose of illustration for teaching or scientific research, as long as the source is indicated and to the extent justified by the non-commercial purpose to be achieved;
    (c) where there is use for the purposes of public security of for the purposes of an administrative or judicial procedure; (d) where other exceptions to copyright which are traditionally authorized under national law are involved, without prejudice to points (a), (b) and (c).
3. In accordance with the Berne Convention for the protection of Literary and Artistic Works, this Article may not be interpreted in

such a way as to allow its application to be used in a manner which unreasonably prejudices the rightholder's legitimate interests or conflicts with normal exploitation of the database.

Chapter III—Sui Generis Right

Article 7—Object of Protection

1. Member States shall provide for a right for the maker of a database which shows that there has been qualitatively and/or quantitatively a substantial investment in either the obtaining, verification or presentation of the contents to prevent extraction and/or re-utilization of the whole or of a substantial part evaluated qualitatively and/or quantitatively, of the contents of that database.
2. For the purposes of this Chapter:
    (a) "extraction" shall mean the permanent or temporary transfer of all or a substantial part of the contents of a database to another medium by any means or in any form;
    (b) "re-utilization" shall mean any form of making available to the public all or a substantial part of the contents of a database by the distribution of copies, by renting, by on-line or other forms of transmission. The first sale of a copy of a database within the Community by the rightholder or with his consent shall exhaust the right to control resale of that copy within the Community. Public lending is not an act of extraction or re-utilization.
3. The right referred to in paragraph 1 may be transferred, assigned or granted under contractual license.
4. The right provided for in paragraph 1 shall apply irrespective of the eligibility of that database for protection by copyright or by other rights. Moreover, it shall apply irrespective of eligibility of the contents of that database for protection by copyright or by other rights. Protection of databases under the right provided for in paragraph 1 shall be without prejudice to rights existing in respect of their contents.
5. The repeated and systematic extraction and/or re-utilization of insubstantial parts of the contents of the database implying acts which conflict with a normal exploitation of that database or which unreasonably prejudice the legitimate interests of the maker of the database shall not be permitted.

Article 8—Rights and Obligations of Lawful Users

1. The maker of a database which is made available to the public in whatever manner may not prevent a lawful user of the database from extracting and/or re-utilizing insubstantial parts of its contents, evaluated qualitatively and/or quantitatively, for any purposes whatsoever. Where the lawful user is authorized to extract and/or re-utilize only part of the database, this paragraph shall apply only to that part.
2. A lawful user of a database which is made available to the public in whatever manner may not perform acts which conflict with normal exploitation of the database or unreasonably prejudice the legitimate interests of the maker of the database.
3. A lawful user of a database which is made available to the public in any manner may not cause prejudice to the holder of a copyright or related right in respect of the works or subject matter contained in the database.

Article 9—Exceptions to the Sui Generis Right

Member States may stipulate that lawful users of a database which is made available to the public in whatever manner may, without the authorization of its maker, extract or re-utilize a substantial part of its contents:

(a) in the case of extraction for private purposes of the contents of a non-electronic database;

(b) in the case of extraction for the purposes of illustration for teaching or scientific research, as long as the source is indicated and to the extent justified by the non-commercial purpose to be achieved;

(c) in the case of extraction and/or re-utilization for the purposes of public security or an administrative or judicial procedure.

Article 10—Term of Protection

1. The right provided for in Article 7 shall run from the date of completion of the making of the database. It shall expire fifteen years from the first of January of the year following the date of completion.
2. In the case of a database which is made available to the public in whatever manner before expiration of the period provided for in paragraph 1, the term of protection by that right shall expire

fifteen years from the first of January of the year following the date when the database was first made available to the public.

3. Any substantial change, evaluated qualitatively or quantitatively, to the contents of a database including any substantial change resulting from the accumulation of successive additions, deletions or alterations, which would result in the database being considered to be a substantial new investment, evaluated qualitatively or quantitatively, shall qualify the database resulting from that investment for its own term of protection.

Article 11—Beneficiaries of Protection Under the Sui Generis Right

1. The right provided for in Article 7 shall apply to database whose makers or rightholders are nationals of a Member State or who have their habitual residence in the territory of the Community.
2. Paragraph 1 shall also apply to companies and firms formed in accordance with the law of a Member State and having their registered office, central administration or principal place of business within the Community; however, where such a company or firm has only its registered office in the territory of the Community, its operations must be genuinely linked on an ongoing basis with the economy of a Member State.
3. Agreements extending the right provided for in Article 7 to databases made in third countries and falling outside the provisions of paragraphs 1 and 2 shall be concluded by the Council acting on a proposal from the Commission. The term of any protection extended to databases by virtue of that procedure shall not exceed that available pursuant to Article 10.

Chapter IV—Common Provisions

Article 12—Remedies

Member States shall provide appropriate remedies in respect of infringements of the rights provided for in this Directive.

Article 13—Continued Application of Other Legal Provisions

This Directive shall be without prejudice to provisions concerning in particular copyright, rights related to copyright or any other rights or obligations subsisting in the data, works or other materials incorporated into a database, patent rights, trade marks, design rights, the protection of national treasures, laws on restrictive practices and unfair competition, trade secrets, security, confidentiality, data protection and privacy, access to public documents, and the law of contract.

Article 14—Application over Time

1. Protection pursuant to this Directive as regards copyright shall also be available in respect of databases created prior to the date referred to Article 16 (1) which on that date fulfill the requirements laid down in this Directive as regards copyright protection of databases.
2. Notwithstanding paragraph 1, where a database protected under copyright arrangements in a Member State on the date of publication of this Directive does not fulfill the eligibility criteria for copyright protection laid down in Article 3 (1), this Directive shall not result in any curtailing in that Member State of the remaining term of protection afforded under those arrangements.
3. Protection pursuant to the provisions of this Directive as regards the right provided for in Article 7 shall also be available in respect of databases the making of which was completed not more than fifteen years prior to the date referred to in Article 16 (1) and which on that date fulfill the requirements laid down in Article 7.
4. The protection provided for in paragraphs 1 and 3 shall be without prejudice to any acts concluded and rights acquired before the date referred to in those paragraphs.
5. In the case of a database the making of which was completed not more than fifteen years prior to the date referred to in Article 16 (1), the term of protection by the right provided for in Article 7 shall expire fifteen years from the first of January following that date.

Article 15—Binding Nature of Certain Provisions

Any contractual provision contrary to Articles 6 (1) and 8 shall be null and void.

Article 16—Final Provisions

1. Member States shall bring into force the laws, regulations and administrative provisions necessary to comply with this Directive before 1 January 1998.

When Member States adopt these provisions, they shall contain a reference to this Directive or shall be accompanied by such reference on the occasion of their official publication. The methods of making such reference shall be laid down by Member States.

2. Member States shall communicate to the Commission the text of the provisions of domestic law which they adopt in the field governed by this Directive.

3. Not later than at the end of the third year after the date referred to in paragraph 1, and every three years thereafter, the Commission shall submit to the European Parliament, the Council and the Economic and Social Committee a report on the application of this Directive, in which, inter alia, on the basis of specific information supplied by the Member States, it shall examine in particular the application of the sui generis right, including Articles 8 and 9, and shall verify especially whether the application of this right has led to abuse of a dominant position or other interference with free competition which would justify appropriate measures being taken, including the establishment of non-voluntary licensing arrangements. Where necessary, it shall submit proposals for adjustment of this Directive in line with developments in the area of databases.

Article 17

This Directive is addressed to the Member States.

Section II
Libraries and Copyright

Chapter Six
Preservation and Copyright[*]

by
Robert L. Oakley

Director of the Law Library & Professor of Law
Georgetown University Law Center

I. Introduction

Preservation is one of the fundamental purposes of libraries. Asked what they do, often librarians say that they acquire and preserve information, organize it, and make it available to their users. Preservation is central to the profession and central to the obligation to our parent institutions and to society at large. It is what we do to ensure that our collections are not only available now, but will continue to be available to future generations of users.

In the past, preservation meant protecting a work through such mechanisms as binding it in a sturdy cover, storing it in suitable conditions, and repairing it when necessary. Unfortunately, preservation

---

has recently taken on a new dimension as well as a greater urgency because the acidic paper used for about the last 150 years of publishing has resulted in library shelves full of increasingly brittle materials. Preservation of the written record—and for that matter, the video and audio record as well—has taken on the proportions of a national historical and cultural crisis because without such an effort, we face the ultimate loss of 150 years of recorded history.

Because of the scope of the problem, preservation no longer means just binding, storage, and repair. As libraries deal with large quantities of brittle books in their collections, preservation is more likely to mean reformatting the item into microform, or more recently, into some digital format. But, without any question, what libraries call reformatting is copying, i.e., reproduction; most likely, it is even multiple copying.

Widely accepted standards for preservation copying require the creation of at least three newer generation copies: an archival master to be stored in a secure location, a use master from which the use copies are made, and a use copy.[1] These standards arose in the pre-digital era, when, in most cases, the original was destroyed in the process of filming, and where use copies could be lost or could deteriorate from exposure to light or other environmental conditions. Under such circumstances, a new use copy could be made from the use master when it was necessary to replace a damaged copy. Only if both the use copy and the use master were damaged would the archival master ever be used.

Nothing in the digital era has changed so as to eliminate the need for the three preservation copies. The original will still either be destroyed in the act of preserving it, or it is likely to be so far deteriorated that one could not expect to go back and copy it again. Moreover, electronic use copies are actually more susceptible to damage and deterioration than their microfilm predecessors. Stray magnetic fields can wipe out an entire disk instantaneously, and the life expectancy of most digital media

---

1. *See generally Research Libraries Group Archives Microfilming Guidelines and American National Standard for Information and Image Management—Recommended Practice for Microfilming Public Records on Silver-Halide Film, ANSI/AIIM MS48-1990,* § 7.1, at 4. National Endowment for the Humanities grants requirements refer to both RLG guidelines and ANSI/AIIM: "[a] first generation preservation master, a second-generation duplicating master, and a third-generation service master must be produced."

is far shorter (10 to 15 years) than either paper (75 to 100 years) or microfilm (300 to 400 years for high-quality silver halide film). With digital techniques, then, it is not only important to make the initial preservation copies, it is also necessary to go back and "refresh" the digital original—the archival master—at periodic intervals.

When the Copyright Act[2] was passed in 1976, an effort was made to accommodate the preservation needs of libraries. Unfortunately, the standards had not fully evolved by then, and it was generally thought that a single copy would suffice. We now know that that is not correct and, accordingly, the Copyright Act needs to be updated to accommodate the needs of libraries to preserve their collections using digital as well as microfilm techniques.

II. The Law on Preservation Today

There are several provisions in the Copyright Act that are relevant to preservation. Some of these provisions are general in nature; others are specific to the preservation problem.

A. The Term of Copyright

A work that is not protected by copyright may be copied for preservation purposes at will or for any other purpose. Unprotected works include works of the United States government,[3] works which did not follow the requisite formalities under the old Copyright Act,[4] and works whose term of protection has expired. The term of copyright is, therefore, critical for library preservation programs, and most large-scale programs have focused their attention primarily on works that are old enough to have lost their protection and come into the public domain.

There are a series of detailed rules in the 1976 Copyright Act setting out the length of the copyright term under various circumstances.[5] The basic rule, however, is that any work created after

---

2.　17 U.S.C. §§ 101–1101 (1994).

3.　*Id.* § 105.

4.　*E.g.,* works that were published without the requisite copyright notice. *See* 17 U.S.C. §§ 10, 19 *et seq.* (1909 Act) *in* MELVILLE B. NIMMER & DAVID NIMMER, NIMMER ON COPYRIGHT (1996).

5.　*See generally* 17 U.S.C. §§ 302–305 (1994).

January 1, 1978 is protected for the life of the author plus 50 years. For anonymous or pseudonymous works, protection lasts for 75 years from the date of first publication or for 100 years from the date of creation, whichever is earlier. The soonest any such published works could come into the public domain, therefore, is 2028 for an author who published a work in 1978 and died that same year.

For older works, the situation is more complicated because the original term was only 28 years, but if it was renewed the owner received an additional term of 47 years for a total potential term of 75 years. This means that materials published in 1921 or earlier clearly are now in the public domain, and can safely be digitized or preserved and distributed in any manner the librarian deems appropriate. Works published later than 1921 but before the new Act took effect might or might not be protected, depending on whether the original copyright was renewed.[6]

With all this in mind, and being somewhat risk averse, many librarians working on preservation projects have adopted a rolling cutoff date for their projects and will only convert older materials. Although such an approach allows the librarians to make progress on the older works in their collections, it forces them to ignore newer works that are also deteriorating, and it places works from the 1920s and 1930s into serious jeopardy.

B. Preservation Sections 108(b) and 108(c)

Although the Act gives copyright owners the exclusive rights to reproduce and distribute their works,[7] the Act also limits those rights in the section on fair use and in a series of specifically enumerated exemptions,[8] including a number of exemptions for specific library purposes set out in section 108.

In the discussions that led up to the passage of the Copyright Act of 1976, preservation copying for unpublished works and manuscripts

---

6. See *infra* Appendix L (p. 545) for a chart prepared by Laura N. Gasaway entitled "When Works Pass into the Public Domain."
7. For the complete list of the exclusive rights granted to a copyright owner, see 17 U.S.C. § 106 (1994).
8. *See id.* §§ 108–120 (1994).

was the first exemption created for libraries.[9] The importance of such a section for unique works that might otherwise be lost or destroyed was obvious, and the ready acceptance of such a provision demonstrated a recognition that such copying was highly unlikely to infringe on any existing economic interests.

In January 1969, S. 543 introduced the basic structure and elements of section 108 as we know it today, including preservation copying for both unpublished works in section 108(b) and for published works in section 108(c). Unlike many of the other sections related to library copying, the record shows that there was never any real dispute over adding these limited exemptions for preservation. These sections now state:

> (b) The rights of reproduction and distribution under this section apply to a copy or phonorecord of an unpublished work duplicated in facsimile form solely for the purposes of preservation and security or for deposit for research use in another library or archives . . . if the copy or phonorecord reproduced is currently in the collection of the library or archives.

> (c) The right of reproduction under this section applies to a copy or phonorecord of a published work duplicated in facsimile form solely for the purpose of replacement of a copy or phonorecord that is damaged, deteriorating, lost, or stolen, if the library or archives has, after reasonable effort, determined that an unused replacement cannot be obtained at a fair price.

Both of these sections permit the making of a single copy in facsimile form. Facsimile form is not defined in the statute, but it appears that the intention of the section was to limit reproduction to analog copies, rather than to extend it to copies in a digital format.[10]

---

9.   An early draft of the bill provided:

Notstanding [sic] the provision of section 106, it is not an infringement of copyright for a nonprofit institution, having archival custody over collections of manuscripts, documents, or other unpublished works of value to scholarly research, to reproduce, without any purpose of direct or indirect commercial advantage, any such work in its collection in facsimile copies or phonorecords for purposes of preservation and security, or for deposit for research use in any other such institution.

See Report of the Register of Copyrights, Library Reproduction of Copyrighted Works (17 U.S.C. § 108) 38 n.53 (1983).

10. The House Report specifically states that such reproduction is limited to microfilm or electrostatic process. *See* H.R. REP. NO. 94-1476, 94th Cong., 2d. Sess. (1976), *reprinted in* 17 OMNIBUS COPYRIGHT REVISION LEGISLATIVE HISTORY 75 (1977).

Such a limitation was not a major problem when the Act was passed, but as digital technology has become more widespread, it now constrains what libraries can do.

The purposes of the copying permitted under the two sections differ slightly. For unpublished works (section 108(b)), the copying may be for purposes of preservation and security or for deposit for research use in another institution. For published works (section 108(c)), the only purpose is for the replacement of a copy that is damaged, deteriorating, lost, or stolen. Some libraries have expressed a desire to digitize their journal collections as new issues arrive in the library. This, they say, is to make the digital copy into the use copy in order to "preserve" the paper original. Despite the long-term preservation goal of such a project, it does not fit within the terms of section 108. First, the copies are digital rather than "facsimile." Second, the copy is not replacing the original; it is being kept along with the original, and both may, in fact, be used. Third, if the copy is of a relatively new work in new or in very good condition, it is not a copy of a work that is damaged, deteriorating, lost, or stolen, except in the general sense that everything is deteriorating with the passage of time.

For published works, before a library may reproduce it at all, the library must also make a reasonable effort to determine that an unused replacement cannot be obtained at a fair price. Such an investigation clearly is intended to ensure that a preservation program does not interfere with the anticipated market of the copyright owner. For most works which remain in print for a relatively short period of time, this is never an issue. Moreover, for works whose pages are brittle with age, the chance of finding an unused replacement in better condition is almost non-existent. As a result, many libraries may check with the publisher or in *Books in Print*, but they inevitably find that a thorough search is not likely to be productive.

Although these sections were important milestones when the Act was first passed, they contain limitations that are problematic today. First, the single-copy limitation makes it unlawful to follow the nationally accepted standards. Virtually every funding agency that gives grants for preservation projects requires that the three-copy standard discussed above be followed. Yet, such a standard plainly exceeds the plain language of section 108. Moreover, the restriction to facsimile form limits the ability of libraries to use digital techniques. As the technology has developed in the years since the Act was passed, libraries have begun to experiment with imaging technology as a way to preserve and even enhance the stored image for the benefit of future generations of library users. Eventually, if it were not for the legal restrictions, digital imaging could replace microform as the standard for all preservation programs. Finally, only unpublished works as opposed to published ones may be "deposited in another library." This provision, together with the provision in section 108(g)(2) that proscribes "the related or concerted reproduction or distribution of multiple copies . . . of the same material . . . " makes it difficult, if not impossible, for libraries to develop cooperative preservation projects in which one library makes a copy of a deteriorated work and then makes additional copies of that work for other libraries that also wish to replace their deteriorated copy. The magnitude of the national brittle books program makes cooperative preservation projects imperative.

C. Fair Use

When a library exceeds the safe harbor of section 108, it runs the risk of liability unless the copying is found to be a fair use, as defined in section 107 of the Act. That section permits the fair use of a work,[11] but calls for the court to look at the situation on a case-by-case basis, evaluating four criteria:

1. the purpose and character of the use, including whether such use is of a commercial nature or is for nonprofit educational purposes;
2. the nature of the copyrighted work;
3. the amount and substantiality of the portion used in relation to the copyrighted work as a whole; and
4. the effect of the use upon the potential market for or value of the copyrighted work.

Preservation as a fair use is by no means certain, but a strong case can be made for it. First, the copying is clearly non-commercial, since the goal is collection preservation, not making a profit. Even if libraries were to make extra copies of items for their sister institutions which had a similar need, they would still be meeting a preservation goal, even if they charged a fee to recover some of the cost. On the other

---

11.   See section 108(f)(4) (1994), which states that nothing in section 108 affects the library's right of fair use.

hand, if a library did decide to re-publish a selection of titles as a means of bringing in some income, that new activity would change the analysis. But as long as the purpose of the copying was pure preservation, the first factor would weigh in favor of the library.

On nature of the copyrighted work, the analysis could go either way. But for the most part, library preservation programs are focusing are older scholarly works, esoteric journals, and other works for which there is little demand. The legislative history states that one consideration concerning this factor is whether the work is out of print.[12] Most likely, then, the second factor would also go in favor of the library.

The third factor clearly cuts the other way. Preservation programs by their very nature are designed to copy complete works, including complete books and even complete runs of journals. Libraries cannot argue that they are only copying a small portion of the work in question; therefore, this factor would weigh in favor of the copyright owner.

Perhaps the key provision in the analysis is the fourth factor—the effect on the market. If, as argued before, the works copied really are old and esoteric with essentially no commercial value, then this factor, too, would weigh in favor of the library. If, on the other hand, libraries choose to preserve classic texts in a given discipline, texts that have been reprinted and that together constitute a marketable core collection for the discipline, then copyright owners may well be able to contend that the library's activity interferes with their market to reprint or otherwise make available the older important materials. This part of the analysis will always be examined on a case-by-case basis, looking at the particular titles involved and analyzing whether there is any continuing viable market for the works in question.

In general, then, there is a strong case to be made that preservation copying—even preservation copying in excess of the narrow provisions of section 108—that does not interfere with the ongoing market of the copyright owner is fair use. Unfortunately, the lack of certainty in the fair use analysis leaves many librarians uneasy. Preservation programs are expensive and take a long time to plan and execute. Many are funded with outside support, and most of them exceed the narrow confines of

---

12.   S. Rep. No. 93-946, 93d Cong., 2d Sess. (1974), *reprinted in* 13 Omnibus Copyright Revision Legislative History 115 (1977).

section 108, either because of the number of copies made, or because of the use of digital techniques, or because they are undertaken in a cooperative effort with other libraries and additional copies are made available to the project partners. For such an intensive and expensive endeavor, most libraries are not willing to incur the significant risk entailed in an uncertain reliance on fair use. As a result, despite the need to preserve even newer materials, almost all large-scale library preservation programs have focused solely on older materials known to be in the public domain.

III. The White Paper, CONFU, and the NII Bill

These issues were discussed seriously before the Working Group on Intellectual Property, in the meetings of CONFU,[13] and in private sessions beyond CONFU while the White Paper was under development. In a statement before the Working Group on Intellectual Property, the library community expressed their concern about the single-copy limitation and then continued:

> The preservation problem has captured the attention of librarians, scholars, and historians nationwide. . . . Although today microfilm is still the medium of choice for preservation, it is clear that the technology is moving rapidly toward the time when preservation will be done electronically. The law should be amended to accommodate the newest preservation technology.
>
> Digital works of enduring value will also need to be preserved. Experience shows that electronic publishers, like print publishers will not keep a particular work available beyond the time when there is an economic incentive to do so. . . . The life-expectancy of most works in digital formats is only 15–20 years—much shorter than the life expectancy of paper. In the case of digital works— whether online, on tape, or on CD—preservation takes the form of "refreshing" or copying the work onto a duplicate of the medium or even moving it to the next technological generation. The current law—by its limitation of preservation copying to copying in facsimile form—does not accommodate this increasingly important need.[14]

---

13. Conference on Fair Use convened by the Patent and Trademark Office, Oct. 1994 through Nov. 1996.

14. Statement of Robert L. Oakley on Behalf of Several Library and Education Associations before the Working Group on Intellectual Property of the Information Policy Committee of the National Information Infrastructure Task Force, Nov. 18, 1993.

As a general matter, print publishers support the need to preserve their materials. Indeed, Nicolas Veliotes, formerly the head of the Association of American Publishers, served as an advisor to the Commission on Preservation and Access. Furthermore, there is no serious difficulty about the need to make three microfilm copies instead of just one. Most publishers are not going to bring a lawsuit against a library just because the library made three copies of a work, instead of one, for preservation purposes. But publishers are unwilling to concede that such copying might be a fair use under section 107 of the Act. During discussions at CONFU, they made clear that any attempt to formulate a fair use guideline for preservation was not going to be acceptable. They were willing, however, to talk about a narrowly focused amendment to section 108.

In the discussions regarding a possible amendment to section 108, it became clear that publishers become very uneasy when the discussion moves beyond microfilm copies of print originals and turns toward the preservation of digital originals or the preservation of print originals using electronic formats. They fear that preserving a work electronically could undo some potential market they might wish to exploit in the future. Nonetheless, consistent with their commitment to a narrowly defined preservation program, there is some willingness within the publishing community to allow a single electronic copy to be made. But they are not at all sure what should happen after then. Use masters from which perfect copies can be made might eliminate a market for reprints or for subsequent editions. Use copies connected to a campus network create the potential for many students to use a work simultaneously when only one copy was purchased. Copies of preserved works made available over the Internet, for example, as a direct form of interlibrary loan, could erode even basic markets for the sale of publications. Those are the worries that are on the minds of publishers.

In the end, publishers reluctantly were willing to see a single electronic copy made for preservation purposes, so long as the use of that copy was tightly controlled. They even suggested that the electronic copy could only be used like the original book—one at a time and only on site. In this day of the library without walls and highly developed networks, such limitations seem artificial and unduly restrictive to most librarians.

The outcome of these discussions was a proposal in the White Paper to accommodate the preservation needs of libraries through an amendment to section 108 of the Act.[15] The White Paper along with the subsequent proposed legislation[16] would allow libraries to make three copies of a work, so long as only one copy was in use while the others were archived. It would also explicitly allow libraries to use digital techniques for preservation purposes. Quite naturally, then, although the library groups suggested a different way to craft the language, they did support this part of the NII proposal even while objecting strenuously to other parts.

Although the library community supported the preservation amendments, the language of the bill actually went further than the library community wanted or needed, and it made a rather basic conceptual change to the underlying philosophy of section 108. Libraries want and need to be able to make three copies of works for preservation purposes. The draft language of the bill puts the three-copy provision in section 108(a) which would make it applicable to all the other subsections, not just the preservation sections. Such a change goes further than is necessary, and the library community has suggested moving the three-copy provision back into subsections (b) and (c).

As it turned out, the preservation section was one of the least controversial parts of the whole NII proposal. It was supported by the Register of Copyrights, and no opposition to it surfaced from the publishing community. It was so non-controversial, in fact, that at the end of the Congress, there was talk about separating out the preservation sections of the bill and passing them on their own. Unfortunately, that did not happen.

IV. Term Extension

The preservation issue also arose in the last Congress in the context of a proposal to extend the term of copyright. As discussed earlier, most preservation programs currently underway in libraries are proceeding only with materials now in the public domain because their term of copyright has expired. Any proposal to extend the term, therefore, has a direct impact on libraries and their ongoing preservation efforts.

---

15.   INTELLECTUAL PROPERTY AND THE NATIONAL INFORMATION INFRASTUCTURE: THE REPORT OF THE WORKING GROUP ON INTELLECTUAL PROPERTY RIGHTS 226–27 (1995).

16.   The NII Protection Act of 1995, H.R. 2441 and S. 1284, 104th Cong., 1st Sess. (1995).

The term of copyright was originally a 14-year, renewable term. Over the years, however, the term has become longer and longer— first to a 28-year renewable term, and then up to 75 years, total. Now, it is life of the author plus 50 years (or 75 years for corporate works).[17] To many outside the copyright owner community, a term of this length seems well beyond what is needed to be an incentive to create, beyond being a reasonable period to exploit a work, and beyond being a limit on the rights of creators. Now, it is just a limit on the ability of the heirs to benefit from the work of their ancestor.

Nonetheless, despite the fact that the copyright term is already well beyond the life of the creator, a bill was introduced in the 104th Congress to extend the term by an additional 20 years—to the life of the author plus 70 years (95 years for anonymous or corporate works). For older works, the new maximum would be 95 years, and works published in the 1920s and 1930s would not come into the public domain for an additional 20 years.[18]

From a preservation perspective, a change from 75 to 95 years makes a critical difference. The life expectancy of a book is about 75 years plus or minus (maybe) 25 years, depending on the original quality of the paper, wear and tear, and a host of other factors. Nonetheless, at 75 years of age, most library materials are showing significant signs of brittleness and deterioration. An additional 20 years of protection will put more library materials at greater risk than ever before.[19]

The stated reason behind this proposal was "international harmonization." Some European countries have already extended their term of copyright, and several others are considering proposals to do so. The United States needs to do likewise, it is argued, because with the reciprocal nature of international copyright, we will place our own authors at a disadvantage in overseas markets if the country fails to keep pace with changes in Europe.

The international dimension of the issue may be one reason behind the proposal, but a more important reason is probably the fact that some valuable properties from the 1920s will soon enter the public domain. Specifically, the Disney Company and the Gershwin estate

---

17.   17 U.S.C. § 302 (1994).

18.   H.R. 989 & S. 483, 104th Cong., 1st Sess. (1995).

19.   For a thorough discussion of term extension, see *supra* Chapter Three (p. 33), "The Term of Copyright," by Dennis S. Karjala.

have some important properties dating from that period. Many wonderful Gershwin tunes were written in the 1920s, and even the venerable Mickey Mouse will soon lose his copyright protection if nothing is done. These interests have placed some powerful forces behind the proposed term extension, and from the beginning it appeared that the bill had an excellent chance of passage.

Because of the impact of such a proposal on preservation and other library activities, the library community responded by proposing that library uses should be exempt from the impact of the longer term on the uses of its collections. Such an exemption would allow libraries to make copies of older works without restriction for purposes such as research, scholarship, and distance learning, in addition to preservation.

The library proposals led to a series of negotiations between the industry and the library community about how best to meet the needs of libraries without undermining the potential markets of the industry. The key issue was whether a particular work still had market value. To get at that issue, the industry proposed that before a library could take advantage of the exemption, it would have to ascertain that the work has not been commercially exploited within the last several years. The precise number of years was never agreed upon, but the need to do such an investigation could present serious pragmatic problems for libraries.

Eventually, even though the proposal about commercial exploitation originated from the industry, it became clear that it would present serious problems for a company that markets its products in the way that Disney does. Disney deliberately withholds works for long periods of time and then re-releases them for short periods with a high level of promotion. A provision that looked for a period of non–exploitation clearly could interfere with that kind of marketing strategy. Moreover, some representatives of the film industry indicated that they simply did not want anyone else preserving their works.

At the same time, some print publishers stated that commercial exploitation would have to include licensing, whether the copyright owner had possession of the work or not. If they had made a work available by license arrangement, such as through the Copyright Clearance Center, that was sufficient to constitute commercial exploitation and remove it from this provision. From the library perspective, such broad exclusion would make the whole library exemption a nullity.

At the conclusion of the talks, there had been no resolution of the issues. The Register of Copyrights, Mary Beth Peters, attempted to craft some compromise language:

> Section 108 of title 17, United States Code, is amended by redesignating subsection "(h)" as subsection "(I)" and by inserting the following new subsection:
>
>> (h) For purposes of this section, during the last 20 years of any term of copyright of a published work, a library or archives, including a nonprofit educational institution that functions as such, may preserve, reproduce, distribute, display or perform in facsimile or digital form a copy or phonorecord of such work, or portions thereof, for purposes of scholarship or research if such library or archives has first determined on the basis of a reasonable investigation that the work:
>>
>>> (1) is not subject to normal commercial exploitation; or
>>> (2) cannot be obtained at a reasonable price.
>>
>> No reproduction, distribution, display or performance under this subsection is authorized if the copyright owner or its agent provides notice pursuant to regulations promulgated by the Copyright Office to an entity described in this subsection that either of the conditions set out in paragraphs (1) and (2) does not apply.
>
> This exemption does not apply to any subsequent uses by users other than such library or archives.[20]

Such an exemption would not solve the preservation problem of the library community generally. It would, however, permit libraries to preserve at least the older works in the 20-year period of an extended term, using digital a well as microfilm techniques.

V. Conclusion

In the end, none of these proposals passed Congress. In the course of all the discussions, however, it became very clear that, with the possible exception of the film industry, preservation of library materials is still not a controversial matter. With that in mind, it should be possible to craft language to achieve that narrow goal early in the 105th Congress and to avoid weaknesses in the bills proposed in the White Paper.

---

20.   Memorandum of May 22, 1996, from Mary Beth Peters to Ed Damich, Chief Intellectual Property Counsel, Senate Committee on the Judiciary.

Chapter Seven
Library Reserve Collections: From Paper to Electronic Collections

by
Laura N. Gasaway[*]

Director of the Law Library & Professor of Law
University of North Carolina

I. Introduction

For years libraries have maintained restricted collections. Such collections were created for several reasons, among them, to remove heavily used items from the general collection to ensure their availability to a greater number of users. Since materials in the general collection can be checked out to users, often they are not available to others, at least temporarily. Librarians began to respond to increased demand for certain books and materials by placing them in a restricted area for in-library use or permitted them to circulate for a much shorter time

*   © 1997 Laura N. Gasaway.

than the usual check-out period. Although the reserve circulation period varied from library to library, two to four hours was normal. Thus, several patrons could use the same title within a day, and the library was able to satisfy the need by simply removing a title from general circulation and placing it in the "reserve collection." The actual book or bound journal volume itself was placed on reserve.

Reserve collections exist in all types of libraries, but they are used especially in school and academic libraries as an adjunct to the classroom to house assigned reading materials. Public libraries also created reserve collections, but often it was to meet the needs of school children who rely on the public library's collection to complete their school assignments.

When photocopy machines became common in libraries, librarians recognized that they need not put an entire bound journal volume on reserve when users were seeking only a particular article. So, journal articles, book chapters, and other short works were photocopied and the reproductions were placed on reserve. This permitted the original volume to be circulated or used while still ensuring an adequate number of copies of the needed item were available on reserve.

The advent of digital technology offered libraries an alternative to handling the large collections of photocopied materials that now make up a huge proportion of library reserve collections. Some academic law libraries began to scan the materials that they had previously photocopied for reserve and to store the reproductions on a server to create an electronic library or electronic collections. Electronic reserve collections benefit both users and libraries. Users can access reserve materials from a computer system maintained by the library or from anywhere within the academic institution that is connected to the campus network. They can read the material on the screen, download the item to a disk, or produce a printed copy. Thus, electronic reserve collections are more flexible for the user. For libraries, electronic collections are easier to manage and maintain. Electronic reserves (e-reserves) reduce both the amount of space required by the collection and the staff needed to service it. No longer do items have to be retrieved from the collection and checked out to individual users; instead, users can access them directly. Further, multiple users can access the same copy simultaneously from different locations.

There are copyright concerns in the creation of both photocopy and electronic reserve collections. The digital environment presents an opportunity to address anew these concerns, but, to date, there has been little agreement between publishers and users of copyrighted works about the contours any new agreements on e-reserves should take.

II. Traditional Reserve Collections

A. Placing Original Volumes on Reserve

Before libraries had lending collections, the entire library, in effect, was a reserve collection. Since nothing left the premises of the library, all materials were used in situ. There was no reason to create separate reserve collections during this era.

It is unclear when the first true reserve collections were created in libraries, but as libraries began to establish lending collections, the need arose to remove heavily used items from general circulation. When only a few novels and other types of general reading materials circulated, the need still was not great. But as non-fiction works began to circulate, and demands on collections increased, libraries had to find ways to extend the use of a small number of copies of important works. Libraries never have had sufficient funds to duplicate materials in unlimited copies despite increased demands to use copyrighted works for research and scholarship in addition to demands for circulating works for general reading. At some point, libraries responded to this demand by removing works from the general circulating collection and placing them in a separate non-circulating collection or in one with a short circulation period. Initially, the books and materials placed on reserve were those that the library identified as heavily used. Two purposes are served by creating a separate reserve collection: (1) more users could have access to the work if the circulation period was made very short; and (2) the materials themselves were protected.

In many libraries, standard works that are likely to be consulted by many people are placed on reserve. For example, a college library often places standard texts, monographs, and treatises on reserve. This collection is often referred to as "permanent reserves" indicating that the library has selected the materials to be placed on reserve and that it intends for the works to remain in the protected collection indefinitely.

In many academic institutions, one copy of each assigned textbook is placed on reserve in the library to assist students who forget to bring their copies on a particular day, or for students who cannot afford to purchase the assigned textbook. Although these are not necessarily part of the permanent reserve collection, they also are original works that are placed on reserve. To supplement textbooks assigned for specific courses, faculty members have long assigned additional readings. Sometimes these additional readings were required, and sometimes they could be read and reviewed for extra credit in the course. The faculty member provided a bibliography of these readings either separately or as a part of the course syllabus. To ensure availability, these materials were placed in a reserve room or collection.

Additionally, librarians often responded to temporary course demands by placing original volumes on reserve for the class term. When a faculty member assigned a chapter of a book and the library determined that there was demand for the work, it was placed on reserve. Often this included bound volumes of journals or a single volume from a longer set or from a multi-volume treatise.

The first mention of a reserve room in library literature was in 1878 when Harvard College reported that professors commonly gave the library a list of books to which they intended to refer their students during the class term. The library would then remove these books from the circulating collection to preserve their use for the class.[1] A decade later Melville Dewey stated that many books were placed "behind the circulation desk in closed shelves" in some academic libraries. The reason for such restricted access was because students took the books and thereby denied access to others.[2] Writing in the 1930s, Charles Harvey Brown stated that reserve rooms are mainly a creation of the 20th century. Interestingly, he also reported that there was some indication that the use of "defined reading" was decreasing and was being replaced by assignment of topics for investigation.[3] He described the gradual movement from closed to open shelves for reading rooms and cited particularly Columbia University and Vassar as institutions that maintained open shelves in their reserve rooms. The University of Nebraska went from closed to open reserve shelves between 1902 and 1910.[4] Other libraries reported a combination of open and closed shelves for

---

1.   3 LIBR. J. 271, 271 (1878).
2.   Charles Harvey Brown, CIRCULATION WORK IN COLLEGE AND UNIVERSITY LIBRARIES 19 (1933), citing 2 LIBR. NOTES 216, 216 (1887).
3.   Id. at 80. Few librarians have noted much declines in reserve collections; in fact, quite the opposite has occurred during the past quarter century.
4.   Id. at 84.

their reserves, and the University of Chicago even established a rental collection for reserve materials. For a "moderate fee" students could check out reserve materials and take them home. This system did not replace the reserve room but apparently did reduce the number of duplicate copies that the library purchased.[5]

B. Photocopies on Reserve

Often a library had difficulty meeting the needs for course reserves because it did not have enough copies of a work to satisfy the demand. Primarily for course reserves, libraries began to take advantage of reprography to make multiple copies of book chapters and articles that faculty members assigned to their students. Referred to as "course reserves," these collections consist of a number of photocopies of articles and chapters placed on reserve at the request of an individual faculty member. These course reserve materials are almost always made available under the name of the course or the faculty member's name.

It is easy to think that reprography began only in the early 1960s when photocopiers commonly began to appear in libraries. In discussing the fact that many academic libraries would not place periodical volumes on reserve unless duplicates were available, in 1933 the following statement appeared: "[I]f numbers are in print, additional copies are purchased. If the numbers are out of print, typed or Photostatted copies of articles are made."[6] Also, if the material was rare or scarce, "Sometimes certain sections of a rare book is Photostatted or mimeographed and duplicate pages are thus made available."[7] Thus, reproducing articles and other works for reserve collection is not a new phenomenon.

A student requests the item at the reserve desk and then has two options: (1) read the photocopy checked out at the reserve desk or (2) make an additional copy of the photocopy to read later. Exactly what percentage of students make copies of the photocopied item is unknown, but practicing librarians believe that it is high. Making a copy of a reserve item does not necessarily mean that the student reads the material, however. In fact, one recent study of reserve collections found that only 40 percent of the students in a class even retrieved

---

5. *Id.* at 88.
6. *Id.* at 89.
7. *Id.* at 162.

items placed on reserve.[8] There was no indication of how many of the 40 percent *read* the item!

In recent years, there have been some reports of abuse of traditional photocopy reserve collections. Some faculty members began to put photocopies of all of the readings for a course on reserve and did not require students to purchase a textbook or other materials. Thus, reserve collections grew tremendously, and the original purpose of such collections was altered. Actually, complaints about abuse of reserve collections are not new. In 1938 the following complaint was published:

> In my humble judgment, some professors have simply lost their sense of proportion. They have become so enamored of the reserved book system that they feel they could not give their favorite course unless there were from 500–1000 books on reserve, specifically ticketed with the name and number of their course.[9]

While this comment dealt with placing originals on reserve, many librarians would make the same complaint about photocopied materials today.

III. Copyright Basics and the ALA Model Policy

Traditional reserve collections in which only original volumes are placed into a special collection raise no copyright concerns. In the United States, there is no restriction on the right to read, and copyright holders are not entitled to any royalties when books are loaned by libraries.[10] Copyright concerns arise only when materials are *reproduced* for library reserve collections.

---

8. Statement of Mary Jackson, Association of Research Libraries, at Conference on Fair Use, October 25, 1995.

9. Theodore W. Koch, *A Symposium on the Reserve Book System in* COLLEGE AND UNIVERSITY LIBRARY SERVICE: TRENDS, STANDARDS, APPRAISAL, PROBLEMS 73, 74 (1938).

10. 17 U.S.C. § 109(a) (1994). In several European countries, there is a public lending right which generates royalties for copyright holders. The United States has not enacted such a provision, nor is it likely to do so. *See* LAURA N. GASAWAY & SARAH K. WIANT, LIBRARIES AND COPYRIGHT: A GUIDE TO COPYRIGHT LAW IN THE 1990s 199–216 (1994) [hereinafter GASAWAY & WIANT].

A. Copyright Basics

Under the Copyright Act of 1976,[11] original works of authorship that are fixed in tangible media of expression are entitled to copyright protection.[12] Copyright holders get a bundle of five rights: reproduction, distribution, adaptation, performance, and display.[13] In reserve collections comprised in whole or in part of photocopied materials, it is the reproduction and distribution rights that are involved. When a library photocopies articles and book chapters and places them on reserve, it has engaged in reproduction. In making the copies available to students who then check out the reproduced copies from the reserve collection, the library is not necessarily distributing that copy, however. Distribution typically envisions a change in ownership of the copy, but in the reserve collection situation, a student simply borrows the copy. That user may indeed make an additional photocopy, but the library's photocopy is returned to the library. Even if the distribution right is implicated along with the reproduction right, the library has not necessarily infringed the copyright.

The five exclusive rights of the copyright holder are tempered by a number of limitations or exceptions found in the statute,[14] the most important of which is fair use.[15] Often called the "safety valve" of copyright, fair use excuses activity that normally would be infringement. When a use is a fair use, the user does not have to seek permission from the copyright holder or pay royalties. The law simply recognizes that some uses of copyrighted works have social value and are excused. Section 107 of the Copyright Act provides that:

> [T]he fair use of a copyrighted work, including such use by reproduction in copies . . . for purposes such as criticism, comment, news reporting, teaching (including multiple copies for classroom use), scholarship, or research, is not an infringement of copyright. . . . [16]

To determine whether a use is fair, the statute directs that the following factors be considered: (1) purpose and character of the use;

---

11.   17 U.S.C. §§ 101–1101.
12.   *Id.* § 102(a).
13.   *Id.* § 106.
14.   *See id.* §§ 107–121.
15.   *Id.* § 107.
16.   *Id.*

(2) nature of the copyrighted work; (3) amount and substantiality used; and (4) effect on the potential market for or value of the work. One of the difficulties with fair use is that only a court can determine authoritatively whether a particular use is fair. Thus, it is not only a limitation on the exclusive rights of the copyright holder, but it is also a defense to copyright infringement. Further, there are no "bright line" rules for judging fair use, but there are some principles that can be used to help evaluate a particular use and whether it qualifies as a fair use. Courts balance these four factors in making a fair use determination.

The first factor, *purpose and character of the use*, focuses on whether the use is for scholarship or commercial gain. Nonprofit educational uses generally are more likely to be a fair use than are commercial ones.[17] Courts also favor so-called productive or transformative uses over simple reproductions. An example of a transformative use is when a critic quotes extensively from a book in a literary criticism of the book.[18] Clearly, photocopying materials for reserve collections involves no such transformative use. The use, however, is for nonprofit educational purposes, so the use for reserve collections satisfies one prong of the first factor but not the other; however, this may be enough.

Nature of the copyrighted work, the second fair use factor, requires an examination of the copyrighted work itself. Each work must be judged separately on this factor. The legislative history states that there is a definite difference between making a copy of a short news note and reproducing an entire musical score. Further, by their nature some works have no fair use rights; this includes standardized tests and work booklets, which are works that are meant to be consumed.[19] As a general rule, uses of factual works are more likely to be a fair use than are uses of creative works.[20] Other considerations for this factor include whether the work is unpublished or is out of print.[21] To rely on this factor in a fair use determination for materials placed on reserve thus requires looking at each item individually.

---

17.   PAUL GOLDSTEIN, COPYRIGHT § 10.2.2.1 (2d ed. 1996) [hereinafter GOLDSTEIN].

18.   American Geophysical Union v. Texaco, Inc., 37 F.3d 881, 890–92 (2d Cir. 1994).

19.   S. REP. NO. 93-976, 93d Cong., 2d Sess. (1974), *reprinted in* 13 OMNIBUS COPYRIGHT REVISION LEGISLATIVE HISTORY 117 (1977) [hereinafter S. REP. NO. 93-976].

20.   *Texaco*, 37 F.3d at 893.

21.   S. REP. NO. 93-976, *supra* note 19.

The third factor, *amount and substantiality used*, focuses on how much of the copyrighted work is reproduced. Generally, the smaller the amount used, the more likely the use will be found to be a fair use. This quantitative determination is very dependent on how "the work" is defined. In section 108(d), for example, libraries are told that they can reproduce a single copy of an article from a periodical issue or other contribution from a collective work. This indicates that the copyrighted work is the journal issue, and certainly librarians had never considered otherwise until the *Texaco* decision held that the individual article was the copyrighted work.[22] Thus, outside of section 108, reproduction of an article may constitute copying 100 percent of a copyrighted work. While short portions of a book might be used, it is unlikely that only portions of articles would be placed on reserve. It is possible, but not the most likely situation for either higher or secondary education. Thus, the entire work is usually copied if the work is defined as an article or a separately authored chapter of a book.

Amount and substantiality is a qualitative test as well. If the alleged infringer takes the heart of the work, regardless of the amount used quantitatively, the use will not be a fair one. Determining the heart of a work is not difficult with some works, but it is very difficult with others. The classic example is a 30-minute videotape of the eruption of a volcano, only one minute of which depicts the actual eruption. The remainder of the tape records events leading up to the eruption and then the aftermath. If the alleged infringer has reproduced the one-minute segment containing the actual eruption, he has copied only one-thirtieth of the tape, but that is the heart of the work, and thus would not be a fair use.[23]

The final fair use factor, *market effect*, focuses on the effect the use has on the potential market for or value of the use. This is the economic test for the copyright holder. In *Harper & Row*,[24] the Supreme Court indicated that the fourth factor was the most important factor,[25]

---

22. *Texaco*, 37 F.3d at 893–94.
23. See Harper & Row Publishers, Inc. v. The Nation Enters., 471 U.S. 539, 566 (1985), for a case in which the qualitative part of this factor was critical to the holding that the use was not a fair one.
24. 471 U.S. 539 (1985).
25. *Id.* at 566.

but this was changed in *Campbell v. Acuff-Rose Music, Inc.*[26] when the Supreme Court held that no one factor was more important than another.[27]

Nonetheless, a series of cases indicates that publishers have an economic interest in the right to license to photocopy and that avoiding paying those royalties, even for research and educational uses, is not a fair use. In *Texaco*, the Second Circuit Court of Appeals held that making single photocopies of articles by a Texaco scientist who archived the copies for later use was not a fair use.[28] Both the archiving and the fact that the publishers had provided a mechanism for licensing through the Copyright Clearance Center, coupled with the court's holding that the publishers had lost the right to license to photocopy because Texaco had opted not to pay royalties for these copies meant that the use was not a fair use.[29] Two cases dealing with the reproduction of coursepacks for college courses by commercial photocopy services but at the request of a faculty member are *Basic Books, Inc. v. Kinko's Graphics Corp.*[30] and *Princeton University Press v. Michigan Document Services.*[31] They also recognize that the loss of royalties for reproduction in coursepacks fails the market-effect test.

B. Classroom Guidelines

When the Copyright Act was being debated, the need to use copyrighted works in nonprofit education was recognized. An agreement negotiated by representatives of publishers, authors, and educational associations and was presented to Congress. Called the "Classroom Guidelines," the agreement covers classroom copying of books and periodicals in nonprofit educational institutions. These guidelines were published in the House Report that accompanied the Act,[32] and Congress recognized the agreement with approval.

---

26.   510 U.S. 569 (1994).

27.   *Id.* at 578.

28.   *Texaco*, 37 F.3d at 899.

29.   *Id.* at 898–99.

30.   758 F. Supp. 1522 (S.D.N.Y. 1991).

31.   99 F.3d 1381 (6th Cir. 1996).

32.   H.R. REP. NO. 94-1467, 94th Cong., 2d Sess. (1976) *reprinted in* OMNIBUS COPYRIGHT LAW REVISION LEGISLATION 68–71 (1977) [hereinafter H.R. REP. NO. 94-1467].

The guidelines[33] detail conditions and tests that should be met when a teacher reproduces multiple copies of copyrighted works to use in the classroom. Although the guidelines indicate that they are minimum rather than maximum guidelines, many educational institutions apply them as if they are maximums. The guidelines also deal with single copying by teachers for their own use in teaching and research,[34] but for purposes of this chapter, it is the multiple-copying portions that are important. Teachers are permitted to make multiple copies of copyrighted works and distribute one copy to each student in the class if certain tests are satisfied: (1) brevity; (2) spontaneity; (3) cumulative effects; and (4) a copyright notice appearing on each copy.[35]

The guidelines define brevity very specifically. For an article, brevity means an article of 2500 words or fewer or an excerpt of 1000 words or 10 percent, whichever is less (but with a minimum of 500 words). For poetry, the guidelines permit the poem to be copied if it is 250 words or fewer in length and is printed on two pages or fewer. If the copyrighted work is a graphic work, it meets the brevity test.[36] These word limitations are problematic for higher education, and the American Association of University Professors and the Association of American Law Schools failed to endorse these guidelines, considering them too restrictive to be workable for colleges and universities.

Spontaneity means that the copying is done at the instigation of the individual teacher and is not directed by "higher authority." Further, the decision to reproduce the work must be made so late in the class term that there is no opportunity to obtain permission from the copyright owner.[37] The spontaneity requirement indicates that the purpose of the multiple copying for classroom use is for filling in, presenting late-breaking news, or for using material of which the faculty member previously was unaware. In other words, it is not a coursepack.

There are several parts to cumulative effects. First, the copying may be done for only one course. If a teacher has multiple sections of a course, however, this is still one course. Second, the teacher may not repeat with respect to the same item from term to term. Such repeated

---

33. For the text of the Classroom Guidelines, see *infra* Appendix B (p. 485).
34. H.R. REP. NO. 94-1467, *supra* note 32, at 68.
35. *Id.* at 68–69.
36. *Id.*
37. *Id.* at 69.

copying cannot meet the spontaneity test for use of the same material in subsequent class terms. Third, teachers may use only one article or other contribution from an author, or two excerpts from an author during the class term, and no more than three from a periodical volume or other collective work. The fourth cumulative effect actually appears later in the guidelines, but it actually is the ultimate cumulative effect: no more than nine instances of such copying during the class term.[38]

Additionally, there may be no charge to the students for the photocopies beyond the actual cost of copying. Further, each reproduced copy must contain a notice of copyright on the first page.[39] Teachers are prohibited from using the guidelines to produce anthologies or to reproduce consumable works (such as standardized tests, answer sheets, or workbooks).[40]

Considerable criticism has been levied at the guidelines from the academic community. In fact, in their active opposition, the American Association of University Professors wrote to Congress encouraging rejection of inclusion of the guidelines in any part of the legislative history.[41] Despite this opposition, many schools have made the guidelines their own by including them in campus copyright policies.[42]

The guidelines have been litigated, but not in a case specifically dealing with reproduction and distribution of photocopies to students in a class by a teacher. The coursepack cases did discuss the guidelines with approval, however. In 1991, the Second Circuit Court discussed the guidelines in *Kinko's* because defendant Kinko's raised the Classroom Guidelines as a defense to the copying it was doing. The court cited and discussed the guidelines with approval even though it found them inapplicable to Kinko's since it is a commercial copying service and the guidelines apply only to nonprofit educational institutions.[43] The Sixth Circuit court sitting en banc also cited the guidelines with approval in

---

38.   *Id.*

39.   *Id.* at 70.

40.   *Id.* at 69.

41.   *See* John C. Stedman, *The New Copyright Law: Photocopying for Educational Use,* 63 AAUP BULL. (1977), at 5, 15.

42.   KENNETH D. CREWS, COPYRIGHT, FAIR USE, AND THE CHALLENGE FOR UNIVERSITIES: PROMOTING THE PROGRESS OF HIGHER EDUCATION 68 (1993) [hereinafter CREWS].

43.   *Id.* at 1535–37.

Michigan Document Services[44] when it reversed the earlier holding of its three-judge panel.[45] It discussed the guidelines and also indicated that they applied to nonprofit educational institutions, which MDS was not. The majority classified MDS as a commercial copying service.[46] One dissenting judge stated that had the individual students made the copies or had the individual faculty members made multiple copies to distribute to the students, it would not have been infringement.[47]

Unfortunately, these cases appear to convert these "safe harbor" guidelines into maximum guidelines. They still have not been litigated with a proper defendant, however, i.e., a teacher who exceeds the guidelines or an educational institution that does direct the copying by individual teachers. Nonetheless, courts have cited the guidelines with approval.

C. ALA Model Policy

After January 1, 1978, the effective date of the Copyright Act, libraries realized that nothing in either section 107 or section 108 clearly dealt with library reserves of photocopies of copyrighted works made to support individual classes, most often at the request of an individual faculty member. Many authorities argued in favor of a broad right for libraries to reproduce copies for reserve based on the Classroom Guidelines. Emeritus Professor of Law John C. Stedman of the University of Wisconsin–Madison stated that the provisions of the Classroom Guidelines should give considerable comfort to reserve collection managers. "[I]f it is permissible to make 'multiple copies for classroom use,' it would seem follow logically that one could make a smaller number for use under the restrictive conditions that typically apply to a library reserve program."[48] He also stated that normally educational institutions would not photocopy entire works for reserve since it would be more economical to purchase the works; thus, the market effect of the copying would be minimal.[49] This contrasts with the *Texaco* holding which found that the

---

44.   99 F.3d 1381 (6th Cir. 1996)
45.   74 F.3d 1528 (6th Cir. 1996).
46.   *MDS*, 99 F.3d at 1390–91.
47.   *Id.* at 1395 (Merritt, J., dissenting).
48.   John C. Stedman, *Academic Library Reserves, Photocopying and the Copyright Law*, 39 COLL. & RES. LIBR. NEWS 263, 265 (1978) [hereinafter Stedman].
49.   *Id.*

right to license to photocopy was an important right that caused negative market impact to the publishers when one in the for-profit sector avoids paying royalties.[50] Stedman did warn libraries to be careful to "avoid unreasonable and excessive photocopying."[51]

In 1982, because of questions from its members, the American Library Association issued its *Model Policy Concerning College and University Photocopying for Classroom, Research and Library Reserve Use*.[52] These guidelines are the least authoritative of any issued in connection with the new Act in that they have no stamp of Congress whatsoever. Further, they do not represent negotiations between copyright holders and users; instead, they are merely the opinion of a library association, albeit the largest library organization. On the other hand, publishers apparently did not object to the guidelines since they have instituted no litigation against libraries that adhere to the ALA Reserve Guidelines.[53]

The guidelines begin with a statement that libraries may photocopy and place materials on reserve "in accordance with guidelines similar to those governing formal classroom distribution for face-to-face teaching. . . ."[54] This view specifically was rejected by the Register of Copyrights, however.[55] The Reserve Guidelines go on to state that the library reserve room functions as an extension to the classroom and that photocopying for reserve for convenience of the student simply reflects the individual student's right to copy materials for herself for class preparation, research, and the like, which is permitted under fair use. The Reserve Guidelines state that the Classroom Guidelines are in many ways inappropriate for colleges and universities since requirements like "brevity" simply cannot mean the same thing for higher education as they do for grade school. If the faculty member's request is for only one copy to be placed on reserve, then the library may copy an entire article, book chapter, or poem.[56]

---

50.   *Texaco*, 37 F.3d at 897–99.

51.   Stedman, *supra* note 48, at 267.

52.   *Reprinted in* 43 Coll. & Res. Lib. News 127–31 (1982) [hereinafter Reserve Guidelines]. The text of the guidelines appears as Appendix F, *infra* p. 497.

53.   *See* Gasaway & Wiant, *supra* note 10, at 148–49.

54.   Reserve Guidelines, *supra* note 52, at 127.

55.   James D. Heller & Sarah K. Wiant, Copyright Handbook 28–29 (1984).

56.   Reserve Guidelines, *supra* note 52, at 129.

The guidelines themselves are divided into two parts. The first part restates some of the requirements from the Classroom Guidelines and states that, in general, materials photocopied for reserve should follow the "standard guidelines," then the following are listed:

1. The distribution of the same materials does not occur every semester.
2. Only one copy is distributed for each student.
3. The material includes a copyright notice on the first page of the portion of the material photocopied.
4. The students are not assessed any fee beyond the actual cost of the photocopying.[57]

For requests to place multiple copies on reserve, the ALA Reserve Guidelines state that these guidelines should be met:

1. The amount of material should be reasonable in relation to the total amount of material assigned for one term of a course taking into account the nature of the course, its subject matter, and level, 17 U.S.C. § 107(1) and (3).
2. The number of copies should be reasonable in light of the number of students enrolled, the difficulty and timing of assignments, and the number of other courses which may assign the same material, 17 U.S.C. § 107(1) and (3).
3. The material should contain a notice of copyright, 17 U.S.C. § 401.
4. The effect of photocopying the material should not be detrimental to the market for the work. (In general, the library should own at least one copy of the work.) 17 U.S.C. § 107(4).[58]

Based on these statements, clearly library reserves are not meant to supersede the need for a textbook which students purchase or a coursepack for which permission is sought and royalties paid when requested. Materials photocopied for reserve may be assigned reading or they may also be optional reading; in either event, they are intended to complement a textbook and/or coursepack and not replace them. The second statement concerning the number of copies of the repro-duced material that are placed on reserve leads to the conclusion that the library is better suited to make this decision than the faculty member. The effect of the photocopying should not be detrimental to

---

57. *Id.*
58. *Id.*

the market for the work, and the only way judge the effect on the market is to examine the parent work. If a faculty member requests that five chapters from a book be placed on reserve, the library needs to know how many chapters are in the book before it can make a determination about the market impact. In other words, five chapters from a six- or eight-chapter book is such a large portion that the faculty member should have the students purchase the book. But if the book is comprised of 35 chapters, five is such a small number that the professor likely would not require students to purchase the book.

The part of the Reserve Guidelines that garners the most criticism is the statement from the Classroom Guidelines that "the distribution of the same photocopied material does not occur every semester." Many libraries simply believe this is too restrictive based on fair use.

A large number of college and university libraries have developed reserve policies that carefully comply with the Reserve Guidelines. Some libraries are very conservative and never go beyond the guidelines, while others are more expansive in their interpretation.[59] Too often, libraries have been the passive recipients of requests from faculty for reserve materials. Librarians have not made the necessary inquiries to determine whether the faculty member's request satisfied the Reserve Guidelines. Further, after the *Kinko's* decision, librarians accepted coursepacks for reserve when faculty members determined that their coursepacks were too expensive when permission was sought and royalties paid, so they began to put the coursepack material on reserve in the library for students to copy themselves. Libraries that accepted this material violated both the spirit and the provisions of the Reserve Guidelines. The huge majority of academic libraries, however, either follow the ALA Reserve Guidelines or have their own similar policies.

Despite compliance with the Reserve Guidelines and other library attempts to comply with fair use for reserve copying, publishers have recently stated that they never agreed to the guidelines. Additionally, they believe that reproducing entire articles is too much.[60]

---

59.   CREWS, *supra* note 42, at 87–88.

60.   The statements were made by publishers' representatives including Carol Risher of the Association of American Publishers and Harriet Goldberg of Simon & Schuster at various sessions of the Conference on Fair Use, Oct. 1994 through Nov. 1996. *See infra* text accompanying notes 70–73.

IV. Electronic Reserve Collections

It was only natural that libraries would turn to technology to solve a variety of problems caused by reserve collections. First, reserve collections occupy considerable space and are not easy to manage. Second, because the individual photocopied items are unbound pieces, they have to be placed in folders or some other cover to prevent loss and to keep them with other reserve items for that course. Many libraries resort to file cabinets and file folders to maintain the materials. Others use pamphlet boxes or other method of storing them on shelves. Third, because faculty members tend to re-use items, the library often has to photocopy the material again each semester as the copies are worn, marked on, etc. Fourth, the items have to be checked out and back in as users retrieve and use them. Lastly, the library has to determine what to do with the items at the end of the semester. Some libraries return all items to the faculty member while others retain them in the reserve collection. Still others hold onto the photocopies but do not permit them to circulate after conclusion of the semester.

E-reserve systems are of several different types, but all include producing a digital copy of an existing print work and then making the item available to students through a workstation. Some libraries permit only in-library use, but more either currently or soon will permit access from anywhere with a network connection.

A. Benefits of Electronic Reserve Systems

Regardless of the decisions the library makes, the management and storage of the collection is a problem for most libraries. As libraries began to have computers and scanning technology available to them, it was natural that they would begin to envision converting paper reserve collections to digital format. An electronic system solves many but not all of the problems inherent in paper reserve collections. For example, an e-reserve system greatly reduces the space required to maintain the collection. It requires scanning only one time rather than repeated copying by the library, it reduces the necessity of finding storage means such as folders, pamphlet boxes, etc., and staff members no longer have to check in and out reserve items.

An e-reserve system provides additional benefits to the library and to the user. For the user, the methods of accessing the material are greatly increased, not only through the ability to search the items on the system in a variety of ways, but also since most e-reserve systems are established over the campus network. Thus, students can retrieve materials not only in the library (as with a paper reserve collection) but also from their dormitory rooms or wherever there is access to the network. With a paper collection, students can either read the photocopy they check out or make a photocopy of that copy to take with them for later reading and study. An electronic system adds an additional possibility. The student may not only read the item on the computer screen or print out a copy but also may download the item to a disk, make notes right on the disk copy, and rearrange the materials to facilitate study.

An electronic system provides additional benefits for the library also. It can manage the collection better, provide better bibliographic access to the materials on reserve, maintain permission records more efficiently, and store the items efficiently when the course is not being taught while still not permitting student access. It relieves demand for seating space within the library and generally delivers reserve items more efficiently.

B. Copyright Concerns Unique to Electronic Reserves

Electronic reserve collections raise all of the copyright concerns that exist for a paper reserve collection but raise new ones as well. Many libraries determined that they would not attempt to obtain permission but would instead try to follow the ALA Reserve Guidelines as a way to deal with the copyright.[61] Others established their systems but decided that they would seek permission for every item scanned into the e-reserve system.[62] A few libraries experimented with e-reserve systems but did not place anything in the system other than items in which the requesting faculty member held the copyright.[63]

---

61.   Duke University Library initially took this approach when it initiated its electronic reserve system in 1992.

62.   One of the first electronic reserve systems implemented was at San Diego State University (SDSU), which seeks permission and pays royalties if requested for each item in the system. For an article that describes the SDSU system, see Richard J. Goodram, *The E-RBR: Confirming the Technology and Exploring the Law of "Electronic Reserves": Two Generations of the Digital Library System at the SDSU Library*, 22 J. ACAD. LIBR. 118 (1996).

63.   The University of Pittsburgh Library chose this alternative as it began to adopt electronic reserves.

Creating an e-reserve system also raises unique copyright problems. Clearly, an item is reproduced when it is scanned and placed into the system, but it is also reproduced whenever a student prints or downloads the item. At least one recent case indicates that simply reading the item on the screen makes a copy of the copyrighted item.[64] Thus, an electronic system makes more copies of a work than are made in a photocopied collection. Further, publishers argue that the copy made is basically not a copy but is an original. In other words, there is no diminution in the quality of the copy when it is reproduced either through printing or downloading to disk as currently occurs when a photocopy is further reproduced. On the other hand, when the use is made for nonprofit educational purposes, it may be a fair use.

Because of the ease of further reproduction once an item is digitized, publishers fear uncontrolled reproduction. They believe students are likely to upload reserve items onto listserves, and "with a few keystrokes, transmit the work to 100,000 people."[65] This is not a possibility with paper reserve systems since the item is not in digital format. While it is not possible to ensure absolutely that such uncontrolled distribution will not occur, the library can take steps to try to prevent this. For example, each item copyrighted work included in the e-reserve system should display the notice of copyright along with an additional statement to the effect that no further distribution of the copyrighted work is permitted.

Another possible copyright problem is that an e-reserve system that is accessed in a public area may also infringe the display right of copyright owners. It is only the right of public display that is an exclusive right of the owner. A public display is defined as one that occurs in a place that is open to the public or where a substantial number of persons outside the normal circle of family and friends is gathered.[66] Thus, displaying a digital copy on a computer screen in public area of the library may be a problem. On the other hand, how

---

64. MAI Sys. Corp. v. Peak Computer, Inc., 991 F.2d 511 (9th Cir. 1993). Many scholars disagree with this holding and believe that transitory copies do not equate with a true reproduction of a copyrighted work. That copy is viewed as incidental to the use.

65. Carol Risher, Vice President for Copyright, Association of American Publishers, statement at the Conference on Fair Use, Jan. 4, 1995.

66. 17 U.S.C. § 101 (1994).

likely is it that a group of students or members of the public are going to be so interested in a reserve item that they flock to a computer workstation in a public area of the library to view a display of an item on reserve? It is very unlikely.

Copyright holders are also concerned that access and use of the material will increase which will reduce their sales of the parent volume or royalties they would otherwise receive for photocopying. This concern has two aspects. One is that ease of access to the electronic system will increase the number of people who use the reproduction of the copyrighted work. This certainly could be the case if the library simply makes all reserve items available over the campus network since individuals outside of the college or university also can access the campus network over the Internet. The library can insure that this does not occur by restricting access to the materials reproduced in the system to students, faculty, and staff of the institution or to students who are actually enrolled in that course.

The other aspect is that the electronic system can easily provide increased bibliographic access points if individual articles and chapters are cataloged and entered into online catalog. This concern easily can be met by simply avoiding cataloging to the article-specific level unless all journals are so cataloged in the library. In other words, bibliographic entry points should be under the name of the faculty member and the number and/or name of the course.

When a library obtains a work in digital format only (as opposed to converting a paper copy to digital), the license agreement that accompanies the work will control whether portions of the work can be included in an e-reserve system. While there still will be fair use, the library exemption contains a statement that nothing "affects any contractual obligations assumed at any time by the library or archives when it obtained a copy or phonorecord of a work in its collection."[67] This indicates that license valid agreements trump section 108 copying.

---

67.   Id. § 108(f)(4).

V. Electronic Reserve Guidelines

When the report on intellectual property in the national information infrastructure, the White Paper,[68] called for a Conference on Fair Use (CONFU) to determine whether it was possible to develop guidelines for the fair use of copyrighted works in the digital environment,[69] many librarians assumed that electronic reserves would be one of these issues. Beginning in October 1994, CONFU met regularly and worked on a series of guidelines, among them e-reserves. The E-Reserve Guidelines ultimately were completed by a small working group, and they recognized that materials included in an e-reserve system should constitute an ad hoc or supplemental source for students and should not take the place of a textbook, coursepack, or other materials.

Despite initial support for the Electronic Reserve Guidelines, ultimately neither most library associations nor the Association of American Publishers (AAP) endorsed them,[70] and they were not included in the final report of CONFU. A number of organizations including the American Council of Learned Societies, the American Association of Law Libraries, Special Libraries Association, and the Association of American University Presses did endorse the guidelines, however. The E-Reserve Guidelines certainly address the important issues.[71] Those library associations that decided not to endorse the guidelines stated that they were too restrictive on libraries. The AAP states that the guidelines "fail to provide any clear guidance on limitations on the use of copyrighted material."[72] The guidelines were criticized as going far beyond fair use since they permit reproduction of entire articles and chapters, rather than small portions.[73]

A. The Guidelines

The guidelines attempt to differentiate between the primary materials assigned for a course and the complementary or supplementary

---

68. INTELLECTUAL PROPERTY AND THE NATIONAL INFORMATION INFRASTRUCTURE: THE REPORT OF THE WORKING GROUP ON INTELLECTUAL PROPERTY RIGHTS (1995).

69. *Id.* at 83–84.

70. AAP Statement on E-Reserves, presented at CONFU, May 26, 1996 [hereinafter AAP Statement].

71. For the text of the Electronic Reserve Guidelines, see *infra* Appendix G (p. 499).

72. AAP Statement, *supra* note 70.

73. *Id.*

readings of copyrighted articles and chapters that might be found in a reserve collection. It equates digitizing the materials with placing them in a collection of photocopies for course reserves and thus permits reproduction of entire journal articles and book chapters. As Peter Grenquist, Executive Director of the Association of American University Presses, stated, "There are costs on both sides. Publishers will have to bear some of the costs and so will libraries."[74] Publishers may receive reduced royalties because of this one-term use without permission, but libraries bear the cost of managing the system and implementing certain restrictions.

The guidelines detail several requirements that should alleviate some of the copyright concerns of the copyright owner community. These limitations include: (a) use of an article or chapter in an e-reserve system only one term without obtaining permission from the copyright holder; (b) restricting access to the e-reserve materials to students enrolled in the course; (c) including admonishments that no further distribution of the material is permitted; and (d) no more detailed bibliographic access to the material than is provided for other journal articles.

1. One-Time Use. The ALA Reserve Guidelines indicate that photocopied materials should be placed on reserve only for one semester. The Electronic Reserve Guidelines contain the same limitation. Because a digital copy of a work is, in effect, an original, and because each copy printed from the digital copy also is an original, the one-time use limitation attempts to balance the rights of the copyright holder with the rights of the nonprofit educational user. It recognizes that repeated use likely is beyond what can be considered a fair use. Librarians must recognize that a digital copy may be different from a photocopy, and for this reason one-time use is a fair restriction. The AAP states that it believes even one-time use is not fair, however.[75]

2. Restricting Access to Enrolled Students. Because there is a possibility of abuse, making the e-reserve course materials available only to students enrolled in the course goes a long way to reduce the potential for abuse. While the likelihood that others outside of the course will be

---

74.   Statement made at CONFU meeting, Washington, DC, May 30, 1996.

75.   AAP Statement, *supra* note 70.

interested in reading the materials on course reserve is slight, this limitation is one of the costs that the library or school must bear.

Students access can be restricted in a variety of ways with varying technological methods. Each institution can select its own method for verifying that the student who seeks access to the material is enrolled in the course. The library can control this verification method entirely and needs little sophistication to do this. One of the simplest methods would be to assign each course an access number that is distributed only to students in the course. Only when the access number is entered into the system would the student be granted access to the electronic course reserve materials. At the other end of the technology scale would be a system adopted by a college or university that automatically verifies course enrollment when the student enters a PIN number. There are institutions which already have the technology to implement this.

3. Statement Prohibiting Further Distribution. The Electronic Reserve Guidelines dictate that each copyrighted item in the digital system should contain notice of copyright. This complies with the Classroom Guidelines and with the ALA Reserve Guidelines. Because of the fairly low level of retrieval of reserve materials generally, the likelihood that students will upload the work onto a listserve seems remote. It appears that many students, however, do not recognize that the copyright notice means works should not be transmitted to others through a listserve, etc. Therefore, including a statement to the effect that "further transmission of this work is prohibited" helps to alert students that such transmission is multiple reproduction of the copyrighted work. If such a statement appears along with the copyright notice, the student is alerted that further transmission or copying is also an infringement of copyright. This is another of the costs that the institution should bear, and it is not burdensome.

4. Bibliographic Access. The problem with bibliographic access was discussed above. The Electronic Reserve Guidelines dictate that libraries should not provide bibliographic access at any greater level of detail than is done for other journal articles and book chapters. This means that the bibliographic access should be limited to course name and number, and name of the faculty member. This reduces the likelihood that other students not enrolled in the course will be encouraged to seek access to the materials.

B. Other Issues

The Copyright Clearance Center (CCC), which collects royalties for copying in excess of fair use photocopying, now handles royalties for digital copying by some of its annual authorization licensees. The CCC has indicated that it would be willing to handle the permissions and royalty collection and distribution issues for e-reserve copying beyond the one-term use. If the E-Reserve Guidelines are followed, then there actually may be more seeking permission and payment of royalties than will occur otherwise. Thus, the CCC's system for reserves will make it considerably easier for both libraries and for copyright holders.

VI. Conclusion

The availability of digital technology presents an excellent opportunity for both libraries and copyright holders to reexamine their policies and determine how reserve collections can take advantage of this new technology and still recognize the legitimate rights and interests of copyright holders. The copyright law is focused not on benefiting the owners of copyrights but on the public good. The law exists to "promote the progress of science and the useful arts,"[76] not to ensure economic rewards to authors and publishers.[77] Promotion of learning is thus a constitutional purpose, and one way it is facilitated is through nonprofit educational uses of copyrighted works. Reserve collections help ensure that materials are available in the library to support courses taught by the institution. E-reserve collections simply adapt new technology for old reserve collections. Because of the differences in digital works and photocopies, however, there must be some controls on libraries' abilities to digitize works and make them available.

Rejection of the E-Reserves Guidelines by the AAP is perhaps understandable, but university presses have signed on to the guidelines. University presses comprise about 18 percent of the membership of the AAP, and materials published by university presses makes up a large portion of the materials reproduced for reserve collections. Publishers may assume that libraries will not place their materials into e-reserve collections if the AAP rejects the guidelines, and this may be accurate.

---

76.   U.S. CONST. art. I, § 8, cl. 8.

77.   Feist Publications, Inc. v. Rural Tel. Serv. Co., 499 U.S. 340, 349 (1991).

It may also mean that the publishers' materials are no longer used for course reserves and the publisher loses too, along with the students who would have been exposed to the ideas in the works and now will not be so enlightened.

Practicing librarians constantly ask for guidance and help in managing reserve collections. The ALA Reserve Guidelines are not completely applicable to the digital world; the E-Reserve Guidelines deal with the specific issues regarding e-reserves and with the concern of both publishers and libraries. Why many library associations have determined that they will not endorse the guidelines is interesting. Some state that they believe libraries can just apply the four fair use factors and make their own determinations. This is well and good, but practicing librarians do not agree. When confronted by a faculty member who demands that his or her course material be placed in the digital system, a librarian may not have time or the ability to apply fair-use factors. The E-Reserve Guidelines provide this cushion for managing reserve collections and the problems compounded by e-reserves.

At least one university library implemented the E-Reserve Guidelines for their library reserve system in the fall of 1996. While it is too early to evaluate completely the success of the Cornell system, preliminary evaluations are positive. It remains to be seen whether the AAP will issue a legal challenge to an institution that follows the E-Reserve Guidelines, but there is some indication that it might do so.

As has already occurred, some libraries will follow the E-Reserve Guidelines regardless of the position library associations take. But without endorsement of the E-Reserve Guidelines libraries are left with little help from their library associations. There often is strength in numbers, and the failure to endorse the guidelines abandons libraries and practicing librarians who seek help from their professional organizations in determining rules of good practice.

Chapter Eight
Resource Sharing and Copyright Among Library Consortia Members[*]

by
David Ensign

Law Librarian and Professor of Law
University of Louisville School of Law

I. Introduction

The library ideal of owning all information resources needed by its patrons is no longer viable for several reasons. One is that the cost of materials has risen dramatically in recent years.[1] At the same time, the

---

1.   According to the price index sponsored by the American Association of Law Libraries, the mean cost per title of legal monographs rose from $11.16 in the 1973–74 academic year to $70.16 in 1993–94. Using 1973–74 as the base year, the index value rose to 628.94 during that period. For all serials including legal periodicals, the mean cost per title rose from $50.08 in 1973–74 to $278.70 in 1993–94, for an index value of 556.51. Bettie Scott, *Price Index for Legal Publications 1993–94*, 86 L. LIBR. J. 837, 838 (1994).

information explosion has increased the number of resources available to libraries.[2] The proliferation of media on which information can be stored has also increased. In the mid-1970s, libraries purchased information primarily in hardcopy sources such as monographs, periodicals, and looseleaf services, or on microforms. Lockheed Dialog and SDC/ORBIT were the primary online services, but little information was available full text. Because the personal computer had not yet been developed, information was not yet available on CD-ROM or other magnetic media. The result of technological developments is that libraries must purchase information on a broader range of media, and at greater cost.

Today, these budgetary constraints, coupled with the increase in availability of information and information resources, have driven libraries to find creative ways to provide the information that patrons demand. Library consortia have arisen as one way for libraries to share resources. There is no one, formal arrangement of consortia, and considerable variety exists among them.[3] One of the purposes that library consortia have in common is to engage in cooperative projects that will ultimately result in improved service to patrons. There are at least two ways to accomplish this. One would be for consortia to enable libraries and their patrons to access information that might not be available if each library had to rely on its own resources; the second is for libraries to gain access to information that they might otherwise access, but at a lower cost. The resulting cost savings can then be used to provide additional sources for patron use.

---

2.   Book title output peaked in 1987, with a total of 56,027 titles. Then output fell for three successive years to 46,743 titles. Output has rebounded since then, showing gains each year with a total of 49,757 titles in 1993, the last year for which complete figures are available at the time this is written. Preliminary figures for book title output for 1994 indicated another modest increase. Gary Ink, *Book Title Output and Average Prices: 1993 Final and 1994 Preliminary Figures*, BOWKER ANNUAL 1995 510 (1995).

3.   Law library consortia run a wide gamut, from informal groups whose "chair" is the rotating host of the next irregularly scheduled meeting to formally incorporated I.R.C. 501(c)(3) organizations with bylaws, dues, and perhaps even a salaried administrator, and from a membership of two or three neighboring law schools to a roster of hundreds of libraries of all types throughout the world.

      Gregory E. Koster, *Introduction to Law Library Consortia: The State of the Art*, 85 LAW LIBR. J. 763 (1993).

Whenever libraries belonging to a consortium undertake to engage in resource sharing as part of a cooperative effort, they need to take care that information is not used in such a way as to violate provisions of the 1976 Copyright Act.[4] This chapter explores ways that library consortia may use information without infringing copyright.

II. The Copyright Act

Section 106 of the Copyright Act conveys certain exclusive rights to the author or owner of a work protected by copyright:

> Subject to sections 107 through 120, the owner of copyright under this title has the exclusive rights to do and to authorize any of the following:
>
> (1) to reproduce the copyrighted work in copies or phonorecords;
> (2) to prepare derivative works based upon the copyrighted work;
> (3) to distribute copies or phonorecords of the copyrighted work to the public by sale or other transfer of ownership, or by rental, lease, or lending;
> (4) in the case of literary, musical, dramatic, and choreographic works, pantomimes, and motion pictures and other audiovisual works, to perform the copyrighted work publicly; and
> (5) in the case of literary, musical, dramatic, and choreographic works, pantomimes, and pictorial, graphic, or sculptural works, including the individual images of a motion picture or other audiovisual work, to display the copyrighted work publicly.[5]

Section 106 reserves to the owner of the copyright such rights as the making of reproductions, copies, or photocopies of a work, and the distribution of those copies except under specific circumstances.[6] The purpose of extending these rights is to encourage creative effort by insuring that the owner of a copyright will derive any benefit to be had from the effort. The author or owner of the copyright is not granted the exclusive right to control all use of a work, however. The first sentence of section 106 recognizes that subsequent sections of the Copyright Act devolve rights to the public, including libraries, in the use of creative works. In particular, section 107 defines fair use of copyrighted material. Anyone may assert fair use as a defense to an allegation of infringement. The

---

4. 17 U.S.C. §§ 101–1101 (1994).
5. 17 U.S.C. § 106 (1994).
6. Section 106A defines artists' moral rights, which is outside the scope of this chapter.

purpose of fair use is to ensure that the public will have access to information to facilitate scholarship and learning.[7]

Section 107 provides:

> Notwithstanding the provisions of sections 106 and 106A, the fair use of a copyrighted work, including such use by reproduction in copies or phonorecords or by any other means specified by that section, for purposes such as criticism, comment, news reporting, teaching (including multiple copies for classroom use), scholarship, or research is not an infringement of copyright. In determining whether the use made of a work in any particular case is a fair use the factors to be considered shall include
>
> (1) the purpose and character of the use, including whether such use is of a commercial nature or is for nonprofit educational purposes;
> (2) the nature of the copyrighted work;
> (3) the amount and substantiality of the portion used in relation to the copyrighted work as a whole; and
> (4) the effect of the use upon the potential market for or value of the copyrighted work.
>
> The fact that a work is unpublished shall not itself bar a finding of fair use if such finding is made upon consideration of all the above factors.[8]

Fair use grants to users and to libraries the ability to use information in ways that might otherwise be reserved to copyright holders under section 106. The first sentence of the section indicates that fair use is not an infringing act that has been forgiven. Rather, activity that can be characterized as fair use is not an infringement at all. Fair uses are legitimate uses and do not require the user to seek permission from the copyright holder.

In addition to fair use, under section 108 libraries may take advantage of special exemptions from rights granted to copyright owners under section 106. In particular, section 108 allows a library to make

---

7.   Art. I, § 8, cl. 8 of the U.S. Constitution provides that the purpose of copyright in the United States is "To promote the Progress of Science and useful Arts, by securing for limited Times to Authors and Inventors the exclusive Right to their respective Writings and Discoveries." Therefore, protection of works is not the primary emphasis of copyright; it is just the means of promoting scholarship. The fact that section 107 specifically mentions "purposes such as criticism, comment, news reporting, teaching . . . scholarship, or research" as examples of fair use is further indication that these are activities favored by copyright.

8.   17 U.S.C. § 107 (1994).

a copy of material available to a patron through photoreproduction.[9] Section 108 also permits a library to engage in routine interlibrary loan activity.[10] Limitations apply to the extent to which copies of a work may be made by libraries. On the other hand, section 108 does not grant to libraries the privilege of unrestricted copying from copyright-protected works.

III. Interlibrary Loan

Interlibrary loan involves the lending of an original copy of material, or the reproduction of material, at the request of a patron at a library that does not own the requested title. Traditionally, libraries participating in consortia arrangements have entered into agreements whereby members of the consortium might direct interlibrary loan requests to each other first, perhaps not charging fees to each other for

---

9.　Section 108 reads:

> (a) Notwithstanding the provisions of § 106, it is not an infringement of copyright for a library or archives, or any of its employees acting within the scope of their employment, to reproduce no more than one copy or phonorecord of a work, or to distribute such copy or phonorecord, under the conditions specified by this section if—
>> (1) the reproduction or distribution is made without any purpose of direct or indirect commercial advantage;
>> (2) the collections of the library or archives are (I) open to the public, or (ii) available not only to researchers affiliated with the library or archives or with the institution of which it is a part, but also to other persons doing research in a specialized field; and
>> (3) the reproduction or distribution of the work includes a notice of copyright.

Id. § 108(a).

10.　Interlibrary loan is governed by section 108(g) which reads:

> (g) The rights of reproduction and distribution under this section extend to the isolated and unrelated reproduction and distribution of a single copy or phonorecord of the same material on separate occasions, but do not extend to cases where the library or archives, or its employee—
>> (2) engages in the systematic reproduction or distribution of single or multiple copies or phonorecords of material described in section (d): Provided, That nothing in this clause prevents a library or archives from participating in interlibrary arrangements that do not have as their purpose or effect, that the library or archives receiving such copies or phonorecords for distribution does so in such aggregate quantities as to substitute for a subscription to or purchase of such work.

Id. § 108(g)(2).

completing interlibrary loan transactions to reimburse the lending library for expenses incurred in handling the transaction.

It is always permissible for a library to lend an original copy of material to another library. Under the first-sale doctrine of the Copyright Act, the owner of a legitimate copy of a copyright-protected work is free to lend that copy to others.[11] Under some circumstances, individuals and institutions may not be permitted to lend or lease computer programs or sound recordings, but specific provisions included in the Copyright Act permit nonprofit libraries and educational institutions to lend these items to one another.[12]

Making photocopies of journal articles, chapters from monographs, and other hardcopy information for the purpose of fulfilling interlibrary loan requests potentially infringes the copyright owner's reserved right to reproduce materials but for express statutory language. Section 108 specifically permits libraries to make copies to satisfy interlibrary loan requests, as long as the requests are not made "in such aggregate quantities as to substitute for subscription to or

---

11. The first-sale doctrine reads:

> (a) Notwithstanding the provisions of section 106(3), the owner of a particular copy or phonorecord lawfully made under this title, or any person authorized by such owner, is entitled, without the authority of the copyright owner, to sell or otherwise dispose of the possession of that copy or phonorecord.

Id. § 109(a).

12. The section 109 limitations state:

> (b)(1)(A) Notwithstanding the provisions of subsection (a), unless authorized by the owners of copyright in the sound recording or the owner[s] of copyright in a computer program . . . neither the owner of a particular phonorecord nor any person in possession of a particular copy of a computer program . . . may, for the purposes of direct or indirect commercial advantage, dispose of . . . the possession of the phonorecord or computer program . . . by rental, lease, or lending, or by any other act or practice in the nature of rental, lease, or lending. Nothing in the preceding sentence shall apply to the rental, lease, or lending of a phonorecord for nonprofit purposes by a lawfully made copy of a computer program by a nonprofit library or nonprofit educational institution. The transfer of possession of a lawfully made copy of a computer program by a nonprofit educational institution to another nonprofit educational institution or to faculty, staff, and students does not constitute rental, lease, or lending for direct or indirect commercial purposes under this subsection.

Id. § 109(b)(1)(A).

purchase of such work."[13] The problem of how to determine the number of copies that might substitute for subscription or purchase was answered in part by the report of the Commission on New Technological Uses of Copyrighted Works (CONTU). Congress appointed CONTU when the 1976 Copyright Act was under consideration. The CONTU report includes guidelines which purport to define minimum levels of photocopying for interlibrary loan activity.[14] Although the guidelines define minimum and not maximum levels of interlibrary borrowing, libraries that stay within the guidelines' limitations are presumed not to be infringing copyright owners' rights.

Libraries within a consortium are free to borrow original materials from each other, and they may engage in interlibrary loan activity as permitted under section 108(g)(2). Libraries, however, should be aware of lending limitations under the guidelines. It is the responsibility of the borrowing institution to keep track of the number of requests made from each title during the year. Libraries should not be tempted to exceed the limits regularly because they are borrowing from "friendly sources."[15]

IV. Cooperative Collection Development

Cooperative lending agreements coupled with cooperative collection development efforts can lead to potential problems with copyright infringement. One way for members of a library consortium to reduce collection development costs is to enter into an agreement that would designate titles or subject areas to be purchased by individual libraries with the understanding that other consortium members needing information from those titles could receive reproductions of the information requested. Other consortium members would either refrain from purchasing titles related to the subject, or might even cancel existing

---

13.   *Id.* § 108(g)(2).

14.   With respect to journal articles, a library may annually request copies of five articles published within the past five years from any journal title. Copies of five excerpts from other types of materials may be requested within a calendar year. Conf. Rep. No. 1733, 94th Cong., 2d Sess. 72–73 (1976), *reprinted in* 1976 U.S.C.C.A.N. 5810, 5813–14. This level of reproduction permitted under the guidelines to satisfy interlibrary loan requests is referred to hereafter as the "suggestion of five."

15.   For a discussion of interlibrary loan generally, see *infra* Chapter Nine (p. 173), "Interlibrary Loan in the Electronic World," by Lucretia W. McClure.

subscriptions to use the savings to collect new titles within their designated subject. On the surface, this appears to be a standard interlibrary loan arrangement. Since interlibrary loans are permitted under section 108(g)(2), it would stand to reason that libraries within the consortium would be able to request copies of other titles owned within the consortium, commensurate with the limitations of the interlibrary loan guidelines.

There is an argument that the cooperative collection development agreement changes the nature of these arrangements, however. One of the requirements of section 108(g) is that reproduction and distribution of materials under the section be on an "isolated and unrelated" basis, and not be "systematic."[16] The legislative history of the Copyright Act of 1976 shows that the Senate specifically anticipated library reproduction in response to arrangements such as these, and disapproved of it as an example of systematic copying.[17] If the Act conditions a library's ability to borrow a limited number of reproductions each year under interlibrary loan guidelines to borrowing that is isolated and unrelated, then members of library consortia with cooperative collection development agreements arguably may not request even one photocopy of an article pursuant to such an agreement. Systematic copying is not permitted under section 108, and photocopying to fill interlibrary loan requests is permitted only when it is isolated and unrelated. Therefore, some copyright owners would argue that the guidelines cannot apply under these circumstances.

Moreover, a library may not be able to fall back on section 107 fair use as a means of supplying copies under cooperative collection development agreements. One of the factors in determining fair use is "the amount and substantiality of the portion used in relation to the copyrighted work as a whole."[18] In general, the greater the proportion of an entire copyrighted work that is reproduced, the less likely the reproduction will be considered a fair use. So, for example, one court held that reproduction of approximately 10 percent of a copyright-protected book was an infringement not protected by fair use.[19] In another case,

---

16.   17 U.S.C. § 108(g) (1994).
17.   S. REP. No. 94-473, 94th Cong., 1st Sess. 70 (1975). For a more detailed discussion of this, see *infra* text accompanying notes 34–37.
18.   17 U.S.C. § 107(3) (1994).
19.   Radji v. Khakbaz, 607 F. Supp. 1296, 1302 (D.D.C. 1985).

reproduction of a 22-page chapter of a book, representing 5 percent of the entire work comprised of 419 pages in 15 chapters "weigh[ed] heavily against defendant" in a fair use determination.[20]

Guidelines that apply to copying by educators which is permitted under fair use are similarly restrictive.[21] For scholarly research, teachers could copy a chapter from a book, an article from a periodical or newspaper, or a short story, a short essay, or short poem. More specific and restrictive limitations apply to multiple copying permitted for classroom use. For example, no more than 250 words of poetry nor more than 1,000 words or 10 percent of a prose work, whichever is less, may be reproduced for classroom distribution.[22]

Fair use is determined on a case-by-case basis, however. All of the four factors of section 107 must be considered in concert, rather than individually, and so the amount and substantiality of the portion used will not by itself determine whether a use is a fair use. At times, courts have determined that copying an entire copyrighted work is nevertheless a fair use.[23] The result is that while section 107 may permit greater latitude in the purpose for reproducing information (scholarship and research, generally) than section 108, at the same time section 107 may impose limitations on the amount of information that may be reproduced. Those limitations under fair use may not be conducive to resource sharing among libraries.

Copyright owners' and publishers' organizations will argue that sections 107 and 108 do not endow library consortium members sufficient authority to enter into cooperative collection development agreements, and to exchange reproductions from titles to satisfy requests in

---

20.   Basic Books, Inc. v. Kinko's Graphics Corp., 758 F. Supp. 1522, 1527 (S.D.N.Y. 1991).

21.   Agreement on Guidelines for Classroom Copying in Not-For-Profit Educational Institutions with Respect to Books and Periodicals. H.R. Rep. No. 94-1476, 94th Cong., 2d Sess. 68, *reprinted in* 1976 U.S.C.C.A.N. 5659, 5681–83. These guidelines were accepted by the House and Senate conferees to Senate bill 22; H.R. Conf. Rep. No. 1733.

22.   *Id.*

23.   Photocopying entire journal articles for scholarly research was permitted as fair use in Williams & Wilkins Co. v. United States, 487 F.2d 1345 (Cl. Ct. 1973), *aff'd*, 420 U.S. 376 (1975). *But see* American Geophysical Union v. Texaco, Inc., 60 F.3d 913 (2d Cir. 1994), which found that articles were entire works and thus failed the fair use test. Reproduction of an entire television program by videotaping could be considered fair use. Sony Corp. of Am. v. Universal City Studios, 464 U.S. 417, 449–50 (1984).

furtherance of the terms of those agreements, absent obtaining permission or paying royalties. Arguments can be made on behalf of libraries that such restrictions may be invalid, and that even if they are not, the distinctions between legitimate and illegitimate consortium activity may be slight enough to be artificial.

V. Exchanging Reproductions Among Consortium Members Is Non-infringing Activity

A. The Purpose and Effect of Consortium Arrangements

Libraries legitimately may reproduce one copy of a work at the request of a user.[24] If a patron of Library A (which belongs to a consortium) walked into Library B, which also belongs to the consortium, and requested a photocopy of a work not owned by Library A, Library B could supply that copy provided the requirements of section 108 were met. Yet, copyright holders argue that because of the consortium agreement, the reproduction could not be made by Library B and sent to Library A to be given to the user. The patron's use of the reproduced material could be the same in both instances. The extent of the material reproduced also may be no different. The nature of the work that is copied, and whether the work is reproduced for scholarship and study, or profit or nonprofit activity may not vary depending on which library supplies the copy to the patron. In short, only the conditions under which the delivery occurs change. If the patron obtains her copy from Library A, the copy will be made at Library B and sent to Library A to be given to him. If the patron goes directly to Library B, he must travel to a distant location to obtain the information he needs. The first situation is clearly interlibrary loan. The latter is not.

Once the patron arrives at Library B, he may choose to photocopy the material himself using a self-service, coin-operated photocopier rather than availing himself of a photocopy service operated by library staff.[25] In these cases, it is not the collection development agreement

---

24.   17 U.S.C. § 108(a) (1994).

25.   *Id.* Section 108(f)(1) provides: "Nothing in this section shall be construed to impose liability for copyright infringement upon a library or archives or its employees for the unsupervised use of reproducing equipment located on its premises: *Provided,* That such equipment displays a notice that the making of a copy may be subject to the copyright law."

itself that creates a potential for infringement. The only practical difference between sending the copy to the user and informing him as to the location of the original, so that he can go to make his own copy, is patron convenience. If the user can reproduce and use information legally under one circumstance, then it is artificial to suggest that providing an identical copy for the same purpose under another circumstance is an infringement. Such also contravenes common sense.

Does the consortium agreement itself create a potential for infringement? Arguably not. Before imaging technology and telefax made document delivery among consortium members relatively simple and instantaneous, it was a common practice for libraries within a consortium to develop union lists of holdings, so that the libraries might know which titles were being held by other libraries within the consortium. Libraries could review the union list to determine subject strengths of other institutions within their group. These union lists might provide a basis for establishing a priority in determining where to direct interlibrary loan requests, or they might provide one factor for determining local collection development practices. Even absent a cooperative collection development agreement, Library A might decide independently not to purchase titles on a particular topic if it knew that Library B had a strong collection on that topic. Library A and Library B might have an agreement not to charge a fee for interlibrary loan transactions, but no formal collection development agreement, wherein Library A agreed to buy titles related to a specific topic, and Library B agreed to purchase titles related to another topic, and the two libraries agreed to provide copies to each other upon request.

Absent the collection development agreement, the two libraries within the consortium legitimately could exchange copies of materials consistent with the interlibrary loan guidelines. Each library could fashion its own collection development policy, in part, by noting the strengths of other libraries, choosing to concentrate its collection development efforts on materials that otherwise might be unavailable to its users. Under these circumstances, Library A and Library B should be able to request copies of journal articles, for example, consistent with the suggestion of five outlined in the CONTU guidelines.

Again, the question must be asked regarding the practical effect of the arrangement. Libraries may participate in consortia; section 108(g)(2) specifically permits interlibrary arrangements. Clearly, libraries within a consortium may exchange information regarding holdings. If libraries within a consortium that has no formal collection development agreement may copy materials consistent with the interlibrary loan guidelines, there is no difference to the copyright holder if libraries within a consortium guided by a formal collection development policy do likewise. Copyright holders may respond that the problem with these collection development arrangements is that they result in fewer copies of a title being sold. The argument is that Library A may refrain from purchasing a title that it otherwise might purchase, because the collection development agreement provides that Library B will purchase titles within a subject area. Worse, because of the agreement, Library A may cancel a subscription for a title, and rely on Library B to provide copies of needed information.

In truth, it is doubtful that cooperative collection development agreements will result in any significant effect on the market for or value of a work. Libraries tend to purchase titles that their users demand. While interlibrary loan and document delivery will suffice to provide information that is seldom needed, patrons and libraries still prefer that information be available on-site.

There are some practical limitations to the extent to which interlibrary loan can substitute for on-site ownership of a title. Interlibrary loan transactions are expensive to libraries.[26] By the time a library completes five interlibrary loan transactions allowed under the guidelines within a calendar year, the cost of interlibrary loan easily could exceed the average cost of purchasing a title.[27] Thus, a library whose patrons consistently request copies from a specific title ultimately is likely to purchase the title. Further, users and libraries greatly prefer instantaneous availability, and borrowing from elsewhere is far slower than retrieving a work from the shelf in Library A to satisfy the request of a user in Library A.

Publishers may argue that they are losing revenue in the form of royalties if libraries do not pay for copying to satisfy consortium

---

26.   The average interlibrary loan transaction costs approximately $30 to complete. Marilyn M. Roche. ARL/RLG INTERLIBRARY LOAN COST STUDY: A JOINT EFFORT BY THE ASSOCIATION OF RESEARCH LIBRARIES AND THE RESEARCH LIBRARIES GROUP (1993).

27.   The average price of a hardback monograph (all subject areas) in 1993 was $35.00. Adrian Alexander, *Prices of U.S. and Foreign Published Materials*, BOWKER ANNUAL 1995 489 (1995). The mean cost of a monographic title in the subject of law for 1994–95 was $71.24. The mean cost of legal serial titles for the same year was $282.77. Bettie Scott, PRICE INDEX FOR LEGAL PUBLICATIONS, 1995 (1996).

requests. This is a circular argument. A copyright owner may ask for royalties when the requested reproduction otherwise would be an infringement. No royalties must be paid for non-infringing acts. The title to section 107 indicates that fair use is a limitation to the exclusive rights given to copyright owners.[28] The introductory text to section 107 states:

> Notwithstanding the provisions of sections 106 and 106A, the fair use of a copyrighted work, including such use by reproduction in copies and phonorecords or by any other means specified by that section, for purposes such as criticism, comment, news reporting, teaching (including multiple copies for classroom use), scholarship, or research, is not an infringement of copyright.[29]

If the copies requested by consortium members can be characterized as fair use, then no royalties are due to the copyright owner. If no royalties are due, then the copyright owner cannot complain that the market for or value of the work is affected because royalties were not paid.

> The title to § 108 similarly indicates that the section is a limitation on the exclusive rights of copyright owners.[30] Again, the introductory text to the section clearly indicates that library copying consistent with § 108 is not an infringement.
>
> Notwithstanding the provisions of § 106, it is not an infringement of copyright for a library or archives, or any of its employees acting within the scope of their employment, to reproduce no more than one copy or phonorecord of a work, or to distribute such copy or phono-record, under the conditions specified by this section. . . . [31]

If photocopying incident to consortium agreements is consistent with § 108, then it is not an infringement. No permission need be sought, and no royalties are due the copyright holder.

Normally, no commercial purpose underlies copying incident to consortium requests. The libraries involved are most often public libraries, school libraries, or university libraries that are nonprofit institutions. Either their agreements provide that the libraries will reciprocate in not charging each other's patrons for photocopying, or the agreements provide that photocopy fees will be on a cost-recovery

---

28.   17 U.S.C. § 107 (1994).

29.   *Id.*

30.   *Id.* § 108.

31.   *Id.* § 108(a).

basis. Thus, the library receives no benefit from providing copies requested by consortium members, and the copyright holder (publisher) loses no revenue to which it is entitled.

What is the underlying use of material copied because of consortium arrangements? Libraries have no obligation to ask a patron what his or her intended use of information will be. A library and its employees may reproduce requested material consistent with the provisions of section 108, as long as they do not know, and have no good reason to know, that the patron's use will be infringing.[32] Teaching, scholarship, and research uses are favored in the copyright law and are more likely to be regarded as fair use.[33] There has been much debate as to the impact of the introductory language to section 107 and its effect on the activities that are cited. While not all uses related to education, scholarship, and research are automatically fair use, nevertheless the language in section 107 plainly favors those activities.

Library users commonly engage in scholarship and research. It must be remembered that requests from consortium libraries come from patrons who are likely to be engaged in scholarship or research of some sort. If it is true that activity underlying consortium requests is likely to be a favored use, and if it is true that libraries are unlikely to forgo purchasing or subscribing to materials that are requested, then it makes little sense that consortium requests would be prohibited.

B. Legislative History

Publishing interests point out that in considering the 1976 Copyright Act, the Senate considered this point and explicitly determined that the provision of photoduplications under cooperative collection development agreements illustrates systematic copying that would be prohibited.

> While it is not possible to formulate specific definitions of "systematic copying", the following examples serve to illustrate some of the copying prohibited by subsection (g).
>
> (1) A library with a collection of journals in biology informs other libraries with similar collections that it will maintain and build its own collection and will make copies of articles from these journals available to them and their patrons on request. Accordingly, the other libraries discontinue or refrain from purchasing subscriptions

---

32.   *Id.* § 108(d)(1).

33.   *Id.* § 107; *see supra* text accompanying note 7.

to these journals and fulfill their patrons requests for articles by obtaining photocopies from the source library.[34]

In comparing the House Report with the earlier Senate Report, it is clear that in general, the Senate had a more restrictive view of library photocopying than did the House. For example, while the Senate Report was concerned with systematic copying by libraries, the House Report, which did not mention intra-system lending, introduced the suggestion that photocopying to fulfill interlibrary loan requests should be permissible.[35]

Indeed, the interlibrary loan guidelines themselves, which are incorporated within the Conference Report, strongly suggest that photocopying to fulfill interlibrary loan requests is just one instance in which one library may reproduce materials at the request of another library. The introduction to the guidelines provides:

> Subsection 108(g)(2) of the bill deals, among other things, with limits on *interlibrary arrangements* for photocopying. It prohibits systematic photocopying of copyrighted materials but permits *interlibrary arrangements* "that do not have, as their purpose or effect, that the library or archives receiving such copies or phonorecords for distribution does so in such aggregate quantities as to substitute for a subscription to or purchase of such work."
>
> These guidelines are intended to provide guidance in the application of section 108 to the most frequently encountered interlibrary case: a library's obtaining from another library, in lieu of interlibrary loan, copies of articles from relatively recent issues of periodicals— those published within five years prior to the date of the request.[36]

It is significant that the introduction provides that "interlibrary arrangements" for photocopying are permissible, as long as those arrangements do not substitute for a subscription to or purchase of such work. The words "interlibrary arrangements" suggest that interlibrary loans would

---

34. S. Rep. No. 94-473, 94th Cong., 1st Sess. 70 (1975).

35. The House bill amended § 108 to make clear that, in cases involving inter-library arrangements for the exchange of photocopies, the activity would not be considered systematic as long as the library or archives receiving the reproductions for distribution does not do so in such aggregate quantities as to substitute for a subscription to or purchase of the work.

Conf. Rep. No. 1733, 94th Cong., 2d Sess. 71 (1976), *reprinted in* 1976 U.S.C.C.A.N. 5810, 5812.

36. *Id.* at 72 (emphasis added).

constitute just one type of such arrangements. The introduction describes interlibrary loans as being "the most frequently encountered interlibrary case," strongly suggesting that other interlibrary arrangements might be permissible as well, and would not be regarded as systematic copying that would be prohibited, as long as the copying does not substitute for subscription to or purchase of the work. Indeed, the title for the guidelines is "PHOTOCOPYING—INTERLIBRARY ARRANGEMENTS" (as opposed to "interlibrary loans"), even though the guidelines themselves refer to the more narrow term of interlibrary loans.[37]

This language, incorporated within the Conference Report, suggests that other types of interlibrary arrangements might also qualify for the library exemptions described in section 108 of the Act. Interlibrary lending is just one such interlibrary arrangement. Photocopying to fulfill user requests among libraries belonging to a consortium might also qualify as such an interlibrary arrangement, even if the libraries within the consortium are parties to a cooperative collection development agreement. The test for determining whether this activity is permissible should be the same as it is for interlibrary loans, i.e., whether the number of requests for photocopies rises to the level of substituting for the subscription to or purchase of the original work. While the level of activity described within the guidelines applies specifically to interlibrary loan requests, the requesting of photocopies among libraries belonging to a consortium is so similar to interlibrary loans that it would be reasonable to apply the same restrictions.

In fact, the argument can be made that lending among consortium members *is* interlibrary lending. The only difference is the formal arrangement for cooperative collection development. If, because the Conference Report adopts a less-restrictive view of systematic copying, the existence of the agreement itself does not define "systematic," but rather the number of requests determines what is "systematic," then the level of copying specified by the guidelines applies directly to consortium photocopying activity, even when a cooperative collection development agreement exists.

The language of the Conference Report shows that Congress intended for the interlibrary loan guidelines to apply to a broad range of activity among libraries, as opposed to a very narrow range. Wisely,

---

37.   Id.

Congress recognized that the scope of interlibrary activity in the future could not be fixed at the point in time when the 1976 Copyright Act was being considered. Thus, the guidelines provide a framework that libraries can apply to any conduct or activity that is similar in nature.

> The conference committee understands that the guidelines are not intended as, and cannot be considered, explicit rules or directions governing any and all cases, now or in the future. It is recognized that their purpose is to provide guidance in the most commonly-encountered interlibrary photocopying situations, that they are not intended to be limiting or determinative in themselves or with respect to other situations, and that they deal with an evolving situation that will undoubtedly require their continuous reevaluation and adjustment. With these qualifications, the conference committee agrees that the guidelines are a reasonable interpretation of the proviso of section 108(g)(2) in the most common situations to which they apply today.[38]

The question, then, is whether a cooperative collection development agreement among libraries within a consortium is enough to remove their interlibrary photocopying activity from the guidelines that define the suggestion of five, and instead prohibit all requests for photocopies among those consortium libraries because they are systematic rather than isolated and unrelated. Given that the same activity clearly would be permissible absent the cooperative collection development agreement, even if union holdings lists were available for consortium members to consult, and given that photocopying activity within the limits defined within the guidelines is presumed to be permissible because it has not risen to the level of substituting for subscription to or purchase of the original work, the activity should be regarded as permissible and the guidelines should apply.

C. Technology

Does the availability of new technology, such as imaging workstations that facilitate the reproduction and distribution of materials among libraries, remove the activity from the section 108 exemptions? Publishing interests are likely to argue that use of such equipment increases the ability of libraries to infringe copyright, and therefore should make such activity impermissible. This argument has been raised twice before. Most recently, software publishers have argued that personal computers and

---

38.   *Id.* at 71–72.

computer networks enable users to easily reproduce and distribute information in ways that clearly would infringe copyrights. As a result, amendments to the 1976 Copyright Act have been proposed that would provide additional protection to commercial information made available on the National Information Infrastructure.[39]

A similar argument was made at the time that photocopiers made reproduction of information from copyrighted sources more practical.[40] The mere fact that inexpensive and improved photocopiers made infringement of copyright easier did not mean that the use of such copiers necessarily resulted in infringement. Section 108(g)(2) and the guidelines do not specify by what method materials that satisfy interlibrary loan requests must be reproduced and distributed. New technology can facilitate non-infringing uses as well as infringing uses. As long as there is a substantial likelihood that equipment can be used

---

39.   The White Paper states:

> Authors are wary of entering this market [the NII] because doing so exposes their works to a higher risk of piracy and other unauthorized uses than any of the traditional, current modes of dissemination. Therefore, authors may withhold their works from this environment. Further, even if authors choose not to expose their works to this more risky environment, the risk is not eliminated. Just one unauthorized uploading of a work onto a bulletin board, for instance—unlike, perhaps, most single reproductions and distributions in the analog or print environment—could have devastating effects on the market for the work.

INTELLECTUAL PROPERTY AND THE NATIONAL INFORMATION INFRASTRUCTURE: THE REPORT OF THE WORKING GROUP ON INTELLECTUAL PROPERTY RIGHTS 10 (1995).

40.   The fact that photocopying by libraries of entire articles was done with hardly any (and at most very minor) complaint until about 10 or 15 years ago, goes a long way to show both that photoduplication cannot be designated as infringement per se, and that there was at least a time when photocopying, as then carried on, was fair use. There have been, of course, considerable changes in the ease and extent of such reproduction, and these developments bear on fair use as of today, but the libraries can properly stand on the proposition that they photocopied articles for many years, without significant protest, and that such copying was generally accepted until the proliferation of inexpensive and improved copying machines, less than two decades ago, led to the surge in such duplication. The question then becomes whether this marked increase in volume changes a use which was generally accepted as "fair" into one which has now become "unfair."

Williams & Wilkins Co. v. United States, 87 F.2d 1345, 1356 (Ct. Cl. 1973), aff'd by an equally divided court, 420 U.S. 376 (1975).

for legitimate purposes, a presumption should not arise that its use results in an infringing act.[41]

The delivery of copies using a fax machine may require that a photocopy of the original work be made that can be fed into the fax to facilitate transmission. Because section 108 requires that copies made by libraries at patron request become the property of the patron, the lending library should not retain its copy after completing transmission.

VI. Conclusion

The extent to which library consortium members may engage safely in interlibrary lending will depend on the circumstances. Under the first-sale doctrine, it should always be permissible for libraries to send an original copy of a copyrighted title to a requesting library. And, it is clear that consortium members that have not entered into cooperative collection development agreements may request photocopies of materials through interlibrary loan, consistent with the limitations of section 108(g)(2) and the guidelines.[42]

What is most in contention is the notion that libraries belonging to a consortium that has executed a cooperative collection development agreement should be permitted to provide photocopies of materials in response to patron requests consistent with the CONTU guidelines. A case can be made that the CONTU Guidelines in the Conference Report, which are broader in scope and permit libraries to engage in a variety

---

41.   *See, e.g.,* Sony Corp. of Am. v. Universal City Studios, 464 U.S. 417 (1984) (suit for contributory infringement against manufacturer of videocassette recorders dismissed, based in part on the fact that while it was possible to use the equipment to infringe copyright, the equipment could also be used for many legitimate purposes).

42.   The Association of American Publishers (AAP) would dispute this:

> The situation today is that the advent of post-1976 technologies—fax machines, computer networks, low-priced scanners and CD-ROMs—has facilitated the interlibrary delivery of photocopies of articles and chapter-length excerpts from books and generated services focussed [sic] on this conduct. Some facilities have begun to charge service fees for providing the copies while not paying royalties to publishers because the copying is, according to them, "interlibrary loan and permissible under the CONTU guidelines." However, as stated above, this copying is far beyond that permitted under CONTU and therefore, may be done only with the permission of copyright holders.

ASSOCIATION OF AMERICAN PUBLISHERS, STATEMENT OF THE ASSOCIATION OF AMERICAN PUB-LISHERS (AAP) ON COMMERCIAL AND FEE-BASED DOCUMENT DELIVERY 5 (1992).

of "interlibrary arrangements," supersede the language describing "systematic copying" in the Senate Report. The suggestion of five insures that the activity does not rise to such a level that it substitutes for subscription to or purchase of the original work. Publishing interests have made it clear, however, that they regard such arrangements to be prohibited as systematic copying.[43]

The divergent positions of copyright holders and information providers such as libraries and educators make a negotiated compromise unlikely. Litigation and congressional action probably will not produce satisfactory results for the information community, given the disparity in power between the two groups.[44] Until there is a pronouncement, librarians find themselves in the uneasy position of following CONTU guidelines and risking becoming a test case, or needlessly straining their budgets and restricting services to patrons in assuming a conservative

---

43.   The AAP Statement posits:

> Additionally, librarians have vigorously promoted resource sharing which amounts to nothing less than the Senate's third example of forbidden co-ordinated subscription buying to save money by filling patron needs from source libraries. This copying and document delivery far exceeds the scope of interlibrary lending contemplated by Congress or CONTU in permitting interlibrary loan arrangements under the proviso. When the push for resource sharing and the development of consortia recombined with the new networks and even the existing inter-university network (Internet), one sees a formula for the erosion of publishing revenues in this country, from: (1) lost book and journals subscription sales, (2) lost royalty income from licensing, and (3) lost new product opportunities. The revenue base that now supports publishing relies on multiple opportunities to exploit a product such as income from sales, subscriptions, and licenses. The interlibrary copying without permission and other non-authorized document delivery denies the copyright owner its rights under the law.

       Id.

44.   Educators were at a disadvantage recently when trying to negotiate with copyright owners fair use guidelines for information published electronically:

> [W]hen the issue of electronic access and remote instruction came to a head in the multimedia negotiations, it underscored a perception that academic leaders were often being outmaneuvered by copyright owners' organizations. Those groups usually send a bevy of lawyers to the drafting sessions, while higher education has often seemed content to let representatives of their national associations carry the ball.

       Robert L. Jacobson, *The Furor Over "Fair Use": Educators Seem to Be Outgunned in Negotiations with Copyright Holders*, CHRON. HIGHER EDUC., May 10, 1996, at A30.

position. And yet, if libraries do not fully exercise their rights under section 108 and under section 107 fair use, they risk losing those rights. Thus, in the name of service to patrons and protecting the rights of users, libraries have little choice but to assume the risk.

Chapter Nine
Interlibrary Loan
in the Electronic World

by
Lucretia W. McClure*

Librarian Emerita
Edward G. Miner Library
University of Rochester Medical Center

Sharing books and journals is a long-established practice among scholars and libraries. Monks once loaned precious manuscripts so they could be hand copied at other monasteries. History is replete with authors and other individuals borrowing and loaning books from each other. By 1876, when the first issue of *Library Journal* appeared, interlibrary loan was already a topic of discussion. Writing in that first issue, Samuel S. Green, Librarian of the Worcester Free Public Library, described the importance of sharing.[1] By 1917 the first American

---

*   © 1997 Lucretia W. McClure.

1.   Samuel S. Green, *The Lending of Books to One Another by Libraries*, 1 LIBR. J. 1, 15–16 (1876).

Library Association Interlibrary Loan Code was produced, and it was officially adopted in 1919.[2] Even individual readers appreciated the value of sharing. A slender book, *The Gentle Art of Book Lending*, was first published in 1895. The author, George S. Layard, called for the pooling of private libraries to provide better collections for use by citizens.[3] One of the basic tenets of scholarship is the obligation to impart knowledge. Teachers, scholars, scientists, and others acknowledge the work of those who have gone before them and, in turn, make known their new knowledge. Without willingness to share information and knowledge, learning could not take place, since all scholars build on the work of others. Authors want their works to be read and discussed; scientists want their experiments to be replicated and used as the basis for further developments.

The purpose of this chapter is to review the changes in technology that have played a role in the lending/borrowing practices in libraries and to consider the impact of the latest, the digital technology. For years interlibrary loan (ILL) was literally a loan. Libraries that received requests for materials physically wrapped the needed volume and sent it along to the borrowing library by mail. Of necessity, this was slow and labor intensive. Further, volumes were often lost in the mail or damaged in transit. More importantly, when the volume was sent to another library to satisfy an ILL request, it was unavailable to users at the lending library. Thus, libraries often refused to lend anything in even moderate demand by its primary clientele. The fear of loss restricted ILL to non-serial items, since the potential loss of a bound journal was too devastating for the lending library to consider. Many libraries even restricted the service to faculty and graduate students.

The development of the photocopier forever changed the way patrons use a library. The custom of reading, taking notes, and studying in the library was turned on its head with the arrival of the mechanical copier. In essence, the way people studied and learned changed significantly. The advent of the photocopier also seemed the answer to the increasing volume in the mail room and the concern about damage caused by mailing heavy volumes. Articles could be copied and sent; needed journals did not leave the library.

---

2.   L.C. GILMER, INTERLIBRARY LOAN THEORY AND MANAGEMENT 24 (1994) [hereinafter GILMER].

3.   GEORGE S. LAYARD, THE GENTLE ART OF BOOK LENDING: A SUGGESTION (2d ed. 1902).

Photocopying soon became the preferred method of staff for filling ILL requests. Users frequently made a photocopy of needed material from a loaned volume or took notes from it anyway, so a time-consuming step was eliminated for users.

Other factors played an important part in the development of interlibrary loan services. Over the years, various tools and resources were created to provide users with an indication of the location of publications. Such union lists and catalogs became an essential part of ILL operations. In 1967, the establishment of the bibliographic utility OCLC provided the electronic database that both enhanced cataloging practices and served as a location finder for libraries across the country. OCLC soon added an interlibrary loan subsystem. To these earlier tools have been added many online library catalogs also available through the Internet. These further facilitate ILL by making it easy for libraries and users to identify what is available and where.

The rapid expansion of the literature that began in the 1960s also had an impact on the growth of interlibrary loan. The number of publications increased while, at the same time, library budgets decreased. The cost of serials, especially those in science and technology, skyrocketed, and libraries found their buying power greatly diminished due both to inflation and to the devaluation of the dollar in international markets. Interlibrary loan became one solution. The slogan "access not ownership" became the watchword of those who saw the ease of access to articles in journals not held by the library as the answer to the high cost of low-use periodicals. It was simply more economical for libraries to request copies of articles from little-used journals through ILL than to subscribe to, bind, and house the journal. Further enhancements to ILL came by way of improved telefacsimile technology and the ability of scanners to convert print documents into digital format.[4] Interlibrary loan still is not fast, however.

I. Fair Use

For the first time in the history of libraries, the 1976 Copyright Act[5] includes a section on libraries that exempted from copyrighted infringement many activities of a library. Generally known as "the library

---

4.   A good overview of the development of ILL is found in GILMER, *supra* note 2.

5.   17 U.S.C. §§ 101–1101 (1994).

exemption" or "library reproduction," section 108 covers most of the copying that a library might do to meet the needs of its users. Additionally, the 1976 Act codified the concept of fair use in section 107. Under fair use, reasonable use of a copyrighted work without permission is allowed for specific purposes including scholarship, teaching, research, and criticism. This is vitally important since the freedom to use knowledge and information is essential in a democratic society.

Throughout the history of copyright in this country, there has been need to create a balance between the intellectual property interests of authors, publishers, and copyright owners and society's need for the free and open exchange of ideas. The right to read, study, browse, listen to, or view copyrighted material is critical to researchers and students seeking to create new knowledge, to faculty in the classroom, and to the general public wishing to advance their own knowledge.

U.S. District Judge Pierre N. Leval describes fair use as a "fundamental policy of the copyright law."

> The stimulation of creative thought and authorship for the benefit of society depends assuredly on the protection of the author's monopoly. But it depends equally on the recognition that the monopoly must have limits.[6]

Libraries and library organizations must continue to use fair use vigorously in support of their users needs.

II. Rights of Users

The 1976 Copyright Act acknowledges the right of libraries to participate in certain circumstances in the interlibrary arrangements that do not have as their purpose or effect the use of these arrangements as a substitute for subscribing or purchasing a work.[7] Because more guidance was needed for both libraries and the copyright owner community, Congress sought a method for developing guidelines on ILL that would provide direction to practicing librarians and detail a safe harbor as to limitations on section 108's exemption for library copying. To that end, Congress established the National Commission on New Technological Uses of Copyrighted Works (CONTU) which was

---

6.   Pierre N. Leval, *Fair Use or Foul?* 36 J. COPYRIGHT SOC'Y 167, 180 (1989).
7.   17 U.S.C. § 108(g)(2) (1994).

charged to develop ILL guidelines that would define what is "such aggregate quantities as to substitute for subscription to or purchase of a work." CONTU completed its work, and the ILL guidelines were published in the Conference Report that accompanied the Act.[8] While the guidelines are not the law, they enjoy a fair degree of congressional support since they were developed by a commission it appointed for that purpose.[9]

The guidelines deal with reproduction of works in lieu of loaning the original; they state that within a calendar year, borrowing libraries may request copies of five or fewer articles from a specific journal title published within the past five years. Articles older than five years do not fall within the guidelines. In fact, the guidelines state that they take no position on materials older than five years. Thus, libraries have to track requests for copies under the guidelines. Also required of the borrowing library is the maintenance of records of all copying done under the guidelines for a period of three calendar years. For non-serial items, a library may make five requests per year for the life of the copyright. Borrowing libraries need to determine how they will handle requests for materials older than five years. Additionally, it is clear that forming consortia to evade the ILL guidelines violated section 108(g)(2).

These guidelines provide excellent guidance to libraries in meeting the information needs of their users. They also have been a factor in a library's decision to continue to subscribe to a title. The slashing of library budgets and the ever-increasing cost of journals, especially in science and technology, present a bleak picture for scholars, faculty, students, and researchers whose access to scholarly articles has been diminished.

Libraries have used the CONTU guidelines as a "safe harbor" for borrowing materials. Keeping records of what is borrowed provides the library a view of users' interests, alerts the collection development/ acquisitions staff about titles that should be acquired, and helps determine how best to fill user needs. Libraries have also taken the opportunity to explain to users why the suggestion of five must be honored,

---

8.   CONF. REP. NO. 1733, 94th Cong., 2d Sess. (1976), *reprinted in* 17 OMNIBUS COPYRIGHT REVISION LEGISLATIVE HISTORY 72–74 (1977).

9.   LAURA N. GASAWAY & SARAH K. WIANT, A GUIDE TO COPYRIGHT LAW IN THE 1990s 53–55 (1994).

the rights and responsibilities of users are under fair use, and libraries' rights and responsibilities under section 108. ILL within the guidelines has permitted libraries to meet the research needs of their users without having to purchase expensive subscriptions that the library cannot support. The suggestion of five has worked relatively well for libraries, and most work hard to stay within the safe-harbor guidelines.

Lending libraries have one responsibility under the guidelines, and that is to supply ILL requests only if the borrowing library has provided a representation that the request is within the guidelines. Another acceptable certification is that although the request is not within the guidelines, the borrowing library is paying royalties beyond the fifth request for the title.

Upon receiving the sixth request from a user, the borrowing library must make a choice. It can deny the user's request, or it can suggest that the user delay the request until after January 1 of the next calendar year. Other options include: (1) ordering the article from an authorized document delivery service (which pays the royalties); (2) requesting the item through ILL and paying the royalty to the Copyright Clearance Center or directly to the publisher; (3) entering a subscription to the title; or (4) very rarely, going beyond the suggestion of five.[10]

Borrowing from other libraries is not a substitute for building an adequate collection for use by an institution's primary clientele. An item borrowed for one user stays with that user; it neither enriches the collection nor enhances any other individual's knowledge. It is, however, a necessary avenue for supplying resources not available in a collection, for titles that are out of print and cannot be purchased, or those beyond the scope of a library's subject area. When a library cannot or should not purchase an item, borrowing through ILL may be the answer.

III. The Digital Environment

Copyright has always been a difficult subject for most librarians. The changes being brought by the digital environment make it even more complex. A representative of the publishing community states that

---

10.   *Id.* at 54–55.

> Our current problem is that technology has outstripped our procedures and definitions. In the past it was technologically difficult to copy full texts of books, full color illustrations of paintings, or full musical performances and to distribute such copies widely. This meant that publication was beyond the means of most people; only a few organizations could serve as publishers. With new electronic methods, we can more easily copy those items and send them all around the world. Technology has made it easy for us to bypass the proprieties of the past. It is easier to copy than to request permission to the detriment of authors and publishers and eventually the public.[11]

To consider changes in the copyright law to accommodate the digital environment, a Working Group on Intellectual Property and the National Information Infrastructure was appointed in 1993 with Bruce A. Lehman, the Assistant Secretary of Commerce and Commissioner of Patents and Trademarks, as chair. The Lehman Working Group, made up of employees from a variety of federal agencies and a few other appointed members, published a preliminary report in July 1994. Hearings were held on the report in Washington in September of that year.

At the hearings, librarians and educators made clear their position that the draft report (the "Green Paper") minimized the importance of fair use. The draft emphasized the protection of proprietary interests to the detriment of users. The final report of the Working Group on Intellectual Property Rights was issued in September 1995, and it pays even less attention to the rights and needs of users of copyrighted works. The report, *Intellectual Property and the National Information Infrastructure* (the White Paper), allows some use of resources in the digital format but leaves a number of contentious issues unresolved.

A Fair Use Conference was convened following the hearings. The Fair Use Conferees, a group representing some sixty organizations— publishers, software manufacturers, lawyers, libraries, universities, scholarly societies, etc., have been meeting regularly since September 1994. The Fair Use Conferees are charged with finding common ground and developing guidelines for the fair use of information and resources in the digital environment for libraries and educational

---

11.   Arly Allen, *Electronic Publication and Copyright: An Interview with Arly Allen and Carol Risher*, 18 CBE VIEWS 126, 126 (1995).

institutions. When completed, the guidelines will be included in the legislative history of the copyright law revision.[12]

A. CONFU Working Group on Interlibrary Loan

The Working Group on Interlibrary Loan is a subgroup of the Fair Use Conferees. Its purpose is to develop guidelines for the practice of interlibrary sharing in the digital environment. In considering how interlibrary loan will function in the digital world, the Copyright Act provides some guidance. Section 101 of the Copyright Act of 1976 defines "copies" as "material objects, other than phonorecords, in which a work is fixed by any method now known or later developed, and from which the work can be perceived, reproduced, or otherwise communicated, either directly or with the aid of a machine or device, and in the form in which the work is first fixed."[13]

Section 108 includes the circumstances in which libraries or archives may reproduce and distribute copies or phonorecords. Gasaway points out that subsections (b) and (c), the two instances in which a library is permitted to copy for itself, i.e., to preserve an unpublished work or to replace a published lost, damaged, stolen, or deteriorating work, use the words "in facsimile form." She goes on to declare that an electronic image is a facsimile, an exact copy, and that sections (d) and (e) of section 108 permit a library to reproduce one copy for a user and the words "copy" and "phonorecord" are used. Thus, she states, "either photocopies or electronic copies may be used to satisfy the user request."[14]

The law does not specify format other than material or phonorecord. In fact, one goal of the 1976 Act was to be technology neutral. Sharing resources is traditional in education and research and is accepted within the Act of 1976 and the CONTU guidelines. Sharing is not unbounded, however; the suggestion of five imposes a fair limit both for library users and for copyright holders.

The final report, the White Paper, outlines some changes that will have an impact on library and educational activities, including interlibrary lending and borrowing. The White Paper offers statements to bring comfort to all interested groups. On the one hand it appears to

---

12.   INTELLECTUAL PROPERTY AND THE NATIONAL INFORMATION INFRASTRUCTURE: THE REPORT OF THE WORKING GROUP ON INTELLECTUAL PROPERTY RIGHTS (1995) [hereinafter White Paper].

13.   17 U.S.C. § 101 (1994).

14.   Laura N. Gasaway, *Document Delivery*, 14 COMPUTERS IN LIBR. 25 (May 1994).

endorse ILL's use of digital copies, and then it seems to pull back on this view. According to the section on interlibrary loan, the ease with which licensing can be instituted through the NII changes the playing field. "Indeed, a publisher's license to access or download all or a portion of the aggregated copyrighted works on a server might be viewed as the online equivalent of a subscription." The report continues: "This 'publication on demand' might become an effective and economic substitute for interlibrary loan on the NII."[15] The report suggest that the CONTU Guidelines cannot be generalized to "borrowing" electronic publications.

In the next paragraph, however, the Working Group emphasizes that the existence of systems for the supply of licensed copies of works or portions of works by electronic means "does not negate the privileges conferred on libraries in Section 108(g)(2), nor do they limit 'borrowing' permitted under existing voluntarily negotiated guidelines or such guidelines to set rules for interlibrary loan via the NII that may be negotiated in the future." While it is clear that "Section 108 does not authorize unlimited reproduction of copies in digital form, it is equally clear that Section 108(g)(2) permits 'borrowing' in electronic form for interlibrary loan in the NII environment, so long as such 'borrowing' does not lead to 'systematic' copying."[16]

The Conferees are urged to provide libraries with a safe borrowing guide and to protect the interests of both copyright owners and libraries. If such guidelines are not forthcoming, the report suggests that a regulatory or legislative solution may be appropriate.

The Working Group on Interlibrary Loan clearly has impetus to provide the guidelines. The dilemma stems from two startlingly different points of view. Many publishers and other copyright owners believe that increased use of licenses will eliminate the need for interlibrary loan. The suggestion is that licenses will be so easy and cheap that libraries can afford to pay for all uses in electronic format. There is also an abiding fear on the part of producers that ease with which material can be transmitted on the Internet will mean loss of control of their publications and the income that could derive from its sale. Librarians take the opposite view and vigorously defend the need for ILL in the digital world.

---

15.   White Paper, *supra* note 12, at 88.
16.   *Id.* at 89.

B. The Current Interlibrary Loan Picture

A number of publishers have expressed concern that libraries are using interlibrary loan to avoid purchase. Statistics from a variety of sources refute that idea. Further, the publishing community seems to think that ILL is rapid, even instantaneous, and cheap. Quite the contrary, an ARL study found that it takes days, not hours, for lending libraries to satisfy ILL requests. Moreover, the cost exceeds $30 per transaction. It cost research libraries $18.62 to borrow an item and $10.93 to lend, making the total $29.55.[17] During a meeting of the CONFU Interlibrary Loan Working Group, Mary Jackson of the Association of Research Libraries framed interlibrary loan with these statistics.

1. Although no accurate totals exist, it is estimated that there are between 25 and 30 million interlibrary loans transacted annually.
2. In the 119 ARL libraries, the total interlibrary loan traffic is just two percent of circulation.
3. OCLC, RLIN, WLN, and DOCLINE are the major utilities by which requests are sent from one library to another, but these systems do not transmit full-text/full-image of requested documents.
4. OCLC is the major system for transmitting interlibrary loan requests, seven million by all types and sizes of libraries.
5. Of those seven million OCLC requests, 50 percent are for book loans and other returnables (90 percent book loans in public libraries).
6. Two-thirds of the lending by research libraries is for photocopies, but half of that is for articles more than five years old.[18]

The ARL statistics for 1994–95 indicate that interlibrary borrowing has increased 39 percent from 1991 through 1995.[19] The decline in library budgets, the increase in the amount of material published, and the improved knowledge of location through electronic catalogs all play strong roles in this increase. It does not mean that libraries are spending less to support and expand their collection. The ARL figures show that research libraries doubled expenditures for serials while buying 8 percent fewer titles since 1986. During the last decade, libraries

---

17.   MARILYN M. ROCHE, ARL/RLG INTERLIBRARY LOAN COST STUDY; A JOINT EFFORT BY THE ASSOCIATION OF RESEARCH LIBRARIES AND THE RESEARCH LIBRARIES GROUP 12 (1993).

18.   Mary Jackson, Oral Report to the CONFU Interlibrary Loan Working Group at the Library of Congress, Washington, DC (Mar. 27, 1976).

19.   ASSOCIATION OF RESEARCH LIBRARIES, STATISTICS, 1994–95: A COMPILATION OF STATISTICS FROM THE ONE HUNDRED NINETEEN MEMBERS OF THE ASSOCIATION OF RESEARCH LIBRARIES 8–11 (1996).

reduced the number of monograph purchases by 23 percent while the unit price for monographs increased by 58 percent. Since 1986 an annual average increase of 11.4 percent for serials and 5.9 percent for monographs was certainly higher than the general inflation in this country for the same period.[20]

Another source of data is from the National Library of Medicine study of interlibrary loan. The library analyzed the data for all interlibrary loan requests for journal articles in 1992. That year NLM used 13,318 unique journal titles to fill 205,746 requests. "Twenty percent of the requests were filled with just 100 titles; however, 500 titles were needed to fill 40% of the requests, 1,000 to fill half, and another 12,318 journal titles to fill all requests."[21]

Another part of this study involved investigating the potential for incorporating imaging technology into the document-delivery process. The purpose of the trial was to determine whether a system linking NLM's interlibrary loan service through DOCLINE so that "requests for articles from titles that were preserved on optical disk could be identified, retrieved, and transmitted automatically from NLM to the requesting library." The results of the pilot project demonstrated that "converting journal articles to electronic images and storing them in anticipation of repeated requests would not meet NLM's objective of improving ILL services." The study showed that to be impractical since the most heavily requested titles change from year to year.[22]

These statistics illustrate that interlibrary loan in many venues is still just that—a loan of a purchased volume or item from one library to another. They also indicate that scholars, students, and academic researchers need older material as much as the most recent and that many articles are requested only once. Not just once by a particular library, but once period. Interlibrary lending and borrowing is increasing because it is becoming easier to find where titles are held throughout the world, because electronic request systems speed the transaction, and because the volume of publishing continues to grow. It is not increasing because libraries wish to avoid purchase of titles for their collections.

---

20.   *Id.*

21.   E. M. Lacroix, *Sail: Automating Interlibrary Loan*, 82 BULL. OF MED. LIBR. ASS'N 171, 174 (1994).

22.   *Id.* at 172.

Another issue that must be addressed in this equation is the difference between ILL and document delivery.[23] ILL traditionally has been library-to-library lending. Document delivery, on the other hand, envisions a library supplying copies of works from its collection to users either on the same campus or to distant users. The key to ILL has been that it is a mediated request. The borrowing library makes the request from another library on behalf of a user. The advent of systems that permit end-user requests to go to a distant library without mediation from that user's primary library disturbs this balance.

There are two possibilities. The first possibility is that such activity is not ILL at all and the suggestion of five is inapplicable. Thus, only general fair use by the user would govern the transaction. On the other hand, it could be that the creation of systems to permit the user to interact with a distant library could mean that copying materials to satisfy his request rises to the level of "systematic copying" and is thus prohibited under section 108(g)(1). A second possibility is that end-user requests are tracked by that individual's primary library and are counted with that library's suggestion of five. This would mean that every user would have to designate a primary library which would be easy for faculty and students but more difficult for others who use public libraries. The down side of this option for libraries is that they would incur the obligation to pay royalties beyond the fifth request from the most recent sixty months of a journal title. The library would have no control since end users who designated that as their primary library would be making requests and obligating the library for the payment. Further, most primary libraries would insist that users first determine whether items are available locally before making ILL requests directly from other libraries for which that primary library might be liable for royalties. Clearly, most libraries designated as primary libraries would have to find some way to charge back the royalty payments to the user.

IV. The Electronic Publishing Dilemma

Part of the ILL Working Group's difficulty arises from the great uncertainty about how electronic publishing will develop. With the systems

---

23.   *See infra* Chapter Ten (p. 189), "The Impact of Recent Litigation on Interlibrary Loan and Document Delivery," by James S. Heller.

available today, each author could become a publisher by making his own writings available via the Internet or on a web site. Universities are reviewing their policies that govern copyright ownership by their faculties, who traditionally have given up all copyrights to publishers in order to have the work published. Commercial publishers that have ventured into electronic journal publishing have not yet found a satisfactory way to charge fees.

What will happen as electronic journals become "increasingly interconnected"? According to one writer, readers will be able to move from one item to another, regardless of who published the original work. The amazing array of exciting images and links that are possible in electronic publishing are wonderful for readers, but pose many questions for publishers. The "interactive powers of the Internet to turn journals into perpetual electronic conferences" can foster online discussion groups and commentary. Already a mouse click can take a subscriber from "one article to related articles in the same journal, other journals, and resources such as databases of DNA sequences, protein structures, or galaxy images."[24]

There are seemingly endless ways to use audio and visual enhancements, to provide an author's raw data, or to link to NLM's MEDLINE database or genes in the GenBank. What has not been determined is how articles and data can be kept uncompromised, the mechanism by which an individual user can pay for use, how a subscription could be sold for one title when links to other journals are involved, and what to do about society's information "have nots." All of these questions are pertinent to the way fair use will function in the electronic environment.

V. Conclusion

Clearly, electronic publishing is still developing and at the same time changing. The Interlibrary Loan Working Group believes that it is premature to develop guidelines for materials originating in digital format. Neither libraries nor publishers are ready. Instead, the group plans to start with guidelines for the print to digital mode. As publishers, authors, universities, libraries, and others move forward into the digital environment, ways must be found to maintain the balance between creators and users.

---

24. Gary Taubes, *Science Journals Go Wired*, 271 SCIENCE 764, 764 (1996).

To maintain the highest quality of scholarship, libraries must be able to obtain copies of works for their users. For little-used materials, ILL is the best method. Subscription income is not lost by publishers, and knowledge is advanced. To maintain the highest quality of research, scientists must have access to the resources of other institutions. To maintain an educated democracy, the citizens of this country must be able to utilize information and knowledge. Sharing resources, regardless of format, must continue if we are to reach and maintain these goals in the future. Douglas C. Bennett, Vice President of the Council of Learned Societies, makes this plea for a common intellectual realm:

> The marketplace and entrepreneurial activity certainly will have central places in the development of a national information infrastructure. But a sole focus on profitable undertakings is unlikely to serve well scholarly communities, higher education, or democracy. This is why the concept of fair use is well worth adapting to the new circumstances. Authors and publishers should be compensated for their work in most cases. No doubt we can work out technical and financial strategies which gain permission and pay royalties for most uses most of the time. But it would be chilling to have to ask permission for all uses of copyrighted materials. For a healthy climate of free inquiry, it will continue to be important *not* to have to ask permission to quote and criticize or to parody a published work.
>
> Let me simply name a broader and more formidable challenge. We need an environment in which all can be aware of what others *can* know. This does not mean everyone should have free access to everything that is published. Rather, it means that everyone should be able to be aware of what is available. For genuinely free inquiry we need a *common* intellectual realm: to publish is to make public. We achieved this in the print world via a complex array of institutions and practices: public education supporting widespread literacy, libraries, bookstores, daily newspapers, and more. What institutions and practices will we need to achieve this in a digital, networked environment? This is a problem that will take our most constructive joint efforts.[25]

The present Copyright Act makes provision for library borrowing and lending; the final report of the Lehman Working Group acknowledges that there can be interlibrary loan in the digital environment.

---

25.   Douglas C. Bennett, *Fair Use in an Electronic Age: A View from Scholars and Scholarly Societies, in* COPYRIGHT, PUBLIC POLICY, AND THE SCHOLARLY COMMUNITY 13–14 (Michael Matthews & Patricia Brennan eds., 1995).

Library and educational association members of the CONFU Interlibrary Loan Working Group also agree that fair use applies in the digital world. It is part of the way in which copyright advances the progress of science and art.

Chapter Ten
The Impact of Recent Litigation on Interlibrary Loan and Document Delivery[*]

by
James S. Heller
Director of the Law Library and Professor of Law
College of William and Mary

I. Introduction

In 1994 two federal appellate courts rendered decisions that may have significant repercussions for interlibrary lending and library document delivery activities even though the cases did not directly involve libraries. In *Campbell v. Acuff-Rose Music, Inc.*,[1] the U.S. Supreme Court held that the rap group 2 Live Crew's parody of Roy Orbison's "Oh Pretty

---

[*]   © 1997 James S. Heller. An earlier version of this chapter appeared in the volume 88, spring 1996 issue of *Law Library Journal*.
1.   114 S. Ct. 1164 (1994).

Woman" qualified as a fair use under section 107 of the Copyright Act of 1976. Most significant was the unanimous Court's analysis of the fair use doctrine itself, and guidelines on how courts should analyze the fair use defense in future copyright infringement cases. Shortly after *Acuff-Rose*, the U.S. Court of Appeals for the Second Circuit handed down its decision in *American Geophysical Union v. Texaco, Inc.*[2] In a 2-to-1 decision, the court held that Texaco's systematic institutional policy of multiplying the available number of copies of copyrighted journal articles by circulating the journals among Texaco's scientists who then made copies of articles was not fair.

For many years librarians have used interlibrary lending and document delivery to provide information to their patrons. Focusing on the fair use (§ 107) and library exemption (§ 108) provisions of the Copyright Act of 1976, this chapter discusses how the *Acuff-Rose* and *Texaco* decisions may affect interlibrary loan and library document delivery activities.[3]

Two definitions are in order. For the purposes of this chapter, "interlibrary lending" describes requests for copies of works not held by the library, from another library, for the requesting library's primary clientele—the patrons they serve directly. These include students and faculty served by a university library, company employees served by a corporate library, judges served by a court library, and the like. "Document delivery" refers to services to those not affiliated with the library or its parent institution, such as a university library providing copies of articles to corporate researchers.

Applying copyright law to library activities remains as difficult—and hot—an issue today as it was two decades ago when Congress was completing its revision of the 1909 Copyright Act. When it comes to document delivery, temperatures rise a few more degrees. And when the discussion turns to transmitting documents electronically, the dialogue gets even hotter. As one might expect, some librarians view interlibrary lending and document delivery as an entitlement that should have few, if any, limitations. They see copyright law as an impediment that unjustly limits their perceived right to copy documents for anyone, at any time. Thankfully, few librarians fall into this category. On the other side

---

2.   60 F.3d 913 (2d Cir.), *amending and repealing decision*, 37 F.3d 881 (2d Cir. 1994).

3.   For a general discussion of interlibrary loan, see *supra* Chapter Nine (p. 173), "Interlibrary Loan in the Electronic World," by Lucretia W. McClure.

is the Association of American Publishers (AAP). The AAP sees document delivery as a serious threat to publishers' economic well-being, which they apparently believe is the whole reason for the existence of copyright law.

In 1992 the AAP released a position paper quite correctly stating that *commercial* document delivery services must secure permission from, and (if requested) pay royalties to, the copyright holder.[4] To be sure, for-profit document deliverers can copy and deliver copyrighted works only with permission. The AAP took a giant leap, however, and claimed that fee-based document delivery services in libraries "are indistinguishable in purpose and effect from those of commercial document delivery suppliers," and also must receive permission or pay royalties.[5] This is not supported by either the law or the legislative history.

The AAP also has expressed its concern over the practice of scanning printed works. In a 1994 position paper it wrote that "copyright owners are greatly concerned about the conversion of a document into digital form, since the impact of this practice differs from and goes beyond even the existing damage from unauthorized photocopying."[6] The AAP asserted that distributing copyrighted works among libraries already results "in lost subscription revenue and lost royalty income . . . [and that] unauthorized scanning can easily increase such losses."[7] The publishing industry is concerned with both the ease with which digitized versions of copyrighted works can be re-transmitted to large numbers of recipients and also with how easily digitized works can be manipulated.[8]

The publishers have a strong ally in the Information Industry Association (IIA), which represents more than 500 companies that pursue business opportunities associated with the creation, distribution, and use of information. The IIA believes that libraries that provide document

---

4. ASSOCIATION OF AMERICAN PUBLISHERS, STATEMENT OF THE ASSOCIATION OF AMERICAN PUBLISHERS (AAP) ON COMMERCIAL AND FEE-BASED DOCUMENT DELIVERY 1 (1992).

5. *Id.*

6. ASSOCIATION OF AMERICAN PUBLISHERS, AAP POSITION PAPER ON SCANNING 2 (1994).

7. *Id.* at 3.

8. One commentator has suggested that telefacsimile transmission should not present a threat to publishers and authors so long as libraries observe restrictions within the Copyright Act and the CONTU Guidelines. David Ensign, *Copyright Considerations for Telefacsimile Transmission of Documents in Interlibrary Loan Transactions*, 81 L. LIBR. J. 805, 812 (1989).

delivery services without paying royalties have an unfair advantage over commercial information brokers who do pay, because libraries can price their services lower. The IIA asserts that libraries that promote and offer fee-based services beyond their primary patron base are engaged in commercial copying, and are not protected by fair use or the library exemption.[9]

A. Interlibrary Lending

Section 108 permits a library, under certain circumstances, to make a single copy of a periodical article or small excerpt of a larger work (such as a book chapter) upon the request of a user, or in response to a request from another library on behalf of *that* library's patron. This right is subject to two conditions. Subsection (g)(1) of section 108 prohibits a library from engaging in related or concerted copying or distribution of either single or multiple copies of the same material on one occasion or over a period of time. Subsection (g)(2) prohibits a library from engaging in the systematic reproduction of single or multiple copies of articles or short excerpts. Libraries may, however, participate in interlibrary arrangements that do not have as their purpose or effect the receipt of copies in such aggregate quantities as to substitute for a subscription to or purchase of a work. Section 108 rights, therefore, encompass isolated and unrelated copying and distribution of single copies of the same or different materials on separate occasions. Interlibrary loan substitutes

---

9.   The IAA position was stated as:

   I think the economic pressures on libraries to come up with additional revenues have pushed them into exercising some essentially commercial enterprises in functioning like these information retailers that I was describing. . . . What that essentially has done is create two kinds of information delivery services at that retail level: the commercial firms that recognize that they have to pay copyright, and the libraries which deny that they have to pay copyright. It creates basically an unfair competition between the two entities. . . . I hope your report would foreclose the possibility that an interpretation of § 108, or § 107 for that matter, could lead to the sanctioning of commercial-like photocopying within mainly large research libraries.

   U.S. Library of Congress, Copyright Office, *Public Hearings on the Report of the Register of Copyrights on the Effects of 17 U.S.C. 108 on the Rights of Creators and the Needs of Users of Works Reproduced by Certain Libraries and Archives*, April 8-9, 1987 (Appendix II, Hearings Transcript) 142–43 (testimony of Paul Zurkowski, President, Information Industry Association).

for a subscription when it is systematic or when it serves as a substitute for purchase or subscription.

Congress failed to define "systematic" copying in the Act, nor do the committee reports that make up the legislative history explain it. In 1976, however, the National Commission on New Technological Uses of Copyrighted Works (CONTU) developed guidelines governing practices under section 108(g)(2).[10] Sometimes called the "Rule of Five," but more appropriately the "suggestion of five," the CONTU Guidelines suggest that a library uses interlibrary loan as a substitute for a subscription to a journal when, in any one calendar year, it requests more than five copies of articles from the same journal title published within the last five years (i.e., the most recent sixty months). Libraries are to maintain three full calendar years of records of requests made and filled. Although CONTU did not specify the content of those records, they probably should include the date of the request; the title, volume, and publication date of the journal issue; the name of the article; its pagination; and the requester's name and institutional affiliation.

The guidelines are addressed primarily to libraries that request copies of articles, but they also speak to libraries that receive requests for copies from other libraries. Under the guidelines, a library should not provide copies absent attestation by the requesting library that the request complies with the guidelines.[11] (As a general matter, a requesting library alternatively may attest that the request complies with the fair use provision of the Act).

B. Document Delivery

About a decade ago, some large academic research libraries began expanding their services to patrons not affiliated with the library or its parent institution by providing copies of articles, chapters, and the like for a fee. Referred to as "document delivery," other libraries followed

---

10. The guidelines were included in the Conference Report, and are part of the legislative history of the Act. CONF. REP. NO. 1733, 94th Cong., 2d Sess. 73 (1976), *reprinted in* 1976 U.S.C.C.A.A.N. 5810, 5812.

11. Guideline 3 states: "No request for a copy or phonorecord of any material to which these guidelines apply may be filled by the supplying entity unless such request is accompanied by a representation by the requesting entity that the request was made in conformity with these guidelines."

suit, and today a large number of libraries offer such services.[12] Demand for these services expanded as developing technologies—tele-facsimile beginning in the 1980s, and scanning in the 1990s—enabled remote users to receive documents from libraries in minutes, rather than days.

Just as libraries are of various sizes and types, so are document-delivery operations. Although most libraries seek merely to recoup their actual costs, some hope to make a profit from document delivery to help fund other services. Some large-scale services function as a separate division within large (usually university) libraries and operate with revenues generated by the service. Less-ambitious libraries usually provide document delivery through their interlibrary loan department.

Whether libraries can engage in fee-based document delivery services without obtaining permission from the copyright owner or payment of royalties depends on the answers to several questions, including who requested the copy; how the requester will use the copy; what is the nature of the material copied; how much of it is copied; what does the library charge for the copy; how does the library use its revenue; and how much aggregate copying does the library conduct? How these questions are answered will help determine whether library document delivery is permitted under either section 107 or section 108 of the Act or, instead, whether permission or payment of royalties is required.

II. Section 108—The Library Exemption

A library must meet three threshold requirements (contained in subsection (a)) to qualify for the section 108 exemptions. The first requirement, which has generated much controversy, is that the copying must be done without a purpose of direct or indirect commercial advantage. A library that profits from its document delivery activities, or which establishes a separate document delivery unit that so profits, cannot qualify for the section 108 exemption. The publishing industry, as noted earlier, considers fee-based library services indistinguishable from commercial services, regardless of whether a profit is made.

---

12. THE FISCAL DIRECTORY OF FEE-BASED RESEARCH AND DOCUMENT SUPPLY SERVICES (County of Los Angeles Public Library/American Library Association, 1993) (lists more than 100 library document providers).

Publishers mistakenly contend that these libraries lose section 108 protection even if they do not profit from their activities. Concededly, a library whose fees exceed its direct and indirect costs—allowing it to expand its collection, for example—loses protection under section 108. But a library that merely recoups its costs (including equipment, labor, utilities, supplies, postage, and other overhead) does not so profit, and it is not automatically disqualified from the section 108 exemption.

Section 108 also requires that a library be open to the public or to persons doing research in a specialized field. There is some debate as to whether libraries in for-profit institutions closed to the general public meet this requirement. A former register of copyrights concluded that the open access requirement, along with the prohibition against copying for the purpose of direct or indirect commercial advantage mentioned above, limits the ability of libraries in for-profit institutions to qualify under section 108.[13] That interpretation seems contrary to the intent of Congress, however; Congress did not intend to limit section 108 to public or university libraries as evidenced by the following language from the House Report that accompanied the Act:

> Similarly, for-profit libraries could participate in interlibrary arrangements for exchange of photocopies so long as the production or distribution was not "systematic" These activities, by themselves, would ordinarily not be considered for direct or indirect commercial advantages; since the "advantage" referred to in this clause must attach to the immediate commercial motivation behind the reproduction or distribution itself, rather than to the ultimate profit-making motivation behind the enterprise in which the library is located.[14]

A library that permits other researchers access to its collections through interlibrary lending should also qualify for the section 108 exemption so long as it meets the other requirements of that section.[15]

Section 108 also requires that a notice of copyright appear on all copies distributed under this section. A library should either reproduce the formal notice that often appears within the publication, or

---

13. U.S. COPYRIGHT OFFICE, REPORT OF THE REGISTER OF COPYRIGHTS: LIBRARY REPRODUCTION OF COPYRIGHTED WORKS (17 U.S.C. § 108) 75–86 (1986).

14. H.R. REP. No. 94-1476, 94th Cong., 2d Sess. 74–75 (1976), *reprinted in* 1976 U.S.C.C.A.A.N. 5810, 5815–16 [hereinafter H.R. REP. No. 94-1476].

15. LAURA N. GASAWAY & SARAH K. WIANT, LIBRARIES AND COPYRIGHT: A GUIDE TO COPYRIGHT LAW IN THE 1990s 45 (1994) [hereinafter GASAWAY & WIANT].

alternatively, stamp the document with the following notice recommended by the American Association of Law Libraries: "This material is subject to the United States Copyright law: Further reproduction in violation of that law is prohibited."[16]

Under section 108(d) a library may copy articles from copyrighted works under certain circumstances. First, a library may reproduce only a single copy of one article from a journal issue or chapter of a book at any one time, and that copy must become the property of the user. Librarians should observe this straightforward rule as if delivered from the heavens: never send more than one copy of a copyrighted work to a requester, and never retain a copy of an article sent.

The library also must have no notice that the copy sent will be used for a purpose other than "private study, scholarship, or research." Although there is no affirmative duty to ascertain the requester's intended use of the materials, to remain safe a library should avoid making copies for for-profit information brokers.

Some might argue that section 108 does not encompass providing copies to employees of for-profit companies, but that interpretation is unduly restrictive. Clearly, Congress did not intend to exclude for-profit libraries from section 108.[17] Moreover, the exemption applies both to libraries that supply copies as well as to those that receive copies. The *Texaco* decision does *not* prohibit a library from copying an article for a corporate employee, nor does it limit an employee's right to receive such articles. Not only is *Texaco* limited to the specific facts of that dispute—and therefore does not directly implicate library document delivery activities—it was decided under the fair use provision of the Act rather than section 108. Moreover, as a decision from the Second Circuit, it affects directly only those in Connecticut, New York, and Vermont.

As noted above, a library's right to send or receive copies of journal articles is not without limits. Section 108(g)(1) prohibits related or concerted reproduction of single or multiple copies of the same article. A library that provides single copies of the same article to a variety of

---

16. *See* JAMES S. HELLER & SARAH K. WIANT, COPYRIGHT HANDBOOK 16–17 (1982). It concludes that law libraries also should use this language or the actual copyright notice.

17. *See* H.R. REP. NO. 94-1476, *supra* note 14, at 74–75, and *infra* text accompanying note 20.

independent users does not run afoul of this provision if each act of copying is isolated and unrelated. Libraries are not required to maintain records of internal copying, and even if several users ask for a copy of the same item over time, the library still may make the copies. This right is not unfettered, however.

Subsection (g)(2), which directly implicates library document delivery, prohibits the systematic copying or distribution of multiple *or single* copies of subsection (d) materials, such as articles. This proviso is designed to prevent a reduction in the value of or market for a work—a subscription to a journal, a journal issue, or a single article. From the copyright owner's standpoint there is direct or potential economic value for each. Because subsection (g)(2) prohibits the systematic copying of the same article *or different* articles from the same journal, former Register of Copyrights David Ladd stated that large-scale library copying services that employ full-time staff, advertise, and make lots of copies probably engage in systematic copying.[18] There is no clear answer as to the point at which a library's activities become "systematic," however, and there has been only one reported decision involving library copying that may implicate section 108, and it was decided prior to the 1976 copyright revision legislation.

In *Williams & Wilkins Co. v. United States*,[19] the U.S. Supreme Court upheld by a 4-to-4 vote a 1973 U.S. Court of Claims decision that large scale copying by the National Library of Medicine (NLM) and the National Institute of Health (NIH) was fair use. *Williams & Wilkins* deals with fair use (rather than with section 108, which did not exist until 1976). It is worthwhile to make one point now, however. Although NIH copied only for its own staff, about 12 percent of NLM'S requests came from private or commercial organizations, drug companies in particular. In other words, NLM engaged in document delivery.

The National Commission on New Technological Uses of Copyrighted Works (CONTU) convened a few years after the *Williams & Wilkins* decision. CONTU did not examine large-scale, fee-based library document delivery, probably because such services did not exist in

---

18. U.S. Copyright Office, Report of the Register of Copyrights: Library Reproduction of Copyrighted Works (17 U.S.C. 108) 140 (1983).

19. 487 F.2d 1345 (Ct. Cl. 1973), *aff'd by an equally divided court*, 420 U.S. 376 (1975).

1978 when it submitted its report.[20] But the Commission did discuss nonprofit copying centers established for the exclusive purpose of providing copies of articles.

CONTU first questioned whether centers such as the British Library Lending Division would qualify as a library or archives under the 1976 Act, and, therefore, might qualify for the section 108 exemption. Concluding that they were not, and did not so qualify, the Commission proceeded to state that other libraries could not receive photocopies of articles from such copy centers under section 108.[21] In other words, not only must nonprofit centers established for the specific purpose of providing copies secure authorization prior to copying, but other libraries could not receive copies from such "document supply centers" under section 108.

The *Texaco* decision should not directly impact library copying under section 108. Because the parties agreed that the dispute would be decided under section 107, any statements by the court on section 108 would be considered dictum.[22] Still, District Court Judge Pierre Leval commented that Texaco's copying was not permitted under section 108. His analysis was mistaken for several reasons.

Judge Leval commented that Texaco makes photocopies solely for commercial advantage, and he therefore concluded that Texaco could not meet the section 108 requirement that copies be made without the purpose of direct or indirect commercial advantage. The legislative history to the Act says otherwise—for-profit companies *may* qualify for the section 108 exemption.

> Isolated, spontaneous making of single photocopies by a library in a for-profit organization, without any systematic effort to substitute photocopying for subscriptions or purchases, would be covered by section 108, even though the copies are furnished to the employees of

---

20.   NATIONAL COMMISSION ON NEW TECHNOLOGICAL USES OF COPYRIGHTED MATERIAL, FINAL REPORT (1978).

21.   "If such nonprofit copying centers are not libraries or archives within the meaning of the 1976 Act, other libraries would not have the benefits of Section 108(d) and its extension in the Section 108(g)(2) proviso and the CONTU guidelines in securing photocopies of articles from them." *Id.* at 162.

22.   District Court Judge Pierre Leval wrote that "[i]t is questionable whether lawfulness under Section 108 comes within the scope off this trial which, by stipulation, covers only the issue [sic] fair use. Fair use is covered by Section 107. Section 108 is a separate special statutory exemption governed by an entirely different set of standards." 802 F. Supp. 1, 28 n.26 (S.D.N.Y. 1992).

the organization for use in their work. . . . These activities, by themselves, would ordinarily not be considered "for direct or indirect commercial advantages," since the "advantage" referred to in this clause must attach to the immediate commercial motivation behind the reproduction and distribution itself, rather than to the ultimate profit-making motivation behind the enterprise in which the library is located.[23]

Judge Leval also wrote that "[a] library that qualifies under § 108 could deliver a maximum of one copy of a particular item to Texaco. . . . If Chickering [the Texaco researcher] obtains a copy of an article, there is no procedure barring his Texaco colleagues from copying the same article."[24] Under Leval's analysis, when one Texaco scientist received a copy of an article under section 108, no other scientists could ever receive a copy of that same article.

This approach cannot be justified in the Act or its legislative history. The subsection (g)(1) and (g)(2) provisos prohibit related and concerted reproduction, as well as systematic copying; they do not prohibit two individuals from the same organization from receiving copies of the same article. For that matter, neither do the CONTU Guidelines. Not surprisingly, the appellate court did not discuss section 108, but neither did it point out Judge Leval's mistakes.

The scope of permissible library document delivery under section 108 remains unsettled. Although CONTU provided some guidance for libraries that *receive* copies of articles, few objective criteria exist to determine the permissible scope of library document delivery. Any such analysis would, in all likelihood, require answers to the several questions posed earlier. Those answers—as well as a finding whether the copyright owner was harmed by the copying—also will help determine whether the copying is permitted under section 107, the fair use provision of the Act.

III. Section 107—Fair Use

Section 107 provides that the fair use of a copyrighted work is not an infringement of copyright. Applying section 107 to library document delivery appears to warrant a two-part analysis. Because a library

---

23.   H.R. REP. No. 94-1476, *supra* note 14, at 75.

24.   802 F. Supp. at 28.

arguably acts as the agent for the requester, one may contend that the library should be able to do for the requester what the requester him or herself may do. (Conversely, a library may be prohibited from making copies for a requester when the requester may not do so).[25] As the entity that makes the copy, the library also must justify *its* copying under fair use. In *Williams & Wilkins* the Court of Claims found that copying by the National Institute of Health and the National Library of Medicine aided scientific research, a purpose the court did not want to impede. The court appropriately focused its attention on the purpose of the libraries that supplied the copies; as a secondary matter they looked at the activities of the requesters. Thus, it is important to look at fair use from the perspective of both the requester and of the supplying library.[26]

A. The First Fair Use Factor: The Purpose and Character of the Use

Congress mandated that courts consider no fewer than four factors in determining whether a use is fair. The first factor examines the purpose and character of the use, including whether the use is of a commercial nature or, instead, for nonprofit educational purposes. (Nonprofit educational uses are favored over commercial uses). Libraries provide document delivery to assist in disseminating information for the needs of distant users. When copies are made for individuals

---

25.   Note the very different analyses by the *Williams & Wilkins* Court of Claims judges. The majority stated that "[t]he NIH and NLM systems . . . are close kin to the current Library of Congress Policy . . . of maintaining machines in the library buildings so that readers can do their own copying. The principal extension by NLM and NIH is to service requesters who cannot conveniently come to the building, as well as out-of-town libraries." 487 F.2d at 1355. Compare the dissent: "There is no showing that these alleged . . . principles have any say in the formulation of the policies and practices of the photocopying operation. . . . The essential elements of agency are wholly lacking." 487 F.2d at 1367.

26.   The initial decision of the Sixth Circuit took this approach in Princeton University Press v. Michigan Document Services, 74 F.3d 1528 (6th Cir. 1996). In examining whether a commercial copyshop's making coursepacks for use by college students was fair, the court examined the actions of both the copyshop that made the copies and the students who purchased (and used) them. That decision, however, was vacated. When the entire panel decided the later case, it wrote that for-profit users may not "stand in the shoes of their customers making nonprofit or noncommercial uses." 99 F.3d 1381, 1388 (citing W. Patry, Fair Use in Copyright Law 420 n.34).

outside the library's primary client base—even when academic libraries serve the corporate sector—the purpose, although not nonprofit educational, is at worse benign. As for the *requester's* fair use rights, section 107 clearly favors copying by educators, students, and non-profit researchers. (Indeed, the preamble to section 107 expressly identifies copying for scholarship or research purposes as within the ambit of fair use). Copyright owners might argue that because *Texaco* limits the right of corporate researchers to rely on fair use for making copies of articles, it follows that libraries cannot provide those researchers the same materials through document delivery.

When examining the first factor, courts today consider whether the use is "productive" or "transformative." In *Campbell v. Acuff-Rose Music, Inc.*,[27] the Supreme Court commented that the central purpose of the first factor is whether the new work merely supplants the original (non-transformative) or, instead, whether it "adds something new, with a further purpose or different character, altering the first with new expression, meaning or message."[28] In considering this element of the first factor, the *Texaco* court found that the Texaco researcher copied the articles to create his own mini-library or archive: "The dominant purpose of the use is 'archival'—to assemble a set of papers for future reference, thereby serving the same purpose for which additional subscriptions are normally sold, or . . . for which photocopy licenses may be obtained."[29] The court also reasoned that copying articles to engage in *future* research was not transformative, even though the researcher who made the copy might use information from that article to create an entirely new work.[30]

---

27.   114 S. Ct. 1164 (1994).

28.   *Id.* at 1171. Some might consider this a significant change from a decade earlier. In 1984 the Court said that "Congress has plainly instructed us that fair use analysis calls for a sensitive balancing of interests. The distinction between 'productive' and 'unproductive' uses may be helpful in calibrating the balance, but it cannot be wholly determinative." Sony Corp. of Am. v. Universal City Studios, 464 U.S. 417, 544 n.40 (1984). Although many thought *Sony* discredited the productive use test, the Court merely clarified that it was one of several factors to be considered. In fact, both the *Campbell* and *Sony* Courts concluded that the respective uses were fair.

29.   *Texaco*, 60 F.3d at 892.

30.   Moreover, the concept of a "transformative" use would be extended beyond recognition if it was applied to Chickering's copying simply because he acted in the course of doing research. The purposes illustrated in section 107 refer primarily to the work of authorship alleged to be a fair use, not to the

Acuff-Rose emphasized that specific facts by themselves will not dictate whether the first factor favors the plaintiff or defendant. A commercial use by the defendant, by itself, does not mean that the first factor will favor the plaintiff. Neither will a non-productive use by itself preclude a finding that this factor favors the defendant.[31]

The *Texaco* court found that copying by a corporate researcher was for a commercial purpose and non-transformative, and it concluded that the first factor clearly favored the plaintiff. The court did not indict *all* corporate-sector copying, however. It emphasized that its holding rested on the specific facts of the case: systematic copying and archiving that resulted from wide-scale routing of journals to which Texaco subscribed.[32] The court stated:

> The parties and many of the *amici curiae* have approached this case as if it concerns the broad issue of whether photocopying of scientific articles is fair use. . . . Such broad issues are not before us. Rather, we consider whether Texaco's photocopying by 400 or 500 scientists . . . is fair use. This includes the question whether such institutional, systematic copying increases the number of copies available to scientists while avoiding the necessity of paying license fees or for additional subscriptions. We do not deal with the question of copying by an individual, for personal use in research or otherwise (not for resale), recognizing that under the fair use doctrine or the *de minimis* doctrine, such a practice of an individual might well not constitute infringement.[33]

---

        activity in which the alleged infringer is engaged. Texaco cannot gain fair use insulation for Chickering's archival photocopying of articles (or books) simply because such copying is done by a company doing research.
     Id.

31.   A recent federal district court decision stated that in examining the "purpose," a court should consider whether the use was commercial or non-commercial, including whether the use was for one of the favored purposes mentioned explicitly in the preamble to section 107. Examining the "character" of the use requires a determination whether the use was transformative or productive. College Entrance Examination Bd. v. Pataki, 889 F. Supp. 554, 567 (N.D.N.Y. 1995). The court also noted the possible tension inherent in the purpose and character elements of the first factor. Finding that the "purpose" was non-commercial, but that the "character" was non-transformative, the court concluded that the first factor favored neither party.

32.   "Our ruling is confined to the institutional, systematic, archival multiplication of copies revealed by the record—the precise copying that the parties stipulated should be the basis for the District Court's decision now on appeal. . . ." *Texaco*, 60 F.3d at 931.

33.   *Id.* at 916.

The *Texaco* court did *not* say that a corporate employee could not occasionally copy articles for his or her own research. Nor did it say that a corporate researcher could not request from a library a single copy of an article from a journal to which the corporation does not subscribe. The court took great care to limit its holding to the specific facts of the case; librarians and their institutions ought not jump to conclusions that the court itself chose not to reach.

B. The Second Factor: Nature of the Work Copied

A fair use analysis also requires consideration of the nature of the work copied. In practice, one may more readily copy factual or informational works than creative works.[34] Even the *Texaco* court concluded that this factor favored the defendant.[35] Document deliverers rarely copy creative works (such as fiction or poetry), and thus the second factor would likely work in their favor.[36]

---

34. "Under this factor, the more creative a work, the more protection it should be accorded from copying; correlatively, the more informational or functional the plaintiff's work, the broader should be the scope of the fair use defense." MELVILLE B. NIMMER & DAVID NIMMER, NIMMER ON COPYRIGHT, § 13.05[A][2][a] (1995). *See also* the brief discussion in *Campbell*, 114 S. Ct. 1164, at 1175, *citing* Stewart v. Abend, 495 U.S. 207, 237–38 (1990), Sony Corp. of Am. v. Universal City Studios, 464 U.S. 417, 455 n.40 (1984), and Feist Publications, Inc. v. Rural Tel. Serv. Co., 499 U.S. 340, 348–51 (1991).

35. *Texaco*, 60 F.3d at 925. A court also is likely to examine whether the original work is published or unpublished. Although a 1992 amendment to section 107 provides that the unpublished nature of a work will not bar a finding of fair use, there is less freedom to copy unpublished works under this section. A section 108 library, however, may copy an unpublished work "in facsimile form solely for purposes of preservation and security or for deposit for research use in another [section 108] library . . . if the copy . . . is currently in the collections of the library or archives." 17 U.S.C. § 108(b) (1994).

36. In Encyclopedia Britannica v. Crooks, 542 F. Supp. 1156 (W.D.N.Y. 1982), a federal district court held that large-scale copying and distributing of videotapes of educational television programs by a nonprofit educational cooperative was infringing, notwithstanding the educational purpose and informational nature of the works copied. The key point for the court was both the systematic copying of entire works by the school system (as many as 10,000 copies in one year), *id.* at 1181; but also that in copying films prepared for the school market, the defendant inhibited plaintiff's ability to sell or license the films to other educational institutions, *id.* at 1178.

C. The Third Factor: The Amount Copied

Fair use also requires consideration of the amount of the work copied. As a general matter, the more that is copied, the less the use is likely to be considered fair. Because libraries typically copy and distribute entire journal articles, each of which is copyrightable, this factor leans against a fair use finding.[37] (Indeed, courts may find infringement even for the use of very small portions of copyrighted works.[38]) Noting that the Texaco researcher copied entire articles from the *Journal of Catalysis*, the *Texaco* court concluded that this factor clearly favored the plaintiff.[39] One suspects that a court could reach the same conclusion in a case involving library document delivery, even though Congress expressly permits libraries to copy entire articles under the section 108 library exemption.

D. The Fourth Factor: Harm to the Copyright Owner

A common denominator synthesizing court decisions throughout the 1980s and into the 1990s has been a determination whether the copyright owner was harmed by the copying. This fourth factor is described in the Act as "the effect of the use on the potential market for or value of the copyrighted work." For several years this factor was considered the most important of the four.[40] The *Acuff-Rose* Court, however, recently commented that courts should not attach any greater significance to any factor: "All are to be explored, and the results weighed together, in light of the purposes of copyright."[41]

---

37.   When an author transfers copyright to the publisher, the publisher has copyright in each individual article and also in each issue as a collective work. The *Texaco* court noted that "each of the eight articles in *Catalysis* was separately authored and constitutes a discrete 'original work of authorship'." *Texaco*, 60 F.3d at 926.

38.   Recent decisions, however, emphasize less the quantity appropriated and more the significance of the portion copied. *See, e.g.,* Harper & Row Publishers, Inc. v. The Nation Enters., 471 U.S. 539 (1985); Basic Books, Inc. v. Kinko's Graphics Corp., 758 F. Supp. 1522 (S.D.N.Y. 1991).

39.   *Texaco*, 60 F.3d at 926.

40.   *See* Harper & Row Publishers, Inc. v. The Nation Enters., 471 U.S. 539, 566 (1985).

41.   *Acuff-Rose*, 114 S. Ct. at 1171. In reversing the appellate court judgment, the Supreme Court stated that

       [i]t was error for the Court of Appeals to conclude that the commercial nature of [the parody] rendered it presumptively unfair. No such evidentiary presumption is available to address either the first factor, the

Both *Acuff-Rose* and *Texaco* stated that the fourth factor requires an examination of more than the market impact of the copying by the individual defendant. Courts must "consider not only the extent of market harm caused by the particular action of the alleged infringer, but also 'whether unrestricted and widespread conduct of the sort engaged in the by the defendant . . . would result in a substantially adverse impact on the potential market' for the original."[42] Courts are much more likely to find infringement when the copyright owner incurs financial harm due to unauthorized (or uncompensated) copying. Under a two-part analysis, one would examine whether the library's activities harm the value of or market for the copyrighted work, and then consider whether the requester's use of that work harms the copyright owner.

Before *Texaco* one might have asserted confidently that an individual—whether a university professor or a corporate researcher—could make a single copy of a journal article under fair use. As long as the individual, or his employer, did not profit directly from making that copy—by reselling it, for example—that single act of copying did not appear to harm the value of the work copied. Similarly, a library's copying and distributing a single copy of an article on request does not, on its face, harm the value of the *particular* work copied. The publishing industry maintains, however, that harm occurs in both instances. In *Texaco* they argued successfully that the copyright owner was denied royalties or license fees because Texaco should have made royalty payments through the Copyright Clearance Center for the copied articles.

It is not difficult to see that every act of copying harms the copyright owner *if* recipients of articles always had to purchase reprints or pay royalties for every instance of copying. This circular reasoning, as noted in the dissent in *Texaco*, makes fair use disappear.[43] But fair use

---

character and purpose of the use, or the fourth, market harm, in determining whether a transformative use, such as parody, is a fair one.

Id. at 1179.

42.   *Acuff-Rose*, 114 S. Ct. at 1177, *citing in part*, 3 NIMMER ON COPYRIGHT § 13.15[A][4] (1995). The *Texaco* court commented that "[t]he fourth factor is concerned with the category of a defendant's conduct, not merely the specific instances of copying." *Texaco*, 60 F.3d at 927 n.12.

43.   For a thoughtful discussion of this point, see Judge Jacobs' dissent in *Texaco*:

(and section 108, for that matter) are very real, and Congress intended those sections to have *some* teeth.

The fourth factor also presents another element: whether the plaintiff must prove that their market was harmed by the copying, or instead, whether the defendant must show it was not so harmed. In 1982 the *Sony* Court said "[i]f the intended use is for commercial gain, that likelihood [of harm to the market for the work] may be presumed. But if it is for a noncommercial purpose, the likelihood must be demonstrated."[44] The Supreme Court revised this approach in *Acuff-Rose*.

The *Acuff-Rose* Court stated that the burden should not shift so quickly; a court will presume harm—and require the defendant to demonstrate that the market for the work copied was *not* harmed— only in circumstances of verbatim copying for commercial purposes.[45] Under either approach, a publisher that charges a nonprofit library with infringement would carry the burden of demonstrating market harm so long as the library did not profit from its document delivery activities. (By contrast, harm would be presumed in an action against a commercial information broker).

Having concluded earlier (when examining the first factor) that Texaco's copying was for a commercial purpose, the Second Circuit found that the burden fell upon Texaco to demonstrate that the market for the *Journal of Catalysis* from which their researcher made copies was not

---

> In this case the only harm to a market is to the supposed market in photocopy licenses. The CCC scheme is neither traditional nor reasonable; and its development into a real market is subject to substantial impediments. There is a circularity to the problem: the market will not crystallize unless courts reject the fair use argument that Texaco presents; but under the statutory test, we cannot declare a use to be an infringement unless (assuming other factors also weigh in favor of the secondary user) there is a market to be harmed. At present, only a fraction of journal publishers have sought to enact these fees. I would hold that this fourth factor decisively weighs in favor of Texaco, because there is no normal market for photocopy licenses, and no real consensus among publishers that there ought to be.

> 60 F.3d at 937 (Jacobs, J. dissenting).

44.   *Sony*, 464 U.S. at 451.

45.   A court should not presume market harm in "a case involving something beyond mere duplication for commercial purposes. . . . [W]hen a commercial use amounts to mere duplication of the entirety of an original, it clearly 'supersede[s]' the objects' . . . of the original and serves as a market replacement for it. . . ." *Acuff-Rose*, 114 S. Ct. at 1177.

harmed. Texaco could not meet this burden. The court found that the publisher lost sales of additional journal subscriptions, back issues, and back volumes, and also licensing revenue and fees that Texaco could pay directly to them or through the Copyright Clearance Center.[46]

The approach would be little different in the case of non-commercial library document delivery. *Acuff-Rose* says that a plaintiff claiming infringement must prove harm when the defendant copied for non-commercial purposes, the situation that applies in the case of non-profit libraries. A *Texaco*-like analysis ensures that copyright owners will have little trouble meeting this burden.

One may speculate whether courts might indeed accept the AAP's argument that little distinguishes for-profit information brokers from library document deliverers. It is not inconceivable that courts might consider the for-profit/nonprofit distinction legally insignificant when analyzing the first fair use factor. The other fair use factors appear identical. Equally plausible, however, courts might distinguish large document delivery operations from smaller ones. Libraries that promote their services widely to outside users—particularly the corporate sector—maintain separate records, employ a large staff whose wages are paid from document delivery proceeds, and function as a separate unit within the library. These services might be less likely to survive a fair use analysis than libraries that receive only occasional requests from outside users.

But even large-scale library document delivery may be fair. Although the fourth fair use factor no longer remains the single most important element of fair use,[47] the *Texaco* court implied that the first (purpose of the use) and fourth (market harm) factors are more important than the second (nature of the copyrighted work) and third (the amount copied).[48] Nonprofit libraries (especially public libraries), that provide document delivery at or below their cost ought not be likened to profit-motivated information brokers. This fundamental difference may convince a court that some level of library document delivery falls within fair use.

---

46. *Texaco*, 60 F.3d at 926–31.

47. Harper & Row Publishers, Inc. v. The Nation Enters., 471 U.S. 539, 566 (1985).

48. "We conclude that three of the four statutory factors, including the important first and fourth factors, favor the publishers." *Texaco*, 60 F.3d at 931.

The *Williams & Wilkins* case is also relevant here. Because an equally divided Supreme Court affirmed the Court of Claims decision, some contend that *Williams & Wilkins* has limited precedential value; others criticize the decision or believe it no longer has continued viability.[49] In any event, the *Texaco* court implied that the copying done by NLM and NIH would not be permitted today, particularly considering the ease with which royalties may be paid through the Copyright Clearance Center.[50]

Acuff-Rose, however, reminds everyone that Congress intended to restate the common law when it enacted section 107: "Congress meant § 107 to 'restate the present judicial doctrine of fair use, not to change, narrow, or enlarge it in any way,' and intended that courts continue the common law tradition of fair use adjudication. H.R. Rep, No. 94-1476, p.66 (1976). . . . "[51] *Williams & Wilkins was* the common law in 1976, and Congress arguably sanctioned the type and level of copying done by NLM and NIH when it passed the 1976 Act.

It is important to remember that NLM and NIH employed policies that limited to some extent the number and nature of copies made, although the libraries themselves admitted that they often granted exceptions. NIH made only a single copy of an article requested, limited copying to no more than one article per issue (and never more than half of an issue), and generally limited copying to 40 or 50 pages. NLM provided only one copy of an article on request, and it would not copy more than one article from an issue or three articles from a volume. NLM also would not copy from 104 journals on a "widely available" list, and it would not honor an excessive number of requests from one individual or institution. At the very least, libraries should develop

---

49.   *See, e.g.,* HOWARD B. ABRAMS, THE LAW OF COPYRIGHT § 15.05[D][3] (1995); MELVILLE B. NIMMER & DAVID NIMMER, 3 NIMMER ON COPYRIGHT § 13.05[e][4][c] (1995).

50.   Texaco contends that Chickering's photocopying constitutes a use that has historically been considered "reasonable and customary." We agree with the District Court that whatever validity this argument might have had before the advent of the photocopy licensing arrangements discussed below in our consideration of the fourth factor, the argument today is insubstantial. As the District Court observed, "To the extent the copying practice was 'reasonable' in 1973 [when *Williams & Wilkins* was decided], it has ceased to be 'reasonable' as the reasons that justified it before the CCC have ceased to exist." 802 F. Supp. at 25.

      60 F.3d at 924.

51.   *Acuff-Rose,* 114 S. Ct. at 1170.

policies that provide some limits on their document delivery activities, perhaps along the lines of those established by NLM and NIH.

IV. Electronic Copying

The publishing industry is understandably concerned that the electronic age makes it easier for libraries to digitize materials and distribute them electronically. Publishers worry that libraries can more easily perform document delivery—which may lead to more copying—and also recognize that scanning enables libraries to create databases of digitized works. Additionally, recipients of digitized documents can retain those documents indefinitely in their own databases and easily re-distribute them inside and outside of their organizations.

The section 108 library exemption does not address library scanning and digitizing print materials. Because the Copyright Act is technologically neutral, some contend that "[i]f it is permissible for a library to make a copy of a work under section 108, it is permissible to make an electronic copy. As libraries move beyond photocopying for a user, then it is permissible to scan a copy and transfer it electronically to the user."[52]

It is important to remember that copies distributed by libraries under section 108 must become the property of the user.[53] A library should never retain a scanned copy in a database; it should delete the digitized copy immediately after transmission.[54] This is similar to the rule libraries should apply to copies transmitted by telefacsimile: after the fax transmission, destroy the photocopy.[55]

The possibility that recipients of lawful copies might subsequently violate copyright should not restrict activities permitted under the

---

52.   Gasaway & Wiant, *supra* note 15, at 43.

53.   17 U.S.C. § 108(d)–(e) (1994).

54.   When the library retains a scanned copy and creates a database of article, it is the equivalent of retaining photocopies which clearly is not permitted under the Act. If the library wished to retain the scanned copy, then it must seek permission from the copyright holder to do so and pay royalties if requested. This is precisely what commercial document delivery services such as CARL/UnCover are doing.

Gasaway & Wiant, *supra* note 15, at 51.

55.   *Id.* at 50.

Act.[56] Publishers' uneasiness that digitization makes it easier for recipients to make and distribute additional unlawful copies should not limit library and user rights under sections 107 and 108.

One other matter warrants mention. The CONTU Guidelines provide that libraries which receive requests from other libraries should not send copies absent attestation that the request complies with the guidelines.[57] Even though this is a requirement that virtually defies enforcement, librarians should not neglect the attestation requirement for requests made by telephone or electronically.

V. Possible Liability

Conceivably even large-scale document delivery is permissible under fair use or the library exemption. But what if a court concluded that the copying was *not* permitted under section 107 or 108? A library generally would be liable for infringing acts of its employees performed within the scope of their employment. An aggrieved copyright owner may recover actual damages and profits from the infringer or alternatively elect to recover statutory damages to be determined by the court. Statutory damages may range from $500 to $20,000 for each work infringed. If the infringement was willful, damages may be as high as $100,000.[58]

Congress is much more forgiving of innocent infringers, however. If the infringer was not aware and had no reason to believe that his or her acts were infringing, statutory damages may be reduced to not less

---

56.   The *Sony* court refused to hold the Betamax manufacturer vicariously liable. "The Betamax can be used to make authorized and unauthorized uses of copyrighted works, but the range of its potential use is much broader than the particularly infringing use. . . ." 464 U.S. at 436–37. If vicarious liability is to be imposed on Sony in this case, it must rest on the fact that it has sold equipment with constructive knowledge of the fact that its customers may use that equipment to make unauthorized copies of copyrighted materials. *Id.* at 439. The sale of copying equipment, like the sale of other articles of commerce, does not constitute contributory infringement if the product is widely used for legitimate, unobjectionable purposes. Indeed, it need merely be capable of substantial noninfringing uses. *Id.* at 442.

57.   Guideline 3 states: "No request for a copy or phonorecord of any material to which these guidelines apply may be fulfilled by the supplying entity unless such request is accompanied by a representation by the requesting entity that the request was made in conformity with these guidelines." Note that CONTU Guidelines focus on *interlibrary* arrangements for photocopying, and therefore apply to requests received from other *libraries*.

58.   17 U.S.C. § 504(c)(1)–(2) (1994).

than $200. Further, a court will not award statutory damages if the infringer was an employee of a nonprofit educational institution, library, or archives who acted within the scope of his or her employment and believed and had reasonable grounds for believing that the copying was a fair use under section 107.[59]

VI. Library Practices

Notwithstanding all the literature on libraries and copyright,[60] librarians who operate fee-based document delivery services remain uncertain about whether they must pay royalties. Many libraries do not, under the theory that making a single copy on request is either a fair use or permitted under section 108. Still, some of these libraries pay royalties under certain circumstances, such as when a requester affirmatively asks that royalties be paid (in which case the requester reimburses the library for the payment), or if the copying is excessive, such as a request for several articles from the same journal issue.

Some libraries do pay royalties for external document delivery. Many of these libraries have joined the Copyright Clearance Center and make royalty payments on a routine basis through the CCC. Although some libraries pay royalties for every copy made, others do so only when they can make payments conveniently through the CCC. On first glance, this appears a curious practice. One might think that when royalties are appropriate—if the copying is not permitted under the Act—they are *always* due, and not only when it is convenient to pay them through the CCC. This practice does not seem so odd, however, when one observes the importance of the CCC to both the trial and appellate courts in the *Texaco* litigation.

In the trial court decision the judge stated that "[t]he monumental change since the decision of *Williams & Wilkins* in 1973 has been the cooperation of users and publishers to create workable solutions to the problem. . . . Most notable has been the creation of the CCC, and its

---

59.   *Id.* § 504(c)(2).

60.   For example, in the last few years a number of copyright books have been published, such as: JANIS H. BRUWELHEIDE, THE COPYRIGHT PRIMER FOR LIBRARIANS AND EDUCATORS (2d ed., 1995); LAURA N. GASAWAY & SARAH K. WIANT, LIBRARIES AND COPYRIGHT: A GUIDE TO COPYRIGHT LAW IN THE 1990s (1994); ARLENE BIELEFIELD & LAWRENCE CHEESMAN, LIBRARIES AND COPYRIGHT (1993); RUTH H. DUKELOW, THE LIBRARY COPYRIGHT GUIDE (1992).

establishment of efficient licensing systems."[61] Although Texaco argued that the CCC was irrelevant to the action, the court disagreed. "Reasonably priced, administratively tolerable licensing procedures are available that can protect the copyright owners' interests without harming research or imposing excessive burdens of users."[62] The appellate court concurred: "Though the publishers still have not established a conventional market for the direct sale and distribution of individual articles, they have created, primarily through the CCC, a workable market for institutional users to obtain licenses for the right to produce their own copies of individual articles via photocopying."[63]

Alternatively, a library might resolve the uncertainty by deciding to enforce the CONTU "suggestion of five" on behalf of those who use the library's document delivery service. Remember that the numerical guidelines apply to *requesters*; the guidelines suggest that when in a single year a library requests more than five copies of articles published within the last five years from the same journal title, it is likely using interlibrary loan as a substitution for purchase of that title. By enforcing the guidelines on behalf of its clients, the sending library would pay royalties after it copies five articles from the same journal title in one calendar year for the same client.

VII. Guidelines, Please

Libraries that provide document delivery should, regardless of their size, have in place a written copyright policy. At the risk of offending everyone—libraries, their clients, and the publishing industry—the following guidelines are proposed for library document deliverers.

✦ The library will pay royalties whenever appropriate regardless of whether a specific title is registered with a licensing organization such as the Copyright Clearance Center. Royalties may be paid either to the licensing organization or directly to the copyright owner.

✦ The library will make only one copy of a requested item at one time for a requester without payment of royalties or permission.

---

61. American Geophysical Union v. Texaco, Inc., 802 F. Supp. 1, 24 (S.D.N.Y. 1992).
62. *Id.* at 25.
63. *Texaco*, 60 F.3d at 930.

✦ The library will make multiple copies of the same item for the same user (including the user's institution), whether made simultaneously or over a period of time, only with permission of the copyright owner or upon payment of royalties.

✦ The library will not copy more than one-half of a periodical issue without first receiving permission to copy or payment of royalties regardless of whether the entire issue consists of only one article.

✦ The library need not ask the requester how he or she plans to use the copy. However, the library will not fill a request if it knows that the requester plans to sell the copy for a profit (i.e., commercial information brokers) absent permission to copy or payment of royalties.

✦ If the library first photocopies materials for subsequent transmission by telefacsimile, the library will destroy the photocopy after the transmission is complete.

✦ If the library downloads text to disk to prepare a copy for transmission to a requester, the library will destroy the electronic copy after the transmission is complete. The library will communicate to the recipient that no further copying or transmission is permitted.

✦ A library that requests materials from other libraries to fill its own clients' requests will follow the CONTU Guidelines regarding number requested and records maintained. Records will include the name of the requester and his or her institutional affiliation, the item copied, the number of copies made, and the date of the transaction. These records shall remain confidential and shall be destroyed three calendar years after the end of the year in which the request was made.[64]

✦ The library may fill requests from other libraries that include an attestation that the request complies with the Copyright Act or the CONTU Guidelines. The library will not provide copies if it knows that the request exceeds fair use or the section 108 exemption absent such attestation, or attestation that the requester has received permission or will pay royalties.

---

64. Many states have enacted legislation to ensure the confidentiality of certain library records. *See, e.g.,* VA. CODE. ANN § 2.1.342(B)(8) (Michie 1995).

✦ The library will include with the copy the "notice of copyright" if
   that notice is readily available. The library will stamp all copies as
   follows: "This material may be protected by Copyright Law (Title
   17, U.S. Code). Further reproduction in violation of that law is
   prohibited."

Chapter Eleven
The Circulation of Software by Libraries*

by
Anne Klinefelter
Head of Public Services
University of Miami School of Law Library

I. Software in the Library Collection

If a public library patron wants to borrow a book about making a will or about learning Spanish, he or she should be able to check out the book from the library. But what if the latest books on these topics came with software containing forms or exercises? Should the inclusion of software prevent the patron from borrowing the material from the library?

The Computer Software Rental Amendments Act of 1990 preserved the right of nonprofit libraries and educational institutions to lend copies of software for nonprofit purposes.[1] The law requires that the

---

*   © 1997 Anne Klinefelter.

1.   Pub. L. No. 101-650, 104 Stat. 5134 (1990).

software be accompanied by a warning that copying such software would constitute a violation of copyright law.[2] So, if the nonprofit library patron had a computer at home which could read the will-writing forms or Spanish-language exercises, or if the library had a computer for such use, the patron should be able to move into the digital era without losing any access to information.

The software in the book, however, may be sealed in plastic containing what is known as a "shrinkwrap" license with terms restructuring the rights established in federal copyright law. While shrinkwrap licenses have received uneven treatment by the courts, they remain widespread and are endorsed in a draft model law by the American Law Institute and the National Conference of Commissioners on Uniform Laws. Even if software shrinkwrap licenses gain some validity through revised state contract law, though, they may be preempted by the federal copyright laws.

Libraries must stay vigilant to remain relevant in the electronic environment because the traditional needs for information persist through the technological transformations of the book. The needs may, in fact, be greater as the cost of information grows and threatens to separate American society into information "haves" and information "have nots." The purpose of this chapter is to explore the legal context for software in library collections, especially nonprofit library collections, to offer librarians guidance about circulating software, and to challenge librarians to articulate and defend the role of libraries as software products expand, replace, and transform many of the information sources in library collections.

II. How Does Copyright Law Apply to Library Circulation of Software?

The first hurdle in discussing software is defining the term. The federal copyright statute does not define "software." The Computer Software Copyright Act of 1980[3] added a definition of "computer programs" to federal copyright law and made clear that computer programs would be considered copyrightable material.[4] While many aspects of the definition

---

2.   17 U.S.C. § 109(b)(2)(A) (1990); 37 C.F.R. § 201.24 (1991).

3.   Act of Dec. 12, 1980, Pub. L. No. 96-517, § 10, 94 Stat. 3028.

4.   17 U.S.C. § 101 (1994).

of "computer program" plague software developers,[5] the most important definitional issue for library collections is the distinction between the legal phrase "computer program" and the vernacular term "software."

"Software" is defined in federal copyright law only as it relates to the phrase "computer program." Computer program is defined as "a set of statements or instructions to be used directly or indirectly in a computer in order to bring about a certain result."[6] "Software" may be generally understood to cover a broader range of things connected with the running of a computer or a particular computer application, and distinguished from "hardware."[7]

The Computer Software Rental Amendments Act of 1990 continued the use of the phrase "computer program" in simultaneously forbidding the renting or lending of software generally and exempting lending by nonprofit libraries and educational institutions.[8] This Act was passed to prevent the loss of software sales which might result from unlawful copying of software lawfully rented or loaned. The Act seeks to achieve this goal by curtailing the first-sale doctrine,[9] an area of copyright law which forms the basis for library lending of any copyrighted materials and which allows anyone to dispose of a legally obtained copy of copyrighted material in whatever way he or she chooses. The first-sale doctrine provides users' rights restricting the otherwise exclusive right of copyright holders to distribute their works. The Computer Software Rental Amendments Act reflected the opinion that software piracy was rampant and growing because copying of software was much easier and achieved with much less loss of quality than was possible with any other medium of expression.[10]

The first-sale doctrine which this Act sought to restrict is a well-established legal concept deriving from the idea that the physical copy

---

5.   *See* Randall Davis, Pamela Samuelson, Mitchell Kapor & Jerome Reichman, *A New View of Intellectual Property and Software*, 39 COMM. OF THE ACM 21 (1996).

6.   17 U.S.C. § 101 (1994).

7.   MICHAEL D. SCOTT, SCOTT ON COMPUTER LAW 201 (2d ed. 1992, Supp. 1995).

8.   Computer Software Rental Amendments Act of 1990, Pub. L. No. 101-650, 104 Stat. 5089, tit. VIII (codified as amended in various sections of 17 U.S.C.).

9.   *Id.* § 106 (1994). The five rights of the copyright holder are reproduction, distribution, adaptation, performance, and display.

10. S. REP. NO. 101-265 (Apr. 19, 1990), to accompany S. 101-198, as amended. 101st Cong., 2d Sess. (1990).

of intellectual property was controlled by tangible property principles.[11] The U.S. Supreme Court recognized the first-sale doctrine in 1908, and statutory copyright law has preserved the right since 1909.[12]

The exemption for nonprofit libraries in the Computer Software Rental Amendments Act of 1990 is accompanied by a provision requiring the register of copyrights to prepare a report for Congress evaluating whether the exemption "has achieved its intended purpose of maintaining the integrity of the copyright system while providing nonprofit libraries the capability to fulfill their function."[13] The register must also provide Congress any information or recommendations which he or she considers necessary to carry out the intended purposed of the exemption.[14] The acting register prepared this report in March 1994 and found insufficient evidence to justify further narrowing of the nonprofit library's lending right.[15]

III. Printed Warning Requirement

The Computer Software Rental Amendments Act authorized the register of copyrights to develop a regulation requiring a printed warning on every physical copy of software that a nonprofit library distributed.[16] The required warning reads:

> Notice: Warning of Copyright Restrictions
>
> The copyright law of the United States (Title 17, United States Code) governs the reproduction, distribution, adaptation, public performance and public display of copyrighted material.
>   Under certain conditions of the law, nonprofit libraries are authorized to lend, lease, or rent copies of computer programs to patrons on a nonprofit basis for nonprofit purposes. Any person who makes an unauthorized copy or adaptation of the computer program, or redistributes the loan copy, or publicly performs or displays the

---

11.   Zechariah Chafee, *Equitable Servitudes on Chattels*, 41 HARV. L. REV. 945, 982 (1928).

12.   PAUL GOLDSTEIN, 2 COPYRIGHT § 5.6.1 (2d ed. 1996).

13.   17 U.S.C. § 109(2)(B) (1994).

14.   *Id.*

15.   THE COMPUTER SOFTWARE RENTAL AMENDMENTS ACT OF 1990: THE NONPROFIT LIBRARY LENDING EXEMPTION TO THE "RENTAL RIGHT": A REPORT OF THE ACTING REGISTER OF COPYRIGHTS 94 (1994) [hereinafter Register's Report].

16.   37 C.F.R. § 201.24 (1994).

computer program, except as permitted by Title 17 of the United States Code, may be liable for copyright infringement.

This institution reserves the right to refuse to fulfill a loan request, if in its judgment, fulfillment of the request would lead to violation of the copyright law.[17]

Librarians have expressed mild complaints about the size of the warning which may have fit more neatly on the older, larger 5¼-inch disks but which become unwieldy or too fine a print on the newer 3½-inch disks.[18] Some librarians have adjusted by attaching the warning to a folder in which the software is distributed.[19] These complaints may gain strength as more software is incorporated into nonprofit library collections.[20]

Other practical problems are associated with the printed warning requirement. Some nonprofit libraries load the software onto laptop computers and circulate the bundled package. Some nonprofit libraries are circulating software by electronic transmission rather than by handing the user a physical copy of the disk. The register of copyrights has noted these options and the libraries' innovations in providing warnings which automatically appear on screen as the software is activated and in providing warnings on in-library computers.[21]

The loading of software onto a file server for in-library or remote access raises the issue of multiple users "borrowing" the software at the same time. Librarians should be careful that such arrangements allow only one user at a time to access the software if the library is relying on the copyright law for circulation rights. Section 117 of the Copyright Act allows an owner of a copy of a computer program to copy or adapt it if to do so is an essential step in using the software or if the copy or adaptation is for archival purposes. Additional copying or reading might

---

17.   37 C.F.R. § 201.24 (1994).

18.   LAURA N. GASAWAY & SARAH K. WIANT, LIBRARIES AND COPYRIGHT: A GUIDE TO COPYRIGHT LAW IN THE 1990s 127 (1994) [hereinafter GASAWAY & WIANT]; E-mail Comment from Instructional Materials Center at the University of Wisconsin-Madison; Register's Report, *supra* note 15, at 47.

19.   Register's Report, *supra* note 15, at 44–45.

20.   E-mail Comment from the University of Southern California; Register's Report, *supra* note 15, at 46.

21.   Joint Libraries Comments from the Association of Research Libraries, the American Association of Law Libraries and the Special Libraries Association; Register's Report, *supra* note 15, at 41, 47–50; GASAWAY & WIANT, *supra* note 18, at 127.

be legitimate as fair use under section 107 or for interlibrary loan under section 108, but significant multiple-use activity would stretch beyond the boundaries of these categories. If the nonprofit library wishes to load software for multiple concurrent-user access, then the library should purchase a copy for each desired simultaneous use, negotiate a network multiple-user license, or do something similar. Another practical effect of the Computer Software Rental Amendments Act of 1990 is that some of the material packaged with computer programs may not be subject to the general restrictions of the Act. In the 1994 report on the effects of the library lending of software, the register of copyrights noted that documentation describing a computer program may be a software component which is not subject to any special restrictions applying to library software lending.[22]

This distinction between "computer programs" and software materials in general means that libraries which do not qualify as nonprofit may still lend software components such as manuals which are not the actual computer program. As more products integrate a book and accompanying software, this separation may become more important to the non-exempted libraries which will be allowed to circulate the printed component but not the computer program component.

Libraries that do not qualify as nonprofit are not entirely unable to add software to their collections; they simply cannot rely on copyright law and the first-sale doctrine. A special library, such as a corporate or law firm library, must negotiate with the software copyright holder or locate an acceptable shrinkwrap product for licensing terms which address who may use the software and where they may use it. Network, multiple-user, and multiple-terminal language is relevant to how the non-exempted library may provide access to the computer program.

IV. Why Is Software Important to Libraries and Library Patrons?

What types of software are appropriate for library collections? The 1994 American Library Association's guide to acquiring electronic publications suggests that a "significant portion of [the software] market falls outside of the collecting interests of most libraries. Programs that provide specific applications, such as those used to manage medical and dental

---

22.   Register's Report, *supra* note 15, at 80.

offices, banks, retail sales, etc., are rarely collected by most libraries."[23] Of course, one type of software that may be of great interest to library patrons and which presents no copyright or other legal obstacles to library lending is shareware. Shareware is software that is intended to be copied and distributed at no cost, sometimes as a marketing mechanism. Usually, shareware contains a message asking for registration and fee payment for use beyond an initial evaluation.[24] The ALA guide notes that shareware is available in regular computer diskette format and as CD-ROM.[25] It is also available electronically from the Internet and through both bulletin board and commercial online services. During the late 1980s and early 1990s, many libraries purchased and made available shareware from the front-runner in this market, PC-SIG. Many others have entered this market, and libraries continue to purchase and offer access to this type of software.[26]

But while much software is not attractive to libraries and other software comes with permission to copy and evaluate, many programs that appeal to libraries and their patrons are copyrighted (and often shrinkwrapped) commercial products. Journal articles and newspaper reports show that libraries are acquiring software as part of the in-library or circulating collection. Liverpool Public Library in New York reports offering software for either in-library or take-home use covering a the following topics:

> [E]ducational, which includes arithmetic and reading games, S.A.T. sample tests, foreign language materials and other related items; recreational, which includes arcade and adventure games, interactive fiction simulations, etc.; and utility, which includes graphics, clip art, integrated database/spreadsheet/work processing packages, desktop publishing programs and more.[27]

---

23. STEPHEN BOSCH ET AL., PUBLICATIONS COMMITTEE OF THE ACQUISITION OF LIBRARY MATERIALS SECTION, ASSOCIATION FOR LIBRARY COLLECTIONS & TECHNICAL SERVICES, AMERICAN LIBRARY ASSOCIATION, GUIDE TO SELECTING AND ACQUIRING CD-ROMS, SOFTWARE, AND OTHER ELECTRONIC PUBLICATIONS, ACQUISITIONS GUIDELINES NO. 9, 8 (1994) [hereinafter BOSCH].

24. Patrick R. Dewey, *Software for Patron Use: Case Studies from Public Libraries*, 40 LIB. TRENDS 139, 143 (1991).

25. *Id.*

26. Karl Beise, *Shareware Galore: The New PC-SIG Library* 106 ONLINE 106 (1992); Erik Delfino, *Shareware: Still a Viable and Economical Alternative*, 90 DATABASE 90 (1992).

27. Karen S. Cullings, *The Public Library as Cornerstone of the Community*, 16 COMPUTERS IN LIBR. 30, 31 (1996) [hereinafter Cullings].

Washington, DC–area public libraries reported success providing in-library access to computer programs such as *Baily's Book House*, a reading game for preschoolers and a CD-ROM product on mammals produced by National Geographic.[28] In an issue of *Library Trends* devoted to "Software for Patron Use in Libraries" in 1991, authors of an article exploring the challenges of physical access concluded: "[T]he recognition of computer software as part of the generic book as well as other evolving formats is important. Making them appropriately accessible to the library's clientele is an equally important issue."[29]

Software, then, is increasingly an important part of library collections. Growth in software collections appears to vary from library to library. Some libraries are reluctant to collect and circulate software because of copyright law confusion while others find the cost of the products and of staff training to be prohibitive.[30] Libraries recognize that software purchases must be made carefully. The ALA guide to selecting electronic materials warns: "Money spent on unused software is wasted as the shelf life of most software is very short. The purchase decision should not be based on a possibility of future use."[31]

As software products expand and replace many of the traditional media for creative expression, the library should be able to embrace this new technology and provide user support in the same way it has provided intellectual access through indexing, cataloging, and reference assistance and through provision of the targeted information or materials. In exploring the modern role of the public library, R. Kathleen Molz notes that public libraries need to advocate collectively their position as unique contributors in the changing technological environment.

> [A]s Theodore Roszak has observed, the public library is the "missing link of the information age." Pointing to the fact that librarians are already skilled intermediaries in handling reference and referral questions, that the profession as a whole is based on a strong ethic of public service, and that public libraries, operated as public utilities, afford one of the few, if not the only, means by which poor people

---

28. Sandra Evans, *Bookworms Go Electronic: Children Flock to the Library for Computers*, WASH. POST, May 22, 1995, at A1 [hereinafter Evans].

29. Mary Louise Brady et al., *Software for Patron Use in Libraries: Physical Access*, 40 LIBR. TRENDS 63, 81 (1991).

30. Register's Report, *supra* note 15, at 35–36, 40. *See generally* Linda J. Piele, *Reference Services and Staff Training for Patron-Use Software*, 40 LIBR. TRENDS 97 (1991).

31. BOSCH, *supra* note 23, at 12.

can have access to the new technology and to the information resources it makes available. Roszak concluded that "If computerized information services have any natural place in society it is in the public library. There, the power and efficiency of the technology can be maximized, along with its democratic access."[32]

In addition to serving an important role in an information society, nonprofit public and educational libraries play an important role in the balance of rights which form the constitutional basis for U.S. copyright law.

Copyright law in this country is different from most other countries' copyright laws in that it rests not on the idea that creators should be rewarded but that by offering a limited monopoly creators will continue to create and society will be the beneficiaries.[33] The Constitution provides:

[T]he Congress shall have Power . . . to promote the Progress of Science and useful Arts, by securing for limited Times to Authors and Inventors the exclusive Right to their respective Writings and Discoveries.[34]

As one librarian has written, "[i]t is important to recognize that the premise of copyright is consistent with the overall mission and goals of librarianship."[35] Duane Webster, Executive Director of the Association of Research Libraries (ARL) focuses on the basis of American copyright law:

[T]he purpose and character of the provisions of the Copyright Law are to serve social interests and the public welfare by encouraging learning, free speech, and the advancement of knowledge. The core concept of copyright is the granting of special and exclusive, but limited, rights to authors as an incentive to create and distribute their works. These exclusive rights are limited to ensure that copyright does not become an undue obstacle to learning. Fair use and the economic

---

32.   R. Kathleen Molz, *The Public Library Inquiry as Public Policy Research*, 20 Libr. & Culture 61, 71, 93 (1994) (quoting *The Public Library: Democracy's Resource: A Draft Statement of Principles*, Pub. Libr., Winter 1981, at 112).

33.   Melville Nimmer & David Nimmer, 1 Nimmer on Copyright § 1.03[A] (1995) (citing Sony Corp. of Am. v. Universal City Studios, Inc., 464 U.S. 417, 429 (1984), Fox Film Corp. v. Doyal, 286 U.S. 123, 127 (1932); Twentieth Century Music Corp. v. Aiken, 422 U.S. 151, 156 (1975))).

34.   U.S. Const. art. 1, § 8, cl. 1, 8.

35.   Richard B. Schockmel, *The Premise of Copyright, Assaults on Fair Use, and Royalty Use Fees*, 22 J. Acad. Libr. 15, 15 (1996).

incentive to publish are both recognized in the Copyright Law as integral to social discourse and the general benefit of society; market share and profitability of the publisher are not.[36]

V. Legal Challenges to Libraries' Circulation of Software

A. Shrinkwrap Licenses

Although software circulation rights for nonprofit libraries are preserved in section 109 of the Copyright Act of 1976, with related provisions for an archival copy and essential adaptations in section 117, libraries may confront conflicting language in shrinkwrap licenses accompanying new copies of software. The shrinkwrap license is so named because a plastic seal covering a new software package is integral to the fiction of a contract between the purchaser and the software producer. Most shrinkwrap licenses are inside the box of the software, while a notice visible through the plastic seal declares that opening of the seal constitutes agreement to the license terms. Most such licenses allow the purchaser to return the opened package for a full refund if the terms are unacceptable. Software producers have been using shrinkwrap-type licenses on mass-marketed software in an attempt to strengthen their position regarding copyright protection and warranty responsibilities.

One of the key components of shrinkwrap licenses is that the transaction is characterized as a license agreement permitting specified uses of the software and not as a sale. By avoiding a sale, the software producer avoids giving the customer the rights awarded by section 117 of the Copyright Act. The archival copy and adaptation copies necessary as an essential step in using software are rights of "owners" of a copy of a computer program according to section 117. The terms of the shrinkwrap license preclude the customer becoming an owner and gaining these rights. The right to make an archival copy is important to all libraries, whether nonprofit or in the for-profit sector, as this right protects the purchaser against damage to the functioning copy. The adaptation necessary as an essential step may involve something

---

36.   Duane E. Webster, *Promoting the Principles of Copyright*, 169 ARL: A BIMONTHLY NEWSL. OF RES. LIBR. ISSUES & ACTIONS, July 1993, at 3, *quoted in* Richard B. Schockmel, *The Premise of Copyright, Assaults on Fair Use, and Royalty Use Fees*, 22 J. ACAD. LIBR. 15 (1996).

as simple and necessary as converting disk size to accommodate available equipment.[37]

Other license terms may alter warranty obligations or may limit the number of machines or users of the software. Any of the terms of the license may be of questionable validity under analysis of state contract law. A few cases have found that such terms materially altered what was a prior contract and sale, requiring express assent beyond the opening and using of the software.[38] A recent opinion from the Seventh Circuit, however, found that a shrinkwrap license was valid under existing standard contract law and was not in conflict with federal copyright law.[39]

Even if a nonprofit library expressly assents to a general shrinkwrap license by signing and returning a listing of terms, section 109 library circulation rights may be preserved. Section 109(b)(2) does not restrict the circulation rights to libraries who are "owners."[40] Of course, the shrinkwrap terms may explicitly restrict use that would allow the nonprofit library to circulate the software, and the library should choose not to sign such an agreement.

B. Efforts to Validate Shrinkwrap under Contract Law

Because mass-marketed software shrinkwrap licenses have been attacked by scholars and some courts as invalid under the Uniform Commercial Code, the American Law Institute and the National Conference of Commissioners on Uniform State Laws have been drafting a proposed article 2B which would provide new support for these licenses under the Uniform Commercial Code (UCC).[41]

---

37. GASAWAY & WIANT, *supra* note 18, at 119.

38. Arizona Retail v. Software Link, Inc., 831 F. Supp. 759 (D. Ariz. 1993); Step-Saver Data Systems, Inc. v. Wyse Technology, 939 F.2d 91 (3d Cir. 1991).

39. ProCD, Inc. v. Zeidenberg, 86 F.3d 1447 (7th Cir. 1996).

40. "Nothing in this subsection shall apply to the lending of a computer program for nonprofit purposes by a nonprofit library. . . ." 17 U.S.C. § 109(b)(2)(A) (1994).

41. Section 2B-103 introduces the scope of the article as applying

> to licenses of information and software contracts whether or not the information exists at the time of the contract or is to be developed or created in accordance with the contract. The article also applies to any agreement related to a license or software contract in which a party is to provide support for, maintain, or modify information.

Although still in draft form, the May 5, 1997, version of article 2B reflects a strong movement toward clarification of many issues regarding licensing of information, including validation of mass-market and shrinkwrap-style licenses. A key component in the article's validation of mass-market licenses is the provision establishing how and when a purchaser agrees to the licensing contract. The sections on "manifesting assent" require that the purchaser complete some desig-nated affirmative act such as using the material or signing the license form after having an opportunity to review all the terms of the con-tract.[42] The article provides that after having an opportunity to review the terms of the license, the purchaser must have the option to return the product for a full refund.[43] Under the article 2B framework, certain terms of the contract could be determined by a court to be excluded and not enforced if the preparer of the contract should know that this term "would cause an ordinary reasonable person acquiring this type of information in the mass market to refuse the license."[44] A further limitation recognizes that any terms which are actually negotiated between the purchaser and the producer would override conflicting terms in the standard form contract.[45]

Unfortunately, article 2B does nothing to prevent such licenses from restricting fair use and first-sale rights awarded under copyright. Furthermore, libraries probably fall outside of the consumer-oriented protections for mass-market licenses when the software or other information product exceeds a certain dollar amount.[46]

The reality is that proposed article 2B assumes that software producers should be able to alter the balance created in the copyright law between users and copyright holders in terms of copying, distri-buting, and creating derivative works under the provisions of sections 109 and 117. Obviously, changing this balance is unacceptable to libraries, both nonprofit libraries seeking to take advantage of their section 109 rights to circulate software and to all libraries expecting,

---

PROPOSED ARTICLE 2B, UNIFORM COMMERCIAL CODE (May 5, 1997 Draft) [hereinafter Article 2B May 1997 Draft].

42.   Id. at 2B-112.

43.   Id. at 2B-113.

44.   Id. at 2B-308(b)(1).

45.   Id. at 2B-308(b)(2).

46.   Id. at 2B-102(a)(26).

at a minimum, section 117 ownership rights to an archival copy and essential adaptations.

C. Preemption of Contracts by Federal Copyright Law

Even if contract law is changed to recognize shrinkwrap licenses for software, courts may invalidate the licenses on federal copyright pre-emption grounds. Preemption means that a law is invalid because it has been preempted by another statute. Preemption of state laws by federal laws is based generally on the supremacy clause of the U.S. Constitution,[47] though the Copyright Act of 1976 contains a specific preemption clause in section 301. Preemption under section 301 is often described as a two-prong test. The first prong requires that the material fall within the "subject matter" of copyright. The second prong requires that the rights in question are equivalent to any of those listed in section 106 of the copyright statute.[48]

Some courts and commentators indicate that the preemption threat to shrinkwrap licenses is a strong one. The Fifth Circuit Court of Appeals in 1988 found a shrinkwrap license invalid due to preemption by federal copyright law.[49] In June 1996, however, the Seventh Circuit Court of Appeals held that federal copyright preemption did not pre-vent state law enforcement of a shrinkwrap license.[50] Many com-mentators have argued persuasively that shrinkwrap licenses should fail under preemption analyses.[51] So, it is no means clear that article 2B will stand up to judicial scrutiny even if it becomes part of the UCC.

What should a library do? The register of copyrights has noted that some shrinkwrap licenses do attempt to prohibit rental or lending while others restrict use to a single machine.[52] A number of libraries are quite concerned that shrinkwrap licenses may take away the non-profit library lending right preserved in the Computer Software Rental

---

47. U.S. CONST. art 6, cl. 2.

48. 17 U.S.C. § 301 (1994).

49. Vault Corp. v. Quaid Software Ltd., 847 F.2d 255 (5th Cir. 1988) (finding a shrink-wrap license to be an impermissible contract of adhesion and finding that the Louisiana law validating the contract was preempted by federal copyright law).

50. ProCD, Inc. v. Zeidenberg, 86 F.3d 1447 (7th Cir. 1996).

51. Mark A. Lemley, *Intellectual Property and Shrinkwrap Licenses*, 68 S. CAL. L. REV. 1239 (1995); Mary Brandt Jensen, *The Preemption of Shrink Wrap License in the Wake of Vault Corp. v. Quaid Software Ltd.*, 8 COMPUTER L.J. 157 (1988).

52. Register's Report, *supra* note 15, at 89.

Amendments Act of 1990.[53] Even though shrinkwrap licenses may be invalid under contract or federal preemption laws, the consistent inclusion of these contracts in mass-marketed software continues to tip the balance in favor of the software producers and away from the user. As two attorneys stated:

> [T]hough of doubtful enforceability in many circumstances, traditional shrinkwrap licenses are nonetheless universally included in mass-market software. They are basically costless and if enforced they offer valuable protection to software vendors. If not enforceable, they at least may have some residual deterrent effect.[54]

The Software Publishers Association (SPA) and the Business Software Alliance (BSA) assured the register of copyrights for the March 1994 Report that they had "no interest in asserting that shrinkwrap licenses override the capability of nonprofit libraries under section 109(b) to lend copies of computer programs for nonprofit purposes."[55] This assurance led the register to suggest that the question is resolvable without legislative action. "We hope this information is correct, and the Office is prepared to bring the parties together to discuss the issue further."[56]

The nonprofit library is left with several options if it chooses to make software available to its patrons. The American Library Association counsel has recommended that when ordering directly from a publisher, libraries should place an explanation or warning of the intention to circulate the software somewhere in the order.[57] Another option is to contact the publisher and attempt to negotiate alteration of the terms of a shrinkwrap license.[58] The Association of Research Libraries has published a booklet with a checklist of issues which academic and research libraries can use in negotiating licenses of electronic resources.[59] Two librarians writing for the American Association of Law Libraries' Committee on Relations with Information

---

53.   *Id.* at 259–60, 278, 294–95.

54.   Gary H. Moore & J. David Hadden, *On-Line Software Distribution: New Life for "Shrinkwrap" Licenses?* 13 COMPUTER L. 1, 1–3 (1996).

55.   Register's Report, *supra* note 15, at 90.

56.   *Id.*

57.   *Id.* at 89.

58.   GASAWAY & WIANT, *supra* note 18, at 122–23.

59.   PATRICIA BOSCH ET AL., LICENSING ELECTRONIC RESOURCES: STRATEGIC AND PRACTICAL CONSIDERATIONS FOR SIGNING ELECTRONIC INFORMATION DELIVERY AGREEMENTS (1997).

Vendors have also advocated and provided guidance on negotiating changes in standard license agreements.[60] The option of accepting the license terms is also available to librarians, particularly if the terms reasonably accommodate the purpose of the purchase. While the shrinkwrap license may stipulate that the opening of the wrap (and the non-return for refund of the product) constitute acceptance, signing an agreement may be a practical requirement for obtaining any updates to the software or other correcting information.

License terms that should trigger a librarian's suspicion include prohibitions against section 117 rights to make an archival copy, making adaptations necessary for running the program, and allowing borrowers to make adaptations necessary for running the program. Nonprofit libraries should be wary of restrictions of the section 109 allowance for circulating the software to patrons.[61]

VI. Why Should Nonprofit Libraries Be Permitted to Circulate Software?

The arguments against restrictions on nonprofit library lending of software are numerous. First, library lending of software and other copyrighted material is a perfectly legitimate activity. As Bruce Kennedy argued for the American Association of Law Libraries in a hearing before a congressional committee considering what became the Computer Software Rental Amendments Act of 1990, library lending of software is an innocent activity. Kennedy testified that without the nonprofit library exemption, the Rental Amendments Act "broadly restricts innocent libraries for the possibility of thwarting a few guilty library users."[62] The first-sale doctrine is a significant factor in preserving a respected balance in copyright and tangible property law by allowing purchasers of copies of copyrighted works to dispose of them as they choose or to loan them as libraries do.

---

60.   Lovisa Lyman & Gary Hill, *Terms of Estrangement: CD-ROM, Computer Diskette, and Internet Database Licenses*, 19 CRIV SHEET 5, inserted in AALL SPECTRUM (May 1997).

61.   R.S. Talab, *Copyright and Other Legal Considerations in Patron-Use Software*, 40 LIBR. TRENDS 85, 88 (1991).

62.   *Computer Software Rental Amendments Act of 1989: Hearings Statement on Behalf of the American Association of Law Libraries, by Bruce M. Kennedy Before the Subcomm. on Patents, Copyrights & Trademarks of the Senate Comm. on the Judiciary on S. 198*, 101st Cong., 1st Sess. 67 (Apr. 19, 1989).

The first-sale doctrine as applied to libraries, particularly, protects a valuable activity supporting lofty yet practical democratic values. Testimony from at least as early as the 1909 Copyright Act identified library lending as a necessary limitation on the exclusive rights secured to copyright owners.[63] Library service to society is in keeping with the constitutional basis for copyright which targets society's progress rather than creators' rewards.

The acting register of copyrights noted in her March 1994 Report to Congress that there continues to be no evidence showing library lending of software leads to software piracy.[64] Even so, as required by the Computer Software Rental Amendments Act, nonprofit libraries must place or embed warnings against illegal copying on the software to assist in protecting the software industry.

Software lending may in some ways actually stimulate software purchases. Of course, every time a library buys software for its collection, the software producer can tally that purchase. For library patrons who will never have the resources to purchase software and/or hardware, this purchase is an added rather than a substitute sale. Many have also suggested that library circulation of software actually develops the copyright owner's market, because borrowers tend to try before they buy.[65]

The focus on software piracy problems can obscure similarities between the historical tension between book producers and public libraries. The book trade's perception of libraries as everything from

---

63. The New York Bar Association submitted a criticism of the enumeration of exclusive rights.

> It is insisted that this section, strictly construed, would prevent the purchaser of a copyrighted book from reselling it, or lending it, or giving it away, and the letting for hire of any such book, thus putting an end to circulating libraries—a concededly valuable and important factor in the education of the people.

Memorandum of the Comm. of Copyright and Trademark of the Association of the Bar of the City of New York. Prepared for the Joint Comm. of the Senate and House in Reference to the Pending Copyright Bill, S. 6330; H.R. 19853, Dec. 1906.

64. "The answers suggest that there is little or no direct evidence and that suppositions are based on convictions rather than fact." Register's Report, *supra* note 15, at 50.

65. Matthew C. Miller, *Software Collections: Circulation Guidelines; Special Section: Document Delivery*, 14 COMPUTERS LIBR. 18, 19 1994; Cullings, *supra* note 27, at 32; statements by library representatives and software publisher Phil Shapiro included in Register's Report, *supra* note 15, at 59–62.

diverters of sales to a sizable market to a marketing tool is very like the current opinions held by software producers. While library association representatives have rightly conceded the problem of easy, high-quality copying of software creations, the underlying tension between creators and libraries is not entirely surprising and not unanticipated in the constitutional balancing for copyright rights.[66]

Libraries have maintained a special place in American copyright law even though book sellers have from time to time viewed book lending as a threat to their market. When the free public libraries were first developing in the United States in the early to mid-19th century, they had an uneasy relationship with booksellers, if not book publishers.[67] Initially benefiting from discounts from booksellers, libraries suffered a short-lived loss of discounts as booksellers expressed dismay at the perceived loss of sales due to library availability of their stock. Soon libraries persuaded sellers that exposure to the books through library circulation only increased sales. This logic and the opportunity to compete for large library orders led dealers to reinstate discounts.[68] By the beginning of the 20th century, librarians believed that the Carnegie gifts to libraries had developed a library trade so large that American book publishers were trying to find ways, such as restricting importing of books, to maximize their share in the library market.[69] The point is that software piracy problems should not become an opportunity for publishers to gain more in the software market than has been carefully allocated through traditional first-sale balancing.

If lending rights of even nonprofit libraries are allowed to be swallowed by restrictive shrinkwrap licenses, this country might find itself approaching a de facto "public lending right" for software and other information products. While other countries have established such

---

66. *Computer Software Rental Amendments Act of 1989, Hearings Before the Subcomm., on Patents, Copyright and Trademarks, Senate Judiciary Comm.* 101st Cong., 1st Sess. (Apr. 19, 1989) (statements by W. David Laird, Director, Library, University of Arizona, representing the American Library Association, p. 60–66; Bruce M. Kennedy, Chair, Copyright Committee, American Association of Law Libraries, p. 67–73).

67. SIDNEY H. DITZION, ARSENALS OF A DEMOCRATIC CULTURE 30–50 (1947).

68. *Id.* at 165–66.

69. *Arguments on the Bills S. 6330 and H.R. 19853, to Amend and Consolidate the Acts Respecting Copyright" Hearings Before the Comm. on Patents, House of Representatives* (June 6, 1906), *in* 4 LEGISLATIVE HISTORY OF THE 1909 COPYRIGHT ACT 65–66 (E. Fulton Brylawski & Abe Goldman eds., 1976) (statement of William P. Cutter, Esq., of the Forbes Library, Northampton, MA).

laws requiring payment of fees to copyright owners for every library lending of their copyrighted works, the United States has never passed such a law.[70] Similarly, widespread use of standardized shrinkwrap licenses which restrict sections 109 and 117 have the effect of private legislation rendering congressional legislation practically irrelevant.[71] As software such as the National Geographic CD-ROM on mammals finds its way into libraries like those in the Washington, DC area, copyright law should preserve the rights of patrons to use these materials just as they use books.[72] Although software is now but a small part if any of many library collections, the market is bound to grow, augmenting and replacing many materials which might have been created as traditional books.

While the publishing industry moves toward electronic media, the library still has a unique and important contribution to make in gathering and offering resources to the general public.[73] We must avoid the unfortunate irony of libraries becoming less valuable as information becomes more so.

---

70. Denmark, Norway, Sweden, Finland, Iceland, The Netherlands, West Germany, New Zealand, Australia, the United Kingdom, Canada, and Israel have some form of subsidy to creators, or their assignees, based on library usage of their creations. Gerald Dworkin, *Public Lending Right—The UK Experience*, 13 COLUM.-VLA J.L. & ARTS 49, 50. (1988); GASAWAY & WIANT, *supra* note 18, at 199–216; PAUL GOLDSTEIN, 2 COPYRIGHT, § 5.6.1, p. 5:114 (2d ed. 1996); Jennifer M. Schneck, *Closing the Book on the Public Lending Right*, 63 N.Y.U. L. REV. 878 (1988).

71. Robert P. Merges, *Intellectual Property and the Costs of Commercial Exchange: A Review Essay*, 93 MICH. L. REV. 1570, 1611–13 (1995).

72. Evans, *supra* note 28.

73. See WILLIAM F. BIRDSALL, THE MYTH OF THE ELECTRONIC LIBRARY: LIBRARIANSHIP AND SOCIAL CHANGE IN AMERICA (1994), warning that the commercialization which accompanies most interpretations of the library of the electronic age runs counter to many important library traditions, including teaching patron self-sufficiency and promoting the widest possible access to information.

Chapter Twelve
Defining the Quiet Zone:
Library and Educational Perspective
On the White Paper[*]

by
Arnold P. Lutzker, Esq.

Fish & Richardson, P.C.
Washington, DC

I. Introduction

In September 1995, with much fanfare and public expectation, the
Commerce Department released its long awaited White Paper on intel-
lectual property laws. The Report of the Working Group on Intellectual
Property Rights (the White Paper),[1] which is part of the Information
Infrastructure Task Force (IITF), provides an extensive discussion of

---

1.   INTELLECTUAL PROPERTY AND THE NATIONAL INFORMATION INFRASTRUCTURE: THE REPORT OF THE
      WORKING GROUP ON INTELLECTUAL PROPERTY RIGHTS (1995) [hereinafter White Paper].

current laws and policies, most notably copyright, but also patent, trademark, and trade secret law, as they relate to digital information. Reforms that the Working Group urges are needed to maintain a legal structure conducive to exploitation of the new technology.

Because of the mandate to the IITF from the Clinton administration to review U.S. laws and recommend whatever changes are necessary to foster the full utilization of the wondrous digital technology now in the marketplace or under development, the White Paper has become the focal point for hearings in the U.S. Congress and discussions in international forum.

In its most elemental terms, the thesis of the Working Group is that "unless the framework for legitimate commerce is preserved and adequate protection for copyrighted works is ensured, the vast communications network will not reach its full potential as a true, global marketplace."[2] The Working Group believes copyright law is not an obstacle to enhancing the information infrastructure, but rather that it is an essential component in making works available. While the report determines that current laws are substantially adequate for the task of advancing the national and global information infrastructures (the "NII" and the "GII"), some modest adjustments are necessary to deal with uncertainties which have materialized.

The primary determinant for the Working Group's recommendations is the belief that our intellectual property laws are designed to support commerce and the economic mandate of copyright. Copyright law is, after all, the grant of exclusive rights to authors to exploit their works during a limited time. Economic incentives lie at the heart of copyright policy. Decisively applying this theological tenet to legal reform for cyberspace, however, will have a subtle yet deleterious impact on libraries and educational institutions. By enshrining the economics of copyright, the White Paper fails to balance the public's interest in accessibility to copyrighted works under the principle of fair use for teaching, scholarship, research, and historic preservation, what I call "the quiet zone" of copyright law.

Fair use analysis, which is an equally vital part of copyright theology, balances the constitutional respect for free speech and governmental interest in education with the economic interests of copyright

---

2.   *Id.* at 16.

owners. In other words, both are important goals of the U.S. copyright law. The White Paper's weighted emphasis on economics underscores what could become the increasing difficulty of nonprofit institutions to secure works for free or low cost and, in turn, to permit the public to have access to them.

The tension has been more evident in recent years, as educational innovations, such as digital databases, distance learning, and multimedia create new learning demands for copyrighted works. In educational environs expanded by technology, the White Paper endorses a commercial form of electronic fencing—accessibility regulated by licensing, encryption, and digital signatures. What is needed in our copyright policy is a recognition that the law cannot treat these issues as black or white; there is also a quiet zone, drawn in shades of gray, which needs to be defined.

II. Proposed Statutory Amendments and Their Impact on Educational Institutions and Libraries

A. Transmission as a Distribution

The principal proposal of the White Paper is that Congress clarify the Copyright Act of 1976,[3] as amended, to define "transmission of a work" as a "distribution," exclusively controlled by the copyright owner.[4] In more formal terms, the report proposes that Congress amend section 106(3) of the Act to recognize expressly that copies or phonorecords of works can be distributed to the public by transmission, and that such transmissions fall within the exclusive distribution right of the copyright owner. Related amendments would expand the definitional section of the Act—

a) to recognize publication by transmission, and
b) to indicate that distributing a copy by a device or process so that it can be fixed at a distant location constitutes a transmission.[5]

The Working Group is explicit in its belief that a transmission of a copyrighted work from a server to a remote computer where it is

---

3.   17 U.S.C. §§ 101–1101 (1994).
4.   White Paper, *supra* note 1, at 213.
5.   *Id.* at 217–19.

stored constitutes a public distribution, even if the work is not viewed.[6] The White Paper also suggests that the storage implicates the reproduction and public performance rights. The amendment, however, would remove legal uncertainty as to whether transmissions are distributions under copyright law.

Comment: While the proposed amendments appear modest, they are based on the premise that all transmissions are within the exclusive domain of the copyright proprietor. If that assumption were carried to logical conclusion, it would establish a threshold burden for libraries and educational institutions seeking many public uses of digital works.

To the extent that the educational exemptions in section 110 are limitations on the *performance right*, for example, they may not be recognized as exceptions to the *distribution right*. As a result, the impact of these changes could be dramatic on distance learning, where classroom teaching is not only performed live, but which also is transmitted to remote locations and stored for future review.[7] If third-party works are incorporated in distance learning classes and transmitted to remote locales where they are independently recorded without prior clearance, that downloading could be held to violate the newly clarified "distribution right."

Further, if one library has a work in a digital form on its server, could another library call up the library and "borrow" that digital copy? Not without the consent of the copyright owner, White Paper advocates would contend. Fair use might allow the transmission, of course, but the fair use analysis is fact-specific, and the conclusion could vary from work to work. Such a situation would leave the average librarian at a complete loss when determining what to do. The safest course would be to deny the soliciting library access to the work. The way to correct these problems would be to add the newly expanded distribution right to the categories covered by these time-honored exemptions so that fair use includes distribution via transmission.

B. Library Exemption Amendments

In a bow to the needs of libraries and archives to work in the 21st century with technology, the White Paper recommends some changes

---

6.   *Id.* at 213.
7.   See 17 U.S.C. § 110(2) (1994) for the current law on instructional broadcasting.

to the section 108 library exemptions to preserve their role in a digital era. While proposing to modernize certain archival, preservation, and lending activities, the White Paper's fix does not work effectively.

Under current law, and subject to a number of pre-conditions, libraries (and their staff) may:

(a) reproduce and distribute one copy of an unpublished work in their collection *in facsimile form* for preservation or research[8];

(b) reproduce *in facsimile form* one copy of a published work to replace a damaged, deteriorated, lost, or stolen copy, which is not available at a fair price[9]; and

(c) reproduce and distribute one copy of an article from a library collection to a qualified researcher, or an entire work when it is determined that the work cannot be acquired at a fair price.[10]

The report's recommendations would allow libraries and archives to prepare three copies of works for preservation purposes, only one of which could be publicly used.[11] It would also recognize that the copyright notice libraries must include on copies they reproduce under section 108(a)(3) is no longer mandatory.[12]

The Working Group also discusses interlibrary loan and recognizes the need for institutions to allow reasonable, shared access to copyrighted works.[13] In instances where the fair use doctrine or other exemptions would apply, that access may be for no fee, even when borrowing is of the electronic version of a work.[14] But because it believes there is questionable applicability to electronic transactions of CONTU guidelines (which clarify section 108(g)(2) and provide guidance on the number of copies a library may request through interlibrary loan), the White Paper urges copyright owners to develop "special, institutional licenses" for schools and libraries as they do in the print domain to facilitate public access.[15]

---

8.   *Id.* § 108(b).
9.   *Id.* § 108(c).
10.   *Id.* § 108(d)–(e).
11.   White Paper, *supra* note 1, at 227.
12.   *Id.*
13.   *Id.* at 226.
14.   *Id.* at 89.
15.   *Id.* at App. 1, 4.

Comment: The White Paper intends to change copyright law to allow preservationists in libraries and archives to do what is common practice, that is to make three copies—an archive copy, a master from which others may be made, and a working copy. While the statutory recommendations expand the number of copies in section 108(a), however, the White Paper ignores section 108(b)–(c), which also need a "three copy" rule to ensure the proposed status for preservation, security, and replacement of damaged works.

More fundamentally, however, the White Paper hedges on the rights of libraries to engage in the real-world use of digital works; namely, permitting digitally acquired (or created) copies to be sufficiently accessible to the public for research, scholarship, and criticism. In the proposed amendment, for example, the Working Group would specifically modify section 108(b) to permit the making of a *facsimile or digital* copy of any unpublished work for preservation, but it would allow only a *facsimile* copy for deposit for researchers.[16] With increased reliance on computer research, this limitation no longer makes any sense. Moreover, while libraries and archives may make a copy of a work which is damaged or is in deteriorating condition, there is a developing need to permit the reproduction of a work when its format becomes obsolete. Otherwise, the statute would not be technology neutral, and copyright law reform would be required every time enterprise leaps into new medium of expression.

While these proposed changes could easily have been recommended in the White Paper, they are inconsistent with certain principles espoused by the Working Group, which emphasize the commerce of copyright. Thus, for the educational and library community, the sobering message of the report is this: As long as the commercial marketplace has established a metered, encrypted system for access, the ability of libraries to serve a public mission, which allows for *no fee* access to published and unpublished works, may be diminished if not totally eliminated.

C. New Exemption for Works for the Visually Impaired

The White Paper proposes establishment of a new exemption for non-profit organizations to reproduce and distribute works to the visually

---

16.   *Id.*

impaired, at cost, provided that the copyright owner has not entered that market during a period of at least one year after first publication.[17]

Comment: If the works are made available commercially by the copyright owner within one year of initial publication, this right would be negated. In other words, unless the copyright owner authorizes preparation of these works for the visually impaired, the benefits of access could be delayed at least one year until the copyright owner's plans become known. After negotiations, a compromise proposal, that eliminated the one-year rule but which requires the use be "exclusively" for the blind or other disabled persons, was introduced in May 1996.[18]

D. Strengthening Legal Sanctions Against Anti-copy Defeating Devices

Also central to the task of the White Paper is the goal of challenging technology which facilitates infringement. The Working Group would ban the importation, manufacture, or distribution of any device or product, or the provision of any service, the primary purpose or effect of which is to defeat anti-copy devices or technology, or to violate the rights of copyright owners.[19]

Comment: This recommendation has a certain logic to it. Who could be in favor of the devices of copyright thievery? However, when machines serve dual copyright purposes—legitimate preservation or duplication of works as well as pirating copyrights in cyberspace—which "purpose" takes priority? Like the ubiquitous photocopy machine or the ever-popular VCR, new technology can offer ways to copy for private or scholastic use as well as mass marketing of pirated works. Which is the "primary purpose"?

An outright ban on equipment used for certain purposes could severely discourage the manufacturer of innovative equipment from its conception. Some members of the copyright owner community may consider that desirable, but it may not be in the public interest. A clearer understanding of the implications of this concept must be made and controls established to allow the benefits of the technology to reach the marketplace.

---

17.   *Id.* at 227–28.
18.   H.R. 104-2441, 104th Cong. 2d Sess. (1996).
19.   White Paper, *supra* note 1, at 230.

The report also recommends criminalization of the mere "offer" or "perform[ance]" of "any service, the primary purpose of effect of which is to avoid, bypass, remove, deactivate, or otherwise circumvent" technology that is intended to inhibit copyright violations.[20] While a sound concern, the troubling aspect of the proposed language is that it does not distinguish exemptions or fair uses from outright violations. The nature and scope of "the offer or performance of any service" is vague and could place libraries or educational institutions at criminal risk if they acquire and use equipment with multi-purpose capabilities or attempt novel exercise of their statutory exemptions.

E. Creation of a Copyright Management Information System

One of the key concepts in the White Paper's recommendations is creation of a Copyright Management Information System (CMIS)—copyright ownership data that would be imbedded in digital works. The value of this information is so important that the Working Group would make it a crime knowingly to alter or remove this information.[21]

Comment: Although the Copyright Act no longer requires copyright notice to secure rights in the United States (a requirement of our joining the Berne Convention), the White Paper foresees the imbedding of copyright ownership information within the digital code as an important tool to protect copyright rights.[22] Tampering with that information would be made a crime.

For libraries, the capacity to access source information facilitates the cataloging function and the creation of CMIS could enhance the researcher's ability to authenticate works. This task has been made more difficult by the end to formalities, including registration. However, copyright management information can change over time. If a copyright is sold, for example, the name of the owner has changed. The recommendations create a potential for liability if libraries correct the imbedded CMIS data to convey new information. That result does not make sense from either a legal or practical perspective. Whether CMIS would square with our Berne obligations not to establish

---

20.   *Id.* at App. 1, 6.

21.   *Id.* at 235–36.

22.   *Id.* at 235.

"formalities" as a prerequisite to copyright ownership is also a matter of some debate.

F. Endorsement of Public Performance Right for Sound Recordings

The White Paper supports pending legislation to establish a public performance right for sound recordings.[23] While the creators of songs and lyrics and their publishers have enjoyed all copyright rights of section 106, owners of sound recordings, i.e., masters from which records, tapes, and CDs are made, have enjoyed only limited rights. Most particularly, they are not entitled to the rights of public performance and public display. First protected in 1972 to prevent tape duplication or record piracy, the key issue in the case of sound recordings has been the absence of a "performance right." Pending legislation would grant the performance right (the ability to collect royalties for digital broadcast or other transmission of recordings). The Working Group would prefer to see the right extended to all recordings, not just digital works.[24]

Comment: The broadcast industry, which pays hundreds of millions of dollars to composers and music publishers for the right to perform music on radio and television, has fought the notion of granting additional music rights to the makers of the tapes, and CDs now played on the air because it would mean millions more in royalties. By the legislation, however, all venues that publicly perform digital works would be liable to the sound recording owners, not simply broadcasters.

For libraries and educational institutions, the expansion of this right could mean that unless use is exempted, covered by fair use or licensed for a fee set by the record companies, there would be greater exposure to a claim of infringement. Any library or educational institution that pays performance societies today for use of music on CDs, could face cost increases if the sound recording owners' rights are enlarged.

G. Criminalize Willful Infringements with Value of More than $5,000

One of the loopholes in copyright law was spotlighted when a free spirit on the Internet made a software program available for free to thousands of online recipients. A court concluded that absent any

---

23.　*Id.* at 225.

24.　*Id.* at 225, *citing* S. 227, 104 Cong., 1st Sess. (1995); H.R. 1506, 104th Cong., 1st Sess. (1995).

monetary gain to the defendant, no criminal action against him was possible.[25] Reacting to the potential destruction of software publishers entire market by such willful acts, the Working Group endorsed a pending bill which would make it a crime willfully and without authority to transmit or reproduce copyrighted works with retail value of $5,000.[26]

Comment: By establishing a $5,000 threshold, the intent of this provision is to criminalize larger-scale distribution of computer programs or copyrighted works, not incidental, individual exploitation. It would not matter that the defendant failed to make a profit. As long as the aggregate value of the works exceeded $5,000, the criminal sanctions would apply.

How this provision would interplay with the fair use doctrine remains unclear. Because a library or educational institution could intentionally distribute copyrighted works on a belief that fair use or another exemption applies, if the limitation was rejected and if the dissemination resulted in widespread copying, could a finding of infringement trigger the criminal sanctions? Clarification to prevent criminalization of such behavior would be appropriate.

III. The Role of Technology and the Implications for Fair Use

The Working Group expresses confidence in the marketplace to develop strong protections against infringements. There is an extensive discussion of technological solutions at the server levels—by encryption, digital signatures, and stenography (digital watermarking). It rejects statutory licensing schemes and argues strongly for creative licensing in the online environment. To facilitate licensing, the White Paper suggests that the Uniform Commercial Code expressly should recognize the validity of agreements entered online or electronically.[27]

At the same time, the White Paper does not advocate any refreshing of the fair use doctrine to explain the rights of users in the digital marketplace. Rather, the Working Group has left to a Conference on

---

25.   United States v. LaMacchia, 871 F. Supp. 535 (D. Mass. 1994).
26.   White Paper, *supra* note 1, at 229, discussing S. 1122, 104th Cong., 1st Sess. (1995).
27.   *Id.* at 59.

Fair Use (CONFU) to discuss the need for any strategy to update the fair use doctrine.[28]

Comment: The Working Group's faith in technology poses a dilemma for educational institutions and libraries. To the extent that the commercial owners control transmissions of works as a public distribution, copy, or display, and are encouraged to develop and employ technological envelopes to restrict unauthorized, non-compensated access to works, those in the public sector who wish enhanced access to copyrighted works may be stymied.

In the print and analog world, fair use fulfills certain statutory goals, including serving education, comment, criticism, scholarship, teaching, and the like. The criteria at the heart of a fair use analysis are the nature of the use (commercial or non-commercial), the nature of the work, the substantiality of the portion used as a percent of the whole, and the impact of the use on the marketplace value of the original.[29]

It is important to understand that the fair use doctrine posits criteria—tools of analysis—and not absolute standards. The fair use analysis is "fact driven." This means that how works are acquired may also be reviewed; for example, if a work is sealed technologically, does that mean that work is *not* subject to fair use? If so, all a copyright owner would have to do is place figurative fence around a work and warn the public that *no use* is allowed without express permission and compensation. That result could negate the statutory doctrine.

Opening a technologically sealed envelope has more ominous connotations as a copyright violation than photocopying or other technological activities. Although the fair use doctrine allows that notwithstanding the exclusive grant of copyright to creators of works, use may be made of a work without the copyright owner's express consent (e.g., no-fee use), access could be dealt a severe blow by the technological fixes. As long as a paid mechanism for access exists, the commercial vendors may challenge any claim to fair use.

The report's treatment of fair use seems to encourage the challenge. The references to the doctrine as being a "murky" limitation, to metering as a way of tracking use, and to the *Texaco* case,[30] which

---

28.   *Id.* at 83–84.

29.   17 U.S.C. § 107 (1)–(4) (1994).

30.   American Geophysical Union v. Texaco, Inc., 37 F.3d 881 (2d Cir. 1994).

found liability by a commercial researcher where a photocopy was found to be available at "reasonable cost" through the Copyright Clearance Center, suggests an interest in constricting fair use.[31] Libraries and educational institutions should be very attentive to these discussions and watchful over any effort to diminish fair use.

In sum, if the White Paper's thorough embrace of technology as an answer to digital copying and distribution takes hold, applying the fair use doctrine and the policies behind the library and educational exemptions would become more difficult. A more balanced approached is needed. If the White Paper's proposals move forward, while CONFU participants debate fair use but fail to reach agreement, critical leverage would be lost. If the benefits offered to content owners by the White Paper do not have a fair use counterbalance, the doctrine may be diminished in the electronic environment. Fair use is too important to the educational community to leave to afterthoughts and legislative cleanup.

IV. International Considerations

The White Paper frankly acknowledges the importance of intellectual property to international trade and places the debate in an international context.[32] The GII is developing as fast as the NII, and the exposure of copyrighted works to infringement internationally is perhaps a greater threat than domestically. The Commerce Department makes clear that the United States should take the lead in the development of international standards for the information infrastructure along the lines proposed in the White Paper.[33]

Comment: Internationally, the Working Group sees harmonization as a theme, with the goal of bridging differences between common law and civil law systems. There is a subtle problem in this aspect of the White Paper, however, and that is who sets policy first.

The Commerce Department was a leading advocate for the convening of a diplomatic conference to reform international copyright standards. The conference, held in Geneva in December 1996, resulted in the adoption of two treaties—one to reform the venerable Berne

---

31.   White Paper, *supra* note 1, at 82.
32.   *Id.* at 130–32.
33.   *Id.* at 147–55.

Convention, and the other to grant new rights to performers and producers of sound recordings.

The Berne amendments expanded protection for computer programs and granted authors rights relating "to making works available to the public," rental, and communications. Additionally, the treaty adopted variations of the White Paper's proposals for a system of rights management information and for treatment of anti-copy defeating devices.

Although some of the central tenets of the White Paper's agenda were proferred (especially defining electronic transmissions as distributions, and granting owners explicit control over RAM copies), the international forum refused to approve those recommendations. Similarly, a new treaty designed to protect a new class of copyrightable works—databases—was tabled. As a result, the treaties (which must be adopted by the U.S. Congress to be enforceable) leave some of the most contentious issues open to legislative debate without the pressure of having to reject a treaty as a way of expressing disapproval on those matters.

V. Online Technology and Service Provider Liability

The White Paper contains numerous discussions of the impact of copyright and related legal principles on the evolving online/Internet environment. The Working Group's most fundamental conclusion is that it is premature to relieve those who use the NII to transmit information (e.g., bulletin board operators and online or Internet service providers) of legal responsibility for the transmissions on their network.[34]

*Comment:*While some courts have split on the issue of service provider liability for copyright infringement, libel, and other legal offenses and calls for legal reform have been heard, the Working Group does not agree. It believes that current law should find the service provider responsible for the works it transmits and that it is in the most practical position to correct copyright abuses online.[35]

The question of online and Internet provider liability was the focus during eight months of intense negotiations among content owners, OSPs and ISPs (firms that fit into both camps), and libraries and

---

34.   *Id.* at 122.

35.   *Id.* at 117.

educators.[36] The thoughtful discussions have yielded much light on the complexity of the issues. A principle that has emerged is one which encourages, but does not obligate, content owners to notify OSPs/ISPs of infringing uses of copyrighted works to facilitate a quick "take down" of the protected work and to shut off of the offending source. Prompt compliance with the take-down request would provide the OSP/ISP an exemption from contributory or vicarious liability. "Good Housekeeping" provider practices, such as educating users and terminating repeat offenders, would be part of the package.

The impact of service provider liability for libraries and educators could be profound. The number of works accessible in an interconnected educational universe is staggering, and the liability for copyright infringement unimaginable. How should libraries and educators sustain their educational mission in this new world and apply the fair use doctrine and other authorized exemptions equitably? These parts of the quiet zone are ignored in the White Paper and in its legislative proposals.

In the online negotiations, educational and library representatives have underscored the importance to academic freedom of not blindly establishing a "take-down regime" as the standard, which could prejudice the rights of scholars, students, and other users. Maintaining the existence and validity of the fair use doctrine and other educational limitations for educational and library service providers is essential to the balance of any reform affecting the Internet and online use.

VI. First-sale Doctrine

In the preliminary draft of this report, the so-called "Green Paper,"[37] the Working Group proposed a change in the "first-sale doctrine."[38] This copyright doctrine acknowledges that the physical copy of a work is different from its copyright and that the copyright owner should not control redistribution of lawfully acquired copies.[39] In other words, when one purchases a book, one "owns" that copy, even though one does not own the copyright to the work. Under the first-sale doctrine,

---

36. The author has represented a coalition of library association at these negotiations.
37. INTELLECTUAL PROPERTY AND THE NATIONAL INFORMATION INFRASTRUCTURE: A PRELIMINARY DRAFT OF THE REPORT OF THE WORKING GROUP ON INTELLECTUAL PROPERTY RIGHTS (1994).
38. Id. at 124–25.
39. 17 U.S.C. § 109(a) (1994).

the copyright owner is given very substantial freedom to choose the first medium of sale of a work; however, once the work is publicly distributed, anyone who acquires a lawful copy is free to sell, give away, or otherwise dispose of that copy.

Reconciling the first-sale doctrine to the issues of transmissions was the subject of the Green Paper proposal. In that case, the Working Group proposed to exempt disposing of a copy *by transmission* from the first-sale doctrine. In the White Paper, the Working Group has retreated from the recommendation that first-sale provision of the Copyright Act be amended. Rather, it discusses the doctrine as it applies in practice and concludes that there are sufficient safeguards for owners under the rights of reproduction, distribution, and display (including specific language limiting the doctrine as it relates to computer programs and sound recordings) so that no change is required.[40]

Comment: The retreat on the change to the first-sale doctrine is not as dramatic as might appear at first blush. In the text of the report, the Working Group establishes several legal theories under current law that suggest transmissions of works would violate copyright rights of owners, despite the protective shell of the first-sale doctrine.[41] This leaves the first-sale doctrine vulnerable in cyberspace. It suggests that there is no right to transfer lawfully acquired works electronically. Such a result would effectively deny application of first-sale rights of owners of copies to anything but physical copies.

Of special importance to libraries is the matter of how to display works lawfully acquired and transfer them to others without running afoul of the doctrine. The most restrictive interpretation—that only one copy might be displayed at a given time and if a work were transferred from a computer to a computer, the first computer owner would have to erase the work in the hand-off—would leave the library community with limited room to maneuver in the digital world.

VII.   Related Areas of the Law

The report reviews patent, trademark, and trade secret law. Although it makes no recommendations for changes in these areas of intellectual property law, it acknowledges that the NII will have an important

---

40.   White Paper, *supra* note 1, at 93.
41.   *Id.* at 92–95.

impact. Since the NII will make much more information publicly available, for example, it could trigger reassessment of patent grants, which are dependent upon review of publicly available data (so-called "prior art").[42]

With regard to trademark law, the White Paper acknowledges that there may be increased potential for international conflicts over domain names and confusion in reaching the right data sources. Further, the Working Group encourages changes in the international classification scheme to ensure the status of goods and services for information technology.[43]

Trade secret law operates on a common law or state statutory system, not a federal basis. The most direct impact of the NII on this body of law will be the capacity of those concerned with trade secrets to utilize the NII as a secure means of communication.[44]

VIII. Summary and Conclusions

After almost two years of consideration and hearings, the White Paper is one of the most comprehensive assessments of legal issues and online/digital technology. While its legal initiatives appear modest, the core thrust of the report is far-reaching. It posits the thesis that copyright is an economic right of owners to be exploited. In its view, the copyright law as a code of regulation should facilitate economic exploitation of works which is in the commercial interests of the United States and its citizenry. It defines copyright law as a flexible statute which needs only minor, definitional tinkering to greet the digital era.

Although the report makes some positive recommendations to enhance the capacity of libraries to copy certain works in a digital format, the broader impact of the White Paper should not be lost. Since the pervasive theme of the recommendations is enhancement of the economic exploitation of copyrighted works, less heed is paid to the public interest aspects of copyright law or established exceptions to copyright rights. There is also a strong article of faith that technology

---

42.   *Id.* at 163–64.
43.   *Id.* at 169–70.
44.   *Id.* at 174.

can solve current problems, through the wizardry of encryption, digital signatures, stenography, and the like.

The weakest part of the report is its assessment of the relationship of fair use to digital use. Although the Working Group will await the recommendations of CONFU before tackling this thorny question, those who cherish the rights of users ought to be vigilant and ensure that alterations made to accommodate new technology are balanced by the public interest in access to works in library and educational settings.

Chapter Thirteen
Coalitions:
Building Partnerships for Change[*]

by
Prudence S. Adler

Assistant Executive Director
Federal Relations and Information Policy
Association of Research Libraries

I. Pressures for Change

Stimulating the growth and development of the national information infrastructure (NII) is a priority of the Clinton administration and many diverse interests.[1] These interests range from telecommunications companies to libraries and from scholarly societies to

---

[*]   © 1997 Prudence S. Adler.

[1]   The NII is described as "a seamless web of communications networks, computers, databases, and consumer electronics." INFORMATION INFRASTRUCTURE TASK FORCE, NATIONAL TELECOMMUNICATIONS AND INFORMATION ADMINISTRATION, NATIONAL INFORMATION INFRASTRUCTURE AGENDA FOR ACTION (1993).

computer hardware and software companies. Although these varied constituencies, associations, and companies may have a slightly differing vision of how the NII, indeed global information infrastructure (GII), will ultimately evolve, these interests share a common appreciation that a robust and interactive GII is central to each of these sectors' future. And, integral to the evolution of the GII are issues relating to copyright and intellectual property.

Recognizing the importance of intellectual property and copyright issues to the development of the NII, a Working Group on Intellectual Property Rights was established by the Clinton administration to explore the application and effectiveness of copyright law and the NII, with a particular emphasis on promoting commerce.[2] Chaired by Bruce Lehman, Assistant Secretary of Commerce and Commissioner of Patents and Trademarks, the Working Group sponsored a series of activities to solicit input on copyright issues and the NII. These included public hearings, and in June 1994, a draft NII report was circulated for comment and review (known as the Green Paper). Part of the review process included three hearings (held in Los Angeles, Chicago, and Washington, DC) hosted by the Working Group,[3] where members of the stakeholder community presented statements of reaction to the Green Paper.[4] More than 2,000 pages of comment were filed in response to the Green Paper, and a wide range of interests were represented in testimony during the hearings.[5]

From the outset it was clear that there was the widespread criticism of the Green Paper by a diversity of interests, both public and private. In reviewing many of the comments filed in addition to statements before the Working Group, library, education, scholarly, not-for-profit segments, and segments of the commercial sectors expressed serious reservations with many of the proposals included in the Green Paper. Equally clear was the general support for these proposals from other parts of the commercial sector, particularly the commercial

---

2. The Working Group was established by the Information Infrastructure Task Force and was housed within the Patent and Trademark Office, Department of Commerce.

3. INTELLECTUAL PROPERTY AND THE NATIONAL INFORMATION INFRASTRUCTURE: THE REPORT OF THE WORKING GROUP ON INTELLECTUAL PROPERTY RIGHTS 4 (1995) [hereinafter White Paper].

4. INTELLECTUAL PROPERTY AND THE NATIONAL INFORMATION INFRASTRUCTURE: A PRELIMINARY DRAFT OF THE REPORT ON THE WORKING GROUP ON INTELLECTUAL PROPERTY RIGHTS (1994).

5. White Paper, *supra* note 3.

content creator community. Banding together, this community established the Creative Incentive Coalition, the purpose of which was to support the White Paper recommendations and to lobby Congress for enactment of the recommendations as amendments to the Copyright Act of 1976.[6] Members of this coalition include the Association of American Publishers, the Business Software Alliance, McGraw Hill Inc., Microsoft Corporation, the Motion Picture Industry of America, Time Warner Inc., Viacom, the Information Industry Association, and related commercial partners.

In September 1995, the final report of the Working Group, Intellectual Property and the National Information Task Force was released. Known as the White Paper, it contains recommendations to amend the Copyright Act of 1976 and presents a lengthy legal analysis of current copyright law.

Key recommendations in the White Paper include the following:

✦ Network transmission is a means of distributing works to the public that falls within the exclusive right of the copyright owner;

✦ Library exemptions in section 108 with a particular focus on preservation issues apply in the digital environment;

✦ Copyright protection systems and copyright management information (CMI) would impose penalties on those who attempt to circumvent or tamper with CMI systems; and

✦ A new exemption for the visually impaired permitting, under certain circumstances, nonprofit organizations to reproduce and distribute works.

The White Paper failed to make recommendations regarding several critical issues including:

✦ Rules to govern the liability of service providers for online copyright infringements committed by their users or subscribers;

✦ The place of "fair use" and "first-sale" doctrines in the world of digital copyright; and

✦ The impact of new regimes of liability on existing cultural exemptions, such as those found in section 110(2), relating to distance education.

---

6.   17 U.S.C. §§ 101–1101 (1994).

Although characterized as only "minor changes" to the Copyright Act, if implemented the recommendations would dismantle the current balance between the rights of copyright owners and users of copyrighted works. Also of concern to many were the legal analyses included in the final report; some of which appeared to do an "end run" around existing court decisions. Additionally, the legislative recommendations and conclusions in the narrative of the White Paper have implications well beyond copyright and intellectual property issues. The proposed legislation and discussion in the White Paper raise a host of issues relating to privacy, confidentiality, and the potential liability of institutions and online service providers in the delivery of information in the networked environment. Finally, the White Paper recommendations and conclusions were seen as a template for a new international legal regime to govern the GII.[7]

The recommendations of the White Paper were included in House and Senate bills, the NII Copyright Protection Act of 1995 (H.R. 2441 and S. 1284) introduced in late September 1995. The introduction of these bills signaled the continuing commitment by the Clinton administration to update the copyright law to meet the digital age. The introduction of this legislation also indicated a strong interest by members of Congress to pursue a similar "digital agenda." The combination of the commitment by the administration, the leadership in Congress (bipartisan as well), and extensive support from the Creative Incentive Coalition posed a formidable challenge to any constituency that disagreed or sought modification with any aspect of the legislation and the White Paper.

II. Formation of the Digital Future Coalition

Responding to this press for change to the Copyright Act, members of the academic law, library, commercial sectors, not-for-profit, and public-interest communities convened a meeting in October 1995 to consider the White Paper and legislative provisions from a variety of perspectives. Although many of these groups had been evaluating and responding to the various reports and hearings, there had been little if

---

7.   For a review of the White Paper from the perspective of libraries and education, see *supra* Chapter Twelve (p. 233), "Defining the Quiet Zone: Library and Educational Perspective on the White Paper," by Arnold P. Lutzker.

any collaboration across communities. Thus, the October meeting presented a venue for different stakeholders and interested parties to consider the impact of the White Paper proposals on a number of communities, well beyond a single interest. It is also fair to say that most if not all of those attending the October session felt a keen sense of frustration with the Working Group process. Members participated in hearings, commented on the Green Paper and met with administration officials, yet few changes were evident in the final report to reflect these deep concerns.

In opening the meeting, Peter Jaszi, Professor of Law, American University noted:

> that it may be far too early in the digital era to rewrite the rules of copyright in as fundamental a way as that envisaged in the White Paper. And it remains to be seen, however, what sort of new copyright regime for the electronic information environment will best fulfill that potential. At the very least, the public and the Congress need more information about the bargain the Administration's National Information Infrastructure Task Force has proposed.[8]

From this one-day session in Washington, the Digital Future Coalition (DFC) emerged. From the outset, five themes dominated these and subsequent DFC discussions:

1. The overriding need to retain the balance between interests which today's carefully crafted copyright law reflects;
2. The depth and breadth of concerns regarding the NII copyright proposals on the part of the DFC constituencies were significant and not limited to a single issue;
3. Many changes to the U.S. copyright regime were increasingly driven by international trade concerns rather than sound intellectual property and copyright policies;
4. Some changes to the Copyright Act may be appropriate, but a full and complete discussion and debate were required before any changes could be made; and
5. The DFC would provide alternative legislative proposals to stimulate constructive dialog and debate.

---

8. Peter Jaszi, invitational letter, Oct. 9, 1995.

Professor Peter Jaszi has noted that in all of the previous copyright debates and revisions, there has never been a forum where the needs of all users in both the public and private sectors are represented. The DFC is such a forum. As a membership organization, it is truly unique in its scope of members—library associations, scholarly societies, computer and communications associations, consumer groups, public-interest organizations, and more. The membership reflects how copyright and intellectual property issues are of significant, indeed critical, importance to each of these constituencies. There is also the fundamental understanding that identifying common ground on these issues is key to influencing the outcome of the copyright debates on both the domestic and international fronts.

III. Strategies for Change

Members of both the House and Senate indicated an interest in moving the NII copyright bills forward on a "fast track." Historically, changes to the Copyright Act have occurred at a relatively slow pace and with a great deal of input from all affected constituencies. Thus a priority for members of the Digital Future Coalition was to quickly educate members of Congress, congressional staff, and others in the administration and beyond, that copyright and intellectual property issues were important to many different communities and groups. These were complex issues which merited a full and complete debate and any action on the NII copyright proposals was premature.

Many note that discussions of copyright and intellectual property issues makes participants' eyes glaze over. It has proven very difficult to translate the importance of copyright and intellectual property issues to those outside of the legal field. It is fair to say that the importance of intellectual property and copyright issues to many communities is not well understood. Indeed, whereas the contributions of sound intellectual property policies to the U.S. economy have been well documented, the importance of copyright and fair use to the research and education sectors as well as other commercial sectors, are just as notable but not widely understood. A further complicating factor is that a whole host of new players such as online service providers have become actively engaged on these issues. And, because the reach of the White Paper goes well beyond copyright and intellectual property, new, "non-copyright community" players have been drawn into the debate. As a consequence, a priority for the DFC was the development of resource packets with "one pagers," i.e., one-page documents which identified and described problem or issue areas and presented alternative legislative proposals to those under consideration.

The DFC suggested seven alternative legislative proposals to those included in the House and Senate bills. These proposals restore the balance lacking in the legislative provisions as introduced or, as in the case of the proposals regarding fair use and distance education, present alternative language to critically important areas about which the White Paper and subsequent legislation was either silent or the attention devoted to the issues was negligible. The seven issues proposed to amend the NII Copyright Protection Act of 1995 include facilitating browsing and networking (§ 106), clarifying and reaffirming that the fair use doctrine is applicable to the digital age (§ 107), updating the rights of libraries and archives with regards to preservation of resources (§ 108), reaffirming the first-sale doctrine in the networked environment (§ 109), fostering distance education (§ 110), balancing protection and progress with regards to anti-circumvention devices (§ 1201), and amending the copyright management proposals (§ 1202).

A primary means to alert and educate members of the Congress and the public to complex and potentially contentious issues is through the press—print, electronic, and radio. Days prior to the first hearing on the House and Senate bills, the DFC published in *Roll Call* (a Capitol Hill newspaper) an open letter to Congress. The DFC expressed the interest in "assuring that the coming Congressional debate over how the law of intellectual property can and should change in a digital age is thorough, broad, and balanced." The DFC also stated:

> Specifically, the DFC believes that the legal regime envisioned in the White Paper, and reflected in S. 1284 and H.R. 2441, is one that could:
>
> ✦ delay or even prevent the emergence of new commercial technologies which "add value" to digital information by increasing copyright owners' effective control over data resources;
> ✦ pick "winners" and frustrate competition in the marketplace for digital goods and services by favoring established companies with large holdings of copyrighted works over innovative "startup" enterprises;
> ✦ stifle innovation and job creation in the private sector with over-broad prohibitions against manufacture and sale of legitimately useful consumer electronic devices, and by severely restricting

reverse analysis of hardware and software for purposes of achieving interoperability;

✦ invite invasion of the privacy of digital information users (including students and library patrons), and expose online/internet service providers to unspecified legal liability, by failing to address the unique circumstances of these new communications media;

✦ threaten the growth of new electronic educational techniques, such as "distance learning" programs vital to rural communities, by imposing potentially prohibitive copyright clearance costs on academic innovators;

✦ reduce educators' and the public's access to digital information by creating a new "transmission right" which would make electronic communications "distributions" within the meaning of the Copyright Act, and by categorizing even "browsing" as a potentially infringing "reproduction";

✦ undermine writers, artists and other individual creators by ignoring their concerns about intellectual property ownership in the digital environment;

✦ increase the gap between information "haves" and "have-nots" by creating new protections for copyright holders without providing balancing safeguards for users; and

✦ erode the traditional concepts and practices of "fair use" by failing to reaffirm their importance in the digital environment.[9]

The DFC letter also highlighted the international ramifications of the intellectual property and copyright debates.[10] The White Paper was simultaneously released in Washington and at the September 1995 meeting of the World Intellectual Property Organization (WIPO) in Geneva. Commissioner Lehman of the Patent and Trademark Office continues to state that the White Paper is intended to serve as a model for the global "rules" of the information superhighway (or a template for intellectual property and copyright issues on a global scale).

To this end, the U.S. delegation to WIPO took the proposals contained in the NII copyright bills and in H.R. 3931, the Database Investment and Intellectual Property Antipiracy Act of 1996, to WIPO sessions in Geneva. Throughout the spring and fall, these proposals were under active consideration by WIPO and were the focus of negotiations during the WIPO diplomatic conference to amend the Berne Convention in December 1996.[11] Responding to this international

---

9.   Digital Future Coalition, *An Open Letter to Congress*, ROLL CALL, Nov. 9, 1995.

10.   *Id.*

11.   For a summary of the WIPO accomplishments, see *infra* Appendix III (p. 281).

challenge, the DFC called upon Congress to "not let this international agenda determine the shape of domestic intellectual property law."

In later correspondence to Vice President Gore, members of DFC formally requested that the administration:

+ modify the portfolio of the administration's delegation to WIPO's December 1996 Diplomatic Conference in Geneva; and

+ formally propose that, at the December 1996 Diplomatic Conference, WIPO adopt a timetable for future discussion and action on the "Digital Agenda" that will permit its careful consideration by the 104th and 105th Congresses, and that will permit the United States' delegation to take congressional action into account in subsequent treaty negotiations; and

+ affirmatively work to assure in all appropriate WIPO bodies that no proposals related to the Digital Agenda are acted upon prior to Congress' full evaluation of these important issues.[12]

The DFC was not alone in expressing serious reservations regarding the administration's position. The Ad Hoc Copyright Coalition, an organization comprised of manufacturers and online service providers, sent a similar letter to President Clinton and Vice President Gore.[13] Congressman Rick Boucher (D-VA) and Carlos J. Moorhead (R-CA), chair of the Subcommittee on Courts and Intellectual Property and sponsor of the NII legislation, also wrote to the chair of the WIPO Experts Committee, Jukka Liedes. Congressman Moorhead commented that the "Congressional hearings raised some issues for consideration in addition to those addressed in the legislative recommendations contained in the 'White Paper,' H.R. 2441, and S. 1284."[14] Congressman Boucher noted that

> given the deep division of interests over the issues raised by the Digital Agenda in the United States, I believe that more time is needed both domestically and internationally to assess their effect and to formulate changes in copyright law that properly balance the needs of content owners, users and electronic service providers. The

---

12.   Letter from the Digital Future Coalition, to Vice President Al Gore (July 12, 1996).

13.   Letter from the Ad Hoc Copyright Coalition, to President Clinton and Vice President Gore (July 12, 1996).

14.   Letter from Congressman Carlos J. Moorhead, to Jukka Liedes, Chairman, WIPO Experts Committee (Aug. 1, 1996).

recommendations . . . advanced by the "White Paper," submitted by the U.S. Patent Office and under consideration in your discussions, have been rejected by the U.S. Congress. The final resolution of these matters by the U.S. Congress will take a form very different from the "White Paper" formulations.[15]

Thus the education campaign undertaken by the DFC focused on reaching multiple constituencies, domestic and abroad. Members of the DFC participated in numerous visits to members of the House and Senate, and to officials in the administration. The DFC was asked to submit testimony before the House Subcommittee on Intellectual Property and provided testimony before the Senate Committee on the Judiciary. The invitation to testify before the Senate Committee on the Judiciary was a clear indication that the DFC educational effort was successful. Members of DFC made numerous presentations to different audiences in addition to sponsoring a press conference prior to scheduled activity on H.R. 2441.

Another measure of success is the large and growing number of newspaper, journal, and radio stories on this issue. The *Washington Post*, the *Columbus* (Ohio) *Dispatch*, the *Los Angeles Times*, and other newspapers published editorials on the legislation. Professor Pamela Samuelson, a founder of the DFC, participated in a National Public Radio piece evaluating the legislation. There were many thoughtful articles in the *New York Times*, the *National Journal*, and beyond. Several universities and consortia such as the University of Wisconsin and the Committee on Institutional Cooperation endorsed statements expressing serious reservations with the legislation.[16] Thus, the DFC quickly emerged as an important voice which understands and reflects the views of multiple and very diverse communities.

Finally, the DFC is an active proponent of the Internet. The DFC's home page[17] includes a wealth of information on copyright issues such as an analysis of the international situation, links to the DFC membership, and the DFC alternative legislative proposals to the White Paper. The World Wide Web site is used as a communications tool to members and interested users of the Internet.

---

15.   Letter from Congressman Rick Boucher, to Jukka Liedes, Chairman, WIPO Experts Committee (July 23, 1996).

16.   World Wide Web address: <http://www.cedar.cic.net/cic/cic/html>.

17.   World Wide Web address: <http://www.ori.net/dfc>.

IV. Conclusion

By the summer of 1996, it was clear that the legislation was stalled in the U.S. Congress. Although progress was made on several contentious issues through separate negotiation sessions (e.g., online service provider liability issues), many members of Congress agreed with Congressman Robert W. Goodlatte (R-VA) that "the problem is that there were just too many contingencies to build the necessary support to pass the underlying legislation."[18] And Congressman Howard L. Berman (D-CA) concluded that "if ever you wanted to do a case study of Congress dealing with legislation it doesn't understand, this is it."[19]

With congressional action increasingly unlikely in the near term, the DFC focus is the international arena. The U.S. delegation's continuing support for the White Paper and the sui generis database proposals[20] raises the possibility that there could be international adoption of some of these proposals without full and complete domestic consideration of these critical copyright and intellectual property issues. For many members of WIPO such as Canada, this could mean that there will be no domestic discussion of a digital agenda. Commenting on the U.S. delegation's position, Commissioner Lehman stated,

> The beauty of our NII legislation, the White Paper, is that it provides us with a template for that international system. So we are going to Geneva in December [1996]. We are going to see if we can't negotiate some new international treaties and get that straightened out. Now it may be that those treaties will require some legislative implementation. They will certainly have to be ratified by the Senate in any event, but they also might have to be implemented and that gives us a sort of second bite of the apple.[21]

In less than a year, the Digital Future Coalition has emerged as a leading voice on issues relating to intellectual property and copyright in the networked environment. The Coalition continues to grow and

---

18.   *Cyberspace Bill Appears Dead*, CONG. Q., June 22, 1996, at 1752.

19.   *Id.*

20.   For a discussion of database protection, see *supra* Chapter Five (p. 85), "Facing Facts: The Database Protection Dilemma," by Jonathan A. Franklin.

21.   *PTO Chief Remains Optimistic About NII Copyright Bill; Offers Views on Database Right, Domain Name Squabbles*, ELECTRONIC INFO. POL'Y & L. REP. (BNA) June 21, 1996, at 264.

include new commercial and not-for-profit interests in its activities.[22] The work of the DFC complements, indeed, extends the work of other related coalitions such as that of the library community (members include the American Association of Law Libraries, American Library Association, the Association of Research Libraries, the Medical Library Association, and the Special Libraries Association) and the Ad Hoc Copyright Coalition (online service providers including America Online, AT&T, MCI, U.S. West, and others). Throughout its first year, the five themes of the DFC guided discussions and all activities. Through close collaboration with many communities, members of the DFC continue to advocate for balanced and equitable copyright policies.[23] Any new legislation or international treaty that eventually emerges from this critically important set of discussions should not disrupt the current balance between the rights of owners and users of copyrighted materials if all communities are to realize the full benefits of the national information infrastructure and the global information infrastructure.

---

22.   A list of the 31 member organizations appears at the end of this chapter as Appendix I, *infra* p. 263.

23.   DFC's testimony appears at the end of this chapter as Appendix II, *infra* p. 264.

Appendix I
Digital Future Coalition Members

Alliance for Public Technology

American Association of Law Libraries

American Committee for Interoperable Systems

American Council of Learned Societies

American Historical Association

American Library Association

Art Libraries Society of North America

Association of American Geographers

Association of Research Libraries

Committee of Concerned Intellectual Property Educators

Computer & Communications Industry Association

Conference on College Composition and Communication

Consortium of Social Science Associations

Consumer Federation of America

Consumer Project on Technology

Electronic Frontier Foundation

Electronic Privacy Information Center

Home Recording Rights Coalition

Medical Library Association

Modern Language Association

National Association of Legal Publishers

National Council of Teachers of English

National Education Association

National Humanities Alliance

National Initiative for a Networked Cultural Heritage

National School Boards Association

National Writers Union

People for the American Way Action Fund

Special Libraries Association

Society of American Archivists

Visual Resources Association

Appendix II
Digital Future Coalition Testimony on the "NII Copyright Protection Act of 1995"

United States Senate Committee on the Judiciary
Presented by Professor Robert L. Oakley
May 7, 1996

Executive Summary

The Digital Future Coalition supports the goal of the "NII Copyright Protection Act" (S. 1284 & H.R. 2441) to update the Copyright Act for the digital future and has proposed a package of amendments to the bill addressing the problems identified below. These changes will assure that any new legislation is a watershed for American businesses of all sizes, schools, libraries, consumers and scholars.

Who We Are and What We Believe . . .

The Digital Future Coalition—representing over 2 million Americans—is a deep, broad and unique group of leading business, library, educational, consumer and technology organizations committed to copyright law and policy that rewards creativity.

264

The DFC believes that the Copyright Act must continue to promote creativity in the future, as it has for hundreds of years in the past, by preserving the balance between strong intellectual property protection and robust access to information for all innovators, including those in business, libraries and education. Content control without access assurance will preclude the "Progress" that the Framers sought and the Constitution requires.

The "NII Copyright Protection Act" Should be Amended To . . .

Provide certainty to the libraries, schools, educators and businesses that will build the NII and make it available to the nation as to when they will—and will not—be liable for infringing the Copyright Act by virtue of doing what they do best: maximizing the benefits of Internet technology for all Americans. Maintain the fundamental balance between ownership and access now in the law by "clarifying" both the scope of owner's rights in electronic transmissions (Section 106 of the Copyright Act) and users' ability to access copyrighted information (Section 107).

Assure libraries' and archives' ability to preserve our cultural heritage by maximizing their ability under the Copyright Act to preserve our nation's cultural heritage and make the Act technology neutral.

Reaffirm the First Sale Doctrine's applicability in "cyberspace" to allow a legally acquired digital copy of a work to be passed on electronically if the original is not also retained.

Foster "distance learning" especially critical to rural communities and the disabled by amending the Copyright Act to permit educators and their students, young and old, to realize the full potential of the NII.

Preserve and protect America's international competitive edge by striking the legislation's dangerously overbroad restrictions on device and component manufacture, import and distribution in favor of technology-specific, industry-developed anti-theft solutions.

Target for civil and criminal liability only those who intend to defeat copyright management information systems—not innocent distributors, libraries and schools.

To Preserve its Prerogatives, Congress Must Urge the Executive Branch NOW To . . .

Withdraw its calls for the World Intellectual Property Organization to conclude treaty negotiations in December 1996 on the same "Digital Agenda" now before Congress.

Instruct the U.S. delegation to WIPO to assure that no such action is taken internationally until a domestic consensus forms on these complicated issues, and Congress exercises its Constitutional power to set domestic copyright policy.

The Digital Future Coalition looks forward to working with Members of the Committee and their staffs to calibrate S. 1284 and the Copyright Act to preserve the critical balance traditionally at its core.

Presentation by Prof. Robert L. Oakley

Good morning, Mr. Chairman, Sen. Biden, and Members of the Committee. My name is Robert Oakley. I am a Professor of Law at the Georgetown University Law Center and Director of the Law Center's Library. I also serve as Washington Affairs Representative for the American Association of Law Libraries, a member of the Digital Future Coalition.

I am honored and pleased to appear before the Committee today on behalf of the Digital Future Coalition to share with you not only our large and diverse group's broad views on copyright and the National Information Infrastructure ("NII"), but to offer for the record a specific, seven-point package of amendments to S. 1284. The DFC respectfully requests that its proposals be considered and incorporated into S. 1284 before that legislation is reported out of this Committee.

Introduction

Before detailing the DFC's legislative package, Mr. Chairman, it is important that the Committee know who and what the Digital Future Coalition is, and what we stand for. If I may say, our very existence and the diversity of our membership are testimony themselves to the importance, breadth and complexity of the issues raised by S. 1284.

The Digital Future Coalition includes many public and private organizations that have been instrumental in building, and that will continue to expand, the Internet and broader NII now emerging.

We are, most simply, over two dozen distinct organizations with a cumulative membership of well over 2 million Americans.

We are also, through our organizational members: major technology and telecommunications corporations; educators; the nation's school boards and libraries; nationally recognized consumer advocates; scholars and teachers of many disciplines, including intellectual property; and leading experts on privacy, the First Amendment and on information technology's pitfalls and potential.

We are—to a member—corporations and organizations with a bedrock commitment to intelligent and balanced copyright law made after substantial scrutiny by Congress. That means on the one hand, Mr. Chairman, that we respect and support strong copyright protection and, on the other hand, that we are committed to equally strong statutory respect for the Constitutional objective that undergirds all of copyright law: "the Progress of Science and useful Arts," and to the principle of Fair Use.

We agree that copyright is at root about promoting creativity. As creators ourselves, however, we understand that creativity results not just from the financial incentive for authors and inventors codified in Title 17 of the U.S. Code, but from that same statute's guarantee of access to copyrighted information. The truest and best measure of our copyright law's success is whether it succeeds in fairly balancing those equal priorities in the service of the Framer's commitment to the broad dissemination of knowledge and information in a Democracy.

Overview of Proposals

The Digital Future Coalition understands, Mr. Chairman, that you, Sen. Leahy and this Committee are eager to get down to the "brass tacks" of assuring that the development and marketplace deployment of 21st century information technology is not hindered by a 20th century statute. The DFC wishes to be absolutely clear that it shares that goal.

Our Coalition is also convinced, however, that—in pursuit of that end—Congress now has an opportunity (and a responsibility) to bring ALL of the critical precepts at the core of copyright law into the digital future together and in balance. In practical terms:

That means that, if the nature and scope of the monopoly rights granted to copyright holders is to be "clarified" by changing the U.S.

Code, then the nature and scope of a key counterbalance to those rights—the Fair Use Doctrine—must be made equally clear in the law;

It means that, even as the Fair Use Doctrine is philosophically re-affirmed, Congress must practically assure that the continued ability of Americans in business, academia and the public at large to rely on and use copyrighted information—and to develop new business models for its distribution—are not precluded by overbroad restrictions on the manufacture of devices and systems needed to make fair use rights real;

It also means, Mr. Chairman, that Congress must deal directly in S. 1284 with the issue of who should be liable, when, and to what extent if a commercial, academic or library computer network carries copyrighted information without the author's permission. Without increased certainty in this critical area of the law, however, both com-mercial and non-commercial use of the NII and GII will be dramatically chilled by the potential for crippling litigation and liability.

Precluding Premature International Action on a "Digital Agenda"

The Digital Future Coalition is also critically concerned, Mr. Chairman, that—unless checked—activities by the Executive Branch in the inter-national arena could moot the Legislative Branch's policy making prerogatives in this critical area of the law. Proposals virtually identi-cal to those now before this Committee have already been presented by the U.S. delegation to the World Intellectual Property Organization by the United States' delegation, which confirmed just days ago that it intends to continue to call for a diplomatic conference to draft treaty language prior to the end of this year which would, in effect, codify the pending legislation in international law.

That call will next be heard from the U.S. delegation in Rome starting tomorrow as the "Stockholm Group" of industrialized nations meets for three days to consider and potentially endorse the U.S. agenda for a December 1996 diplomatic conference to be held in Geneva. The Governing Body of WIPO itself will meet in Geneva on May 20, less than two weeks from now, to cast plans for the confer-ence in concrete. The DFC believes that the Framers would take a dim view of such de facto preemption of Congress' sole authority to make copyright policy. That possibility, however, now looms large on the international horizon.

Accordingly, Mr. Chairman, we urge you, the Committee and the Senate to immediately send a strong message to the Executive Branch that: (1) the Administration's "Digital Agenda" is premature for consideration by WIPO pending the formation of a domestic consensus and the conclusion of Congressional action on the legislation before us; and (2) the United States' delegation to WIPO should work affirmatively to assure that any such "Digital Agenda" is not placed before a 1996 or early 1997 diplomatic conference intended to amend the Berne Convention for the first time in 25 years.

Legislative Proposals

Turning now to the DFC's specific legislative proposals, I would like to request, Mr. Chairman, that they be incorporated in the record of these hearings at the conclusion of my remarks, together with relevant explanatory materials. These proposals, for the record, have been expressly endorsed by the undersigned members of the Digital Future Coalition. Thank you, Mr. Chairman. In sum, the DFC proposes:

> that new provisions concerning the Fair Use and First Sale Doctrines, distance education and ephemeral digital reproductions of copyrighted works be added to S. 1284;
> that Section 1201, regarding "Circumvention of Copyright Protection Systems," simply be stricken from the bill in favor of technology-specific solutions based on negotiated solutions among those most concerned; and
> that proposed changes in two of the remaining provisions of the legislation be modified to better assure that the critical "balance" in copyright law just described is maintained. (Those provisions concern preservation activities addressed in Section 108, and "copyright management information" systems covered by new Section 1202.)

In addition, the undersigned DFC members urge the Committee not to approve S. 1284 unless and until it is amended to clarify and define the scope of network service providers' liability under the Copyright Act in a manner that does not require or encourage such providers to compromise the privacy rights of their users.

For the Committee's convenience, I will address the undersigned DFC members' proposed amendments in the order of the statutory sections to which they relate, beginning with Section 106 of the Copyright Act.

Section 106: Ephemeral Digital Reproductions

As introduced, S. 1284 would amend Section 106 of the Copyright Act to provide for a "transmission" right as an aspect of the "distribution" right already identified in subsection (3). If such a right is made explicit in the Act, however, further clarification of the statute is needed to assure that the mere act of reading a digital document will not constitute copyright infringement.

Such liability could well be imposed if the new transmission right is interpreted by courts to support a finding that every temporary reproduction of a work in a computer's random access memory (RAM) or "cache" storage (incidental to its use on a computer system) is a technical "copy" for all purposes under the Copyright Act. Under this construction of the law, activities that can now be undertaken without risk of liability in the analog environment would become a potential source of liability in the digital one.

While a few courts have considered "RAM" reproduction to be "copying" under the Copyright Act (see particularly Ninth Circuit decisions, such as MAI v. Peak, 991 F.2d 511 [9th Cir. 1993]), this interpretation has been substantively addressed only in a few jurisdictions and has not been reviewed by the Supreme Court. It is, therefore, far from being settled law. It is, however, one of the central tenets of the White Paper on "Intellectual Property and the National Information Infrastructure" and thus clouds all discussions of rights and wrongs in cyberspace.

The "NII Copyright Protection Act" offers the Congress an opportunity to definitively clarify that the mere fact that a work in digital form is loaded into the random access or cache memory of a computer—creating temporary electronic versions of the work destined for automatic erasure—does not constitute the sort of "copying" with which the law of copyright is now or need be concerned. Accordingly, the DFC proposes that—in addition to modifying Section 106(3)—S. 1284 be broadened to amend the description of the "reproduction right" in Section 106(1) of the Copyright Act as follows:

For the purposes of this subsection, the ephemeral reproduction of a work in temporary computer memory or digital storage, which is incidental to the otherwise lawful use of that work, and which does not lead to the making of a permanent reproduction, is not a copy. This language is intended to apply only to necessary and incidental reproduction of digital works in connection with their use on computer systems. It will have no application to situations in which permanent electronic copies, such as those made on a computer's disks (or other permanent or semi-permanent storage media) are made.

Section 107: Fair Use

As noted earlier in these remarks, it is critical that the copyright law strike an appropriate balance between protecting the rights of copyright owners and otherwise promoting "Progress in Science and the useful Arts." In the scheme of American copyright, "fair use" safeguards our collective interest in the flow of information—which is, in turn, a source of economically valuable knowledge.

Fair use, in addition to reflecting in copyright law First Amendment-based principles of free speech, provides the basis for many of our most important day-to-day activities in scholarship and education. Moreover, it is no less vital to American industries, which lead the world in technological innovation. It is also of tremendous value to the Judiciary in dealing with the challenge of precisely such innovation, and repeatedly has been recognized by the Supreme Court as essential to the work of writers and others who creatively transmogrify the earlier works of others in the alchemy that we call "Art."

The maintenance of a robust Fair Use Doctrine in the new legal environment of cyberspace thus remains a high priority of the Digital Future Coalition and, we respectfully submit, should rank among Congress' highest priorities, as well.

S. 1284 proposes to "clarify" that transmission is a form of distribution under the Copyright Act, one of the "bundle of rights" granted to copyright holders by Section 106 of the Act. Many also consider the proposed language an expansion of those rights. Under either interpretation, the Digital Future Coalition believes that a comparable change is necessary and appropriate in the "Fair Use" portion of the statute (Section 107) in order to assure that the scope of fair use parallels the scope of the rights to which it relates. Including such language in the pending legislation and the Act also will reaffirm Congress' commitment to the vibrancy of the Fair Use Doctrine in the digital future.

To those ends, the DFC proposes that the introductory paragraph of Section 107 be amended to read as follows (with proposed new language indicated by italics):

Notwithstanding the provisions of Sections 106 and 106A, the fair use of a copyrighted work, including such use by reproduction in copies or phonorecords, *by transmission*, or by any other means specified by that section, for purposes such as criticism, comment, news reporting, teaching (including multiple copies for classroom use), scholarship, or research is not an infringement of copyright.

Section 108: Library Exemptions

The transformation of the information environment gives rise to both challenges and opportunities for many important social institutions, including libraries. The undersigned members of the Digital Future Coalition agree with you and Sen. Leahy, Mr. Chairman, that a "digital update" to Section 108 of the Copyright Act is required if the needs of libraries and researchers are to be met. Moreover, such an update is vital to libraries' ongoing and uphill efforts to solve a preservation problem which now ranks as nothing short of a national intellectual and historical crisis.

The Digital Future Coalition supports technical revisions to S. 1284 advanced by several of its member organizations (the American Association of Law Libraries, the American Library Association, the Association of Research Libraries, the Medical Library Association, and the Special Libraries Association) and supported by the Register of Copyrights. These revisions would make Sec. 108 "technology-neutral" throughout, thus allowing libraries to use the best and newest technology platform to carry out the activities authorized by Section 108.

Our proposal would also add an important new subsection designed to help the library community meet the special preservation challenges posed by digital works in obsolete formats (i.e., works which can no longer be accessed by the technologies that produced them because such technologies are no longer reasonably available).

Specifically, the DFC proposes that Section 108 be revised in a manner largely consistent with S. 1284 to read as follows (proposed new language in italics; deletions in square brackets):

(a) Except as otherwise provided, notwithstanding the provisions of Section 106, it is not an infringement of copyright for a library or archives, or any of its employees acting within the scope of their employment, to reproduce no more than one copy or phonorecord of a work, or to distribute such copy or phonorecord, under the conditions specified by this section, if—

{Subsections 1 and 2 remain unchanged};

(3) The reproduction or distribution of the work includes a notice of copyright if such notice appears on the copy or phonorecord that is reproduced under the provisions of this section.

(b) The rights of reproduction and distribution under this section apply to [one copy] *three copies* or phonorecords of an unpublished work duplicated [in facsimile form] solely for purposes of preservation and security or for deposit for research use in another library or archives of the type described by clause (2) of subsection (a), if the copy or phonorecord reproduced is currently in the collections of the library or archives.

(c) The right of reproduction under this section applies to [one copy] *three copies* or phonorecords of a published work duplicated [in facsimile form] solely for the purpose of replacement of a copy or phonorecord that is damaged, deteriorating, lost, or stolen, *or if the existing format in which the work is stored has become obsolete,* if the library or archives has, after a reasonable effort, determined that an unused replacement cannot be obtained at a fair price.

Section 109: The First Sale Doctrine

It has long been recognized in American law that someone who legally obtains a book or video cassette, for example, may—without the permission of the owner or fear of liability—give, sell or otherwise transfer possession of that work to someone else. Library lending, for example, is a direct outgrowth of this "First Sale Doctrine" now codified at Section 109(a) of the Copyright Act.

The Digital Future Coalition rejects the suggestion, made in the report on "Intellectual Property and the National Information Infrastructure" (produced by the Working Group on Intellectual Property Rights of the President's Information and Infrastructure Task Force) and elsewhere, that the First Sale Doctrine applies only to the *physical* transfer of an actual object and does not apply to the electronic transmission of a work under any circumstances. Such analysis, in any event, misses the critical point that Congress now has the opportunity to determine whether some digital equivalent to the traditional "first sale" doctrine, as it exists in the analog information environment, should apply in cyberspace. We believe that it should.

Historically, the ability to pass on lawfully obtained copies of works has been important to libraries, scholars, and ordinary information consumers. It has also be a crucial factor in the emergence of new business models. Just as "first sale" in the past has given us everything from lending libraries to video rental outlets, we believe that the digital equivalent of "first sale" could be the basis for important new cultural and economic developments in cyberspace. One means to that end would be to add to Section 109 of the Copyright Act the following new subsection:

> (f) The privilege set forth in subsection (a) extends to any transmission of a single copy or phonorecord so long as the transmitter erases or destroys his or her copy or phonorecord at substantially the same time. The reproduction of a work, to the extent required to exercise this privilege, is not an infringement.

If adopted, this proposal would codify a standard with which responsible users of the NII may reasonably be expected to comply, and one which would be no more difficult to enforce than a flat prohibition on all retransmissions of lawfully acquired digital copies of copyrighted works. Indeed, content providers could take advantage of increasingly sophisticated technological means to make it difficult, if not practically impossible, to forward such copies without simultaneously deleting them.

Sections 110 and 112: Distance Education

"Distance Education" is one of the most exciting and potentially productivity-enhancing trends in American education today. Using television and other technologies, educators are increasingly able to deliver non-profit educational services critical to success in the global economy to students in rural communities, disabled individuals, adults enrolled in continuing education programs, and many other special communities of learners. Literally millions of Americans benefit from these efforts. The Digital Future Coalition is concerned, however, that if the current law and pending legislation are not modified, the tremendous educational and social benefits of distance learning will be lost to millions of children and adults across the nation.

Students today enjoy the benefits of distance education in large part because of provisions contained in Sec. 110(2) of the Copyright Act of 1976, which allow for the "performance or display" of certain works delivered by means of "transmission" in non-profit educational settings. Today, that typically means television. Increasingly, however, distance educators will want and need to make use of digital transmissions over local networks and the Internet in order to maximize the reach and effectiveness of their services.

Under S. 1284, however, Sec. 106(3) of the Copyright Act would be amended to define transmissions of copyrighted works by means of digital networks as "distributions" of copies. The existing exemptions for education in Sec. 110, however, do not apply to the "distribution right." S. 1284, as written, thus promises to clarify and expand the rights of copyright proprietors while narrowing the continued ability of distance educators (in both government and non-profit institutions) to use the latest and best technology to carry on their crucial work.

Furthermore, unlike the broadcast technologies of the mid-1970's, digital networks make it possible to deliver distance non-profit educational services to students individually and outside traditional classroom settings through individual computer terminals. At present, however, the locations to which educators may deliver "distance ed" programming are limited under Sec. 110(2) of the Copyright Act. Moreover, the limitations of the Sec. 110(2) exemptions to certain classes of copyrighted works are increasingly outdated in an era of digital "convergence" and "multimedia" presentations.

Ideally, the best way to assure that the technologies of learning continue to flourish in the digital age would be to engage in a comprehensive rethinking of the relationship between educational practice and copyright, starting from first premises. Such an effort, however, would take time. If there is to be legislation in the near term to adapt copyright to the networked information environment, the undersigned DFC members believe it is essential that any such legislation include language that addresses these important distance education issues.

Specifically, the DFC proposes amending Sec. 110(2)—and its companion Sec. 112(b)—to bring distance education into the digital age by adding "distribution" to the list of conditionally exempt educational uses. Sec. 110 should be further updated by eliminating current restrictions the kinds of places in which exempt transmissions may legally be received, and on the kinds of works subject to the exemption. Finally, to help assure that these provisions are not abused, the DFC also proposes new restrictive language which would limit the scope of Sections 110 and 112 to transmissions primarily intended for the use of "officially enrolled" students. As modified according to our suggestions, Secs. 110(2) and 112(b) would read as follows:

Section 110(2):

2) performance, display or distribution of a work by or in the course of transmission—if

(A) the performance, display or distribution is a regular part of the systematic instructional activities of a governmental body or a nonprofit educational institution, and

(B) the performance, display or distribution is directly related and of material assistance to the teaching content of the transmission, and

(C) the transmission is made primarily for reception by students officially enrolled in the course in connection with which it is offered, or

(D) the transmission is made primarily for reception by officers or employees of governmental bodies as a part of their official duties or employment;

Section 112(b):

Notwithstanding the provisions of section 106, it is not an infringement of copyright for a governmental body or other nonprofit organization entitled to perform, display or distribute a work by or in the course of a transmission, under section 110(2) or under the limitations on exclusive rights in sound recordings specified by section 114(a) to make no more than thirty copies or phonorecords of a particular transmission program embodying the performance, display or distribution, if—

[the balance of the statute as in the original. . . .]

Proposed Section 1201:
Circumvention of Copyright Protection Systems

The Digital Future Coalition does not take lightly, and does not believe frivolous, the concern of many in the entertainment and information industries that digital technology creates new dilemmas. The DFC does, however, take strong issue with the suggestion that proposed Section 1201 is an appropriately measured and balanced response to this concern.

As representatives of entertainment industries now readily admit, similar concerns over technological innovation have proven unfounded in the past. Originally viewed as a deadly threat to the motion picture industry, for example, the VCR actually spawned a new and previously unenvisioned market for that industry which now accounts for the majority of its domestic revenues.

Despite that experience (and positive experience in the past with narrow device-specific "black box" prohibition laws aimed at satellite signal piracy) the NII Working Group has offered Congress a vague and sweeping provision—one which would, in effect, overturn the Supreme Court's decision that made the VCR industry viable and established the public's fair use right to "time shift" programs by recording them for private use.

In the Betamax decision, the Supreme Court held that because the Betamax is "capable of substantial noninfringing uses, Sony's sale of such equipment to the general public does not constitute contributory infringement of respondents' copyrights." Since Section 1201, as drafted, could outlaw devices that have substantial noninfringing uses if they do not also respond to all anticopying technology, we believe it reverses the Supreme Court's decision.

Moreover, because Section 1201 covers components as well as devices, it could be used by courts to outlaw entirely the sale of a variety of products including recording devices with substantial noninfringing uses. Such products should not be expected to comply with anti-copying encoding that would prevent fair use copying, would distort regular TV pictures, would require expensive licenses, or otherwise would frustrate consumers.

Members of the DFC do not advocate allowing consumers to circumvent properly protected copyright works through such systems as "black boxes" that have no commercially significant use other than to circumvent copy protection. But our members do support the right of consumers to continue to make legal, fair use reproductions of copyrighted works. We therefore recommend that Congress not adopt Section 1201. Rather, we urge Congress, working with concerned industries, to address copying issues on a more specific basis in terms of devices and technologies.

Technically expert DFC member organizations look forward to sharing with the Committee additional information regarding the viability of relying on technology to guard against the unauthorized use of copyrighted digital works in a manner consistent with the Fair Use Doctrine.

Section 1202: Copyright Management Information

The Digital Future Coalition is similarly concerned that proposed Section 1202, as incorporated in S. 1284, goes too far in attempting to further the laudable purpose of counteracting piracy by forbidding the misrepresentation of "copyright management information." Clearly, the development of systems and programs intended to provide consumers and other information users with information about who holds the rights to a copyrighted work, how to contact the rights holder, and (if permission to use the work is legally required) under what terms it may be obtained are not inherently objectionable. Penalizing individuals who remove or alter such information in order to further actual copyright infringement also seems appropriate.

As drafted, however, proposed Section 1202(a) also would penalize a potentially wide range of non-infringing activities. For example, a legitimate wholesaler which acquired several thousand copies of a copyrighted book or videotape each of which included accurate "copyright management information" (CMI) at the time of the acquisition might subsequently learn through the trade press that the rights to those works had been transferred as part of a major corporate acquisition. Under Section 1202(a), because the wholesaler knew that the CMI imbedded in each copy in his inventory had now been rendered "false" by market events outside its control, he or she would risk liability for redistributing them in the normal course of otherwise lawful business activities. Similar liability would be faced by libraries and educators.

This certainly unintended result would obtain because the only requirement for liability under Section 1202(a) is mere knowledge that false CMI has been distributed. Nonsensically, the distributor's intent and the reason that the information is or became inaccurate are irrelevant.

Section 1202(b), by contrast, speaks to the true heart of the problem—the wrongful alteration or removal of such information. By incorporating a similar concept in Section 1202(a) the inadvertent sweep of the provision will be appropriately narrowed. Specifically, we propose that liability for transmitting false copyright management information be imposed only on those who do so in furtherance of actual copyright infringement. So modified, Sec. 1202(a) would read as follows:

> False Copyright Management Information.—No person shall knowingly provide copyright management information that is false, or knowingly publicly distribute or import for public distribution copyright management information that is false, in furtherance of infringement.

The DFC also is concerned that, by making the definition of "copyright management information" ("CMI") open-ended, S. 1284 effectively delegates to the Copyright Office the authority to define what will and will not be a criminal offense. Such determinations, the Coalition believes should continue to be made by Congress itself. In addition, if broadly defined, it is clear that CMI systems will be capable not only of providing information users with information about copyright proprietors, but will furnish such proprietors with data about the information user (see *Chronicle of Higher Education*, March 22, 1996, p. A23). Absent effective privacy safeguards (such as the development of anonymous payment mechanisms), serious privacy problems will result.

For both of these reasons, the DFC strongly urges that detailed hearings be conducted on the appropriate scope of the definition of CMI for purposes of the pending legislation. Not incidentally, such hearings also will afford authors an opportunity to be heard as to how CMI technology may best advance their significant interests in the digital information marketplace.

Online Service Provider Liability

Finally, the DFC wishes to highlight for the Committee an additional issue of very substantial concern to its members. While we are not presently proposing a legislative solution in deference to ongoing multiparty negotiations, the Digital Future Coalition believes that S. 1284 should not be reported out of the Judiciary Committee (or, certainly, approved by the Senate) unless it is explicitly amended to define the circumstances under (and the extent to) which Internet access providers, bulletin board operators, libraries, educational institutions, and other system operators will be held liable for violations of the new "transmission" right for copyright infringement by subscribers and other end-users. Such legislation is needed for many reasons, including the protection of privacy. Given the uncertain and fluid state of case law in this area, absent clear lines of liability service providers may have no practical defense to crippling damages but the invasive monitoring and supervision of their subscribers' private communications.

Conclusion

Like most participants in the networked information environment, the members of the Digital Future Coalition are creators of copyrighted works, as well as consumers of information. As such, we believe strongly in the importance of providing appropriate copyright protection in cyberspace for large content providers and individual authors alike. The new "transmission" right included in S. 1284 may be an appropriate means to this end. As we have indicated, however, the DFC is gravely concerned that the codification of that right—without other compensating adjustments to the Copyright Act—may miscalibrate the traditional balance of interests reflected in the Copyright Act today.

Such imbalance not only threatens consumer interests and to inhibit or preclude the emergence of new business models in cyberspace, but also promises to retard the very "Progress in Science and the useful Arts" that led the Framers of the Constitution to grant Congress the power to award copyrights over two centuries ago.

The undersigned members of the Digital Future Coalition appreciate this opportunity to present our views on S. 1284. We look forward to working with the Committee and its staff to craft legislation which honors the Constitution by reaffirming and guarding the balance at copyright's core.

Thank you again, Mr. Chairman.

Alliance for Public Technology
American Association of Law
    Libraries
American Committee for Inter-
    operable Systems
American Council of Learned
    Societies
American Historical Association
American Library Association
Art Libraries Society of North
    America
Association of American
    Geographers
Association of Research Libraries
Committee of Concerned
    Intellectual Property Educators
Computer & Communications
    Industry Association

Conference on College Composition
    and Communication
Consortium of Social Science
    Associations
Consumer Federation of America
Consumer Project on Technology
Electronic Frontier Foundation
Electronic Privacy Information
    Center
Home Recording Rights Coalition
Medical Library Association
National Council of Teachers of
    English
National Education Association
National Humanities Alliance
National School Boards Association
People for the American Way
    Action Fund
Special Libraries Association

WIPO: Summary and Key Accomplishments

The World Intellectual Property Organization (WIPO) completed consideration of three treaties in a Diplomatic Conference convened in December 1996 in Geneva, Switzerland. Delegates from 160 countries met to consider proposed changes to copyright law with a particular focus on the digital environment. The treaties sought to update copyright law concerning works delivered in digital form, to enact protections for performers in and producers of sound recordings, and to enact a new intellectual property regime to protect databases.

At the close of the Diplomatic Conference, the delegates adopted two new versions of the three treaties that had been originally proposed. These treaties include substantive changes from those circulated in the fall of 1996. Consideration of the third treaty regarding database protection was deferred with the recommendation that WIPO convene another session early in 1997 to consider a schedule for future discussions on database protection. Overall, the work of the WIPO conference resulted in a more balanced approach to copyright issues than had been true of the draft proposals. The efforts of representatives of the Digital Future Coalition, the Home Recording Rights Coalition, International Federation of Library Associations, the Computer

Communications Industry Association, and others were instrumental in achieving this balanced approach.

Reproduction Right

The original WIPO proposal would have placed libraries at risk for the activities of their patrons because it would have extended the right of reproduction (the right of the copyright owner) to all temporary copies, including ephemeral images captured in a computer's random access memory. When coupled with the right of communication to the public called for in the draft treaties, there would have been a chilling effect on the ability of libraries and library users to access needed information resources due to serious concerns over liability.

This proposal was dropped from the Copyright Treaty, as were references to temporary copying from the second Phonograms Treaty.

Communication to the Public

The draft WIPO proposal included a new exclusive "right of communication to the public." When coupled with the right of reproduction, this would have significantly increased the exposure of online service providers, including libraries, to copyright infringement liability.

Although the Conference retained this proposal, it was significantly modified with accompanying language that noted that "the mere provision of physical facilities for enabling or making a communication does not in itself amount to communication." This limits, although does not eliminate, concerns about indirect liability for activities of patrons and other users.

Fair Use and Related Educational Exceptions

The draft WIPO proposal would have undermined many of the exceptions created by Congress in support of education and library activities. In particular, the proposal could have limited the applicability of these exceptions to the digital environment.

The treaties permit current limitations and exceptions to continue in the print and digital environments. With the support of the U.S. delegation, the Conference adopted an "agreed upon statement" making clear that the two treaties "will permit application of fair use in the digital environment, and should be understood to permit Contracting

Parties to devise new exceptions and limitations as appropriate in the digital environment." The addition of "new exceptions and limitations" and language in the treaty preamble which recognizes "the need to maintain a balance between the rights of authors and the larger public interest, particularly education, research and access to information," is significant progress in reaching a balance between the interests of users and owners of copyrighted works in the digital environment.

Technological Measures, Anti-circumvention

The draft WIPO proposal would have imposed liability for devices that had the "primary purpose or effect" of circumventing any technology used to protect copyrighted works (e.g. VCRs). Such language would have precluded libraries from engaging in lawfully permitted activities in support of research, education, and public access to information. For example, if a manufacturer developed a device that enabled a library to circumvent copy-protection systems for the purpose of making "lawful" archival copies, the manufacturer could have been held liable if a court determined that the manufacturer should have expected that at least one user would also use the device to make an infringing copy.

The treaties include only a general obligation to protect technologies against the act of circumvention for unlawful purposes. As a consequence, there is no longer a "threat" to the manufacturer of such devices nor ultimately to the current and future market for such devices nor to the end user who employs them for fair use, archiving, or related educational purposes.

Rights Management Information

The WIPO draft treaties would have protected rights management information (terms and conditions, information regarding authors and more), from alteration, deletion, indeed any changes including legitimate changes.

The WIPO treaties include language that rights management information will be protected but only when the information is knowingly altered for the purpose of enabling infringement.

Section III
Education and Copyright

Chapter Fourteen
Myths and Misperceptions from Perspectives of Educators and Copyright Owners[*]

by
Janis H. Bruwelheide

Professor of Education
Montana State University–Bozeman

I. Introduction

The subject of copyright is one that often baffles and confuses educators. Part of the problem is the complexity of the matter, and another part is a rapidly changing environment which appears to have outgrown current law, guidelines, and interpretations. There is little help available at most educational institutions to assist educators in making decisions regarding use of copyrighted works for educational purposes. Moreover, it is very difficult to seek permission or obtain clarification from

---

copyright owners, when they can be located, or to extend use beyond what is generally considered a fair use. Educators often believe that copyright owners do not understand how teachers and faculty work in a daily classroom or instructional environment. Copyright owners may think that educators want to abuse fair use and other privileges to escape payment or the hassles of seeking permission.

Current copyright law and guidelines provide educators with some flexibility. Newer technologies push the envelope, and guidelines for mixed media, imaging, and distance education are badly needed. The Conference on Fair Use (CONFU) offers some promise of guidelines if a majority of users and copyright owners can reach agreement on them.

President Clinton formed the Information Infrastructure Task Force in 1993 to explore issues and to develop and implement a plan for the administration's vision for the national information infrastructure (the NII). The Working Group on Intellectual Property Rights in the Electronic Environment was established to examine intellectual property issues for the NII and make recommendations concerning changes to U.S. intellectual property law and policy. A public hearing was held by the Working Group in November 1993, and written comments were solicited until December 10, 1993.[1] After a review period the Working Group released a draft report in July 1994.[2] The Working Group heard testimony during September 1994, and read comments during the next four months. The White Paper, released in September 1995, set forth the Working Group's examination, analyses, and recommendations for each major area of intellectual property law and focused heavily on copyright law.[3] The White Paper has been described by educators and librarians as very pro–copyright owner, and it is controversial. After its release, the White Paper's recommendations were introduced as amendments to the Copyright Act, and they are wending their way through the legislative process.[4]

---

1. INTELLECTUAL PROPERTY AND THE NATIONAL INFORMATION INFRASTRUCTURE: THE REPORT OF THE WORKING GROUP ON INTELLECTUAL PROPERTY RIGHTS 1–2 (1995) [hereinafter White Paper].

2. INTELLECTUAL PROPERTY AND THE NATIONAL INFORMATION INFRASTRUCTURE: A PRELIMINARY DRAFT OF THE REPORT OF THE WORKING GROUP ON INTELLECTUAL RIGHTS (1994) [hereinafter Green Paper].

3. White Paper, *supra* note 1, at 4.

4. *See* H.R. 2441 and S. 1284, 104th Cong., 1st Sess. (1996).

The Conference on Fair Use (CONFU) was convened by the Commissioner of Patents and Trademarks to bring together representatives of library and education associations and copyright owners to discuss issues related to fair use and possibly develop guidelines for uses of copyrighted materials by educators and librarians.[5]

CONFU participants began meeting in September 1994, and talks continued through fall 1996. After considerable discussion, six areas of educational fair use were identified as potentials for the development of guidelines and consideration by smaller working groups: multimedia, electronic reserves, software, distance learning, interlibrary loan, and visual images. To date, negotiations and discussions have proceeded at an erratic pace with varying degrees of success. According to one report summarizing the recent meetings,[6] electronic reserves negotiations were described as the most troubled. The subsequent draft document lacked support from larger user organizations as well as from publisher groups and will not be sent forward as CONFU guidelines. As of December 1996, some of the proposed guidelines are on schedule and in near final form: multimedia, distance learning, and visual images. The interlibrary loan group has reported that it is too soon to develop guidelines on interlibrary lending of digital works.

Perhaps a clearer understanding of both the education and copyright owner perspective is needed. This chapter explores common myths and misperceptions held by many educators and copyright owners (which perhaps impede progress), and makes suggestions for consideration by both sides. The term "educator" is used to encompass teachers and faculty in not-for-profit educational environments, kindergarten through adult students. Before identifying and discussing the myths, sections of the copyright law that are particularly relevant for education are discussed to ensure a common basis for understanding.

---

5.   Green Paper, *supra* note 2, at 4.
6.   Georgia Harper, CONFU: The Conference on Fair Use (web page), 1996;
     <http://www.utsystem.edu/OGC/IntellectualProperty/mds>.

II. The Copyright Act of 1976[7]

A. Exclusive Rights of Copyright Holder

Copyright owners are afforded certain exclusive rights under the copyright law. In exchange for making their works available to the public, copyright owners may sell or give away these rights, whether in whole or in part. Unless the copyright holder grants permission, other uses of copyrighted materials are an infringement absent fair use or other exemption. Five exclusive rights belong to the copyright owner:

1. To reproduce the copyrighted work in copies or phonorecords;
2. To prepare derivative works;
3. To distribute copies or phonorecords of the copyrighted work to the public;
4. In the case of literary, musical, dramatic, and choreographic works, pantomimes, motion pictures and other audiovisual works, to perform the copyrighted works publicly; and
5. For literary, musical, dramatic, and choreographic works, pantomimes, and pictorial, graphic or sculptural works, including the individual images of a motion picture or other audiovisual work, to display the copyrighted work publicly.[8]

B. Fair Use

The copyright law provides for the limited use of a copyrighted work without obtaining the copyright holder's permission. This use includes reproduction of portions of the work and is called "fair use" for the purposes of criticism, comment, news reporting, teaching, scholarship, or research.[9]

Four factors are applied to determine whether use of a copyrighted work is a fair use:

1. The purpose and character of the use, including whether such use is of a commercial nature or is for nonprofit educational purposes;
2. The nature of a copyrighted work;

---

7.   17 U.S.C. §§ 101–1101 (1994).
8.   17 U.S.C. § 106 (1994).
9.   *Id.* § 107.

3. The amount and substantiality of the portion used in relation to the copyrighted work as a whole; and
4. The effect of the use upon the potential market for or value of the copyrighted work.[10]

While all four factors are supposed to be considered equally when deciding whether a use is fair, some cases demonstrated that the fourth factor appears to be more heavily weighted.[11]

In recent cases, however, the U.S. Supreme Court seems to have reconsidered the issue somewhat.[12]

C. Face-to-Face Teaching Activities

One of the best but nevertheless most frustrating parts of the current Act is the section referred to as the classroom exemption.[13]

The "face-to-face" teaching activities limitations on exclusive rights exempts from copyright liability instructors and pupils involved in "face-to-face" instruction in a nonprofit educational institution. Any part of a work may be displayed or performed in class whenever there is face-to-face teaching activity. The statute requires that copies of audiovisual works used are lawfully made copies or originals. Students and teacher must be present simultaneously in the same general area although not necessarily in sight of each other. Some legal entities have interpreted this situation to mean that the activity can occur on the same physical plant as long as the buildings are joined together. Entertainment and recreation applications are excluded from using the section 110 exemption. The House Report uses the terminology that the instruction must take place in a classroom or similar place devoted to instruction which is being used as a classroom for systematic instructional activities.[14] Under these conditions, authorization is given to students and instructors engaged in face-to-face instructional activities to use copyrighted works. Most schools take the position that when in doubt, an instructor should ask permission. Permission is not extended to

---

10. *Id.*
11. *See* Harper & Row Publishers, Inc. v. The Nation Enters., 471 U.S. 539 (1985).
12. *See* Campbell v. Acuff-Rose Music, Inc., 114 S. Ct. 1164 (1994).
13. 17 U.S.C. § 110(1) (1994).
14. H.R. REP. NO. 94-1476, 94th Cong., 2d Sess., *reprinted in* OMNIBUS COPYRIGHT LEGIS-LATIVE HISTORY OF THE COPYRIGHT ACT OF 1976 82 (1977) [hereinafter H.R. REP. NO. 94-1476].

transmitting these materials via networks such as interactive television or satellite, however, without the copyright holder's approval.

According to the House Report, "broadcasting or other transmissions from an outside location into classrooms . . . whether open or closed circuit" is prohibited.[15]

Attorneys for various organizations within higher education are very divided on this issue as it applies to distance education, so readers should consult legal counsel for clarification and support and make sure that a policy statement exists. There is nothing in this section of the Act which gives permission to tape at a remote site for archival or review purposes.

III. The Myths

A. Myths Held by Educators

1. Coursepacks may be freely compiled and used for educational reasons.
2. The "10-percent rule" is part of the law and applies to all types of materials.
3. Absence of a copyright notice means that the material is in the public domain.
4. Educators may preserve or make archival (backup) copies of all types of media, print and nonprint.
5. Anything from the Internet may be freely used and "pasted" into new works.
6. Photographs and images may be scanned and used on any Web page.
7. "Home Use" videos may be used for entertainment purposes in a classroom.
8. No publisher will pay any attention to what is done in this institution since it is just a small community college.
9. There is no problem with placing materials on reserve in the library in lieu of using a coursepack since the royalties for coursepacks are so high.

---

15.   *Id.* at 81.

10. There is nothing wrong with copying computer software that another teacher purchased since both will be using it for educational purposes.
11. Since nonprofit music performances by the school choir are exempted, there is no problem with recording the concert and distributing copies of the recording to performers and their parents.
12. As long as it is for educational purposes, there is no problem with scanning and using anything in a multimedia product.
13. There is no difference in distance learning and face-to-face teaching when it comes to the use of copyrighted materials.
14. Cartoon characters may be used freely to illustrate lessons, decorate classroom bulletin boards, newsletters, art projects, etc.
15. Any use of copyrighted material can be considered appropriate in an educational setting as long as there is no charge for it.
16. States, state agencies, and their employees cannot be sued for copyright infringements.

B. Myths Held by Copyright Owners

1. Educators want to deprive copyright owners of rightful profits.
2. Educators have plenty of lead time and assistance to request permission to use materials beyond what can be considered to be a fair use.
3. The complaints that educators make concerning lack of funding to pay user fees are unfounded.
4. Educators want to create new works from copyrighted works without seeking permission or paying fees.
5. Educators want to archive (backup) all audiovisual media automatically because they do not want to pay for additional copies or rentals.
6. The classroom copying guidelines were intended to be interpreted as maximum standards for educational fair use copying, not as minimum standards.
7. The only classroom is one in which an educator is physically face-to-face and present under the same roof as the students.
8. Publishers make it easy and cost effective to obtain licenses for the use of copyrighted works beyond the classroom exemption.
9. Virtually anything a teacher might want to use is covered by the Copyright Clearance Center.

10. Educators are constantly finding ways to avoid paying royalties for coursepacks or for materials placed on reserve in the library.
11. The only uses a teacher may make of copyrighted works are covered under the classroom guidelines and the face-to-face teaching exemption.
12. No copying of sheet music or recorded music is permitted under any circumstances, even for educational use.
13. There is no need for teacher- or student-developed multimedia products since publishers will produce those products for sale to the education market.

C. Educators' Myths: The Reality

1. Coursepacks and Anthologies May Be Freely Compiled and Used for Educational Reasons as a Fair Use Substitute for a Textbook. Scanners and photocopiers make it so easy to duplicate materials that surely it is permissible to create coursepacks, or so educators would like to believe. The *Kinko's*[16] case provided publishers with ammunition for elimination of coursepacks unless permission is sought, fees are paid, and guidelines are followed. While the case was not an outright indictment against the creation of coursepacks and anthologies at the request of faculty members, it brought home the point that flagrant copying of copyrighted materials under a fair use claim would not be upheld. Since that time, many universities and colleges require their faculty to seek permission.

In February 1996, the Sixth Circuit reversed a lower court opinion and found that defendant Michigan Document Services (MDS) had made a fair use of copyrighted materials when it created coursepacks for students and professors in its vicinity.[17] Facts in the case were similar to the *Kinko's* case except that the defendant is not a nationwide chain. Rumors and misinformation about the overturning of the *Kinko's* decision spread quickly to educational institutions via the Internet and other means. The court reheard the case *en banc* and upheld the district court's decision that the copying by MDS was not

16. Basic Books, Inc. v. Kinko's Graphics Corp., 758 F. Supp. 1522 (S.D.N.Y. 1991).
17. Princeton Univ. Press v. Michigan Document Servs., Inc., 1996 WL 54741, at 12 (6th Cir. Feb. 12, 1996).

fair use.[18] One crucial issue in the case is whether the for-profit copy shop's uses of coursepacks is fair. Publishers did *not* argue, however, that the same coursepacks, if prepared by the faculty or students, would not have been a fair use.[19]

The Guidelines For Classroom Copying were published in the House Report.[20] Although they are not the law, these guidelines provide teachers and librarians with *minimum* guidelines as to the fair use of copyrighted materials reproduced from books and periodicals for classroom use as agreed to by publishers and some education associations.[21] It should be noted that fair use may justify copying beyond the minimum guidelines.[22] These guidelines apply to multiple copying of protected works for distributing one copy to each student in a class.

There are three tests that must be applied under the guidelines: brevity, spontaneity, and cumulative effect. Current news periodicals, newspapers, and current news sections of periodicals are not affected by the tests for spontaneity and cumulative effect. The test for brevity defines parameters for length. The classroom guidelines for prose delineate minimum standards for copying by and for educators. The limit may be extended slightly to permit completion of a line or paragraph.[23] Brevity includes the following: "Prose: (a) Either a complete article, story or essay of less than 2,500 words, or (b) an excerpt from any prose work of not more than 1,000 words or 10 percent of the work, whichever is less, but in any event a minimum of 500 words."[24]

There are two parts to the test for spontaneity. The first is that copying is done only at the instigation of the teacher. In other words, a higher authority cannot require the teacher to reproduce a

---

18. Michigan Document Servs., Inc. v. Princeton Univ. Press, 99 F.3d 1381 (6th Cir. 1997).
19. Georgia Harper, Coursepacks and Fair Use: Issues Raised by the Michigan Document Services Case (web page) (Apr. 16, 1996) <http://www.utsystem.edu/OGC/IntellectualProperty/mds>.
20. H.R. REP. NO. 94-1476, *supra* note 14, at 68.
21. The National Education Association and the American Association of University Professors were signatories.
22. H.R. REP. NO. 94-1476, *supra* note 14, at 68. Circular 21 from the Copyright Office, *Reproduction of Copyrighted Works by Educators and Libraries* (1992) contains excerpts of testimony as well as the guidelines that are useful for educators.
23. H.R. Rep. No. 94-1476, *supra* note 14, at 69.
24. *Id.* at 68.

copyrighted work. Secondly, the decision to use the work for maximum effect is so spontaneous that it is not realistic to expect a reply to a permissions request.

Section II deals with cumulative effect for multiple copying.

  (i)   The copying of the material is for only one course in the school in which the copies are made.
  (ii) Not more than one short poem, article, story, essay or two excerpts may be copied from the same author, nor more than three from the same collective work or periodical volume during one class term.
  (iii) There shall not be more than nine instances of such multiple copying during one class term.[25]

Several prohibitions are also set forth in section III of the guidelines, and these have been used by foes of coursepacks.

  (A) Copying shall not be used to create or to replace or substitute for anthologies, compilations, or collective works.
  (B) There shall be no copying of or from works intended to be "consumable."
  (C) Copying shall not:
       (a) substitute for the purchase of books, publishers' reprints or periodicals;
       (b) be directed by higher authority;
       (c) be repeated with respect to the same item by the same teacher from term to term.
  (D) No charge shall be made to the student beyond the actual cost of the photocopying.[26]

2. The "10% Rule" Means I May Copy 10% of a Work; This Is Part of the Law and Applies to All Types of Materials. The "10-percent rule" has been commonly followed by many educators as a guideline for reproducing copyrighted materials. *There is no such rule,* however, either as a part of the statute or case law. A clause in section 107, which is a continual source of friction and confusion, is the third factor: the amount and substantiality used of the copyrighted work. The guidelines for classroom copying and educational use of music suggest that copying 10 percent or less of the total work is fair use. If the amount is a "substantial portion" or represents the essence of the work which

---

25.   *Id.* at 69.
26.   *Id.* at 69–70.

might affect sales if copied and distributed, then the use is not considered to be a fair use. Further, in the classroom guidelines, the quantitative measure for prose is 2500 words or less if a complete article is reproduced, or 1000 words, or an excerpt of 10 percent, whichever is less.[27] While the guidelines indicate 10 percent of a short work that is no more than 1000 words is fair use, 10 percent of a 500-page book may not be fair use. It certainly is not prudent to apply this percentage to various forms of multimedia materials until appropriate new guidelines are developed.

Another source of this myth is Guidelines for Educational Uses of Music also published in the House Report.[28] The Music Guidelines also contained a reference to using no more than 10 percent of a whole work. Many educational organizations have implemented a 10-percent rule as an administrative guideline for educators. Although it is not part of the law, it often is used as a rule of thumb in some institutions. The Music Guidelines' mention of 10 percent extends only to a single copy of a non-performable unit for academic purposes, however.[29]

Schools that rely on a 10-percent rule should be aware that there is a risk in assuming that 10 percent automatically is fair use. Neither the classroom nor music guidelines provide much support for an absolute 10-percent rule.

3. *Absence of a Copyright Notice Indicates That the Material Is in the Public Domain.* Until March 1, 1989, lack of the notice was some indication that a work was in the public domain. When the United States joined the Berne Convention in 1988, however, the copyright owner no longer had to affix a copyright notice to a work.[30] Removal of this formality certainly makes it more difficult to determine whether a work is protected by copyright. It means that one must assume everything fixed in a tangible medium is copyrighted unless it is a U.S. government publication or the work specifically says there is no claim of copyright.

---

27.   *Id.* at 68.
28.   *Id.* at 70.
29.   *Id.* at 71.
30.   17 U.S.C. § 401 (1994).

4. Educators May Preserve or Make Archival (Backup) Copies of All Types of Media, Both Print and Nonprint. This myth is a common one and stems primarily from section 117 of the Copyright Act[31] which applies only to computer programs and, unfortunately, does not extend to other forms of media. There are two instances where duplication of a copyrighted computer program is permissible by the lawful owner of a copy of that program. The first instance is when use of the program requires creation of a copy as an essential step to permit the software to run on a specific computer.

The second instance, which is the primary source of this myth, permits the making of a copy for archival (backup) reasons only. The intent of this provision is for the archival copy of a computer software program to be stored in case the original becomes damaged. It may not serve as a second copy. Only one archival copy is to exist at one time. Of course, licensing agreements could extend these privileges. Software publishers differ tremendously in their provision of rights and must always be consulted for their policies.

Another source of this myth is found in section 108(c) for libraries and archives, which deals with replacement of published deteriorating, lost, damaged, or stolen materials.[32] A library may replace such an item with a reproduction if an unused copy cannot be located at a fair price. This also applies to media such as videotapes, but the reproduction cannot be made until after the loss or deterioration has occurred. This seems ridiculous to educators who usually cannot replace a copy with a new, unused copy because one often is no longer available. Further, they have to borrow a copy from elsewhere to reproduce since their copy is now damaged or destroyed and cannot be used to duplicate another copy.

5. Anything Found on the Internet May Be Freely Used, Reposted, and "Cut" and "Pasted" into New Works. There is a common misperception that works distributed and available on the Internet are there to be used in any way and for any reason and that copyright does not apply. Such is not the case. Elimination of the copyright notice requirement is one explanation for the confusion. Many people still believe that only works which contain a copyright notice are protected. Another reason is the

---

31.   *Id.* § 117(2).
32.   *Id.* § 108(c).

ease of access and copying for users of the Internet and its various browsers. Because works on the Internet are obviously fixed in a tangible medium, items found on listservs, Usenet, e-mail, or in any other area are copyrighted unless there is specific language to the contrary on the work. On the other hand, fair use provisions apply to materials found on the Internet. Users should ask permission before reposting anything beyond fair use since distribution is one of the rights of copyright owners. Some groups post messages as to the status of postings and subscription instructions also may contain some information. Sometimes individuals who post messages and information put a disclaimer at the end or beginning of a posting, which is helpful. Publishers are very concerned about potential abuse because of the ease of reproducing these works and the ease of electronic manipulation.

6. Photographs and Images May Be Scanned and Used on Any Web Page. Easy access and copying capability as well as the lack of copyright notice are likewise possible explanations for this myth. People seem to believe that because it is so easy to duplicate copyrighted works that it is also permissible to do so. Educators do not always understand that photographs and images are copyrighted especially when they appear in a collection of works or are readily available in formats such as post cards and the like which seem to be freely distributed. Absent a transfer of rights, the photographer holds the copyright. Photographs are subject to fair use considerations just as anything else. Lack of notice can make it difficult to determine who really owns the copyright. Educators often are unsure about when to seek permission to use photographs and how to go about the task, but this does not relieve them of the responsibility. Royalty-free photograph collections are becoming more available, which will perhaps simplify the use of this medium.

7. "Home Use" Videos May Be Used for Entertainment Purposes in Classrooms. This myth is widespread and is an issue of contention with copyright owners and users as well. The two-tier terminology of "home use videos" and "videos with public performance rights" is very confusing to members of the education community. Section 110(1) of the Act exempts the performance and display of works for face-to-face teaching and covers most educational uses of videos as well as other media.[33]

Where section 110(1) does not apply, the fair use doctrine may permit other showings as long as the video is part of an instructional lesson plan. The use of a video for entertainment without performance rights, however, whether for rewards or after school programs is not permitted. Because of the confusion, some educational entities have taken an extreme position and completely prohibited use of videos labeled "home use" or rented from stores. Such a position certainly deprives educators of flexibility and prevents students from using video formats in instructional ways. Other entities do not place this restriction on video use since they believe that section 110(1) trumps the "home use only" provision.[34]

8. No Publisher Will Pay Any Attention to What Is Done in this Institution Since It Is Just a Small Community College. Often comments are made that the size of an institution or its geographical location (isolation) provides some protection from violation detection. However, this certainly is not the case. Organizations that investigate copyright violations, such as the Software Publishers Association and the Association for Information Media and Equipment, have investigated violations and found infringing activities in a wide variety of locations and types of institutions. When the author queried an employee at the Association of American Publishers concerning coursepack detection, she was told that the Association employs people who scan college and university bookstores looking for coursepacks which may be infringements. Occasionally a disgruntled or fed-up employee of an institution will report situations that can lead to investigations. Advertisements have been placed in periodicals and on videocassettes offering possible rewards for reports of violations. For these reasons it is important to show a record of compliance and maintain a paper trail.

9. There Is No Problem with Placing Materials on Reserve in the Library in Lieu of Using a Coursepack Since the Royalties for Coursepacks Are So High. Library reserves are a way to supplement classroom activities

---

33. *Id.* § 110(1).
34. *See* LAURA N. GASAWAY & SARAH K. WIANT, LIBRARIES AND COPYRIGHT: A GUIDE TO COPYRIGHT IN THE 1990s 104 (1994).

and are often viewed as an extension of the classroom. Almost fifteen years ago the American Library Association published the *Model Policy Concerning College and University Photocopying for Classroom, Research, and Library Reserve Use*[35] to provide suggestions on using photocopied materials for reserve collections. The Model Policy is accepted widely and followed by libraries, and although publishers say they never agreed to them, the guidelines have never been litigated. There are some problems with the Model Policy and its practical application for libraries, however. Examples include restrictions on copying that do not meet the needs of undergraduate and graduate students, ambiguity of terms such as "reasonable amount," and referral of users to the classroom guidelines. The classroom guidelines contain provisions simply not applicable to reserve rooms. Thus, it is not surprising that coursepacks look attractive as an alternative. The reserve guidelines are not to be used in this fashion, however. A coursepack is a coursepack no matter how it is packaged.

The Model Policy focuses on reasonability. The amount of material placed on reserve should be reasonable in relation to the other materials assigned for the course. This indicates that all of the material for a course should not be placed on reserve instead of having students purchase a textbook or a coursepack. Further, the number of copies placed on reserve should be reasonable; reasonable in relation to the number of students in the class, how quickly the material has to be read, and what else is assigned.[36]

What is clear is that reproductions of most copyrighted materials such as journal articles should not be placed on reserve indefinitely without permission unless the publisher grants blanket permission for educational purposes. Normally, these publications will contain a statement to this effect. Readers should monitor outcome of the CONFU meetings and negotiations on electronic reserve guidelines which may provide guidance on establishing and maintaining reserve collections in digital format if the guidelines are finally adopted and accepted.

---

35.   AMERICAN LIBRARY ASSOCIATION, MODEL POLICY CONCERNING COLLEGE AND UNIVERSITY PHOTOCOPYING FOR CLASSROOM RESEARCH AND LIBRARY RESERVE USE (1982).

36.   *Id.* For the ALA Reserve Guidelines, see *infra* Appendix F (p. 497).

10. There Is Nothing Wrong with Copying Computer Software That Another Teacher Purchased Since Both Will Be Using It for Educational Purposes. Copying illegally is wrong—the purpose is irrelevant. If another teacher purchases the software, then he or she is the one who may exercise the archival copying provision according to the law. The backup cannot be used as a second copy. The purchaser of copyrighted software purchased the right to make a copy of the software when it is a necessary step to utilize it on his or her machine, such as to load it on the hard drive.[37] Other reproduction of the software to use the copy is prohibited unless the copyright owner permits the copying. Most software is governed by license agreements, and librarians and educators should consult the license agreement when in doubt about uses or reproduction of the software. If the use or copying is not mentioned in the license, then check with the software publisher.

11. Because Nonprofit Music Performances by the School Choir Are Exempted, There Is No Problem with Recording the Concert and Distributing Copies of the Recording to Performers and Their Parents. Performing the music is not the same issue as recording and distributing copies of the performance. Recording the music and distributing the copies would likely require permission and/or royalties whether copies are given away or sold. Usually fees would be levied on *all* copies distributed and not just ones which were sold. The same interpretation would apply to videotaping a school concert or holiday performance which contained music. If the instructor wanted to tape the performance for the purposes of aural exercise, evaluation, or examination, a single copy can be made under the Guidelines on the Educational Uses of Music.[38] The guidelines allow for a single copy of student performances to be made for evaluation and rehearsal purposes. Either the teacher or institution may retain the copy.[39]

Certain performances of music in schools and libraries are not infringements under section 110. For example, music may be performed without seeking permission or paying royalties under the face-to-face classroom exemption.[40] If certain requirements are met, music may be

---

37.   17 U.S.C. § 117 (1994).
38.   H.R. Rep. No. 94-1476, *supra* note 14, at 71.
39.   *Id.*
40.   17 U.S.C. § 110(1).

performed royalty free in instructional broadcasting.[41] It may also be performed in nonprofit performances where there is no payment of fees to anyone involved in organizing the performance or performing the music if no admission is charged. If admission is charged, proceeds must be used for educational or charitable purposes.[42] The music guidelines also provide guidance for the reproduction of sheet music.[43]

12. As Long As It Is for Educational Purposes, There Is No Problem with Scanning and Using Anything in a Multimedia Product. For use in face-to-face teaching where the product is not leaving the classroom, there is reason to believe that there should be leeway under fair use especially if the item was not a permanent one and only small portions of a copyrighted work are used. Section 110(1), however, permits performance but not reproduction of the works. Moreover, once an item leaves the classroom, it would lose the fair use privileges. If the work becomes fixed, it might even be viewed as a derivative work. The medium is not usually the issue: copying or performing of the work is the concern. Therefore, under existing law, permissions must be sought.

Seeking permissions can be very difficult because of the wide range of materials that might be used in a multimedia product, and costs can be prohibitive. Usually there is no single entity that owns the rights to all of the works needed to create a multimedia program. To produce a single multimedia work, for example, rights might be needed from at least the following entities: the music publisher, record company, artists, photographers, print publisher, television producer, movie producer, and others. Additionally, a developer must think not only of the rights a work and its potential users will need to consider in licensing negotiations, but also what additional possible future uses for the work, such as online distribution, may require. To further complicate the matter, the publisher of a journal may only own the one-time right to use a photograph and each photographer would consequently have to be contacted by the multimedia developer.

New guidelines for faculty-developed multimedia produced by the Coalition of College and University Media Centers with input from CONFU provide guidance for the creation and in-class use of

---

41.   *Id.* § 110(2).

42.   *Id.* § 110(4).

43.   H.R. REP. NO. 94-1476, *supra* note 14, at 70.

multimedia products.[44] These guidelines limit use to two years and have strict portion limitations such as how many seconds of a movie may be used, the number of photographs from one photographer, etc. Any efforts to share the multimedia product with other teachers (except to display it at a conference) or efforts to commercialize it is outside of these guidelines.[45]

13. There Is No Difference Between Distance Learning and Face-to-face Teaching; They Are Exactly the Same Thing When It Comes to the Use of Copyrighted Materials. How educators wish this were true. There are several gray areas in copyright, and distance learning is a big one. Many people believe that if the performance of a copyrighted work for distance learning occurs within a building but not outside of it, there is no problem. Other individuals argue that students and teachers must be present simultaneously in the same general location. There are also opposite opinions concerning how much copyrighted material may be transmitted or broadcast over a distance-education network without proper written permission or licensing agreements.

The reality is that it falls somewhere in the middle under current law. Section 110(2) provides that for "instructional broadcasting," a teacher may perform a nondramatic literary or musical work or display a work for nonprofit distance education if certain conditions are met. These conditions include that the performance be part of systematic instruction and that reception be in a classroom or similar place normally devoted to instruction.[46] Thus, the Act treats different types of works differently and focuses on the place of reception[47] as being important.

CONFU also has developed distance-learning guidelines which basically extend the face-to-face teaching exemption to the one-time performance of even an entire work to enrolled students in all types of

---

44.   For the Multimedia Guidelines, see *infra* Appendix H (p. 505).

45.   *See also* DIANE J. BRINSON & MARK F. RADCLIFFE, THE INTELLECTUAL PROPERTY LAW PRIMER FOR MULTIMEDIA DEVELOPERS (1994). An abridged version is available online at: <http://www.eff.org>.

46.   17 U.S.C. § 110(2) (1994).

47.   For a discussion of distance learning and copyright, see *infra* Chapter Seventeen (p. 377), "Copyright and Distance Education: Displays, Performances, and Limitations of Current Law," by Kenneth D. Crews.

distance-learning programs except asynchronous computer network delivery.[48]

14. Cartoon Characters May Be Used Freely to Illustrate Lessons, Decorate Classroom Bulletin Boards, Newsletters, Art Projects, Etc. The Classroom Guidelines provide permission to use copies of cartoon characters in a limited sense. For example, you can make multiple copies of a single illustration to distribute to a class if the requirements of the guidelines are met.[49] Also, a cartoon may be posted, i.e., displayed on a bulletin board or to a class, but section 110(1) does not permit reproduction of the work.[50]

Using cartoons in other ways is likely to be considered a derivative work, and this right belongs to the copyright owner. Changing a cartoon into a graphical image for a bulletin board, newsletter, or poster is such a derivative work. Rights to use graphics in this fashion would need to be acquired and usually this process is very costly. Owners of the rights to cartoon characters zealously protect these rights—they must do so to protect ownership. Disney, for example, has tenaciously pursued schools for using its characters beyond the parameters of fair use. The same rules apply to the use of slogans and trademarked images.

15. Any Use of Copyrighted Material Can Be Considered Appropriate in an Educational Setting as Long as There Is No Charge for It. Charging for copies of the material is not the issue. What matters is the reproduction, performance, and display of copyrighted works. Rights of copyright owners are infringed whether a charge is made or not. A potential market for sales and/or licensing may be harmed.

16. States, State Agencies, and Their Employees Cannot Be Sued for Copyright Infringements. The issue of sovereign immunity was clarified in 1990. For many years there was debate as to whether state entities and employees were immune or could be held liable for copyright infringements under the Eleventh Amendment of the U.S. Constitution. Legislation was unclear and courts were divided in opinion. In November 1990, a new section was added to the Copyright Act which clarified the issue. It stated that state entities, agencies, and employees *were not*

---

48.   For the Distance Learning Guidelines, see *infra* Appendix J (p. 535).

49.   H.R. REP. NO. 94-1476, *supra* note 14, at 68.

50.   17 U.S.C. § 110(1) (1994).

immune from suits for copyright infringements and could be held liable for copyright violations.[51] A recent case has again raised some question about whether states are immune to suit,[52] but the matter is far from clear. Before assuming that an institution is immune from suit, educators should consult their university counsel.

D. Copyright Owners' Myths: The Reality

1. Educators Want to Deprive Copyright Owners of Rightful Profits. Perhaps the key to understanding the origin of this myth is in the word "rightful." The majority of educators do not object to paying a fair price for materials with reasonable rights. Often, however, copyright owners make it difficult or impossible to obtain permissions, demand outrageous fees for use, and do not respond to inquiries in a timely fashion. Educators may believe that if they request permission for the use but do not receive answer, then they can go ahead and use the work. They do not always see the problem if no commercial use is being made of the materials and since section 107 specifically mentions teaching as an exemplary of fair use.

2. Educators Have Plenty of Lead Time and Assistance to Request Permission to Use Materials Beyond Fair Use. Educators do plan instruction ahead of time but must be sensitive to issues such as the teachable moment, relevancy, and other miscellaneous factors which can alter a lesson plan or class with little advance notice. Thus, the teachable moment might be lost if postponed to a future time and the copyrighted materials might lose relevancy. Plans change, new events occur, and timing is everything. So there may not be sufficient lead time to seek permission or wait for an answer.

The issue of currency is a critical one for education. The Classroom Guidelines include a statement on spontaneity:

(i)   The copying is at the instance and inspiration of the individual teacher, and

(ii) The inspiration and decision to use the work and the moment of its use for maximum teaching effectiveness are so close in time

---

51.   *Id.* § 511.

52.   *See* Seminole Tribe of Florida v. Florida, 116 S. Ct. 1114 (1996).

that it would be unreasonable to expect a timely reply to a request for permission.[53]

Usually there is little to no assistance or support provided to educators to handle the permissions process, which can be extremely time consuming and intimidating. Access to information concerning how to seek permissions is often unavailable, and it requires extensive knowledge about where to go and how to seek permission.[54]

For coursepacks, the Copyright Clearance Center's (CCC) Academic Permissions Service (APS) and the availability of blanket permissions with more than 4000 publishers has helped considerably. The CCC's home page further facilitates permissions requests when the fees are posted for that work. The APS, however, only deals with coursepacks for printed works, and teachers use a much wider variety of types of works in their teaching.

3. The Complaints That Educators Make Concerning Lack of Funding to Pay Fees Are Unfounded. According to a recent survey, the United States spends an average of $125 per K through 12 student each year on copyrighted materials and textbooks.[55] Because an average figure was used and not the more indicative mean, this indicates clearly that many districts spend less. When considering the wide variety of content and the importance of currency and timeliness, this money does not go very far. Higher education is in a similar condition, but costs are usually passed on to the students. University and college textbook prices may be very expensive depending on the field.

Funds for educational materials are not unlimited. Educators have endured very tight budgets since the 1980s. Legislators are not loosening their purse strings, nor are the voters. Further, in many public school districts, materials must be provided to students free of charge. Thus, schools, themselves underfunded, have no source for funds to pay permission fees.

---

53. H.R. REP. NO. 94-1476, *supra* note 14, at 69.
54. *See* Campbell v. Acuff-Rose Music, Inc., 114 S. Ct. 1164 (1994).
55. David Rothman, *Copyright and K-12: Who Pays in the Network Era* (June 1996) <http://www.ed.gov/Technology/futures/rothman.html>.

4. Educators Want to Create New Works from Copyrighted Works Without Seeking Permission or Paying Fees. This often stems from lack of understanding concerning copyright and fair use for education. Another possible explanation is because technology makes it so easy to create new formats and compilations, educators may not see that it violates owners' rights. In any event, this use may be a so-called productive or transformative use that the courts often approve.[56]

Productive use implies a use in creating a new work—for example, in criticism or scholarship—but it is not simply compiling works into something like a coursepack. Some believe that it would be very difficult to teach or learn if transformative uses were not permitted under fair use.

On the other hand, most teachers are very law abiding. They want to be fair to copyright owners but still want to perform their duties to educate students.

5. Educators Want to Archive (Back up) All Audiovisual Media Automatically Because They Do Not Want to Pay for Additional Copies or Rentals. This myth is rooted mostly in an idea that teachers lack understanding and have bad information. Because section 108 of the Act provides limited copying for libraries, and because section 117 permits archival copying of computer software, the idea of archival copying has been over generalized to all formats. Maybe educators want to do this, but they are learning that they cannot. Since budgets are limited, two copies of media seldom are permitted by the budget. Further, accidents do happen to audiovisual media whether mechanical or human in origin, and publishers should realize that by the time a second copy is needed, the item is often out of print and unavailable. Thus, the content of the media is lost for all practical purposes.

Under section 108 a library may replace a lost, damaged, stolen, or deteriorating audiovisual work with a reproduction after the library first tries to obtain an unused copy. Additionally, the unused copy must be available at a fair price.[57] The problem, however, is that the reproduction can be made only after the damage has occurred. In the interim, while searching for a copy to purchase, the teachable moment may be lost.

---

56.   *Acuff-Rose*, 114 S. Ct. at 1164.
57.   17 U.S.C. § 108(c), (g) (1994).

6. The Classroom Copying Guidelines Were Intended to Be Interpreted as Maximum Standards for Educational Fair Use Copying, Not as Minimum Standards. The legislative history accompanying the Act states clearly that the purpose of the guidelines is to state the minimum and not the maximum standards of educational fair use under section 107.[58] Parties who agreed to the guidelines suggested a more lenient approach to copying instead of the narrower approach some parties attempt to impose today.

7. The Only Classroom Is One in Which the Educator Is Physically Face-to-face and Present under the Same Roof as the Students. Today's two-way interactive technologies make it possible for students and educators to be separated geographically but still face-to-face, such as in desktop videoconferencing or two-way interactive television. Increasingly, courses are being delivered via distance learning, and the future will be away from the traditional classroom because of the flexibility technology offers in teaching methodology. Section 110(2) of the Act deals with transmission of certain types of copyrighted works over a network if particular conditions are satisfied, but it excludes other types of works. CONFU has produced distance learning guidelines which recognize the change in the way courses are delivered.[59]

8. Publishers Make It Easy and Cost Effective to Obtain a License for the Use of Copyrighted Works Beyond the Classroom Exemption. Section 110(2) permits instructional broadcasting of displays of any work and performances of nondramatic literary and musical works, if certain conditions are met.[60] Thus, no license to use these works in their entirety, even repeatedly, is needed.

It is counterintuitive to teachers to require them to seek permission to use a work for distance education when they can use the work in face-to-face teaching. Distance learning is a new way to deliver educational content, and it is here to stay. An educator can be "face-to-face" with students electronically, so why should the same provisions not apply to this medium as to the traditional classroom? Admittedly, some environments are less susceptible to people outside the class tuning in

---

58. H.R. Rep. No. 94-1476, *supra* note 14, at 68.
59. For the Distance Learning Guidelines, see *infra* Appendix J (p. 535).
60. 17 U.S.C. § 110(2) (1994).

than others. For example, interactive television or desktop videoconferencing, which is usually "closed" except to class participants, should enjoy the same privileges as a "regular" classroom. Satellite-transmitted courses are more open and may need additional permissions or licenses. One wonders if the problem is the use of copyrighted materials over the distance education network or the possibility of illegal taping at remote sites or by outsiders. Distance learning guidelines provide helpful information for this area.

For repeated performance of works besides nondramatic literary and musical works, a license is needed. It is very difficult and time consuming to obtain permissions and licenses for such uses, particularly for nonprint media. Often the time spent tracking down copyright owners leads to a dead end. Sometimes the owners do not even respond to queries from educators and librarians. Costs can seem very out of proportion for what is sometimes a one-time use request. Usually there is no help at an institution, particularly in the K through12 environment, to conduct the work. Also, the classroom teacher usually has no knowledge of how to proceed in most circumstances.

9. Virtually Anything a Teacher Might Want to Use Is Covered by the Copyright Clearance Center. How we wish this were the case! Journal formats are covered quite well, as are some books, but this is not the case with nonprint media. The CCC is beginning to negotiate to include photographs, but there seems to be little movement to consolidate the licensing of other types of works for use in multimedia in the CCC or a similar organization.

10. Educators Are Constantly Finding Ways to Avoid Paying Royalties for Coursepacks or for Materials Placed on Reserve in the Library. Perhaps some individuals do try to avoid paying royalties, but the majority of educators do not. The problem stems from lack of understanding and clear guidelines. There are also conflicting opinions and interpretations. Reasonable royalties and a mechanism for collecting them are needed when fair use or the reserve guidelines do not apply. The CCC has expressed a willingness to deal with royalties for electronic reserves beyond any guidelines.

11. The Only Uses a Teacher May Make of Copyrighted Works Is under the Classroom Guidelines and the Face-to-face Teaching Exemption. There are a variety of guidelines such as the Music Guidelines and the Off-Air Taping Guidelines[61] that may be used by teachers in addition to the classroom guidelines. CONFU has produced newer guidelines for the electronic media. There also are statutory sections that provide a basis for use of works in education, including section 110, face-to-face teaching. Further, section 107 provides a broad fair use exemption that must be applied on a case-by-case basis.

12. No Copying of Sheet Music or Recorded Music Is Permitted under Any Circumstances Even for Educational Use. Fair use applies to some reproduction of music. The music guidelines definitely provide two instances where sheet music can be copied, and they are quite clear. Emergency copying to replace purchased copies which are not available for an imminent performance is permitted. Further, single or multiple copies of excerpts may be made for study as long as they do not comprise a performable unit or exceed 10 percent of the work. The guidelines also state that a recording may be made for evaluative purposes and retained by the teacher or the institution. Copies may be made for student aural exercises as well.[62]

13. There Is No Need for Teacher- or Student-developed Multimedia Products Since Publishers Will Produce Those Products for Sale to the Education Market. If this were not a myth, the creativity and learning horizons of students and teachers would be severely limited. Publishers are not omnipotent and cannot possibly anticipate every curricular need and application. There always has been and always will be a need for teachers to design some of their own curriculum products. Teachers themselves know their students' best instructional climate, learning styles, and which resources are needed to complement offerings from publishers. Timeliness is also an important consideration. Publishers' offerings can be too dated in some subject areas which are changing rapidly.

---

61.   127 CONG. REC. E4750–52 (1981).
62.   *Id.* at 71.

Moreover, increasingly students will prepare multimedia projects in lieu of formal papers. They must be given the leeway to explore this new technology without having to seek advance permission.[63]

IV. Recommendations

In light of these myths and misperceptions, the following recommendations would help educators and copyright owners to comply more easily with copyright considerations and to understand the other's perspective.

✦ Educators must be responsible when using copyrighted materials, but must follow the educational exemptions or risk the chance of losing privileges or seeing more restrictions develop.

✦ Additional training and education about copyright must be provided to help educators understand a complex subject and be able to apply the law to their daily work.

✦ Copyright owners must make it easier for educators to seek permission and must reply in a timely fashion.

✦ Fees for licensing, reprints, and copying need to be examined to ensure that they are reasonable for education and educators. Affordability is an important issue.

✦ Copyright owners should explore options to make it more affordable for educators to purchase additional copies of a work such as a video or periodicals to use in nontraditional environments and to protect deteriorating copies which may contain irreplaceable content.

✦ A clearing house for nonprint media permissions should be developed similar to the Copyright Clearance Center.

✦ Copyright notices should be displayed more often, or appropriate notices posted on Internet listservs, newsgroups, or Web pages to indicate whether copyright rights are being exercised or whether items are being placed in the public domain. Another suggestion is that list operators post a notice as part of the subscription which asks participants to indicate whether materials are free to be reposted.

---

63. *See infra* Appendix H (p. 505). The Multimedia Guidelines do permit student use of copyrighted works to produce multimedia projects and further allows retention in the student's portfolio.

✦ The networked environment must be utilized to compensate copyright owners appropriately while maintaining easy use and access for educational purposes.

✦ Publishers should consider the electronic environment as an opportunity to supplement their curriculum offerings while making them more timely and perhaps reducing production costs for updating materials through traditional means. Costs to students and educators must be reasonable. If the costs are reasonable and it is easy to obtain permission and pay royalties when due, then there will be little reason for educators not to seek permission when needed. Educators generally have neither the time nor the desire to look for ways to "beat the system."

✦ Teachers and librarians must seize the opportunity to become part of the negotiation process concerning fair use and reasonable compensation schemes. If they do not, they and millions of students will have to live with the consequences.

✦ Guidelines and pending legislation must not ignore the legislative history of the current copyright law which suggested clearly that future guidelines and changes should be cognizant of generous fair use privileges for educators and students. After all, when the current law was drafted, some of the same conversations took place. There were concerns, for example, that photocopiers would prove to be the death of the publishing industry. Concerns then must have been similar among owners and users yet it was possible to draft guidelines which have proven to be very workable and have stood the test of time. Technologies are different today and the environment is certainly more sophisticated, but the use made of copyrighted works remains the same as does the purpose: to educate students. However, the same needs for educators to use copyrighted materials and for owners to receive reasonable returns are still the focal points for discussion.

To cope with growing pains of an increasingly sophisticated technological environment in an era where information is a key to success, there must be a way for educators and copyright owners to work together so that both sides win. Students must not be the losers. After all, a well-educated populace is the foundation for a strong country and a vital economy. Both sides will surely agree on that matter. Providing good education is impossible without current materials and resources that can be used in a variety of instructional environments when and where they are most appropriate. The creativity which produces these resources must be rewarded and encouraged. Growing pains must not be allowed to stunt growth. We must use the opportunity to work together for the common goal of a healthy, information-rich environment supported by a strong educational framework. This way both sides will win.

Chapter Fifteen
Users' Rights to Photocopy:
The Impact of *Texaco*
and *Michigan Document Services*[*]

by
Sarah K. Wiant[**]

Director of the Law Library and Professor of Law
Washington and Lee University

I. Introduction

American copyright law protects the rights of authors, publishers, and users.[1] The law vests authors and publishers with the right to control the reproduction, adaptation, distribution, performance, and display of their

---

[*]   © 1997 Sarah K. Wiant.

[**]   The author is indebted to research assistants Lance McNaughton and Chris Meyer for their many contributions in the preparation of this chapter.

1.   L. RAY PATTERSON & STANLEY W. LINDBERG, THE NATURE OF COPYRIGHT: A LAW OF USERS' RIGHTS 4 (1991) [hereinafter PATTERSON & LINDBERG].

works.[2] This includes the limited right to license or prohibit photo-copying of copyrighted works. Copyright law also vests users with the right, in certain circumstances, to make photocopies without obtaining prior permission and without paying licensing fees. Section 108 of the Copyright Act allows library and archive photocopying and for such things as interlibrary loan at the request of a user;[3] and section 107 allows all users, including libraries and archives,[4] to make fair use of copyrighted materials.[5] While the extent and protections of section 108 are fairly well defined, section 107's protections for unauthorized photocopying are vague and uncertain. This chapter addresses the problem of applying the fair use doctrine to photocopying in the wake of two major photocopying infringement cases: *American Geophysical Union v. Texaco, Inc.*[6] and *Princeton University Press v. Michigan Document Services,*[7] and the impact of these decisions on libraries.

Texaco brought to boil a long-simmering conflict between users and publishers. Texaco, a major international petroleum refiner, maintained a large research laboratory in Beacon, New York. As a part of its research, Texaco subscribed to numerous scientific journals and allowed its researchers to photocopy articles to keep in their files or to use in the labs.[8] Several journal publishers brought suit claiming that Texaco had infringed on their copyrights; Texaco responded that, among other things, its use was a fair use.[9]

For the sake of convenience and efficiency the *Texaco* case focused on eight items (four articles, two notes, and two letters to the editor) copied from Academic Press's *Journal of Catalysis* by Texaco scientist Dr. Donald Chickering.[10] By agreement of the parties, the only issue before the court was fair use.[11] The District Court for the Southern

---

2. 17 U.S.C. § 106 (1994); *see generally* LAURA N. GASAWAY & SARAH K. WIANT, LIBRARIES AND COPYRIGHT: A GUIDE TO COPYRIGHT LAW IN THE 1990s 19–20 (1994).

3. 17 U.S.C. § 108 (1994).

4. *Id.* § 108 (f)(4).

5. *Id.* § 107.

6. 60 F.3d 913 (2d Cir. 1994).

7. No. 94-1778, 1996 WL 54741 (6th Cir. Feb. 12, 1996), *vacated and reh'g granted en banc*, 74 F.3d 1528 (6th Circ. 1996).

8. American Geophysical Union v. Texaco, Inc., 802 F. Supp. 1, 4 (S.D.N.Y. 1992).

9. *Texaco*, 60 F.3d at 914–15.

10. *Texaco*, 802 F. Supp. at 6.

11. *Id.* at 5 n.1.

District of New York and the Court of Appeals for the Second Circuit (in a 2-to-1 decision) found that Texaco's use was not a fair use, but instead represented what the court of appeals called "institutional, systematic, multiplication of copies."[12] Texaco appealed this ruling to the U.S. Supreme Court, but settled the case before the Court decided whether to hear it. Accordingly, the case stands as good law in the Second Circuit (Connecticut, New York, and Vermont) and may have influential weight on courts in other circuits. The case greatly narrows the fair use exception as applied to photocopying by for-profit corporations and may have further negative ramifications for application of fair use in new media such as the Internet and World Wide Web.

The influence of *Texaco* may be lessened by *Princeton University Press v. Michigan Document Services* (*MDS*) if the decision in the rehearing *en banc* reaffirms the panel decision. In *MDS*, several publishers sued a copy shop that prepared "coursepacks," comprised of excerpts from copyrighted works, which were designed for use by students at the University of Michigan.[13] MDS raised the fair use defense, but the district court rejected the defense and instead found MDS guilty of willful infringement, assessing damages of more than $350,000.[14] A three-judge panel for the Sixth Circuit Court of Appeals (in a 2-to-1 decision) reversed the district court, finding a fair use.[15] The publishers petitioned the court of appeals for a rehearing *en banc* (a hearing by all fourteen judges of the Sixth Circuit), which was granted.[16] The panel decision has been vacated,[17] which means that it has no legal effect, and the full court had reheard the case.[18] Whatever the result, either party can then appeal to the U.S. Supreme Court. If fair use is finally found in *MDS*, it will greatly expand the fair use exception for

---

12. *Texaco*, 60 F.3d at 931.
13. Princeton Univ. Press v. Michigan Document Servs., 855 F. Supp. 905, 907 (E.D. Mich. 1994).
14. *Id.* at 912; Princeton Univ. Press v. Michigan Document Servs., 869 F. Supp. 521, 524 (E.D. Mich. 1994). These damages included statutory damages, attorney fees and costs.
15. Princeton Univ. Press v. Michigan Document Servs., No. 94-1778, 1996 WL 54741, at 12 (6th Cir. Feb. 12, 1996), *vacated and reh'g granted en banc*, 74 F.3d 1528 (6th Cir. 1996).
16. Princeton Univ. Press v. Michigan Document Servs., 74 F.3d 1528 (6th Cir. 1996).
17. *Id.*
18. See Addendum to this chapter, *infra* p. 342.

photocopying, especially in educational and nonprofit contexts. If the copy shop loses, however, the result will reinforce and extend *Texaco's* narrowing of the fair use exception for photocopying.

II. The Fair Use Doctrine

Fair use has been called, among the more polite descriptions, "perhaps the most debated and least understood principle of copyright law."[19] The uncertainty surrounding the doctrine is especially troubling because fair use, as codified in section 107 of the Copyright Act, is the primary section that protects users' rights under copyright law. The effect of this uncertainty on individuals has been minimal, since individuals are rarely the target of copyright infringement actions.[20] On the other hand, the effect of the uncertainty on corporations, universities, and libraries has been severe.[21] Uncertain about the protections afforded by fair use, institutions have been forced to craft policies that do not fit the law's protections or prohibitions. Some, such as AT&T's Bell Labs, have chosen to pay for all uses, including photocopying, in hopes of avoiding potential liability for copyright infringement.[22] Others, such as Texaco, have chosen to risk liability and bear the costs of litigation, only to find that the courts disagree with their fair use analysis.[23] While AT&T and Texaco can afford to pay millions of dollars for blanket copying licenses or to fight an infringement suit in court (and then pass these costs on to consumers), most American

---

19.   PATTERSON & LINDBERG, *supra* note 1, at 66.

20.   For exceptions to this general proposition, see Withol v. Crow, 309 F.2d 777 (8th Cir. 1962); Marcus v. Rowley, 695 F.2d 1171 (9th Cir. 1983).

21.   These costs exceed simple monetary losses. Restrictive application of authors' and publishers' rights can hamper the basic purposes of copyright law to advance the useful arts and sciences. Kenneth Crews notes that the problem became especially acute for universities after NYU's 1983 settlement of a copyright infringement suit:

> The settlement received widespread attention and fueled a growing awareness that copyright law can directly impede teaching and research—the fundamental pursuits of higher education. Universities were thrown into a quandary. They needed to avoid infringement liability, but they also had to minimize impediments on their very reasons for existing.

KENNETH D. CREWS, COPYRIGHT, FAIR USE AND THE CHALLENGE FOR UNIVERSITIES 3 (1993).

22.   Louise Schaper & Alicja Kawecki, *Towards Compliance: How One Global Corporation Complies with Copyright Law*, ONLINE, Mar. 1991, at 15–21.

23.   American Geophysical Union v. Texaco, Inc., 60 F.3d 913 (2d Cir. 1994).

corporations, libraries, universities, law firms, and hospitals cannot afford the time and expense of these alternatives. Because the fair use determination can be made only by a court after copying has occurred and an infringement action is brought, decision makers responsible for developing a workable and cost-effective photocopying policy for their institutions need to take proactive steps to minimize potential liability. The first step is a recognition of the problem. The second step requires development of photocopying policies based on a thorough under-standing of fair use, the impact of *Texaco*, and the potential impact of *MDS* on fair use as applied to photocopying.

Despite the continued and profound disagreements concerning fair use and its application in these cases, there is method to the fair use madness. Congress, primarily at the urging of educators, incorporated a fair use test into the Copyright Act of 1976.[24] Section 107 provides a basis for reasoned decision making in developing photocopying policies and even in deciding whether to make a single copy. The section lists four factors courts must consider in deciding whether a particular use is fair:

> [T]he factors to be considered shall include—(1) the purpose and char-acter of the use, including whether such use is of a commercial nature or is for non-profit educational purposes; (2) the nature of the copy-righted work; (3) the amount and substantiality of the portion used in relation to the copyrighted work as a whole; and (4) the effect of the use upon the potential market for or value of the copyrighted work.[25]

This test assumed critical importance in both *Texaco* and *MDS* and must serve as the starting point for anyone trying to anticipate whether making a copy will be an inexpensive fair use or a potentially costly infringement.

In addition to being the starting point for the fair use analysis, the section 107 factors or test is also the source for much of the fair use confusion. First, the Supreme Court has ruled that the test cannot "be simplified with bright-line rules, for the statute, like the doctrine it recognizes, calls for case-by-case analysis."[26] This means that where a court might recognize a fair use when an individual photocopies an

---

24.   17 U.S.C. § 107 (1994).
25.   *Id.* § 107(1)–(4).
26.   Campbell v. Acuff-Rose Music, Inc., 114 S. Ct. 1164, 1170 (1994).

article for his or her own personal use, that same court might reject the fair use defense when the copy is made by an individual for use in his or her employment. Second, courts have at different times put different weight on each of the four factors. Third, each of the four statutory factors have uncertain definitions; courts have been unable to agree, for example, on the meaning of commercial use. Finally, after having addressed the four statutory factors, courts are allowed to consider other factors such as privacy interests of the copyright holder and good faith of the user.[27] Professor Paul Goldstein argues that at bottom the fair use test "attempts no more than to balance the benefits and losses produced by particular uses."[28] Because the relative weight given to each fair use factor varies from case to case, cautious decision makers need a thorough understanding of how the test has been applied by the courts.

III. The Fair-use Doctrine Applied

A. Purpose and Character of the Use

Two simple rules of thumb guide interpretation and application of the first factor. First, commercial use weighs against a finding of fair use.[29] Second, a duplicative or superseding use such as photocopying weighs against a finding of fair use, while a transformative or productive use such as criticism or parody weighs in favor of a finding of fair use.[30] Hence, a company that photocopied the most recent John Grisham novel and sold it for a profit to the public would certainly lose on the first factor. The use is superseding because it replaces the need for the original, and it is commercial because it is an exploitation of the copyrighted material itself. Most companies and institutions are not faced with situations that are quite so clear, and the problem with the simple rules of thumb described above has been that the courts have been unable to

---

27. WILLIAM F. PATRY, THE FAIR USE PRIVILEGE IN COPYRIGHT LAW 568–69 (2d ed. 1995) [hereinafter PATRY].

28. PAUL GOLDSTEIN, 2 COPYRIGHT § 10.2, at 10:18 (2d ed. 1996).

29. *Acuff-Rose*, 114 S. Ct. at 1174. The opinion makes clear, however, that the purpose of the use is not dispositive: "Accordingly, the mere fact that a use is educational and not for profit does not insulate it from a finding of infringement, any more than the commercial character of a use bars a finding of fairness." *Id.*

30. Pierre N. Leval, *Toward A Fair Use Standard*, 103 HARV. L. REV. 1105, 1111 (1990) [hereinafter Leval].

agree on the definitions for commercial, nonprofit educational, transformative, productive, duplicative, and superseding uses. The different conclusions in *Texaco* and *MDS* on the issues of commercial purpose and transformative character illustrate the problem well.

1. Commercial or Nonprofit Educational Purposes. Texaco argued that its use was for scientific (nonprofit educational) purposes.[31] The publishers argued, in response, that Texaco's use was primarily commercial.[32]

Although one commentator who worked closely with the publishers in *Texaco* has labeled Texaco's nonprofit argument "fatuous,"[33] Texaco made a strong case that its use could be seen as being for nonprofit purposes under section 107. Texaco argued that the use had to be distinguished from the user. The company's argument focused on the fact that Dr. Chickering, the scientist whose copying was at issue, copied the articles "for the purpose of advancing scientific research."[34] Texaco downplayed the fact that Dr. Chickering's scientific research was aimed at improving the company's products and profitability.[35]

The publishers countered Texaco's arguments by defining commercial use as "an attempt by the user to profit by using the copyright owner's property."[36] The publishers claimed Texaco directly profited from the photocopies made by Dr. Chickering: "Texaco uses photocopies as an integral part of the research and development activities that it conducts to 'maximize profitability.' Texaco's use of photocopies also produces immediate cost savings."[37] Not surprising, the publishers also minimized Texaco's argument that Dr. Chickering's copying advanced socially beneficial research. They argued that "[a]ny public benefits from Texaco's research activities . . . are simply

31. Fair Use Trial Brief of Texaco at 46–55, American Geophysical Union v. Texaco, Inc., 802 F. Supp. 1 (S.D.N.Y. 1992) (No. 85 Civ. 3446 (PNL)).

32. Plaintiff's Post-Trial Memorandum Concerning Fair Use at 72–86, American Geophysical Union v. Texaco, Inc., 802 F. Supp. 1 (S.D.N.Y. 1992) (No. 85 Civ. 3446 (PNL)).

33. *See* PATRY, *supra* note 27, at 227.

34. Fair Use Trial Brief of Texaco at 43, *Texaco*, 802 F. Supp. at 1.

35. *Id*. at 48.

36. Plaintiff's Post-Trial Memorandum Concerning Fair Use at 73, *Texaco*, 802 F. Supp. at 1.

37. *Id*. at 76.

secondary by-products of Texaco's commercial activities and are not the motivation for Texaco's activities."[38]

District Court Judge Pierre Leval favored the publishers' arguments and found that Texaco's use was a commercial use: "Granted, the copiers are scientists, they are using their copies to assist in socially valuable scientific research and they do not resell the copies. Nonetheless their research is being conducted for commercial gain."[39] Throughout its analysis the court repeatedly refers to Texaco as the user and weighs this factor heavily in its acceptance of the publishers' arguments that Texaco's use is a commercial use.[40]

Judge Leval's consideration of the for-profit character and motivation of the user skews his first factor analysis. The purpose of copyright law is to "promote the Progress of Science and useful Arts."[41] Copyright law does not inquire into whether the user seeking to advance science and the useful arts is a profit making or nonprofit corporation. Indeed, copyright's chosen method for advancing science and the useful arts is the profit motive. Instead, the Supreme Court has said that the real question is whether the user is attempting to profit directly from the exploitation of the copyright itself: "The crux of the profit/non-profit distinction is not whether the sole motive of the use is monetary gain but whether the user stands to profit from exploitation of copyrighted material without paying the customary price."[42] There is no argument in *Texaco* that Dr. Chickering's purpose was to sell the copied works publicly or to otherwise make a profit from the copyright itself.[43] His primary use was to photocopy articles that may have been useful in his research. At most, Chickering's use was a secondary or derivative commercial use rather than an infringing exploitation of the copyrighted material.

On appeal, Texaco attacked the district court's commercial use finding, arguing specifically that Judge Leval "inappropriately focused on the character of the user rather than the nature of the use in

---

38.   *Id.*

39.   *Texaco*, 802 F. Supp. at 16.

40.   *Id.*

41.   U.S. Const. art. I, § 8, cl. 8.

42.   Harper & Row Publishers, Inc. v. The Nation Enters., 471 U.S. 539, 562 (1985).

43.   *Texaco*, 802 F. Supp. at 16.

labeling Texaco's copying as commercial."[44] The court of appeals agreed with this analysis, in part, but it too characterized Texaco as the user and considered the company's for-profit status as an important element in finding a commercial use:

> Texaco's photocopying for Chickering could be regarded simply as another "factor of production" utilized in Texaco's efforts to develop profitable products. Conceptualized in this way, it is not obvious why it is fair for Texaco to avoid having to pay at least some price to copyright holders for the right to photocopy the original articles.[45]

Judge Jacobs dissented from the court's conclusion, however, noting that Texaco had paid at least some price:

> Finally, the circulation of *Catalysis* among a number of Texaco scientists can come as no surprise to the publisher of *Catalysis*, which charges double the normal subscription rate to institutional subscribers. The publisher must therefore assume that, unless they are reading *Catalysis* for pleasure or committing it to memory, the scientists will extract what they need and arrange to copy it for personal use before passing along the institutional copies.[46]

Whether the reasoning in *Texaco* is flawed, it remains the law in the Second Circuit. The case expands the definition of "commercial" to include not only uses of the copyright but also uses of the work itself by focusing on the user and the user's reasons for copying a particular work. The case also creates up a presumption that if a researcher works for a profit-seeking entity, that researcher's use will be viewed as the institution's use and will weigh towards a finding of commercial use. Corporations (and perhaps all profit-seeking institutions in the Second Circuit and in those circuits that adopt *Texaco's* reasoning) must rely heavily on the other factors in the fair use analysis to overcome this presumption. *MDS* may ameliorate the worst effects of *Texaco's* commercial presumption, however.

Michigan Document Services' use was clearly commercial. University professors selected the materials they wanted to assign for their courses and then gave the materials to MDS. MDS copied the

---

44. *Texaco*, 60 F.3d at 920.
45. *Id.* at 922.
46. *Id.* at 936 (Jacobs, J., dissenting).

materials, bound them, and sold them to students for a profit.[47] The District Court for the Eastern District of Michigan called MDS's actions "pure copying for profit."[48] Although the three-judge panel of the Sixth Circuit Court of Appeals acknowledged that MDS's actions were commercial, that court came to a different conclusion on the first factor. The court concluded that the commercial use in the case did not weigh against a finding of fair use because the copy shop was acting as the agent for professors and students whose use was "entirely nonprofit educational."[49]

The panel's findings directly contradict the holding in another case construing whether the reproduction of materials for coursepacks constitutes copyright infringement. In *Basic Books, Inc. v. Kinko's Graphics Corp.*,[50] the U.S. District Court for the Southern District of New York also acknowledged that there were two uses in its coursepack case: the students' nonprofit educational use and Kinko's for-profit use.[51] The *Kinko's* court used the Supreme Court's ruling in *Harper & Row Publishers, Inc. v. The Nation Enterprises* to conclude that Kinko's profited "from the exploitation of the copyrighted material without paying the customary price."[52] In contrast, the *MDS* court found that "MDS does not 'exploit' copyrighted material within the meaning of *Harper & Row*."[53] The *Kinko's* court found that Kinko's use of advanced photocopying technologies and its aggressive marketing actually supplanted the copyright holder's right which was commercially valuable. Further, this was Kinko's intended purpose.[54] The *MDS* court found that the "business of producing and selling coursepacks is more properly viewed as the exploitation of professional

---

47.   Princeton Univ. Press v. Michigan Document Servs., 855 F. Supp. 905, 907 (E.D. Mich. 1994).

48.   *Id.* at 909. Indeed, at first blush the only difference between the commercial nature of the enterprises in *Texaco* and *MDS* is the size of the corporate entity.

49.   Princeton Univ. Press v. Michigan Document Servs., 1996 WL 54741, at 7 (6th Cir. Feb. 12, 1996), *vacated and reh'g granted en banc*, 74 F.3d 1528 (6th Cir. 1996).

50.   758 F. Supp. 1522 (S.D.N.Y. 1991).

51.   *Id.* at 29.

52.   *Id.* at 1532 (quoting Harper & Row Publishers, Inc. v. The Nation Enters., 471 U.S. 539, 562 (1985)).

53.   *MDS*, 1996 WL 54741, at 7.

54.   *Kinko's*, 758 F. Supp. at 1531 (quoting Harper & Row Publishers, Inc. v. The Nation Enters., 471 U.S. 539, 562 (1985)).

copying technologies . . . not the exploitation of copyrighted creative materials."[55]

It must be emphasized again that the *MDS* court's holding has been vacated and has no legal effect.[56] Additionally, even if the entire Sixth Circuit reaffirms the panel's decision, the case will not overrule *Kinko's* which was decided by a district court in the Second Circuit. Accordingly, *Kinko's* is still good law in that Second Circuit district, and coursepacks there are likely to be found to be unfair commercial exploitation. Until *MDS* is finally decided, *Kinko's* also remains the only major coursepack case, and potential copiers, especially those within the Second Circuit, should be aware of the *Kinko's* court's finding of a strong commercial purpose.

The *MDS* case may also prove important outside the context of coursepacks, as its treatment of the character of the use stands in stark contrast to the treatment accorded this factor in *Texaco*. Where the *Texaco* courts found Texaco's commercial status as a strong force weighing against fair use, the *MDS* court looked beyond MDS's commercial status and profit motivation to consider the nature of the use itself. If the panel decision is reaffirmed by the *en banc* court, the case could ameliorate the *Texaco's* treatment of the character of the user as more important than the character of the use. Of course, a clear resolution to the conflict on this factor will likely come only when the Supreme Court deals with the issue in a photocopying infringement suit against a for-profit corporation (such as MDS).

2. *Transformative or Productive Character of the Use.* The absence of a transformative or productive use weighs against a finding of fair use.[57] Former Policy Planning Advisor to the Register of Copyrights William Patry argues that the essence of such transformative uses is the creation of a new or derivative work.[58] Examples of such new or derivative works include parody, news reporting, and criticism. Both the district court and the court of appeals in *Texaco* found that the photocopying of entire copyrighted works was not transformative or productive. In contrast, the *MDS* court found that the photocopying of

---

55. *MDS*, 1996 WL 54741, at 7.
56. *MDS*, 74 F.3d at 1528.
57. 3 NIMMER ON COPYRIGHT § 13.05[A][1][b] at 13-161 (1996) [hereinafter NIMMER].
58. *See* PATRY, *supra* note 27, at 231.

excerpts from larger works and their assembly into course packs was slightly transformative.

Texaco argued that Dr. Chickering's use was productive because it advanced science and was transformative because it converted the articles into a more useable form.[59] Judge Leval dismissed the productivity argument, declaring that productive use meant production of "something new and different from the original."[60] He dismissed Texaco's transformation argument because in his view the copies made by Chickering superseded the originals. He noted that even if some transformative use was found "that use is overshadowed by the primary aspect of the copying, which is to multiply copies."[61] The court of appeals agreed with Judge Leval. It first noted that "[t]o the extent that the secondary use involves merely an untransformed duplication, the value generated by the secondary use is little or nothing more than the value that inheres in the original."[62] The court of appeals did find that the conversion of the articles from their journal format to photocopies could add some value by making them more useable.[63] The court concluded, however, that "the predominant archival purpose of the copying tips the first factor against the copier, despite the benefit of a more useable format."[64]

Once again, the district court and the court of appeals relied on their characterization of Texaco as the user to negate Texaco's argument that Dr. Chickering's use was transformative rather than duplicative or superseding. The district court found that the main feature of the photocopying was that it gave multiple Texaco scientists their own copies from the original that Texaco had purchased and these copies "supersede the original and multiply its presence."[65]

The court of appeals amplified this point by saying that such copying was part of a "systematic process" to encourage company researchers to reproduce articles and thereby multiply available copies

---

59.   *Texaco,* 802 F. Supp. at 13–14.

60.   *Id.* at 14.

61.   *Id.* at 15.

62.   *Texaco,* 60 F.3d at 923.

63.   *Id.* at 923–24.

64.   *Id.* at 923.

65.   *Texaco,* 802 F. Supp. at 14–15.

without compensating the copyright owner.[66] The impact of the district court's and court of appeal's finding that this copying was institutional and systematic cannot be underestimated.

The district court noted that if Chickering were an individual subscriber and was the only user of the subscription, then making the argument that making a copy to use in the lab or to mark it up was a transformative use might be persuasive.[67] Because both the district court and the court of appeals found that Texaco was the user rather than Dr. Chickering, both rejected the claim that Chickering's use was primarily individual and transformative.

Judge Jacobs, writing in dissent to the court of appeal's decision in *Texaco*, argued that the institutional setting of Dr. Chickering's work and copying was irrelevant to the fair use analysis. The corporate setting does not change the character of the copying nor does the selection of the articles by a scientist make the copying systematic. Further, it does not become systematic just because others in the organization may be doing the same thing.[68] The weight given by both the district court and the court of appeals to the institutional use by Texaco raises serious concerns. If the *Texaco* approach is adopted in other circuits, institutions will have to be very careful concerning copying done by researchers and employees because of the potential that the courts will view isolated copying by individuals as a systemic or institutional policy of exploiting authors' and publishers' copyrights. Profit-seeking institutions must be especially wary. The impact of the opinion on mixed institutions[69] such as teaching hospitals is unclear, however. Is the hospital primarily commercial because it seeks profits or is it primarily nonprofit because it teaches new doctors? How would a court decide whether copying by a resident of an article from a $12,000 medical journal was for institutional purposes or personal enrichment? Is a copy of a medical journal article made in a for-profit hospital and attached to a patient's chart a fair use copy? *Texaco* leaves these questions and many others like them unanswered.

---

66.   *Texaco*, 60 F.3d at 920.

67.   *Texaco*, 802 F. Supp. at 14.

68.   *Texaco*, 60 F.3d at 935 (Jacobs, J., dissenting).

69.   A teaching hospital has both nonprofit educational uses of copyrighted works for teaching as well as uses by doctors who may be affiliated with the hospital but who individually are for-profit. Thus, it is a "mixed institution."

The Sixth Circuit concluded that MDS's use was slightly trans-formative. The court found creative content in the assembly of materi-als in a new format and arrangement customized for the professor and consisting of portions of other works.[70] The court also noted that pub-lishers do not offer customized materials of this nature, nor are they equipped to do so.[71] Once again, the *Michigan Document Services* court's findings directly contradict the findings of the *Kinko's* court which found that Kinko's coursepacks were a mere repackaging.[72] The *Kinko's* court ruled that this did not pass the transformative use test set out by Judge Leval in his 1990 article on fair use: "The use . . . must employ the quoted matter in a different manner or for a different purpose from the original. A quotation of copyrighted material that merely repackages or republishes the original is unlikely to pass the test."[73] The split between the courts is plain.

The court of appeals in *Texaco* embraced the Supreme Court's holding in *Acuff-Rose* that transformative uses are generally favored over non-transformative uses because transformative uses further the constitutional purpose of copyright.[74] In *MDS*, the Sixth Circuit acknowledged *Acuff-Rose's* force but still found some transformative value in the creation of coursepacks. The dissent in *MDS* was probably correct in arguing that the majority had misconstrued *Acuff-Rose*.[75] Copiers and decision makers should not rely on *MDS's* finding of a slightly transformative value in coursepacks in their own fair use analysis, but instead should recognize that in *Kinko's, Acuff-Rose,* and *Texaco,* the courts have favored productive uses.

B. Nature of the Copyrighted Work

Works that contain a highly creative content are ordinarily given greater copyright protection than predominantly factual material.[76] In

---

70.   *MDS*, 1996 WL 54741, at 6.

71.   *Id.*

72.   *Kinko's*, 758 F. Supp. at 1530.

73.   Leval, *supra* note 30, *quoted in Kinko's*, 758 F. Supp. at 1530.

74.   *Acuff-Rose*, 114 S. Ct. at 1171 (internal citation omitted).

75.   *MDS*, 1996 WL 54741, at 15 (Nelson, J., concurring in part and dissenting in part). "This kind of mechanical 'transformation' bares [sic] little resemblance to the creative metamorphosis accomplished by the parodists in the *Campbell* case." *Id.*

76.   *See* NIMMER, *supra* note 57, § 13.05[A][2][a], at 13-172, 173.

Acuff-Rose, the Supreme Court noted that "creative expression for public dissemination falls within the core of the copyright's protective purposes."[77] Since facts along with ideas are not copyrightable (only their expression is), they fall outside the core of copyright's protective purposes; factual and informational materials such as medical journals, scientific studies, and historical treatises are generally subject to greater copying under fair use.[78] The preference for fair use of factual materials also is drawn from the belief that "the risk of restraining the flow of information is more significant with informational work. . . ."[79] Courts and commentators generally disagree, however, over the definition of factual and creative works and over the degree of protection which each is entitled to receive.

In *Texaco*, the district court found that the material copied by Dr. Chickering was primarily factual, "consisting of reports on scientific experimental research. The texts describe procedures followed and characterize the results found. Results are expressed largely in tables and graphs."[80] Although the court noted that these works were the kinds of works that copyright law was designed to protect and that copyright protection is vital to the success of scientific journals,[81] the district court concluded that the predominantly factual nature of the articles weighed in favor of Texaco.[82] The publishers challenged this finding on appeal stressing the need for broad copyright protection to foster journal production.[83] While the court of appeals acknowledged that "a significant measure of creativity"[84] went into the writing of the articles, the court warned against too expansive of an application of the argument that copyright protection is vitally necessary to protect journals. Although the court recognized the importance of strong copyright production to provide sufficient incentives for the creation of scientific works, nearly every category of copyrightable works could

---

77.   *Acuff-Rose*, 114 S. Ct. at 1175.

78.   *See* NIMMER, *supra* note 57, § 13.05[A][2][a], at 13-172.

79.   Consumers Union v. General Signal Corp., 724 F.2d 1044, 1049 (2d Cir. 1983), *cert. denied*, 469 U.S. 823 (1984).

80.   *Texaco*, 802 F. Supp. at 17.

81.   *Id*. at 16.

82.   *Id*. at 17.

83.   *Texaco*, 60 F.3d at 925.

84.   *Id*.

plausibly assert that broad copyright protection was essential to the continued vitality of that category of works.[85] The district court's and the court of appeal's analysis of this factor are consistent with general application of the second fair use factor.

While the works taken in *Texaco* were predominantly factual, the *MDS* court found that the works copied by MDS contained original analysis and creative theories.[86] The court also took the opportunity to note that creative nonfiction as well as fictional works are entitled to copyright protection.[87]

The results on the second factor in *Texaco* and *MDS* are entirely consistent with past fair use interpretations, and prospective copiers can use these decisions as a guide to whether they are copying primarily factual works or primarily creative works. Courts recognize that the purpose of copyright is to advance science and useful arts.[88] This is particularly important in a field such as scientific research: "Though scientists surely employ creativity and originality to develop ideas and obtain facts and thereafter to convey the ideas and facts in scholarly articles, it is primarily the ideas and facts themselves that are of value to other scientists in their research."[89] Science is a syncretic process. A researcher who makes a discovery announces it to the world often through a journal article. While the peculiar expression of his findings are embodied in the announcement, the facts and ideas enter the public domain. Then other researchers test and report on the findings. Each step of new analysis and research builds on the previous step. A broad application of fair use is necessary to ensure the free flow of information. Even predominantly factual materials are entitled to some measure of copyright protection, however, and the nature of the work must still be considered along with the other fair use factors.

---

85.   *Id.*

86.   *Id.* at 8 (quoting Feist Publications, Inc. v. Rural Tel. Serv. Co., 499 U.S. 340, 344–48 (1991) (internal quotation marks omitted).

87.   *MDS*, 1996 WL 54741, at 8.

88.   U.S. CONST. art. I, § 8, cl. 8.

89.   *Texaco*, 60 F.3d at 925 n.11.

C. Amount and Substantiality of the Portion Used in Relation to the Copyrighted Work as a Whole

Put simply, the more you use, the less likely your use is fair. Despite this seemingly logical guide, copying even a small portion of a text has been found unfair. In *Harper & Row v. Nation Enterprises*,[90] *The Nation* magazine printed unauthorized excerpts from former President Gerald Ford's memoirs. Although the excerpts taken represented only a small portion (about 300 words) of the memoirs, the district court concluded that *The Nation* took the heart of the work.[91] The Supreme Court weighed this factor along with the fact that *The Nation* had violated Harper & Row's fundamental right to first publication and found that it weighed heavily against the magazine.[92] Thus, in assessing whether a particular use is fair, an analysis under the third factor must take into account both quantitative and qualitative considerations.[93]

Texaco's initial argument on the third factor of the fair use analysis focused on a quantitative analysis. The company argued that Dr. Chickering's copying represented only a small portion of the overall work copied. The thrust of Texaco's argument was that the entire journal issue represented the copyrighted work.[94] Texaco argued that the amount and substantiality used was insignificant, averaging 0.26 percent of the number of pages published in the journal during the year.[95]

The district court and the court of appeals rejected Texaco's reasoning on the third factor. Judge Leval noted initially that in *Sony Corp. v. Universal City Studios*, the Supreme Court ruled that copying an entire copyrighted work ordinarily militates against a finding of fair use.[96] Calling Texaco's argument "imaginative lawyering," the district court found that each individual article within the *Journal of Catalysis* was a separately authored work carrying its own copyright.[97] The court of

---

90.   471 U.S. 539 (1985).

91.   *Id.* at 564–65 (citing Harper & Row Publishers, Inc. v. The Nation Enters., 557 F. Supp. 1067, 1072 (S.D.N.Y. 1983)).

92.   *Id.* at 565–66.

93.   *See* NIMMER, *supra* note 57, § 13.05 [A][4], at 13-183.

94.   Fair Use Trial Brief of Texaco at 65, *Texaco*, 802 F. Supp. 1.

95.   *Id.* at 66 (internal quotation marks omitted).

96.   *Texaco*, 802 F. Supp. at 17 (quoting Sony Corp. of Am. v. Universal City Studios, 464 U.S. 417, 450 (1984) (internal quotation marks omitted)).

97.   802 F. Supp. at 17.

appeals concurred with the district court's conclusion, calling Texaco's argument "superficially intriguing" but ultimately rejecting it.[98] The court found that the fact that Texaco photocopied the entirety of the eight articles at issue persuasive that the primary purpose and character of the use was to establish a personal library of pertinent articles for Chickering.[99]

The clearest points to emerge from *Texaco* is that the copying of an entire work weighs heavily against a finding of fair use and that an article is an entire work. Prospective copiers must be aware that cover-to-cover copying generally is not countenanced and can lead to heavy penalties for infringement. The clearest recent examples of this are companies that have been found to have infringed on publishers' copyrights by making multiple copies of newsletters rather than purchasing multiple subscriptions.[100] Even this rule is not absolute. In *Williams & Wilkins Co. v. United States*,[101] the Court of Claims found the photocopying of thousands of journal articles by the National Institutes of Health and the National Library of Medicine to be a fair use.[102] The Supreme Court found that the taping of entire television programs for the purpose of time shifting was a fair use in *Sony Corp. v. Universal City Studios*.[103] Ordinarily, however, cover-to-cover copying is a heavy weight against fair use.

The question in *MDS* was not whether the copy shop copied entire articles but whether the copy shop copied so much of the works that the copies superseded the originals. Once again the differences between the decision in *MDS* and *Kinko's* are substantial. First, the *Kinko's* court found that in that case the amount of the copying as a portion of the whole works ranged from approximately 5 percent to 25 percent of each work[104]; in *MDS* each individual excerpt was between 5 percent

---

98.   *Texaco*, 60 F.3d at 925.

99.   *Id.* at 926.

100. Pasha Publications v. Enmark Gas Corp., 1992 U.S. Dist. LEXIS 2834 (N.D. Tex. Mar. 10, 1992); Television Digest v. United States Tel. Ass'n, 841 F. Supp. 5 (D.D.C. 1993).

101. 487 F.2d 1345 (Ct. Cl. 1973), *aff'd*, 420 U.S. 376 (1975).

102. *Id.* at 1362.

103. 464 U.S. 417, 454–55 (1984).

104. *Kinko's*, 758 F. Supp. at 1533.

and 30 percent of the total.[105] The *Kinko's* court found that "the portions copied were critical parts of the books copied, since that is the likely reason the college professors used them in their classes."[106] In contrast, the *MDS* court decided that there was no evidence, even with respect to the copying of 30 percent of one book, that the professors had directed the copying of the heart of the work instead of just the portions that were relevant to their classes.[107]

The third prong will continue to play an important role in any analysis of fair use and is closely tied to the first factor. In *Acuff-Rose*, the Court noted that "the extent of permissible copying varies with the purpose and character of the use."[108] This is the best guide available to determine whether a particular use is fair, and it requires prospective copiers to ask three questions. First, is a whole work being copied or only a part? *Texaco* establishes that, at least, in the context of a for-profit corporation, copying of an entire work is a serious strike against a finding of fair use. Second, if only part is being copied, is that part the heart of the work? Taking the heart of a work is less fair than taking a less important part of the work, although determining what is the heart of the work is tricky as the courts continue to use different standards. Finally, copiers should ask whether the copy will satisfy the need for the original. If the copy can be used as an adequate replacement for the original, a court will be less likely to find fair use.

D. Effect of the Use upon the Potential Market for or Value of the Copyrighted Work

The fourth fair use factor requires a complex, multi-step analysis to determine the effect of a particular use on both the market for the work and on the work's potential value. At least one authority has suggested that if you look at the results of the fair use cases, rather than to their stated rationale, market emerges as the most important factor.[109] In *Acuff-Rose*, however, the Supreme Court encouraged a move away from placing undue emphasis on the any one factor,

---

105.   *MDS*, 1996 WL 54741, at 9.

106.   *Kinko's*, 758 F. Supp. at 1533.

107.   *MDS*, 1996 WL 54741, at 9.

108.   *Acuff-Rose*, 114 S. Ct. at 1175.

109.   *See* NIMMER, *supra* note 57, § 13.05[A][4], at 13-185 (internal citations omitted).

including the fourth.[110] In both *Texaco* and *MDS*, the fourth factor continues to hold critical importance and likely will continue to play a critical role in future fair use analyses.

Prospective copiers need to be aware of two markets protected under the fourth factor of the fair use analysis. First, the market for the work itself must be considered. Copying which replaces the work in its original form clearly weighs against a finding of fair use under the fourth factor because it interferes with the copyright holder's right to exploit the work itself. In *Pasha Publications v. Enmark Gas Co.*,[111] a gas company that ordered a single subscription to an industry newsletter and then created multiple copies for employees directly interfered with the market for the work itself, and the court found that its use was not a fair use.[112] The copyright holder's right to produce or license derivative works is also protected under the fourth factor.[113] The protection of derivative markets, however, extends to "only those that the creators of original works would in general develop or license others to develop."[114] For example, parodies and criticism generally are not considered derivative protected markets.[115] The effect on the value of the work is also closely tied to the analysis of potential markets. Copying that supersedes the market for the work diminishes the value of the work itself and is likely to be found unfair.[116]

The plaintiff publishers in *Texaco* declared that they were primarily worried about a speculative kind of harm to their copyrights, the losses that they and other publishers of scientific and technical journals would suffer as a result of the widespread photocopying practices among for-profit, research-oriented corporations.[117] The publishers also contended that Texaco's failure to pay licensing fees for the copied articles caused actual harm to the value of the copyrighted articles.[118] Finally, the

---

110.   *Acuff-Rose*, 114 S. Ct. at 1170–71.
111.   1992 U.S. Dist. LEXIS 2834 (N.D. Tex. Mar. 10, 1992).
112.   *Id.* at 4.
113.   *Harper & Row*, 471 U.S. at 568.
114.   *Acuff-Rose*, 114 S. Ct. at 1178.
115.   *Id.*
116.   *See* PATRY, *supra* note 27, at 560.
117.   Plaintiffs' Post-Trial Memorandum Concerning Fair Use at 109, *Texaco*, 802 F. Supp. 1.
118.   *Id.* at 111.

plaintiffs argued that Texaco's photocopying practices cost the plaintiffs lost revenue from sales of back issues and reprints.[119] The district court accepted all of these arguments, putting the predominant weight on the plaintiff's claimed right to licensing permissions and fees.

The district court divided its analysis of the fourth factor into two separate inquiries: the impact on the sales of entire journals and the impact on the value of and market for the individual copied articles. The district court concluded that while Texaco would not replace photocopying by greatly increasing journal subscriptions, Texaco would still increase the number of subscriptions somewhat.[120] The court of appeals agreed with the district court that Texaco would not greatly increase its subscriptions, but held that this only tipped the fourth factor slightly in favor of the publishers.[121] The district court and the court of appeals found that the impact of Dr. Chickering's copying on the loss of actual and potential licensing revenues and fees weighted the fourth factor heavily against Texaco.[122] Both courts found the existence of the Copyright Clearance Center (CCC) to be a critical factor which weighed against fair use in *Texaco*.[123]

The Copyright Clearance Center was established in 1977 as a not-for-profit organization that collects photocopying and royalty remittance fees.[124] The CCC is a voluntary organization, and as such, it serves as the agent for a number of publishers and their works.[125] While the number of participating publishers is significant, the CCC is not comprehensive, and it is distinctly lacking in areas such as law.[126] Users of copyrighted works join the CCC and can pay royalties for covered publishers and works to the CCC, which then distributes them back to publishers.

---

119.   *Id.* at 118.
120.   *Texaco*, 802 F. Supp. at 19.
121.   *Texaco*, 60 F.3d at 929.
122.   *Texaco*, 802 F. Supp. at 19; *Texaco*, 60 F.3d at 931.
123.   *Id.*
124.   *Id.* at 7. The CCC began collecting fees in 1978. *See* LAURA N. GASAWAY & SARAH K. WIANT, LIBRARIES AND COPYRIGHT: A GUIDE TO COPYRIGHT LAW IN THE 1990s 68 (1994) [hereinafter GASAWAY & WIANT].
125.   GASAWAY & WIANT, *supra* note 124, at 68.
126.   *Id.*

Corporate CCC members may choose two types of licenses: a transaction reporting service (TRS) license and an annual authorization service (AAS) license.[127] The TRS license requires copiers to make notation of each copy made and to keep records of royalties and payments owed to the publishers. The AAS is a blanket license negotiated between a corporation and the CCC that allows the company to copy at will CCC publications to which the company subscribes.[128] Texaco was a member of the CCC and paid through the TRS but did not pay for all the photocopies which it made.[129] The primary reason Texaco was targeted for suit was because the fees it paid to the CCC were significantly below those paid by other major oil companies.[130]

The district court found that if Texaco's copying was held not to be a fair use that the company would still have to find an efficient way to get copies of the articles for its scientists.[131] The court concluded that Texaco would still make photocopies as long as there was some inexpensive and non-burdensome way to do so.[132] The court believed that the CCC was not excessively burdensome.[133]

The court of appeals accepted the district court's conclusion that Texaco's copying significantly affected the publishers revenue in the form of licensing fees.[134] The court reached this conclusion despite accepting Texaco's argument that it is not always appropriate for a court to find against fair use based on potential licensing revenues. Only traditional, reasonable, or likely-to-be-developed markets should be legally cognizable when evaluating the impact on potential licensing for a copyrighted work.[135] Texaco argued that the CCC was not "a fair, reasonable and convenient method for payment of license fees for copying. . . ."[136] The court of appeals came to an opposite conclusion, however, noting that although the publishers still have not established

---

127.   *Texaco*, 802 F. Supp. at 6–7.

128.   *See* GASAWAY & WIANT, *supra* note 124, at 69–70.

129.   *Texaco*, 60 F.3d at 930.

130.   *See* GASAWAY & WIANT, *supra* note 124, at 60.

131.   *Texaco*, 802 F. Supp. at 18.

132.   *Id.*

133.   *Id.*

134.   *Texaco*, 60 F.3d at 930.

135.   *Id.*

136.   Fair Use Trial Brief of Texaco at 96, *Texaco*, 802 F. Supp. 1.

a conventional market for the direct sale and distribution of individual articles, they have created a workable market for licensing photo-copying.[137] The court of appeals ruled that since section 106(1) grants copyright holders the exclusive right to reproduce their works and section 106(3) gives copyright holders the exclusive right to distribute their works and because the market for licensing individual journal articles is viable, it was appropriate to consider lost licensing fees in the fair use analysis.[138]

Both courts' conclusions concerning the fourth fair use factor are troubling. Both found that since the publisher was willing to accept payment for the articles copied and that because there was a mechanism in place for collecting photocopying fees, Dr. Chickering's copying caused damage or was likely to cause damage to a potential market. Fair use, however, does not turn on a publisher's willingness to accept payment, or even on the existence of a mechanism to collect fees. If a particular use is not a fair use, royalties or licensing fees are owed whether the copyright holder has established a mechanism to collect those fees. In contrast, if a particular use is a fair use, royalties or licensing fees are not owed even though the copyright holder desires payment and a mechanism for collecting those royalties exists. The court of appeals noted the danger of circular reasoning lurking behind its opinion, but it dismissed the challenge by holding that reasoning is circular only if the availability of payment is conclusive against fair use.[139] Since the fourth factor weighs heavily in the fair use determination, however, circular reasoning on the fourth factor can improperly skew the entire fair use analysis.

In *MDS* the Sixth Circuit confronted the circularity problem head on. "It is circular to argue that a use is unfair and a fee therefore required, on the basis that the publisher is otherwise deprived of a fee."[140] The *MDS* court ruled that there was no proof in the record which indicated a negative impact on either the market for the original or for derivative works.[141] The court relied on the affidavits of the professors who commissioned the coursepacks to be made by MDS to

---

137.   *Texaco*, 60 F.3d at 930.
138.   *Id.*
139.   *Id.* at 930–31.
140.   *MDS*, 1996 WL 54741, at 11.
141.   *Id.* at 9.

conclude that there was no damage to the market for originals.[142] Indeed, the court speculated that, if anything, the use of excerpted materials could actually enhance the chance that a student might later purchase original works.[143] The panel found for MDS on the fourth factor. If the decision in the rehearing *en banc* affirms the panel, then the impact of *Texaco's* influence on the fourth factor may be lessened.

Prospective copiers should take two lessons from *Texaco* and *MDS*. First, use of a work, whether in whole or in part, in such a way that it replaces the original in the market or greatly decreases the value of the original generally is not a fair use. Second, the existence of the CCC, other licensing organizations, and document delivery services may be held against for-profit copiers in the fair use analysis. The existence of the Copyright Clearance Center weighed heavily in finding no fair use in *Texaco*. Because publishers stand to collect significant revenues from the CCC, document delivery services, and other licensing organizations, a court that accepts *Texaco's* reasoning likely will find against the copier under the fourth fair use factor. Although the Sixth Circuit initially rejected the CCC's existence as a relevant factor in the fair use analysis, the potential treatment to be given by other circuits is still uncertain and bears careful watching.

E. Fair Use as an Equitable Rule of Reason

Courts begin their treatment of the fair use defense with an analysis under the four statutory factors described above. As noted throughout this chapter, however, fair use does not lend itself to a quick, tidy and regular analysis. Even the framers of section 107 noted this problem:

> Although the courts have considered and ruled upon the fair use doctrine over and over again, no real definition of the concept has ever emerged. Indeed, since the doctrine is an equitable rule of reason, no generally applicable definition is possible and each case raising the question must be decided on its own facts.[144]

After courts complete the four factor analysis, many also will consider equitable factors. The *Texaco* courts rejected several equitable claims

---

142.   *Id.* at 11.

143.   *Id.*

144.   H. R. REP. NO. 94-1476, 94th Cong., 2d Sess., at 65 (1976); Kenneth D. Crews, *What Qualifies as "Fair Use"?*, CHRON. OF HIGHER EDUC., May 17, 1996, at B1–2.

made by Texaco, including the company's argument that its copying simply constituted time-shifting, allowing scientists to copy articles for future reading[145] (much like Sony allowed time-shifting by consumers who recorded television programs for future viewing).[146] The court rejected this argument and other equitable arguments advanced by the company.[147]

Decision makers trying to develop institutional policies on photocopying also must consider any equitable factors which may make their copying more or possibly less fair. William Patry notes several examples of these equitable factors, including "privacy interests, defendant's good faith or lack thereof, wrongful denial of exploitative conduct towards the work of another, commission of error and the plaintiff's misuse of his or her copyright to suppress unfavorable comment."[148] Nonetheless, the bread and butter of the fair use analysis remains the four statutory factors and should remain the focus of all persons concerned about potential liability for copyright infringement.

IV. Impact on Libraries

Texaco attempted to defend its copying as a fair use by relying on support from the legislative history on section 108's protections for library photocopying.[149] The district court first dismissed Texaco's argument that its copying met the statutory requirements of section 108.[150] Then, in an important footnote, the court also noted that the case was by stipulation a fair use case under section 107 and it was questionable whether section 108, which covers library and archive photocopying, was within the scope of the trial.[151] The court of appeals applied section 108 only to buttress its conclusion that Congress "has impliedly suggested that the law should recognize licensing fees for photocopying as part of the potential market for or value of journal articles."[152] *MDS*

---

145. *Texaco*, 802 F. Supp. at 22.
146. Sony Corp. of Am. v. Universal City Studios, 464 U.S. 417, 454–55 (1984).
147. *Texaco*, 802 F. Supp. at 22–23. In fact, time shifting has been found to satisfy the fourth factor only by the *Sony* court.
148. *See* PATRY, *supra* note 27, at 568–69 (citations omitted).
149. Fair Use Trial Brief of Texaco at 46–48, *Texaco*, 802 F. Supp. 1.
150. *Texaco*, 802 F. Supp. at 27–28.
151. *Id*. at 28 n.26.
152. *Texaco*, 60 F.3d at 931.

never touches on section 108 or on library photocopying generally. Thus, the only substantive impact of these cases on library photocopying is the extent to which they modify the standards for fair use and photocopying under section 107.[153]

V. Impact of *Texaco* and *MDS* on New Media

Neither *Texaco* nor *MDS* directly implicate media or uses beyond photocopying. As mentioned above, the fair use doctrine is applied on a case-by-case basis, and each case tends to be limited strictly to the facts at issue. The Supreme Court's decision in *Acuff-Rose* heavily favors productive uses in the fair use analysis, and *Texaco's* reliance on the productive use factor does not augur well for duplicative or reproductive uses.[154] The recent emergence of the Internet and World Wide Web as mainstream communication and publication technologies raise serious copyright and fair use concerns. Both the Internet and the Web rely heavily on verbatim duplication of text and reproduction of sound, images, and video. Although the Copyright Act is technologically neutral, if Judge Leval's less-than-neat distinction between productive and non-productive uses holds, this could either stunt the growth of the Internet, or more likely, force Internet service providers, corporations, and libraries to choose between obtaining licenses or risking liability for potential infringements.

The other factors in the fair use analysis in *Texaco*, including commercial use and effect on potential markets, also could chill emerging new media such as the Internet. If it stands, the *MDS* holding likely will lessen these dangers especially regarding nonprofit educational uses. Because of the continued uncertainty, however, decision makers must be confident but cautious when assessing potential liability and defenses for both photocopying and similar duplicative technologies.

---

153.   17 U.S.C. § 108(f)(4) (1994) provides that nothing in section 108 "in any way affects the right of fair use as provided by § 107." The Special Libraries Association contends that the rights and benefits granted by section 108 are in addition to the protections of fair use. The Association of American Publishers argues that section 108 is the exclusion section protecting library photocopying. *See generally* Gasaway & Wiant, *supra* note 124, at 57–59.

154.   *See* Laura G. Lape, *Transforming Fair Use: The Productive Use Factor in Fair Use Doctrine*, 58 Alb. L. Rev. 677, 679 (1995).

VI. Conclusion

Texaco and *MDS* may affect nonprofit educational institutions and libraries, but their primary impact is on for-profit corporations. *Texaco's* greatest effect on nonprofit educational institutions, including libraries, is in its focus on the user rather than the use. Copying done by a professor for a class at the university may be ascribed to the university rather than to the professor's personal use under *Texaco's* reasoning. *MDS* may expand fair use for nonprofit educational purposes by extending the protection given to copies made for academic purposes.

Personal use of a copyrighted work is not affected by these cases. Indeed, Professors Ray Patterson and Stanley Lindberg argue that personal use is not even subject to the fair use exception:

> An individual's use of a copyrighted work for his or her own private use is a personal use, not subject to fair use restraints. Such use includes use by copying, provided that the copy is neither for public distribution or sale to others nor a functional substitute for a copyrighted work currently available on the market at a reasonable price.[155]

On the other hand, *Texaco's* treatment of the company rather than the researcher as the user may severely limit application of the personal use exception in both for-profit and educational institution cases.

The law of fair use and photocopying after *Texaco* is unsettled and, at least for the present, *MDS* is unlikely to clarify matters. Fair use in photocopying is likely to remain unsettled until the U.S. Supreme Court has an opportunity to deal with the issue. This uncertainty should not, however, lead decision makers and copiers to overly cautious or, alternatively, reckless responses. In many fields, such as in for-profit scientific research, there are compelling reasons to photocopy.[156] Decision makers should apply the fair use test (with due regard to the treatment in *Texaco* and *MDS*) and may want to consult their corporate counsel to decide whether their uses are likely to be fair uses. Except in very unusual circumstances, institutions need not forbid all photocopying. To aid in making these determinations, the American Association of Law Libraries has developed a sample photocopying policy which may help in developing corporate photocopying

---

155. L. RAY PATTERSON & STANLEY W. LINDBERG, THE NATURE OF COPYRIGHT: A LAW OF USERS' RIGHTS 194 (1991) (italics omitted).

156. *Texaco*, 802 F. Supp. at 18.

policies (see appendix following this chapter). Applicability of these decisions to digital copying is unknown. Although many scholars believe that digital copying is permitted by libraries since the law is technologically neutral, others disagree. Regardless of the approach taken, however, decision makers must remember that copyright law protects the user's right to make copies of copyrighted works.

VII. Addendum

On November 8, 1996, a divided court sitting *en banc* in *Michigan Document Services (MDS)*[157] found the copying of substantial portions of copyrighted books for coursepacks sold to students by a for-profit off-campus copy shop was not fair use. The decision reversed the February 12, 1996, three-judge panel that found such use fair. Judge Nelson (the lone dissenter on the three-judge panel), writing for the majority, and joined by seven of his colleagues, upheld the summary judgment granted by the lower court.[158]

The majority noted that the language in the doctrine of fair use[159] contained in the statute does not provide blanket immunity for "multiple copies for classroom use." Further, the court said, "It is true that the use to which the materials are put by the students who purchase the coursepacks is non-commercial in nature."[160] The publishers are not challenging student use. Rather, the publishers are challenging the reproduction and sale of copyrighted works by a for-profit company maximizing its profits by refusing to pay requested royalties.[161]

The second fair use factor, the nature of the work, was not at issue. On the third factor, the amount and substantiality of the use, the court found that the amounts used were not insubstantial.[162] Finally, the court determined that the burden of proof of the effect on the market was on

---

157.   Princeton Univ. Press v. Michigan Document Servs., 74 F.3d 1528 (6th Cir. 1996), *rev'd en banc*, 99 F.3d 1381 (6th Cir. 1996).

158.   *Id.*

159.   17 U.S.C. § 107 (1994).

160.   *MDS*, 99 F.3d at 1385.

161.   *Id.*

162.   *Id.* at 1389.

the alleged infringer if the use was found to be commercial.[163] The court found the defendant's use to be commercial.[164]

The *en banc* court took issue with the finding of willful infringement. It remanded the case to state more precisely the scope of the injunction.[165]

Judge Boyce (dissenting) complains that the majority focused improperly on the identity of the person operating the copier.[166] Judge Merritt held that the plain language of the statute allows multiple copies for classroom use.[167] Finally, in a lengthy dissent nearly one-third longer than the majority opinion, Judge Ryan (who wrote the vacated opinion) complained about the circularity problem on permission fees in evaluating market effect.[168] He insists that the use to be considered is that of the student and faculty member, not the use by MDS.[169]

On March 31, 1997, the U.S. Supreme Court denied certiorari and declined to hear the appeal of MDS.[170] A nationwide answer to the issue of commercial coursepack reproduction would have been very useful to both educators and copyright holders. Whether the reasoning is flawed, *MDS* remains the law in the Sixth Circuit. The result reinforces the *Kinko's* decision and extends *Texaco's* narrowing of the fair use exception for photocopying.

---

163.   *Id.* at 1385.
164.   *Id.* at 1386.
165.   *Id.* at 1392.
166.   *Id.* at 1393.
167.   *Id.* at 1394.
168.   *Id.* at 1407.
169.   *Id.* at 1400–01.
170.   99 F.3d 1381 (6th Cir. 1996), *cert. denied,* 117 S. Ct. 1336 (1997).

Appendix
American Association of Law Libraries'
Model Law Firm Copyright Policy
October 10, 1996

Introductory Statement

Reproducing copyrighted materials is governed by the Copyright Act of 1976, 17 United States Code. AALL reaffirms the application of the fair use provision (17 U.S.C. § 107) and the library exemption (17 U.S.C. § 108) in the law firm environment. These Guidelines are intended solely for the consideration of law firm libraries as suggested procedures in complying with copyright law. Firmwide implementation should be done with the input and advice of firm management.

Firm Statement

[Firm] does not condone the unauthorized reproduction of copyrighted materials, in any format. Unauthorized reproduction includes copying beyond that which is permitted under the Copyright Act that is done without permission and/or payment of royalties.

Responsibility Statement

Compliance with the Copyright Act is the individual responsibility of every employee, including partners, associates, paralegals, and staff members.

Sources of Copies

Under these Guidelines, sources of copies should be the lawfully obtained original copyrighted work, whether found in the library, obtained through ILL from a lending library, or retrieved from an online service or document delivery service which pays royalties to the copyright owner.

Definitions

1. Copy: For purposes of these Guidelines, a copy is either 1) a photo reproduction of text or images via a copier; 2) transmission or downloading of text or images from a computer; or 3) any other replication by way of electronic means, or other form of transcription, of text or images subject to copyright restrictions.
2. Reproduction equipment: Reproduction equipment includes photocopiers, microform reader/printers, network workstations, scanners and other electronic transmission devices. It is not intended that copyright notices be posted on individual computer workstations throughout the firm.
3. Reproduction centers: Reproduction centers include areas of the firm staffed by personnel, either employed by the firm or by a third party, who have the primary responsibility for attending to copiers and other reproduction equipment. Reproduction centers that are staffed by third party vendors likely fall outside the § 108 library exemption. However, the personnel staffing these Centers work closely with firm personnel and the firm Librarian in accepting reproduction requests, and should therefore be included in the scope of these Guidelines.

Signage

Notice on Equipment

The firm should post the following signs on all reproduction equipment: *"The Making of a Copy May Be Subject to the United States Copyright Law* (Title 17 United States Code)." Alternatively, the firm may elect to use the following notice recommended by the American Library Association: *"The Copyright Law of the United States* (Title 17 U.S. Code) *Governs the Making of Photocopies or Other Reproductions of Copyrighted Material. The Person Using this Equipment Is Liable for Any Infringement"* or the notice that appears below under "Signage: Notice Where Orders are Placed and on Request Form."

Notice on Copies

The following notice should be stamped on or affixed to the first page of every copyrighted item reproduced by the library or reproduction center if the page does not contain the copyright notice: *"This Material Is Subject to the United States Copyright Law; Further Reproduction in Violation of That Law Is Prohibited."*

Notice Where Orders Are Placed and on Request Form

The Library or reproduction center should display the following sign where copying orders are placed, and should include this notice on the actual copying request form:

NOTICE

WARNING CONCERNING COPYRIGHT RESTRICTIONS

The copyright law of the United States (Title 17, United States Code) governs the making of photocopies or other reproduction of copyrighted material.

Under certain conditions specified in the law, libraries and archives are authorized to furnish a photocopy or other reproduction. One of these specified conditions is that the photocopy or reproduction is not to be "used for any purpose other than private study, scholarship or research." If a user makes a request for, or later uses, a photocopy or reproduction for purposes in excess of "fair use", that user may be liable for copyright infringement.

This institution reserves the right to refuse to accept a copying order if, in its judgment, fulfillment of the order would involve violation of copyright law.

ROUTING AND LIBRARY REPRODUCTION: The Library may route originals and/or copies of tables of contents. When the length of the routing list becomes excessive, the firm should purchase additional copies of a copyrighted work.

The library or reproduction center may make one copy of an article in response to a specific request from an employee or partner for individual scholarship, research or educational use. Recipients are cautioned against systematic reproduction of articles for later (rather than current) use and creating personal libraries. Although in most instances making subsequent copies from the original copy requires permission, circumstances may exist—such as making a single copy for one client or co-counsel, or for submission to a court (see *Nimmer on Copyright* § 13.05[D][2])—where the copying may be a fair use.

The Library or reproduction center should not, nor should individuals, make multiple copies of articles, or cover-to-cover copies of newsletters, periodical issues or volumes. This practice should be observed for both standard library materials and materials obtained from online services. *Note:* Because of the typically short length of newsletters, the library or reproduction center, as a general rule, may reproduce only small portions of newsletters subject to copyright protection.

INTERLIBRARY LENDING/DOCUMENT DELIVERY: The library typically may borrow or lend only lawfully obtained original copies of copyrighted materials, or the original copyrighted work.

Lending: In response to requests from other libraries, the library may make one copy of an article so long as the requester attests, and the library reasonably believes, that the request complies with the Copyright Act or the CONTU guidelines.

Borrowing: In requesting materials from other libraries, the library may request a single copy of an article or brief excerpts from a book, so long as the request complies with the Copyright Act or the CONTU guidelines. (CONTU suggests that a library subscribe to a journal title if it requests photocopies of articles published in the periodical within five years prior to the date of the request more than five times within a given year).

COMPUTER PROGRAMS: According to section 117 of the Copyright Act, the firm may make one archival copy of software it has purchased, and may also adapt purchased software so that it can be used on firm equipment. Firm personnel should not load any unauthorized copy of any computer program, or portion thereof, onto any computer, file server, or other magnetic or electronic media storage device belonging to the firm. License agreements should be strictly followed with regard to the use of all authorized copies of software programs.

PERMISSIONS AND ROYALTIES: These guidelines express minimum standards of fair use. Circumstances may exist where copying beyond these guidelines is permitted under the Copyright Act. However, reproducing material beyond that which is permitted by these guidelines generally will require permission, and, when necessary, payment of royalties. Royalties may be made directly to the copyright owner or other alternative mechanisms such as the Copyright Clearance Center.

QUESTIONS/FOR MORE INFORMATION: Please direct any copyright concerns to [Librarian and/or Intellectual Property Attorney].

NOTES

1. Review and Implementation: Firm management should review the copyright law—particularly 17 U.S.C. §§ 107–108—as well as firmwide copying and other copyright related activities before implementing policy. At a minimum level, this should include a review of *Copyright Office Circular R21: Reproduction of Copyrighted Words by Educators and Librarians*, the Heller/Wiant *Copyright Handbook*, and Gasaway/Wiant *Libraries and Copyright: A Guide to Copyright Law in the 1990s*.

2. Management should review carefully all firmwide online database, CD-ROM and software contracts.

3. Management should consider reviewing such seminal cases as:
   Sony Corporation of America v. Universal City Studios Inc., 464 U.S. 417 (1984).
   Washington Bureau Information v. Collier, Shannon & Scott, No. CA 91-0305-A (D.C. Va. filed 2/26/91). (Parties settled; no court decision. *But see* 41 Pat. Trademark & Copyright J. (BNA) 389 (case announced and described); 42 Pat. Trademark & Copyright J. (BNA) 619 (settlement announced))

Basic Books v. Kinko's Graphics, 758 F. Supp. 1522 (S.D.N.Y. 1991).

Pasha Publications v. Enmark Gas, 22 U.S.P.Q.2d. (BNA) 1076, 1991–1992 Copyright L. Dec. (CCH) ¶ 26,881 (N.D. Tex. 1992).

Television Digest v. U.S. Telephone Ass'n, 841 F. Supp. 5 (D.D.C. 1993).

Campbell v. Acuff-Rose Music, 114 S. Ct. 1164 (1994).

American Geophysical Union v. Texaco, 60 F.3d 913 (2d Cir. 1994).

Chapter Sixteen
Fair Use for Teaching and Research: The Folly of *Kinko's* and *Texaco**

by
L. Ray Patterson
Pope Brock Professor of Law
University of Georgia

> The very object of publishing a book . . . is to communicate to the
> world the useful knowledge which it contains. But this object would
> be frustrated if the knowledge could not be used without incurring
> the guilt of the piracy of the book.[1]

I. Introduction

The copyright statute provides that "the fair use of a copyrighted
work, including such use by reproduction in copies . . . for purposes
such as . . . teaching (including multiple copies for classroom use),

---

1.   Baker v. Selden, 101 U.S. 99, 103 (1879).

scholarship, or research, is not an infringement of copyright. . . ."[2] Despite this language, *Basic Books, Inc. v. Kinko's Graphic Corp.*[3] held that a copyshop infringes when it makes for a teacher multiple copies of materials for classroom use; and *American Geophysical Union v. Texaco, Inc.*[4] held that the payment of $2484 for three subscriptions to a scholarly journal does not entitle a scientist to reproduce an article from the journal for research purposes without paying a license fee.

The position here is that *Kinko's* and *Texaco* are wrong. Whether you agree with this conclusion will depend largely upon whether you prefer the result, a preference normally dictated by self-interest. What is needed then is a test to determine the appropriateness or inappropriateness of the rulings.

One such test is the collateral fact test. Did the courts use and rely on collateral facts to reach and support their conclusions? A disinterested person would conclude that they did. In *Kinko's*, the court relied on the fact that a commercial copyshop made the classroom copies, and in *Texaco*, that the scientist who made the copies for research was an employee of a for-profit corporation. A more fundamental—and thus more important—test is the nature-of-fair-use test. Fair use is a derivative concept of copyright and thus depends upon copyright's function (defined by the copyright statute) and purpose (defined by the copyright clause of the U.S. Constitution) for its meaning.

By these measures, *Kinko's* and *Texaco* are not only nonsense, they are dangerous nonsense. To prove the point, I discuss the purpose and function of copyright and fair use, and then examine *Kinko's* at the district court level (after which it was settled) and *Texaco* at the district court and court of appeals level. I then consider why the two cases are unfortunate instances of intellectual and legal folly.

II. The Relationship of Copyright and Fair Use

Without the copyright monopoly there would be no need for fair use, which is why it is derived from copyright. When Congress changed the nature of copyright, as in the 1976 Act, it also changed fair use by codifying it. Courts, however, continue to apply fair use precedent

---

2.   17 U.S.C. § 107 (1994).

3.   758 F. Supp. 1522 (S.D.N.Y. 1991).

4.   802 F. Supp. 1 (S.D.N.Y. 1991); 60 F.3d 913 (2d Cir. 1994).

decided under prior statutes when fair use was only a judicial and not a statutory doctrine.

Courts that do so presumably take comfort in the language of the House Report that the codification of fair use was not intended to change the doctrine in any way.[5] You can infer, however, that this was the statement of a less-than-sophisticated congressional staffer, because the statement is illogical and the fact is impossible, as demonstrated by an understanding of the origin of fair use and the change in the nature of copyright made by the 1976 Act.

Under the 1831 Copyright Act,[6] in force when Joseph Story created the fair use doctrine in *Folsom v. Marsh*,[7] copyright protected a book only as it was printed. This meant that another author could take the first author's copyrighted book and, without infringing the copyright, abridge, translate, or dramatize it and create—in copyright terms—a new work entitled to its own copyright. Story did not like the "fair abridgment" doctrine, as he made clear in cases prior to *Folsom*, because it meant that copyright protection was too narrow.[8] Consequently, he broadened the protection by laying down a rule that no longer could a second author use the entire work of another author in creating his own. The second author was limited to using only an amount of the work that was fair.

The object of the fair use doctrine thus was the printed book and its subject was the rights of competing authors, not the rights of individual users who purchased copies of the work. Eaton Drone made the point abundantly clear in his 19th century classic on copyright law[9]; that fair use did not affect the rights of individuals who used a book

---

5.   H.R. Rep. No. 94-1476, 94th Cong., 2d Sess. 66 (1976).

6.   4 Stat. 436–39 (1846).

7.   9 F. Cas. 342 (C.C.D. Mass. 1841).

8.   *See, e.g.,* Gray v. Russell, 10 F. Cas. 1035, 1038 (C.C.D. Mass. 1839) (No. 5,728) ("Although the doctrine is often laid down in the books, that an abridgment is not a piracy of the original copyright; yet this proposition must be received with many qualifications").

9.   It is a recognized principle that every *author, compiler, or publisher* may make certain uses of a copyrighted work, in the preparation of a rival or other publication. . . . [I]t would be a hindrance to learning if every work were a sealed book to all subsequent *authors*. The law, therefore, wisely allows a "fair use" to be made of every copyrighted production. . . .

   Easton S. Drone, A Treatise on the Law of Property in Intellectual Productions 286 (1879) (emphasis added).

for its intended purpose is confirmed by a ruling of Justice Brewer of the U.S. Supreme Court on circuit.[10]

The point is important because the subject of the original fair use doctrine—the rights of authors—is the basis for the "transformative" doctrine, which remains relevant only when the rights of two authors are in issue. (Thus, contrary to *Kinko's* and the district court in *Texaco*, the transformative doctrine is irrelevant to making multiple copies for classroom use or a single copy for research.)

The 1976 Act changed the nature of copyright from a concept to protect books in their printed form to a concept to protect works of authorship in manuscript as well as in print, and the change is more fundamental than has been recognized. This is because it eliminates publication as a condition for copyright, provides protection from the moment of fixation,[11] and gives the copyright owner the right to reproduce the work in copies.[12] This change narrowed the copyright monopoly in one sense and broadened it in another.

It narrowed copyright by limiting it to the original components of works[13]; it broadened copyright in the sense that copyright provided protection from the moment of fixation of the original components.[14] Logically, then, fair use could not, as a statutory doctrine, remain the same as it was when it was a judicial doctrine. As a judicial doctrine, it was limited to authors; as a statutory doctrine, fair use is broadened to encompass personal use which does not require the creation of a new work.

Copyright owners have embraced the broadening but not the narrowing of copyright. They interpret the extended protection to the time of fixation to apply to unoriginal as well as original components of the copyrighted work in order to require a license for personal use

---

10.   [T]he effect of a copyright is not to prevent any reasonable use of the book which is sold. . . . I buy a book which has been copyrighted. I may use the book for reference, study, reading, lending, copying passages from it at my will. I may not duplicate that book, and thus put it upon the market, for in so doing I would infringe the copyright. But merely taking extracts from it, merely using it, in no manner infringes upon the copyright.

    Stover v. Lathrop, 33 F. 348, 349 (C.C.D. Colo. 1888).
11.   17 U.S.C. § 102(a) (1994).
12.   *Id.* § 106(1).
13.   *Id.* § 103; *see* Feist Publications, Inc. v. Rural Tel. Serv. Co., 499 U.S. 340 (1991).
14.   17 U.S.C. § 102(a) (1994).

of the work. And they have succeeded in getting the *Kinko's* and *Texaco* courts to accept this interpretation, presumably because of what can be called the simplistic principle: If the application of statutory rules becomes too complex, then the solution is to simplify them and apply them in a simplistic manner. Even if copyrighted works contain un-copyrightable material, for example, courts can ignore that fact in applying the fair use doctrine; and even though the rule is that fair use must be determined on a case-by-case basis, this is too complicated and courts can treat copyrighted works as a class. And, because the judicial fair use doctrine does not include personal use, neither does the statutory fair use doctrine. This, of course, is precisely the effect of the court's rulings in *Kinko's* and *Texaco*.

As the above comments suggest, the fair use doctrine is a complex rule that the *Kinko's* and *Texaco* courts simplified in the interest of expedience and to the benefit of publishers. There are two difficulties that the two courts seem to have had in understanding these points. One is that they do not appreciate the fact that fair use is not a single rule but a doctrine of several rules. Thus section 107 of the Copyright Act, the fair use section, consists of two major paragraphs, the first of which provides exemplars of fair use[15] (which all three opinions under discussion either ignore or reject). The second paragraph states four non-exclusive factors to be used in determining whether a use is fair: the purpose of the use, the nature of the work, the amount used, and the impact of the use upon the market.[16] Logic dictates that these factors be applied on a work-by-work basis, but the logic eluded both *Kinko's* and *Texaco*.

The second difficulty is that these judges did not understand that the purpose of the *statutory* fair use doctrine is the reverse of the *judicial* fair use doctrine. The right to publish a book, the extent of the author's copyright under the 1831 Act (in force when the fair use doctrine was promulgated) is much narrower than the right to reproduce the work in copies under the 1976 Act. The original judicial fair use doctrine thus enhanced the narrow statutory copyright monopoly; the statutory fair use doctrine is intended to limit the broad statutory monopoly.

---

15.   17 U.S.C. § 107 (1994).

16.   *Id.* § 107(1)–(4).

Congress' concern that without the fair use limitation publishers would seek to enhance the copyright monopoly beyond its statutory limits was justified, a point proven by the publishers' current goal: to replace the fair use doctrine with a licensing system for copying any excerpt from a book.[17] *Kinko's* and *Texaco* are major steps toward that goal, and their harm emerges clearly only in light of copyright fundamentals: the function (the means of implementing a goal) and purpose (the goal itself) of both copyright and fair use.

A. The Function of Copyright and Fair Use

The function of copyright is to provide rewards to copyright owners to encourage them to provide access to their work. Copyright is thus a monopoly regulated in the public interest. This is why copyright is a statutory grant that is a series of limited rights to which a given work is subject for a limited period of time.[18] The grant is made only upon conditions precedent (the creation and fixation of an original work of authorship),[19] and the protected work is subject to fair use by others and to compulsory licenses, e.g., the compulsory recording license.[20]

The regulation of copyright exists because its subject matter— materials of learning—are vested with a large public interest. Learning, of course, requires access to the information and ideas to be learned. This need explains the access function of copyright. And it bears repeating that until the 1976 Act, copyright was not available until the copyright claimant *published* the book to be protected, thereby ensuring the right of access.

Without publication as a condition precedent of copyright, it was clear to Congress that copyright owners could seek rewards that have

---

17.   The only proof the point needs is the current fad in copyright notices. You need only check the copyright notice of almost any recent publication to learn that no one may copy any portion of the book for any reason by any means at any time without the written permission of the publisher. For "permission," read "a license for a fee."

18.   17 U.S.C. § 106 (grant of rights); *id.* §§ 107–18 (statement of limitations); *id.* §§ 302, 304 (duration of copyright); the grant is made only upon conditions precedent (the creation and fixation of an original work of authorship, *id.* § 102(a)), and the protected work is subject to fair use by others, *id.* § 107, and to compulsory licenses, e.g., the compulsory recording license, *id.* § 115.

19.   *Id.* § 102(a).

20.   *Id.* § 115.

the effect of inhibiting access to copyrighted materials, such as through a licensing system, in the private interest of profit over the public interest in learning. The expanded scope of the copyright monopoly thus required a general limitation that the requirement of publication had theretofore served. Fair use is that general limitation and it is intended to prevent the abuse of copyright by owners. Therefore, consistent with the function of copyright to reward copyright owners for providing access, the function of fair use is to protect the right of access once the works are published or made public.

B. The Purpose of Copyright and Fair Use

The right of access that fair use protects is a corollary of the purpose of copyright, which is to promote learning, as the copyright clause clearly establishes "The Congress shall have power . . . To Promote the progress of Science, . . . by securing, for limited times, to Authors . . . the exclusive Right to their . . . writings. . . ."[21] The purpose of copyright, then, is to promote learning, and the purpose of fair use, derived from this purpose and consistent with its function, is *to prevent copyright censorship.*[22] Thus, fair use provides the public with a right of access that copyright owners might otherwise wish to deny. The anti-censorship purpose of fair use, however, is not readily apparent, and it is helpful to develop the idea at some length.

We start with the point that the constitutional clause not only grants a congressional power, it also limits that power in the form of three constitutional policies of copyright: (1) the promotion of learning, because the language so states; (2) the protection of the public domain, because copyright can subsist only for a limited time and only for original writings; and (3) the benefit to the author, who is entitled to the exclusive right. It is not clear, however, what the "exclusive

---

21. U.S. CONST. art. I, § 8, cl. 1, 8. The Copyright Clause is contained in the Intellectual Property Clause, which also includes the Patent Clause. Only the Copyright Clause is quoted here.

22. For a case in which fair use served the purpose of anti-censorship, although the court did not discuss the point, see Belmore v. City Pages, Inc., 880 F. Supp. 673 (D. Minn. 1995). A newspaper reprinted in full a "fable" by a police officer published in a monthly newspaper of the Police Officers' Federation of Minneapolis. Defendant considered the fable to be racist and inappropriate and published it to make the point. In an action for copyright infringement, court granted summary judgment on the basis of fair use.

right" entails; nor is it clear what "to promote the progress of science" means. It is on these points that copyright history is instructive.

The "exclusive right" that the Constitution empowers Congress to grant to authors is the exclusive right of publication, a point the Supreme Court repeatedly has made clear.[23] The Court's rulings make sense because in 1787 copyright was available only for printed books, which, of course, were necessary for learning.

The meaning of "the progress of science" phrase, however, requires more than a sentence, because it has been ignored and apparently not litigated. The conclusion is that the phrase is to prevent Congress from granting a copyright to be used for censorship purposes, a conclusion supported by publication as a condition precedent for the Anglo-American copyright for more than two and a half centuries (from 1710 to 1978).

Copyright history, which dates from the 1550s in England, makes clear the anti-censorship purpose of the promotion of learning. The original copyright, created by the London Company of the booktrade, the Stationers' Company,[24] was a trade copyright known as the stationers' copyright,[25] and for a century and a half it served in two capacities: It was an instrument of monopoly and a device of censorship.[26]

---

23. Stephens v. Cady, 55 U.S. (14 How.) 528, 530 (1852) (copyright "is an incorporeal right to print and publish the map"); Stevens v. Gladding, 58 U.S. (17 How.) 604 (1854) (reconsidering and affirming *Cady*); Baker v. Selden, 101 U.S. 99, 103 (1879) (copyright of a book secures only "the exclusive right of printing and publishing" the book); Holmes v. Hurst, 174 U.S. 82, 85 (1899) (copyright is "the right of author to a monopoly of his publication under the copyright act"); American Tobacco Co. v. Werckmeister, 207 U.S. 284, 297 (1907) (purpose of copyright is "to secure a monopoly having a limited time, of the right to publish the production which is the result of the inventor's thought"); 17 U.S.C. § 10 (1909) ("Any person entitled thereto by this title may secure copyright for his work *by publication of the work with notice. . . .*") (emphasis added); 17 U.S.C. § 106(1) (right to reproduce in copies); § 106(3) (right to distribute copies to the public). *See* L. Ray Patterson, *Copyright and the "Exclusive Right" of Authors*, 1 J. INTELL. PROP. L. 1 (1993).

24. See C. BLAGDEN, THE STATIONERS' COMPANY, A HISTORY, 1403–1959 (1960) for a comprehensive treatment.

25. The stationers' copyright is the direct ancestor of the American copyright by way of the first English copyright statute, the Statute of Anne of 1710, 8 Anne, c. 19, the model for the first U.S. copyright statute, the 1790 Copyright Act. 1 Stat. 124 (1790).

26. Early records of the Stationers' Company that have been transcribed prove the points. A TRANSCRIPT OF THE REGISTERS OF THE COMPANY OF STATIONERS OF LONDON 1554–1640 A.D. 5 vols., Privately Printed (Edward Arber, ed. 1875–94); [hereinafter

Various Star Chamber Decrees[27] and their successor, the Licensing Act of 1662, made the printing of a book in violation of the stationers' copyright as much of an offense as printing a book without the licenser's imprimatur.[28]

The important point for present purposes is that the statutory copyright that superseded the trade copyright of the publishers was designed to prevent the continued use of copyright for either monopolistic or censorship purposes.[29] The anti-monopoly, anti-censorship

---

TRANSCRIPT]; EYRE & RIVINGTON, A TRANSCRIPT OF THE REGISTERS OF THE WORSHIPFUL COMPANY OF STATIONERS; FROM 1640–1708 A.D., 3 vols., Privately Printed (1913–14); RECORDS OF THE COURT OF THE STATIONERS COMPANY, 1576 TO 1602 (W.W. Greg & E. Boswell eds., 1930); RECORDS OF THE COURT OF THE STATIONERS' COMPANY 1602 TO 1640 (William A. Jackson ed., 1957).

27.   The most notable were the Star Chamber Decrees of 1586 and 1637, *reprinted in* L. RAY PATTERSON, COPYRIGHT IN HISTORICAL PERSPECTIVE (1968), Appendix II [hereinafter PATTERSON, COPYRIGHT IN HISTORICAL PERSPECTIVE]. The 1637 Decree was codified in the form of the Licensing Act of 1662, 13 & 14 Car. II, c. 33. There were also ordinances of censorship during the Interregnum, the Ordinances of 1643, 1647, and 1649, *reprinted in* C.H. FIRTH & R.S. RAIT, ACTS AND ORDINANCES OF THE INTERREGNUM (1911), the reason for John Milton's anti-censorship tract, *Areopagitica*.

28.   The Licensing Act of 1662, 13 & 14 Car. II, c. 33, 8 Stat. 137, provided in par. III:

> That *no private person* or persons whatsoever *shall* at any time hereafter *print*, or cause to be printed *any book* or pamphlet whatsoever, *unless the same . . . be first entered in the book of the register of the company of stationers of London*; . . . and shall be first lawfully licensed . . . [by officials designated the purpose] (emphasis added).

In par. VI, the Act provided:

> That *no person* or persons *shall* within this kingdom, or elsewhere, *imprint* or cause to be imprinted, nor shall import or bring in, or cause to be imported or brought into this kingdom . . . *any copy or copies, book or books, . . . which any person or persons have . . .* by force or virtue of *any entry* thereof duly made or to be made *in the register-book of the said company of stationers . . .* (emphasis added).

29.   *See* PATTERSON, COPYRIGHT IN HISTORICAL PERSPECTIVE, *supra* note 27. The best material to demonstrate this point is found in *Proceedings in the Commons on the Booksellers Copy-Right Bill*, in 17 WILLIAM COBBETT, THE PARLIAMENTARY HISTORY OF ENGLAND 1077–1110 (1813).

Shortly after the adverse decision of the House of Lords in Donaldson v. Beckett, 4 Burr. 2408, 98 Eng. Rep. 257 (1774), the booksellers sought to overturn the case with new legislation and failed.

A typical comment against the booksellers was one made by Mr. Attorney General Thurlow: "[H]e said, they were a set of impudent monopolizing men, that they had combined together and raised a fund of upwards of 3,000£ in order to file bills in Chancery against any person who should endeavor to get a livelihood as

nature of the new statutory copyright is most clearly shown by the title of its source, the Statute of Anne of 1710. The title read: "An act for the encouragement of learning, by vesting the copies of printed books in the authors or purchasers of such copies, during the times therein mentioned."[30]

The anti-censorship purpose is seen in the encouragement of learning and its implementation in the fact that copyright was only for "printed books," which no longer required the licenser's imprimatur; and the anti-monopoly component is seen in "the times therein mentioned," that is, limited times.[31]

The relevance of this history is that the framers adopted the limitations of the English statute for the U.S. Constitution, as shown by the fact that the title of the Statute of Anne was the source of the Copyright Clause, which reads:

> Congress shall have Power . . . To promote the Progress of Science . . . by securing for limited Times . . . to Authors . . . the exclusive Right to their . . . Writings.

Given the background of this language, one can infer that the "promotion of science" requirement was placed in the copyright clause for the same reason that "the encouragement of learning" was placed in the title of the Statute of Anne: to prevent the continued use of copyright as a device of censorship.

The history of copyright, however, never did run smoothly, and before accepting that conclusion, it is helpful to consider briefly the post–Statute of Anne history of copyright in 18th century England. That history consists largely of the efforts of the booksellers, from 1731 to 1774, to override the Statute of Anne with judicial legislation, the same thing that contemporary publishers seek to do with judicial

---

well as themselves. . . ." 17 COBBETT'S PARLIAMENTARY HISTORY 1086 (1813). The similarity to the action of contemporary publishers is evident.

30.   Statute of Anne of 1710, 8 Anne, c. 19.

31.   There is one other point that is not obvious in the title. The fact that the stationers' copyright was perpetual meant that prior to the Statute of Anne there was no public domain, a condition antithetical to a regime of press control. The demise of censorship meant the availability of a public domain, and its creation was one of the happy consequences of the first copyright statute.

rulings overriding the fair use doctrine. The 40-year episode was known as the "Battle of the Booksellers."[32]

For present purposes, as to the trade copyright, it is important to note only that: (1) it was limited to members of the Stationers' Company (which excluded authors as copyright owners); (2) it did not require printing (the registration of the title of a work secured the copyright); (3) it was ideal for monopolizing the booktrade; and (4) it was protected by decrees and acts of censorship (the *quid pro quo* for the stationers' service as policemen of the press).

As to the new statutory copyright, it is important to note that there were important differences: (1) it was made available to anyone entitled thereto, that is, *authors* and their assigns; (2) it could exist only for two terms of 14 years each (not in perpetuity); (3) it was available only for *printed* books; and (4) its condition precedent was a new writing (not a licenser's imprimatur).

The Statute of Anne thus struck two fatal blows to the booksellers' monopoly: The new copyright was no longer limited to publishers and it did not exist in perpetuity. Therefore, the publishers did not like it and they did what they always do when they do not like statutory provisions. They went to court to override them—in this instance, the limited term of copyright—to get judicial rulings giving the author a perpetual common law copyright under the natural law by reason of the act of creation, a copyright that could, of course, be assigned to a bookseller.

The booksellers created a fund for suing recalcitrant booksellers to obtain injunctions in chancery (and succeeded), before resorting to the common law courts. For present purposes, however, only two cases are important, *Millar v. Taylor*,[33] a King's Bench decision that gave the booksellers what they wanted, i.e., judicial recognition of a common law copyright in perpetuity; and *Donaldson v. Beckett*,[34] a House of Lords' decision, which took away the judicially created perpetual common law copyright.

Only five years separated *Millar* and *Donaldson*, and it is important to understand the booksellers' argument that the court in *Donaldson* rejected for two reasons: (1) that case is, in effect, an annotation of the

---

32.   PATTERSON, COPYRIGHT IN HISTORICAL PERSPECTIVE, *supra* note 27, at 151–79.

33.   4 Burr. 2303, 98 Eng. Rep 201 (K.B. 1769).

34.   2 Bro. P.C. 129, 1 Eng. Rep. 837, 4 Burr. 2408, 98 Eng. Rep. 257 (H.L. 1774); 17 WILLIAM COBBETT, PARLIAMENTARY HISTORY OF ENGLAND 954–1003 (1813).

copyright clause; and (2) the Supreme Court used it as guiding precedent in its first copyright case, *Wheaton v. Peters*.[35] The booksellers' argument was based on the fact that the Statute of Anne provided copyright only for printed books. It was logical to argue: (1) that before printing the manuscript, the author had a common law copyright in his or her creations under the natural law; and (2) that the printing of the work did not take away that copyright, since the statutory copyright was only security for making the work available to the public.

The House of Lords accepted the first part of the booksellers' argument, but not the second. Thus, it held that an author does have a common law copyright in his or her creations prior to publication; but after publication, the sole remedy is found in the copyright statute. The ruling was sound in view of the history of copyright's use for both censorship and monopolistic purposes prior to the Statute of Anne. That history is the basis for saying that the promotion of knowledge phrase in the copyright clause is to prevent copyright from being used as a device of censorship. There are, however, other compelling arguments.

The first argument is regarding what the phrase does not mean. It does not mean that every copyrighted work must be a contribution to learning. For if a work must advance learning as a condition for copyright protection, courts must evaluate and rule on the quality of the work's contents and thus act as censors. The result would be a content-based copyright, a violation of the First Amendment that would also create a conflict between two constitutional provisions.[36] Second, since the framers did not waste words, we can assume that the phrase "promote the progress of science" must have significant meaning, and one is justified in assuming that its purpose is to prevent copyright from being used to control access (the essence of censorship) to copyrighted works and thus is consistent with the First Amendment. Third, the "exclusive right" in the copyright clause only can have meant the exclusive right of publication (the only existing means

---

35.   33 U.S. (8 Pet.) 591 (1834).

36.   This explains why Justice Holmes, in Bleistein v. Donaldson Lithographing Co., 188 U.S. 239 (1903), read out of the statute one of the few attempts of Congress to provide a content-based copyright, the fine arts limitation ("in the construction of this act, the words 'engraving', 'cut', and 'print' shall be applied only to pictorial illustrations or works connected with the fine arts").

of widespread non-oral communication in the 18th century) and publication was the means of ensuring public access to promote learning. Finally, the Supreme Court's many rulings that copyright exists primarily to serve the public interest is evidence that publishers, once they have sold a book, should not be able to use copyright to control access to the information and learning that the book may contain.[37]

The anti-censorship role of fair use in the copyright scheme thus follows logically. For if the purpose of copyright is to promote learning, and if learning requires uninhibited access to the material to be learned, and if fair use is the only limitation on the copyright owner's rights in order to ensure access, it follows that the purpose of fair use is to prevent copyright censorship. The conclusions can be summed up by saying that the rule is *fair use*, the principle is the *right of access*, and the policy is the *promotion of learning*.

With this background, one can more intelligently assess the quality of the courts' reasoning and understanding of copyright in the opinions in *Kinko's* and *Texaco*.

III. *Kinko's* and *Texaco*

The folly of *Kinko's* and *Texaco* is that they give publishers the power of copyright censorship by enabling them to establish a licensing system as a substitute for fair use.[38] They are, in short, examples of judicial legislation, the effect of which is to amend the copyright statute and a cause of which is oversight of two basic propositions of

---

37. *See, e.g.,* Fox Film Corp. v. Doyal, 286 U.S. 123, 127 (1932) (primary objective in conferring the monopoly of copyright lies in the general benefits derived by public from labors of authors); United States v. Paramount Pictures, Inc., 334 U.S. 131, 158 (1948) (copyright law makes reward to author secondary consideration); Twentieth Century Music Corp. v. Aiken, 422 U.S. 151, 156 (1975) (copyright primarily to benefit public, secondarily to benefit author); Sony Corp. of Am. v. Universal City Studios, 464 U.S. 417, 429 (1984) (the limited grant of copyright is a means by which an important public purpose may be achieved).

38. The publishers' efforts apparently have been directed primarily to the academic community. *See* QUESTIONS AND ANSWERS ON COPYRIGHT FOR THE CAMPUS COMMUNITY (National Ass'n of College Stores, Inc., The Ass'n of American Publishers, Inc. & The Ass'n of American University Presses, Inc. 1994). The pamphlet can best be described as a compendium of disinformation intended to create a climate that makes copyright censorship appear to be normal. Students, of course, present a captive market for licensing fees [hereinafter NACS, QUESTIONS AND ANSWERS].

copyright law: (1) not all copyrights are created equal; and (2) there is a distinction between the work and the copyright in the work.

The first proposition is apparent from the fact that originality is a constitutional condition for copyright[39] and that Congress has provided copyright protection for original works that may contain uncopyrightable material.[40] Section 102(a) works, creative works (e.g., novels and dramas) receive plenary copyright protection, but section 103 works, compilations and derivative works "receive only limited protection," and the compilation copyright does not protect "the facts or information conveyed."[41]

The second proposition follows from the first and is manifested in the limited term of copyright, because the work goes into the public domain after the copyright has expired.[42] Thus, a long-established rule of copyright law is that the work is separate from the copyright.[43]

The rule, of course, is necessary to limit the copyright monopoly according to the scope of protection. Its importance, however, is that the varying measures of copyright protection deter copyright censorship by publishers. This is because an important condition for copyright censorship—and a concomitant licensing system to implement it—is a copyright that provides uniform protection as a proprietary monopoly so that all copyrights can be treated as members of one class.[44] Thus, variable-protection copyrights protect against censorship.

Because the two courts overlooked these basic propositions, the cases promote the publishers' goal of creating a nationwide licensing system to control the use of books for education and research.

A. Kinko's

The opinion in Kinko's reads as if it were a conclusion in search of reasons. Its comment that "American law has protected intellectual property rights through the copyright law" for almost 300 years can be

---

39.   Feist Publications, Inc. v. Rural Tel. Serv. Co., 499 U.S. 340 (1991).

40.   17 U.S.C. § 103 (1994).

41.   *Feist*, 499 U.S. at 359.

42.   17 U.S.C. §§ 302, 304 (1994).

43.   *See supra* note 23.

44.   Note the logic of licensing. Under the Licensing Act of 1662, if any portion of a book was offensive, the licenser's imprimatur was denied; under the publishers' plan, if any portion of a book is copyrightable, the publishers' imprimatur is required.

faulted on two counts.[45] First, intellectual property is not limited to copyright law; it also includes patents and trademarks. Second, since the United States had not had its 300th birthday in 1991 (when the statement was made), it is difficult to see how American law could have provided protection during that time. The first U.S. Copyright Act, in fact, was not enacted until May 1791, almost exactly 200 years—less one month—from the date of the *Kinko's* case, March 28, 1991.

Apparently the court used the 300-year figure to refer to English law, because it said "the protection derives from the English Statute of Anne (8 Anne, c. 19, 1710), the first statute to recognize the rights of authors."[46] The court more properly could have said that the protection derives from the U.S. Constitution by way of the stationers' copyright through the Statute of Anne.

The court's most puzzling statement, however, is this:

> The copyright law, *through the fair use doctrine*, has promoted the goal of encouraging creative expression and integrity by ensuring that those who produce intellectual works may benefit from them.[47]

How the fair use doctrine aids in "ensuring that those who produce intellectual works may benefit from them" is unclear, as fair use is a right of users.

The court then discussed the common disagreement as to the application of the four factors in section 107, and noted:

> This case is distinctive in many respects from those which have come before it. It involves multiple copying. The copying was conducted by a commercial enterprise which claims an educational purpose for the materials. The copying was just that copying—and did not "transform" the works in suit, that is, interpret them or add any value to the material copied, as would a biographer's or critic's use of a copyrighted quotation or excerpt. Because plaintiffs specifically allege violation of both, this court has the task of evaluating the copying under fair use doctrine and the "Agreement on Guidelines for Classroom Copying in Not-For-Profit Educational Institutions."[48]

---

45. 758 F. Supp. at 1529.
46. *Id.*
47. *Id.* at 1529–30 (emphasis added).
48. *Id.* at 1529.

The paragraph is a culmination of the court's faulty reasoning. True, the case "involves multiple copying," but the copies were made for classroom use and section 107 specifically says that the fair use of a copyrighted work for a purpose such as "teaching (including multiple copies for classroom use)" is not an infringement. Nor does the statute require that the copies be made by the individual teacher or student. Copying by a commercial enterprise does not, of course, alter the purpose for which the materials are copied, that is, for use in the classroom.

The plaintiffs' allegation that the copying violated the classroom guidelines suggests that their counsel took advantage of an uninformed court. Most disinterested copyright scholars recognize that: (1) the guidelines are not law; (2) the guidelines provide safe-harbor provisions that do not preempt the right of fair use[49]; and (3) if the copying exceeds the guidelines, the issue is fair use, not violation of the guidelines. Thus, if copying is within the guidelines, there is no issue of either infringement or fair use; if copying exceeds the guidelines, the only issue is infringement or fair use.

The court's discussion of the four fair use factors reads like a parody of an answer to a law school exam. In dealing with the first factor, purpose and character of the use, the court discusses transformative use and commercial use. The emphasis on transformative use is misplaced, and the use of Judge Leval's test—that " '[t]hat the use . . . must employ the quoted matter in a different manner or for a different purpose from the original,' "[50]—was error. As the Supreme Court recognized in *Acuff-Rose*,[51] Congress defined the use in issue (multiple copies for classroom use) to be one as to which the transformative requirement is irrelevant. Thus, the fact that "Kinko's work cannot be categorized as anything other than a mere repackaging" is relevant, but not for the reason the court thought. Multiple copies of excerpts are the kind of repackaging that Congress authorized in section 107.

---

49.   The Agreement provides: "Moreover, the following statement of guidelines is not intended to limit the types of copying permitted under the standards of fair use under judicial decision and which are stated in Section 107. . . ." H.R. REP. No. 94-1476, 94th Cong., 2d Sess. 68 (1976).

50.   758 F. Supp. at 1530.

51.   Campbell v. Acuff-Rose Music, Inc., 114 S. Ct. 1164 (1994).

As to commercial use, the court admitted that the packets "in the hands of the students, was no doubt educational. However, the use in the hands of Kinko's employees is commercial."[52] This, of course, is like saying that the telephone company makes use of a work that a professor faxes to a student and the service provider is therefore an infringer, even though the professor is not. The point can be made more directly. Kinko's is a non-discretionary service provider which had no say as to the content of the materials it copied. In making Kinko's a commercial user of the work, the court was clearly reaching for a reason to support its conclusion, and not using reason to determine what the conclusion should be.

As to the nature of the work, the second factor, the court found in favor of Kinko's because "The books infringed in suit were factual in nature," as if all such books are members of a single class.[53] The constitutional requirement of originality, however, means that a determination of the copyrightability of works must be made on a book-by-book basis, and not all factual works meet this requirement.

It is in the amount and substantiality of the portion used, the third factor, where the court's analysis fails it completely. Although admitting that the availability of the work is an appropriate factor, the court noted that "plaintiffs in this case convincingly argue that damage to out-of-print works may in fact be greater since permissions fees may be the only income for authors and copyright owners."[54] The court followed this statement with a classic example of bootstrap reasoning: "This court finds and concludes that the portions copied were critical parts of the books copied, since that is the likely reason the college professors used them in their classes."[55]

As to the fourth factor, market effect, the court had little trouble finding that it favored the publishers. Noting that Kinko's "produced 300- to 400-page packets at a cost of $24 to the student," and that one packet which "contained excerpts from 20 different books, totalled 324 pages, and cost $21.50,"[56] the court found "that Kinko's copying unfavorably impacts upon plaintiffs' sales of their books and collection

---

52. *Kinko's*, 758 F. Supp. at 1530.
53. *Id.* at 1532.
54. *Id.* at 1533.
55. *Id.*
56. *Id.*

of permissions fees."[57] The court, however, did not explain whether, in the absence of the coursepacks, a professor would have required students to purchase 20 books for one course. But apparently it deemed this irrelevant, because the adverse impact "is more powerfully felt by authors and copyright owners of the out-of-print books, for whom permissions fees constitutes a significant source of income."[58] Presumably the out-of-print books had been sold, and it is worth noting that the copyright statute gives the copyright owner the right *either* to sell *or* to lease (not both) copies of the work.[59] The court, in short, was saying that not receiving fees to which the copyright owner is not entitled is harm that creates an infringement action.

The court's treatment of other defenses—copyright misuse, estoppel and acquiescence, and failure to record—manifests the same quality of reasoning as does the fair use discussion. The remedy granted, however, should be noted.

In granting an injunction to prevent the copying of future works, the court ignored the fact that copyrighted works may contain uncopyrightable materials and thereby overlooked two simple and irrefutable propositions: (1) the injunction provides copyright protection without regard to statutory (or constitutional) requirements and thus creates a federal common law copyright; and (2) under the Constitution, only Congress has the authority to grant copyrights.

The analytically deficient opinion in *Kinko's* could be ignored as an unfortunate sport, except for two things: (1) its holding is widely trumpeted by publishers as proof of the correctness of their claim that a license scheme is an appropriate substitute for the fair use doctrine[60]; and (2) few people bother to read the opinion and therefore pass up the opportunity to understand that its holding is neither sound nor correct. The court, having substituted argument and inference for the actual words of the statute, foolishly rendered a holding that amends the Copyright Act.

Kinko's was followed by an equally intellectually egregious opinion, *Texaco*. On the district court level, *Texaco* is a product of a

---

57.   *Id.* at 1534.

58.   *Id.*

59.   17 U.S.C. § 106(3) (1994).

60.   *See* Association of American Publishers, Questions and Answers on Copyright for the Academic Community (1994).

little knowledge; on the appellate level, it is simply a classic case of intellectual dishonesty.

B. *Texaco* in the District Court

Texaco, said the district court, "spends in excess of $80,000,000 a year in research," a fact that seems to have a mesmeric effect on the court and explains the judge's bias favoring the publishers.[61] The point apparently is that publishers are entitled to their fair share of these funds. Presumably, the $828 for each of three subscriptions to the periodical at issue (for a total of $2484 a year) that Texaco paid was weighed and found wanting; therefore Texaco must pay an additional fee to copy an article from any one of the three subscription copies, delivered and paid for, for purposes of research.[62]

The ruling shows again the truth of the maxim about a little knowledge.[63] To prove the point, it is necessary to discuss only the judge's misreading of the "progress of science" phrase in the copyright clause along with his misunderstanding of the relationship of the transformative doctrine to the fair use doctrine.

1. The Promotion of Learning. The judge quoted the copyright clause of the Constitution and announced that "The theory espoused by this constitutional provision is that the advancement of public good, through growth of knowledge and learning, is to be obtained by securing the private commercial interests of authors."[64] In support of this conclusion, he stated four reasons:

1. "If authors are guaranteed the opportunity to profit from their writings, they will have an incentive to create, and the public will ultimately reap the resulting expansion of human knowledge."[65]

---

61. 802 F. Supp. at 4.
62. *Id.* at 7.
63. An example is the court's statement, "The copyright entered the law of England through the Statute of Anne in 1710." *Id.* at 8. The judge ignored the 150-year history of the stationers' copyright, the predecessor of, and model for, the statutory copyright.
64. *Id.* at 9.
65. *Id.* at 10.

2. "If there were no copyright protection, authors would find it difficult to earn a living from their writings because others could freely copy the works."[66]
3. "[T]he public's right to appropriate the works of authors would make the public poorer through loss of the benefit of authors' endeavors."[67]
4. The energies of authors "would be diverted to other pursuits by the need to feed their families."[68]

All of the propositions are manifestations of concern about the welfare of authors, presumably based on the notion that without copyright to protect their works, authors will not, or cannot afford to, write. The facts of the case, however, showed: (1) the authors received no pay for the works in issue[69]; and (2) the publisher required an assignment of the copyright as a condition for publishing the article. So much for the argument that authors will have to engage in other "pursuits by the need to feed their families" if publishers are not allowed to license the copying of articles from periodicals they have sold!

2. Fair Use and Transformative Use. The judge's argument: "[T]he public's right to appropriate the works of authors would make the public poorer through loss of the benefit of authors' endeavors," is misleading at best and nonsensical at worst. It almost surely derives from confusion as to the relationship of fair use and transformative use. The irony of the judge's position is that he would allow one author to take another author's work, transform it, and put it on the market as a matter of fair use. But he would not allow an individual to copy one article from a periodical for research, because that would be infringement as an appropriation of the work of the author.

There comes a time, however, when even judges should use a little bit of common sense. One does not appropriate the work of an author simply by making a single copy for personal use. And if a thousand or even a hundred thousand persons each makes a single copy of the periodical for which they have paid, the publisher is hurt not one bit.

---

66. *Id.*
67. *Id.*
68. *Id.*
69. *Id.* at 16.

This follows from the nature of copyright: an intangible right attached to a physical object, e.g., a book, which is intended to be used by another, whether reader, researcher, or scholar. Thus, one should not confuse the use of the work with the appropriation of the copyright. Use of the work is permissible, appropriation of the copyright is not. The basis of this confusion is the unarticulated premise of the argument that the "author" owns both the work and the copyright. But copyright is only an incorporeal right, a point recognized since the 1769 ruling of the Court of King's Bench in *Millar v. Taylor*.

The district court opinion can be faulted both as a matter of logic and a little knowledge, but the Second Circuit compounded the problem by affirming the case in an opinion that is intellectually dishonest.

C. *Texaco* in the Second Circuit

The only manufacturer in the free-market system which sells a product and then claims the right to license its use for its intended purpose is the publisher. The point is well demonstrated by the fact that a subscriber who pays $2484 annually for three subscriptions to a periodical, as did Texaco, must pay the publisher a licensing fee to copy a single article. The ruling defies common sense. The Second Circuit in *Texaco*, however, substituted rationalization in using a classic technique to reach a result it desired rather than accept the result that the plain meaning of the statutory language mandated. It simply reframed the question. The parties briefed the case on the issue of whether a scientist's copying of articles from scholarly journals for research purposes was fair use. The appellate court changed the issue so that a scientist's copying for research purposes became institutional copying for archival purposes.

Section 107, of course, deals with neither institutional nor archival copying, and the reformulation of the issue enabled the court to avoid the plain language of the first paragraph of section 107 and to concentrate on the four fair use factors of the second paragraph. Thus, in a lengthy opinion, the court totally ignores the first paragraph of section 107 in its discussion.

1. The Second Circuit Misread the Copyright Clause. The Second Circuit's cavalier disregard of the Copyright Clause is shown by its willingness to engage in judicial legislation and amend the copyright statute by judicial action. Thus, in its footnote 19, the court suggested a judicially created compulsory license. "If the dispute is not now settled, this appears to be an appropriate case for exploration of the possibility of a court-imposed compulsory license," a proposition for which it cited *Nimmer on Copyright.* Apparently it did not occur to the court—or to Nimmer—that such a ruling might well be unconstitutional under the Copyright Clause and Supreme Court precedent.[70] The court's most grievous error in reading the Copyright Clause, however, occurred when it said:

> Ultimately, *the monopoly privileges conferred by copyright protection and the potential financial rewards therefrom are* . . . *to motivate publishers to produce journals* . . . It is the prospect of such dissemination that contributes to the motivation of these authors.[71]

The court was wrong. And in assuming the power to redefine the rights and duties of copyright owners that Congress has legislated, the court misread the Copyright Clause. The Copyright Clause does not empower Congress to reward publishers, only authors. And for a court to say copyright benefits publishers directly in order to benefit authors indirectly is unwise. Until the Copyright Clause is amended, Congress can enact copyright statutes only to benefit authors.

2. The Second Circuit Misread the Copyright Act. The Second Circuit also misread the Copyright Act, for its willingness to amend the statute by judicial ruling is based on "legislative" facts as a substitute for the words of the statute. As if it were speaking of the results of a study, for example, the court concluded that photocopying constitutes a threat to the sanctity of copyright, explaining in conclusory fashion that, "the invention and widespread availability of photocopying technology threatens to disrupt the delicate balances established by the Copyright Act."[72]

The comment is disingenuous. The court surely knew that photocopying machines were in widespread use in 1976; and only a failure to read and analyze the first paragraph of section 107 could enable it to avoid the fact that Congress did take that into account. The terms "copying" and "copies" in the first paragraph clearly do not refer to

---

70. Globe Newspaper Co. v. Walker, 210 U.S. 356, 367 (1908) (since "Congress has prescribed the remedies . . . 'no others can be resorted to.' ")

71. 60 F.3d at 927 (emphasis added).

72. *Id.* at 916.

handwritten copies. Since scriptoria are not a feature of modern-day life, it is photocopy machines that enable teachers to use the right to make "multiple copies for classroom use." So, instead of the availability of photocopying, it is the court's reliance on an unproven legislative fact that "threatens to disrupt the delicate balances established by the Copyright Act."

The court gave its reason for its willingness to engage in judicial legislation: "Congress has thus far provided scant guidance for resolving fair use issues involving photocopying, legislating specifically only as to library copying, and providing *indirect* advice concerning classroom copying."[73] The facts are that: (1) Congress specifically provided that "the fair use of a copyrighted work, including such use by reproduction in copies . . . for purposes such as . . . teaching (including multiple copies for classroom use), scholarship, or research, is not an infringement of copyright"; and (2) the classroom guidelines have no relevance to a case involving copying by a research scientist for a corporation.

Perhaps the court's most unfortunate misreading of the statute is seen in this statement: "It is indisputable that, as a general matter, a copyright holder is entitled to demand a royalty for licensing others to use its copyrighted work, see 17 U.S.C. 106 (copyright owner has exclusive right 'to authorize' certain uses). . . ."[74]

The court was wrong again. The statute gives the copyright owner the option of distributing copies "by sale . . . *or* by rental, lease, or lending."[75] It does not, as the court implied, give the copyright owner the right to sell books and then lease the use of that copy to the purchaser (and others) in return for royalty payments.

The *Texaco* court's unwitting candor about copyright aiding publishers over authors brings the central issue to the forefront. Can courts ignore the First Amendment and the Copyright Clause and amend the copyright statute "by judicial action" and do what Congress cannot? That is, can courts empower publishers to leverage their single-source monopoly into a licensing scheme so they can exercise copyright censorship over materials that students must have for learning?

---

73. *Id*. at 917 (emphasis added).

74. *Id*. at 929.

75. 17 U.S.C. § 106(3) (1994).

IV. Conclusion: The Folly of *Kinko's* and *Texaco*

That the two cases in their folly fail the test of common sense is beyond question. Indeed, they can be said to be decisions of extreme dumbness for one simple reason: *Kinko's* and *Texaco* establish the predicate for copyright censorship.[76] The fault that led to this folly, apparently, was a lack of imagination, the inability to see through the cant and hypocrisy of copyright owners and understand the impact of their decisions. The decisions give the manufacturer of books the right to sell its product and then to license its use for its intended purpose, a form of double dipping that the free market has generally eschewed. The surprising thing is not that publishers would make the claim, but that any court would agree with them, which raises the question of why *Kinko's* and *Texaco* fail the test of common sense.

There is no definitive answer, but it is useful to note that the publishing industry is a powerful one that has three major advantages in the copyright arena. Professor Jessica Litman has articulated them with clarity in her article on copyright changes sought for the National Information Infrastructure. As she has demonstrated, copyright owners: (1) exercise great influence on the legislative process in Congress[77]; (2) control the media and inform the public about copyright law as it serves their purpose[78]; and (3) control the media and create a culture about copyright and property rights to aid them in misleading courts.[79]

---

76.   To see the publishers' promiscuous use of *Kinko's* in their campaign for copyright censorship, see NACS, QUESTIONS AND ANSWERS, *supra* note 38, at 6–9. The publishers also cite the district court order in this case to support their campaign.

77.   "Congress, for its part, has, since the turn of the century been delegating the policy choices involved in copyright matters to the industries affected by copyright." Jessica Litman, *The Exclusive Right to Read*, 13 CARDOZO ARTS & ENT. L. REV. 29, 33 (1994); *see also* Jessica Litman, *Copyright Legislation and Technical Change*, 68 OR. L. REV. 275 (1989).

78.   "[B]y asserting that what members of the public think of as ordinary use of copyrighted works was, in fact, flagrant piracy . . . copyright owners may well have won a rhetorical battle the rest of the country never realized was being fought." Jessica Litman, *The Exclusive Right to Read*, 13 CARDOZO ARTS & ENT. L. REV. 29, 36 (1994).

79.   "[B]ecause the assumptions underlying copyright owners' claims to expansive control over the works they create and disseminate crept into our discourse without much examination at a time when the price of acknowledging them was only nominal, we have so far allowed important policy choices to be made without serious debate." *Id.* at 37.

The result is what can be called the halo effect. Copyright is viewed as a special type of property that involves learning, which provides it with an immunity from normal rules; indeed, the copyright owner is to be honored for its sacrifice in making learning available to the masses, and is thus entitled to special consideration because profit is deemed to be a secondary consideration. Copyright owners use the halo effect to good advantage, claiming that they are entitled to govern the copyright monopoly by their own rules—for example, with overly broad copyright notices—not the law as duly enacted by Congress. *Kinko's* and *Texaco* are products of the halo effect.[80] By treating copyright as a common law proprietary monopoly in lieu of the statutory public-interest monopoly the Constitution authorizes, the courts gave publishers the power to establish their licensing system.

The major value of the halo effect for publishers is that it makes effective their implied threat of withholding books from the market if their wishes are not granted. Few judges recognize how time-worn the threat is; it has been used at least since the 17th century when, to protect their monopoly, booksellers in 1643 petitioned Parliament for censorship legislation.[81] The halo effect thus obscures the *Kinko's-Texaco* fallacy: One is harmed by not receiving that to which he is not entitled.

Congress made "multiple copies for classroom use" and research fair use of copyrighted works to protect students and scholars engaged in research from the very market claims that (in disregard of the Constitution) *Kinko's* and *Texaco* purported to legalize. Fortunately, there are other courts not located in the center of the publishing industry that can avoid the folly of *Kinko's* and *Texaco*, and can save the country from copyright censorship which the publishers' licensing system requires.

---

80. The fact that the publishing industry is centered in New York City, the home of the *Kinko's* and *Texaco* courts, is irrelevant as a matter of law, but not of common sense.

81. The argument was "Many mens studies carry no other profit or recompense with them, but the benefit [copyright] of their Copies; and if this be taken away, many Pieces of great worth and excellence will be strangled in the womb, or never conceived at all for the future." Stationers' Petition of April 1643, I TRANSCRIPT, *supra* note 26, at 584, 587 (brackets in original).

Chapter Seventeen
Copyright and Distance Education: Displays, Performances, and the Limitations of Current Law[*]

by
Kenneth D. Crews

Associate Professor, Indiana University School of Law—Indianapolis
IU School of Library and Information Science
Director, Copyright Management Center

I. Introduction

Instructors utilize a wealth of different materials in the classroom, whether teaching in a face-to-face setting or through distance learning. Many of the materials that teachers use are protected by copyright, and

---

common uses in the classroom or in distance learning can give rise to copyright implications. Showing a chart or picture or playing a video-tape or music recording can be a "display" or a "performance" under the law. Public displays and performances are among the exclusive rights held by copyright owners. The simple showing of these works in the classroom setting could be a copyright infringement, absent an exemption. Fortunately, the copyright law also includes exceptions or limitations on the rights of owners, the best known of which is fair use.[2] But the U.S. Copyright Act of 1976[3] has many other, more specific, exceptions. Of particular relevance for this chapter is section 110 and its allowance of some performances and displays for face-to-face teaching and distance learning.[4] Those exceptions are not sweeping and, especially for distance learning, the law is often a convolution of arcane details leading ultimately to a delineation of works that may be performed and ones that may not. Often the line drawn by the statute defies logic and bears little relation to the needs of education.

Copyright law in the United States exists by Act of Congress, and the U.S. Constitution authorizes Congress to make this law: "The Congress shall have Power . . . To promote the Progress of Science and useful Arts, by securing for limited Times to Authors and Inventors the exclusive Right to their respective Writings and Discoveries."[5] The law fundamentally grants copyright privileges to authors, but does so with the purpose of promoting knowledge and learning. The law is based on the premise that granting rights to creators of new works will encourage that creativity and encourage the investment and risk associated with publishing and disseminating new works. Exclusive rights allowed to copyright owners include rights to reproduce, distribute, perform, or display publicly, and to make derivative works from the copyrighted material.[6] Most academicians undoubtedly have encountered these rights when they have sought to make copies of book

---

2. 17 U.S.C. § 106 (1994).
3. *Id.* §§ 101–1101 (1994).
4. *Id.* § 110(1)–(2) (applicable to displays and performances in face-to-face teaching and in distance learning).
5. U.S. CONST. art. I, § 8, cl. 1, 8.
6. 17 U.S.C. § 106 (1994).

chapters and other materials for classroom distribution,[6] or when they were required to assign rights to a publisher in exchange for having their articles appear in some scholarly journals.[7]

Fair use and other public rights are an essential balance to those exclusive rights, with the purpose of encouraging socially beneficial activities and the advancement of knowledge. Thus, fair use generally applies to pursuits such as teaching, research, criticism, and news reporting.[8] Fair use is today codified in section 107 of the Copyright Act, which provides little specificity and few details about the scope and range of fair use under particular circumstances. Whether an activity is fair use depends on the balancing of four ambiguous and flexible factors. Other statutory limitations on owners' rights are, by comparison, highly detailed and clearly defined. Section 110 is one such provision.

Section 110 includes a variety of exceptions to the exclusive rights of display and performance otherwise held by the proprietor. It addresses such seemingly disparate circumstances as hymns sung during church services[9] and background music played in record stores to generate sales of music recordings.[10] It also addresses educational uses in face-to-face teaching and in distance learning. This chapter explores those provisions and evaluates them in accord with educational needs. It demonstrates the broad reach of the face-to-face provisions, but it underscores the confines of the distance-learning rules. This chapter also highlights alternatives and options available to teachers and administrators who seek to use copyright protected materials, but who encounter the barriers set forth in the law. Finally, this chapter outlines the law's shortcomings for meeting educational needs and proposes areas in need of revision.

---

6.   A 1991 court ruling against Kinko's for making photocopied coursepacks underscored that fair use for classroom handouts will have limits, even though the ruling was limited to the making of systematic coursepacks for commercial profit. Basic Books, Inc. v. Kinko's Graphics Corp., 758 F. Supp. 1522 (S.D.N.Y. 1991).

7.   17 U.S.C. § 201(d) (1994).

8.   According to the fair use section, the law generally applies to "criticism, comment, news reporting, teaching (including multiple copies for classroom use), scholarship, or research. . . ." *Id.* § 107.

9.   *Id.* § 110(3).

10. *Id.* § 110(7).

II.   Displays and Performances and the Copyright Act

A. Public Displays and Performances

The terms "display" and "performance" are defined in the Copyright Act. To display something includes the simple showing of a work, whether it is a picture, a page of text, a book cover, a chart, or other material.[12] To perform something includes to recite, play, or act the work, or to show sequentially images from an audiovisual work, or to make audible the accompanying sounds.[13] Distance learning necessarily involves displays and performances whenever an instructor shows a chart, picture, or video clip and the images are transmitted to students at other locations.

The rights of the copyright owner, however, extend only to displays and performances that are "public."[14] Under the law, much of what occurs in class is "public." The statutory definition provides four possibilities that would make the activity public. First, the performance or display is "at a place open to the public." Many classrooms and other learning environments are open to the public, whether the public chooses to enter or not. Second, the activity is "at any place where a substantial number of persons outside of a normal circle of a family and its social acquaintances is gathered." That definition describes most groups of students enrolled in a course. Third, the works are transmitted or communicated to a place as described in the first two situations. Fourth, the transmission or communication is to the public, even if it is received at different times or at different places. The notion of "public" in this last example would most likely borrow the concept of "substantial" numbers of persons beyond friends and family. These four possibilities encompass nearly every common situation involving face-to-face and distance teaching.

---

12.   *Id.* § 101. ("To 'display' a work means to show a copy of it, either directly or by means of a film, slide, television image, or any other device or process or, in the case of a motion picture or other audiovisual work, to show individual images nonsequentially").

13.   *Id.* § 101. ("To 'perform' a work means to recite, render, play, dance, or act it, either directly or by means of any device or process or, in the case of a motion picture or other audiovisual work, to show its images in any sequence or to make the sounds accompanying it audible").

14.   *Id.* § 101.

B. Face-to-Face Teaching

In traditional face-to-face teaching, nearly all displays and performances are allowed under a specific exception to the owners' rights. Section 110(1) allows almost any "performance" or "display" in the nonprofit educational context, when the activities are in the classroom or
other similar location. In particular, the following activities are explicitly not infringements under this statute:

> [P]erformance or display of a work by instructors or pupils in the
> course of face-to-face teaching activities of a nonprofit educational
> institution, in a classroom or similar place devoted to instruction,
> unless, in the case of a motion picture or other audiovisual work, the
> performance, or the display of individual images, is given by means
> of a copy that was not lawfully made under this title, and that the
> person responsible for the performance knew or had reason to believe
> was not lawfully made. . . .[14]

This provision sets the barest and the most reasonable of any
condition for use: Any copy of an audiovisual work must be "lawfully
made."[15] Even the requirement of "face-to-face" is not burdensome and
apparently does not have to be read literally. The House Report, which
accompanied passage of the 1976 Act, states:

> The concept does not require that the teacher and students be able to
> see each other, although it does require their simultaneous presence
> in the same general place. Use of the phrase "in the course of face-to-
> face teaching activities" is intended to exclude broadcasting or other
> transmissions from an outside location into classrooms, whether radio
> or television and whether open or closed circuit. However, as long as
> the instructor and pupils are in the same building or general area, the
> exemption would extend to the use of devices for amplifying or
> reproducing sound and for projecting visual images.[16]

---

14. *Id.* § 110(1).

15. Taking the statute apart word for word, it actually contains several conditions.
One major treatise isolates four distinct conditions. PAUL GOLDSTEIN, 2 COPYRIGHT,
§ 5.8.1.1 (2d ed. 1990) [hereinafter GOLDSTEIN]. The condition of "lawfully made"
refers to copies made pursuant to "this title," that is, pursuant to Title 17 of the
United States Code, which is the entire Copyright Act. Thus, copies made under a
rightful exercise of fair use, for example, would also be "lawfully made."

16. H.R. REP. No. 94-1476, 94th Cong., 2d Sess. (1976), *reprinted in* 17 OMNIBUS COPY-
RIGHT REVISION LEGISLATIVE HISTORY 81 (1977) [hereinafter H.R. REP. No. 94-1476].

This explanation may mean that Congress intended to permit displays and performances of works through some closed-circuit system that delivers images and sounds to other nearby locations on campus—a common need for popular classes, where all students are unable to meet in one room.

That capability is crucial for campuses lacking large auditoriums for basic and popular courses. Nevertheless, the argument remains that any communication of a performance or display to a place beyond their origination constitutes a transmission—even if only a short distance—and is no longer face-to-face teaching. By that reasoning, transmission of the works subjects the activities to the limitations and restrictions applicable to distance learning.

C. Transmission of Classroom Activities

Section 110(2) allows for the "transmission" of a performance or display, but only within rigorous limits. The law defines "transmit" to mean a communication of a performance or display "by any device or process whereby images or sounds are received beyond the place from which they are sent."[18] By the vision of Congress, teaching occurs in the face-to-face classroom, or it occurs by transmission from place of origin to remote locations. That vision might have been sufficient and even all-encompassing when Congress enacted section 110 in 1976, but it hardly captures the rapidly evolving nature of teaching and learning, nor does it embrace the range of technologies available today for organizing and delivering the learning experience. Yet "transmission" is the characteristic that separates distance education from traditional teaching, and transmission triggers the application of section 110(2).

Section 110(2) may be understood in two parts. First, the statute sets forth some ground rules for its applicability to any situation. Those ground rules define the allowable reasons for the transmission of works and the places where, or the persons to whom, the works may be transmitted. Second, even upon full compliance with those conditions, the law narrowly circumscribes the range of copyright protected works that may be used in distance learning. These statutory rigors stand in sharp contrast to the more open opportunities for displays and performances in the traditional classroom.

---

18.   17 U.S.C. § 101 (1994).

III. The Ground Rules for Distance Education

A. Conditions to Using Section 110(2)

Section 110(2), subparts (A), (B), and (C) set forth requirements for enjoying the benefits of the statute, and many distance-learning courses from established colleges and universities will often qualify. But these ground rules do not adequately anticipate the growing diversity of "distance-learning" experiences, whereby students may learn on their own pace, at home, or by accessing prepared materials on the World Wide Web or other networked system.

Subsection (C)(I) requires that the transmission be "primarily" for "reception in classrooms or similar places normally devoted to instruction. . . ." This language easily anticipates closed-circuit systems that send signals to a classroom or other place used as instruction. The language need not be read so strictly as to confine education only to customary classrooms—educators should be able to send the signal to any facility set aside for instruction at that time. The House Report makes explicit that such places may include studios, libraries, and other facilities, as long as they are used for instructional purposes at some designated times.[18] The report makes no mention of an individual's house or dormitory room as a place of instruction, although the report refers frequently to educational television and radio of such a nature that their signals are routinely received at home. That language would support the argument that the home is increasingly a place "devoted to instruction" for many students.

The statutory language, of course, is not explicit, leaving room for concerned and well-meaning educators to curtail what might otherwise be lawful and beneficial strategies for teaching. The lack of precision in the statute is also an open door for detractors to argue that the statute means only what it narrowly purports on its face, and that transmission to private homes is not permitted. That interpretation would effectively eliminate all uses of copyrighted works in the conduct of distance learning, except with permission and the likely royalty fees that would ensue.

A related issue arises from (C)(ii), which requires that the transmission be "primarily" for students who are unable to attend in the

---

18.   H.R. Rep. No. 94-1476, *supra* note 16, at 82.

classroom because of their "disabilities or other special circumstances." Why are colleges and universities offering distance-learning programs? If the reason is simply for the ease and convenience of students, that may not be a "special circumstance" which prevents their attendance. If the reason is because students are unable—because of work, family obligations, or personal conditions—to attend class at the appointed time, then academics may have a good case for using the rights of section 110(2). The House Report endorses this view:

> Accordingly, the exemption is confined to instructional broadcasting that is an adjunct to the actual classwork of nonprofit schools or is primarily for people who cannot be brought together in classrooms such as preschool children, displaced workers, illiterates, and shut-ins.
>
> There has been some question as to whether or not the language in this section of the bill is intended to include instructional television college credit courses. These telecourses are aimed at undergraduate and graduate students in earnest pursuit of higher educational degrees who are unable to attend daytime classes because of daytime employment, distance from campus, or some other intervening reason. So long as these broadcasts are aimed at regularly enrolled students and conducted by recognized higher educational institutions, the committee believes that they are clearly within the language of section 110(2)(C)(ii). Like night school and correspondence courses before them, these telecourses are fast becoming a valuable adjunct of the normal college curriculum.[20]

Readers should note that the subparts under (C) are stated in the alternative, with the connector "or," not "and." Thus, for example, if one satisfies subsection (I) regarding the place of receiving the transmission, one need not satisfy subsection (ii) regarding "special circumstances."

B. Open- vs. Closed-circuit Transmission

The statute states that the transmission must be "primarily" for reception by the certain categories of students described above. Closed-circuit systems are able to limit access to the defined groups. But transmission via cable or public broadcast enables other members of the public to view the class and consequently to receive the transmissions of copyrighted works. Does access by non-students reduce the ability

---

20.   *Id.* at 84.

of the university to utilize section 110(2)? According to the House Report, apparently not:

> In all three cases, the instructional transmission need only be made "primarily" rather than "solely" to the specified recipients to be exempt. Thus, the transmission could still be exempt even though it is capable of reception by the public at large. Conversely, it would not be regarded as made "primarily" for one of the required groups of recipients if the principal purpose behind the transmission is reception by the public at large, even if it is cast in the form of instruction and is also received in classrooms. Factors to consider in determining the "primary" purpose of a program would include its subject matter, content, and the time of its transmission.[20]

Hence, an instructor can broadcast via open-circuit system, but the content and other circumstances should be clearly oriented toward creating a learning environment and not toward making a performance of a work of general interest available to public viewers.

C. Transmissions Not Part of Regular Courses

Many colleges or universities use distance-learning facilities to transmit instructional material that may not be part of the regular curriculum. These broadcasts might be continuing education programs or other special offerings. According to the House Report, the rights of section 110 still apply:

> The concept of "systematic instructional activities" is intended as the general equivalent of "curriculums," but it could be broader in a case such as that of an institution using systematic teaching methods not related to specific course work. A transmission would be a regular part of these activities if it is in accordance with the pattern of teaching established by the governmental body or institution. The use of commercial facilities, such as those of a cable service, to transmit the performance or display, would not affect the exemption as long as the actual performance or display was for nonprofit purposes.[21]

IV. Displays and Performances Allowed

Once stating all the "ground rules" for section 110(2), the law then proceeds to confine the types of materials that may be included in the

---

20.   *Id.* at 83.
21.   *Id.*

transmission. One key phrase captures the limitation by allowing "performance of a nondramatic literary or musical work or display of a work. . . ."[23] This brief excerpt from the statute allows displays of all works, but performances of only certain types. In particular, section 110(2) limits the allowed performance to a "nondramatic literary or musical work." The terms "dramatic" and "nondramatic" are not defined in the Copyright Act, but according to the House Report, "the copyright owner's permission would be required for the performance on educational television or radio of a dramatic work, of a dramatico-musical work such as an opera or musical comedy, or of a motion picture."[24] Following are some examples of allowed and disallowed activities in "transmission" or distance learning:

Allowed:

✦ Showing a photograph, chart, table or a still from a motion picture. These are "displays" of works.

✦ Performances of musical works and literary works, but only if they are "nondramatic" works. "Literary works" are defined to encompass "works, other than audiovisual works, expressed in words, numbers, or other verbal or numerical symbols or indicia. . . ."[25] Motion pictures and videos are specifically excluded from the scope of "literary works." "Musical work" is also not defined in the statute.

Not Allowed:

✦ Performances of any dramatic work, whether musical or textual.

✦ Performances of any work that is neither "musical" nor "literary." Hence, all audiovisual works are excluded from the specific right of use in distance learning. Audiovisual works include motion pictures, videotapes, and even animated screen displays from many computer programs.

---

23.   17 U.S.C. § 110(2) (1994).

24.   H.R. REP. NO. 94-1476, *supra* note 16, at 83.

25.   17 U.S.C. § 101 (1994).

Some Examples:

+ A professor may read from the book *Moby Dick*, but may not show a clip from the motion picture starring Gregory Peck for distance education.

+ A professor may read an excerpt from the novel *Witness for the Prosecution*, but may not recite lines or create a dramatic performance of the stage play of the same name. The professor also may not show the motion picture for distance education, although he could do so for face-to-face teaching.

+ Because only nondramatic works qualify, the professor may play a popular song, but not an operatic stage musical work. Some works are both dramatic and nondramatic. "Pinball Wizard" is a popular song and an opera piece. "Hey There" is one of the best-selling popular songs of the early 1950s, but it is also from a Broadway musical. Whether such songs qualify might depend on the context of their use—whether the course is the study of popular music or stage productions—and on the selection of the recording used—whether the recording is from the dramatic work or a popular version.

+ The statute alone does not specify whether members of the class may simply recite lines from a dramatic work or make a dramatic reading of a nondramatic work—such as a novel. The House Report sheds some light on congressional intent: "a performer could read a nondramatic literary work aloud under section 110(2), but the copyright owner's permission would be required for him to act it out in dramatic form."[25]

The law forces a distinction between "dramatic" and "nondramatic" works that yields results bearing no relationship whatsoever to educational objectives. The distinction is rooted in concepts of "grand" and "small" rights sometimes associated with certain copyrighted works. "Grand" rights include the use of a work in a dramatic performance, while "small" rights are the nondramatic performances of the same

---

25. H.R. Rep. No. 94-1476, *supra* note 16, at 83. This provision also means that the educational use should not be used to make a derivative dramatic work from a nondramatic work. *See* GOLDSTEIN, *supra* note 15, § 5.8.1.2. *See also* MELVILLE B. NIMMER & DAVID NIMMER, 2 NIMMER ON COPYRIGHT, § 8.15 [C][2] (1995) ("an acting out of the novel in dramatic form would not be exempt").

work. Traditionally, composers retained grand rights, but allowed agencies such as the American Society of Composers, Authors and Publishers (ASCAP) to license small rights on their behalf.[27] Section 110(2) is a vestige of that arcane distinction, but that dichotomy of works in the distance-learning environment is irrelevant and unproductive. Moreover, section 110(2) distinguishes dramatic and nondramatic works, not merely circumstances under which they are performed.

V. Making Copies of the Transmission

Most universities will want to make copies of the transmission, and those copies are commonly used by students who missed a class and by faculty who want to review the session and improve their teaching methods. The copies are also used for further broadcast by the originating institution, and by other organizations that also qualify for the section 110(2) opportunities.

Section 112(b) of the Copyright Act expressly allows a nonprofit institution that makes a transmission containing a display or performance allowed under section 110(2) to make no more than 30 copies of such transmission, if: (1) no further copies are made from those copies; and (2) those copies are destroyed within seven years after the date of the first transmission, except one copy may be preserved for archival purposes.[28] Keep in mind that this provision applies if the copyrighted works included without permission in the distance-learning program are limited to only those works within section 110(2)'s purview: displays of works or performances of nondramatic literary or musical works.

If the transmission does not include anyone else's copyrighted materials, then the right to duplicate the tapes will be determined solely by the university and the individual faculty member. If the transmission includes works beyond those allowed under section 110(2), the right to make copies will depend on either a fair use analysis or a license agreement with the owner of the copyright to the included works.

A practical procedure for implementing this provision would be to number the copies of the tapes in succession from 1 to 30. Each tape

---

27.   Paul Goldstein, Copyright's Highway: From Gutenberg to the Celestial Jukebox 71 (1994).

28.   17 U.S.C. § 112(b) (1994).

should be labeled to indicate its place of origin and date of first transmission. The label should, of course, include other information about
the tape's content and copyright status. If section 112(b) applies, the
House Report details that the 30 copies may be used for future
transmissions by the original source, or they may be exchanged with
other broadcasters for their transmission.[28]

VI. What If a Program Does Not Fit These Requirements?

What if an instructor wants to include an AV work in a distance-
learning broadcast? What if he or she wants to make more than 30
copies, or keep them for longer than seven years? The Copyright Act
gives no reliable alternatives, although the most probable course of
action would take one of the following forms:

I. Apply "Fair Use" to the Situation

Section 107 of the Copyright Act sets forth the general framework of
fair use, and it offers only four general and vague factors to apply for
determining whether an activity is allowable or is an infringement. The
law is utterly without specifics. Neither the fair-use statute nor any
court decision addresses any situation directly related to distance education. Deciphering fair use is beyond the scope of this overview, but any
fair-use determination is inherently a complex judgment call.[29] Nevertheless, academics must continue to make reasonable determinations
of fair use in a wide range of circumstances.

2. Secure the Copyright Owner's Permission

Anytime the intended use exceeds rights allowed to the public under
copyright law, one recourse is to obtain permission from the copyright
owner. The request for permission should carefully describe all anticipated uses of the work—in other words, be sure the permission fills
expected needs.

---

28.   H.R. REP. NO. 94-1476, *supra* note 16, at 104 ("exchanges of recordings among
       instructional broadcasters are permitted").

29.   For a general study of fair use and its implications for education, see KENNETH D.
       CREWS, COPYRIGHT, FAIR USE, AND THE CHALLENGE FOR UNIVERSITIES (1993).

3. Purchase the Needed Materials under Favorable Terms that Allow Use in Distance Learning

Many copyrighted works are subject to a "license." That agreement is both a restriction on use, and it is an opportunity to negotiate provisions that serve anticipated needs. For example, a letter accompanying the order form for the purchase of commercial videotapes might include a provision allowing distance-education use. In particular, the purchase might specifically allow public performance and transmission rights for educational purposes.

4. Seek Alternatives to the Intended Use

A cinema instructor can sometimes replace clips with "stills" from a movie. In so doing, the instructor has replaced a "performance" of an audiovisual work with a lawfully permitted "display." If an AV work may not be shown at all through distance education, then several copies may be purchased and placed on reserve at various locations for student viewing.

These alternatives may not be ideal, and they may at times prove costly or cumbersome, but pursuing these or other alternatives may be the best resolution when an instructor encounters limitations raised under the current Copyright Act.

VII. Future Directions and Statutory Revision

Distance learning will continue to be a growing part of college and university planning for the future. Elementary and high schools are also beginning to provide distance-learning courses. The arcane and complex language of section 110(2) poses severe problems for the reasonable and beneficial uses of copyrighted works in the modern "classroom" experience. Some materials that are not allowed for use under the law will be available under license terms from the copyright owner. But licenses are controlled by the owner, who may impose a high fee or undue restrictions, or who may simply reject the request for permission outright. Most importantly, the law establishes a range of conditions and limitations triggered simply by the "transmission" of the work. The end use and the ultimate value of the work for educating the public, however, are unchanged regardless of whether the teaching is face to face or over distance. Congress recognized the importance of teaching and learning when it adopted section 110(1), and it recognized the importance of the use of materials in furtherance of the constitutional objective of promoting "the Progress of Science and the useful Arts." Yet concerns that the transmission of works may reach beyond the intended audience of students has led to restrictions on all transmissions and has led to total elimination of some types of works from distance learning.

The delineations in the statute may have made some sense in 1976 and may have served some legitimate objectives at that time, but they make little sense to educators today. Section 110 is one of the least-known copyright provisions, even among teachers and administrators responsible for distance learning, and it will continue to be generally avoided and disregarded as long as it persists in forcing distinctions that test logic and that require convoluted legal introspection. Copyright law, copyright owners, and the educational community deserve better. Section 110(2) is ripe for many changes, and those changes should effectuate the balance between protection for copyright owners and the encouragement of learning, all as intended by the U.S. Constitution.

To enhance distance learning and to strengthen respect for copyright, Congress should amend the statutes to achieve these results:

✦ Materials allowed for use in distance learning should not be restricted by type. The distinction in the current law makes the teaching of entire subjects and disciplines prohibitive. A course on music history, for example, could include symphonies and popular music, but would have to ignore opera and stage musicals. Eradicating half of history leaves students only half educated.

✦ Audiovisual materials must be allowed in distance learning. Good pedagogy rarely requires use of lengthy videotapes and other works in the limited time allowed for class; that practical necessity should be the real limit on the use of materials. Instructors should not be barred from using short clips from feature films and educational programs. In fact, the performance of entire works should be permitted if that performance furthers educational objectives.

✦ Transmission to private residences and offices should be explicitly permitted. The House Report implies that Congress anticipated home reception of transmissions, but the language of the statute has enough ambiguity to deter well-meaning instructors and perhaps to fuel legal attacks on innovative educational programs. Transmission to houses is increasingly essential as colleges and universities reach students who are unable to attend in classrooms, and as educators seek creatively to meet new obligations under the Americans with Disabilities Act.

✦ The right to retain and utilize copies of the transmission under section 112(b) should permit copies of transmissions that embody more than the narrow scope of materials allowed under the present section 110(2). The best resolution would be to eliminate the narrowness of section 110, but short of that change, section 112(b) should allow copies of transmissions that include materials used pursuant to fair use under section 107.

✦ Congress should make clear that fair use law allows uses of materials that do not qualify under section 110(2). Whether section 110 is a floor or a ceiling on public rights of use in distance learning is a question open to ongoing debate.

✦ The Copyright Act should address and allow educational experiences other than the traditional face-to-face or distance-learning environments. Distance learning increasingly is taking place on flexible schedules and in innovative formats, such as through multimedia production or by means of the Internet.

Recognizing the shortcomings of the law and the uncertainty of fair use, the task of negotiating "guidelines" for understanding this law has fallen upon the Conference on Fair Use (CONFU).[31] CONFU is an informal gathering of stakeholders—publishers, authors, educators, librarians, and others—who are seeking to develop fair-use guidelines applicable to a wide range of situations.[32] CONFU participants first convened in late 1994, and in December 1996 an "Interim Report" included draft guidelines for fair use associated with multimedia development, visual images, and distance learning.[33] At this writing, interested parties are assessing the proposed guidelines and submitting comments. Some

---

31.   CONFU is an outgrowth of a suggestion from the Information Infrastructure Task Force in a report issued in July 1994. *See* INTELLECTUAL PROPERTY AND THE NATIONAL INFORMATION INFRASTRUCTURE: A PRELIMINARY DRAFT OF THE REPORT OF THE WORKING GROUP ON INTELLECTUAL PROPERTY RIGHTS 133–34 (1994).

32.   For this author's analysis of CONFU and its struggle with the issues surrounding electronic reserves, see Kenneth D. Crews, *What Qualifies as "Fair Use"?* CHRON. OF HIGHER EDUC., May 17, 1996, at B1–B2.

33.   *The Conference on Fair Use: An Interim Report to the Commissioner* 31–56 (1996) (available at <http://www.uspto.gov/web/offices/dcom/olia/confu/>).

education groups appear to favor the distance-learning guidelines, while many do not. Their viability and implications are unknown at this time, but these guidelines nevertheless are one possibility for softening the consequences of a seemingly irrational statute. The guidelines also are an earnest recognition that fair use can encompass distance learning, despite the rigors of a statute of specific applicability. Yet any such guidelines necessarily will entail a recognition of competing concerns and a likely compromise of views.

The concerns of copyright owners and of educators are real and may demand consideration of various reasonable allowances and restrictions. Perhaps instructors could accept limits on the proportion of a lengthy work that may be utilized or agree to perform entire works only once without permission. Perhaps instructors could encode certain transmissions so only enrolled students likely would receive them. Perhaps colleges and universities could accept the requirement to post cautionary notices about copyright and actively deter students from making copies of the transmission for distribution.[33] Such options must be explored more fully for their feasibility and effectiveness, but any restrictions should be aimed specifically to prevent uses reaching beyond educational needs. In the end, an understanding of the law must allow practical implementation of teaching innovations and serve the needs of students. Most of all, any restrictions must be balanced against expanded rights of use, all in furtherance of the constitutional objective: to encourage the creation and the utilization of new works to promote the progress of knowledge and learning.

Unfortunately, the trend in Congress may be in exactly the opposite direction. The "White Paper" from the Information Infrastructure Task Force makes little comment about section 110 and distance learning, but the report's proposed revisions in the Copyright Act would give copyright owners exclusive rights of "transmission" of their works, even if the transmission does not include the making of copies.[34] Critics of the proposal warn that it could inhibit or restrict

---

33. Warning notices posted on copy machines and copy request forms are an important and familiar aspect of the copying exemption available to many libraries. 17 U.S.C. § 108(d)(2), (e)(2), (f)(1) (1994).

34. INTELLECTUAL PROPERTY AND THE NATIONAL INFORMATION INFRASTRUCTURE: THE REPORT OF THE WORKING GROUP ON INTELLECTUAL PROPERTY RIGHTS 95–96, 213–18 (1995).

even those transmissions allowed under the existing section 110(2).[36] Current law already establishes tight limits on the use of copyrighted works in distance learning; colleges and universities have a duty to learn and understand those limits, and they have a responsibility to identify their deficiencies and take action with their congressional delegations to advocate reasonable and crucial changes.

---

36.   *See, e.g.*, Statement of Members of the Digital Future Coalition on H.R. 2441: The NII Copyright Protection Act of 1995, Subcomm. on Courts and Intell. Property of the House Comm. on Hearings before the Judiciary, Feb. 15, 1996 (available at <http://www.ari.net/dfc/legislat/copyrigh.html>).

Chapter Eighteen
A Picture
Is Worth a Thousand Words:
Copyright and the Use of Image Archives
and Collections for Research, Teaching,
and Scholarship in the Digital Age[*]

by
Barbara Hoffman, Esq.
New York, New York

I. Introduction

The new information technologies have pushed to the forefront the use of images for commercial purposes; for example, software companies have an expanded appetite for images search to acquire rights to scan photographs or paintings digitally in libraries, archives, and museum collections worldwide. Bill Gates' Corbis has amassed more than

---

200,000 images in its collection, about 25,000 of which are fine art, with the strategy of providing two products: (1) a multimedia stock agency; and (2) a series of databases available either via CD–ROM or through an electronic network.

In educational institutions, museums, archives, and libraries, where images have long played a central role, the future use of digital imagery in teaching and research has emerged as one of the central concerns. As art historian Charles S. Rhyne noted:

> In conducting research, art historians browse photographs, slides, reproductions in books, and other images as avidly as statisticians study numbers. . . . For the great majority of art historians, who consider the visual experience of the work of art an essential part of its study, no image can fully satisfy. . . . In contrast, artists most intensively press the demand for free manipulation and innovative use of computer images. . . . The best education, like the best research, requires flexibility and free exploration. . . . Images on most CD-ROM's and photo CD's become educationally useful when they are copied onto institutional file servers, where thousands of images can be accessed by many different viewers at the same time. . . . In large classes where expensive art books cannot be assigned for study, computer images offer for the first time the possibility of assigning high quality color images for student study. . . . But it may eventually be in the seemingly prosaic provision of an immense number of new, higher quality images, not entirely dependent on but stimulated by the new technology, that digital imagery makes its most significant contribution.[1]

The electronic revolution is taking educational institutions, museums, archives, and libraries into unchartered legal and technological terrain, causing concerns particularly in the museum and higher education community about the intellectual, aesthetic, and institutional implications of converting visual images to electronic form. Museums are rethinking concepts basic to their operations such as "stewardship" and "exhibition" as well as copyright, connoisseurship, and control, while universities, archives, libraries, and study centers are reexamining issues such as the development of international standards for the capture, storage, transmission, and description of images along with the resolution of the complex issues of copyright and fair

---

1.   Charles S. Rhyne, *Computer Images for Research, Teaching, and Publication in Art History and Related Disciplines*, 12 VISUAL RESOURCES 19, 20–36 (1996) [hereinafter Rhyne].

use.[2] Image archives are both a gold mine and a mine field of intellectual property.

How can images be distributed over networks without compromising their integrity? In the new electronic world, will students be able to incorporate freely into a class report images of works in their local museum? Will museums and archives be able to share with local educational institutions in their community a database of images in their collection made available via a networked environment or on CD-ROM? Will such sharing take place internationally and on what terms? Who are the rights holders and what are the appropriate mechanisms for managing rights to use images and compensating rights holders for their use?

In theory, the use of images in the new media raises the same thorny and as yet unresolved issues as in the traditional print media. For example, one aspect of the rise of cinema studies as an academic discipline has been a new concern to illustrate articles and books with frame enlargements. The legal status of the use of such frames has remained problematic. Does the use of the enlargement violate copyright? Should the scholar contact the copyright holder to obtain permission?[3] Can a scholar use an image in an exhibition catalog without requesting permission or use it for a discussion of a photographer's work when the photographer has denied permission because she disagrees with the article?

Yet, the nature of digital images makes more obvious the legal and ethical problems that are still unresolved in the print media. Michael Ester, CEO of Luna Imaging, observes that "the fees paid for reproduction rights in scholarly as opposed to commercial publications, the use by universities of photographs and slides taken from books, and the sharing and copying of slide collections are undercurrent issues that become difficult to dismiss.[4]

The new digital technologies permit image, sound, and text to be digitized into zeros and ones; stored and replicated with ease in copies as

---

2.   *Id.* at 35.

3.   *See generally* Kristin Thompson, *Report of the Ad Hoc Committee of the Society For Cinema Studies, 'Fair Usage Publication of Film Stills,'* 32 CINEMA J., Winter 1993, at 3.

4.   Michael Ester, *Draft White Paper on Digital Imaging in the Arts and Humanities,* Getty Art History Information Program Initiative on Electronic Imaging and Information Standards 3–4, Mar. 1994, Santa Monica, CA.

perfect as the original; permit existing works to be incorporated into new works; and increase the potential for unauthorized alteration and appropriation of copyrighted work. To a far greater extent than photo-copying, the digital technologies have eroded traditional roles and boundaries among authors and users, content owners, service providers, producers, publishers, and distributors, making it imperative to seek a balance between access to images and protection of authors' and publishers' economic and moral rights. During the past decade, computer technology itself has forced judges to reconsider and in some cases re-define copyright doctrine in such areas as originality, authorship, fixation, substantial similarity, and the idea/expression dichotomy.

Robert A. Baron, a museum computer consultant, has written that:

> Central to all work in the visual arts and the key to our electronic future is the process of finding and using images. We need to know how our on-line age will affect the range and depth of access, how mundane affairs such as researching images and obtaining permission to use those images will be affected, and how the *mores* of a digital and electronic present will affect how we use customary resources in the future. One of the core issues is best discussed from the student's perspective. In preparing his dissertation, the doctoral student under-goes a rite of passage that leads him from university womb into the harsher realities of so-called "real life," and with ever increasing frequency, students are being exposed during it to marketplace actualities. Universities are asking their doctoral students to honor claims of copyright in their use of images and resources. Dissertation publishers such as University Microfilms International (UMI), require dissertations for publication to comply with the laws that govern commercial use of images in published works.[5]

The global information infrastructure and the World Wide Web have facilitated the merging of massive data storage with interactive hyper-media. Information technology is providing the ability to digitalize via high-speed international networks the cultural and academic libraries of the world, to transmit images across the globe, and to provide scholars and educators with remote access to the treasures of these libraries. It may be unclear how copyright and other intellectual property rules apply, since such simultaneous transmission of digital images to computers worldwide will often implicate inconsistent legal regimes.

---

5.   Robert A. Baron, *Digital Fever: A Scholar's Copyright Dilemma*, 15 MUSEUM MGMT. & CURATORSHIP 49, 50 (1996).

This chapter discusses the special legal concerns and issues in building electronic image archives and collections and the use of such image archives for teaching, research, publication, and artistic production in the field of art and architectural history. The issues discussed herein also have relevance for other disciplines, particularly the sciences which are developing their own uses for digital imagery. While the focus and discussion of the significant issues is filtered through the lens of the U.S. copyright law, the digital information environment cannot be contained within U.S. borders; inevitably, the full exploitation by museums, archives, and educational institutions of the new technologies will require links to an extensive global network. Thus, an understanding of the various national laws that provide the legal framework which governs the use and display of images for research, teaching, and scholarship is both instructive and necessary.[6]

II. The International Legal Context

The Berne Convention, Article 9, and the laws of member nations, including the United States, guarantee authors and copyright owners certain exclusive rights, including the right of reproduction. In the digital environment, the right of reproduction could become a global-use right which is all encompassing. In the United Kingdom, for example, the Software Act of 1980 confirms that input into a computer memory is an act of reproduction, while in the United States, the

---

6.   The European Union is developing two telecommunications computer networks, one linking libraries, the other linking museums and technical partners. A Visual Arts Network for the Exchange of Cultural Knowledge (VAN-EYCK, <http://www.bbk.ac.uk/Departments/HistoryOf Art/van_eyck.html>) will provide cross-library access to art history photographic archives and texts. It will link The Witt Library, Courtauld Institute of Art, London; The RKD (Rijksbureau Voor Kunsthistorische Documentatie), The Hague; Cruickshank-Glin Archive, Trinity College, Dublin; Birkbeck College, London; Utrecht University, and Vasari Ltd. Telecommunications links to be used include EURO ISDN and academic research telecommunications facilities. A European Museums Network will provide cross-museum access to images of works in the participating museum collections with accompanying text. It will link museums in Lisbon, Madrid, Paris, The Hague, Bremen, Bremerhaven, Copenhagen, and Hamburg, and provide interactive multimedia access for museum visitors. *See* Rhyne, *supra*, note 1, at 44 n.24; Achim Lipp, *Towards The Electronic Kunst und Wunderkammer: Spinning on the European Museums Network EMN*, 10 Visual Resources, 101, 101–18 (1994).

White Paper[7] takes the position that a screen display stored only in a computer's RAM is a copy and thus implicates the reproduction right, making "browsing" a potential act of infringement. Although several computer law cases support the notion that copies in RAM are sufficiently stable to be considered reproductions under certain circumstances, that conclusion has been challenged on technical grounds.[8] Regarding distribution rights, there is uncertainty in several countries as to whether online transmission is covered by current statutes which speak of rights to reproduce, publicly perform, display, or distribute copies of the work to the public.

Not surprisingly, in both the United States' and the United Kingdom's systems of copyright law, based on economic incentive rather than author's rights, there is less protection for what are called moral rights or droit moral. Sourced in the continental system, these rights of a non-pecuniary nature include the author's personal, non-economic interest in receiving attribution for a work and in maintaining the integrity of the work even after the work has been transferred or sold.

In the United States, moral rights are limited to works protected by the Visual Artists Rights Act of 1990 (VARA),[9] which amends the copyright law to provide for limited rights of attribution and integrity. Thus, moral rights are given greater protection in continental Europe, while the contours of fair use, based on judicial decision, are broader in the United States.

The Berne Convention and various national laws provide exemptions and limitations on the rights of copyright owners, including exemptions for teaching, private copying, and the general fair use or fair dealing exceptions of common law countries.[10] The Berne Convention, for example, includes a general authorization to member countries to permit reproduction for educational purposes (Article 10.2). Article 10.2 provides:

---

7.   INTELLECTUAL PROPERTY AND THE NATIONAL INFORMATION INFRASTRUCTURE: THE REPORT OF THE WORKING GROUP ON INTELLECTUAL PROPERTY RIGHTS (1995).

8.   *See generally* Ira L. Brandriss, *Writing in Frost on a Window Pane: E-Mail and Chatting on RAM and Copyright Fixation*, 43 J. COPYRIGHT SOC'Y 237 (1996).

9.   17 U.S.C. § 106A (1994).

10. The U.S. fair use concept is somewhat more liberal and susceptible of broader interpretation than is the concept of fair dealing in U.K. and Canadian law.

It shall be a matter for legislation in the countries of the Union, and for special agreements existing or to be concluded between them, to permit the utilization, to the extent justified by the purpose, of literary or artistic works by way of illustration in publications, broadcasts or sound or visual recordings for teaching, provided such utilization is compatible with fair practice.[11]

The French Code of Intellectual Property excerpts from copyright infringement "analyses and brief quotes justified by the critical, polemical, pedagogical, scientific or informational character of the work in which they are incorporated."[12]

In theory, if a reproduction or display of a copyrighted image does not qualify under one of the exemptions, an infringement of copyright has occurred.

As the European Commission says in its Green Paper, it is clear that the intellectual property law applying to digital dissemination or transmission will have to be harmonized . . . "to a degree adequate for achieving interpretability between legal systems."[13]

Clearly, there will have to be a better understanding of how the copyright laws of various countries can function together whenever

---

11. Jane C. Ginsburg, *Reproduction of Protected Works for University Research or Teaching*, 39 J. COPYRIGHT SOC'Y 181, 185–86 (1992) [hereinafter Ginsburg], states:

This text prompts three pertinent questions: 1. To what kinds of works does it apply; 2. How much of any given work may be reproduced; 3. How many copies may be made? With respect to the first question, the text makes fairly clear that all works protected by the Convention are subject to this exception to the exclusive right of reproduction. Answers to the second and third questions emerge less readily. The phrase "to the extent justified by the purpose" might set some limitation on the amount that may be copied from any given work; it is not always necessary to copy the whole of the work in order to convey the information required for the teaching purpose. On the other hand, the phrase does not preclude the whole of a work in appropriate circumstances. Similarly, the phrase "by way of illustration" may also suggest a limitation on the amount to be copied, but does not clearly prohibit reproducing the entirety of a work. . . . Moreover, Professor Ricketson has stated that Article 10.2 also permits the preparation for teaching purposes of compilations anthologizing all or parts of a variety of works.

12. C. Prop. Intell. art. L. 122-5.3.a. (Fr.); *see also* Spain, Copyright Act of 1987, art. 32; Italy, Copyright Act of 1941, art. 70; Belgium, Copyright Act of 1994, art. 13.

13. *The Outlook for Intellectual Property Rights Within the Context of New Dissemination Techniques*, C-INFO (Finnish Copyright Society), extra issue, Sept. 1995, at 3.

copyrighted material is uploaded from one country and downloaded, distributed, and copied in another. Questions include: When does infringement occur? Who will have a cause of action to sue? What national law will apply? What will be the role of national treatment?

Harmonization of international ideas concerning the Internet have begun to appear. The European Commission recommends that national legislatures establish clearly that the act of digitalization (or scanning) constitutes a reproduction of a copyright work and therefore is an act controllable by the copyright owner. The European Community, the United States, Australia, and WIPO are considering the introduction of a right to transmit material digitally.[14]

In the United States in 1996, bills were introduced in both the House and the Senate proposing:

> (1) a group of related amendments intended to make clear that one of the ways in which copies of a work can be distributed to the public is by transmission; and (2) a broadening of the exemptions available to users, specifically, allowing libraries to make digital copies of works in certain circumstances for preservation purposes, and permitting nonprofit reproduction of works in a format accessible to the visually impaired.[15]

The subtext of any international harmonization effort on the part of the United States, however, is based on two important factors in the development of this country as the world's leading technological innovator: (1) strong protection of intellectual rights; and (2) the fact that the United States is a major producer and exporter of copyrighted materials and high-technology products. This consideration is present implicitly, if not explicitly, in all discussion regarding copyright and the new technologies.

To bring the international copyright system into the digital networked age, the World Intellectual Property Organization (WIPO), an arm of the United Nations, convened in Geneva, Switzerland, with representatives of 160 nations for a three-week conference to decide whether to ratify three controversial international treaty instruments: (1) the draft Protocol to the Berne Convention for the Protection of literary and artistic works; (2) a "New Instrument" treaty on the

---

14.   Anna Booy, Artistic License in the Digital World, Address at EVA '96: Electronic Imaging and the Visual Arts, London, July 25, 1996.

15.   Hon. Marybeth Peters, *The National Information Infrastructure: A Copyright Office Perspective*, 20 COLUM.-VLA J. L. & ARTS 341, 348 (1996).

rights of performers and producers of music and protection of music recordings; and (3) a new treaty for the protection of databases. As this is published, discussion on the latter treaty has been tabled. The proposals noted above and introduced as changes in the legislation called the National Information Infrastructure Copyright Protection Act of 1995. The U.S. Patent and Trademark Office says that its proposals are necessary to protect the financial assets of information service providers. "Freely accessible, yes; free of charge, no" are words attributed to Bruce Lehman, the Assistant Commerce Secretary and U.S. Commissioner of Patents and Trademarks, head of the U.S. delegation. The three treaty proposals would set a system of rules with massive implications for both the shape of the information system and its economic haves and have nots. The fair use doctrine, for one, has been hotly contested and will affect what will be available at low cost or for free in such venues as libraries, schools, and universities.

Critics of the administration's proposals say that the proposals would decidedly tilt access to information away from users and define copyright violations too broadly. A November 7, 1996 letter to the White House from James H. Billington (U.S. Library of Congress), said that major library associations in the United States felt deep concern that the proposed treaties would hurt education and the public's access to information.

III. Copyright Basics in U.S. Law

The basis of congressional power to enact copyright laws is found in the U.S. Constitution. According to this provision, "Congress shall have Power . . . To promote the Progress of Science and useful Arts, by securing for limited Times to Authors . . . the exclusive Right to their respective Writings."[16]

For progress in science and the useful arts to occur, the courts have stated that others must be permitted to build upon and refer to the creations of prior thinkers. Accordingly, three judicially created doctrines have been fashioned to limit the copyright monopoly and promote its purpose. First, copyright law does not protect ideas but only their creative expression; second, facts are not protected, regardless of the labor expended by the original author in uncovering them; and, third,

---

16.   U.S. CONST. art I, § 8, cl. 1, 8.

the public may make "fair use" of the copyrighted works. The Supreme Court has acknowledged repeatedly "the inherent tension in the need simultaneously to protect copyrighted material and to allow others to build upon it."[17] As Justice Sandra Day O'Connor wrote:

> The primary objective of copyright is not to reward the labor of authors, but "[t]o promote the progress of Science and useful Arts." To this end, copyright assures authors the right to their original expression, but encourages others to build freely upon the ideas and information conveyed by a work. . . . This result is neither unfair nor unfortunate. It is the means by which copyright advances the progress of science and art.[18]

Congress has implemented its constitutional mandate in Title 17 of the United States Code known as the 1976 Copyright Act.[19] As Mary Levering of the Copyright Office noted in an address to the College Art Association:

> The genius of United States copyright law is that it balances the intellectual property rights of authors, publishers, and copyright owners with society's need for the free exchange of ideas. Taken together, fair use and other exemptions allowing certain uses of copyrighted works without permission, were incorporated in the Copyright Act of 1976, and constitute indispensable legal doctrines for promoting the dissemination of knowledge, while ensuring authors, publishers, and copyright owners protection of their creative works and a return on their economic investments. The preservation and continuation of this balance in the new digital environment is essential to the free flow of information and the development of an information infrastructure that serves the public interest. The loss or diminution of these provisions in the emerging information infrastructure would harm scholarship, teaching, and the operation of a free society.[20]

A. Rights of the Copyright Owner in a Copyrighted Work

To be protected under current U.S. copyright law, a work "must be an original work of authorship fixed in a tangible medium of expression."[21] Works of visual art—a painting, a photograph, a sculpture—

---

17. Campbell v. Acuff-Rose Music, Inc., 114 S. Ct. 1164, 1169 (1994).

18. Feist Publications, Inc. v. Rural Tel. Serv. Co., 499 U.S. 340, 349 (1991).

19. 17 U.S.C. §§ 101–1101 (1994).

20. Mary Levering, College Art Association Annual Meeting, San Antonio, Texas, Jan. 21, 1995.

21. 17 U.S.C. § 102(a) (1994).

are protected by copyright. Thus, the simple act of creating an original work in a "fixed" medium, including the electronic, gives the author copyright in the work. Under section 106 of the Copyright Act, the copyright owner has the exclusive right to (1) reproduce the work in copies or phonorecords; (2) prepare derivative works based on the copyrighted work (which includes the right to recast, transform or modify); (3) distribute copies by sale or other ownership transfer, or to rent, lease or lend copies; (4) perform the work publicly; (5) display the work publicly[22]; and (6) authors of works of visual art protected under section 106A have the right to claim authorship (attribution) and prevent the use of their name in conjunction with certain modifications of the work and the right to prevent alteration of their work (integrity). Architectural plans and drawings were originally protected under the 1976 Copyright Act. Other forms of architectural works received protection only on passage of the Architectural Works Copyright Protection Act of 1990.[23]

A copyright owner may divide monopoly rights in the work in a number of ways: *inter alia* by the type of use and/or media, exclusivity or non-exclusivity, territory, or duration and thus may only grant a right to a specific media (e.g., platform CD-ROM for IBM) or a specific location (i.e., a site license). Copyright holders are customarily reluctant to agree to broad transfers of rights to future unknown technologies. The grant of rights to an educational institution to use an image in one media or for one purpose does not necessarily permit its use in other ways. In particular, ownership of a copy does not necessarily include any of the bundle of intangible rights of copyright and without such grant of rights, a license, or an available defense or exception to those rights, the owner of a copy can not reproduce, alter, or publicly display the copy. When museums, stock houses, galleries, archives, or publishers permit use of an image, often they are

---

22. *Id.* § 106. To "display a work" is defined to mean "to show a copy of it, either directly or by means of a film, slide, television, image or any other device or process or, in the case of a motion picture or other audiovisual work, to show individual images nonsequentially." *Id.* § 101.

23. *Id.* § 102(a)(8). An "architectural work" is defined as "the design of a building as embodied in any tangible medium of expression, including a building, architectural plans, or drawings." It includes the overall form as well as the "arrangement and composition of spaces and elements" in the design of the building, but does not include overall standard features. *Id.* § 101.

providing access to a particular copy of the image, on certain terms and conditions. The underlying rights in the work, if any, may be held by the author. A rights holder is often concerned with control over the exploitation of the image not only to benefit from future technologies, but also, as with the custodians of art and architectural images, to preserve the integrity and authenticity of the image.

B. Authors' Rights in Cyberspace

Authors and copyright holders, in theory, enjoy the same copyright protection in cyberspace as in other media; digital image files are equivalent to paintings, photographs, and other works and, if displayed or copied without permission, implicate the right of reproduction and display. However, this simple fundamental concept is not so easily applied in cyberspace. What constitutes the making of a copy? Reproduction under section 106(1) is to be distinguished from "display" under section 106(5). For a work to be reproduced, its fixation in tangible form must be "sufficiently permanent or stable to permit it to be perceived, reproduced, or otherwise communicated for a period of more than transitory duration."[24] Thus, the showing of images on a screen or tube might not be a violation of section 106(1), although it might come within the scope of section 106(5). Is the mere display of an image on a video monitor a technical violation of the copyright law? Is the transitory storage of an image in a computer memory a copy? What rights of adaptation and reproduction exist for users who download images? Does the right to display accompany transmission of a digital image?[25] How will the law distinguish between an artist's electronic snatches of pieces of art, a

---

24.   *Id.* § 102(a).

25.   Playboy Enters., Inc. v. Frena, 839 F. Supp. 1552 (M.D. Fla. 1993), is one of the first U.S. cases to consider the issue. In finding that an operator of a subscription computer billboard infringed *Playboy* magazine's display right, the court held that "the display right precludes unauthorized transmission of the display from one place to another, for example, by a computer system. . . . 'Display' covers any showing of a 'copy' of the work, 'either directly or by means of a film, slide, television image or any other device or process.' " 17 U.S.C. § 101.

  For there to be copyright infringement, however, the display must be public. "A 'public display' is a display 'at a place open to the public or . . . where a substantial number of persons outside of a normal circle of family and its social acquaintances is gathered.' " MELVILLE B. NIMMER, 2 NIMMER ON COPYRIGHT § 8.14(C) at 8–169 (1993). A place is "open to the public" in this sense even if access is limited to paying customers. *Id.* at 1557.

software publisher's creating a textbook, or a digitally altered image incorporated into a new work of art?

Must a subsequent appropriation or collage acknowledge its sources? Does the first sale doctrine apply to a lawfully acquired digital-transmission? As noted previously, the White Paper concludes that temporary storage of a computer file in memory constitutes copying for the purposes of copyright, as does "scanning," "uploading," and "downloading." The proposed amendment to the copyright law which creates a right of distribution by transmission and blurs the distinction between the right of display, reproduction, and performance.[26] Thus, the copyright owner's exclusive rights to reproduce the work, to display a work publicly, and to distribute the work by transmission are implicated in many transactions using the National Information Infrastructure (NII). If the underlying image is protected, is permission needed to create copies and derivative works? When is there sufficient added authorship to a public domain work to create a protected derivative work as in some digitalization or photography processes? While current legal analysis supports the conclusion that digital scanning of images constitutes the making of a copy and thus infringement, there is no clear legal precedent that establishes whether an intermediate copy may be considered fair use if the end use is fair, or whether an intermediate digital copy is an infringement if the final work is not substantially similar.[27]

IV. Special Copyright Concerns and Issues in Building Electronic Image Archives

Visual images can be original works, reproductions of other works, or if a reproduction includes original elements, they can be both. Often, a digital image is many generations removed from the original work

---

26. *See* H.R. 2441 and S. 1284, 104th Cong., 1st Sess. (1996).

27. *See* Sega Enters., Ltd. v. Accolade, Inc., 977 F.2d 1510 (9th Cir. 1992). The court found that defendant Accolade, a manufacturer of video game cartridges, disassembled the copyrighted computer program of the plaintiff, a video game console manufacturer. Using the "object code" it obtained, Accolade manufactured video game cartridges compatible with Sega's "Genesis" video game console. *Id.* at 1514–15. The Ninth Circuit found the first factor to favor Accolade. *Id.* at 1522. In words directly applicable here, it stated that the use at issue "was an *intermediate* one only and thus any commercial 'exploitation' was *indirect* or *derivative*." *Id.* (emphasis added).

that it reproduces. For example, a digital image may have been scanned from a slide that was copied from a published book which contained a photographic transparency that reproduced an original work of art. The term "surrogate" is often used in practice to define a reproduction of an original visual image. Each stage of reproduction in this chain may involve an additional layer of rights.

An original visual image is a work of art or an original work of authorship (or a part of a work), fixed in digital or analog form, and expressed in a visual medium. Examples include graphic, sculptural, and architectural works, as well as stills from motion pictures or other audiovisual works. A reproduction is a copy of an original visual image in digital or analog form. The most common forms of reproductions are photographic, including prints, 35mm slides, and color transparencies. The original visual image shown in a reproduction is often referred to as the "underlying work." A published reproduction is a reproduction of an original visual image appearing in a work distributed in copies and made available to the public by sale or other transfer of ownership, or by rental, lease, or lending. Examples include a plate in an exhibition catalog that reproduces a work of art or a digital image appearing in CD-ROM or online. A copy of a published reproduction is a subsequent copy made of a published reproduction of an original visual image, for example, a 35mm slide which is a copy of an image in a book.[28]

As previously noted, images in archives, museums, libraries, and collections may have multiple layers of authorship: the underlying copyrighted work, the photograph of the original work, or its digitization. Obtaining rights to one does not automatically grant rights to use another, and therefore all must be considered when analyzing the rights connected with an image. Determining the copyright status of an underlying image may be difficult for several reasons. Even if an institution owns an original work of art, it does not necessarily hold copyright to the work of art. One must conceptually separate ownership of the material object and ownership of copyright. Works of art transferred subsequent to the Copyright Act of 1976 do not transfer any of the rights of copyright unless accompanied by a written transfer of such rights. Prior to 1978, however, under the *Pushman* doctrine, an artist

---

28. Proposed Educational Fair Use Guidelines for Digital Images. For the text of these guidelines, see *infra* Appendix I (p. 519).

was presumed to have transferred common law copyright at the time the original work of art was sold unless the artist specifically reserved copyright ownership. Even prior to the 1976 Act, in New York and California statutes were enacted revising the presumption of the *Pushman* doctrine.[29]

Rights to use images will vary depending not only on the identities of the layers of rights holders but also on other factors such as the terms of any bequest or applicable license. If a museum, archive, library, or collection reproduces a work of art, it must obtain the consent of the copyright owner to reproduce the work and, if it is to be a copyright claimant, must add a non-trivial and original contribution not found in the original work of art. One area of dispute between rights holders and users is whether photographs of public domain works contain sufficient originality to be entitled to copyright protection. Whether a photograph of a painting displays sufficient originality to qualify for copyright is a close question. According to a leading copyright authority, a photograph of a two-dimensional object like a painting or drawing may lack this quantum of originality.[30] Alternatively, a photograph of a sculpture or other three-dimensional object that involves the photographer's judgment in selecting camera angles and lighting is a clearer case of sufficient original authorship.[31] There was sufficient added authorship to a public domain work of art to entitle a small-scale reproduction of Rodin's "Hand of God" to obtain copyright protection. In the case of *Alva Studios, Inc. v. Winninger*,[32] the court held that the reproduction embodies and results from Alva's skill and originality in producing an accurate scale reproduction of the original. The court emphasized the difference in size, the different treatment of the base, and the quality control exercised by the

---

29.   Pushman v. New York Graphic Soc'y, 39 N.E.2d 249 (N.Y. 1942).

30.   1 NIMMER ON COPYRIGHT § 208[E][2] at 2-131 (1996).

31.   For cases involving originality in photographs, see Gross v. Seligman, 21 F. 930 (2d Cir. 1914) (where photographer, after sale of photograph and copyright, took later picture with same model and pose but with addition of a smile on her mouth and a cherry in her teeth, held an infringement); and the related case of Franklin Mint Corp. v. National Wildlife Art Exch., 575 F.2d 62 (3d Cir. 1978) (holding that later painting by artist of same subject not infringement, as similarity reflected the common theme).

32.   177 F. Supp. 265 (S.D.N.Y. 1959). *See also* L. Batlin & Son, Inc. v. Snyder, 536 F.2d 486 (2d Cir. 1976); *see generally* Rhoda L. Berkowitz & Marshall A. Leaffer, *Copyright and the Art Museum*, 8 COLUM.-VLA J. L. & ARTS 249 (1984).

museum's curatorial staff. Simply because an underlying work may have fallen into the public domain does not necessarily mean that a reproduction is in the public domain or can be copied.

Whether digitalization of a public domain image is properly considered a process or idea, or a mere trivial variation and thus not entitled to copyright protection, or whether it is of sufficient originality and skill to warrant copyright protection is unresolved by any court decision. The U.S. Copyright Office has accepted digitized versions of public domain works for copyright registration; however, what the Copyright Office requires for registration purposes should not be confused with what the courts have determined or will determine is necessary for copyright protection.

Is the image in the public domain? A source of visual images free of copyright concerns is the public domain. If an image is in the public domain, one may freely use, copy, adapt, distribute, and display it without fear of copyright infringement. This explains the mustache on the Mona Lisa or a Van Gogh self-portrait wearing headphones. Works in the public domain are not protected by copyright, even when incorporated into a copyrighted work. Nevertheless, as discussed above, an artist may make a new or derivative version of a public domain art work which may itself be copyrightable if sufficiently original. The public domain consists of materials that do not enjoy copyright protection as a matter of law. A significant part of the public domain consists of works that once were protected by copyright but which have lost that protection by expiration, forfeiture, or abandonment. A work enters the public domain when its copyright protection has expired. The duration of a copyright depends on whether the work is governed by the 1909 Act or the 1976 Act. The duration of copyright in works created as of 1978 is the life of the author plus 50 years; no copyright in works created under the 1976 Act will expire before the end of 2028.[33] For works published before 1978, the duration depends on whether the work was published or unpublished.[34] Generally speaking, the copyright on works published prior to 1922 has expired.

Copyright protection for works of art created prior to 1988 may also have been lost for failure to follow the copyright formalities,

---

33.   17 U.S.C. § 302 (1994).

34.   For a chart depicting when works enter the public domain, see *infra* Appendix K (p. 545).

primarily the omission of notice on "published" copyrighted works. Works like old photographs, however, that have no affixed copyright notice may not be in the public domain since, if the photographs were never published, neither the 1909 Act nor the 1976 Act required the affixation of any copyright notice. In 1992, Congress amended the Copyright Act to provide that pre-1978 works then in their first term of copyright would be automatically renewed. As a result, copyright in works published between 1964 and 1977 will expire 75 years from initial publication. Recently, by virtue of the Uruguay Round of GATT, President Clinton signed certain implementing legislation which resurrected foreign copyright in works which had entered the public domain in this country for omission of notice or failure to renew. Such works will have the copyright restored for the remainder of the term the foreign work would otherwise have had in the United States if the work had not entered the public domain.

The concept of publication was an important concept both under the 1909 Act (where publication without copyright notice injected the work into the public domain) and under the 1976 Copyright Act, although of somewhat reduced importance, until U.S. adherence to the Berne Convention in 1989. Under the 1909 Act, the law was not entirely clear on whether a non-commercial display of a work of art constitutes publication. Particularly when works have been sold many times, and records are inadequate to establish the publication history of the work, it may be difficult to determine the copyright status of the work. Similarly, limited distribution was held not to constitute publication under the 1909 Act. Many photographs, publicity stills for films, and other images of limited distribution or images provided to archives without limitation may be considered unpublished and therefore not required to have a copyright notice. In general, unpublished works not only have a different duration under current copyright law, but they may be treated differently under continental legal systems and in fair use analysis.

A. Limitations and Exemptions on the Copyright Owner's Exclusive Rights

A copyright owner's rights are limited in several respects under existing law. The "first-sale" doctrine permits the owner of a copy of a work to sell or otherwise dispose of the work without further payment of royalties to the copyright holder. Thus, the owner of a CD-ROM of the Barnes Collections masterpieces would be free to sell the CD-ROM, but not to copy the copyrighted images on the disk. One limitation on the display right is closely related to the first-sale doctrine: The owner of a work of visual art may display it to the public at the place where it is located. The statute provides:

> Notwithstanding the provisions of section 106(5) [which grants copyright owners the exclusive right to display publicly copies of a work], the owner of a particular copy lawfully made under this title, or any person authorized by such owner, is entitled, without the authority of the copyright owner, to display that copy publicly, either directly or by the projection of no more than one image at a time, to viewers present at the place where the copy is located.[35]

Section 110(1) permits the performance or display of a copyrighted work in the course of face-to-face teaching activities in a classroom or similar place of instruction. The privilege to display applies only to those who own the work. Due to its "face-to-face teaching" requirement, this provision may not protect the telecommunications, transmission, and subsequent digitalization of programs embodying copyrighted works. Thus, if an audiovisual work accompanying a museum exhibition is broadcast by closed circuit television from one museum to another location, the exemption would not apply.

Section 110(2) permits the performance of a nondramatic literary or musical work or display of a work, by or in the course of a transmission, if—

(A) the performance or display is a regular part of the systematic instructional activities of a governmental body or a nonprofit educational institution; and

(B) the performance or display is directly related and of material assistance to the teaching content of the transmission; and

(C) the transmission is made primarily for—
(i) reception in classrooms or similar places normally devoted to instruction, or
(ii) reception by persons to whom the transmission is directed because their disabilities or other special circumstances[36] prevent

---

35.   17 U.S.C. § 109(a) (1994).

36.   "Special circumstances" include daytime employment and distance from campus that may interfere with daytime attendance at regular classes. According to the legislative history:

their attendance in classrooms or similar places normally devoted to instruction, or

(iii) reception by officers or employees of governmental bodies as a part of their official duties or employment.[37]

This means that copyrighted drawings, slides, maps, or art prints may be transmitted to a remote site without constituting an infringement; movies, videos, and other audiovisual works may not. Audio tapes of musical performances would be allowed, but not audiovisual tapes of musical performances. Section 110(2) does not apply to the performance of an "audiovisual work."[38]

The situation in which audiovisual works could be transmitted on an electronic network despite section 110(2) is where the use and the portion of the work transmitted is such that it meets the fair use provisions of section 107. Fair use applies concurrently with section 110(2). There appears to be some consensus that section 107 applies to all of the exclusive rights of the copyright holder, but that because of the specific limitations contained in section 110, there may be a higher burden of demonstrating fair use beyond section 110(2).[39] Neither section 110 nor fair use under current interpretations provide complete insulation for universities wishing to completely digitize copyrighted images and produce multimedia works for distribution, subsequent copying, and lending to students for later viewing and future use as well.

There has been some question as to whether or not the language in this section of the bill is intended to include instructional television college credit courses. These telecourses are aimed at undergraduate and graduate students in earnest pursuit of higher educational degrees who are unable to attend daytime classes because of daytime employment, distance from campus, or some other intervening reason. So long as these broadcasts are aimed at regularly enrolled students and conducted by recognized higher educational institutions, the committee believes that they are clear within the language of § 110(2)(C)(ii).

H.R. REP. NO. 94-1476, 94th Cong., 2d Sess. (1976), *reprinted in* 17 OMNIBUS COPYRIGHT REVISION LEGISLATIVE HISTORY 84 (1977) [hereinafter H.R. REP. NO. 94-1476].

37. 17 U.S.C. § 110(2) (1994).

38. "Audiovisual works" are defined as "works that consist of a series of related images which are intrinsically intended to be shown by the use of machines or devices such as projectors, viewers, or electronic equipment, together with accompanying sounds, if any, regardless of the nature of the material objects, such as films or tapes, in which the works are embodied." *Id.* § 101.

39. For the Proposed CONFU Distance Learning Guidelines, *see infra* Appendix J (p. 535).

The balancing of the Copyright Act is apparent in the special exemptions for libraries and archives in section 108 and proposed amendments permitting digitization of images for archival and preservation purposes. Many have expressed concern that the special section 108 exemptions for libraries are no longer relevant in the digital era. Libraries, of course, may make fair use of copyrighted works pursuant to the provisions of section 107. Section 108, however, provides additional exemptions specifically for libraries and archives. On the one hand, there are those who believe that since licensing of transaction of works in digital form will be a feature of the digital distribution systems of the future, there is no need for library exceptions. Each copying transaction will be cheap and libraries can simply pay for all of the copying in which they engage. On the other hand, there are those who believe that unrestricted copying in libraries should be the rule, without the special conditions and limitations set forth in section 108.[40] Legislation introduced in both the House and Senate based on the White Paper has attempted to preserve this balance in the proposed legislation. The bill amends the current exemption for libraries to allow the preparation of three copies of works in digital format, and it authorizes the making of a limited number of digital copies by libraries and archives for purposes of preservation.[41]

B. Fair Use

The most significant and perhaps murkiest of the limitations on a copyright owner's exclusive rights is the doctrine of fair use. Fair use is both a limitation and an affirmative defense to an action for copyright infringement. It is potentially available with respect to all manners of unauthorized use of all types of works in any media. When fair use exists, the user is required neither to seek permission from the copyright owner nor to pay a license fee for the use.

Permissions have generally been sought by publishers for the use of reproductions of art images. Actual practice in the area of illustrating film-related publications has been confused and inconsistent. Museums' positions on fair use often depend on the nature of their

---

40. *See* Doug Bennett, Fair Use in Digital Environment: The Work of the Conference on Fair Use, Address to the National Federation of Abstracting and Information Services, Philadelphia, PA (Feb. 27, 1996) [hereinafter Bennett].

41. H.R. 2441 and S. 1284, 104th Cong., 1st Sess. (1996).

collections, with modern art or contemporary museums taking a strong fair use stance vis-à-vis artists' collecting societies like ADAGP,[42] VAGA[43] and ARS.[44] In developing visual resources collections, slide curators usually have not sought permission for a number of reasons, including the difficulty in establishing copyright ownership, the nature of the use and the user, and because the use of the visual materials was limited to one individual or institution. When slides have been available through vendors, restrictions imposed by such vendors generally have been adhered to, although the impact of such restrictions is not clear. In a statement issued in May of 1983, slide vendors stated:

> All slides of art of architecture—whether originals of duplicates—are the original creation of the company producing them, and/or the owning institution, artist and photographer. These slides are thus protected under International Copyright Laws. Such slides are sold under the express condition that they are to be used for teaching and studying purposes only and may be projected via normal slide projector for classroom and lecture use. No purchased slides may be reproduced or transmitted by any other means, electronic or mechanical, including photocopy, slide duplicator, video recording, or any information storage and retrieval system now known to be invented, without permission in writing from the producer.
>
> As a further clarification, since these slides are produced for the specific purpose of teaching, scholarship and research, the normal "fair use" clause allowing single copies to be made by individuals for these purposes does *not* apply. Since virtually the only market for these slides is comprised of the very teachers, students, scholars, and visual resource people who would be interested in copies, and any copying activity whatsoever is a form of direct damage to the producer of the original image. Therefore, any unauthorized copying of slides must be considered in violation of copyright law and in violation of professional ethics. Any authorized copying must be agreed upon in writing.[45]

In 1988 the International Group of Scientific Technical & Medical Publishers adopted a formal policy on electrocopying that said, in part: "[W]herever and whenever STM and its members are represented, no

---

42.   Association es arts graphiques et plastiques.

43.   Visual Artists and Gallery Association.

44.   Artists' Rights Society.

45.   VISUAL RESOURCES ASSOCIATION, SLIDE BUYERS' GUIDE; AN INTERNATIONAL DIRECTORY OF SLIDE SOURCES FOR ART AND ARCHITECTURE xviii (6th ed. 1990).

electronic storage of information will be permitted without written authorization. The concepts of 'fair use' and 'private research' that exist in current legislation should not be applied to electronically stored information."[46]

The Association of American University Presses (AAUP) was approached by STM to sign onto this policy statement. The result was a policy issued in February 1989 the final part of which, paralleling the STM statement, said: "[E]lectrocopying of copyrighted works is permissible without authorization only in special limited circumstances where application can legitimately be made of the concept of 'fair use' (and similar concepts that exist in other national legislations)."[47]

Based originally on judicial decision, Congress codified the doctrine in the Copyright Act of 1976. Section 107, the fair use section of the Act, does not define fair use. Instead, the preamble to section 107 sets forth certain illustrative examples such as teaching, scholarship, and research as examples of a fair use and instructs that this use be considered together with four interrelated factors to determine whether the use made of a work in any particular case constitutes fair use. The mere fact that an image may be used for broad purposes of education does not mean that a use is "fair." The Supreme Court stated in *Campbell v. Acuff Rose Music, Inc.*[48] that all four statutory factors must be considered without favoritism and that fair use must be considered on a case-to-case basis.[49] The doctrine is described as an "equitable rule of reason" in the legislative history of section 107 and the embodiment of the delicate balance of the statutory scheme to promote free dissemination of information, "thereby benefiting the public by allowing

---

46. 20th General Assembly, Frankfurt, Germany, Oct. 1988. These publishers are often referred to as "STM publishers."

47. Sandy Thatcher, Copyright and Optical Scanning in the Distributed Digital Library, Policy Statement, New England Library Association, May 5, 1995 (on file with author).

48. 114 S. Ct. 1164 (1994).

49. *Id.* at 1170–71.

the second author through a good faith productive use of the first author's work . . . [to create] a new, original work."[50]

The contours of fair use in the academic environment currently have been shaped by carefully selected test cases brought by book and journal publishers to establish broad principles in areas where substantial license revenues were at stake. Such decisions as *Kinko's*[51] and *Texaco*[52] placed a limited interpretation on the application of fair use in the context of learning and research. As Association of American Publishers letter to copyshop owners advises "that *Kinko's* means that absent permission from the copyright holders, the copying of excerpts from copyrighted works into course anthologies which are distributed to students infringes the copyright in the works excerpted."[53] This trend toward limiting fair use was recently reversed by the Supreme Court in *Acuff-Rose*.[54] The U.S. Court of Appeals for the Sixth Circuit in *Princeton University Press v. Michigan Document Services, Inc.*[55] on the precedents of *Feist*[56] and *Acuff Rose*,[57] permitted as fair use coursepack copying on much the same facts as *Kinko's*. The reasoning of that case has been criticized by many copyright scholars and the Sixth Circuit, having agreed to reconsider the decision en banc,[58] affirmed the district court judgment dismissing the fair use claim, relying on the reasoning of *Kinko's* and *Texaco*.[59]

The fair use of materials for academic purposes is rarely the subject of judicial consideration, and university counsel appear relatively risk adverse in their application and analysis of the few precedents to date.

---

50.   H.R. Rep. No. 90-83, 90th Cong., 1st Sess. 29–30 (1967). The Report of the Committee on the Judiciary of the House noted that any precise definition of fair use was impossible and said that the endless variety of situations and combinations of circumstances that can arise in particular cases precludes the formulation of exact rules in the statute.

51.   Basic Books, Inc. v. Kinko's Graphics Corp., 758 F. Supp. 1522 (S.D.N.Y. 1991).

52.   American Geophysical Union v. Texaco, Inc., 60 F.3d 913 (1994).

53.   Letter circulated in 1991 following the *Kinko's* decision (on file with author).

54.   114 S. Ct. 1164 (1994).

55.   99 F.3d 1381 (6th Cir. 1996).

56.   Feist Publications, Inc. v. Rural Tel. Serv. Co., 499 U.S. 340, 349 (1991).

57.   114 S. Ct. 1164, 1169 (1994).

58.   For a discussion of these decisions, see *supra* Chapter Fifteen (p. 315), "User's Right to Photocopy: The Impact of *Texaco* and *Michigan Document Services*," by Sarah K. Wiant.

59.   99 F.3d 1381 (6th Cir. 1996).

There are few cases to date analyzing the fair use of visual images for teaching, scholarship, criticism, or research.[60]

The application of section 107 requires an analysis of both of its two paragraphs. The second paragraph lists four *non-exclusive* factors for determining whether a use is fair. They include: (1) the purpose and character of the use, including whether commercial or nonprofit education; (2) the nature of the copyrighted work; (3) the amount and substantiality of the portion used; and (4) the effect of the use upon the potential market for or value of the copyrighted work. The four fair use factors are to be weighed together, in light of the objectives of copyright to promote the progress of science and the useful arts.[61]

As Judge Pierre N. Leval noted at a 1994 meeting of the College Art Association on the subject of appropriation art:

> As to the first and second factors, the statute tells us nothing about what kind of purpose and character of the secondary use, and what kind of nature of the copyrighted work, will favor or disfavor a finding of fair use. In my view (which is not necessarily shared by other judges and copyright scholars), a study of the pattern of decisions reveals that courts have placed great importance on the first factor—the purpose and character of the secondary use. An important question has been: Does this appropriation fulfill the objective of the Copyright Law to stimulate creativity for public instruction? Is the appropriation transformative? Does it use the appropriate matter in a different way or for a different purpose from the original? Appropriation that merely repackages the original will not pass the test. If, on the other hand, the appropriate use adds to the original, if the original is transformed in the creation of new information, new attitudes, new aesthetics, insights and understandings, that is the type of appropriation that the fair use doctrine intends to protect. . . .
>
> Many other types of critique and commentary also fairly require quotation to communicate their message. An art historian or critic

---

60.   *See* Ferrato v. Castro, 888 F. Supp. 33 (S.D.N.Y. 1995), granting plaintiff's motion to dismiss with prejudice and holding that the incorporation by defendant of photographic images of plaintiff's copyrighted photographs in a mixed-media collage under the supervision of the Whitney Museum Independent Studies Program of New York City without plaintiff's permission for the purposes of exhibition in a show entitled "The Subject of Rape" and subsequently included in the exhibition catalog was fair use. The court refused to consider whether other uses not before it were fair use.

61.   *See Acuff-Rose*, 114 S. Ct. at 1171.

who seeks to make a point about an artist's work cannot effectively do so without showing illustrations.[62]

1. *Purpose and Character of the Use*. Who is the user? What are the uses—cataloging, teaching, scholarship, research, or criticism?

The courts have placed great importance on the purpose and character of the secondary use and whether the use is "transformative" and consistent with the goals of copyright law to stimulate creativity. The U.S. Supreme Court has said that "[t]he inquiry here may be guided by the examples given in the preamble of § 107. . . . "[63]

In *Twin Peaks Productions, Inc. v. Publications Int'l Ltd.*,[64] the court was called upon to determine whether a book of comment and criticism that summarized in great detail the plots of eight episodes of the television series *Twin Peaks* constituted fair use.[65] With respect to the "purpose" element of this factor, the court noted that "purpose" in fair use analysis is not an all-or-nothing matter. The issue is not simply whether a challenged work serves one of the non-exclusive purposes identified in section 107, such as criticism, comment, news reporting, teaching (including multiple copies for classroom use), scholarship, or research, but whether it does so to an insignificant or a substantial extent.

Turning to the "character" element, Chief Judge Newman in *Twin Peaks* focused upon the transformative nature of the allegedly infringing use. The court explained, for example, that such a transformative use would occur "if a plot was briefly described for purposes of adding significant criticism or comment about the author's plotting technique."[66]

Recent cases emphasize that the factor one analysis also must involve some qualitative measure of the value generated by the secondary use of the copyrighted material and the manner in which it is used. The more transformative the new work, the less will be the significance of other factors like commercialism.

---

62. Panel on Appropriation Art at the Annual Meeting of the College Art Association, New York, NY, Feb. 16, 1994.

63. *Acuff-Rose*, 114 S. Ct. at 1170.

64. 996 F.2d 1366 (2d Cir. 1993).

65. *Id.* at 1374.

66. *Id.* at 1375.

Ralph Oman, former register of copyrights, noted:

[I]n the use of a few frame enlargements to illustrate a classroom lecture versus the reproduction in a book of frame enlargements. The latter would be construed with less latitude from the user's standpoint in a "fair use" analysis than the former. The fact that a university press is "non-profit" will not be dispositive if the work in question would threaten the potential market value for any work that the copyright owner wants to publish—for example, a book about the film by the copyright owner—even if the copyright owner has never released such a book in the past.[67]

The courts have placed great importance on the purpose and character of the secondary use and whether the use is "transformative" and consistent with the goals of the copyright law to stimulate creativity. The U.S. Supreme Court has said that "[t]he inquiry here may be guided by the examples given in the preamble of § 107."[68] Since the preamble lists as an example "teaching (including multiple copies for classroom use)," and since whether or not the use is "for nonprofit educational purposes" is listed in factor one, this factor favors the educator who makes, or has another make, copies including single art images, only for classroom use.

Educational use promotes the progress of knowledge and the public interest, so the use of copyrighted material including images for teaching, research, and criticism is more likely to be considered fair use under factor one. Nevertheless, there is no general exemption for education, and the first factor must be analyzed in conjunction with other factors. For example, many artists, photographers, and illustrators may gain substantial revenues from licensing images for textbooks at the secondary and college level. Other classic examples of "transformative" copying concern art criticism, artistic parody (but not necessarily), and appropriation.[69] Courts have rejected fair use where there is only "piracy" or a quotation to highlight or enliven without any critical comment on the subject. In 1841 in *Folsom v. Marsh*,[70] the leading early American decision on the fair use defense,

---

67.   Ralph Oman, Letter to David Bordwell (Jan. 7, 1992), 32 CINEMA J., Winter 1993, at 17.

68.   *Acuff-Rose*, 114 S. Ct. at 1170.

69.   *See generally* Rogers v. Koons, 960 F.2d 301 (2d Cir. 1992).

70.   9 Fed. Cas. 342 (1841).

Justice Storey stated that the second work must contain "real, substantial condensation of the materials and intellectual labor and judgment thereupon; and not merely the facile use of the scissors; or extracts of the essential parts constituting the chief value of the original work."[71]

In the *Texaco* case, the court found that factor one tipped against Texaco because, citing *Folsom,*

[Th]e photocopying "merely supersedes the objects of original creation". . . . We do not mean to suggest that no instance of archival copying would be fair use, but the first factor tilts against Texaco in this case because the making of copies . . . is part of a systematic process of encouraging employee researchers to copy articles so as to multiply available copies while avoiding payment.[72]

2. Nature of the Copyrighted Work. The second factor is a recognition of the fact that there are three types of copyrightable works: (1) creative or predominantly original works; (2) compilations; and (3) derivative works. Thus, the Supreme Court has ruled in *Acuff-Rose* that factor two "calls for recognition that some works are closer to the core of copyright protection than others. . . ."[73] Copyright law gives greater protection to certain classes of works that embody more creativity, such as fiction, photographs, poetry, and art images, compared with more factual materials. The more creative a work is, the greater it is protected.

When it comes to original works of art, factor two will almost always go against a finding of fair use because of the innately creative nature of art. Also, if a work is unpublished, copying it is less likely to be considered a fair use (though the fact that it is unpublished does not by itself bar a finding of fair use if such a finding is made upon consideration of all the other factors taken together).[74] On the other hand, the status of a digitally photographed public domain work or "curatorial photography" is unclear. As noted previously, digital image archives are composed of many different types of works. Each category of work is more appropriately analyzed separately. For example,

---

71.   *Id.* at 345.
72.   *Texaco,* 60 F.3d at 920.
73.   *Acuff-Rose,* 114 S. Ct. at 1175.
74.   17 U.S.C. § 107 (1994).

a photograph of a renaissance work of art or other examples of "thin copyright" might provoke a different analysis than a photograph by Dianne Arbus or Richard Avedon, or a photograph of a work by Pablo Picasso, Faith Ringgold, or Richard Serra. Finally, of interest with respect to this factor, a U.S. district court judge in New York has recently held, with respect to the analysis of the second factor, that:

> Anyone who has seen any of the great pieces of photojournalism— for example, Alfredo Eisenstadt's classic image of a thrilled sailor exuberantly kissing a woman in Times Square on V-J Day and the stirring photograph of U.S. Marines raising the American flag atop Mount Surabachi on Iwo Jima—or, perhaps in some eyes, more artistic, but nevertheless representational, photography—such as Ansel Adams' work and the portraits of Yousuf Karsh—must acknowledge that photographic images of actual people, places and events may be creative and deserving of protection as purely fanciful creations. Nevertheless, history has its demands. There is a public interest in receiving information concerning the world in which we live. The more newsworthy the person or event depicted, the greater the concern that too narrow a view of the fair use defense will deprive the public of significant information. Moreover, only a finite number of photographers capture images of a given historical event. Hence, without denying for a moment the creativity inherent in the film clips of actual events relating to the Zaire fight, the degree of protection that properly may be afforded to them must take into account that too narrow a view of the fair use defense could materially undermine the ability of other Ali biographers to tell, in motion picture or perhaps still photographic form, an important part of his story. See, e.g., Rosemont Enterprises, Inc., 366 F.2d at 307. This of course is not to say that historical film footage loses all copyright protection, only that its character as historical film footage may strengthen somewhat the hand of a fair use defendant as compared with an alleged infringer of a fanciful work or a work presented in a medium that offers a greater variety of forms of expression.[75]

3. Amount and Substantiality of the Portion Used in Relation to the Copyrighted Work as a Whole. As Judge Leval noted,

> The third and fourth factors direct a court's attention to how much of the work can be taken and how serious a harm has the taking inflicted on the value of the original work. The amount that can be

---

75.   Monster Communications, Inc. v. Turner Broadcasting Sys., 935 F. Supp. 490 (S.D.N.Y. 1996).

copied as a matter of fair use is a logical function of the first two factors, the purpose of the use and the nature of the work.[76]

For private or personal use, there may be occasions when the entire work may be copied.[77]

Normally courts look at both the quantitative and qualitative amount that is taken. The use of a pictorial, graphic, and sculptural work will usually involve the whole work. Nevertheless, the Supreme Court in *Acuff-Rose* recently held that this factor would not necessarily be determinative and must be considered in light of the purpose and use of the new work. The Court suggested that the extent of copying can provide an insight into the primary purpose of copying, and cautioned that there was a need for more particularized inquiry about the amount taken.[78]

The Supreme Court acknowledged in *Acuff-Rose* that the facts bearing on this third factor will also tend to address the fourth factor of market harm.[79]

4. Effect of the Use upon the Potential Market. More important in deciding whether a use is fair is whether the new work that is compiled by using copyrighted material competes with the original work. Prior to *Acuff-Rose*, lower courts deemed this to be the most important of the four factors. Judge Leval stated:

> That last factor has been seen as particularly important. It stresses the commercial nature of the copyright, which seeks to protect the ability of authors and artists to make a living from their work. Copying that interferes with that ability is disfavored; if the copies furnish the public with a substitute for the original artist's work, so that the public will buy the appropriation rather than the original, such copying is unlikely to be found fair use. But where the appropriation is a salute, or a jab, in the direction of an admired or reviled icon, and that salute or jab will not become a commercial substitute for the original, this kind of appropriation may well pass the test of fair use.[80]

---

76.   Judge Pierre N. Leval, Address on Appropriation Art at the Meeting of the College Art Association, New York, NY (Feb. 16, 1994) [hereinafter Leval].

77.   Sony Corp. of Am. v. Universal City Studios, 464 U.S. 417 (1984).

78.   *Acuff-Rose*, 114 S. Ct. at 1175–76.

79.   *Id.* at 1175.

80.   Leval, *supra* note 76.

The Supreme Court made clear in *Acuff-Rose* that market effect is only one of four factors to be considered, and it is to receive no greater weight than the others.[81] The Supreme Court has also stressed the need for evidence about markets for particularized licenses, "the market for potential derivative uses includes only those that creators of original works would in general develop or license others to develop."[82] Thus, the fact that an artist or photographer may license his or her images, but refuses to do so because of negative critical commentary of the image, should not cause this factor to weigh against fair use, since rarely is there a market for licensing for parody or negative critical commentary.[83] Some commentators and decisions have seen fair use as an example of market failure, perceiving a close relationship between a finding of fair use and the copyright owner's inability to implement reasonably priced, administratively tolerable licensing procedures. If the costs of negotiations and seeking out hundreds of copyright owners whose permission might be required proved unreasonable or unduly burdensome, the public interest and good of the copyright system might be thwarted.

The duration of the use and the degree of dissemination are also relevant concerns under the fourth factor. For example, the analysis of factor four considerations may vary as a function of the number of copies and of whether the image is transmitted over the Internet for (a) distance learning; (b) use by other institutions; (c) use by students off-campus.

The four factors are not exclusive, and other relevant factors may be considered. Such factors include whether the work is available. The work may be unavailable because it is out of print or because of excessive price. Under the library exemption, the rights of reproduction apply to the entire work if it is determined "on the basis of reasonable investigation, that an unused copy or phonorecord of the copyrighted work cannot be obtained at a fair price . . ."[84] and the purpose of the reproduction is to replace a lost, damaged, stolen, or deteriorating

---

81.   *Acuff-Rose*, 114 S. Ct. at 1170–71.
82.   *Id.* at 1178.
83.   *Id.*
84.   17 U.S.C. § 108(c) (1994).

work.[85] Images appearing in even the most basic art history textbooks are often unavailable from commercial vendors. While a substantial body of images are sold commercially, still many more, such as plans, maps, diagrams, reconstructions, and the like, are not as available. Images for courses in non-European art are not readily available from vendors. Furthermore, it is often impossible to determine if an image is available from a commercial source because reference tools or indexes to images currently do not exist. As Professor Rhyne notes:

> Because books and magazines are filled with images of so many different works of art, it is not generally realized that most of the world's art has never been photographed, let alone digitized. One sees images of the same paintings, drawings, sculptures, architecture, and other works of art over and over again, and the most famous of these are, of course, the works that are appearing first on commercial compact disks (usually CD-ROMs). Even the largest photo archives for art history research are highly selective, largely dependent on suppliers, and unable to keep pace with the modern discovery and restoration of older art, much less the creation of new. . . . Within the world of architecture, only the most famous buildings have been photographed at all comprehensively; this is even more true with vernacular architecture and industrial archaeology. Likewise with sculpture, only the masterpieces of world art have been photographed from a sufficient number of angles to support detailed study, many photographs of sculpture are not in color, and less famous sculpture and tribal objects are photographed inadequately or not at all.[86]

The relationship between licensing and the doctrine of fair use is critical to the digital networked environment. The concern is that technological means of tracking transactions and licensing will lead to reduced application and scope of the fair use doctrine in a network environment. In *American Geophysical Union v. Texaco Inc.*,[87] the court established liability for unauthorized photocopying based in part on the court's perception that obtaining a license for the right via the CCC was not *unreasonably burdensome*.[88]

---

85. *Id.* § 108(c). Libraries, however, are not permitted to reproduce pictorial or graphic works for users. *Id.* § 108(h).

86. Rhyne, *supra* note 1, at 23–24.

87. 60 F.3d 913 (2d Cir. 1994).

88. *Id.* at 931–32. This reasoning was reaffirmed in Princeton University Press v. Michigan Document Services, 99 F.3d 1381 (1996), with the caveat "only traditional, reasonable or whether to be developed markets are to be considered in this

Professor Jane Ginsberg notes that the WIPO Berne Protocol proposal identifies that whether a use qualifies for a teaching exemption
depends on whether the use conflicts with a "normal exploitation of
the work." The proposal recognizes that if the market for excerpts is
being exploited by means of collective licensing, the free copying of
works for educational purposes poses such a conflict.[89]

The analysis of licensing and the market-effect factor is particularly complex with respect to fair use in the academic environment. As
Robert Baron notes, however, not all issues of licensing involve copyright and fair use. As one museum director stated:

> Copyright laws that have traditionally permitted "fair use" exemp-
> tions for published *copyrighted materials*, when their purpose is educa-
> tional and non-profit, may not be able to withstand the coercive
> mechanics of supply and demand will replace the broader provisions
> of *our laws of copyright and "fair use."*
>
> On-line vendors will be under continual financial pressure to
> remove those items that are never accessed—so as to use their storage
> space better for things that are sure to contribute to their revenue
> stream. In consequence, the on-line scholar will be poorly served by
> the elimination of rarely used but potentially important files. . . . If
> scholarly activity is to be redefined as a commercial endeavor, one
> must also accept a new reality—that there is an economic justification
> for the production of scholarly works. . . .
>
> When scholars must consider the cost of every decision to access a
> work or not, and when they must decide whether to look on-line for
> information resources or not, the long-standing credit of scholarly
> pursuit—freedom of access, freedom of expression—will have already
> been subverted by economic priorities. The conflict between free access
> and copyright is precipitated by the strife that arises when the modern
> scholar dreams of himself and his high calling as part of a worthy and
> venerable tradition outside of economic warrant, while the vendor looks
> at him as just another customer. Consequently, if scholars are forced to
> abandon this ancient vision of their calling, they must inevitably come
> face to face with their uncertain standing as economic beings. The insti-
> tutional scholar, supported by his museum or department, and by uni-
> versity, government or foundation grants, will be given leave to con-
> tinue to live his fiction for a while, but the scholar, pursuing an unsup-
> ported or unsupportable agenda, may soon find that his access to the
> tools and resources available to others is diminishing, not by dint of

---

connection and even the availability of an existing system for collecting licensing
fees will not be conclusive" (quoting *Texaco*, 60 F.3d at 930–31).

89.   Ginsburg, *supra* note 11, at 191 n.24.

diminishing rights of access, but rather because it will be increasingly likely that he cannot afford to use them.

Limitations on photography, contracts with publishers stipulating one-time use, restrictions on the resolution of digital images made available on the Internet or compact discs are all strategies available to museums, archives, and libraries that want to control the use of their images. As long as these strategies are applied to limiting or controlling access to objects in the public domain, copyright law cannot be brought to bear. One might say "it's not fair" but one cannot invoke the doctrine of fair use.[90]

Fair use may be considered along a spectrum of uses. Copying and using copyrighted artwork for commercial purposes or broad distribution—such as replicating an image on a tee shirt, incorporating copyrighted images into commercial multimedia products or illustrations in textbooks for distribution, sale, or display on the World Wide Web, or reproducing the original artwork as a poster or postcard—is much more likely to be considered a copyright infringement than using the same images or works in a classroom room for teaching. Other such uses more likely to be fair uses are: (1) use in a critical, scholarly article which comments on the image in question; (2) digitizing images in research collections for students when most of the images are not sold on the market; (3) creating thumbnail images and making these searchable by field as a bibliographic reference; or (4) using copyrighted images in academic course assignments or in fulfillment of degree requirements for research such as a term paper, thesis, or dissertation. The case for fair use in connection with scholarly, analytical, or critical use of images is a strong one.[91]

There is always the possibility that in copying copyrighted materials one may exceed the limits of fair use and thus infringe the copyright of the copied work. Congress recognized this danger and provided special protection for teachers, librarians, and other employees of nonprofit institutions in the form of a good faith defense. If such a person believes in good faith that the copying is a fair use, neither the copier nor the institution is liable for statutory damages. The Copyright Act provides:

---

90. Unofficial review of draft CONFU Proposed Guidelines by the Association of Art Museum Directors (UAAMD 1/19) (Jan. 22, 1996) (emphasis added).

91. *See* Ferrato v. Castro, 94 Civ. 2009, 888 F. Supp. 33 (S.D.N.Y. 1995).

> The court shall remit statutory damages in any case where an infringer believed and had reasonable grounds for believing that his or her use of the copyrighted work was a fair use under section 107, if the infringer was: (I) an employee or agent of a nonprofit educational institution, library, or archives acting within the scope of his or her employment who, or such institution, library, or archives itself, which infringed by reproducing the work in copies of phonorecords. . . . [92]

Since statutory damages may range from $500 to $20,000, and in the case of willful infringement up to $100,000,[93] the good faith defense is meaningful protection for educators and nonprofit institutions.

Due to the potential ambiguities inherent in a fair use analysis, four sets of guidelines covering educational photocopying and video-taping were agreed to between libraries, educators, and publishers at the time the 1976 Copyright Act was passed and in 1981.[94] The result has been, in certain circumstances, a quantitative gloss on the construction of fair use and library copying privileges. For educational purposes, for instance, the Classroom Guidelines generally permit the copying of short extracts of works, provided that the copying is spontaneously done or requested by the instructor (and the copies are neither used nor remade repeatedly over time).[95] The Classroom Guidelines were the result of negotiation and agreement among the Ad Hoc Committee of Educational Institutions and Organizations on Copyright Law Revision, the Authors League of America, Inc., and the Association of American Publishers. Thus, the Classroom Guidelines are not readily adaptable to the teaching or study of art and art history, which depends on critical discourse in images, in either the print or digital media and where hundreds of images may be used in a single class.

The 1976 "guidelines" are specific in nature, and it is important to understand that they are best viewed as safe-harbor provisions. If an educator does not exceed these guidelines, then there is no issue of infringement, no question of fair use, and good faith exists as a matter of law.[96] If, however, the copying exceeds the guidelines, the educator or librarian must rely on fair use or one of the exceptions or limitations for

---

92.   17 U.S.C. § 504(c)(2) (1994).

93.   *Id.* § 504(c).

94.   All of the guidelines appear in Appendices B through E, *infra.*

95.   H.R. REP. NO. 94-1476, *supra* note 36, at 68–70.

96.   HOWARD ABRAMS, 2 THE LAW OF COPYRIGHT § 15.06(A)(4) (1991).

the right to copy the material. Both the status of the guidelines in relation to fair use and their application to the new technologies are the subject of discussion. The appellate court state in *Texaco* that:

> Though we have been instructed to defer to Congress "when major technological innovations alter the market for copyrighted materials, *Sony*, 464 U.S. at 431, Congress has thus far provided scant guidance for resolving fair use issues involving photocopying, legislating specifically only as to library copying, *see* 17 U.S.C. 108, and providing indirect advice concerning classroom copying. n3. *See generally* 3 Nimmer on Copyright 13.05 [E]. However, we learn from the Supreme Court's consideration of copying achieved by use of a videotape recorder that mechanical copying is to assessed for fair use purposes under the traditional mode of analysis, including the four statutory factors of section 107. *See Sony*, 464 U.S. at 447–56. We therefore are obliged to apply that analysis to the photocopying that occurred in this case.[97]

What is fair use in cyberspace? The Working Group on Intellectual Property Rights in its Green Paper called for the Conference on Fair Use "to determine whether educational or library guidelines of a similar nature [to those developed in 1976] might prove attainable in the NII context."[98] The Working Group added further that "should the participants in the Conference on Fair Use fail to agree on appropriate guidelines, the Working Group may conclude that the importance of such guidelines may necessitate regulatory or legislative action in that area."[99]

Christine Sundt, visual resources curator at the University of Oregon, described the new educational environment thusly:

> Without question, making digital images accessible through electronic networks or the WWW and the distribution and display of such digital images at multiple workstations with the possible downloading and printing of copies of such images raises significant copyright issues. The complexities of the electronic environment and the growing potential for implicating copyright infringements raise the need for a fresh review of fair use. Is the following example merely the digital version of the existing Classroom Guidelines? To what extent can educational institutions digitize existing slide libraries?

---

97.   *Texaco*, 60 F.3d at 917.

98.   INTELLECTUAL PROPERTY AND THE NATIONAL INFORMATION INFRASTRUCTURE: A PRELIMINARY REPORT OF THE WORKING GROUP ON INTELLECTUAL PROPERTY RIGHTS 134 (1994).

99.   *Id.* at 84.

NEW SCENARIO: An educator may display digital images stored in the school's digital image archive and accessed through a campus network to the classroom where instruction is taking place.

DESCRIPTION OF THE SCENARIO: An art history survey class is being taught in an "electronic classroom." The students enrolled in the course meet with the instructor just as they did in the traditional classroom, but instead of showing slides to present the artwork under discussion, the students view digital images projected by an LCD viewer connected to the instructor's laptop computer. The computer is connected to the university's network through an internal Ethernet card that provides her with access to the school's digital image collection, housed in another building on the campus. The instructor has a list of image numbers that she has preprogrammed on her laptop that serves as an interface to the image collection management software. The instructor also has the option of calling up additional images from the digital image collection, as needed, using the software's browsing tool/search engine feature. These additional (unplanned) images would be used to answer a student's question triggered by one of the images seen in the lecture (e.g. a student asks: "Last week you showed us a building with 'swirly' columns. Do you think Rubens may have known or seen these columns because it looks to me like he copied them in this painting!" At this point the instructor can access the view of the building she showed last week that includes the columns to compare them with the Rubens work on the screen), or to provide other artworks when the students need more examples of the concept or style being presented (e.g. the students are having a difficult time understanding the concept of "Mannerism" as it differs from "Baroque" art. The instructor can bring in other examples immediately, via the network, from the image archive, while the student's interest is peaked rather than waiting until the next lecture, as would have been required if she had been using slides).

After class, the students go to the reserve room of the library and review the images shown in class. The same slide list that the instructor prepared for her lecture has been put "on reserve" for as long as she determines is sufficient time for the students to review the materials and prepare for their scheduled exams, typically a mid-term and final.[100]

V. Conference on Fair Use (CONFU)

The Conference on Fair Use was facilitated by the Patent and Trademark Office as an outgrowth of recommendations in the White Paper

---

100.   Letter from Professor Christine L. Sundt, Visual Resources Curator, University of Oregon (Apr. 4, 1996) (on file with author).

that representatives of the school and library communities meet with representatives of the copyright-holder community to see if guidelines for fair use in public libraries and schools could be developed.

The meetings began in September 1994 and continued monthly until 1996, when meetings of the whole were held less frequently in favor of smaller working groups on several issues such as image archives, distance learning, and electronic reserves. At the first meeting the participants agreed:

> [I]t would not be useful to take the existing guidelines for use of print materials in nonprofit educational institutions, or off-air taping of televisions programs, and simply modify them for the new digital world. They agreed that the electronic environment is very different from the environment in place when the earlier guidelines were drafted in the mid-70s. For instance, several of the existing guidelines refer to use in a classroom—but today's learning environment involves remote locations, dorm rooms, home-based learning, distance learning within a state or region, and the like. Further electronic works have different properties from print and are frequently sold under different terms.[101]

The dynamics of the group meetings was aptly expressed by participant Douglas Bennett, Vice President of the American Council of Learned Societies. Bennett states:

> Several dozen organizations participate in the work on CONFU. It is difficult to give a precise number because new participants continue to arrive and some have drifted away, but perhaps 50 or 60 organizations have been steadily involved. Many are organizations that represent publishers and other copyright holders. Users of copyrighted materials are principally represented by library organizations.
>
> Publishers worry that networks and digital technology open the door to users transmitting millions of illegal, perfect copies across the globe with just a few key strokes. On this worry, fair use is an open door to renegade behavior that will undercut the financial viability of publishers. Librarians have a very basic worry as well. Librarians worry that the new technology will be used to create a world which is strictly pay-per-view. There will not longer be any fair use, nor any sharing of materials among users or institutions. Though seldom expressed in bald form, these two very large worries dominate

---

101.   Carol Risher, Statement of the Association of American Publishers on Scanning (Aug. 1994).

CONFU, one from each side. Their scale and breadth have tended to be corrosive of practical solutions for particular problems.

There are also some seldom-expressed hopes that participants bring with them into the discussions. Publishers hope that the new technology will bring new efficiencies, possibilities for publishing on demand, relief from the need to hold inventory, and new possibilities for deriving additional income from previously-published materials. Librarians hope that the technology will allow them to work out new strategies for sharing materials, and provide a foundation for cooperative collection development. These hopes are rarely expressed for fear of sparking the corresponding worry from the other side.

Something else slowing progress is shared awareness that the technology continues to evolve very quickly. No one wants to enter into an agreement which will be rendered unfavorable to them by a quick shift in what the technology makes possible.[102]

The approach of the CONFU was to have interested parties present a discussion of issues on a particular topic and then proceed to a discussion of scenarios and guidelines on selected issues. More than twenty discrete issues and sub-issues were initially identified for discussion and subsequently were considered by CONFU participants in varying degrees of detail. Six issues were isolated for intensive discussion and negotiation: electronic reserves, interlibrary loan/document delivery, distance learning, multimedia, software use in libraries, and visual image archives. The participants of CONFU established November 30, 1996, as a reasonable target date for either producing separate voluntary guidelines covering each of the six issues noted above or for determining whether it is currently possible to do so. Resulting guidelines and other written materials from CONFU appear in the appendices of this book.

VI. CONFU Guidelines for Digital Image Archives: A Brief Critique

The Proposed Educational Fair Use Guidelines For Digital Images[103] are divided into five parts: (1) Introduction; (2) Image Digitization and Use by Educational Institutions; (3) Image Digitization and Use by Educators, Scholars and Students; (4) Important Reminders and Fair Use

---

102.   Bennett, *supra* note 40.
103.   These guidelines appear as Appendix I, *infra* p. 519.

Limitations under These Guidelines; and (5) Transition Period for Pre-Existing Analog Image Collections.

In addition to a general, unexceptional introduction on fair use,[104] the draft guidelines try to achieve consensus guidelines and solutions in two areas: (1) the digitalization of existing (non-digital) analog slide collections; and (2) fair use of newly acquired analog images. At the time this book was published, it seemed unlikely that the academic user community will agree to the guidelines. In part, this reflects the fact that the guidelines seem more restrictive than current court decisions on fair use warrant. Although fair use is based on a case-by-case analysis, precedents in the application of the fair use doctrine mean that courts do not decide each case on a *tabula rasa*. Recent decisions have argued for a sensitive balancing of all factors in light of achieving the goals of the copyright law. The guidelines reject this sensitive application of the factors and look almost exclusively to the fourth factor and not at all to the second factor. The presumptions rejected by *Campbell v. Acuff-Rose Music, Inc.*[105] are the *deus ex machina* of the guidelines. There are many reasons to predict that in the future a consensual collective licensing model may eventually provide the framework for the use of image archives and collections for research, teaching, and scholarship in the digital age; but for many reasons, at least with respect to art, architecture, and art history, that future has not arrived. In part, criticism of the guidelines stems from the difficult and unworkable burden imposed upon smaller educational institutions, libraries, and archives.

The guidelines have much to recommend them. For example, the agreed-to use by educators, scholars, and students set forth in 3.1.1, 3.1.2, 3.2, and 3.4 clarify the legality of current uses. Many provisions on image digitization and use by educational institutions also seem to achieve a workable balance, particularly the use of thumbnail images. But many sections are, as the comments indicated, unworkable and unsupported by current legal doctrine. For example, a more neutral definition in 3.3 might state:

> These guidelines do not cover reproducing and publishing images in publications, including scholarly publications in print or digital form.

---

104. All of the CONFU guidelines use the same introduction.
105. 114 S. Ct. 1164, 1170 (1994).

Or, in 2.4.2:

> Where the rightsholder of an image is unknown, a digitized image may be used subject to the four-factor fair use analysis (see Section 1.1).

Or:

> Where the rightsholder of an image is unknown, a digitized image may be used (see Section 1.1) for up to three years from first use, provided that a reasonable inquiry (see Section 5.2) is conducted by the institution seeking permission to digitize, retain, and reuse the digitized image. If, after three years, the educational institution is unable to identify sufficient information to seek permission, the use shall be considered a fair use.

The comments of Lelia W. Kinney, Electronic Editor, College Art Association, and Co-Chair, Committee on Electronic Information (CEI), on an earlier draft based on a CAA survey, are similarly apt for the current proposed guidelines:

> We appreciate the improvements in this draft, notably its "decriminalization" of the use of digital imagery for educational and scholarly purposes (though not, regrettably, a straightforward acknowledgment of the legality of fair use), its recognition that digital thumbnails have no intrinsic or commercial value, its allowance for spontaneity in teaching and the corresponding dynamic nature of the digital materials required for classroom use, and its provision for a 7-year transition period for pre-existing collections. However, so many issues remain unresolved that we cannot recommend endorsement. As Jeffrey Muller (Brown University) put it, the bottom line is that "our teaching is going to be hurt." There really was little ambiguity on this basic point: "The guidelines as currently proposed are unworkable and will preclude the market some see to exploit" (David Newman, Brookhaven College).
>
> However, I must stress that this process has, more than anything else, revealed that it is premature to produce any guidelines at this time. The technology is dynamic and evolving, and teaching with digital imagery and producing digital works of art are both in an experimental, rapidly developing phase. Attempting to finalize guidelines before the issues are sorted out in the various educational, commercial, and legal domains would be counterproductive.[106]

Glen Lowry, Director of the Museum of Modern Art, commenting on the proposed guidelines stated:

---

106.   Memorandum from Lelia W. Kinney to College Art Association (Aug. 30, 1996).

However, the Museum of Modern Art is concerned with the AAMD's endorsement of these guidelines, which instead of emphasizing educational uses and open access, greatly favor seeking permissions and/or clearance of rights. Many of the uses covered by the guidelines have been to date freely allowed as being educational both on the part of museums and other scholars. We question whether as a matter of policy, museums and other educational institutions or individual scholars, with limited resources, should be required to now pay for such uses. Moreover, we believe that museums should encourage educational uses by providing other educators with access to images in their collections without undue expense and restriction. Additionally, we believe that these guidelines will particularly affect those museums with modern and contemporary art collections, where the works are largely subject to copyright.

In elaboration, by requiring museums to locate the source of images and to pay for their use, the guidelines will change current industry practice and place an unreasonable burden on museums in terms of time and resources.[107]

The fair use doctrine permits and requires courts to avoid rigid application of the copyright statute when, on occasion, it would stifle the very creativity which the copyright law is designed to foster. A broad view of authors' and artists' rights and the potential licensing of images by such groups as the Getty-inspired Art Museum Consortium (AMICO) is not incompatible with a sensitively contoured concept of fair use.

In short, copyright owners should not be prevented from legitimate exploitation of the market for their product nor control over its uses, but some uses will never be licensed (i.e., "the widow censor") and some uses are reasonable, fair, and require no permission. The proposed guidelines substitute for the indeterminate, flexible boundaries of the fair use doctrine, the very rigidity that the doctrine was designed to eliminate

Museums, educators, and scholars will no doubt benefit in the future from the development of guidelines for the use of digital images. Such guidelines, however, must reflect current practice, economic reality, and the sensitive balance between copyright owners and users that exists under current law.

---

107.   Letter to Mimi Guardieri, Director, Association of Art Museums (Apr. 11, 1997) (on file with author).

Memorandum from Lelia W. Kinney to College Art Association, August 30, 1996, Summarizing Comments

Burden Shifting

The idea of searching for copyright holders in order to secure permissions for use assumes a staff. Our faculty of two art historians (each teaching a 12-hour load) and a half-time slide curator who cannot possibly keep up the demands placed on him leaves no one to do the searching. Again, if we were to adopt the draft guidelines we would simply have to stop using digital images. (William Allen, Arkansas State University, Jonesboro)

It is good that the framers of the guidelines have recognized the value of digitizing pre-existing collections and are aware of the problems of getting permissions for them. What is unclear is how far we really have to go in chasing down the source of an undocumented image, and how much time it will take. . . . Chasing the 139 images down [of 1371 that are included in the course] will be an incredible task since they came from a variety of sources. Some of them were taken out of

436

books, mostly years ago, with no reference kept. There are references for a few of them, which are old plans that were most likely taken from earlier plans published in books that are now in the public domain. . . . Others came from slides purchased over the years in Greece, in Paris, in Rome, etc. If some of these give the name of the company that produced them, most do not have an address. Many do not contain copyright notice: does that mean they are in the public domain? (Kathy Cohen, San Jose State University)

Many of my slides were purchased years ago from slide distributors who are no longer in business. Some were purchased in stores and from vendors off the streets in Rome, Pisa, Florence, Paris, etc. I could type the letters inquiring, but to whom do you mail them? (Necia Miller, CAAH)

Who is going to pick up the costs of the enormous amount of labor involved in seeking permissions? (Jeffrey Muller, Brown University)

Disproportionate Impact on Small Institutions

Let me point out that to some extent (considerable, I suspect) that those institutions with the least sophisticated computer systems and the smallest staffs are also going to be institutions with historically large proportions of minority students and disadvantaged students, institutions in rural areas (institutions, like mine, that serve a large number of first-generation college students), and institutions that are evolving from two-year and/or vocational status to college status (we have three such campuses attached to us and more on the way). (William Allen, Arkansas State University, Jonesboro)

Multiple Use Is Fair Use

There is nothing that I see in the fair use statute stipulating that second uses are not fair uses. Using a single copy multiple times in a lecture or educational situation is not the same as making and distributing multiple copies. . . . The process stipulated for obtaining rights assumes that fair use is equivalent with "first use," and that a second use is not a fair use, even though the facts of the use have not changed. (Robert Baron)

Am I to understand that if we digitize images for study purposes only (low resolution, secured access), they are good only for a one-shot course in one semester, and that afterwards we must obtain permission or license to use them again? If so, the idea is impractical. It took me three months on my own time (unpaid) to digitize images for a course that lasts four months. We are in a state university that certainly couldn't afford licensing fees for the materials that we use, and in the case of one course, the material is not available for student accessibility anywhere else. If this is the case, I can't live with it. What's the point of so much labor-intensive effort if we must then discard it? (Judith Sobre, University of Texas, San Antonio)

I have just finished a complete course for the first semester of the art history survey which I have titled "The Web of Art and Culture." It contains 1371 digitized images plus all the texts for each image divided into 20 computerized lessons which take the place of course lectures. In addition, there is a Study Guide so that students can work independently and come to class once per week for small discussion sections. This has been an unbelievable amount of work, and there is no way that I would just use it for one semester. (Kathy Cohen, San Jose State University)

Time Limitations

Our terms are ten weeks long and there is barely enough time to get the images that the faculty want scanned and the attached data into the system, much less to begin to seek permission. Fair use means not having to ask for permission. . . . Please remember that even if we could find the staff time to see such permissions it does not mean that they will be forthcoming. As you all know, a great many of the illustrations in art books are made from the transparencies supplied by museums. When we are seeking permission to digitize slides made from copywork, the book publishers will refer us back to the museum. (Elizabeth O'Donnell, Dartmouth College)

The Need for Non-commercial Repositories of Imagery

I particularly agree . . . on the inherent danger of our only being able to make available "legal" images in the very narrow and highly commercial sense that the guidelines stipulate. For many years, our incoming students have been given a rather distorted view of the "canon" of art history because such a high percentage of images included in these basic texts have come from a few major museums, especially the national galleries. Are these same images always included because they are truly the most representative pieces of an artist's oeuvre, or because they are the easiest and cheapest to reproduce? (Eileen Fry, Indiana University)

I totally agree that many of the stipulations in this document would be detrimental to the principles of academic freedom. They would not only place undue—in many cases impossible—demands on the academic institution and/or individual faculty member both in terms of time and expense, but they would potentially stifle access to information. Taken to extreme levels this might be considered a *de facto* form of censorship. My collection, a major collection of architecture slides, contains lots of material from printed sources. I would guess that 99% of these images are unavailable commercially either in analog or digital form. Furthermore, there are no plans to make this material available in these ways because, quite frankly, there isn't a profit to be made by providing these images commercially. This situation is mirrored in many slide collections which serve advanced undergraduate and graduate students. Faculty members use the relevant research of any given field to teach ideas and concepts and, thus, need resources that got way beyond the common war horses. (Margaret N. Webster, Cornell University)

Copy Reproductions and Public Domain Imagery

Frankly, I'd like to see CAA take a hard line on this business of copyrighting images made by people who have been dead for hundreds of years—or produced by an anonymous maker. Images should go into the public domain just as written works do. Museums can protect their financial interest in reproductions of objects in their collections by issuing "the only reproduction authorized by" seals of approval. I don't have a problem with museums making money from the process of making and selling reproductions of objects in their collection, but I do feel that copyrighting the reproduction of, say, a 17th-century painting is ridiculous. As others have pointed out, there is no creative content in this kind of reproduction—that is the point—as such, there is nothing copyrightable. (Andrea Pappas, University of Southern California)

As the numbers of layers of rights that exist over the "underlying work" decreases, it is absurd to maintain that the number of layers that must be cleared should increase (with increasing cost) as the quality and fidelity to the original decreases. . . . If works in the public domain cannot be obtained save by license or other contractual means, then there is no meaning in the concept of the public domain. Any fair use analysis of a reproduction of a public domain work in which the creators of the illustration claim copyright status will need to undergo a separate analysis of how much originality and singularity that reproduction brings to the public domain underlying work. (Robert Baron, Museum Computer Consultant)

"Original" Digital Imagery

It is either not included or just not made clear that an image may have been produced entirely on the computer and not be a digitization of any "original" image. If a work is created on the computer, then the term "original" is ambiguous. If there are 10 copies of the digital file, they are identical. How is "original" defined for digital images? This is a basic point. . . . So far it seems that [the guidelines] apply only to the study of art, not its production. (Anne Morgan Spalter, Brown University)

Linking Is Not Discussed

Linking to existing sites is not covered in this agreement, and it is an essential part of the Web. We should encourage museums and libraries to put up their own sites, and then link to them (this would be easiest for everyone). (Cynthia Rubin, University of Vermont)

Distance Learning and Multimedia Guidelines Are Not Incorporated

I am uncomfortable with the fact that both the document for multimedia teaching and long distance learning are not even attached to this document for comparison or further reference. (Nancy Macko, Scripps College)

Distance learning programs are being developed all over this country and many other parts of the world, especially the English speaking one. It needs . . . to be included in the Guidelines. (Jerrold Maddox, Pennsylvania State University)

Chapter Nineteen

Does Faculty Assignment of Copyright Violate the Constitutional Mandate?*

by
Bert R. Boyce

Professor and Dean
School of Library and Information Science
Louisiana State University

I. A Call to Arms

It is time for academic librarians to take a fresh look at copyright issues, but it is even more important, after that look, for all librarians to use whatever leverage is available to influence change in our copyright laws. While all librarians are limited in the service they can provide their patrons by the current law and, as I shall point out, while the progress of science and all learned activity is impeded by that same law, it is the academic librarian and the institution itself that suffers

---

* © 1997 Bert R. Boyce.

the most direct harm. The unconscionable growth in serials budgets and the resulting reduction in availability of serials in local collections is a direct result of the current legal situation. The inability to transfer freely learned literature via electronic means will prove to be an even worse restriction, particularly as electronic distance education grows in popularity and the need to make literature available at remote sites grows with it.

Academic libraries continue to face the unending problem of growing costs of periodical and other serials, and the only solution appears to be shrinking serials collections and moving toward a policy of access on demand rather than actual holding of the material. This solution is a classical sub-optimization. Its lowers the individual library's costs in the short term while maintaining service. As subscriptions fall, however, the publishers will maintain their profits by imposing or increasing charges on electronic display or by charging fees on individual reproduction. The costs for on-demand access to articles will skyrocket soon under the proposed changes in the copyright laws. This sounds very much like pay-per-view television, and this solution of access on demand will certainly fail. It seems quite possible to make the case that it has failed already, when considering that soaring serials budgets have made serious inroads into book purchases as well as serials collecting in all academic libraries.

Faculties are beginning to be concerned about the growing difficulty in obtaining the resources that provide for transfer of scholarship over time and space, and which represent the social record of learned activity. Most of this concern appears in the form of appeals to the administrators in higher education to devote more money to the problem. Since the money is not normally available, we need to look at the whole problem from a new perspective and actively seek new solutions.

II. The Current and Future Copyright Problem

It is difficult to overstate the importance of this problem even though its long-term effects are not generally understood. Learned literature is important to the humanities and to social science but even more to "big science."[1] It is not just that published papers establish priority of discovery, and it is not just that they are a key part of the measurement of success in learned activity—they are exceedingly important in the learning process of new researchers, and they are exceedingly important to established scientists who wish to understand and make use of work somewhat outside their immediate areas of interest. With the rapid growth of knowledge, many academics know a great deal about a very little, and they converse regularly with colleagues who also concentrate on the same fine focus of learning. The literature is the only clear path to broader understanding. Despite initial excitement about the dawn of the information age, all indications are that this path is not about to become a superhighway. It is about to become a toll road where each mile traveled will have a direct cost.

Under the White Paper that is likely to be the basis of the new copyright law, it seems clear that publishers will be able to charge for each electronically produced copy, or partial copy, of an academic's paper.[2] Thus, even if we convert the learned journal communication system to electronic form, our library budgets will be charged for each displayed copy of a learned paper. These funds will not go to the academic who carried out the research, nor will they not go to the institution of higher education which must pay for access to the materials needed by the academic and which paid the academic's salary and provided the laboratory or research materials that supported the work reported. Instead, the funds will go to the publisher that accepted the paper from the academic for no reward. This is, of course, what happens now, but pay-per-view will accelerate the current disastrous situation.

While some academics benefit economically from copyright, the benefit is material only in rare cases. That benefit comes from royalties for books or performance arts, and not from the journal literature. In

---

1. The term "big science" may have originated with Derek de sola Price in his 1963 book *Little Science, Big Science*. The reference is to a sociological phenomena beginning in the 1940s that is characterized by growth in government, number of Ph.D.s, very expensive equipment, and most importantly, cooperative enterprise among investigators. DEREK DE SOLA PRICE, LITTLE SCIENCE, BIG SCIENCE (New York, NY: Columbia Univ. Press 1963).

2. INTELLECTUAL PROPERTY AND THE NATIONAL INFORMATION INFRASTRUCTURE: THE REPORT OF THE WORKING GROUP ON INTELLECTUAL PROPERTY RIGHTS (1995). A portable document format (PDF) file of the report is available on the World Wide Web site of the U.S. Patent & Trademark Office at <http://www.uspto.gov>.

many disciplines, and in particularly the sciences, books are a secondary form of communication of research results, and it is the journal literature that provides a communication channel of record. It is in this area of the learned periodical literature that academic institutions provide services to commercial enterprises at no charge and, at the same time, expend huge and constantly growing sums to maintain their library collections. When journal publishers detail the increasing cost of publications, they start calculating costs upon receipt of the manuscript from the academic author. Content development is not even considered to be a cost of publishing in the learned literature.

If academics were musicians publishing their works or artists recording them, they would share in the payment for every performance of their work. Why is the academic denied the same reward? Why is the institution that supports the academic's work denied cost recovery? This system appears to be an apparent scheme to move taxpayer and student consumer dollars into the hands of private business while choking the life blood of learned activity, the communication system used to educate its next generation and provide the record and authority of its accomplishment.

Why is not the academic community up in arms over this result? Presumably because academics are insulated from the incredible costs academic libraries bear for collection of the learned literature. Scholarly authors also seem unaware of the current changes proposed for the sale of written communication. In any major institution this is a multi-million-dollar annual expenditure rising at far beyond the cost of inflation, and one which will explode if the proposals contained in the current White Paper become law. It is not an exaggeration to say that current big science as we know it in the United States is threatened by these developments.

Because it is the librarians who are on the front line in this battle and who are already suffering the wounds, it is an absolute necessity that librarians pick up what weapons are available and drive back the enemy. Faculty and academic administrators should be natural allies. They, too, are big losers under the current and future copyright laws. Unfortunately, they have not been shown the implications of the path we are following, since the academic library community has focused its energy on coping with providing an acceptable level of service rather than with forcing its masters and patrons to see the implications of the larger picture.

III. Who Pays the Costs of Production?

Academic faculty currently do most of the intellectual work, the content development, of scholarly journal production. In many cases they use their employer's human or software word processors to produce camera-ready copy. This is a huge expenditure of faculty and staff resources for what is viewed as a service to their disciplines. Their intellectual efforts most often are given free to a commercial enterprise. Clearly, the cost of publishing a learned paper begins as soon as the content development begins. The publisher, however, sees the cost of publishing as beginning only upon receipt of the manuscript. This is rather like an oil company saying the cost of a gallon of gasoline begins with the cost of the truck that hauls it to the service station and assuming that the refined fuel appears in the truck without effort or expenditure. The company that priced its product with that sort of cost analysis would not be long in business, unless it could get someone to contribute its exploration and refining costs for free. This, of course, is exactly what the publishers of the learned literature have managed to do.

If faculty were producing patents instead of scholarly articles, we would be talking about technology transfer activities and figuring out just how the institution that supported development could get its share of the rewards. Referees get nothing. Faculty editors get some travel money, and they sometimes receive some support for postage and telephone bills. Who pays the overhead? The institution, of course. Neither the researchers nor the institutions of higher education that bear the costs of the work of scholars receive the slightest economic reward from the publisher who demands the copyright as a condition of publication. Then who buys the publisher's product, the content of which they have just given away for free? The academic institution uses its library's periodical budget to buy back its gifts to others. Just what does copyright law do as it applies to the learned journal literature do for academic institutions and their faculty? Absolutely nothing. There is no economic reward for the content development of learned journal literature.

What is in fact obvious, but for some reason unrealized, is that institutions of higher education have in their power the means to fight this situation. There are at least four possible strategies all bound up in the current and future copyright situation. All require either modification of current copyright law or cooperative action by institutions of higher education to preserve their copyright prerogatives. All require convincing faculty and academic administrators of the danger in, and the remedies for, the current situation.

IV. Strategies for Change

The first of the strategies is to insist that any fee charged for the viewing of materials published by employees of academic institutions be split by the publisher with the institution and perhaps the author. There is precedent for this in the theater and music businesses, where artists receive residual payments each time their work is performed. If there is going to be an organization like the American Society of Composers, Authors, and Publishers (ASCAP) for producers of learned literature, it would best be organized by the academic community, and it should be organized quickly. It may even be that ASCAP could serve in the required capacity, but publishers clearly must be willing to share copyright with the producers of the material. Since they happily receive the material at no cost now, a means to bring pressure will be required.

Another possibility would be to argue that a provision like that for music performance be added to the law providing that any display or reproduction of a copyrighted document by a unit of a not-for-profit educational organization is a fair use when the display is produced for instructional purposes of students enrolled in a class.[3] This might solve the problem of copyright in distance education; but to encourage the development of science, a waiver for research purposes in such an institution would be required. This would certainly be less popular with the publishers.

A second solution would be to revise the law in a manner that required that authors and their institutions retain copyright after publication. For example, any publication of less than 100 pages, the production of which is supported in any way by an institution of higher education, would become the non-transferable property of its author and that institution jointly. The copyright held by them could be without possibility of assignment for its legal duration or for a specified period, such as 25 years, during the term of copyright. This solution would require a major lobbying effort on the part of the academic and library communities. Considering both the monetary costs

---

3.   Robert A. Wynbrandt, *Musical Performance in Libraries: Is a License from ASCAP Required?* 29 PUB. LIBR. 224, 224–25 (1990).

to libraries and the costs to scholarship because of the current trends, such an effort is certainly justified.

If authors and institutions shared the copyright they could control distribution for the benefit of scholarship. If academic institutions are going to have to pay by the use for the work of their own employees and those of the employees of sister institutions, they should at least share in the revenue produced and use it to cover the expenses of access. As long as authors are willing to sign over complete rights to their work to commercial publishers to see their work in print, however, this is not likely to occur.

We need to establish policies that will prevent authors from assigning their copyright to commercial publishers without returning a significant share in residual rights at a minimum. To apply pressure for either of these solutions, universities might, for an example, refuse to consider a publication for the purposes of promotion and tenure unless copyright in the work were equally shared by the author and the employer or if a proper financial agreement were not reached. Perhaps even better, academic institutions should, as a group, insist that the portion of the copyright due to them as the corporate sponsors of the work be assigned to no one without their permission under threat of litigation. This might require an alternate form of publication until the commercial publishers acquiesced. In fact, alternate forms of publication could be considered a third solution as well as a pressure tactic to gain a share in residual revenues. This might ultimately involve nothing less than the institutions of higher education taking control of learned publishing under current laws.[4]

In an important work on the value of scholarly articles, Bennett and Matheson make the point that "academics do not view the articles they write as valuable commodities."[5] Perhaps we in higher education handed over our birthright to commercial publishers because we did not want to have to mess with the gross commercialism of the distribution side of the publishing industry. One writer has said: "Both the trade author and the esoteric author had to be prepared to make a

---

4. Bert R. Boyce, *Meeting the Serials Cost Problem: A Supply-Side Proposal*, 24 AMER. LIBR. 272, 272–73 (1993).
5. Scott Bennett & Nina Matheson, *Scholarly Articles: Valuable Commodities for Universities*, CHRON. HIGHER EDUC. May 27, 1992, at 36.

Faustian bargain with the paper publisher (who was not, by the way, the devil either, but likewise a victim of the bargain.)"[6]

By "esoteric" Harnad means scholarly writing. Times have changed. We currently have the opportunity to move the world of scholarly publication in a different direction. If the commercial publishers will not accept learned literature without copyright protection, then we can do our own publishing. The electronic journal is already on the scene. This is a medium readily available to the academic community, but we are allowing the commercial publishers to take it over. We can change this "[i]f every esoteric author in the world this very day established a globally accessible local ftp archive for every piece of esoteric writing he did from this day forward, the long-heralded transition from paper publication to purely electronic publication (of esoteric research) would follow suit almost immediately."[7]

V. A Commercial Solution

We probably need a bit more structure than that, but a lack of structure does not make a change impossible. All that seems to be required are electronic inter-communication facilities like the Internet and a governance structure which would both retain traditional journal quality filters and induce scholars to utilize this system rather than the extant one. Such a structure might operate as a loosely affiliated consortium of not-for-profit corporations controlled by academic institutions in direct competition with commercial publishers. There would certainly be some management overhead involved. Interestingly, however, the major costs—production and quality control—are already sunk costs in the academic budget.

If one speaks to those who are considering the commercial potential of the Internet, what one hears is that the middleman is likely to be eliminated. Since price information for items on the Net will be available for comparison shopping, why not order a shirt electronically directly from the web page of the south China prisoner factory that

---

6.   Stevan Harnad, *Electronic Scholarly Publication: Quo Vadis?* 2 MANAGING INFO. 31, 31 (1995).

7.   Stevan Harnad, *Implementing Peer Review on the Net: Scientific Quality Control in Scholarly Electronic Journals, in* ELECTRONIC PUBLISHING CONFRONTS ACADEMIA? (Robin P. Peek & Gregory B. Newberry eds., 1995).

made it, rather than pay Sears or Walmart to import the item and put it on their web page catalog with the attendant mark up in price? This is not to say that authors in the scholarly journal literature are in the same situation as slave labor, but considering that the organization that sells their product pays them nothing for their production, and then charges them for its use, the analogy is not totally inappropriate. Academic institutions do not need the middleman publisher either. The only services that the publisher provides that are of value in the journal communication system are either provided to the publishers by academics and their institutions at rates far below cost, or they involve physical production and distribution activities which can be carried out by academic institutions electronically. This is even more true since the producer and the consumer are the same parties, and the middleman provides no useful function in the process.

If universities are to become the publishers of scientific literature in electronic format, tenure and promotion policies may have to be changed to recognize this form of scholarly publishing. There certainly will be resistance, but this is an area in which the academic community has total control. Concerted action by institutions of higher learning would make this change more palatable, but such changes are likely to come in any event.

A recent survey found that university administrators "do not consider the academic community well equipped to take on an enterprise of this kind and would not give it high priority in allocation of university resources."[8] What they fail to understand is that they are already providing the majority of the resources. It is the *benefits* that they are passing on to others. Academic administrators need to be educated in this area if a solution to lower costs and to providing more free dissemination of knowledge is to come about. University administrators have a fiduciary responsibility to minimize the costs of their operation and to maximize the cash flow from university assets. A public university administrator who gives away assets to private industry and fails to use legal remedies to protect the university's budget from private exploitation can only be described a derelict in the performance of duty. But this is exactly what is being done. Further,

---

8.   F. W. Lancaster, *Attitudes in Academia Toward Feasibility & Desirability of Networked Scholarly Publishing*, 43 LIBR. TRENDS 741, 747 (1995).

many state institutions have restrictions that prevent giving away state property. This also is exactly what is being done.

VI. The Death of Copyright: A Final Solution

A final approach is to attack the copyright law directly as it applies to the learned literature on the grounds of its unconstitutional nature.[9] Such an effort could be simply a pressure tactic to achieve one of the other solutions, but could, in fact, be the final solution if copyright for learned literature could be eliminated. In her otherwise excellent review of the interests of readers and authors in scholarly publishing, Carol Tenopir makes the following unfortunate statement. "Copyright laws were made to protect authors' and publishers' investment of time, creativity, and capital."[10] The Constitution of the United States says that "The Congress shall have Power . . . to promote the Progress of Science and useful Arts, by securing for limited Times to Authors and Inventors the exclusive Right to their respective Writings and Discoveries."[11] Note that publishers are not mentioned as the beneficiaries of this largess. From this argument's point of view, what is important is the statement of purpose of copyright, "to promote the progress of Science and useful Arts." In 1991 the U.S. Supreme Court in *Feist Publications, Inc. v. Rural Telephone Service Co.*[12] affirmed the primacy of the advancement of science when it stated "[t]he primary objective of copyright is not to reward the labor of authors but to promote the Progress of Science and useful Arts."[13] In 1994 the Court again recognized the role of the published literature in the advancement of learning when *Campbell v. Acuff-Rose Music, Inc.*[14] mentioned the "inherent tension in the need simultaneously to protect copyrighted material and to allow others to build upon it."[15]

Economists believe that government intervention in property rights in a theoretically free market may be efficient if all costs, including

---

9. Bert R. Boyce, *Copyright Could Be Wrong*, AMER. LIBR., Feb. 1996, at 27, 27–28.

10. Carol Tenopir, *Authors & Readers: The Success or Failure of Electronic Publishing*, 43 LIBR. TRENDS 571, 583 (1995)

11. U.S. CONST. art. I, § 8, cl. 1, 8.

12. 499 U.S. 340 (1991).

13. *Id.* at 349.

14. 114 S. Ct. 1164 (1994).

15. *Id.* at 1169.

transaction costs, are balanced against benefits. The societial benefit of the learned literature is the production of more learned literature and the new knowledge that it represents. The maximization of copies and their wide unfettered distribution is most likely to stimulate this production. The costs of transactions now associated with the copyright intervention clearly outweigh the benefit to the authors of maintaining copying rights. In fact, as pointed out below, these benefits no longer exist. Roger McCain provides an excellent discussion of the copy situation which includes the statement, "Thus, just as the emergence of printing favored a legal system that protected the property rights of producers of information, so the emergence of photocopy technology seems to favor a property rights system that secures the proprietor of a copying machine in his property right to copy whatever he pleases."[16]

The scholarly journal often is described as a natural monopoly, a situation where "average cost falls over the entire range of demand; it is a common occurrence where there are large up-front costs, low per unit costs, and limited substitutability."[17] This means that commercial enterprises must charge beyond marginal cost to avoid loss with a product like a scholarly journal. However, the up-front costs are very questionable today. In fact, these "first copy costs" are a fiction in the modern environment. The Internet has changed the potential cost structure of distribution. The layout, subscription, and distribution costs will now be minimized by electronic distribution, and the other claimed up-front costs, editing and selection, have never been a fact.

Academics write, edit, and referee learned periodicals because both they and their employers see these activities as just what they are, as beneficial to mankind, as important to "the progress of science and useful arts," i.e., learning, in that they promote the communication without which modern science could not function. These activities also are considered important to their careers since the social system of academia bases its rewards to a large extent on success in these efforts. The academic's reward for publication comes not from copyright, but rather from the social and employment situation in which the academic functions. From the academic's point of view, copyright appears

---

16. Roger A. McCain, *Information as Property & as a Public Good: Perspectives from the Economic Theory of Property Rights*, 58 LIBR. Q. 265, 265–82 (1988).

17. David W. Lewis, *Economics of the Scholarly Journal*, 50 C. & RES. LIBR. 674, 674–88 (1989).

largely irrelevant as a means "to promote the progress of science and useful arts." If we can show, as I believe we can, that the current law impedes the progress of science as it applies to the learned journal literature, then on its face, copyright law contradicts the clearly expressed purposes of the authors of the basic law of the United States.

The implication is that institutions of higher learning, as the clearly injured parties, should institute court action to overturn the law, or at very least begin to strongly argue for its modification. A law that meets constitutional requirements should be able to demonstrate that the granting of the exclusive right in some way benefits the authors, and that this grant benefits, and does not in some way impede, the progress of science. All available evidence suggests that the current law meets none of these tests for scholarly journal articles. A key question is whether the current system of learned journal publication, governed as it is by current copyright law, is dedicated to the promotion of learning. It seems quite clear that it is not.

In terms of promoting science, copyright is an impediment, and society would be far better off if copyright did not apply to the learned journal communication system. This would allow free distribution of research results without charges, the benefits from which do not now make their way to the authors and inventors as the Constitution implies they should. From the point of view of promoting learning, the free and easy dissemination of the journal literature is the major concern. A current, clearly written review of what we have learned from past research about the crucial role of the scientific journal communication system demonstrates that formal communication is what makes science work. Modern learning is a social enterprise in which the free exchange of ideas and techniques allows researchers to confirm, modify, and build upon each other's ideas to the overall benefit of learned activity.[18] Anything that restricts that activity works actively to undermine the progress of science and the useful arts.

Current copyright law, as it applies to the learned periodical literature, sorely restricts that activity.

✦ Under current law, publishers claim that distributing copies of academics' papers to their departmental colleagues can be restricted

---

18.   A. C. Schaffner, *The Future of Scientific Journals: Lessons from the Past*, 13 INFO. TECH. & LIBR. 239, 239–42 (1994).

by the publisher. Does this promote the progress of science and the useful arts?

✦ Under current law, publishers claim that academics could be prevented from the public display of figures and graphs of their own papers. Does this promote the progress of science and the useful arts?

✦ Under current law, publishers claim that they could prevent academics from speaking about the results of their research and distributing copies of these academic papers at conferences. Does this promote the progress of science and the useful arts?

✦ Under the proposed changes in the law, each display of a copy of a paper on an electronic medium could result in a charge to the user. Does this promote the progress of science and the useful arts?

✦ Under the current law, the prices of journals will continue to increase because of the inelasticity of demand, forcing academic libraries to collect less and less. Does this promote the progress of science and the useful arts?

If our national goal is to promote science and the useful arts (as the primary law of the land clearly states), then all learned journal literature should be freely available in electronic or printed form to whomsoever wishes to make use of it.

Anything that leads to unimpeded distribution of research results is an unqualified social good in that it leads to the progress of science in the sense of the Founding Fathers and, at least for the learned journal communication system, the First Amendment of the Constitution which favors free distribution should take precedence over Article I, section 8. Current copyright law actively impedes the progress of science and useful arts and therefore subverts the explicitly stated intent of those who drafted of the primary law of the land. The direction of proposed changes certainly will make matters worse. Since it is the institutions of higher education that suffer the main economic loss from this law that appears to run afoul of the Constitution, it is these institutions that should be leading the fight against it. To a large measure, it is academic researchers who are responsible for the progress of science and useful arts. This is particularly true in the learned journal communication system where they carry out the research, write the papers without compensation, edit the journals for virtually no compensation, referee the papers for no compensation, and then are required to use their employers' resources to buy back the product of their own and others' labors at skyrocketing costs so that it can be used by their students and their colleagues. Because the commercial publishers require full transfer of copyright without compensation for the publication of research results, not a penny generated returns to the author or the institution. Only the costs of use are left to the academic institution, and these costs actively interfere with the free flow of information and thus the progress of science and useful arts.

But, of course, it is not just the monetary costs of maintaining collections and routing material to those who need it that restricts progress. Collections of papers cannot be made available legally to students in classes without compensation.[19] Reprints may be circulated to colleagues if they have been purchased, but not if they are copied by the author. Readings for distance-education sites cannot be made available to students electronically even though their assignments and class submissions use that medium. Material may be made available if permission is sought and fees paid through the Copyright Clearinghouse Center, but not without an expenditure of time and money, none of which goes to the producers of the information shared.

The free flow of ideas is necessary for success in modern scholarship. Today's scientist does not work in the tower of a remote castle barring the door against unhappy peasants. Modern scholarship is a cooperative activity where each person's work builds upon that of others. Electronic and written communication are vital to its success. "For scientific work to be effectual, it must be communicated in such a way that it can be assimilated by other scientists and form the basis of their further work. In almost every scientific discipline, the acceptable medium for accomplishing this and establishing priority is the scientific journal article."[20] If scientists cannot share their information, then their work will stop. When one is no longer able to share information freely with a colleague because that information has been published and cannot be reproduced or distributed without fees paid

---

19.   There are guidelines on multiple copying for classroom use, but these require spontaneity as one hurdle and discourage lesson planning. *See* H.R. REP. NO. 94–1476, 94th Cong., 2d Sess. 68 (1976), *reprinted in* 17 OMNIBUS COPYRIGHT REVISION LEGISLATIVE HISTORY 68–71 (1977)

20.   W. D. Garvey & S. D. Gottfredson, *Changing the System: Innovations in the Interactive Social System of Scientific Communication, in* COMMUNICATION: THE ESSENCE OF SCIENCE 300, 302 (1979).

to an entity that has contributed almost nothing to its production, the progress of science and useful arts has not been promoted, it has been actively been impeded.

VII. Conclusion

The whole learned community would be far better off if copyright law did not apply to learned literature. Since the current law impedes the purpose of the Founding Fathers as explicitly stated in the Constitution, it cannot be a constitutional law. The economics of the publishing industry are changing, and pay-by-use electronic access is the very close next step. If those who produce the learned literature, and those who support that production receive no compensation for their labor and investment but are required by inelastic demand to repurchase their own products at ever increasing prices, then it is no exaggeration to predict that academic activity and big science as it exists in the United States today will fall into rapid decline.

This is not in the interest of a country that wishes to maintain itself as a world power. It is not in the interest of the academic community. It is not in the interest of the taxpayers who support the academic enterprise in this country in many ways and who will need to cover these access costs. It is not in the interest of the families that support students who assist in paying for that enterprise. It is not in the interest of those students themselves who are deprived not only of their money but also of unlimited access to the world's knowledge, which they surely deserve. The only beneficiaries of the current law and the social situation that it has produced are a small number of commercial enterprises. They are well aware of the situation and are lobbying hard to preserve their self-interest at the cost of the public good. Unfortunately, they also have the money and the power to win this battle.

The United States cannot afford to maintain the current system. The copyright laws must change their application to the scholarly literature, and they have to change quickly before irreparable harm is done.

Chapter Twenty

The Intellectual Property Dilemma: Proposal for the Creation of an International Scholars Academic Network[*]

by
Jerry D. Campbell

University Librarian and Dean of the University Libraries
The University of Southern California

I. A Difference in Purpose

It may seem obvious to scholars that the fundamental purpose of scholarly publishing is to make ideas known. By making ideas known, scholars share what they have learned, stimulate further inquiry, and

---

[*] © 1997 Jerry D. Campbell. This proposal was first shared in an earlier version in September 1995 for a program session at the CAUSE/CNI regional conference in Greensboro, NC. It was revised in October 1995 for an EDUCOM preconference workshop in Portland, OR. It was revised again to the present form and utilized in February 1996 as a discussion item by the Board of Directors of the Association of Research Libraries.

ultimately promote even more discovery. So committed are scholars to the effort to make ideas known that the great majority of them routinely and freely assign copyright of their writings to publishers. Scholars expect publishers, in turn, to carry out the timely and widespread distribution of their writings. Thus, in the view of scholars, publishing is a servant of scholarship that exists to disseminate knowledge.

This purpose is not so obvious, however, to publishers, or more particularly to commercial publishers. They have naturally developed a different notion of the purpose of scholarly publishing. For them, copyrighted writings have become "intellectual property." This intellectual property, in turn, has acquired value as a commercial commodity. Thus, in the view of commercial publishers, the purpose of scholarly publishing is to generate profitable earnings.

In the best of circumstances, these differing senses of purpose need not create conflict. Indeed, the U.S. government established copyright in the late 18th century to provide a financial incentive for publishers to spread the work of American scholars. As a result, working hand in hand the scholarly and the publishing worlds have, during the past two centuries, fostered an explosion in the growth of knowledge that neither could have achieved without the other. The growth of worldwide literacy and learning has depended in equal portions upon the creation of knowledge by scholars and its distribution by publishers. For decades, the scholarly and the publishing worlds worked in a happy partnership.

A. The Impact of the Information Economy

Over those decades, however, many changes took place. Among the most notable was the increasing role of published work in the credentialing of scholars. As the number of scholars grew, so also did the competition among them. The primary demonstration of a scholar's prowess came to be the publication of high-quality original research. This imperative to publish served to quicken the pace at which scholars worked, to foster tremendous growth in the amount of original research conducted, and to increase the demand for publication.

At the same time, commercial publishing began to change from individually owned operations to multinational corporations. And where the founding proprietors understood and shared the scholars' sense of the purpose of publishing and brought that shared sense to bear on publishing practices and pricing, the great publishing corporations grew distant from the scholarly enterprise, answering rather to the economic interests of holding companies and stock-holders. The great increase in the number of scholars and in the demand for publishing propelled scholarly publishing into a growth industry. As a result, the selling of published knowledge and data became a multi-billion-dollar business, and the great corporate publishers came to view publications strictly as commodities.

These changes in the practices of scholars and publishers were aspects of what has come to be called the information age. Though the information age encompasses many elements of the culture that arose in the first few decades after the introduction of the computer, perhaps its quintessential marks have been the dizzying speed with which knowledge has grown and the value that has been attached to it. The old saying that knowledge is power gave way to the reality that knowledge is money. Particularly in areas of science, technology, and medicine, breakthrough ideas came to be worth millions of dollars as they moved from the university to the commercial marketplace. With the growing recognition of the value of information, the cost of commercial publications escalated in price at a rate that vastly exceeded that of most other U.S. goods.[1] The ironic result was that just as scholars began to depend upon more rapid and precise access to published knowledge to maintain their own research competitiveness, the affordability and, therefore, the availability of published knowledge declined.

B. A Breach in the Historic Partnership

As the scholarly and publishing worlds changed, the differences in their respective views of the purpose of scholarly publishing magnified, and the long-standing harmony between them diminished. Not surprisingly, their differences played out in the legal arena, more specifically in the context of copyright law. The first demonstration of the deepening rift in viewpoints appeared when commercial interests, prompted by the introduction of photocopy technology, called for the strengthening of copyright restrictions in the mid-1970s. Scholars, who had always shared books and journals widely among themselves and their students, found photocopiers to be an extraordinary

---

1. According to the Association of Research Libraries Statistics, the rise in the cost of journals was exceeded only by the rise in medical costs.

enhancement to such sharing. Publishers, who focused on books and journals as assets, regarded such copying and distribution as direct threats to sales. As it sought to recognize the validity of both viewpoints and resolve the matter in the 1976 revision of the Copyright Act,[3] Congress simultaneously tightened restrictions while spelling out specific privileges (referred to as "fair use") for students, teachers, researchers, and libraries.

This resolution was not what commercial publishers had hoped, but it brought an uneasy and temporary truce to the debate over the differing senses of purpose. The maturing of computer technology, however, reawakened the debate with a vengeance. Computers made it possible for scholars to make perfect electronic copies of documents and to distribute them widely and immediately. And, unlike photocopies that lost resolution as copies were made of copies, each successive electronic copy was as perfect as the original. So, where many publishers considered photocopiers to be a threat to the sale of academic publications, they saw computers as a potential commercial death knell.

With its eye on the need for a coherent and well-designed national information infrastructure (NII), the Clinton administration launched a reexamination of the copyright law for NII and assigned to a task force chaired by the secretary of commerce the responsibility to craft a revision especially designed for the networked environment. An effort was undertaken by commercial interests to argue for revised legislation that would treat all electronic publications, including scholarly publications, solely as commercial property by curtailing the fair use provisions. At the same time, the education community argued that fair use practices remain unaltered.

After months of discussion and debate, the view of the primacy of the commercial value of intellectual property held sway within Working Group on Intellectual Property in its White Paper.[4] Thus, the revisions proposed emphasized the commercial rights and values associated with published knowledge and de-emphasized the special status of scholarly knowledge and its use by scholars, students, and libraries.

---

3.   17 U.S.C. §§ 101–1101 (1994).

4.   INTELLECTUAL PROPERTY AND THE NATIONAL INFORMATION INFRASTRUCTURE: THE REPORT OF THE WORKING GROUP ON INTELLECTUAL PROPERTY RIGHTS (1995).

The revisions proposed have caused great concern within the scholarly community and are now pending before both houses of Congress.[4]

It must be understood that while the views of educators and commercial publishers now seem irreconcilable, both are nonetheless valid. Even though copyright was established within U.S. law specifically for the purpose of serving scholarship, scholarship currently accounts for only a small portion of intellectual property generated within the United States. Intellectual property now includes a vast amount of information such as that relating to visual and graphic arts which may be directed to diverse ends, for example, news and entertainment. In this environment, it is unreasonable to establish the basic copyright law on the special purpose for which scholarly knowledge is created. The negative financial implications for other categories of intellectual property, especially works for entertainment, are too great. At the same time, there may be dire consequences for the competitiveness and economy of the United States if published scholarly knowledge is allowed to fall indiscriminately into the category of a commercial commodity.

II. The Intellectual Property Dilemma

The likelihood that fair use will be diminished or eliminated entirely for electronic information poses a serious dilemma for scholars and the education world concerning how best to guarantee the necessary dissemination and use of scholarly knowledge in the digital environment. The fair use doctrine has long protected most scholarly uses of copyrighted works. Fair use is a privilege or a right of someone other than the copyright holder to reproduce and use a copyrighted work in ways that ordinarily would constitute infringement of the copyright except for the existence of certain factors. Fair use, now embodied in the statute, typically favors uses for scholarship, teaching, criticism, news reporting, and the like. [5] If a use is a fair use, the scholar need not seek permission for that use nor pay for the privilege. Under fair use, the custom of scholars has been to use a published document liberally

---

4.   *See* The NII Protection Act of 1995, H.R. 2441 and S. 1284, 104th Cong., 1st Sess. (1995).

5.   17 U.S.C. § 107 (1994). The four fair use factors a court will consider in deciding whether a use is a fair use include: (1) purpose and character of the use; (2) nature of the copyrighted work; (3) amount and substantiality used; and (4) market effect.

within a school once the document has been acquired by the college or university through purchase or interlibrary loan. Over time, important scholarly documents may be used hundreds or thousands of times by a multitude of students and teachers. Consequently, already financially stressed educational institutions are disturbed by the prospect of a pay-per-use (or similarly costly) requirement for the use of scholarly knowledge in electronic form. If the commercial value of scholarly knowledge as a commodity takes precedence, the technology that holds the capacity for making it instantly and ubiquitously available actually may restrict access by inserting requirements for permissions and payments. As a result, materials available for teaching and learning would be artificially limited, the pace of research would slow, and the quality of education in general increasingly would be governed by a school's or an individual scholar's ability to pay. For the world of education, therefore, the loss of fair use promises to impede the effectiveness of the academic process dramatically.

Yet, the dilemma over how legally to treat scholarly knowledge is not simply a scholar's dilemma. In the fast-moving world of knowledge, it is not just the scholars whose work is slowed if a complex system of restrictions, permissions, and payments is imposed upon the scholarly process; it is the whole capacity for the discovery of knowledge and for its movement into marketable products that is also decreased. Indeed, since the United States is now dependent upon its intellectual creativity to maintain international competitiveness, slowing the work of research and discovery strikes at the heart of its capacity to be the world's leader in developing new scientific, technical, and medical (STM) knowledge.

Additionally, since much of the world's STM knowledge is published outside of this country, there is an unexamined question about the wisdom of assigning sole ownership and control of knowledge so crucial to U.S. competitiveness to foreign corporations. Indeed, in recent years the practice of differential pricing often has made it necessary for domestic purchasers to pay comparatively more for foreign publications than purchasers in other countries even when much of the content originated in the United States. The implications of this circumstance for national competitiveness and national security as publishing becomes more electronic have not been considered thoroughly.

Thus, while limiting or eliminating fair use in the digital environment protects the commercial interests of publishers, it clearly places scholarship at a disadvantage and, consequently, may also damage the national interest. Indeed, the financial value of scholarly knowledge made available quickly and inexpensively in the United States as the fuel for more research and discovery vastly outweighs its simple value as an asset to commercial publishers. The national interest would best be served by continuing the fair use provisions for the education world into the digital environment.

A. Solving the Dilemma

Perhaps the best way to solve this dilemma is for schools and scholars to take a leadership role in managing their own intellectual property. This would require that universities adopt copyright policies similar to the patent policies already in place in many institutions. Under such policies, universities and their faculties would retain copyright ownership of the knowledge they create, negotiate limited publication rights with commercial publishers, and become more actively involved in publishing themselves. In serving as publishers, universities would have to assume responsibility for the peer review process, for editing, and for managing the intellectual property that came under their purview. Such academic publishing could best succeed if universities also established a publishing consortium based upon policies, principles, and costs that recognize the primacy of the scholar's sense of purpose in the creation of new knowledge. Such a consortium would retain ownership and control of new scholarly knowledge within the academy and would guarantee ease of access and flexible use by scholars and researchers.

This solution would also provide for the long-term preservation of electronic knowledge within the academy, something that is not guaranteed when unrestricted rights reside with the less-stable commercial world. Additionally, this solution would create an environment in which scholarship would prosper and in which the creativity of the U.S. scholarly community would flourish.

The name suggested for the consortium is the International Scholars Academic Network, or IScAN for short. The stated objectives for the consortium would include the following:

1. To provide a new electronic publishing venue controlled by the academy.
2. To facilitate the rapid dissemination of scholarly knowledge.

3. To establish an environment that encourages the flexible, fair use of published knowledge by researchers, teachers, students, and libraries.
4. To make a positive impact on the cost of disseminating scholarly knowledge.
5. To encourage the creative and effective use of technology in scholarly publishing.
6. To reestablish the feasibility of publishing important but commercially unattractive scholarly items.

To accomplish these ends, the proposed consortium would seek the most cost-effective approaches to achieving its ends. It would, for instance, contract for services wherever possible and premise its own support on cost recovery. What follows is the outline of such a consortium.

B. Proposal for the Creation of an International Scholars' Academic Network (IScAN)

1. Consortium for the Exchange and Dissemination of Scholarly Knowledge
1.1 IScAN will be a nonprofit consortium whose purpose is to promote the exchange and dissemination of scholarly knowledge by means of networking technologies.
1.2 IScAN will be operated on a cost-recovery, non-profit basis.

2. Governance
2.1 IScAN will have a representative governing commission established by the full members of the consortium. The governing commission will establish policy, adopt standards, set fees, authorize contributors, and otherwise administer IScAN.

3. Memberships, Licenses, and Subscriptions
3.1 Membership in IScAN is available to scholarly associations, learned societies, educational institutions, and nonprofit research and cultural institutions. Affiliate membership shall be available to other nonprofit private, public, and governmental agencies.
3.2 Access to the IScAN will be made available for a fee to commercial agencies through a licensing arrangement.
3.3 Independent researchers may apply for personal subscriptions to IScAN.

4. Publications and Publishing Policy

4.1 IScAN will maintain the highest-quality standards for electronic scholarly publications.

4.2 IScAN will be recognized by member colleges and universities as the preferred source for publications that carry status for tenure and promotion.

4.3 Scholarly materials will be contributed to IScAN only by duly authorized members of the consortium. To receive authorization, members must submit their procedures for jurying and editing to the governing commission for review and must meet established standards for quality.

4.4 The Commission will adopt and maintain formatting standards for electronic publishing. Contributing members must comply with all such standards.

4.5 Affiliate members have access to IScAN publications but may not contribute publications directly.

4.6 The intellectual property rights for materials first published by IScAN will be owned and managed by the authors or the members who contributed them. Secondary publication rights may be contracted to commercial publishing agencies, but they must be restricted so as not to affect ongoing access to or use of materials on IScAN.

4.7 IScAN will provide two categories of scholarly publications:

Category One will consist of academic publications added to the network on a cost-recovery basis. All Category One items will be available to subscribers as a benefit of a single IScAN subscription.

Category Two will consist of academic publications offered through the network as individual items. Such items will be optional and will be made available for fees beyond and in addition to the membership fees. Costs for Category Two items will be determined by the contributing members.

4.8 IScAN may provide access to commercially published electronic information under consortial licensing arrangements. Such resources will be optional and will be made available for negotiated fees beyond and in addition to the membership fees

5. Nonprofit Cost Recovery

5.1 Networking costs to be recovered will include the costs of dedicated hardware, software, and staff. It will also include the costs associated with the long-term storage of archived publications.

5.2 Publishing costs to be recovered for Category One items will include all costs incurred in publishing. Such costs will encompass the costs associated with jurying and editing, and the costs of administering publication programs.

5.3 The Commission will adopt guidelines outlining the costs to be recovered and establish standard rates for such costs.

5.4 The operating costs of the Commission and research and development for IScAN will be recovered.

5.5 IScAN will not recover costs associated with the research and authoring of works.

6. Membership Fees and Licensing Costs

6.1 Fees for members and affiliate members will be based on the total costs of operating the network and publishing Category One items and will be set at levels necessary to recover all such costs.

6.2 Membership and affiliate fees will be graduated based on the nature and size of the member agency. Research universities, for instance, will pay a larger membership fee than small public schools.

6.3 License fees will also be graduated based on the nature and size of the agency being licensed. Major commercial corporations, for instance, will pay a higher fee than small family-owned businesses.

6.4 Membership and affiliate membership will entitle agencies of all sizes to unlimited access to IScAN publications. This access will include the right to redistribute publications electronically to the member's primary constituency.

6.5 Access and redistribution rights provided to licensed agencies will be specifically provided in the licenses.

7. Academic Customs and the Progress of Scholarship

7.1 Items published in IScAN may be used by scholars and researchers in accordance with existing academic customs.

7.2   Authors who are from member institutions or who are individual subscribers may cite from texts or excerpt from multimedia objects with attribution in new publications appearing in IScAN without permission or payment in the same fashion as properly attributed citations appear in paper publications.

7.3   Authors may cite from texts or excerpt from multimedia objects with attribution in noncommercial presentations, lectures, and workshops without permission or payment.

7.4   Teachers from member institutions may utilize citations from texts or excerpts from multimedia objects with attribution in classroom and distance-learning presentations without permission or payment.

7.5   Individuals who are from member institutions or who are individual subscribers may make paper copies of IScAN publications for personal use as necessary.

7.6   Electronic coursepacks may be compiled from publications in IScAN and distributed to classes at no cost or on a cost-recovery basis by members without additional permission or payment.

7.7   Paper copies of individual IScAN publications or coursepacks of multiple IScAN publications may be compiled and sold by members to their constituencies on a cost-recovery basis without additional permission or payment.

8. Technology

8.1   The technology infrastructure of IScAN will be dynamic and constantly evolving.

8.2   The technology infrastructure of IScAN will be based in open systems architectures and standards.

8.3   IScAN will be a leader in providing connectivity to other not-for-profit and commercial networks.

8.4   IScAN will maintain the infrastructure necessary to carry out the secure exchange of intellectual property by electronic means. This will include authorization/authentication, secure financial transactions and accounting, and maintaining the integrity of intellectual property.

Appendix A
Selected Statutes

Section 102. Subject Matter of Copyright: In General

(a) Copyright protection subsists, in accordance with this title, in original works of authorship fixed in any tangible medium of expression, now known or later developed, from which they can be perceived, reproduced, or otherwise communicated, either directly or with the aid of a machine or device. Works of authorship include the following categories:

(1) literary works;
(2) musical works, including any accompanying words;
(3) dramatic works, including any accompanying music;
(4) pantomimes and choreographic works;
(5) pictorial, graphic, and sculptural works;
(6) motion pictures and other audiovisual works;

(7) sound recordings; and

(8) architectural works.[1]

(b) In no case does copyright protection for an original work of authorship extend to any idea, procedure, process, system, method of operation, concept, principle, or discovery, regardless of the form in which it is described, explained, illustrated, or embodied in such work.

Section 103. Subject Matter of Copyright: Compilations and Derivative Works

(a) The subject matter of copyright as specified by section 102 includes compilations and derivative works, but protection for a work employing preexisting material in which copyright subsists does not extend to any part of the work in which such material has been used unlawfully.

(b) The copyright in a compilation or derivative work extends only to the material contributed by the author of such work, as distinguished from the preexisting material employed in the work, and does not imply any exclusive right in the preexisting material. The copyright in such work is independent of, and does not affect or enlarge the scope, duration, ownership, or subsistence of, any copyright protection in the preexisting material.

---

1. Section 102(a) was amended by the Architectural Works Copyright Protection Act, Pub. L. No. 101-650, 104 Stat. 5089, 5133, which added at the end thereof paragraph (8).

Section 105. Subject Matter of Copyright: United State Government Works[2]

Copyright protection under this title is not available for any work of the United States Government, but the United States Government is not precluded from receiving and holding copyrights transferred to it by assignment, bequest, or otherwise.

Section 106. Exclusive Rights in Copyrighted Works

Subject to sections 107 through 120, the owner of copyright under this title has the exclusive rights to do and to authorize any of the following:

(1) to reproduce the copyrighted work in copies or phonorecords;

(2) to prepare derivative works based upon the copyrighted work;

(3) to distribute copies or phonorecords of the copyrighted work to the public by sale or other transfer of ownership, or by rental, lease, or lending;

(4) in the case of literary, musical, dramatic, and choreographic works, pantomimes, and motion pictures and other audio-visual works, to perform the copyrighted work publicly; and

(5) in the case of literary, musical, dramatic, and choreographic works, pantomimes, and pictorial, graphic, or sculptural works, including the individual images of a motion picture or other audiovisual work, to display the copyrighted work publicly.

---

2. An exception is provided by the Act of July 11, 1968, Pub. L. No. 90-396, 82 Stat. 339, which the Act states may be cited as the "Standard Reference Data Act." A provision of this enactment amended title 15 of the United States Code, entitled "Commerce and Trade," by authorizing the Secretary of Commerce, at 15 U.S.C. § 290e, to secure copyright and renewal thereof on behalf of the United States as author or proprietor "in all or any part of any standard reference data which he prepares or makes available under this chapter," and to "authorize the reproduction and publication thereof by others." *See also* section 105(f) of the Transitional and Supplementary Provisions, a part of the Act of October 19, 1976, Pub. L. No. 94-553, 90 Stat. 2541.

Section 106A. Rights of Certain Authors to Attribution and Integrity[3]

(a) RIGHTS OF ATTRIBUTION AND INTEGRITY. Subject to section 107 and independent of the exclusive rights provided in section 106, the author of a work of visual art—

(1) shall have the right—
    (A) to claim authorship of that work, and
    (B) to prevent the use of his or her name as the author of any work of visual art which he or she did not create;

(2) shall have the right to prevent the use of his or her name as the author of the work of visual art in the event of a distortion, mutilation, or other modification of the work which would be prejudicial to his or her honor or reputation; and

(3) subject to the limitations set forth in section 113(d), shall have the right—
    (A) to prevent any intentional distortion, mutilation, or other modification of that work which would be prejudicial to his or her honor or reputation, and any intentional distortion, mutilation, or modification of that work is a violation of that right, and
    (B) to prevent any destruction of a work of recognized stature, and any intentional or grossly negligent destruction of that work is a violation of that right.

(b) SCOPE AND EXERCISE OF RIGHTS. Only the author of a work of visual art has the rights conferred by subsection (a) in that work, whether or not the author is the copyright owner. The authors of a joint work of visual art are co-owners of the rights conferred by subsection (a) in that work.

---

3.   A new section 106A was added by the Visual Artists Rights Act of 1990, Pub. L. No. 101-650, 104 Stat. 5128. The act states that, generally, it is to take effect six months after the date of its enactment, that is, six months after December 1, 1990, and that the rights created by section 106A shall apply to—(l) works created before such effective date but title to which has not, as of such effective date, been transferred from the author; and (2) works created on or after such effective date, but shall not apply to any destruction, distortion, mutilation, or other modification (as described in section 106A(a)(3)) of any work which occurred before such effective date.

(c) EXCEPTIONS.
    (1) The modification of a work of visual art which is a result of the passage of time or the inherent nature of the materials is not a distortion, mutilation, or other modification described in subsection (a)(3)(A).
    (2) The modification of a work of visual art which is a result of conservation, or of the public presentation, including lighting and pigment, of the work is not a destruction, distortion, mutilation, or other modification described in subsection (a)(3) unless the modification is caused by gross negligence.
    (3) The rights described in paragraphs (1) and (2) of subsection (a) shall not apply to any reproduction, depiction, portrayal, or other use of a work in, upon, or in any connection with any item described in subparagraph (A) or (B) of the definition of "work of visual art" in section 101, and any such reproduction, depiction, portrayal, or other use of a work is not a destruction, distortion, mutilation, or other modification described in paragraph (3) of subsection (a).

(d) DURATION OF RIGHTS.
    (1) With respect to works of visual art created on or after the effective date set forth in section 610(a) of the Visual Artists Rights Act of 1990, the rights conferred by subsection (a) shall endure for a term consisting of the life of the author.
    (2) With respect to works of visual art created before the effective date set forth in section 610(a) of the Visual Artists Rights Act of 1990, but title to which has not, as of such effective date, been transferred from the author, the rights conferred by subsection (a) shall be coextensive with, and shall expire at the same time as, the rights conferred by section 106.
    (3) In the case of a joint work prepared by two or more authors, the rights conferred by subsection (a) shall endure for a term consisting of the life of the last surviving author.
    (4) All terms of the rights conferred by subsection (a) run to the end of the calendar year in which they would otherwise expire.

(e) TRANSFER AND WAIVER.
    (1) The rights conferred by subsection (a) may not be transferred but those rights may be waived if the author expressly agrees to such waiver in a written instrument signed by the author.

Such instrument shall specifically identify the work, and uses of that work, to which the waiver applies, and the waiver shall apply only to the work and uses so identified. In the case of a joint work prepared by two or more authors, a waiver of rights under this paragraph made by one such author waives such rights for all such authors.

(2) Ownership of the rights conferred by subsection (a) with respect to a work of visual art is distinct from ownership of any copy of that work, or of a copyright or any exclusive right under a copyright in that work. Transfer of ownership of any copy of a work of visual art, or of a copyright or any exclusive right under a copyright, shall not constitute a waiver of the rights conferred by subsection (a). Except as may otherwise be agreed by the author in a written instrument signed by the author, a waiver of the rights conferred by subsection (a) with respect to a work of visual art shall not constitute a transfer of ownership of any copy of that work, or of ownership of a copyright or of any exclusive right under a copyright in that work.

Section 107. Limitations on Exclusive Rights: Fair Use[4]

Notwithstanding the provisions of sections 106 and 106A, the fair use of a copyrighted work, including such use by reproduction in copies or phonorecords or by any other means specified by that section, for purposes such as criticism, comment, news reporting, teaching (including multiple copies for classroom use), scholarship, or research, is not an infringement of copyright. In determining whether the use made of a work in any particular case is a fair use the factors to be considered shall include—

(1) the purpose and character of the use, including whether such use is of a commercial nature or is for nonprofit educational purposes;

(2) the nature of the copyrighted work;

---

4.   Section 107 was amended by the Visual Artists Rights Act of 1990, Pub. L. No. 101-650, 104 Stat. 5089, 5128, 5132, which struck out "section 106" and inserted in lieu thereof "sections 106 and 106A." Section 107 was also amended by the Act of Oct. 24, 1992, Pub. L. No. 102-492, 106 Stat. 3145, which added the last sentence.

(3) the amount and substantiality of the portion used in relation to the copyrighted work as a whole; and

(4) the effect of the use upon the potential market for or value of the copyrighted work.

The fact that a work is unpublished shall not itself bar a finding of fair use if such finding is made upon consideration of all the above factors.

Section 108. Limitations of Exclusive Rights: Reproduction by Libraries and Archives[5]

(a) Notwithstanding the provisions of section 106, it is not an infringement of copyright for a library or archives, or any of its employees acting within the scope of their employment, to reproduce no more than one copy or phonorecord of a work, or to distribute such copy or phonorecord, under the conditions specified by this section, if—

(1) the reproduction or distribution is made without any purpose of direct or indirect commercial advantage;

(2) the collections of the library or archives are (i) open to the public, or (ii) available not only to researchers affiliated with the library or archives or with the institution of which it is a part, but also to other persons doing research in a specialized field; and

(3) the reproduction or distribution of the work includes a notice of copyright.

(b) The rights of reproduction and distribution under this section apply to a copy or phonorecord of an unpublished work duplicated in facsimile form solely for purposes of preservation and security or for deposit for research use in another library or archives of the type described by clause (2) of subsection (a), if the copy or phonorecord reproduced is currently in the collections of the library or archives.

(c) The right of reproduction under this section applies to a copy or phonorecord of a published work duplicated in facsimile form solely for the purpose of replacement of a copy or phonorecord that is damaged, deteriorating, lost, or stolen, if the library or archives has,

---

5. Section 108 was amended by the Copyright Amendments Act of 1992, Pub. L. No. 102307, 106 Stat. 264, 272, which repealed subsection (i) in its entirety.

after a reasonable effort, determined that an unused replacement cannot be obtained at a fair price.

(d) The rights of reproduction and distribution under this section apply to a copy, made from the collection of a library or archives where the user makes his or her request or from that of another library or archives, of no more than one article or other contribution to a copyrighted collection or periodical issue, or to a copy or phonorecord of a small part of any other copyrighted work, if—

    (1) the copy or phonorecord becomes the property of the user, and the library or archives has had no notice that the copy or phonorecord would be used for any purpose other than private study, scholarship, or research; and

    (2) the library or archives displays prominently, at the place where orders are accepted, and includes on its order form, a warning of copyright in accordance with requirements that the Register of Copyrights shall prescribe by regulation.

(e) The rights of reproduction and distribution under this section apply to the entire work, or to a substantial part of it, made from the collection of a library or archives where the user makes his or her request or from that of another library or archives, if the library or archives has first determined, on the basis of a reasonable investigation, that a copy or phonorecord of the copyrighted work cannot be obtained at a [f]air price, if—

    (1) the copy or phonorecord becomes the property of the user, and the library or archives has had no notice that the copy or phonorecord would be used for any purpose other than private study, scholarship, or research; and

    (2) the library or archives displays prominently, at the place where orders are accepted, and includes on its order form, a warning of copyright in accordance with requirements that the Register of Copyrights shall prescribe by regulation.

(f) Nothing in this section—

    (1) shall be construed to impose liability for copyright infringement upon a library or archives or its employees for the unsupervised use of reproducing equipment located on its premises: *Provided,* That such equipment displays a notice that the making of a copy may be subject to the copyright law;

   (2) excuses a person who uses such reproducing equipment or who requests a copy or phonorecord under subsection (d) from liability for copyright infringement for any such act, or for any later use of such copy or phonorecord; if it exceeds fair use as provided by section 107;

   (3) shall be construed to limit the reproduction and distribution by lending of a limited number of copies and excerpts by a library or archives of an audiovisual news program, subject to clauses (1), (2), and (3) of subsection (a); or

   (4) in any way affects the right of fair use as provided by section 107, or any contractual obligations assumed at any time by the library or archives when it obtained a copy or phonorecord of a work in its collections.

(g) The rights of reproduction and distribution under this section extend to the isolated and unrelated reproduction or distribution of a single copy or phonorecord of the same material on separate occasions, but do not extend to cases where the library or archives, or its employee—

   (1) is aware or has substantial reason to believe that it is engaging in the related or concerted reproduction or distribution of multiple copies or phonorecords of the same material, whether made on one occasion or over a period of time, and whether intended for aggregate use by one or more individuals or for separate use by the individual members of a group; or

   (2) engages in the systematic reproduction or distribution of single or multiple copies or phonorecords of material described in subsection (d): Provided, That nothing in this clause prevents a library or archives from participating in interlibrary arrangements that do not have, as their purpose or effect, that the library or archives receiving such copies or phonorecords for distribution does so in such aggregate quantities as to substitute for a subscription to or purchase of work.

(h) The rights of reproduction and distribution under this section do not apply to a musical work, a pictorial, graphic or sculptural work, or a motion picture or other audiovisual work other than an audiovisual work dealing with news, except that no such limitation shall apply with respect to rights granted by subsections (b) and (c), or with respect to pictorial or graphic works published as illustrations, diagrams, or similar adjuncts to works of which copies are reproduced or distributed in accordance with subsections (d) and (e).

Section 109. Limitations on Exclusive Rights: Effect of Transfer of Particular Copy or Phonorecord[6]

(a) Notwithstanding the provisions of section 106(3), the owner of a particular copy or phonorecord lawfully made under this title, or any person authorized by such owner, is entitled, without the authority of the copyright owner, to sell or otherwise dispose of the possession of that copy or phonorecord.

(b)(1)(A) Notwithstanding the provisions of subsection (a), unless authorized by the owners of copyright in the sound recording or the owner of copyright in a computer program (including any tape, disk, or other medium embodying such program), and in the case of a sound recording in the musical works embodied therein, neither the owner of a particular phonorecord nor any person in possession of a particular copy of a computer program (including any tape, disk, or other medium embodying such program), may, for the purposes of direct or indirect commercial advantage, dispose of, or authorize the disposal of, the possession of that phonorecord or computer program (including any tape, disk, or

---

6.   Section 109 was amended by the Act of October 4, 1984, Pub. L. No. 98-450, 98 Stat. 1727, and the Act of November 5, 1988, Pub. L. No. 100-617, 102 Stat. 3194. The 1984 Act redesignated subsections (b) and (c) as subsections (c) and (d), respectively, and inserted after subsection (a) a new subsection (b).

The earlier amendatory Act states that "the provisions of section 109(b). . . shall not affect the right of an owner of a particular phonorecord of a sound recording, who acquired such ownership before . . . [October 4, 1984], to dispose of the possession of that particular phonorecord on or after such date of enactment in any manner permitted by section 109 of title 17, United States Code, as in effect on the day before the date of the enactment of this Act." It also states, as modified by the 1988 amendatory Act, that the amendments "shall not apply to rentals, leasings, lendings (or acts or practices in the nature of rentals, leasings, or lendings) occurring after the date which is 13 years after . . . [October 4, 1984]."

Section 109 was also amended by the Computer Software Rental Amendments Act of 1990, Pub. L. No. 101-650, 104 Stat. 5089, 5134, 5135, which added at the end thereof subsection (e). The amendatory Act states that the provisions contained in the new subsection (e) shall take effect one year after the date of enactment of such Act, that is, one year after December 1, 1990. The Act also states that such amendments so made "shall not apply to public performances or displays that occur on or after October 1, 1995."

other medium embodying such program) by rental, lease, or lending, or by any other act or practice in the nature of rental, lease, or lending. Nothing in the preceding sentence shall apply to the rental, lease, or lending of a phonorecord for nonprofit purposes by a nonprofit library or nonprofit educational institution. The transfer of possession of a lawfully made copy of a computer program by a nonprofit educational institution to another nonprofit educational institution or to faculty, staff, and students does not constitute rental, lease, or lending for direct or indirect commercial purposes under this subsection.

(b)(1)(B) This subsection does not apply to—

(i) a computer program which is embodied in a machine or product and which cannot be copied during the ordinary operation or use of the machine or product; or

(ii) a computer program embodied in or used in conjunction with a limited purpose computer that is designed for playing video games and may be designed for other purposes.

(b)(1)(C) Nothing in this subsection affects any provision of chapter 9 of this title.

(b)(2)(A) Nothing in this subsection shall apply to the lending of a computer program for nonprofit purposes by a nonprofit library, if each copy of a computer program which is lent by such library has affixed to the packaging containing the program a warning of copyright in accordance with requirements that the Register of Copyrights shall prescribe by regulation.

(b)(2)(B) Not later than three years after the date of the enactment of the Computer Software Rental Amendments Ace of 1990, and at such times thereafter as the Register of Copyright[s] considers appropriate, the Register of Copyrights, after consultation with representatives of copyright owners and librarians, shall submit to the Congress a report stating whether this paragraph has achieved its intended purpose of maintaining the integrity of the copyright system while providing nonprofit libraries the capability to fulfill their function. Such report shall advise the Congress as to any information or recommendations that the Register of Copyrights considers necessary to carry out the purposes of this subsection.

(b)(3) Nothing in this subsection shall affect any provision of the antitrust laws. For purposes of the preceding sentence, "antitrust laws" has the meaning given that term in the first section of the

Clayton Act and includes section 5 of the Federal Trade Commission Act to the extent that section relates to unfair methods of competition.

(b)(4) Any person who distributes a phonorecord or a copy of a computer program (including any tape, disk, or other medium embodying such program) in violation of paragraph (1) is an infringer of copyright under section 501 of this title and is subject to the remedies set forth in sections 502, 503, 504, 505, and 509. Such violation shall not be a criminal offense under section 506 or cause such person to be subject to the criminal penalties set forth in section 2319 of title 18.[7]

(c) Notwithstanding the provisions of section 106(5), the owner of a particular copy lawfully made under this title, or any person authorized by such owner, is entitled, without the authority of the copyright owner, to display that copy publicly, either directly or by the projection of no more than one image at a time, to viewers present at the place where the copy is located.

(d) The privileges prescribed by subsections (a) and (c) do not, unless authorized by the copyright owner, extend to any person who has acquired possession of the copy or phonorecord from the copyright owner, by rental, lease, loan, or otherwise, without acquiring ownership of it.[8]

7.　Section 109(b) was amended by the Computer Software Rental Amendments Act of 1990, Pub. L. No. 101-650, 104 Stat. 5089, 5134, in the following particulars: a) paragraphs (2) and (3) were redesignated as paragraphs (3) and (4), respectively; b) paragraph (1) was struck out and new paragraphs (1) and (2) were inserted in lieu thereof; and c) paragraph (4), as redesignated by the amendatory Act, was struck out and a new paragraph (4) was inserted in lieu thereof.

　　The amendatory Act states that section 109(b), as amended, "shall not affect the right of a person in possession of a particular copy of a computer program, who acquired such copy before the date of the enactment of this Act, to dispose of the possession of that copy on or after such date of enactment in any manner permitted by section 109 of title 17, United States Code, as in effect on the day before such date of enactment."

　　The amendatory Act also states that the amendments made to section 109(b) 11 "shall not apply to rentals, leasings, or landings (or acts or practices in the nature of rentals, leasings, or landings) occurring on or after October 1, 1997."

8.　The Act of November 5, 1988, Pub. L. No. 100-617, 102 Stat. 3194, made technical amendments to section 109(d), by striking out "(b)" and inserting in lieu thereof "(c)" and by striking out "coyright" and inserting in lieu thereof "copyright."

(e) Notwithstanding the provisions of sections 106(4) and 106(5), in the case of an electronic audiovisual game intended for use in coin-operated equipment, the owner of a particular copy of such a game lawfully made under this title, is entitled, without the authority of the copyright owner of the game, to publicly perform or display that game in coin-operated equipment, except that this subsection shall not apply to any work of authorship embodied in the audiovisual game if the copyright owner of the electronic audiovisual game is not also the copyright owner of the work of authorship.

Section 110. Limitations on Exclusive Rights: Exemption of Certain Performances and Displays[9]

Notwithstanding the provisions of section 106, the following are not infringements of copyright:

(1) performance or display of a work by instructors or pupils in the course of face-to-face teaching activities of a nonprofit educational institution, in a classroom or similar place devoted to instruction, unless, in the case of a motion picture or other audiovisual work, the performance, or the display of individual images, is given by means of a copy that was not lawfully made under this title, and that the person responsible for the performance knew or had reason to believe was not lawfully made;

(2) performance of a nondramatic literary or musical work or display of a work, by or in the course of a transmission, if—

    (A) the performance or display is a regular part of the systematic instructional activities of a governmental body or a nonprofit educational institution; and

    (B) the performance or display is directly related and of material assistance to the teaching content of the transmission; and

    (C) the transmission is made primarily for—

        (i) reception in classrooms or similar places normally devoted to instruction, or

        (ii) reception by persons to whom the transmission is directed because their disabilities or other special

---

9.   Section 110 was amended by the Act of October 25, 1982, Pub. L. No. 97-366, 96 Stat. 1759, which added paragraph (10).

circumstances prevent their attendance in classrooms or similar places normally devoted to instruction, or

(iii) reception by officers or employees of governmental bodies as a part of their official duties or employment;

(3) performance of a nondramatic literary or musical work or of a dramatico-musical work of a religious nature, or display of a work, in the course of services at a place of worship or other religious assembly;

(4) performance of a nondramatic literary or musical work otherwise than in a transmission to the public, without any purpose of direct or indirect commercial advantage and without payment of any fee or other compensation for the performance to any of its performers, promoters, or organizers, if—

(A) there is no direct or indirect admission charge; or

(B) the proceeds, after deducting the reasonable costs of producing the performance, are used exclusively for educational, religious, or charitable purposes and not for private financial gain, except where the copyright owner has served notice of objection to the performance under the following conditions;

(i) the notice shall be in writing and signed by the copyright owner or such owner's duly authorized agent; and

(ii) the notice shall be served on the person responsible for the performance at least seven days before the date of the performance, and shall state the reasons for the objection; and

(iii) the notice shall comply, in form, content, and manner of service, with requirements that the Register of Copyrights shall prescribe by regulation;

(5) communication of a transmission embodying a performance or display of a work by the public reception of the transmission on a single receiving apparatus of a kind commonly used in private homes, unless—

(A) a direct charge is made to see or hear the transmission; or

(B) the transmission thus received is further transmitted to the public;

(6) performance of a nondramatic musical work by a governmental body or a nonprofit agricultural or horticultural organization, in the course of an annual agricultural or

horticultural fair or exhibition conducted by such body or organization; the exemption provided by this clause shall extend to any liability for copyright infringement that would otherwise be imposed on such body or organization, under doctrines of vicarious liability or related infringement, for a performance by a concessionnaire, business establishment, or other person at such fair or exhibition, but shall not excuse any such person from liability for the performance;

(7) performance of a nondramatic musical work by a vending establishment open to the public at large without any direct or indirect admission charge, where the sole purpose of the performance is to promote the retail sale of copies or phonorecords of the work, and the performance is not transmitted beyond the place where the establishment is located and is within the immediate area where the sale is occurring;

(8) performance of a nondramatic literary work, by or in the course of a transmission specifically designed for and primarily directed to blind or other handicapped persons who are unable to read normal printed material as a result of their handicap, or deaf or other handicapped persons who are unable to hear the aural signals accompanying a transmission of visual signals, if the performance is made without any purpose of direct or indirect commercial advantage and its transmission is made through the facilities of: (i) a governmental body; or (ii) a non-commercial educational broadcast station (as defined in section 397) of title 47); or (iii) a radio subcarrier authorization (as defined in 47 CFR 73.293–73.295 and 73.593–73.595); or (iv) a cable system (as defined in section 111 (f)).

(9) performance on a single occasion of a dramatic literary work published at least ten years before the date of the performance, by or in the course of a transmission specifically designed for and primarily directed to blind or other handicapped persons who are unable to read normal printed material as a result of their handicap, if the performance is made without any purpose of direct or indirect commercial advantage and its transmission is made through the facilities of a radio subcarrier authorization referred to in clause (8) (iii), Provided, That the provisions of this clause shall not be applicable to

more than one performance of the same work by the same performers or under the auspices of the same organization.

(10) notwithstanding paragraph 4 above, the following is not an infringement of copyright: performance of a nondramatic literary or musical work in the course of a social function which is organized and promoted by a nonprofit veterans' organization or a nonprofit fraternal organization to which the general public is not invited, but not including the invitees of the organizations, if the proceeds from the performance, after deducting the reasonable costs of producing the performance, are used exclusively for charitable purposes and not for financial gain. For purposes of this section the social functions of any college or university fraternity or sorority shall not be included unless the social function is held solely to raise funds for a specific charitable purpose.

Appendix B

Agreement on Guidelines for Classroom Copying in Not-for-profit Educational Institutions with Respect to Books and Periodicals

The purpose of the following guidelines is to state the minimum standards of educational fair use under Section 107 of H.R. 2223. The parties agree that the conditions determining the extent of permissible copying for educational purposes may change in the future; that certain types of copying permitted under these guidelines may not be permissible in the future; and conversely that in the future other types of copying not permitted under these guidelines may be permissible under revised guidelines.

Moreover, the following statement of guidelines is not intended to limit the types of copying permitted under the standards of fair use under judicial decision and which are stated in Section 107 of the Copyright Revision Bill. There may be instances in which copying which does not fall within the guidelines stated below may nonetheless be permitted under the criteria of fair use.

Guidelines

I. Single Copying for Teachers

A single copy may be made of any of the following by or for a teacher at his or her individual request for his or her scholarly research or use in teaching or preparation to teach a class:
  - A. A chapter from a book;
  - B. An article from a periodical or newspaper;
  - C. A short story, short essay, or short poem, whether or not from a collective work;
  - D. A chart, graph, diagram, drawing, cartoon, or picture from a book, periodical, or newspaper.

II. Multiple Copies for Classroom Use

Multiple copies (not to exceed in any event more than one copy per pupil in a course) may be made by or for the teacher giving the course for classroom use or discussion; provided that:
  - A. The copying meets the tests of brevity and spontaneity as defined below; and
  - B. Meets the cumulative effect test as defined below; and
  - C. Each copy includes a notice of copyright.

Definitions

Brevity

(i) Poetry: (a) A complete poem is less than 250 words and if printed on not more than two pages; or (b) from a longer poem, an excerpt of not more than 250 words.

(ii) Prose: (a) Either a complete article, story, or essay of less than 2,500 words; or (b) an excerpt from any prose work of not more than 1,000 words or 10 percent of the work, whichever is less, but in any event a minimum of 500 words.

[Each of the numerical limits stated in (i) and (ii) above may be expanded to permit the completion of an unfinished line of a poem or of an unfinished prose paragraph.]

(iii) Illustration: One chart, graph, diagram, drawing, cartoon, or picture per book or per periodical issue.

(iv) "Special" works: Certain works in poetry, prose, or in "poetic prose" which often combine language with illustrations and which are intended sometimes for children and at other times for a more general audience fall short of 2,500 words in their entirety. Paragraph "ii" above notwithstanding such "special works" may not be reproduced in their entirety; however, an excerpt comprising not more than two of the published pages of such special work and containing not more than 10 percent of the words found in the text thereof, may be reproduced.

Spontaneity

(i) The copying is at the instance and inspiration of the individual teacher; and

(ii) The inspiration and decision to use the work and the moment of its use for maximum teaching effectiveness are so close in time that it would be unreasonable to expect a timely reply to a request for permission.

Cumulative Effect

(i) The copying of the material is for only one course in the school in which the copies are made.

(ii) Not more than one short poem, article, story, essay or two excerpts may be copied from the same author, nor more than three from the same collective work or periodical volume during one class term.

(iii) There shall not be more than nine instances of such multiple copying for one course during one class term.

[The limitations stated in "ii" and "iii" above shall not apply to current news periodicals and newspapers and current news sections of other periodicals.]

III. Prohibitions as to I and II Above

Notwithstanding any of the above, the following shall be prohibited:

A. Copying shall not be used to create or to replace or substitute for anthologies, compilations, or collective works. Such replacement or substitution may occur whether copies of various works or excerpts therefrom are accumulated or reproduced and used separately.

B. There shall be no copying of or from works intended to be "consumable" in the course of study or of teaching. These include workbooks, exercises, standardized tests and test booklets, and answer sheets and like consumable material.

C. Copying shall not:
    (a) substitute for the purchase of books, publishers' reprints or periodicals;
    (b) be directed by higher authority;
    (c) be repeated with respect to the same item by the same teacher from term to term.
    (d) No charge shall be made to the student beyond the actual cost of the photocopying.

Agreed March 19, 1976

Ad Hoc Committee on Copyright Law Revision: By Sheldon Elliott Steinbach.

Author-Publishers Group: Authors League of America: By Irwin Karp, Counsel.

Association of American Publishers, Inc.: By Alexander C. Hoffman, Chairman, Copyright Committee.

Appendix C
Guidelines for Educational Uses of Music

The purpose of the following guidelines is to state the minimum and not the maximum and standards of educational fair use under Section 107 of H.R. 2223. The parties agree that the conditional purposes may change in the future; that certain types of copying permitted under these guidelines may not be permissible in the future, and conversely that in the future other types of copying not permitted under these guidelines may be permissible under revised guidelines.

Moreover, the following statement of guidelines is not intended to limit the types of copying permitted under the standards of fair use under judicial decision and which are stated in Section 107 of the Copyright Revision Bill. There may be instances in which copying which does not fall within the guidelines stated below may nonetheless be permitted under the criteria of fair use.

A. Permissible Uses

1. Emergency copying to replace purchased copies which for any reason are not available for an imminent performance provided purchased replacement copied shall be substituted in due course.
2. For academic purposes other than performance, single or multiple copies of excerpts of works may be made, provided that the excerpts do not comprise a part of the whole which would constitute a performable unit such as a selection, movement or aria, but in no case more than 10 percent of the whole work. The number of copies shall not exceed one copy per pupil.
3. Printed copies which have been purchased may be edited or simplified provided that the fundamental character of the work is not distorted or the lyrics, if any, altered or lyrics added if none exist.
4. A single copy of recordings of performances by students may be made for evaluation or rehearsal purposes any may be retained by the educational institution or individual teacher.
5. A single copy of a sound recording (such as a tape, disk, or cassette) of copyrighted music may be made from sound recordings owned by an educational institution or an individual teacher for the purpose of constructing aural exercises or examinations and may be retained be the educational institution or individual teacher. (This pertains only to the copyright of the music itself and not to any copyright which may exist in the sound recording.)

B. Prohibitions

1. Copying to create or replace or substitute for anthologies, compilations, or collective works.
2. Copying of or from works intended to be "consumable" in the course of study or of teaching such as workbooks, exercises, standardized tests, and answer sheets and like material.
3. Copying for the purpose of performance, except as in A(1) above.
4. Copying for the purpose of substituting for the purchase of music, except as in A(1) and A(2) above.
5. Copying without inclusion of the copyright notice which appears on the printed copy.

Appendix D
Interlibrary Loan Guidelines

Guidelines for the Proviso of Subsection 108(g)(2)

1. As used in the proviso of Subsection 108(g)(2), the words "such aggregate quantities as to substitute for a subscription to or purchase of such work" shall mean:

    (a) With respect to any given periodical (as opposed to any given issue of a periodical), filled requests of a library or archive (a "requesting entity") within any calendar year for a total of six or more copies of an article or articles published in such periodical within five years prior to the date of the request. These guidelines specifically shall not apply, directly or indirectly, to any request of a requesting entity for a copy or copies of an article or articles published in any issue of a periodical, the publication date of which is more than five years prior to the date when the request is made. These guidelines do not define the meaning, with respect to such a request, of "such aggregate quantities as to substitute for a subscription to [such periodical]".

    (b) With respect to any other material described in Subsection 108(d), (including fiction and poetry), filled requests of a requesting entity within any calendar year for a total of six or more copies or phonorecords of or from any given work (including a collective work) during the entire period when such material shall be protected by copyright.

2. In the event that a requesting entity—
    (a) shall have in force or shall have entered an order for a subscription to a periodical, or

    (b) has within its collection, or shall have entered an order for, a copy or phonorecord of any other copyrighted work, material from either category of which it desires to obtain by copy from another library or archives (the "supplying entity"), because the material to be copied is not reasonably available for use by the requesting entity itself, then the fulfillment of such request shall be treated as though the requesting entity made such copy from its own collection. A library or archive may request a copy or phonorecord from a supplying entity only under those circumstances where the requesting entity would have been able, under the other provisions of Section 108, to supply such copy from materials in its own collection.

3. No request for a copy or phonorecord of any material to which these guidelines apply may be fulfilled by the supplying entity unless such request is accompanied by a representation by the requesting entity that the request was made in conformity with these guidelines.

4. The requesting entity shall maintain records of all requests made by it for copies or phonorecords of any materials to which these guidelines apply and shall maintain records of the fulfillment of such requests, which records shall be retained until the end of the third complete calendar year after the end of the calendar year in which the respective request shall have been made.

5. As part of the review provided for in Subsection 108(i), these guidelines shall be reviewed not later than five years from the effective date of this bill. [Subsection 108(i) was later repealed].

Guidelines for Off-air Recordings of Broadcast Programming for Educational Purposes

In March 1979, Congressman Robert Kastenmeier, chairman of the House Subcommittee on Courts, Civil Liberties, and Administration of Justice, appointed a Negotiating Committee consisting of representatives of education organizations, copyright proprietors, and creative guilds and unions. The following guidelines reflect the Negotiating Committee's consensus as to the application of "fair use" to the recording, retention, and use of television broadcast programs for educational purposes. They specify periods of retention and use of such off-air recordings in classrooms and similar places devoted to instruction and for homebound instruction. The purpose of establishing these guidelines is to provide standards for both owners and users of copyrighted television programs.

1. The guidelines were developed to apply only to off-air recording by nonprofit educational institutions.

2. A broadcast program may be recorded off-air simultaneously with broadcast transmission (including simultaneous cable retransmission) and retained by a nonprofit educational institution for a period not to exceed the first forty-five (45) consecutive calendar days after date of recording. Upon conclusion of such retention period, all off-air recordings must be erased or destroyed immediately. "Broadcast programs" are television programs transmitted by television stations for reception by the general public without charge.

3. Off-air recordings may be used once by individual teachers in the course of relevant teaching activities, and repeated once only when instructional reinforcement is necessary, in classrooms and similar places devoted to instruction within a single building, cluster or campus, as well as in the homes of students receiving formalized home instruction, during the first ten (10) consecutive school days in the forty-five (45) day calendar day retention period. "School days" are school session days—not counting weekends, holidays, vacations, examination periods, and other scheduled interruptions—within the forty-five (45) calendar day retention period.

4. Off-air recordings may be made only at the request of and used by individual teachers, and may not be regularly recorded in anticipation of requests. No broadcast program may be recorded off-air more than once at the request of the same teacher, regardless of the number of times the program may be broadcasted.

5. A limited number of copies may be reproduced from each off-air recording to meet the legitimate needs of teachers under these guidelines. Each such additional copy shall be subject to all provisions governing the original recording.

6. After the first ten (10) consecutive school days, off-air recordings may be used up to the end of the forty-five (45) calendar day retention period only for teacher evaluation purposes i.e., to determine whether or not to include the broadcast program in the teaching curriculum, and may not be used in the recording institution for student exhibition or any other non-evaluation purposes without authorization.

7. Off-air recordings need not be used in their entirety, but the recorded programs may not be altered from their original content. Off-air recordings may not be physically or electronically combined or merged to constitute teaching anthologies or compilations.

8. All copies of off-air recording must include the copyright notice on the broadcast program as recorded.
9. Educational institutions are expected to establish appropriate control procedures to maintain the integrity of these guidelines.

Appendix F
ALA Model Policy on
Library Reserves[1]

At the request of a faculty member, a library may photocopy and place on reserve excerpts from copyrighted works in its collection in accordance with guidelines similar to those governing formal classroom distribution for face-to-face teaching discussed above. This University [College] believes that these guidelines apply to the library reserve shelf to the extent it functions as an extension of classroom readings or reflects an individual student's right to photocopy for his personal scholastic use under the doctrine of fair use. In general, librarians may photocopy materials for reserve room use for the convenience of students both in preparing class assignments and in pursuing informal educational activities which higher education requires, such as advanced independent study and research.

If the request calls for only *one* copy to be placed on reserve, the library may photocopy an entire article, or an entire chapter from a book, or an entire poem.

---

1.   ALA MODEL POLICY CONCERNING COLLEGE AND UNIVERSITY PHOTOCOPYING FOR CLASSROOM, RESEARCH AND LIBRARY RESERVE USE (March 1982).

The negotiated safe-harbor guidelines for classroom uses are in many ways inappropriate for the college and university level. "Brevity" simply cannot mean the same thing in terms of grade-school readings that it does for more advanced research. Because university professors were not specifically represented in the negotiation of the classroom guidelines, ALA published *Model Policy Concerning College and University Photocopying for Classroom Research and Library Reserve Use* (Model Policy).

In general with respect to classroom uses, the standard guidelines should be followed:

1. The distribution of the same photocopied material does not occur every semester.
2. Only one copy is distributed for each student.
3. The material includes a copyright notice on the first page of the portion of material photocopies.
4. The students are not assessed any fee beyond the actual cost of the photocopying.

Requests for multiple copies on reserve should meet the following guidelines:

1. The amount of material should be reasonable in relation to the total amount of material assigned for one term of a course taking into account the nature of the course, its subject matter, and level, 17 U.S.C. § 107(1) and (3).
2. The number of copies should be reasonable in light of the number of students enrolled, the difficulty and timing of assignments, and the number of other courses which may assign the same material, 17 U.S.C. § 107(1) and (3).
3. The material should contain a notice of copyright, *see,* 17 U.S.C. § 401.
4. The effect of photocopying the material should not be detrimental to the market for the work. (In general, the library should own at least one copy of the work.) 17 U.S.C. § 107(4).

Appendix G
Proposed Fair Use Guidelines
for Electronic Reserve Systems
Revised: March 5, 1996

Introduction

Many college, university and school libraries have established reserve operations for readings and other materials that support the instructional requirements of specific courses. Some educational institutions are now providing electronic reserve systems that allow storage of electronic versions of materials that students may retrieve on a computer screen and from which they may print a copy for their personal study. When materials are included as a matter of fair use, electronic reserve systems should constitute an *ad hoc* or supplemental source of information of students, beyond a textbook or other materials. If included with permission from the copyright owner, however, the scope and range of materials is potentially unlimited, depending upon the permission granted. Although fair use is determined on a case-by-case basis, the following guidelines identify an understanding of fair use for the reproduction, distribution, display and performance of materials in the context of creating and using an electronic reserve system.

Making materials accessible through electronic reserve systems raises significant copyright issues. Electronic reserve operations include the making of a digital version of text, the distribution and display of that version at workstations and downloading and printing of copies. The complexities of the electronic environment and the growing potential for implicating copyright infringements, raise the need for a fresh understanding of fair use. These guidelines are not intended to burden the facilitation of reserve unduly, but instead offer a workable path that educators and librarians may follow in order to exercise a meaningful application of fair use, while also acknowledging and respecting the interests of copyright owners.

These guidelines focus generally on the traditional domain of reserve rooms, particularly copies of journal articles and book chapters and their accompanying graphics. Nevertheless, they are not meant to apply exclusively to textual materials and may be instructive for the fair use of other media. The guidelines also focus on the use of the complete article or the entire book chapter. Using only brief excerpts from such works would most likely also be fair use, possibly without all of the restrictions or conditions set forth in these guidelines. Operators of reserve systems should also provide safeguards for the integrity of the text and the author's reputation, including verification that the text is correctly scanned.

The guidelines address only those materials protected by copyright and for which the institution has not obtained permission before including them in an electronic reserve system. The limitations and conditions set forth in these guidelines need not apply to materials in the public domain such as works of the U.S. government or works on which copyright has expired or to works for which the institution has obtained permission for inclusion in the electronic reserve system. License agreements may govern the uses of some materials. Persons responsible for electronic reserve systems should refer to applicable license terms for guidance. If an instructor arranges for students to acquire a work by some means that includes permission from the copyright owner, the instructor should not include that same work on an electronic reserve system as a matter of fair use.

These guidelines are the outgrowth of negotiations among diverse parties attending the Conference on Fair Use ("CONFU") meetings sponsored by the Information Infrastructure Task Force's Working Group on Intellectual Property Rights. While endorsements of any guidelines by all conference participants is unlikely, these guidelines have been endorsed by the organizations whose names appear at the end. These guidelines are in furtherance of the Working Group's objective of encouraging negotiated guidelines of fair use.

This introduction is an integral part of these guidelines and should be included with the guidelines wherever they may be reprinted or adopted by a library, academic institution, or other organization or association. No copyright protection of these guidelines is claimed by any person or entity and anyone is free to reproduce and distribute this document without permission.

A. Scope of Material

1. In accordance with fair use (Section 107 of the U.S. Copyright Act), electronic reserve systems may include copyrighted materials at the request of a course instructor.

2. Electronic reserve systems may include short items (such as an article from a journal, a chapter from a book or conference proceedings, or a poem from a collected work) or excerpts from longer items. "Longer items" may include articles, chapters, poems and other works that are of such length as to constitute a substantial portion of a book, journal, or other work of which they may be a part. "Short items" may include articles, chapters, poems and other works of a customary length and structure as to be a small part of a book, journal, or other work, even if that work may be marketed individually.

3. Electronic reserve systems should not include any material unless the instructor, the library, or another unit of the educational institution possesses a lawfully obtained copy.

4. The total amount of material included in electronic reserve systems for a specific course as a matter of fair use should be a small proportion of the total assigned reading for a particular course.

B. Notices and Attributions

1. On a preliminary or introductory screen, electronic reserve systems should display a notice, consistent with the notice described in Section 108(f)(1) of the Copyright Act. The notice

should include additional language cautioning against further electronic distribution of the digital work.

2. If a notice of copyright appears on the copy of a work that is included in an electronic reserve system, the following statement shall appear at some place where users will likely see it in connection with access to the particular work—

    The work from which this copy is made includes this notice: [restate the elements of the statutory copyright notice: e.g. Copyright 1996, XXX Corp.]

3. Materials included in electronic reserve systems should include appropriate citations or attributions to their sources.

C. Access and Use

1. Electronic reserve systems should be structured to limit access to students registered in the course for which the items have been placed on reserve and to instructors and staff responsible for the course or the electronic system.

2. The appropriate methods for limiting access will depend on available technology. Solely to suggest and not to prescribe options for implementation, possible methods for limiting access may include one or more of the following or other appropriate methods—
    (a) individual password controls or verification of a student's registration status, or
    (b) password system for each class, or
    (c) retrieval of works by course number or instructor name, but not by author or title of the work, or
    (d) access limited to workstations that are ordinarily used by, or are accessible to, only enrolled students or appropriate staff or faculty.

3. Students should not be charged specifically or directly for access to electronic reserve systems.

D. Storage and Reuse

1. Permission from the copyright holder is required if the item is to be reused in a subsequent academic term for the same course offered by the same instructor, or if the item is a standard

assigned or optional reading for an individual course taught in multiple sections by many instructors.

2. Material may be retained in electronic form while permission is being sought or until the next academic term in which the material might be used, but in no event for more than three calendar years, including the year in which the materials are last used.

3. Short-term access to materials included on electronic reserve systems in previous academic terms may be provided to students who have not completed the course.

Endorsing Organizations

American Association of Law Libraries
Association of American University Presses
American Council of Learned Societies
Indiana Partnership for Statewide Education, Working Group
Music Library Association
National Education Association
National School Boards Association
Special Libraries Association

Appendix H
Proposed Fair Use Guidelines for Educational Multimedia

Prepared by
Consortium of College
and University Media Centers

1. Introduction[1]

1.1 Preamble

Fair use is a legal principle that defines the limitations on the exclusive rights[2] of copyright holders. The purpose of these guidelines is to provide guidance on the application of fair use principles by educators, scholars and students who develop multimedia projects using portions of copyrighted works under fair use rather than by seeking authorization for non-commercial educational uses. These guidelines apply only to fair use in the context of copyright and to no other rights.

---

1. These Guidelines shall not be read to supersede other preexisting educational fair use guidelines that deal with the Copyright Act of 1976.
2. See section 106 of the Copyright Act.

There is no simple test to determine what is fair use. Section 107 of the Copyright Act[3] sets forth the four fair use factors which should be considered in each instance, based on particular facts of a given case, to determine whether a use is a "fair use": (1) the purpose and character of use, including whether such use is of a commercial nature or is for nonprofit educational purposes, (2) the nature of the copyrighted work, (3) the amount and substantiality of the portion used in relation to the copyrighted work as a whole, and (4) the effect of the use upon the potential market for or value of the copyrighted work.

While only the courts can authoritatively determine whether a particular use is fair use, these guidelines represent the participants'[4] consensus of conditions under which fair use should generally apply and examples of when permission is required. uses that exceed these guidelines may or may not be fair use. The participants also agree that the more one exceeds these guidelines, the greater the risk that fair use does not apply.

The limitations and conditions set forth in these guidelines do not apply to works in the public domain—such as U.S. Government works or works on which copyright has expired for which there are no copyright restrictions—or to works for which the individual or institution has obtained permission for the particular use. Also, license agreements may govern the uses of some works and users should refer to the applicable license terms for guidance.

The participants who developed these guidelines met for an extended period of time and the result represents their collective understanding in this complex area. Because digital technology is in a dynamic phase, there may come a time when it is necessary to review these guidelines. Nothing in these guidelines shall be construed to apply to the fair use privilege in any context outside of educational and scholarly uses of educational multimedia projects.

This preamble is an integral part of these guidelines and should be included whenever the guidelines are reprinted or adopted by organizations and educational institutions. Users are encouraged to reproduce

---

3.   The Copyright Act of 1976, as amended, is codified at 17 U.S.C. § 101 *et seq.*

4.   The names of various organizations participating in this dialog appear at the end of these guidelines and clearly indicate the variety of interest groups involved, both from the standpoint of the users of copyrighted material and also from the standpoint of the copyright owners.

and distribute these guidelines freely without permission; no copyright protection of these guidelines is claimed by any person or entity.

1.2 Background

These guidelines clarify the application of fair use of copyrighted works as teaching methods are adapted to new learning environments. Educators have traditionally brought copyrighted books, videos, slides, sound recordings and other media into the classroom, along with accompanying projections and playback equipment. Multimedia creators integrated these individual instructional resources with their own original works in a meaningful way, providing compact educational tools that allow great flexibility in teaching and learning. Material is stored so that it may be retrieved in a nonlinear fashion, depending on the needs or interests of learners. Educators can use multimedia projects to respond spontaneously to students' questions by referring quickly to relevant portions. In addition, students can use multimedia projects to pursue independent study according to their needs or at a pace appropriate to their capabilities. Educators and students want guidance about the application of fair use principles when creating their own multimedia projects to meet specific instructional objectives.

1.3 Applicability of These Guidelines

These guidelines apply to the use, without permission, of portions of lawfully acquired copyrighted works in educational multimedia projects which are created by educators or students as part of a systematic learning activity by nonprint educational institutions. Educational multimedia projects created under these guidelines incorporate students' or educators' original material, such as course notes or commentary, together with various copyrighted media formats including but not limited to, motion media, music, text material, graphics, illustrations, photographs and digital software which are combined into an integrated presentation. Educational institutions are defined as nonprofit organizations whose primary focus is supporting research and instructional activities of educators and students for noncommercial purposes.

For the purposes of the guidelines, **educators** include faculty, teachers, instructors, and others who engage in scholarly, research and instructional activities for educational institutions. The copyrighted works used under these guidelines are **lawfully acquired** if obtained by the institution or individual through lawful means such as purchase, gift or license agreement but not pirated copies. Educational multimedia projects which incorporate portions of copyrighted works under these guidelines may be used only for **educational purposes** in systematic learning activities including use in connection with non-commercial curriculum-based learning and teaching activities including use in connection with non-commercial curriculum-based learning and teaching activities by educators to students enrolled in courses at nonprofit educational institutions or otherwise permitted under Section 3. While these guidelines refer to the creation and use of educational multimedia projects, readers are advised that in some instances other fair use guidelines such as those for off-air taping may be relevant.

2. Preparation of Educational Multimedia Projects Using Portions of Copyrighted Works

These uses are subject to the Portion Limitations listed in Section 4. They should include proper attribution and citation as defined in Sections 6.2.

2.1 By Students

Students may incorporate portions of lawfully acquired copyrighted works when producing their own educational multimedia programs for their own multimedia projects for a specific course.

2.2 By Educators for Curriculum-Based Instruction

Educators may incorporate portions of lawfully acquired copyrighted works when producing their own educational multimedia programs for their own teaching tools in support of curriculum-based instructional activities at educational institutions.

3. Permitted Uses of Educational Multimedia Programs Created Under These Guidelines

Uses of educational multimedia projects created under these guidelines are subject to the Time, Portion, Copying and Distribution Limitations listed in Section 4.

3.1 Student Use

Students may perform and display their own educational multimedia projects created under Section 2 of these guidelines for educational uses in the course for which they were created and may use them in their own portfolios as examples of their academic work for later personal uses such as job and graduate school interviews.

3.2 Educator Use for Curriculum-Based Instruction

Educators may perform and display their own educational multimedia projects created under Section 2 for curriculum-based instruction to students in the following situations:

3.2.1. for face-to-face instruction,

3.2.2. assigned to students for directed self study,

3.2.3. for remote instruction to students enrolled in curriculum-based courses and located at remote sites, provided over the educational institution's secure electronic network in real-time, or for after class review or directed self-study, provided there are technological limitations on access to the network and educational multimedia projects (such as password or PIN) and provided further that the technology prevents the making of copies of copyrighted material.

If the educational institution's network or technology used to access the educational multimedia project created under Section 2 of these guidelines cannot prevent duplication of copyrighted material, students or educators may use the multimedia educational projects over an otherwise secure networks for a period of only 15 days after its initial real-time remote use in the course of instruction or 15 days after its assignment for directed self-study. After that period, one of the two use copies of the educational multimedia project may be placed on reserve in a learning resource center, library or similar facility for on-site use by students enrolled in the course. Students shall be advised that they are not permitted to make their own copies of the multi-media project.

3.3 Educator Use at Peer Conferences

Educators may perform or display their own multimedia projects created under Section 2 of these guidelines in presentations to their peers, for example, at workshops and conferences.

3.4 Educator Use for Professional Portfolio

Educators may retain educational multimedia projects created under Section 2 of these guidelines in their personal portfolios for later personal uses such as tenure review or job interviews.

4. Limitations—Time, Portion, Copying and Distribution

The preparation of educational multimedia projects incorporating copyrighted works under section 2, and the use of such projects under Section 3, are subject to the limitations noted below.

4.1 Time Limitations

Educators may use their educational multimedia projects created for educational purposes under Section 2 of these guidelines for teaching courses, for a period of up to two years after the first instructional use with a class. Use beyond that time period, even for educational purposes, requires permission for each copyrighted portion incorporated in the production. Students may use their educational multimedia projects as noted in Section 3.1.

4.2 Portion Limitations

Portion limitation means the amount of a copyrighted work that can reasonably be used in educational multimedia projects under these guidelines regardless of the original medium from which the copyrighted works are taken. **In the aggregate** means the total amount of copyrighted material from a single copyrighted work that is permitted to be used in an educational multimedia project without permission under these guidelines. These limits apply cumulatively to each educator's or student's multimedia project(s) for the same academic semester, cycle or term. All students should be instructed about the reasons for copyright protection and the need to follow these guidelines. It is understood, however, that students in kindergarten through grade six may not be able to adhere rigidly to the portion limitations in this section in their independent development of educational multimedia projects. In any event, each such project retained under sections 3.1 and 4.3 should comply with the portion limitations in this section.

4.2.1 Motion Media. Up to 10% or 3 minutes, whichever is less, in the aggregate of a copyrighted motion media work may be reproduced or otherwise incorporated as a part of a multimedia project created under Section 2 of these guidelines.

4.2.2 Text Material. Up to 10% or 1000 words, whichever is less, in the aggregate of a copyrighted work consisting of text material may be reproduced or otherwise incorporated as a part of a multimedia project created under Section 2 of these guidelines. An entire poem of less than 250 words may be used, but no more than three poems by the same poet, or five poems by different poets from any anthology may be used. For poems of greater length, 250 words may be used but not more than three excerpts by a poet, or five excerpts from different poets from a single anthology may be used.

4.2.3 Music, Lyrics, and Music Video. Up to 10% but in no event more than 30 seconds of the music and lyrics from an individual musical work (or in the aggregate extracts from an individual work), whether the musical work is embodied in copies, or audio or audiovisual works, may be reproduced or otherwise incorporated as a part of a multimedia project created under Section 2. Any alterations to a musical work shall not change the basic melody or the fundamental character of the work.

4.2.4 Illustrations and Photographs. The reproduction or incorporation of photographs and illustrations is more difficult to define with regard to fair use because fair use usually precludes the use of an entire work. Under these guidelines a photograph or illustration may be used in its entirety but no more than 5 images by an artist or photographer may be reproduced or otherwise incorporated as part of an educational project created under Section 2. When using photographs and illustrations from a published collective work, not more than 10% or 15 images whichever is less, may be reproduced or otherwise incorporated as part of an educational multimedia project created under Section 2.

4.2.5 Numerical Data Sets. Up to 10% or 2500 fields or cell entries, whichever is less, from a copyrighted database or data table may be reproduced or otherwise incorporated as a part of an educational multimedia project created under Section 2 of these guidelines. A field entry is defined as a specific item of information, such as a name or Social Security number, in a record of a database file. A cell entry is defined as the intersection where a row and a column meet on a spreadsheet.

4.3 Copying and Distribution Limitations

Only a limited number of copies, including the original, may be made of an educator's educational multimedia project. For all of the uses permitted in Section 3, there may be no more than two use copies only one of which may be placed on reserve as described in Section 3.2.3.

An additional copy may be made for preservation purposes but may only be used or copied to replace a use copy that has been lost, stolen, or damaged. In the case of a jointly created educational multimedia project, each principal creator may retain one copy but only for the purposes described in Sections 3.3 and 3.4 for educators and Section 3.1 for Students.

5. Examples of When Permission Is Required

5.1 Using Multimedia Projects for Non-Educational or Commercial Purposes

Educators and students must seek individual permissions (licenses) before using copyrighted works in educational multimedia projects for commercial reproduction and distribution.

5.2 Duplication of Multimedia Projects Beyond Limitations Listed in These Guidelines

Even for education uses, educators and students must seek individual permissions for all copyrighted works incorporated in their personally created educational multimedia projects before replicating or distributing beyond the limitations listed in Section 4.3.

5.3 Distribution of Multimedia Projects Beyond Limitations Listed in These Guidelines

Educators and students may not use their personally created educational multimedia projects over electronic networks, except for uses as described in Section 3.2.3, without obtaining permissions for all copyrighted works incorporated in the program.

6. Important Reminders

6.1 Caution in Downloading Material from the Internet

Educators and students are advised to exercise caution in using digital material downloaded from the Internet in producing their own educational multimedia projects, because there is a mix of works protected by copyright and works in the public domain on the network. Access to works on the Internet does not automatically mean that these can be reproduced and reused without permission or royalty payment and, furthermore, some copyrighted works may have been posted to the Internet without authorization of the copyright holder.

6.2 Attribution and Acknowledgment

Educators and students are reminded to credit the sources and display the copyright notice © and copyright ownership information if this is shown in the original source, for all works incorporated as part of the educational multimedia projects prepared by educators and students, including those prepared under fair use. Crediting the source must adequately identify the source of the work, giving a full bibliographic description where available (including author, title, publisher, and place and date of publication), the copyright ownership information includes the copyright notice (©, year of first publication and name of the copyright holder).

The credit and copyright notice information may be combined and shown in a separate section of the educational multimedia project (*e.g.* credit section) except for images incorporated into the project for uses described in Section 3.2.3. In such cases, the copyright notice and the name of the creator of the image must be incorporated into the image when, and to the extent, such information is reasonably available; credit and copyright notice information is considered "incorporated" if it is attached to the image file and appears on the screen when the image is viewed. In those case when displaying source credits and copyright ownership information on the screen with the image would be mutually exclusive with an instructional objective (*e.g.* during examinations in which the source credits and/or copyright information would be relevant to the examination questions), those images may be displayed on the screen. In such cases, this information should be linked to the image in a manner compatible with such instructional objectives.

6.3 Notice of Use Restrictions

Educators and students are advised that they must include on the opening screen of their multimedia program and any accompanying print material a notice that certain materials are included under the fair use exemption of the U.S. Copyright Law and have been prepared according to the multimedia fair use guidelines and are restricted from further use.

6.4 Future Uses Beyond Fair Use

Educators and students are advised to note that if there is a possibility that their own educational multimedia project incorporating copyrighted works under fair use could later result in a broader dissemination, whether or not as a commercial product, it is strongly recommended that they take steps to obtain permissions during the development process for all copyrighted portions rather than waiting until after completion of the project.

6.5 Integrity of Copyrighted Works: Alterations

Educators and students may make alterations in the portions of the copyrighted works they incorporate as part of an educational multimedia project only if the alterations support specific instructional objectives. Educators and students are advised to note that alterations have been made.

6.6 Reproduction or Decompilation of Copyrighted Computer Programs

Educators and students should be aware that reproduction or decompilation of copyrighted computer programs and portions thereof, for example the transfer of underlying code or control mechanisms, even for educational uses, are outside the scope of these guidelines.

6.7 Licenses and Contracts

Educators and students should determine whether specific copyrighted works, or other data or information are subject to a license or contract. Fair use and these guidelines shall not preempt or supersede licenses and contractual obligations.

Appendix A: (as of September 26, 1996)

1. Organizations Endorsing These Guidelines

American Association of Community Colleges (AACC)
American Society of Journalists and Authors (ASJA)
American Society of Media Photographers, Inc. (ASMP)
American Society of Composers, Authors and Publishers (ASCAP)
Association for Educational Communications and Technology (AECT)
Association for Information Media and Equipment (AIME)
Association of American Publishers (AAP)[5]
Harvard University Press
Houghton Mifflin
McGraw–Hill
Simon and Schuster
Worth Publishers
Association of College Research Libraries (ACRL)
Association of American Colleges and Universities (AAC&U)
Association of American University Presses, Inc. (AAUP)
Broadcast Music, Inc. (BMI)
Consortium of College and University Media Centers (CCUMC)
Creative Incentive Coalition (CIC)[6]

---

5. The Association of American Publishers (AAP) membership includes more than 200 publishers.

6. The Creative Incentive Coalition membership includes the following organizations: Association of American Publishers, Association of Independent Television Stations, Association of Test Publishers, Business Software Alliance, General Instrument Corporation, Information Industry Associaiton, Information Technology Industry Council, Interactive Digital Software Association, Magazine Publishers of America, The McGraw-Hill Companies, Microsoft Corporation, Motion Picture Association of America, Inc., National Cable Television Association, National Music Publisher's Association, Newspaper Association of America, Recoding Industry Association of America, Seagram/MCA, Inc., Software Publishers Association, Time Warner, Inc., Turner Broadcasting System, Inc., West Publishing Company, and Viacom, Inc.

Information Industry Association (IIA)
Instructional Telecommunications Council (ITC)
Maricopa Community Colleges/Phoenix
Motion Picture Association of America (MPAA)
Music Publishers' Association of the United States (MPA)
Recording Industry Association of America (RIAA)
Software Publishers Association (SPA)

2. Individual Companies and Institutions Endorsing These Guidelines

Houghton-Mifflin
John Wiley & Sons, Inc.
McGraw-Hill
Time Warner, Inc.

3. U.S. Government Agencies Supporting These Guidelines

U.S. National Endowment for the Arts (NEA)
U.S. Copyright Office

Appendix B: Organizations Participating in Guideline Development

Being a participant does not necessarily mean that the organization has or will endorse these guidelines.

Agency for Instructional Technology (AIT)
American Association of Community Colleges (AACC)
American Association of Higher Education (AAHE)
American Library Association (ALA)
American Sociery of Journal Authors, Inc. (ASJA)
American Society of Media Photographers (ASMP)
Artists Rights Foundation
Association of American Colleges and Universitities (AAC&U)
Association of American Publishers (ACRL)
Association for Educational Communications and Technology (AECT)
Association for Information Media and Equipment (AIME)
Association of Research Libraries (ARL)
Authors Guild, Inc.
Broadcast Music, Inc. (BMI)
Consortium of College and University Media Centers (CCUMC)

Copyright Clearance Center (CCC)
Creative Incentive Coalition (CIC)
Directors Guild of American (DGA)
Europena American Music Distributors Corp.
Educational institutions represented:
    American University
    Carnegia Mellon University
    City College/City University of New York
    Kent State University
    Maricopa Community Colleges/Phoenix
    Penn State Univeristy
    University of Delaware
Information Industry Association (IIA)
Instructional Telecommunictions Council (ITC)
International Association of Scientific, Technical and Medical Publishers
Medical Publishers
Motion Picture Association of America (MPAA)
Music Publishers Association (MPA)
National Association of State Universities and Land Grant Colleges (NASULGC)
National Council of Teachers of Mathematics (NCTM)
National Educational Association (NEA)
National Music Publishers Association (NMPA)
National School Boards Association (NSBA)
National Science Teachers Association (NSTA)
National Video Resources (NVR)
Public Broadcasting System (PBS)
Recording Industry Association of American (RIAA)
Software Publishers Association (SPA)
Time-Warner, Inc.
U.S. Copyright Office
U.S. National Endowment for the Arts (NEA)
Viacom, Inc.

CONFU Proposed Educational Fair Use Guidelines for Digital Images[1]
Draft—December 3, 1996

Table of Contents

---

1. These guidelines shall not be read to supersede other pre-existing educational use guidelines that deal with the 1976 Copyright Act.

Appendix B: Organizations Participating in Development of These Guidelines.

1. Introduction

1.1 Preamble

Fair use is a legal principle that provides certain limitations on the exclusive rights[2] of copyright holders. The purpose of these guidelines is to provide guidance on the application of fair use principles by educational institutions, educators, scholars and students who wish to digitize copyrighted visual images under fair use rather than by seeking authorization from the copyright owners for non-commercial educational purposes. These guidelines apply to fair use only in the context of copyright.

There is no simple test to determine what is fair use. Section 107 of the Copyright Act[3] sets forth the four fair use factors which should be assessed in each instance, based on the particular facts of a given case, to determine whether a use is a "fair use": (1) the purpose and character of the use, including whether such use is of a commercial nature or is for nonprofit educational purposes, (2) the nature of the copyrighted work, (3) the amount and substantiality of the portion used in relation to the copyrighted work as a whole, and (4) the effect of the use upon the potential market for or value of the copyrighted work.

While only the courts can authoritatively determine whether a particular use is fair use, these guidelines represent the endorsers' consensus of conditions under which fair use should generally apply and examples of when permission is required. Uses that exceed these guidelines may or may not be fair use. The endorsers also agree that the more one exceeds these guidelines, the greater the risk that fair use does not apply.

The limitations of conditions set forth in these guidelines do not apply to works in the public domain—such as U.S. government works or works on which copyright has expired for which there are no copyright restrictions—or to works for which the individual or institution has obtained permission for the particular use. Also, license

---

2.   See Section 106 of the Copyright Act.

3.   The Copyright Act of 1976, as amended, is codified at 17 U.S.C. § 101 *et seq*.

agreements may govern the uses of some works and users should refer to the applicable license terms for guidance.

Those who developed these guidelines met for an extended period of time and the result represents their collective understanding in this complex area. Because digital technology is in a dynamic phase, there may come a time when it is necessary to review the guidelines. Nothing in these guidelines should be construed to apply to the fair use privilege in any context outside of educational and scholarly uses of digital images. These guidelines do not cover non-educational or commercial digitization or use at any time, even by nonprofit education institutions. These guidelines are not intended to cover fair use of copyrighted works in other educational contexts such as educational multimedia projects,[4] [distance education, or electronic reserves,] which may be addressed in other fair use guidelines.

This Preamble is an integral part of these guidelines and should be included whenever the guidelines are reprinted or adopted by organizations and educational institutions. Users are encouraged to reproduce and distribute these guidelines freely without permission; no copyright protection of these guidelines is claimed by any person or entity.

1.2 Background: Rights in Visual Images

As photographic and electronic technology has advanced, the making of high-quality reproductions of visual images has become easier, cheaper and more widely accessible. However, the fact that images may be easily available does not automatically mean they can be reproduced and reused without permission. Confusion regarding intellectual property rights in visual images arises from the many ways that images are created and the many sources that may be related to any particular image. Clearing permission, when necessary, requires identifying the holder of the applicable rights. Determining all the holders of the rights connected with an image requires an understanding of the source of the image, the content portrayed and the creation of the image, both for original visual images and for reproductions of images.

---

4.   In general, multimedia projects are stand-alone, interactive programs incorporating both original and pre-existing copyrighted works in various media formats, while visual archives are databases of individual visual images from which images intended for educational uses may be selected for display.

Visual images can be original works or reproductions of other works; in some cases, original works may incorporate reproductions of other works as well. Often, a digital image is several generations removed from the visual image it reproduces. For example, a digital image of a painting may have been scanned from a slide, which was copied from a published book that contained a printed reproduction of the work of art; this reproduction may have been made from a color transparency photographed directly from the original painting. There may be intellectual property rights in the original painting, and each additional stage of reproduction in this chain may involve another layer of rights.

A digital image can be an original visual image, a reproduction, a published reproduction, or a copy of a published reproduction. An original visual image is a work of art or an original work of authorship (or a part of a work), fixed in digital or analog form and expressed in a visual medium. Examples include graphic, sculptural and architectural works, as well as stills from motion pictures or other audiovisual works. A reproduction is a copy of an original visual image in digital or analog form. The most common forms of reproductions are photographic, including prints, 35mm slides, and color transparencies. The original visual image shown in a reproduction is often referred to as the "underlying work." Digital images can be reproductions of either original visual images or of other reproductions. A published reproduction is a reproduction of an original visual image appearing in a work distributed in copies and made available to the public by sale or other transfer of ownership, or by rental, lease, or lending. Examples include a plate in an exhibition catalog that reproduces a work of art, and a digital image appearing CD-ROM or online. A copy of a published reproduction is a subsequent copy made of a published reproduction of an original visual image, for example, a 35mm slide which is a copy of an image in a book. The rights in images in each of these layers may be held by different rightsholders; obtaining rights to one does not automatically grant rights to use another, and therefore all must be considered when analyzing the rights connected with an image. Rights to use images will vary depending not only on the identities of the layers of rightholders, but also on other factors such as the terms of any bequest or applicable license.

1.3 Applicability of These Guidelines

These guidelines apply to the creation of digital images and their use for educational purposes. The guidelines cover (1) pre-existing analog image collections and (2) newly acquired analog visual images. The guidelines do not apply to images acquired in digital form, or to images in the public domain, or to works for which the user has obtained the relevant and necessary rights for the particular use.

Only lawfully acquired copyrighted analog images (including original visual images, reproductions, published reproductions and copies of published reproductions) may be digitized pursuant to these guidelines. These guidelines apply only to educational institutions, educators, scholars, students and image collection curators engaging in instructional, research, or scholarly activities at educational institutions for educational purposes.

1.4 Definitions

Educational institutions are defined as nonprofit organizations whose primary purpose is supporting the nonprofit instructional, research and scholarly activities of educators, scholars and students. Examples of educational institutions include K–12 schools, colleges and universities; libraries, museum, hospitals and other nonprofit institutions also are considered educational institutions under this definition when they engage in nonprofit instructional, research, or scholarly activities for educational purposes. Educational purposes are defined as non-commercial instruction or curriculum-based teaching by educators to students at nonprofit educational institutions, and research and scholarly activities, defined as planned non-commercial study or investigation directed toward making a contribution to a field of knowledge and non-commercial presentation of research findings at peer conferences, workshops, or seminars.

Educators are faculty, teachers, instructors, curators, librarians, archivists, or professional staff who engage in instructional, research, or scholarly activities for educational purposes as their assigned responsibilities at educational institutions; independent scholars also are considered educators under this definition when they offer courses at educational institutions. Students are participants in instructional, research, or scholarly activities for educational purposes at educational institutions.

A digital image is a visual work stored in binary code (bits and bytes). Examples include bitmapped images (encoded as a series of bits and bytes each representing a particular pixel or part of the image) and vector graphics (encoded as equations and/or algorithms representing lines and curves). An analog image collection is an assemblage of analog visual images systematically maintained by an educational institution for educational purposes in the form of slides, photographs, or other stand-alone visual media. A pre-existing analog image collection is one in existence as of [December 31, 1996]. A newly acquired analog visual image is one added to an institution's collection after [December 31, 1996].

A visual online catalog is a database consisting of thumbnail images of an institution's lawfully acquired image collection, together with an descriptive text including, for example, provenance and rights information that is searchable by a browsing display to enable visual identification of records in an educational institution's image collection, is a small scale, typically low resolution, digital reproduction which has no intrinsic commercial or reproductive value.

2. Image Digitization and Use by Educational Institutions

This Section covers digitization by educational institutions of newly acquired analog visual images and Section 6 covers digitization of pre-existing analog image collections. Refer to the applicable section depending on whether you are digitizing newly acquired or pre-existing analog visual works.

2.1 Digitizing by Institutions: Newly Acquired Analog Visual Images

An educational institution may digitize newly, lawfully, acquired analog visual images to support the permitted educational uses under these guidelines unless such images are readily available in usable digital form for purchase or license at a fair price. Images that are readily available in usable digital form for purchase or license at a fair price should not be digitized for addition to an institutional image collection without permission.

2.2 Creating Thumbnail Images

An educational institution may create thumbnail images of lawfully acquired images for inclusion in a visual catalog for use at the institution. These thumbnail images may be combined with descriptive text in a visual catalog that is searchable by a number of fields, such as the source.

2.3 Access, Display, and Distribution on an Institution's Secure Electronic Network

Subject to the time limitations in Section 2.4, an educational institution may display and provide access to images digitized under these guidelines through its own secure electronic network. When displaying digital images on such networks, an educational institution should implement technological controls and institutional policies to protect the rights of copyright owners, and use best efforts to make users aware of those rights. In addition, the educational institution must provide notice stating that digital images on its secure electronic network shall not be downloaded, copied, retained, printed, shared, modified, of otherwise used, except as provided for in the permitted educational uses under these guidelines.

2.3.1 Visual Online Catalog. An educational institution may display a visual online catalog, which included the thumbnail images created as part of the institution's digitization process, on the institution's secure electronic network, and may provide access to such catalog by educators, scholars, and students affiliated with the educational institution.

2.3.2 Course Compilation of Digital Images. An educational institution may display an educator's compilation of digital images (see also Section 3.1.2) on the institution's secure electronic network for classroom use, after-class review, or directed study, provided that there are technological limitations (such as a password or PIN) restricting access only to students enrolled in the course. The institution may display such images on its secure electronic network only during the semester or term in which that academic course is given.

2.3.3 Access, Display, and Distribution Beyond the Institution's Secure Electronic Network. Electronic access to, or display or distribution of, images digitized under these guidelines, including the thumbnail images in the institution's visual online catalog, is not permitted beyond the institution's own electronic network, even for educational purposes. Those portions of the visual online catalog which do not contain images digitized under these guidelines, however, such as public domain images and text, may be accessed, displayed, distributed beyond the institution's own secure electronic network.

2.4 Time Limitation for Use of Images Digitized by Institutions from Newly Acquired Analog Visual Images

An educational institution may use and retain in digital image collections images which are digitized from newly acquired analog visual images under these guidelines, as long as the retention and use comply with the following conditions:

2.4.1 Images Digitized from a Known Source and Not Readily Available in Usable Digital Form for Purchase or License at a Fair Price May Be Used for One Academic Term and May Be Retained in Digital Form While Permission Is Being Sought. Permission is required for uses beyond the initial use; if permission is not received, any use is outside the scope of these guidelines and subject to the four-factor fair use analysis (*see* Section 1.1).

2.4.2 Where the Rightsholder of an Image Is Unknown, a Digitized Image May Be Used for up to 3 Years from First Use, Provided That a Reasonable Inquiry (Section 5.2) Is Conducted by the Institution Seeking Permission to Digitize, Retain, and Reuse the Digitized Image. If, after 3 years, the educational institution is unable to identify sufficient information to seek permission, any further use of the image is outside the scope of these guidelines and subject to the four-factor fair use analysis (see Section 1.1).

3. Use by Educators, Scholars, and Students

Subject to the time limitations in Section 2.4, images digitized under these guidelines may be used by educators, scholars, and students as follows.

3.1 Educator Use of Images Digitized under These Guidelines

3.1.1 An Educator May Display Digital Images for Educational Purposes, Including Face-to-face Teaching of Curriculum-based Courses, and Research and Scholarly Activities at a Non-profit Educational Institution.

3.1.2 An Educator May Compile Digital Images for Display on the Institution's Secure Electronic Network (See Also Section 2.3.2) to Students Enrolled in a Course Given by That Educator for Classroom Use, After-class Review, or Directed Study, During the Semester or Term in Which the Educator's Related Course Is Given.

3.2 Use of Images for Peer Conferences

3.3 Use of Images for Publications

These guidelines do not cover reproducing and publishing images in publications, including scholarly publications in print or digital form, for which permission is generally required. Before publishing any images under fair use, even for scholarly and critical purposes, scholars and scholarly publishers should conduct the four-factor fair use analysis (see Section 1.1).

3.4 Student Use of Images Digitized under These Guidelines

Students may:

+ Use digital images in an academic course assignment such as a term paper or thesis, or in fulfillment of degree requirements.
+ Publicly display their academic work incorporating digital images in courses for which they are registered and during formal critiques at a nonprofit educational institution.
+ Retain their academic work in their personal portfolios for later uses such as graduate school and employment applications.

Other student uses are outside the scope of these guidelines and are subject to the four-factor fair use analysis (see Section 1.1).

4. Image Digitization by Educators, Scholars, and Students for Spontaneous Use

Educators, scholars, and students may digitize lawfully acquired images to support the permitted educational uses under these guidelines if the inspiration and decision to use the work and the moment of its use for maximum teaching effectiveness are so close in time that it would be unreasonable to expect a timely reply to a request for permission. Images digitized for spontaneous use do not automatically become part of the institution's image collection. Permission must be sought for any reuse of such digitized images or their addition to the institution's image collection.

5. Important Reminders and Fair Use Limitations under These Guidelines

5.1 Creation of Digital Image Collections

When digitizing copyrighted images, as permitted under these guidelines, an educational institution should simultaneously conduct the process of seeking permission to retain and use the images. Where the rightsholder is unknown, the institution should pursue, and is encouraged to keep records of, its reasonable inquiry (see Section 5.2). Rightsholders and others who are contacted are encouraged to respond promptly to inquiries.

5.2 Reasonable Inquiry

A reasonable inquiry by an institution for the purpose of clearing rights to digitize and use digital images includes, but is not limited to, conducting each of the following steps: (1) checking any information within the control of the educational institution, including slide catalogs and logs, regarding the source of the image; (2) asking relevant faculty, departments staff, and librarians, including visual resource collections administrators, for any information regarding the source of the image; (3) consulting standard reference publications and databases for information regarding the source of the image; and (4) consulting rights reproduction collectives and/or major professional associations representing image creators in the appropriate medium.

5.3 Attribution and Acknowledgment

Educators, scholars, and students should credit the sources and display the copyright notice(s) with any copyright ownership information shown in the original source, for all images digitized by educators, scholars, and students, including those digitized under fair use. Crediting the source means adequately identifying the source of the work, giving a full bibliographic description where available (including the

creator/author, title, publisher, and place and date of publication) or citing the electronic address if the work is from a network source. Educators, scholars, and students should retain any copyright notice or other proprietary rights notice placed by the copyright owner or image archive or collection on the digital image, unless they know that the work has entered the public domain or that the copyright ownership has changed. In those cases when source credits and copyright ownership information cannot be displayed on the screen with the image for educational reasons (e.g., during examinations), this information should still be linked to the image.

5.4 Licenses and Contracts

Institutions should determine whether specific images are subject to a license or contract; a license or contract may limit uses of those images.

5.5 Portions from Single Sources Such as Published Compilations or Motion Pictures

When digitizing and using individual images from a single source such as a published compilation (including but not limited to books, slide sets, and digital image collections), or individual frames from motion pictures or other audiovisual works, institutions and individuals should be aware that fair use limits the number and substantiality of the images that may be used from a single source. In addition, a separate copyright in a compilation may exist. Further, fair use requires consideration of the effect of the use on the potential market for or value of the copyrighted work. The greater the number and substantiality of images taken from a single source, the greater the risk that the use will not be fair use.

5.6 Portions of Individual Images

Although the use of entire works is usually not permitted under fair use, it is generally appropriate to use images in their entirety in order to respect the integrity of the original visual image, as long as the limitations on use under these guidelines are in place. For purposes of electronic display, however, portions of an image may be used to highlight certain details of the work for educational purposes as long as the full image is displayed with or linked to the portion.

5.7 Integrity of Images: Alterations

To maintain the integrity of copyrighted works, educators, scholars, and students are advised to exercise care when making any alterations in a work under fair use for educational purposes such as criticism, comment, teaching, scholarship, and research. Furthermore, educators, scholars, and students should note the nature of any changes they make to original visual images when producing their own digital images.

5.8 Caution in Downloading Images from Other Electronic Sources

Educators, scholars, and students are advised to exercise caution in using digital images downloaded from other sources, such as the Internet. Such digital environments contain a mix of works protected by copyright and works in the public domain, and some copyrighted works may have been posted to the Internet without authorization of the copyright holder.

6. Transition Period for Pre-existing Analog Image Collections

6.1 Context

Pre-existing visual resource collections in educational institutions (referred to in these guidelines as "pre-existing analog image collections") often consist of tens of thousands of images which have been acquired from a wide variety of sources over a period of many years. Many pre-existing collections lack adequate source information for older images, and standards for accession practices are still evolving. In addition, publishers and vendors may no longer be in business, and information about specific images may no longer be available. For many images there may also be several layers of rightsholders: the rights in an original visual image are separate from rights in a reproduction of that image and may be held by different rightsholders. All these factors complicate the process of locating rightsholders, and seeking permissions for pre-existing collection will be painstaking and time consuming.

However, there are significant educational benefits to be gained if pre-existing analog image collections can be digitized uniformly and systematically. Digitization will allow educators to employ new technologies using the varied and numerous images necessary in their current curricula. At the same time, rightsholders and educational institutions have concerns that images in some collections may have been acquired without permission or may be subject to restricted uses. In either case, there may be rightsholders whose rights and interests are affected by digitization and other uses.

The approach agreed upon the representatives who developed these guidelines is to permit educational institutions to digitize lawfully acquired images as a collection and to begin using such images for educational purposes. At the same time, educational institutions should begin to identify the rightsholders and seek permission to retain and use the digitized images for future educational purposes. Continued use depends on the institutions' making a reasonable inquire (see Section 5.2) to clear the rights in the digitized image. This approach seeks to strike a reasonable balance and workable solution for copyright holders and users who otherwise may not agree on precisely what constitutes fair use in the digital era.

6.2 Digitizing by Institutions: Images in Pre-existing Analog Image Collections

6.2.1 Educational Institutions May Digitize Images from Pre-existing Analog Image Collections During a Reasonable Transition Period of 7 Years (The Approximate Useful Life of a Slide) from [December 31, 1996]. In addition, educators, scholars, and students may begin to use those digitized images during the transition period to support the educational uses under these guidelines. When digitizing images during the transition period, institutions should simultaneously begin seeking the permission to digitize, retain, and reuse all such digitized images.

6.2.2 Digitization from Pre-existing Analog Image Collections Is Subject to Limitations on Portions from Single Sources such as Published Compilations or Motion Pictures (see Section 5.5). Section 6 of these guidelines should not be interpreted to permit the systematic digitization of images from an educational institution's collections of books, films, or periodicals as part of any methodical process of digitizing images from the institution's pre-existing analog image collection during the transition period.

6.2.3 If, after a Reasonable Inquiry (see Section 5.2), an Educational Institution Is Unable to Identify Sufficient Information to Seek

Appropriate Permission During the Transition Period, Continued Retention and Use Is Outside the Scope of These Guidelines and Subject to the Four-factor Fair Use Analysis (see Section 1.1). Similarly, digitization and use of such collections after the expiration of the transition period is outside the scope of these guidelines and subject to the four-factor fair use analysis (see Section 1.1).

Appendix A

Organizations Endorsing These Guidelines

American Association of Museums
Consortium of College and University Media Centers
National Council of Teachers of Mathematics
Special Libraries Association

Appendix B

Organizations Participating in Development of These Guidelines

(Note that participation in the process of drafting these guidelines does not assume the endorsement of any of the participating organizations.)

American Association of Community Colleges
American Association of Museums
American Council of Learned Societies
American Society of Media Photographers
American Society of Picture Professionals
Art Libraries Society of North America
Association of American Publishers
Association of American Universities
Association of Art Museum Directors
Association of Research Libraries
Coalition for Consumers' Picture Rights
College Art Association
Consortium of College and University Media Centers
Corbis Corporation
Creative Inventive Coalition
The J. Paul Getty Trust
Instructional Telecommunications Council

Library of Congress/National Digital Library Project
Medical Library Association
National Council of Teachers of Mathematics
National Endowment for the Arts
National Initiative for a Networked Cultural Heritage
National Science Teachers Association
Picture Agency Council of America
Special Libraries Association
U.S. Copyright Office
Visual Resources Association

CONFU Proposed Educational Fair Use Guidelines for Distance Learning[1]

Performance & Display of Audiovisual and Other Copyrighted Works
December 18, 1996

1.1 Preamble

Fair use is a legal principle that provides certain limitations on the exclusive rights[2] of copyright holders. The purpose of these guidelines is to provide guidance on the application of fair use principles by educational institutions, educators, scholars and students who wish to use copyrighted works for distance education under fair use rather than by seeking authorization from the copyright owners for non-commercial purposes. The guidelines apply to fair use only in the context of copyright.

---

1. The Guidelines shall not be read to supersede other preexisting educational use guidelines that deal with the 1976 Copyright Act.
2. See Section 106 of the Copyright Act.

There is no simple test to determine what is fair use. Section 107 of the Copyright Act[3] sets forth the four fair use factors which should be assessed in each instance, based on the particular facts of a given case, to determine whether a use is a "fair use": (1) the purpose and character of the use, including whether such use is of a commercial nature or is for nonprofit educational purposes, (2) the nature of the copyrighted work, (3) the amount and substantiality of the portion used in relation to the copyrighted work as a whole, and (4) the effect of the use upon the potential market for or value of the copyrighted work.

While only the courts can authoritatively determine whether a particular use is a fair use, these guidelines represent the endorsers' consensus[4] of conditions under which fair use should generally apply and examples of when permission is required. Uses that exceed these guidelines may or may not be fair use. The endorsers also agree that the more one exceeds these guidelines, the greater the risk that fair use does not apply.

The limitations and conditions set forth in these guidelines do not apply to works in the public domain—such as U.S. government works or works on which the copyright has expired for which there are no copyright restrictions—or to works for which the individual or institution has obtained permission for the particular use. Also, license agreements may govern the uses of some works and users should refer to the applicable license terms for guidance.

Those who developed these guidelines met for an extended period of time and the result represents their collective understanding in this complex area. Because digital technology is in a dynamic phase, there may come a time when it is necessary to review these guidelines. Nothing in these guidelines should be construed to apply to the fair use privilege in any context outside of educational and scholarly uses of distance education. These guidelines do not cover non-educational or commercial digitization or use at any time, even by nonprofit educational institutions. These guidelines are not intended to cover fair use

---

3.   The Copyright Act of 1976, as amended, is codified at 17 U.S.C. § 101 *et seq.*

4.   The names of the various participants in this dialog appear at the end of these guidelines and indicate the variety of interest groups involved, both from the standpoint of the users of copyrighted works and also from the standpoint of the copyright holder.

of copyrighted works in other educational contexts such as educational multimedia projects, electronic reserves or digital images which may be addressed in other fair use guidelines.

This Preamble is an integral part of these guidelines and should be included whenever the guidelines are reprinted or adopted by organizations and educational institutions. Users are encouraged to reproduce and distribute these guidelines freely without permission; no copyright protection of these guidelines is claimed by any person or entity.

1.2 Background

Section 106 of the Copyright Act defines the right to perform or display a work as an exclusive right of the copyright holder. The Act also provides, however, some exceptions under which it is not necessary to ask the copyright holder's permission to perform or display a work. One is the fair use exception contained in Section 107, which is summarized in the preamble. Another set of exceptions, contained in Section 110(1)–(2), permit instructors and students to perform or display copyrighted materials without permission from the copyright holder under certain carefully defined conditions.

Section 110(1) permits teachers and students in a nonprofit educational institution to perform or display any copyrighted work in the course of face-to-face teaching activities. In face-to-face instruction, such teachers and students may act out a play, read aloud a poem, display a cartoon or a slide, or play a videotape so long as the copy of the videotape was lawfully obtained. In essence, Section 110(1) permits performance and display of any kind of copyrighted work, and even a complete work, as a part of face-to-face instruction.

Section 110(2) permits performance of a nondramatic literary or musical work or display of any work as a part of a transmission in some distance learning contexts, under the specific conditions set out in that Section. Section 110(2) does not permit performance of dramatic or audiovisual works as a part of a transmission The statute further requires that the transmission be directly related and of material assistance to the teaching content of the transmission and that the transmission be received in a classroom or other place normally devoted to instruction or by persons whose disabilities or special circumstances prevent attendance at a classroom or other place normally devoted to instruction.

The purpose of these guidelines is to provide guidance for the performance and display of copyrighted works in some of the distance learning environments that have developed since the enactment of Section 110 and that may not meet the specific conditions of Section 110(2). They permit instructors who meet the conditions of these guidelines to perform and display copyrighted works as if they were engaged in face-to-face instruction. They may, for example, perform an audiovisual work, even a complete one, in a one-time transmission to students so long as they meet the other conditions of these guidelines. They may not, however, allow such transmissions to result in copies for students unless they have permission to do so, any more than face-to-face instructors may make copies of audiovisual works for their students without permission.

The developers of these guidelines agree that these guidelines reflect the principles of fair use in combination with the specific provisions of Section 110(1)–(2). In most respects, they expand the provisions of Section 110(2).

In some cases students and teachers in distance learning situations may want to perform and display only small portions of copyrighted works that may be permissible under the fair use doctrine even in the absence of these guidelines. Given the specific limitations set out in Section 110(2), however, the participants believe that there may be a higher burden of demonstrating that fair use under Section 107 permits performance or display of more than a small portion of a copyrighted work under circumstances not specifically authorized by Section 110(2).

1.3 Distance Learning in General

Broadly viewed, distance learning is an educational process that occurs when instruction is delivered to students physically remote from the location or campus of program origin, the main campus, or the primary resources that support instruction. In this process, the requirements for a course or program may be completed through remote communications with instructional and support staff including either one-way or two-way written, electronic or other media forms.

Distance education involves teaching through the use of telecommunications technologies to transmit and receive various materials through voice, video and data. These avenues of teaching often constitute instruction on a closed system limited to students who are pursuing educational opportunities as part of a systematic teaching activity or curriculum and are officially enrolled in the course. Examples of such analog and digital technologies include telecourses, audio and video teleconferences, closed broadcast and cable television systems, microwave and ITFS, compressed and full-motion video, fiber optic networks, audiographic systems, interactive videodisk, satellite-based and computer networks.

2. Applicability and Eligibility

2.1 Applicability of the Guidelines

These guidelines apply to the performance of lawfully acquired copyrighted works not included under Section 110(2) (such as a dramatic work or an audiovisual work) as well as to uses not covered for works that are included in Section 110(2). The covered uses are (1) **live interactive distance learning classes** (i.e., a teacher in a live class with all or some of the students at remote locations) and (2) **faculty instruction recorded without students present for later transmission**. They apply to delivery via satellite, closed circuit television or a secure computer network. They do not permit circumventing anti-copying mechanisms embedded in copyrighted works.

These guidelines do not cover asynchronous delivery of distance learning over a computer network, even one that is secure and capable of limiting access to students enrolled in the course through PIN or other identification system. Although the participants believe fair use of copyrighted works applies in some aspects of such instruction, they did not develop fair use guidelines to cover these situations because the area is so unsettled. The technology is rapidly developing, educational institutions are just beginning to experiment with these courses, and publishers and other creators of copyrighted works are in the early stages of developing materials and experimenting with marketing strategies for computer network delivery of distance learning materials. Thus, consideration of whether fair use guidelines are needed for asynchronous computer network delivery of distance learning courses perhaps should be revisited in three to five years.

In some cases, the guidelines do not apply to specific materials because no permission is required, either because the material to be performed or displayed is in the public domain, or because the instructor or the institution controls all relevant copyrights. In other cases, the guidelines do not apply because the copyrighted material is already subject to a specific agreement. For example, if the material was obtained pursuant to a license, the terms of the license apply. If the institution has received permission to use copyrighted material specifically for distance learning, the terms of that permission apply.

2.2 Eligibility

2.2.1 Eligible Educational Institution. These guidelines apply to nonprofit educational institutions at all levels of instruction whose primary focus is supporting research and instructional activities of educators and students but only to their nonprofit activities. They also apply to government agencies that offer instruction to their employees.

2.2.2 Eligible Students. Only students officially enrolled for the course at an eligible institution may view the transmission that contains works covered by these guidelines. This may include students enrolled in the course who are currently matriculated at another eligible institution. These guidelines are also applicable to government agency employees who take the course or program offered by the agency as a part of their official duties.

3. Works Performed for Instruction

3.1 Relation to Instruction

Works performed must be integrated into the course, must be part of systematic instruction and must be directly related and of material assistance to the teaching content of the transmission. The performance may not be for entertainment purposes.

4. Transmission and Reception

4.1 Transmission (Delivery)

Transmission must be over a secure system with technological limitations on access to the class or program such as a PIN number, password, smartcard or other means of identification of the eligible student.

4.2 Reception

Reception must be in a classroom or other similar place normally devoted to instruction or any other site where the reception can be controlled by the eligible institution. In all such locations, the institution must utilize technological means to prevent copying of the portion of the class session that contains performance of the copyrighted work.

5. Limitations

5.1 One Time Use

Performance of an entire copyrighted work or a large portion thereof may be transmitted only once for a distance learning course. For subsequent performances, displays or access, permission must be obtained.

5.2 Reproduction and Access to Copies

5.2.1 Receiving Institution. The institution receiving the transmission may record or copy classes that include the performance of an entire copyrighted work, or a large portion thereof, and retain the recording or copy for up to 15 consecutive class days (i.e., days in which the institution is open for regular instruction) for viewing by students enrolled in the course.[5] Access to the recording or copy for such viewing must be in a controlled environment such as a classroom, library or media center, and the institution must prevent copying by students of the portion of the class session that contains the performance of the copyrighted work. If the institution wants to retain the recording or copy of the transmission for a longer period of time, it must obtain permission from the rightsholder or delete the portion which contains the performance of the copyrighted work.

5.2.2 Transmitting Institution. The transmitting institution may, under the same terms, reproduce and provide access to copies of the transmission containing the performance of a copyrighted work; in addition, it can exercise reproduction rights provided in Section 112(b).

---

5.   Because the class session may include performance of an entire work, the 15 consecutive class day retention and access is imposed.

6. Multimedia

6.1 Commercially Produced Multimedia

If the copyrighted multimedia work was obtained pursuant to a license agreement, the terms of the license apply. If, however, there is no license, the performance of the copyrighted elements of the multimedia works may be transmitted in accordance with the provisions of these guidelines.

7. Examples of When Permission Is Required

7.1 Commercial Uses

Any commercial use including the situation where a nonprofit educational institution is conducting courses for a for-profit corporation for a fee such as supervisory training courses or safety training for the corporation's employees.

7.2. Dissemination of Recorded Courses

An institution offering instruction via distance learning under these guidelines wants to further disseminate the recordings of the course or portions that contain performance of a copyrighted work.

7.3 Uncontrolled Access to Classes

An institution (agency) wants to offer a course or program that contains the performance of copyrighted works to non-employees.

7.4 Use Beyond the 15-day Limitation

An institution wishes to retain the recorded or copied class session that contains the performance of a copyrighted work not covered in Section 110(2). (It also could delete the portion of the recorded class session that contains the performance).

Endorsing Organizations

American Association of Law Libraries
American Council of Learned Societies
American Society of Journalists and Authors
Consortium of College and University Media Centers
National Council of Teachers of Mathematics

National Education Association
National School Boards Association
Sonneck Society for American Music
Special Libraries Association

Organizations Participating in Developing But Not Necessarily Endorsing or Supporting These Guidelines:

American Association of Community Colleges
American Association of Law Libraries
American Council of learned Societies
Association of American Publishers
Association of American Universities
Association of College and Research Libraries
Association of Research Libraries
Broadcast Music, Inc.
City University of New York
Coalition of College and University Media Centers
Creative Incentive Coalition
Houghton Mifflin
Indiana Partnership for Statewide Education
John Wiley & Sons, Inc.
Kent State University
National Association of State Universities and Land Grant Colleges
National Geographic
National School Board Association
Special Libraries Association
State University of New York
U.S. Copyright Office
University of Texas System
Viacom, Inc

Appendix K
When Works Pass into the Public Domain

Date of work	Protected	From Term
Created 1-1-78 or after	When work is fixed in tangible medium of expression	Life + 50 years (or if work of corporate authorship, 75 years from publication, or 100 years from creation, whichever is first)
Published more than 75 year ago	Now in public domain	None
Published between 75 years ago and the end of 1963	When published with notice	28 years + could be renewed for 47 years; if not so renewed, now in public domain
Published from 1964–77	When published with notice	28 years for first term; now automatic extension of 47 years for second term
Created before 1-1-78, but not published	1-1-78, the effective date of the 1976 Act which eliminated common law copyright	Life + 50 years or 12-31-2002, whichever is greater
Created before 1-1-78 but published between then and 12-31-2002	1-1-78, the effective date of the Act which eliminated common law copyright	Life + 50 years or 12-31-2027, whichever is greater

Table of Cases

Table of Statutes

Index